ST/SG/AC.10/1/Rev.23 (Vol.I)

Recommendations on the

TRANSPORT OF DANGEROUS GOODS

Model Regulations

Volume I

Twenty-third revised edition

UNITED NATIONS
New York and Geneva, 2023

© 2023 United Nations
All rights reserved worldwide

Requests to reproduce excerpts or to photocopy should be addressed to the Copyright Clearance Center at copyright.com.

All other queries on rights and licenses, including subsidiary rights, should be addressed to:

United Nations Publications
405 East 42nd Street, S-09FW001
New York, NY 10017
United States of America

Email: permissions@un.org
website: https://shop.un.org

The designations employed and the presentation of the material in this publication do not imply the expression of any opinion whatsoever on the part of the Secretariat of the United Nations concerning the legal status of any country, territory, city or area, or of its authorities, or concerning the delimitation of its frontiers or boundaries.

United Nations publication issued by the United Nations Economic Commission for Europe.

ST/SG/AC.10/1/Rev.23 (Vol. I)

ISBN: 978-92-1-139221-0
eISBN: 978-92-1-001905-7

ISSN: 1014-5753
eISSN: 2412-0820

Sales number: E.23.VIII.3

Complete set of two volumes.
Volumes I and II not to be sold separately.

INTRODUCTION

The *Recommendations on the Transport of Dangerous Goods* are addressed to governments and to the international organizations concerned with safety in the transport of dangerous goods.

The first version, prepared by the United Nations Economic and Social Council's Committee of Experts on the Transport of Dangerous Goods, was published in 1956 (ST/ECA/43-E/CN.2/170).

In response to developments in technology and the changing needs of users, they have been regularly amended and updated at succeeding sessions of the Committee of Experts pursuant to Resolution 645 G (XXIII) of 26 April 1957 of the Economic and Social Council and subsequent resolutions.

At its nineteenth session (2-10 December 1996), the Committee adopted a first version of the *Model Regulations on the Transport of Dangerous Goods*, which were annexed to the tenth revised edition of the *Recommendations on the Transport of Dangerous Goods*. This was done to facilitate the direct integration of the Model Regulations into all modal, national and international regulations and thereby enhance harmonization, facilitate regular updating of all legal instruments concerned, and result in overall considerable resource savings for the Governments of the Member States, the United Nations, the specialized agencies and other international organizations.

By resolution 1999/65 of 26 October 1999, the Economic and Social Council extended the mandate of the Committee to the global harmonization of the various systems of classification and labelling of chemicals which are applicable under various regulatory regimes, e.g.: transport; workplace safety; consumer protection; environment protection, etc. The Committee was reconfigured and renamed "Committee of Experts on the Transport of Dangerous Goods and on the Globally Harmonized System of Classification and Labelling of Chemicals", supported with one sub-committee specialized in transport of dangerous goods and another one addressing the global harmonization of classification and labelling of chemicals.

At its eleventh session (9 December 2022), the Committee adopted a set of amendments to the Model Regulations on the Transport of Dangerous Goods, concerning, *inter alia*:

(a) new UN numbers and provisions regulating the transport of sodium ion batteries, fire suppressant dispersing devices, disilane, gallium contained in articles and trifluoromethyltetrazole-sodium salt in acetone;

(b) a tightening of the conditions for the transport of tetramethylammonium hydroxide, including the creation of a new UN number for concentrations of not less than 25 %;

(c) changes to the provisions for the transport of battery powered vehicles, including the creation of three new UN numbers;

(d) an exemption for the transport of cells or batteries from production runs and pre-production prototypes;

(e) a new special provision to increase the authorized volume for transport in limited quantities of some compressed gases of Division 2.2 without subsidiary hazards;

(f) more specific concentration limits for ammonium nitrate hot concentrated solutions;

(g) exemptions for nitrocellulose membrane filters used in rapid test devices such as those for pregnancy tests, COVID-19 infections, or other infectious diseases;

(h) a clarification concerning pharmaceutical products (such as vaccines) that are packed in a form ready to be administered; and

(i) an update to the requirements for the use of recycled plastics in packagings;

This twenty-second revised edition of the Recommendations takes account of all the amendments which were circulated as document ST/SG/AC.10/50/Add.1.

At its eleventh session, the Committee also adopted a set of amendments to the *Manual of Tests and Criteria* (ST/SG/AC.10/50/Add.2) and the *Globally Harmonized System of Classification and Labelling of Chemicals* (GHS) (ST/SG/AC.10/50/Add.3). The amendments adopted by the Committee will be reflected in the eighth revised edition of the *Manual* (ST/SG/AC.10/11/Rev.8) and the tenth revised edition of the GHS (ST/SG/AC.10/30/Rev.10).

This publication has been prepared by the secretariat of the United Nations Economic Commission for Europe (UNECE) which provides secretariat services to the Economic and Social Council's Committee of Experts.

Additional information, including corrigenda to this publication, if any, may be found on the UNECE Sustainable Transport Division website:

https://unece.org/transport/dangerous-goods

GENERAL TABLE OF CONTENTS

VOLUME I

Recommendations on the Transport of Dangerous Goods

    Nature, purpose and significance of the Recommendations

    Principles underlying the regulation of the transport of dangerous goods

    Classification and definitions of classes of dangerous goods

    Consignment procedures

    Emergency response

    Compliance assurance

    Transport of radioactive material

    Reporting of accidents and incidents

    Data sheet to be submitted to the United Nations for new or amended classification of substances

Annex: Model Regulations on the Transport of Dangerous Goods

    Part 1: General provisions, definitions, training and security

    Part 2: Classification

    Part 3: Dangerous goods list, special provisions and exceptions

    Appendix A: List of generic and N.O.S. proper shipping names

    Appendix B: Glossary of terms

    Alphabetical index of substances and articles

VOLUME II

Annex: Model Regulations on the Transport of Dangerous Goods

    Part 4: Packing and tank provisions

    Part 5: Consignment procedures

    Part 6: Requirements for the construction and testing of packagings, intermediate bulk containers (IBCs), large packagings, portable tanks, multiple-element gas containers (MEGCs) and bulk containers

    Part 7: Provisions concerning transport operations

Table of correspondence between paragraphs, tables and figures in the 2018 edition of the IAEA Regulations for the Safe Transport of Radioactive Material and the twenty-third revised edition of the Recommendations on the Transport of Dangerous Goods

RECOMMENDATIONS ON THE TRANSPORT OF DANGEROUS GOODS

NATURE, PURPOSE AND SIGNIFICANCE OF THE RECOMMENDATIONS

1.   These Recommendations have been developed by the United Nations Economic and Social Council's Committee of Experts on the Transport of Dangerous Goods[1] in the light of technical progress, the advent of new substances and materials, the exigencies of modern transport systems and, above all, the requirement to ensure the safety of people, property and the environment. They are addressed to governments and international organizations concerned with the regulation of the transport of dangerous goods. They do not apply to the bulk transport of dangerous goods in sea-going or inland navigation bulk carriers or tank-vessels, which is subject to special international or national regulations.

2.   The recommendations concerning the transport of dangerous goods are presented in the form of "Model Regulations on the Transport of Dangerous Goods", which are presented as an annex to this document. The Model Regulations aim at presenting a basic scheme of provisions that will allow uniform development of national and international regulations governing the various modes of transport; yet they remain flexible enough to accommodate any special requirements that might have to be met. It is expected that governments, intergovernmental organizations and other international organizations, when revising or developing regulations for which they are responsible, will conform to the principles laid down in these Model Regulations, thus contributing to worldwide harmonization in this field. Furthermore, the new structure, format and content should be followed to the greatest extent possible in order to create a more user-friendly approach, to facilitate the work of enforcement bodies and to reduce the administrative burden. Although only a recommendation, the Model Regulations have been drafted in the mandatory sense (i.e., the word "shall" is employed throughout the text rather than "should") in order to facilitate direct use of the Model Regulations as a basis for national and international transport regulations.

3.   The scope of the Model Regulations should ensure their value for all who are directly or indirectly concerned with the transport of dangerous goods. Amongst other aspects, the Model Regulations cover principles of classification and definition of classes, listing of the principal dangerous goods, general packing requirements, testing procedures, marking, labelling or placarding, and transport documents. There are, in addition, special requirements related to particular classes of goods. With this system of classification, listing, packing, marking, labelling, placarding and documentation in general use, carriers, consignors and inspecting authorities will benefit from simplified transport, handling and control and from a reduction in time-consuming formalities. In general, their task will be facilitated and obstacles to the international transport of such goods reduced accordingly. At the same time, the advantages will become increasingly evident as trade in goods categorized as "dangerous" steadily grows.

PRINCIPLES UNDERLYING THE REGULATION OF THE TRANSPORT OF DANGEROUS GOODS

4.   Transport of dangerous goods is regulated in order to prevent, as far as possible, accidents to persons or property and damage to the environment, the means of transport employed or to other goods. At the same time, regulations should be framed so as not to impede the movement of such goods, other than those too dangerous to be accepted for transport. With this exception, the aim of regulations is to make transport feasible by eliminating risks or reducing them to a minimum. It is a matter therefore of safety no less than one of facilitating transport.

5.   The Model Regulations annexed to this document are addressed to all modes of transport. Modal transport regulations may occasionally apply other requirements for operational reasons.

---

[1]   *In 2001, the Committee was reconfigured and renamed "Committee of Experts on the Transport of Dangerous Goods and on the Globally Harmonized System of Classification and Labelling of Chemicals" (see resolution 1999/65 of 26 October 1999 of the Economic and Social Council).*

CLASSIFICATION AND DEFINITIONS OF CLASSES OF DANGEROUS GOODS

6. The classification of goods by type of hazard involved has been drawn up to meet technical conditions while at the same time minimizing interference with existing regulations. It should be noted that the numerical order of the classes is not that of the degree of danger.

7. The objective of the recommended definitions is to indicate which goods are dangerous and in which class, according to their specific characteristics, they should be included. These definitions have been devised so as to provide a common pattern which it should prove possible to follow in the various national and international regulations. Used with the list of dangerous goods, the definitions should provide guidance to those who have to use such regulations; and they present a notable degree of standardization while retaining a flexibility that allows diverse situations to be taken into account. Classifications for substances in the Model Regulations are made on the basis of consideration of data submitted to the Committee by governments, intergovernmental organizations and other international organizations in the form recommended in figure 1. However the actual data submitted are not formally endorsed by the Committee.

8. The *Manual of Tests and Criteria* (ST/SG/AC.10/11/Rev.8) presents the United Nations schemes for the classification of certain types of dangerous goods and gives descriptions of the test methods and procedures, considered to be the most useful, for providing competent authorities with the necessary information to arrive at a proper classification of substances and articles for transport. It should be noted that the Manual is not a concise formulation of testing procedures that will unerringly lead to a proper classification of products and it assumes, therefore, competence on the part of the testing authority and leaves responsibility for classification with them. The competent authority has discretion to dispense with certain tests, to vary the details of tests and to require additional tests, when this is justified, to obtain a reliable and realistic assessment of the hazard of a product.

9. Wastes should be transported under the requirements of the appropriate class considering their hazards and the criteria presented in the Model Regulations. Wastes not otherwise subject to these Regulations but covered under the Basel Convention[2] may be transported under Class 9.

10. Many of the substances listed in Classes 1 to 9 are deemed as being dangerous to the environment. Additional labelling is not always specified except for transport by sea. Criteria for substances and mixtures dangerous to the aquatic environment are given in chapter 2.9 of the Model Regulations.

11. Many consignments of goods are treated with fumigants that pose a hazard during transport, in particular to workers who may be exposed unknowingly when they open cargo transport units. The Model Regulations address fumigated cargo transport units as consignments that are subject to special documentation and warning sign requirements in the consignment procedures of part 5.

CONSIGNMENT PROCEDURES

12. Whenever dangerous goods are offered for transport certain measures should be taken to ensure that the hazards of the dangerous goods offered are adequately communicated to all who may come in contact with the goods in the course of transport. This has traditionally been accomplished through special marking and labelling of packages to indicate the hazards of a consignment and through the inclusion of relevant information in the transport documents and by placarding of cargo transport units. Requirements in this regard are provided in the Model Regulations annexed to this document.

13. The labels recommended in 5.2.2.2 of the Model Regulations should be affixed on goods or packages. The labelling system is based on the classification of dangerous goods and was established with the following aims in mind:

---

[2] *Basel Convention on the Control of Transboundary Movements of Hazardous Wastes and their Disposal (1989).*

(a) To make dangerous goods easily recognizable from a distance by the general appearance (symbol, colour and shape) of the labels they bear;

(b) To provide, by means of colours on the labels, a useful first guide for handling, stowage and segregation.

14. In certain cases, where the danger of an item of dangerous goods is considered low, or the goods are packed in a limited quantity, exemptions from labelling may be provided. In such cases, marking of packages with the class or division and the packing group number may be required.

15. One of the primary requirements of the transport document for dangerous goods is to convey the fundamental information relative to the hazard of the goods being offered for transport. To achieve this end, it is considered necessary to include certain basic information in the transport document for the dangerous goods consignment unless otherwise exempted in the Model Regulations. It is recognized that individual national authorities or international organizations may consider it necessary to require additional information. However, the basic items of information considered necessary for each dangerous substance, material or article offered for transport by any mode are identified in the Model Regulations.

EMERGENCY RESPONSE

16. The relevant national and/or international organizations should establish emergency provisions to be taken in the event of accidents or incidents during the transport of dangerous goods in order to protect persons, property and the environment. For radioactive material appropriate guidelines for such provisions are contained in "Planning and Preparing for Emergency Response to Transport Accidents Involving Radioactive Material", Safety Standard Series No. TS-G-1.2 (ST-3), IAEA, Vienna (2002).

COMPLIANCE ASSURANCE

17. The competent authority should ensure compliance with these Regulations. Means to discharge this responsibility include the establishment and execution of a programme for monitoring the design, manufacture, testing, inspection and maintenance of packaging, the classification of dangerous goods and the preparation, documentation, handling and stowage of packages by consignors and carriers, to provide evidence that the provisions of the Model Regulations are being met in practice.

TRANSPORT OF RADIOACTIVE MATERIAL

18. The competent authority should ensure that the consignment, acceptance for transport and transport of radioactive material is subject to a Radiation Protection Programme as described in the Model Regulations. The competent authority should arrange for periodic assessments of the radiation doses to persons due to the transport of radioactive material, to ensure that the system of protection and safety complies with the "Radiation Protection and Safety of Radiation Sources: International Basic Safety Standards", IAEA Safety Standards Series No. GSR Part 3, IAEA, Vienna (2014).

REPORTING OF ACCIDENTS AND INCIDENTS

19. The relevant national and international organizations should establish provisions for the reporting of accidents and incidents involving dangerous goods in transport. Basic provisions in this connection are recommended in 7.1.9 of the Model Regulations. Reports or summaries of reports that the States or international organizations deem relevant to the work of the Sub-Committee of Experts on the Transport of Dangerous Goods (e.g., reports involving packaging and tank failures, major release) should be submitted to the Sub-Committee for its consideration and action, as appropriate.

Figure 1

DATA SHEET TO BE SUBMITTED TO THE UNITED NATIONS
FOR NEW OR AMENDED CLASSIFICATION OF SUBSTANCES

Submitted by .... Date ....

Supply all relevant information including sources of basic classification data. Data should relate to the product in the form to be transported. State test methods. Answer all questions - if necessary, state "not known" or "not applicable" - If data is not available in the form requested, provide what is available with details. Delete inappropriate words.

Section 1. SUBSTANCE IDENTITY

1.1   Chemical name ....

1.2   Chemical formula ....

1.3   Other names/synonyms ....

1.4.1 UN number ....   1.4.2 CAS number ....

1.5   Proposed classification for the Recommendations

      1.5.1   proper shipping name (3.1.2[1])..

      1.5.2   class/division .... subsidiary hazard(s) ....

                  packing group ....

      1.5.3   proposed special provisions, if any ....

      1.5.4   proposed packing instruction(s)..

Section 2. PHYSICAL PROPERTIES

2.1   Melting point or range..........°C

2.2   Boiling point or range ....°C

2.3   Relative density at:

      2.3.1   15 °C ....

      2.3.2   20 °C ....

      2.3.3   50 °C ....

2.4   Vapour pressure at:

      2.4.1   50 °C .... kPa

      2.4.2   65 °C .... kPa

2.5   Viscosity at 20 °C[2]   .... m^2/s

2.6   Solubility in water at 20 °C   .... g/100 ml

2.7   Physical state at 20 °C (2.2.1.1[1])   ☐ solid   ☐ liquid[2]   ☐ gas

---

[1]   *This and similar references are to chapters and paragraphs in the Model Regulations on the Transport of Dangerous Goods.*

[2]   *See definition of "liquid" in 1.2.1 of the Model Regulations on the Transport of Dangerous Goods.*

2.8   Appearance at normal transport temperatures, including colour and odour ....
      ....
      ....
      ....

2.9   Other relevant physical properties ....
      ....
      ....
      ....

Section 3. FLAMMABILITY

3.1   Flammable vapour

      3.1.1   Flash point (2.3.3[1]) ....°C oc/cc

      3.1.2   Is combustion sustained? (2.3.1.3[1])   yes/no

3.2   Autoignition temperature ....°C

3.3   Flammability range (LEL/UEL) .... %

3.4   Is the substance a flammable solid? (2.4.2[1])   yes/no

      3.4.1   If yes, give details   ....
      ....
      ....
      ....

Section 4. CHEMICAL PROPERTIES

4.1   Does the substance require inhibition/stabilization or other treatment such as nitrogen blanket to prevent hazardous reactivity?   yes/no

      If yes, state:

      4.1.1   Inhibitor/stabilizer used ....

      4.1.2   Alternative method ....

      4.1.3   Time effective at 55 °C..

      4.1.4   Conditions rendering it ineffective ....

4.2   Is the substance an explosive according to paragraph 2.1.1.1? (2.1[1])   yes/no

      4.2.1   If yes, give details   ....
      ....
      ....
      ....

---

[1]   *This and similar references are to chapters and paragraphs in the Model Regulations on the Transport of Dangerous Goods.*

4.3   Is the substance a desensitized explosive? (2.4.2.4[1])   yes/no

    4.3.1   If yes, give details ....
....
....
....

4.4   Is the substance a self-reactive substance? (2.4.1[1])   yes/no

    If yes, state:

    4.4.1   exit box of flow chart ....

        What is the self-accelerating decomposition temperature (SADT) for a 50 kg package? .... °C

        Is the temperature control required? (2.4.2.3.4[1])   yes/no

    4.4.2   proposed control temperature for a 50 kg package .... °C

    4.4.3   proposed emergency temperature for a 50 kg package .... °C

4.5   Is the substance pyrophoric? (2.4.3[1])   yes/no

    4.5.1   If yes, give details ....
....
....
....

4.6   Is the substance liable to self-heating? (2.4.3[1])   yes/no

    4.6.1   If yes, give details ....
....
....
....

4.7   Is the substance an organic peroxide (2.5.1[1])   yes/no

    If yes state:

    4.7.1   exit box of flow chart ....

        What is the self-accelerating decomposition temperature (SADT) for a 50 kg package? .... °C

        Is temperature control required? (2.5.3.4.1[1])   yes/no

    4.7.2   proposed control temperature for a 50 kg package .... °C

    4.7.3   proposed emergency temperature for a 50 kg package .... °C

4.8   Does the substance in contact with water emit flammable gases? (2.4.4[1])   yes/no

    4.8.1   If yes, give details ....
....
....
....

---

[1]   *This and similar references are to chapters and paragraphs in the Model Regulations on the Transport of Dangerous Goods.*

4.9 Does the substance have oxidizing properties (2.5.1[1])   yes/no

    4.9.1   If yes, give details ....

....

....

....

4.10 Corrosivity (2.8[1]) to:

    4.10.1   mild steel   .... mm/year   at .... °C

    4.10.2   aluminium   .... mm/year   at .... °C

    4.10.3   other packaging materials (specify)

            .... mm/year   at .... °C

            .... mm/year   at .... °C

4.11 Other relevant chemical properties ....

....

....

....

Section 5. HARMFUL BIOLOGICAL EFFECTS

5.1 LD_{50}, oral (2.6.2.1.1[1])   ....mg/kg   Animal species ....

5.2 LD_{50}, dermal (2.6.2.1.2[1])   ....mg/kg   Animal species ....

5.3 LC_{50}, inhalation (2.6.2.1.3[1])   ....mg/litre   Exposure time.. hours

    or   ....ml/m^3 Animal species ....

5.4   Saturated vapour concentration at 20 °C (2.6.2.2.4.3[1]) ....ml/m^3

5.5   Skin exposure (2.8[1]) results   Exposure time .... hours/minutes

            Animal species..

5.6   Other data ....

....

....

....

5.7   Human experience ....

....

....

....

---

[1] *This and similar references are to chapters and paragraphs in the Model Regulations on the Transport of Dangerous Goods.*

Section 6. SUPPLEMENTARY INFORMATION

6.1 Recommended emergency action

    6.1.1 Fire (include suitable and unsuitable extinguishing agents) ....
....
....
....

    6.1.2 Spillage ....
....
....
....

6.2 Is it proposed to transport the substance in:

    6.2.1 Bulk Containers (6.8^1)   yes/no

    6.2.2 Intermediate Bulk Containers (6.5^1)?   yes/no

    6.2.3 Portable tanks (6.7^1)?   yes/no

If yes, give details in sections 7, 8 and/or 9.

Section 7. BULK CONTAINERS (only complete if yes in 6.2.1)

7.1 Proposed type(s) ....

Section 8. INTERMEDIATE BULK CONTAINERS (IBCs) (only complete if yes in 6.2.2)

8.1 Proposed type(s)..

Section 9. MULTIMODAL TANK TRANSPORT (only complete if yes in 6.2.3)

9.1 Description of proposed tank (including IMO tank type if known)..

9.2 Minimum test pressure ....

9.3 Minimum shell thickness ....

9.4 Details of bottom openings, if any ....

9.5 Pressure relief arrangements ....

9.6 Filling ratio/degree of filling, as applicable ....

9.7 Unsuitable construction materials ....

---

[1] *This and similar references are to chapters and paragraphs in the Model Regulations on the Transport of Dangerous Goods.*

Annex

Model Regulations
on the

TRANSPORT
OF
DANGEROUS GOODS

Notes on the structure of the Model Regulations

These Model Regulations consist of seven parts, each of which is divided into chapters. Chapters are numbered sequentially within each part, with the first digit identifying the part in which the chapter is located. For example, the second chapter in part 7 would be designated "Chapter 7.2". Chapters are further divided into sections, which, in turn, are normally divided into a number of paragraphs. Sections and paragraphs are numbered sequentially with the first number always being the number of the chapter in which the section or paragraph is contained (e.g., 7.2.1 would be the first section in chapter 7.2, and "7.2.1.1" would be the first paragraph in that section).

As an exception, and in order to keep a correspondence between the class number and the chapter number in part 2, the first chapter ("Introduction") of part 2 has been numbered "Chapter 2.0".

When references appear in the text to other provisions of these regulations, the reference will normally consist of the full section or paragraph reference, as described above. In certain cases, however, broader reference may be made to an entire part or chapter by noting only the relevant part (e.g., "Part 5"), or the relevant chapter (e.g., "Chapter 5.4").

Recommendations on tests and criteria, which are incorporated by reference into certain provisions of these regulations, are published as a separate manual (*Manual of Tests and Criteria*, ST/SG/AC.10/11/Rev.8).

TABLE OF CONTENTS

VOLUME I

			Page
Part 1	**GENERAL PROVISIONS, DEFINITIONS, TRAINING AND SECURITY**		19
	Chapter 1.1	General provisions	21
		1.1.1 Scope and application	21
		1.1.2 Dangerous goods forbidden from transport	23
	Chapter 1.2	Definitions and units of measurement	25
		1.2.1 Definitions	25
		1.2.2 Units of measurement	36
	Chapter 1.3	Training	39
	Chapter 1.4	Security provisions	41
		1.4.1 General provisions	41
		1.4.2 Security training	41
		1.4.3 Provisions for high consequence dangerous goods	42
	Chapter 1.5	General provisions concerning radioactive material	45
		1.5.1 Scope and application	45
		1.5.2 Radiation protection programme	46
		1.5.3 Management system	47
		1.5.4 Special arrangement	47
		1.5.5 Radioactive material possessing other dangerous properties	48
		1.5.6 Non-compliance	48
Part 2	**CLASSIFICATION**		49
	Chapter 2.0	Introduction	51
		2.0.0 Responsibilities	51
		2.0.1 Classes, divisions, packing groups	51
		2.0.2 UN numbers and proper shipping names	53
		2.0.3 Precedence of hazard characteristics	55
		2.0.4 Transport of samples	57
		2.0.5 Classification of articles as articles containing dangerous goods, N.O.S	58
	Chapter 2.1	Class 1 – Explosives	59
		2.1.1 Definitions and general provisions	59
		2.1.2 Compatibility groups	61
		2.1.3 Classification procedure	63
	Chapter 2.2	Class 2 – Gases	77
		2.2.1 Definitions and general provisions	77
		2.2.2 Divisions	77
		2.2.3 Mixtures of gases	78
		2.2.4 Gases not accepted for transport	79

TABLE OF CONTENTS (cont'd)

VOLUME I

			Page
Chapter 2.3		Class 3 - Flammable liquids	81
	2.3.1	Definition and general provisions	81
	2.3.2	Assignment of packing groups	82
	2.3.3	Determination of flash point	83
	2.3.4	Determination of initial boiling point	84
	2.3.5	Substances not accepted for transport	84
Chapter 2.4		Class 4 - Flammable solids; substances liable to spontaneous combustion; substances which, in contact with water, emit flammable gases	85
	2.4.1	Definitions and general provisions	85
	2.4.2	Division 4.1 - Flammable solids, self-reactive substances solid desensitized explosives and polymerizing substances	86
	2.4.3	Division 4.2 - Substances liable to spontaneous combustion	97
	2.4.4	Division 4.3 - Substances which in contact with water emit flammable gases	98
	2.4.5	Classification of organometallic substances	99
Chapter 2.5		Class 5 - Oxidizing substances and organic peroxides	101
	2.5.1	Definitions and general provisions	101
	2.5.2	Division 5.1 - Oxidizing substances	101
	2.5.3	Division 5.2 - Organic peroxides	104
Chapter 2.6		Class 6 - Toxic and infectious substances	123
	2.6.1	Definitions	123
	2.6.2	Division 6.1 - Toxic substances	123
	2.6.3	Division 6.2 - Infectious substances	129
Chapter 2.7		Class 7 - Radioactive material	135
	2.7.1	Definitions	135
	2.7.2	Classification	136
Chapter 2.8		Class 8 - Corrosive substances	161
	2.8.1	Definition and general provisions	161
	2.8.2	General classification provisions	161
	2.8.3	Packing group assignment for substances and mixtures	161
	2.8.4	Alternative packing assignment methods for mixtures: Step-wise approach	163
	2.8.5	Substances not accepted for transport	166
Chapter 2.9		Class 9 - Miscellaneous dangerous substances and articles, including environmentally hazardous substances	167
	2.9.1	Definitions	167
	2.9.2	Assignment to Class 9	167
	2.9.3	Environmentally hazardous substances (aquatic environment)	169
	2.9.4	Lithium batteries	181
	2.9.5	Sodium ion batteries	183

TABLE OF CONTENTS (cont'd)

VOLUME I

			Page
Part 3	**DANGEROUS GOODS LIST, SPECIAL PROVISIONS AND EXCEPTIONS**		185
	Chapter 3.1	General	187
		3.1.1 Scope and general provisions	187
		3.1.2 Proper shipping name	187
		3.1.3 Mixtures or solutions	189
	Chapter 3.2	Dangerous goods list	191
		3.2.1 Structure of the dangerous goods list	191
		3.2.2 Abbreviations and symbols	192
	Chapter 3.3	Special provisions applicable to certain articles or substances	317
	Chapter 3.4	Dangerous goods packed in limited quantities	359
		3.4.7 Marking for packages containing limited quantities	360
		3.4.8 Marking for packages containing limited quantities conforming to part 3, chapter 4 of the ICAO Technical Instructions for the Safe Transport of Dangerous Goods by Air	360
		3.4.11 Use of overpacks	361
	Chapter 3.5	Dangerous goods packed in excepted quantities	363
		3.5.1 Excepted quantities	363
		3.5.2 Packagings	364
		3.5.3 Tests for packages	364
		3.5.4 Marking of packages	365
		3.5.5 Maximum number of packages in any cargo transport unit	366
		3.5.6 Documentation	366
APPENDICES			367
	Appendix A	List of generic and N.O.S. proper shipping names	369
	Appendix B	Glossary of terms	389
ALPHABETICAL INDEX OF SUBSTANCES AND ARTICLES			401

TABLE OF CONTENTS (cont'd)

VOLUME II

Part 4   **PACKING AND TANK PROVISIONS**

      Chapter 4.1   Use of packagings, including intermediate bulk containers (IBCs) and large packagings

      Chapter 4.2   Use of portable tanks and multiple-element gas containers (MEGCs)

      Chapter 4.3   Use of bulk containers

Part 5.   **CONSIGNMENT PROCEDURES**

      Chapter 5.1   General provisions

      Chapter 5.2   Marking and labelling

      Chapter 5.3   Placarding and marking of cargo transport units and bulk containers

      Chapter 5.4   Documentation

      Chapter 5.5   Special provisions

Part 6.   **REQUIREMENTS FOR THE CONSTRUCTION AND TESTING OF PACKAGINGS, INTERMEDIATE BULK CONTAINERS (IBCs), LARGE PACKAGINGS, PORTABLE TANKS, MULTIPLE-ELEMENT GAS CONTAINERS (MEGCs) AND BULK CONTAINERS**

      Chapter 6.1   Requirements for the construction and testing of packagings

      Chapter 6.2   Requirements for the construction and testing of pressure receptacles, aerosol dispensers, small receptacles containing gas (gas cartridges) and fuel cell cartridges containing liquefied flammable gas

      Chapter 6.3   Requirements for the construction and testing of packagings for Division 6.2 infectious substances of Category A (UN Nos. 2814 and 2900)

      Chapter 6.4   Requirements for the construction, testing and approval of packages for radioactive material and for the approval of such material

      Chapter 6.5   Requirements for the construction and testing of intermediate bulk containers

      Chapter 6.6   Requirements for the construction and testing of large packagings

      Chapter 6.7   Requirements for the design, construction, inspection and testing of portable tanks and multiple-element gas containers (MEGCs)

      Chapter 6.8   Requirements for the design, construction, inspection and testing of bulk containers

      Chapter 6.9   Requirements for the design, construction, inspection and testing of portable tanks with shells made of fibre reinforced plastics (FRP) material

TABLE OF CONTENTS (cont'd)

VOLUME II

Part 7. PROVISIONS CONCERNING TRANSPORT OPERATIONS

    Chapter 7.1   Provisions concerning transport operations by all modes of transport

    Chapter 7.2   Modal provisions

TABLE OF CORRESPONDENCE between paragraphs, tables and figures in the 2018 edition of the IAEA Regulations for the Safe Transport of Radioactive Material and the twenty-third revised edition of the Recommendations on the Transport of Dangerous Goods

PART 1

GENERAL PROVISIONS, DEFINITIONS, TRAINING AND SECURITY

CHAPTER 1.1

GENERAL PROVISIONS

Introductory notes

NOTE 1: *Recommendations on Tests and Criteria, which are incorporated by reference into certain provisions of these Regulations, are published as a separate Manual ("Manual of Tests and Criteria", ST/SG/AC.10/11/Rev.8), the contents of which are:*

> *Part I: Classification procedures, test methods and criteria relating to explosives*
>
> *Part II: Classification procedures, test methods and criteria relating to self-reactive substances, organic peroxides and polymerizing substances*
>
> *Part III: Classification procedures, test methods and criteria relating to various hazard classes*
>
> *Part IV: Test methods concerning transport equipment*
>
> *Part V: Classification procedures, test methods and criteria relating to sectors other than transport*
>
> *Appendices: Information common to a number of different types of tests and national contacts for test details.*

NOTE 2: *Part III of the "Manual of Tests and Criteria" contains some classification procedures, test methods and criteria which are also given in these Regulations.*

1.1.1 Scope and application

1.1.1.1 These Regulations prescribe detailed requirements applicable to the transport of dangerous goods. Except as otherwise provided in these Regulations, no person may offer or accept dangerous goods for transport unless those goods are properly classified, packaged, marked, labelled, placarded, described and certified on a transport document, and otherwise in a condition for transport as required by these Regulations.

1.1.1.2 These Regulations do not apply to the transport of:

(a) Dangerous goods that are required for the propulsion of the means of transport or the operation of its specialised equipment during transport (e.g. refrigeration units) or that are required in accordance with the operating regulations (e.g. fire extinguishers); and

(b) Dangerous goods, packaged for retail sale, that are carried by individuals for their own use.

NOTE 1: *Specific modal provisions for the transport of dangerous goods as well as derogations from these general requirements can be found in the modal regulations.*

NOTE 2: *Certain special provisions of chapter 3.3 also indicate substances and articles which are not subject to these Regulations.*

NOTE 3: *1.1.1.2 (a) above is only applicable to the means of transport performing the transport operation.*

NOTE 4: *For dangerous goods in equipment in use or intended for use during transport, see 5.5.4.*

1.1.1.3   In certain parts of these Regulations, a particular action is prescribed, but the responsibility for carrying out the action is not specifically assigned to any particular person. Such responsibility may vary according to the laws and customs of different countries and the international conventions into which these countries have entered. For the purposes of these Regulations, it is not necessary to make this assignment, but only to identify the action itself. It remains the prerogative of each government to assign this responsibility.

1.1.1.4   In the transport of dangerous goods, the safety of persons and protection of property and the environment are assured when these Regulations are complied with. Confidence in this regard is achieved through quality assurance and compliance assurance programmes.

1.1.1.5   *Exceptions for dangerous goods packed in limited quantities*

Certain dangerous goods packed in limited quantities are exempted from certain requirements of these regulations subject to the conditions laid down in chapter 3.4.

1.1.1.6   *Transport of dangerous goods by post*

In accordance with the Universal Postal Union Convention, dangerous goods as defined in these Regulations, with the exception of those listed below, are not permitted in mail transported internationally. Appropriate national authorities should ensure that provisions are complied with in relation to the international transport of dangerous goods. The following dangerous goods may be acceptable in international mail subject to the provisions of the appropriate national authorities:

(a) Infectious substances, assigned to Category B (UN 3373) only, and solid carbon dioxide (dry ice) when used as a refrigerant for UN 3373; and

(b) Radioactive material in an excepted package conforming to the requirements of 1.5.1.5, the activity of which does not exceed one tenth of that listed in table 2.7.2.4.1.2 and that does not meet the definitions and criteria of classes, other than Class 7, or divisions, as defined in part 2.

For international movement by post additional requirements as prescribed by the Acts of the Universal Postal Union apply.

NOTE: *The Acts of the Universal Postal Union do not apply to the domestic transport of dangerous goods by mail. Domestic transport of dangerous goods in the mail is subject to the provisions of the appropriate national authorities.*

1.1.1.7   *Application of standards*

Where the application of a standard is required and there is any conflict between the standard and these Regulations, the Regulations take precedence. The requirements of the standard that do not conflict with these Regulations shall be applied as specified, including the requirements of any other standard, or part of a standard, referenced within that standard as normative.

NOTE: *A standard provides details on how to meet the provisions of these Regulations and may include requirements in addition to those set out in these Regulations.*

1.1.1.8   *Transport of dangerous goods used as a coolant or conditioner*

Dangerous goods, that are only asphyxiant (which dilute or replace the oxygen normally in the atmosphere), when used in cargo transport units for cooling or conditioning purposes are only subject to the provisions of section 5.5.3.

1.1.1.9   *Lamps containing dangerous goods*

The following lamps are not subject to these Regulations provided that they do not contain radioactive material and do not contain mercury in quantities above those specified in special provision 366 of chapter 3.3:

(a) Lamps that are collected directly from individuals and households when transported to a collection or recycling facility;

(b) Lamps each containing not more than 1 g of dangerous goods and packaged so that there is not more than 30 g of dangerous goods per package, provided that:

    (i) the lamps are certified to a manufacturer's quality management system;

    NOTE: The application of ISO 9001:2008 may be considered acceptable for this purpose.

    and

    (ii) each lamp is either individually packed in inner packagings, separated by dividers, or surrounded with cushioning material to protect the lamps and packed into strong outer packagings meeting the general provisions of 4.1.1.1 and capable of passing a 1.2 m drop test.

(c) Used, damaged or defective lamps each containing not more than 1 g of dangerous goods with not more than 30 g of dangerous goods per package when transported from a collection or recycling facility. The lamps shall be packed in strong outer packagings sufficient for preventing release of the contents under normal conditions of transport meeting the general provisions of 4.1.1.1 and that are capable of passing a drop test of not less than 1.2 m.

(d) Lamps containing only gases of Division 2.2 (according to 2.2.2.1) provided they are packaged so that the projectile effects of any rupture of the bulb will be contained within the package.

NOTE: *Lamps containing radioactive material are addressed in 2.7.2.2.2(b).*

1.1.2 Dangerous goods forbidden from transport

1.1.2.1   Unless provided otherwise by these Regulations, the following are forbidden from transport:

Any substance or article which, as presented for transport, is liable to explode, dangerously react, produce a flame or dangerous evolution of heat or dangerous emission of toxic, corrosive or flammable gases or vapours under normal conditions of transport.

CHAPTER 1.2

DEFINITIONS AND UNITS OF MEASUREMENT

1.2.1 Definitions

NOTE: *This chapter provides definitions of general applicability that are used throughout these Regulations. Additional definitions of a highly specific nature (e.g., terms relating to construction of intermediate bulk containers or portable tanks) are presented in the relevant chapters.*

For the purposes of these Regulations:

Aerosol or aerosol dispenser means an article consisting of a non-refillable receptacle meeting the requirements of 6.2.4, made of metal, glass or plastics and containing a gas, compressed, liquefied or dissolved under pressure, with or without a liquid, paste or powder, and fitted with a release device allowing the contents to be ejected as solid or liquid particles in suspension in a gas, as a foam, paste or powder or in a liquid state or in a gaseous state;

Aircraft

> *Cargo aircraft* means any aircraft, other than a passenger aircraft, which is carrying goods or property;
>
> *Passenger aircraft* means an aircraft that carries any person other than a crew member, a carrier's employee in an official capacity, an authorized representative of an appropriate national authority, or a person accompanying a consignment or other cargo;

Alternative arrangement means an approval granted by the competent authority for a portable tank or MEGC that has been designed, constructed or tested to technical requirements or testing methods other than those specified in these regulations (see, for instance, 6.7.5.11.1);

Animal material means animal carcasses, animal body parts, foodstuffs or feedstuffs derived from animals;

Approval

> *Multilateral approval*, for the transport of radioactive material, means approval by the relevant competent authority of the country of origin of the design or shipment, as applicable, and also, where the consignment is to be transported through or into any other country, approval by the competent authority of that country;
>
> *Unilateral approval*, for the transport of radioactive material, means an approval of a design which is required to be given by the competent authority of the country of origin of the design only;

ASTM means the American Society for Testing and Materials (ASTM International, 100 Barr Harbor Drive, PO Box C700, West Conshohocken, PA, 19428-2959, United States of America);

Bag means a flexible packaging made of paper, plastics film, textiles, woven material or other suitable materials;

Box means a packaging with complete rectangular or polygonal faces, made of metal, wood, plywood, reconstituted wood, fibreboard, plastics or other suitable material. Small holes for purposes such as ease of handling or opening, or to meet classification requirements, are permitted as long as they do not compromise the integrity of the packaging during transport;

Bulk container means a containment system (including any liner or coating) intended for the transport of solid substances which are in direct contact with the containment system. Packagings, intermediate bulk containers (IBCs), large packagings and portable tanks are not included.

A bulk container is:

- of a permanent character and accordingly strong enough to be suitable for repeated use;

- specially designed to facilitate the transport of goods by one or more means of transport without intermediate reloading;

- fitted with devices permitting its ready handling;

- of a capacity of not less than 1.0 m^3.

Examples of bulk containers are freight containers, offshore bulk containers, skips, bulk bins, swap bodies, trough-shaped containers, roller containers, load compartments of vehicles, flexible bulk containers;

Bundle of cylinders means a pressure receptacle comprising an assembly of cylinders or cylinder shells that are fastened together and which are interconnected by a manifold and transported as a unit. The total water capacity shall not exceed 3 000 litres except that bundles intended for the transport of gases of Division 2.3 shall be limited to 1 000 litres water capacity;

Cargo transport unit means a road transport tank or freight vehicle, a railway transport tank or freight wagon, a multimodal freight container or portable tank, or a MEGC;

Carrier means any person, organization or government undertaking the transport of dangerous goods by any means of transport. The term includes both carriers for hire or reward (known as common or contract carriers in some countries) and carriers on own account (known as private carriers in some countries);

CGA means the Compressed Gas Association (CGA, 14501 George Carter Way, Suite 103, Chantilly, VA 20151, United States of America);

Closed cargo transport unit means a cargo transport unit which totally encloses the contents by permanent structures with complete and rigid surfaces. Cargo transport units with fabric sides or tops are not considered closed cargo transport units;

Closed cryogenic receptacle means a thermally insulated pressure receptacle for refrigerated liquefied gases of a water capacity of not more than 1 000 litres;

Closure means a device which closes an opening in a receptacle;

NOTE: *For pressure receptacles, closures are, for example, valves, pressure relief devices, pressure gauges or level indicators.*

Combination packaging means a combination of packagings for transport purposes, consisting of one or more inner packagings secured in an outer packaging in accordance with 4.1.1.5;

Competent authority means any body or authority designated or otherwise recognized as such for any purpose in connection with these Regulations;

Compliance assurance means a systematic programme of measures applied by a competent authority which is aimed at ensuring that the provisions of these Regulations are met in practice;

Composite packaging means a packaging consisting of an outer packaging and an inner receptacle so constructed that the inner receptacle and the outer packaging form an integral packaging. Once assembled it remains thereafter an integrated single unit; it is filled, stored, transported and emptied as such;

Confinement system, for the transport of radioactive material, means the assembly of fissile material and packaging components specified by the designer and agreed to by the competent authority as intended to preserve criticality safety;

Consignee means any person, organization or government which is entitled to take delivery of a consignment;

Consignment means any package or packages, or load of dangerous goods, presented by a consignor for transport;

Consignor means any person, organization or government which prepares a consignment for transport;

Containment system, for the transport of radioactive material, means the assembly of components of the packaging specified by the designer as intended to retain the radioactive material during transport;

Conveyance means

        (a)   For transport by road or rail: any vehicle;

        (b)   For transport by water: any vessel, or any hold, compartment, or defined deck area of a vessel; and

        (c)   For transport by air: any aircraft;

Crate means an outer packaging with incomplete surfaces;

Criticality safety index (CSI) assigned to a package, overpack or freight container containing fissile material, for the transport of radioactive material, means a number which is used to provide control over the accumulation of packages, overpacks or freight containers containing fissile material;

Critical temperature means the temperature above which the substance cannot exist in the liquid state;

Cylinder means a pressure receptacle of a water capacity not exceeding 150 litres;

Defined deck area means the area of the weather deck of a vessel, or of a vehicle deck of a roll-on/roll-off ship or a ferry, which is allocated for the stowage of dangerous goods;

Degree of filling means the ratio, expressed in %, of the volume of liquid or solid introduced at 15 °C into the means of containment and the volume of the means of containment ready for use;

Design, for the transport of radioactive material, means the description of fissile material excepted under 2.7.2.3.5 (f), special form radioactive material, low dispersible radioactive material, package or packaging which enables such an item to be fully identified. The description may include specifications, engineering drawings, reports demonstrating compliance with regulatory requirements, and other relevant documentation;

Design life, for composite cylinders and tubes, means the maximum life (in number of years) to which the cylinder or tube is designed and approved in accordance with the applicable standard;

Dose rate means the ambient dose equivalent or the directional dose equivalent, as appropriate, per unit time, measured at the point of interest.

Drum means a flat-ended or convex-ended cylindrical packaging made of metal, fibreboard, plastics, plywood or other suitable materials. This definition also includes packagings of other shapes e.g. round taper-necked packagings, or pail-shaped packagings. Wooden barrels or jerricans are not covered by this definition;

Elevated temperature substance means a substance which is transported or offered for transport:

        -    in the liquid state at a temperature at or above 100 °C;

        -    in the liquid state with a flashpoint above 60 °C and which is intentionally heated to a temperature above its flashpoint; or

- in a solid state and at a temperature at or above 240 °C;

EN (standard) means a European standard published by the European Committee for Standardization (CEN) (CEN – 36 rue de Stassart, B-1050 Brussels, Belgium);

Exclusive use, for the transport of radioactive material, means the sole use, by a single consignor, of a conveyance or of a large freight container, in respect of which all initial, intermediate and final loading and unloading and shipment are carried out in accordance with the directions of the consignor or consignee, where so required by these Regulations;

Filling ratio means the ratio of the mass of gas to the mass of water at 15 °C that would fill completely a pressure receptacle fitted ready for use;

Freight container means an article of transport equipment that is of a permanent character and accordingly strong enough to be suitable for repeated use; specially designed to facilitate the transport of goods, by one or other modes of transport, without intermediate reloading: designed to be secured and/or readily handled, having fittings for these purposes, and approved in accordance with the International Convention for Safe Containers (CSC), 1972, as amended. The term "freight container" includes neither vehicle nor packaging. However a freight container that is carried on a chassis is included. For freight containers for the transport of radioactive material, a freight container may be used as a packaging.

In addition: Small freight container means a freight container that has an internal volume of not more than 3 m^3. Large freight container means a freight container that has an internal volume of more than 3 m^3.

Fuel cell means an electrochemical device that converts the chemical energy of a fuel to electrical energy, heat and reaction products;

Fuel cell engine means a device used to power equipment and which consists of a fuel cell and its fuel supply, whether integrated with or separate from the fuel cell, and includes all appurtenances necessary to fulfil its function;

GHS means the tenth revised edition of the *Globally Harmonized System of Classification and Labelling of Chemicals*, published by the United Nations as document ST/SG/AC.10/30/Rev.10;

IAEA means the International Atomic Energy Agency (IAEA, P.O. Box 100 – A -1400 Vienna, Austria);

ICAO means the International Civil Aviation Organization (ICAO, 999 University Street, Montreal, Quebec H3C 5H7, Canada);

IMO means the International Maritime Organization (IMO, 4 Albert Embankment, London SE1 7SR, United Kingdom);

Inspection body means an independent inspection and testing body approved by the competent authority;

Intermediate Bulk Container (IBC)

IBC means any rigid or flexible portable packaging, other than those specified in chapter 6.1, that:

(a) has a capacity of:

(i) not more than 3.0 m^3 (3 000 litres) for solids and liquids of packing groups II and III;

(ii) not more than 1.5 m^3 for solids of packing group I when packed in flexible, rigid plastics, composite, fibreboard and wooden IBCs;

(iii) not more than 3.0 m^3 for solids of packing group I when packed in metal IBCs;

(iv) not more than 3.0 m^3 for radioactive material of Class 7;

(b) is designed for mechanical handling;

(c) is resistant to the stresses produced in handling and transport, as determined by tests;

Remanufactured IBC means a metal, rigid plastics or composite IBC that:

(a) is produced as a UN type from a non-UN type; or

(b) is converted from one UN design type to another UN design type.

Remanufactured IBCs are subject to the same requirements of these Regulations that apply to new IBCs of the same type (see also design type definition in 6.5.6.1.1);

Repaired IBC means a metal, rigid plastics or composite IBC that, as a result of impact or for any other cause (e.g. corrosion, embrittlement or other evidence of reduced strength as compared to the design type) is restored so as to conform to the design type and to be able to withstand the design type tests. For the purposes of these Regulations, the replacement of the rigid inner receptacle of a composite IBC with a receptacle conforming to the original design type from the same manufacturer is considered repair. However, routine maintenance of rigid IBCs (see definition below) is not considered repair. The bodies of rigid plastics IBCs and the inner receptacles of composite IBCs are not repairable. Flexible IBCs are not repairable unless approved by the competent authority;

Routine maintenance of flexible IBCs means the routine performance on plastics or textile flexible IBCs of operations, such as:

(a) Cleaning; or

(b) Replacement of non-integral components, such as non-integral liners and closure ties, with components conforming to the original manufacturer's specification;

provided that these operations do not adversely affect the containment function of the flexible IBC or alter the design type;

NOTE: For rigid IBCs, see "Routine maintenance of rigid IBCs".

Routine maintenance of rigid IBCs means the routine performance on metal, rigid plastics or composite IBCs of operations such as:

(a) Cleaning;

(b) Removal and reinstallation or replacement of body closures (including associated gaskets), or of service equipment, conforming to the original manufacturer's specifications, provided that the leaktightness of the IBC is verified; or

(c) Restoration of structural equipment not directly performing a dangerous goods containment or discharge pressure retention function so as to conform to the design type (e.g. the straightening of legs or lifting attachments) provided that the containment function of the IBC is not affected;

NOTE: For flexible IBCs, see "Routine maintenance of flexible IBCs".

IAEA Regulations for the Safe Transport of Radioactive Material means one of the editions of those Regulations, as follows:

(a) For the 1985, 1985 (as amended 1990) editions: IAEA Safety Series No. 6

(b) For the 1996 edition: IAEA Safety Series No. ST-1

(c) For the 1996 (revised) edition: IAEA Safety Series No. TS-R-1 (ST-1, Revised)

(d) For the 1996 (as amended 2003), 2005, 2009 editions: IAEA Safety Standards Series No. TS-R-1

(e) For the 2012 edition: IAEA Safety Standards Series No. SSR-6

(f) For the 2018 edition: IAEA Safety Standards Series No. SSR-6 (Rev.1);

Inner packaging means a packaging for which an outer packaging is required for transport;

Inner receptacle means a receptacle which requires an outer packaging in order to perform its containment function;

Inner vessel, for a closed cryogenic receptacle, means the pressure vessel intended to contain the refrigerated liquefied gas;

Intermediate packaging means a packaging placed between inner packagings, or articles, and an outer packaging;

ISO (standard) means an international standard published by the International Organization for Standardization (ISO - 1, ch. de la Voie-Creuse, CH-1211 Geneva 20, Switzerland);

Jerrican means a metal or plastics packaging of rectangular or polygonal cross-section;

Large packaging means a packaging consisting of an outer packaging which contains articles or inner packagings and which

(a) is designed for mechanical handling; and

(b) exceeds 400 kg net mass or 450 litres capacity but has a volume of not more than 3 m^3;

Large salvage packaging means a special packaging which

(a) is designed for mechanical handling; and

(b) exceeds 400 kg net mass or 450 litres capacity but has a volume of not more than 3 m^3;

into which damaged, defective, leaking or non-conforming dangerous goods packages, or dangerous goods that have spilled or leaked are placed for purposes of transport for recovery or disposal;

Liner means a separate tube or bag inserted into a packaging, (including IBCs and large packagings) but not forming an integral part of it, including the closures of its openings;

Liquid means a dangerous good which at 50 °C have a vapour pressure of not more than 300 kPa (3 bar), which is not completely gaseous at 20 °C and at a pressure of 101.3 kPa, and which has a melting point or initial melting point of 20 °C or less at a pressure of 101.3 kPa. A viscous substance for which a specific melting point cannot be determined shall be subjected to the ASTM D 4359-90 test; or to the test for determining fluidity (penetrometer test) prescribed in section 2.3.4 of annex A of the Agreement concerning the International Carriage of Dangerous Goods by Road (ADR)[1];

Management system, for the transport of radioactive material, means a set of interrelated or interacting elements (system) for establishing policies and objectives and enabling the objectives to be achieved in an efficient and effective manner;

Manual of Tests and Criteria means the eighth revised edition of the United Nations publication bearing this title (ST/SG/AC.10/11/Rev.8);

---

[1] *United Nations publication: ECE/TRANS/326 (Sales No. E.22.VIII.2).*

Maximum capacity as used in 6.1.4 means the maximum inner volume of receptacles or packagings expressed in litres;

Maximum net mass means the maximum net mass of contents in a single packaging or maximum combined mass of inner packagings and the contents thereof and is expressed in kg;

Maximum normal operating pressure, for the transport of radioactive material, means the maximum pressure above atmospheric pressure at mean sea-level that would develop in the containment system in a period of one year under the conditions of temperature and solar radiation corresponding to environmental conditions in the absence of venting, external cooling by an ancillary system, or operational controls during transport;

Metal hydride storage system means a single complete hydrogen storage system, including a pressure receptacle shell, metal hydride, pressure relief device, shut-off valve, service equipment and internal components used for the transport of hydrogen only;

Multiple-element gas container (MEGC) means a multimodal assembly of cylinders, tubes or bundles of cylinders which are interconnected by a manifold and which are assembled within a framework. The MEGC includes service equipment and structural equipment necessary for the transport of gases;

Net explosive mass (NEM) means the total mass of the explosive substances, without the packagings, casings, etc. *(Net explosive quantity (NEQ), net explosive contents (NEC), or net explosive weight (NEW) are often used to convey the same meaning.)*;

Neutron radiation detector is a device that detects neutron radiation. In such a device, a gas may be contained in a hermetically sealed electron tube transducer that converts neutron radiation into a measureable electric signal;

Offshore bulk container means a bulk container specially designed for repeated use for transport of dangerous goods to, from and between offshore facilities. An offshore bulk container is designed and constructed in accordance with the Guidelines for the approval of offshore containers handled in open seas specified by the International Maritime Organization (IMO) in document MSC/Circ.860;

Open cryogenic receptacle means a transportable thermally insulated receptacle for refrigerated liquefied gases maintained at atmospheric pressure by continuous venting of the refrigerated liquefied gas;

Outer packaging means the outer protection of a composite or combination packaging together with any absorbent materials, cushioning and any other components necessary to contain and protect inner receptacles or inner packagings;

Overpack means an enclosure used by a single consignor to contain one or more packages and to form one unit for convenience of handling and stowage during transport. Examples of overpacks are a number of packages either:

    (a)   Placed or stacked on to a load board such as a pallet and secured by strapping, shrink wrapping, stretch wrapping, or other suitable means; or

    (b)   Placed in a protective outer packaging such as a box or crate;

Package means the complete product of the packing operation, consisting of the packaging and its contents prepared for transport;

Packaging means one or more receptacles and any other components or materials necessary for the receptacles to perform their containment and other safety functions;

Portable tank means:

    (a)   For the purposes of the transport of substances of Class 1 and Classes 3 to 9, a multimodal portable tank. It includes a shell fitted with service equipment and structural equipment necessary for the transport of dangerous substances;

(b) For the purposes of transport of non-refrigerated, liquefied gases of Class 2, a multimodal tank having a capacity of more than 450 litres. It includes a shell fitted with service equipment and structural equipment necessary for the transport of gases;

(c) For the purposes of transport of refrigerated liquefied gases, a thermally insulated tank having a capacity of more than 450 litres fitted with service equipment and structural equipment necessary for the transport of refrigerated liquefied gases;

The portable tank shall be capable of being loaded and discharged without the need of removal of its structural equipment. It shall possess stabilizing members external to the shell, and shall be capable of being lifted when full. It shall be designed primarily to be loaded on to a vehicle or vessel and is equipped with skids, mountings or accessories to facilitate mechanical handling. Road tank-vehicles, rail tank-wagons, non-metallic tanks (except FRP portable tanks, see chapter 6.9), gas cylinders, large receptacles, and intermediate bulk containers (IBCs) are not considered to fall within this definition;

Pressure drum means a welded pressure receptacle of a water capacity exceeding 150 litres and of not more than 1 000 litres, (e.g. cylindrical receptacles equipped with rolling hoops, spheres on skids);

Pressure receptacle means a transportable receptacle intended for holding substances under pressure including its closure(s) and other service equipment and is a collective term that includes cylinders, tubes, pressure drums, closed cryogenic receptacles, metal hydride storage system, bundles of cylinders and salvage pressure receptacles;

Pressure receptacle shell means a cylinder, a tube a pressure drum or a salvage pressure receptacle without its closures or other service equipment, but including any permanently attached device(s) (e.g. neck ring, foot ring, etc.);

NOTE: *The terms "cylinder shell", "pressure drum shell" and "tube shell" are also used.*

Quality assurance means a systematic programme of controls and inspections applied by any organization or body which is aimed at providing adequate confidence that the standard of safety prescribed in these Regulations is achieved in practice;

Radiation detection system is an apparatus that contains radiation detectors as components;

Radioactive contents, for the transport of radioactive material, mean the radioactive material together with any contaminated or activated solids, liquids, and gases within the packaging;

Receptacle means a containment vessel for receiving and holding substances or articles, including any means of closing;

Reconditioned packagings include:

(a) Metal drums that:

(i) are cleaned to original materials of construction, with all former contents, internal and external corrosion, and external coatings and labels removed;

(ii) are restored to original shape and contour, with chimes (if any) straightened and sealed, and all non-integral gaskets replaced; and

(iii) are inspected after cleaning but before painting, with rejection of packagings with visible pitting, significant reduction in material thickness, metal fatigue, damage threads or closures, or other significant defects; or

(b) Plastics drums and jerricans that:

(i) are cleaned to original materials of construction, with all former contents, external coatings and labels removed;

(ii) have all non-integral gaskets replaced; and

(iii) are inspected after cleaning with rejection of packagings with visible damage such as tears, creases or cracks, or damaged threads, or closures, or other significant defects;

Recycled plastics material means material recovered from used industrial packagings or from other plastics material that has been pre-sorted and prepared for processing into new packagings, including IBCs. The specific properties of the recycled material used for production of new packagings, including IBCs, shall be assured and documented regularly as part of a quality assurance programme recognized by the competent authority. The quality assurance programme shall include a record of proper pre-sorting and verification that each batch of recycled plastics material, which is of homogeneous composition, is consistent with the material specifications (melt flow rate, density, and tensile properties) of the design type manufactured from such recycled material. This necessarily includes knowledge about the plastics material from which the recycled plastics have been derived, as well as awareness of the prior use, including prior contents, of the plastics material if that prior use might reduce the capability of new packagings, including IBCs, produced using that material. In addition, the packaging or IBC manufacturer's quality assurance programme under 6.1.1.4 or 6.5.4.1 shall include performance of the appropriate mechanical design type tests in 6.1.5 or 6.5.6 on packagings or IBCs, manufactured from each batch of recycled plastics material. In this testing, stacking performance may be verified by appropriate dynamic compression testing rather than static load testing;

NOTE: *ISO 16103:2005 "Packaging – Transport packages for dangerous goods – Recycled plastics material", provides additional guidance on procedures which may be followed in approving the use of recycled plastics material. These guidelines have been developed based on the experience of the manufacturing of drums and jerricans from recycled plastics material and as such may need to be adapted for other types of packagings, IBCs and large packagings made of recycled plastics material.*

Remanufactured IBC (see *"Intermediate Bulk Container (IBC)"*).

Remanufactured large packaging means a metal or rigid plastics large packaging that:

(a) Is produced as a UN type from a non-UN type; or

(b) Is converted from one UN design type to another UN design type.

Remanufactured large packagings are subject to the same requirements of these Regulations that apply to new large packagings of the same type (see also design type definition in 6.6.5.1.2);

Remanufactured packagings include:

(a) Metal drums that:

(i) are produced as a UN type from a non-UN type;

(ii) are converted from one UN type to another UN type; or

(iii) undergo the replacement of integral structural components (such as non-removable heads); or

(b) Plastics drums that:

(i) are converted from one UN type to another UN type (e.g. 1H1 to 1H2); or

(ii) undergo the replacement of integral structural components;

Remanufactured drum is subject to the same requirements of these Regulations that apply to a new drum of the same type;

Repaired IBC (see *"Intermediate Bulk Container (IBC)"*);

Reused large packaging means a large packaging to be refilled which has been examined and found free of defects affecting the ability to withstand the performance tests: the term includes those which are refilled with the same or similar compatible contents and are transported within distribution chains controlled by the consignor of the product;

Reused packaging means a packaging to be refilled which has been examined and found free of defects affecting the ability to withstand the performance tests: the term includes those which are refilled with the same or similar compatible contents and are transported within distribution chains controlled by the consignor of the product;

Routine maintenance of flexible IBC (see "Intermediate Bulk Container (IBC)");

Routine maintenance of rigid IBC (see "Intermediate Bulk Container (IBC)");

Salvage packaging means a special packaging into which damaged, defective, leaking or non-conforming dangerous goods packages, or dangerous goods that have spilled or leaked, are placed for purposes of transport for recovery or disposal;

Salvage pressure receptacle means a pressure receptacle with a water capacity not exceeding 3 000 litres into which are placed damaged, defective, leaking or non-conforming pressure receptacle(s) for the purpose of transport e.g. for recovery or disposal;

Self-accelerating decomposition temperature (SADT) means the lowest temperature at which self-accelerating decomposition may occur in a substance in the packaging, IBC or portable tank as offered for transport. The SADT shall be determined in accordance with the test procedures given in part II, section 28 of the *Manual of Tests and Criteria*.

Self-accelerating polymerization temperature (SAPT) means the lowest temperature at which self-accelerating polymerization may occur with a substance in the packaging, IBC or portable tank as offered for transport. The SAPT shall be determined in accordance with the test procedures established for the self-accelerating decomposition temperature for self-reactive substances in accordance with part II, section 28 of the *Manual of Tests and Criteria*;

Service equipment of a pressure receptacle means closure(s), manifold(s), piping, porous, absorbent or adsorbent material and any structural devices, e.g. for handling;

Service life, for composite cylinders and tubes, means the number of years the cylinder or tube is permitted to be in service;

Settled pressure means the pressure of the contents of a pressure receptacle in thermal and diffusive equilibrium;

Shipment means the specific movement of a consignment from origin to destination;

Siftproof packaging means a packaging impermeable to dry contents including fine solid material produced during transport;

Solid means a dangerous good, other than a gas, that does not meet the definition of liquid in this section;

Tank means a portable tank, including a tank container, a road tank-vehicle, a rail tank-wagon or a receptacle to contain solids, liquids, or gases, having a capacity of not less than 450 litres when used for the transport of gases as defined in 2.2.1.1;

Test pressure means the required pressure applied during a pressure test for qualification or requalification;

Through or into means through or into the countries in which a consignment is transported but specifically excludes countries "over" which a consignment is carried by air, provided that there are no scheduled stops in those countries;

Transport index (TI) assigned to a package, overpack or freight container, or to unpackaged LSA-I or SCO-I or SCO-III, for the transport of radioactive material, means a number which is used to provide control over radiation exposure;

Tube means a pressure receptacle of seamless or composite construction having a water capacity exceeding 150 litres but not more than 3 000 litres;

UNECE means the United Nations Economic Commission for Europe (UNECE, Palais des Nations, 8-14 avenue de la Paix, CH-1211 Geneva 10, Switzerland);

Vehicle means a road vehicle (including an articulated vehicle, i.e. a tractor and semi-trailer combination), railroad car or railway wagon. Each trailer shall be considered as a separate vehicle;

Vessel means any seagoing vessel or inland waterway craft used for carrying cargo;

Wooden barrel means a packaging made of natural wood, of round cross-section, having convex walls, consisting of staves and heads and fitted with hoops;

Working pressure

(a) For a compressed gas, means the settled pressure at a reference temperature of 15 °C in a full pressure receptacle;

(b) For UN 1001 acetylene, dissolved, means the calculated settled pressure at a uniform reference temperature of 15 °C in an acetylene cylinder containing the specified solvent content and the maximum acetylene content;

(c) For UN 3374 acetylene, solvent free, means the working pressure which was calculated for the equivalent cylinder for UN 1001 acetylene, dissolved.

Clarifying examples for certain defined terms

The following explanations and examples are meant to assist in clarifying the use of the some of the packaging terms defined in this section.

The definitions in this section are consistent with the use of the defined terms throughout the Regulations. However, some of the defined terms are commonly used in other ways. This is particularly evident in respect of the term "inner receptacle" which has often been used to describe the "inners" of a combination packaging.

The "inners" of "combination packagings" are always termed "inner packagings" not "inner receptacles". A glass bottle is an example of such an "inner packaging".

The "inners" of "composite packagings" are normally termed "inner receptacles". For example, the "inner" of a 6HA1 composite packaging (plastics material) is such an "inner receptacle" since it is normally not designed to perform a containment function without its "outer packaging" and is not therefore an "inner packaging".

1.2.2 Units of measurement

1.2.2.1 The following units of measurement [a] are applicable in these Regulations:

Measurement of	SI Unit [b]	Acceptable alternative unit	Relationship between units		
Length	m (metre)	--	--		
Area	m² (square metre)	--	--		
Volume	m³ (cubic metre)	l [c] (litre)	1 l	=	10^{-3} m³
Time	s (second)	min (minute)	1 min	=	60 s
		h (hour)	1 h	=	3 600 s
		d (day)	1 d	=	86 400 s
Mass	kg (kilogramme)	g (gramme)	1 g	=	10^{-3} kg
		t (ton)	1 t	=	10^{3} kg
Mass density	kg/m³	kg/l	1 kg/l	=	10^{3} kg/m³
Temperature	K (kelvin)	°C (degree Celsius)	0 °C	=	273.15 K
Difference of temperature	K (kelvin)	°C (degree Celsius)	1 °C	=	1 K
Force	N (newton)	--	1 N	=	1 kg · m/s²
Pressure	Pa (pascal)	bar (bar)	1 bar	=	10^{5} Pa
			1 Pa	=	1 N/m²
Stress	N/m²	N/mm²	1 N/mm²	=	1 MPa
Work		kWh (kilowatt-hour)	1 kWh	=	3.6 MJ
Energy	J (joule)		1 J	=	1 N · m = 1 W · s
Quantity of heat		eV (electronvolt)	1 eV	=	$0.1602 \cdot 10^{-18}$ J
Power	W (watt)	--	1 W	=	1 J/s = 1 N · m/s
Electrical resistance	Ω (ohm)	--	1 Ω	=	1 kg · m² · s⁻³ · A⁻²
Kinematic viscosity	m²/s	mm²/s	1 mm²/s	=	10^{-6} m²/s
Dinamic viscosity	Pa · s	mPa · s	1 mPa · s	=	10^{-3} Pa · s
Activity	Bq (becquerel)				
Dose equivalent	Sv (sievert)				

Notes to 1.2.2.1:

[a] *The following round figures are applicable for the conversion of the units hitherto used into SI Units.*

Force
1 kg = 9.807 N
1 N = 0.102 kg

Stress
1 kg/mm² = 9.807 N/mm²
1 N/mm² = 0.102 kg/mm²

Pressure
1 Pa = 1 N/m² = 10^{-5} bar = 1.02×10^{-5} kg/cm² = 0.75×10^{-2} torr

1 bar = 10^5 Pa = 1.02 kg/cm² = 750 torr
1 kg/cm² = 9.807×10^4 Pa = 0.9807 bar = 736 torr
1 torr = 1.33×10^2 Pa = 1.33×10^{-3} bar = 1.36×10^{-3} kg/cm²

Energy, Work, Quantity of heat

1 J=1 Nm	= 0.278 × 10^{-6} kWh	= 0.102 kgm	= 0.239 × 10^{-3} kcal
1 kWh	= 3.6 × 10^6 J	= 367 × 10^3 kgm	= 860 kcal
1 kgm	= 9.807 J	= 2.72 × 10^{-6} kWh	= 2.34 × 10^{-3} kcal
1 kcal	= 4.19×10^3 J	= 1.16 × 10^{-3} kWh	= 427 kgm

Power   *Kinematic viscosity*

1 W	= 0.102 kgm/s	= 0.86 kcal/h	1 m^2/s	= 10^4 St (Stokes)
1 kgm/s	= 9.807 W	= 8.43 kcal/h	1 St	= 10^{-4} m^2/s
1 kcal/h	= 1.16 W	= 0.119 kgm/s		

Dynamic viscosity

1 Pa·s	= 1 Ns/m^2	= 10 P (poise)	= 0.102 kgs/m^2
1 P	= 0.1 Pa·s	= 0.1 Ns/m^2	= 1.02 × 10^{-2} kgs/m^2
1 kgs/m^2	= 9.807 Pa·s	= 9.807 Ns/m^2	= 98.07 P

[b]   The International System of Units (SI) is the result of decisions taken at the General Conference on Weights and Measures (Address: Pavillon de Breteuil, Parc de St-Cloud, F-92310 Sèvres).

[c]   The abbreviation "L" for litre may also be used in place of the abbreviation "l" when a typewriter cannot distinguish between figure "1" and letter "l".

The decimal multiples and sub-multiples of a unit may be formed by prefixes or symbols, having the following meanings, placed before the name or symbol of the unit:

Factor			Prefix	Symbol
1 000 000 000 000 000 000	= 10^{18}	quintillion	exa	E
1 000 000 000 000 000	= 10^{15}	quadrillion	peta	P
1 000 000 000 000	= 10^{12}	trillion	tera	T
1 000 000 000	= 10^9	billion	giga	G
1 000 000	= 10^6	million	mega	M
1 000	= 10^3	thousand	kilo	k
100	= 10^2	hundred	hecto	h
10	= 10^1	ten	deca	da
0.1	= 10^{-1}	tenth	deci	d
0.01	= 10^{-2}	hundredth	centi	c
0.001	= 10^{-3}	thousandth	milli	m
0.000 001	= 10^{-6}	millionth	micro	µ
0.000 000 001	= 10^{-9}	billionth	nano	n
0.000 000 000 001	= 10^{-12}	trillionth	pico	p
0.000 000 000 000 001	= 10^{-15}	quadrillionth	femto	f
0.000 000 000 000 000 001	= 10^{-18}	quintillionth	atto	a

NOTE: 10^9 = 1 billion is United Nations usage in English. By analogy, so is 10^{-9} = 1 billionth.

1.2.2.2   Deleted.

1.2.2.3   Whenever the mass of a package is mentioned, the gross mass is meant unless otherwise stated. The mass of containers or tanks used for the transport of goods is not included in the gross mass.

1.2.2.4   Unless expressly stated otherwise, the sign "%" represents:

(a)   In the case of mixtures of solids or of liquids, and also in the case of solutions and of solids wetted by a liquid: a percentage mass based on the total mass of the mixture, the solution or the wetted solid;

(b) In the case of mixtures of compressed gases: when filled by pressure, the proportion of the volume indicated as a percentage of the total volume of the gaseous mixture, or, when filled by mass, the proportion of the mass indicated as a percentage of the total mass of the mixture.

In the case of mixtures of liquefied gases and gases dissolved under pressure: the proportion of the mass indicated as a percentage of the total mass of the mixture.

1.2.2.5 Pressures of all kinds relating to receptacles (such as test pressure, internal pressure, safety-valve opening pressure) are always indicated in gauge pressure (pressure in excess of atmospheric pressure); however, the vapour pressure of substances is always expressed in absolute pressure.

CHAPTER 1.3

TRAINING

1.3.1 Persons engaged in the transport of dangerous goods shall be trained in the contents of dangerous goods requirements commensurate with their responsibilities. Employees shall be trained in accordance with 1.3.2 before assuming responsibilities and shall only perform functions, for which required training has not yet been provided, under the direct supervision of a trained person. Training requirements specific to security of dangerous goods in chapter 1.4 shall also be addressed.

1.3.2 Individuals such as those who classify dangerous goods; pack dangerous goods; mark and label dangerous goods; prepare transport documents for dangerous goods; offer or accept dangerous goods for transport; carry or handle dangerous goods in transport; mark or placard or load or unload packages of dangerous goods into or from transport vehicles, bulk packagings or freight containers; or are otherwise directly involved in the transport of dangerous goods as determined by the competent authority; shall be trained in the following:

    (a) *General awareness/familiarization training:*

        (i) Each person shall be trained in order to be familiar with the general provisions of dangerous goods transport requirements;

        (ii) Such training shall include a description of the classes of dangerous goods; labelling, marking, placarding and packaging, segregation and compatibility requirements; a description of the purpose and content of the dangerous goods transport document; and a description of available emergency response documents;

    (b) *Function-specific training*: Each person shall be trained in specific dangerous goods transport requirements which are applicable to the function that person performs;

    (c) *Safety training*: Commensurate with the risk of exposure in the event of a release and the functions performed, each person shall be trained in:

        (i) Methods and procedures for accident avoidance, such as proper use of package-handling equipment and appropriate methods of stowage of dangerous goods;

        (ii) Available emergency response information and how to use it;

        (iii) General dangers presented by the various classes of dangerous goods and how to prevent exposure to those hazards, including if appropriate the use of personal protective clothing and equipment; and

        (iv) Immediate procedures to be followed in the event of an unintentional release of dangerous goods, including any emergency response procedures for which the person is responsible and personal protection procedures to be followed.

1.3.3 Records of training received according to this chapter shall be kept by the employer and made available to the employee or competent authority, upon request. Records shall be kept by the employer for a period of time established by the competent authority.

1.3.4 The training required by 1.3.2 shall be provided or verified upon employment in a position involving dangerous goods transport and shall be periodically supplemented with retraining as deemed appropriate by the competent authority.

CHAPTER 1.4

SECURITY PROVISIONS

Introductory notes

NOTE 1: *This chapter provides requirements intended to address the security of dangerous goods in transport in all modes. Mode specific security provisions can be found in chapter 7.2. National and modal authorities may apply additional security provisions which should be considered when offering or transporting dangerous goods.*

NOTE 2: *For the purposes of this chapter security means measures or precautions to be taken to minimise theft or misuse of dangerous goods that may endanger persons or property.*

1.4.1 **General provisions**

1.4.1.1 All persons engaged in the transport of dangerous goods shall consider security requirements for the transport of dangerous goods commensurate with their responsibilities.

1.4.1.2 Consignors shall only offer dangerous goods to carriers that have been appropriately identified.

1.4.1.3 Transit sites, such as airside warehouses, marshalling yards and other temporary storage areas shall be properly secured, well lit and, where possible, not be accessible to the general public.

1.4.1.4 The provisions of this chapter do not apply to:

    (a) UN 2908 and UN 2909 excepted packages;

    (b) UN 2910 and UN 2911 excepted packages with an activity level not exceeding the A_2 value; and

    (c) UN 2912 LSA-I and UN 2913 SCO-I.

1.4.2 **Security training**

1.4.2.1 The training specified for individuals in 1.3.2 (a), (b) or (c) shall also include elements of security awareness.

1.4.2.2 Security awareness training shall address the nature of security risks, recognising security risks, methods to address and reduce such risks and actions to be taken in the event of a security breach. It shall include awareness of security plans (if appropriate) commensurate with the responsibilities of individuals and their part in implementing security plans.

1.4.2.3 Such training shall be provided or verified upon employment in a position involving dangerous goods transport and shall be periodically supplemented with retraining.

1.4.2.4 Records of all security training received shall be kept by the employer and made available to the employee or competent authority, upon request. Records shall be kept by the employer for a period of time established by the competent authority.

1.4.3 Provisions for high consequence dangerous goods

1.4.3.1 *Definition of high consequence dangerous goods*

1.4.3.1.1　High consequence dangerous goods are those which have the potential for misuse in a terrorist event and which may, as a result, produce serious consequences such as mass casualties, mass destruction or, particularly for Class 7, mass socio-economic disruption.

1.4.3.1.2　An indicative list of high consequence dangerous goods in classes and divisions other than Class 7 is given in table 1.4.1 below.

Table 1.4.1: Indicative list of high consequence dangerous goods

Class 1, Division 1.1	explosives
Class 1, Division 1.2	explosives
Class 1, Division 1.3	compatibility group C explosives
Class 1, Division 1.4	UN Nos. 0104, 0237, 0255, 0267, 0289, 0361, 0365, 0366, 0440, 0441, 0455, 0456, 0500, 0512 and 0513
Class 1, Division 1.5	explosives
Class 1, Division 1.6:	explosives
Division 2.1	flammable gases in bulk
Division 2.3	toxic gases (excluding aerosols)
Class 3	flammable liquids of packing groups I and II in bulk
Class 3 and Division 4.1	desensitized explosives
Division 4.2	goods of packing group I in bulk
Division 4.3	goods of packing group I in bulk
Division 5.1	oxidizing liquids of packing group I in bulk
Division 5.1	perchlorates, ammonium nitrate, ammonium nitrate fertilizers and ammonium nitrate emulsions or suspensions or gels, in bulk
Division 6.1	toxic substances of packing group I
Division 6.2	infectious substances of Category A (UN Nos. 2814 and 2900) and medical waste of Category A (UN 3549)
Class 8	corrosive substances of packing group I in bulk

NOTE: *For the purposes of this table, "in bulk" means transported in quantities greater than 3 000 kg or 3 000 l in portable tanks or bulk containers.*

1.4.3.1.3　For dangerous goods of Class 7, high consequence radioactive material is that with an activity equal to or greater than a transport security threshold of 3 000 A_2 per single package (see also 2.7.2.2.1) except for the following radionuclides where the transport security threshold is given in table 1.4.2 below.

Table 1.4.2: Transport security thresholds for specific radionuclides

Element	Radionuclide	Transport security threshold (TBq)
Americium	Am-241	0.6
Gold	Au-198	2
Cadmium	Cd-109	200
Californium	Cf-252	0.2
Curium	Cm-244	0.5
Cobalt	Co-57	7
Cobalt	Co-60	0.3
Caesium	Cs-137	1
Iron	Fe-55	8000
Germanium	Ge-68	7
Gadolinium	Gd-153	10
Iridium	Ir-192	0.8
Nickel	Ni-63	600
Palladium	Pd-103	900
Promethium	Pm-147	400
Polonium	Po-210	0.6
Plutonium	Pu-238	0.6
Plutonium	Pu-239	0.6
Radium	Ra-226	0.4
Ruthenium	Ru-106	3
Selenium	Se-75	2
Strontium	Sr-90	10
Thallium	Tl-204	200
Thulium	Tm-170	200
Ytterbium	Yb-169	3

1.4.3.1.4   For mixtures of radionuclides, determination of whether or not the transport security threshold has been met or exceeded can be calculated by summing the ratios of activity present for each radionuclide divided by the transport security threshold for that radionuclide. If the sum of the fractions is less than 1, then the radioactivity threshold for the mixture has not been met nor exceeded.

This calculation can be made with the formula:

$$\sum_i \frac{A_i}{T_i} < 1$$

Where:

A_i = activity of radionuclide i that is present in a package (TBq)

T_i = transport security threshold for radionuclide i (TBq).

1.4.3.1.5   When radioactive material possesses subsidiary hazards of other classes or divisions, the criteria of table 1.4.1 shall also be taken into account (see also 1.5.5.1).

1.4.3.2 *Specific security provisions for high consequence dangerous goods*

1.4.3.2.1 In implementing national security provisions competent authorities shall consider establishing a programme for identifying consignors or carriers engaged in the transport of high consequence dangerous goods for the purpose of communicating security related information.

NOTE: *In addition to the security provisions of these Regulations, competent authorities may implement further security provisions for reasons other than safety of dangerous goods during transport. In order to not impede international and multimodal transport by different explosives security markings, it is recommended that such marks be formatted consistent with an internationally harmonized standard (e.g. European Union Commission Directive 2008/43/EC).*

1.4.3.2.2 Security plans

1.4.3.2.2.1 Carriers, consignors and others (including infrastructure managers) engaged in the transport of high consequence dangerous goods (see 1.4.3.1) shall adopt, implement and comply with a security plan that addresses at least the elements specified in 1.4.3.2.2.2.

1.4.3.2.2.2 The security plan shall comprise at least the following elements:

(a) Specific allocation of responsibilities for security to competent and qualified persons with appropriate authority to carry out their responsibilities;

(b) Records of dangerous goods or types of dangerous goods transported;

(c) Review of current operations and assessment of vulnerabilities, including inter-modal transfer, temporary transit storage, handling and distribution as appropriate;

(d) Clear statements of measures, including training, policies (including response to higher threat conditions, new employee/employment verification etc.), operating practices (e.g. choice/use of routes where known, access to dangerous goods in temporary storage, proximity to vulnerable infrastructure etc.), equipment and resources that are to be used to reduce security risks;

(e) Effective and up to date procedures for reporting and dealing with security threats, breaches of security or security incidents;

(f) Procedures for the evaluation and testing of security plans and procedures for periodic review and update of the plans;

(g) Measures to ensure the security of transport information contained in the plan; and

(h) Measures to ensure that the distribution of the transport information is limited as far as possible. (Such measures shall not preclude provision of transport documentation required by chapter 5.4 of these Regulations).

NOTE: *Carriers, consignors and consignees should co-operate with each other and with appropriate authorities to exchange threat information, apply appropriate security measures and respond to security incidents.*

1.4.3.2.3 For radioactive material, the provisions of this chapter and of section 7.2.4 are deemed to be complied with when the provisions of the Convention on Physical Protection of Nuclear Material (INFCIRC/274/Rev.1, IAEA, Vienna (1980)) and the IAEA circular on "Nuclear Security Recommendations on Physical Protection of Nuclear Material and Nuclear Facilities" (INFCIRC/225/Rev.5, IAEA, Vienna (2011)) are applied.

CHAPTER 1.5

GENERAL PROVISIONS CONCERNING RADIOACTIVE MATERIAL

1.5.1 **Scope and application**

1.5.1.1 These Regulations establish standards of safety which provide an acceptable level of control of the radiation, criticality and thermal hazards to people, property and the environment that are associated with the transport of radioactive material. These Regulations are based on the 2018 edition of the IAEA Regulations for the Safe Transport of Radioactive Material. Explanatory material can be found in "Advisory Material for the IAEA Regulations for the Safe Transport of Radioactive Material (2018 Edition)", Safety Standards Series No. SSG-26 (Rev.1), IAEA, Vienna (2019). The prime responsibility for safety shall rest with the person or organization responsible for facilities and activities that give rise to radiation risk.

1.5.1.2 The objective of these Regulations is to establish requirements that must be satisfied to ensure safety and to protect people, property and the environment from harmful effects of ionizing radiation during the transport of radioactive material. This protection is achieved by requiring:

(a) Containment of the radioactive contents;

(b) Control of external dose rate;

(c) Prevention of criticality; and

(d) Prevention of damage caused by heat.

These requirements are satisfied firstly by applying a graded approach to contents limits for packages and conveyances and to performance standards applied to package designs depending upon the hazard of the radioactive contents. Secondly, they are satisfied by imposing conditions on the design and operation of packages and on the maintenance of packagings, including a consideration of the nature of the radioactive contents. Thirdly, they are satisfied by requiring administrative controls including, where appropriate, approval by competent authorities. Finally, further protection is provided by making arrangements for planning and preparing emergency response to protect people, property and the environment.

1.5.1.3 These Regulations apply to the transport of radioactive material by all modes on land, water or in the air, including transport which is incidental to the use of the radioactive material. Transport comprises all operations and conditions associated with and involved in the movement of radioactive material; these include the design, manufacture, maintenance and repair of packaging, and the preparation, consigning, loading, transport including in-transit storage, unloading and receipt at the final destination of loads of radioactive material and packages. A graded approach is applied to the performance standards in these Regulations that are characterized by three general severity levels:

(a) Routine conditions of transport (incident free);

(b) Normal conditions of transport (minor mishaps);

(c) Accident conditions of transport.

1.5.1.4 These Regulations do not apply to any of the following:

(a) Radioactive material that is an integral part of the means of transport;

(b) Radioactive material moved within an establishment which is subject to appropriate safety regulations in force in the establishment and where the movement does not involve public roads or railways;

(c) Radioactive material implanted or incorporated into a person or live animal for diagnosis or treatment;

(d) Radioactive material in or on a person who is to be transported for medical treatment because the person has been subject to accidental or deliberate intake of radioactive material or to contamination;

(e) Radioactive material in consumer products which have received regulatory approval, following their sale to the end user;

(f) Natural material and ores containing naturally occurring radionuclides (which may have been processed), provided the activity concentration of the material does not exceed 10 times the values specified in table 2.7.2.2.1, or calculated in accordance with 2.7.2.2.2 (a) and 2.7.2.2.3 to 2.7.2.2.6. For natural materials and ores containing naturally occurring radionuclides that are not in secular equilibrium the calculation of the activity concentration shall be performed in accordance with 2.7.2.2.4;

(g) Non-radioactive solid objects with radioactive substances present on any surfaces in quantities not in excess of the limit set out in the definition for "contamination" in 2.7.1.2.

1.5.1.5 *Specific provisions for the transport of excepted packages*

1.5.1.5.1 Excepted packages which may contain radioactive material in limited quantities, instruments, manufactured articles and empty packagings as specified in 2.7.2.4.1 shall be subject only to the following provisions of parts 5 to 7:

(a) The applicable provisions specified in 5.1.1.2, 5.1.2, 5.1.3.2, 5.1.5.2.2, 5.1.5.2.3, 5.1.5.4, 5.2.1.7, 5.4.1.5.7.1 (f) (i) and (ii), 5.4.1.5.7.1 (i), 7.1.8.3.1, 7.1.8.4.3, 7.1.8.5.1 to 7.1.8.5.4 and 7.1.8.6.1; and

(b) The requirements for excepted packages specified in 6.4.4;

except when the radioactive material possesses other hazardous properties and has to be classified in a class other than Class 7 in accordance with special provision 290 or 369 of chapter 3.3, where the provisions listed in (a) and (b) above apply only as relevant and in addition to those relating to the main class or division.

1.5.1.5.2 Excepted packages shall be subject to the relevant provisions of all other parts of these Regulations.

1.5.2 **Radiation protection programme**

1.5.2.1 The transport of radioactive material shall be subject to a radiation protection programme which shall consist of systematic arrangements aimed at providing adequate consideration of radiation protection measures.

1.5.2.2 Doses to persons shall be below the relevant dose limits. Protection and safety shall be optimized in order that the magnitude of individual doses, the number of persons exposed and the likelihood of incurring exposure shall be kept as low as reasonably achievable, economic and social factors being taken into account, within the restriction that the doses to individuals are subject to dose constraints. A structured and systematic approach shall be adopted and shall include consideration of the interfaces between transport and other activities.

1.5.2.3 The nature and extent of the measures to be employed in the programme shall be related to the magnitude and likelihood of radiation exposures. The programme shall incorporate the requirements in 1.5.2.2, 1.5.2.4 to 1.5.2.7 and 7.1.8.1.1. Programme documents shall be available, on request, for inspection by the relevant competent authority.

1.5.2.4 For occupational exposures arising from transport activities, where it is assessed that the effective dose either:

(a) Is likely to be between 1 and 6 mSv in a year, a dose assessment programme via workplace monitoring or individual monitoring shall be conducted; or

(b) Is likely to exceed 6 mSv in a year, individual monitoring shall be conducted.

When workplace monitoring or individual monitoring is conducted, appropriate records shall be kept.

NOTE: *For occupational exposures arising from transport activities, where it is assessed that the effective dose is most unlikely to exceed 1mSv in a year, no special work patterns, detailed monitoring, dose assessment programmes or individual record keeping need be required.*

1.5.2.5 In the event of a nuclear or radiological emergency during the transport of radioactive material, provisions as established by relevant national and/or international organizations, shall be observed to protect people, property and the environment. This includes arrangements for preparedness and response established in accordance with the national and/or international requirements and in a consistent and coordinated manner with the national and/or international emergency arrangements.

1.5.2.6 The arrangements for preparedness and response shall be based on the graded approach and take into consideration the identified hazards and their potential consequences, including the formation of other dangerous substances that may result from the reaction between the contents of a consignment and the environment in the event of a nuclear or radiological emergency. Guidance for the establishment of such arrangements is contained in "Preparedness and Response for a Nuclear or Radiological Emergency", IAEA Safety Standards Series No. GSR Part 7, IAEA, Vienna (2015); "Criteria for Use in Preparedness and Response for a Nuclear or Radiological Emergency", IAEA Safety Standards Series No. GSG-2, IAEA, Vienna (2011); "Arrangements for Preparedness for a Nuclear or Radiological Emergency", IAEA Safety Standards Series No. GS-G-2.1, IAEA, Vienna (2007), and "Arrangements for the Termination of a Nuclear or Radiological Emergency", IAEA Safety Standards Series No. GSG-11, IAEA, Vienna (2018).

1.5.2.7 Workers shall be appropriately trained in the radiation hazards involved and the precautions to be observed in order to ensure restriction of their exposure and that of other persons who might be affected by their actions.

1.5.3 Management system

1.5.3.1 A management system based on international, national or other standards acceptable to the competent authority shall be established and implemented for all activities within the scope of these Regulations, as identified in 1.5.1.3, to ensure compliance with the relevant provisions of these Regulations. Certification that the design specification has been fully implemented shall be available to the competent authority. The manufacturer, consignor or user shall be prepared:

(a) To provide facilities for inspection during manufacture and use; and

(b) To demonstrate compliance with these Regulations to the competent authority.

Where competent authority approval is required, such approval shall take into account and be contingent upon the adequacy of the management system.

1.5.4 Special arrangement

1.5.4.1 Special arrangement shall mean those provisions, approved by the competent authority, under which consignments which do not satisfy all the requirements of these Regulations applicable to radioactive material may be transported.

1.5.4.2 Consignments for which conformity with any provision applicable to radioactive material is impracticable shall not be transported except under special arrangement. Provided the competent authority is satisfied that conformity with the radioactive material provisions of these Regulations is impracticable and that the requisite standards of safety established by these Regulations have been demonstrated through means alternative to the other provisions of these Regulations, the competent authority may approve special arrangement transport operations for a single consignment or a planned series of multiple consignments. The overall level of safety in transport shall be at least equivalent to that which would be provided if all the applicable requirements in these Regulations had been met. For international consignments of this type, multilateral approval shall be required.

1.5.5 Radioactive material possessing other dangerous properties

1.5.5.1 In addition to the radioactive and fissile properties, any subsidiary hazard of the contents of a package, such as explosiveness, flammability, pyrophoricity, chemical toxicity and corrosiveness, shall also be taken into account in the documentation, packing, labelling, marking, placarding, stowage, segregation and transport, in order to be in compliance with all relevant provisions for dangerous goods of these regulations.

1.5.6 Non-compliance

1.5.6.1 In the event of non-compliance with any limit in these Regulations applicable to dose rate or contamination:

(a) The consignor, carrier, consignee and any organization involved during transport, who may be affected, as appropriate, shall be informed of the non-compliance:

(i) by the carrier if the non-compliance is identified during transport; or

(ii) by the consignee if the non-compliance is identified at receipt;

(b) The consignor, carrier or consignee, as appropriate, shall:

(i) take immediate steps to mitigate the consequences of the non-compliance;

(ii) investigate the non-compliance and its causes, circumstances and consequences;

(iii) take appropriate action to remedy the causes and circumstances that led to the non-compliance and to prevent a recurrence of the causes and circumstances similar to those that led to the non-compliance; and

(iv) communicate to the relevant competent authority(ies) on the causes of the non-compliance and the corrective or preventive actions taken or to be taken;

(c) The communication of the non-compliance to the consignor and relevant competent authority(ies), respectively, shall be made as soon as practicable and it shall be immediate whenever an emergency exposure situation has developed or is developing.

PART 2

CLASSIFICATION

CHAPTER 2.0

INTRODUCTION

2.0.0 Responsibilities

2.0.0.1 The classification shall be made by the appropriate competent authority when so required or may otherwise be made by the consignor.

2.0.0.2 A consignor who has identified, on the basis of test data, that a substance listed by name in column 2 of the Dangerous Goods List in chapter 3.2 meets classification criteria for a hazard class or division that is not identified in the list, may, with the approval of the competent authority, consign the substance:

(a) Under the most appropriate generic or not otherwise specified (N.O.S.) entry reflecting all hazards; or

(b) Under the same UN number and name but with additional hazard communication information as appropriate to reflect the additional subsidiary hazard(s) (documentation, label, placard) provided that the primary hazard class remains unchanged and that any other transport conditions (e.g. limited quantity, packaging and tank provisions) that would normally apply to substances possessing such a combination of hazards are the same as those applicable to the substance listed.

NOTE: *When a competent authority grants such approvals, it should inform the United Nations Sub-Committee of Experts on the Transport of Dangerous Goods accordingly and submit a relevant proposal of amendment to the Dangerous Goods List. Should the proposed amendment be rejected, the competent authority should withdraw its approval.*

2.0.1 Classes, divisions, packing groups

2.0.1.1 *Definitions*

Substances (including mixtures and solutions) and articles subject to these Regulations are assigned to one of nine classes according to the hazard or the most predominant of the hazards they present. Some of these classes are subdivided into divisions. These classes and divisions are:

Class 1: Explosives

- Division 1.1: Substances and articles which have a mass explosion hazard
- Division 1.2: Substances and articles which have a projection hazard but not a mass explosion hazard
- Division 1.3: Substances and articles which have a fire hazard and either a minor blast hazard or a minor projection hazard or both, but not a mass explosion hazard
- Division 1.4: Substances and articles which present no significant hazard
- Division 1.5: Very insensitive substances which have a mass explosion hazard
- Division 1.6: Extremely insensitive articles which do not have a mass explosion hazard

Class 2: Gases

- Division 2.1: Flammable gases

Division 2.2: Non-flammable, non-toxic gases

Division 2.3: Toxic gases

Class 3: Flammable liquids

Class 4: Flammable solids; substances liable to spontaneous combustion; substances which, in contact with water, emit flammable gases

Division 4.1: Flammable solids, self-reactive substances, solid desensitized explosives and polymerizing substances

Division 4.2: Substances liable to spontaneous combustion

Division 4.3: Substances which in contact with water emit flammable gases

Class 5: Oxidizing substances and organic peroxides

Division 5.1: Oxidizing substances

Division 5.2: Organic peroxides

Class 6: Toxic and infectious substances

Division 6.1: Toxic substances

Division 6.2: Infectious substances

Class 7: Radioactive material

Class 8: Corrosive substances

Class 9: Miscellaneous dangerous substances and articles, including environmentally hazardous substances

The numerical order of the classes and divisions is not that of the degree of danger.

2.0.1.2 Many of the substances assigned to Classes 1 to 9 are deemed, without additional labelling, as being environmentally hazardous.

2.0.1.2.1 Wastes shall be transported under the requirements of the appropriate class considering their hazards and the criteria in these Regulations.

Wastes not otherwise subject to these Regulations but covered under the Basel Convention[1] may be transported under Class 9.

2.0.1.3 For packing purposes, substances other than those of Classes 1, 2 and 7, divisions 5.2 and 6.2 and other than self-reactive substances of Division 4.1 are assigned to three packing groups in accordance with the degree of danger they present:

Packing group I: Substances presenting high danger;
Packing group II: Substances presenting medium danger; and
Packing group III: Substances presenting low danger.

The packing group to which a substance is assigned is indicated in the Dangerous Goods List in chapter 3.2.

---

[1] *Basel Convention on the Control of Transboundary Movements of Hazardous Wastes and their Disposal (1989).*

Articles are not assigned to packing groups. For packing purposes any requirement for a specific packaging performance level is set out in the applicable packing instruction.

2.0.1.4 Dangerous goods are determined to present one or more of the dangers represented by Classes 1 to 9 and divisions and, if applicable, the degree of danger on the basis of the requirements in chapters 2.1 to 2.9.

2.0.1.5 Dangerous goods presenting a danger of a single class and division are assigned to that class and division and the degree of danger (packing group), if applicable, determined. When an article or substance is specifically listed by name in the Dangerous Goods List in chapter 3.2, its class or division, its subsidiary hazard(s) and, when applicable, its packing group are taken from this list.

2.0.1.6 Dangerous goods meeting the defining criteria of more than one hazard class or division and which are not listed by name in the Dangerous Goods List, are assigned to a class and division and subsidiary hazards(s) on the basis of the precedence of hazards in 2.0.3.

2.0.2   UN numbers and proper shipping names

2.0.2.1 Dangerous goods are assigned to UN numbers and proper shipping names according to their hazard classification and their composition.

2.0.2.2 Dangerous goods commonly carried are listed in the Dangerous Goods List in chapter 3.2. Where an article or substance is specifically listed by name, it shall be identified in transport by the proper shipping name in the Dangerous Goods List. Such substances may contain technical impurities (for example those deriving from the production process) or additives for stability or other purposes that do not affect their classification. However, a substance listed by name containing technical impurities or additives for stability or other purposes affecting its classification shall be considered a mixture or solution (see 2.0.2.5). For dangerous goods not specifically listed by name, "generic" or "not otherwise specified" entries are provided (see 2.0.2.7) to identify the article or substance in transport. The substances listed by name in column (2) of the Dangerous Goods List of chapter 3.2 shall be transported according to their classification in the list or under the conditions specified in 2.0.0.2.

Each entry in the Dangerous Goods List is characterized by a UN number. This list also contains relevant information for each entry, such as hazard class, subsidiary hazard(s) (if any), packing group (where assigned), packing and tank transport requirements, etc. Entries in the Dangerous Goods List are of the following four types:

(a) Single entries for well-defined substances or articles e.g.

   1090 ACETONE
   1194 ETHYL NITRITE SOLUTION;

(b) Generic entries for a well-defined group of substances or articles e.g.

   1133 ADHESIVES
   1266 PERFUMERY PRODUCT
   2757 CARBAMATE PESTICIDE, SOLID, TOXIC
   3101 ORGANIC PEROXIDE, TYPE B, LIQUID;

(c) Specific n.o.s. entries covering a group of substances or articles of a particular chemical or technical nature e.g.

   1477 NITRATES, INORGANIC, N.O.S.
   1987 ALCOHOLS, N.O.S.;

(d) General n.o.s. entries covering a group of substances or articles meeting the criteria of one or more classes or divisions e.g.

1325 FLAMMABLE SOLID, ORGANIC, N.O.S.
1993 FLAMMABLE LIQUID, N.O.S.

2.0.2.3　　All self-reactive substances of Division 4.1 are assigned to one of twenty generic entries in accordance with the classification principles and flow chart described in 2.4.2.3.3 and figure 2.4.1.

2.0.2.4　　All organic peroxides of Division 5.2 are assigned to one of twenty generic entries in accordance with the classification principles and flow chart described in 2.5.3.3 and figure 2.5.1.

2.0.2.5　　A mixture or solution meeting the classification criteria of these Regulations composed of a single predominant substance identified by name in the Dangerous Goods List and one or more substances not subject to these Regulations and/or traces of one or more substances identified by name in the Dangerous Goods List, shall be assigned the UN number and proper shipping name of the predominant substance named in the Dangerous Goods List unless:

(a) The mixture or solution is identified by name in the Dangerous Goods List;

(b) The name and description of the substance named in the Dangerous Goods List specifically indicate that they apply only to the pure substance;

(c) The hazard class or division, subsidiary hazard(s), packing group, or physical state of the mixture or solution is different from that of the substance named in the Dangerous Goods List; or

(d) The hazard characteristics and properties of the mixture or solution necessitate emergency response measures that are different from those required for the substance identified by name in the Dangerous Goods List.

In those other cases, except the one described in (a), the mixture or solution shall be treated as a dangerous substance not specifically listed by name in the Dangerous Goods List.

2.0.2.6　　For a solution or mixture when the hazard class, the physical state or the packing group is changed in comparison with the listed substance, the appropriate N.O.S. entry shall be used including its packaging and labelling provisions.

2.0.2.7　　A mixture or solution containing one or more substances identified by name in these Regulations or classified under a N.O.S. entry and one or more substances is not subject to these Regulations if the hazard characteristics of the mixture or solution are such that they do not meet the criteria (including human experience criteria) for any class.

2.0.2.8　　Substances or articles which are not specifically listed by name in the Dangerous Goods List shall be classified under a "generic" or "not otherwise specified" ("N.O.S.") entry. The substance or article shall be classified according to the class definitions and test criteria in this part, and the article or substance classified under the generic or "N.O.S." entry in the Dangerous Goods List which most appropriately describes the article or substance[2]. This means that a substance is only to be assigned to an entry of type c), as defined in 2.0.2.2, if it cannot be assigned to an entry of type b), and to an entry of type d) if it cannot be assigned to an entry of type b) or c)[2].

2.0.2.9　　A mixture or solution meeting the classification criteria of these Regulations that is not identified by name in the Dangerous Goods List and that is composed of two or more dangerous goods shall be assigned to an entry that has the proper shipping name, description, hazard class or division, subsidiary hazard(s) and packing group that most precisely describe the mixture or solution.

---

[2] *See also the "List of generic or n.o.s. proper shipping names" in appendix A.*

2.0.3 Precedence of hazard characteristics

2.0.3.1 The table below shall be used to determine the class of a substance, mixture or solution having more than one hazard, when it is not named in the Dangerous Goods List in chapter 3.2 or to assign the appropriate entry for articles containing dangerous goods N.O.S. (UN Nos. 3537 to 3548, see 2.0.5). For goods having multiple hazards which are not specifically listed by name in the Dangerous Goods List, the most stringent packing group denoted to the respective hazards of the goods takes precedence over other packing groups, irrespective of the precedence of hazard table in this chapter. The precedence of hazard characteristics of the following has not been dealt with in the Precedence of hazards table in 2.0.3.3, as these primary characteristics always take precedence:

(a) Substances and articles of Class 1;

(b) Gases of Class 2;

(c) Liquid desensitized explosives of Class 3;

(d) Self-reactive substances and solid desensitized explosives of Division 4.1;

(e) Pyrophoric substances of Division 4.2;

(f) Substances of Division 5.2;

(g) Substances of Division 6.1 with a packing group I inhalation toxicity[3]:

(h) Substances of Division 6.2;

(i) Material of Class 7.

2.0.3.2 Apart from radioactive material in excepted packages (where the other hazardous properties take precedence) radioactive material having other hazardous properties shall always be classified in Class 7 and the subsidiary hazard shall also be identified. For radioactive material in excepted packages, except for UN 3507, URANIUM HEXAFLUORIDE, RADIOACTIVE MATERIAL, EXCEPTED PACKAGE, special provision 290 of chapter 3.3 applies.

---

[3] *Except for substances or preparations meeting the criteria of Class 8 having an inhalation toxicity of dusts and mists (LC_{50}) in the range of packing group I, but toxicity through oral ingestion or dermal contact only in the range of packing group III or less, which shall be allocated to Class 8.*

2.0.3.3   Precedence of hazards

Class or Division and Packing Group	4.2	4.3	5.1 I	5.1 II	5.1 III	6.1, I Dermal	6.1, I Oral	6.1 II	6.1 III	8, I Liquid	8, I Solid	8, II Liquid	8, II Solid	8, III Liquid	8, III Solid
3 I[a]								3	3	3	–	3	–	3	–
3 II[a]							3	3	3	8	–	3	–	3	–
3 III[a]						6.1	6.1	6.1	3[b]	8	–	8	–	3	–
4.1 II[a]	4.2	4.3	5.1	4.1	4.1	6.1	6.1	4.1	4.1	–	8	–	4.1	–	4.1
4.1 III[a]	4.2	4.3	5.1	4.1	4.1	6.1	6.1	6.1	4.1	–	8	–	8	–	4.1
4.2 II		4.3	5.1	4.2	4.2	6.1	6.1	4.2	4.2	8	8	4.2	4.2	4.2	4.2
4.2 III		4.3	5.1	5.1	4.2	6.1	6.1	6.1	4.2	8	8	8	8	4.2	4.2
4.3 I			5.1	4.3	4.3	6.1	4.3	4.3	4.3	4.3	4.3	4.3	4.3	4.3	4.3
4.3 II			5.1	4.3	4.3	6.1	4.3	4.3	4.3	8	8	4.3	4.3	4.3	4.3
4.3 III			5.1	5.1	4.3	6.1	6.1	6.1	4.3	8	8	8	8	4.3	4.3
5.1 I						5.1	5.1	5.1	5.1	5.1	5.1	5.1	5.1	5.1	5.1
5.1 II						6.1	5.1	5.1	5.1	8	8	5.1	5.1	5.1	5.1
5.1 III						6.1	6.1	6.1	5.1	8	8	8	8	5.1	5.1
6.1 I Dermal										8	6.1	6.1	6.1	6.1	6.1
6.1 I Oral										8	6.1	6.1	6.1	6.1	6.1
6.1 II Inhalation										8	6.1	6.1	6.1	6.1	6.1
6.1 II Dermal										8	6.1	8	6.1	6.1	6.1
6.1 II Oral										8	8	8	6.1	6.1	6.1
6.1 III										8	8	8	8	8	8

[a]   Substances of Division 4.1 other than self-reactive substances and solid desensitized explosives and substances of Class 3 other than liquid desensitized explosives.

[b]   6.1 for pesticides.

–   Denotes an impossible combination.

For hazards not shown in this table, see 2.0.3.

2.0.4   **Transport of samples**

2.0.4.1   When the hazard class of a substance is uncertain and it is being transported for further testing, a tentative hazard class, proper shipping name and identification number shall be assigned on the basis of the consignor's knowledge of the substance and application of:

        (a)   the classification criteria of these Regulations; and

        (b)   the precedence of hazards given in 2.0.3.

The most severe packing group possible for the proper shipping name chosen shall be used.

Where this provision is used the proper shipping name shall be supplemented with the word "SAMPLE" (e.g., FLAMMABLE LIQUID, N.O.S. SAMPLE). In certain instances, where a specific proper shipping name is provided for a sample of a substance considered to meet certain classification criteria (e.g., GAS SAMPLE, NON-PRESSURIZED, FLAMMABLE, UN 3167) that proper shipping name shall be used. When an N.O.S. entry is used to transport the sample, the proper shipping name need not be supplemented with the technical name as required by special provision 274.

2.0.4.2   Samples of the substance shall be transported in accordance with the requirements applicable to the tentative assigned proper shipping name provided:

        (a)   The substance is not considered to be a substance prohibited for transport by 1.1.2;

        (b)   The substance is not considered to meet the criteria for Class 1 or considered to be an infectious substance or a radioactive material;

        (c)   The substance is in compliance with 2.4.2.3.2.4 (b) or 2.5.3.2.5.1 if it is a self-reactive substance or an organic peroxide, respectively;

        (d)   The sample is transported in a combination packaging with a net mass per package not exceeding 2.5 kg; and

        (e)   The sample is not packed together with other goods.

2.0.4.3   *Samples of energetic materials for testing purposes*

2.0.4.3.1   Samples of organic substances carrying functional groups listed in tables A6.1 and/or A6.3 in appendix 6 (Screening Procedures) of the *Manual of Tests and Criteria* may be transported under UN 3224 (self-reactive solid type C) or UN 3223 (self-reactive liquid type C), as applicable, of Division 4.1 provided that:

        (a)   The samples do not contain any:

            (i)   Known explosives;

            (ii)   Substances showing explosive effects in testing;

            (iii)   Compounds designed with the view of producing a practical explosive or pyrotechnic effect; or

            (iv)   Components consisting of synthetic precursors of intentional explosives;

        (b)   For mixtures, complexes or salts of inorganic oxidizing substances of Division 5.1 with organic material(s), the concentration of the inorganic oxidizing substance is:

            (i)   Less than 15 %, by mass, if assigned to packing group I (high hazard) or II (medium hazard); or

            (ii)   Less than 30 %, by mass, if assigned to packing group III (low hazard);

(c) Available data do not allow a more precise classification;

(d) The sample is not packed together with other goods; and

(e) The sample is packed in accordance with packing instruction P520 and special packing provisions PP94 or PP95 of 4.1.4.1, as applicable.

2.0.5 **Classification of articles as articles containing dangerous goods, N.O.S.**

NOTE: *For articles which do not have an existing proper shipping name and which contain only dangerous goods within the permitted limited quantity amounts specified in Column 7a of the Dangerous Goods List, see UN 3363 and special provision 301 of chapter 3.3.*

2.0.5.1 Articles containing dangerous goods may be classified as otherwise provided by these Regulations under the proper shipping name for the dangerous goods they contain or in accordance with this section. For the purposes of this section "article" means machinery, apparatus or other devices containing one or more dangerous goods (or residues thereof) that are an integral element of the article, necessary for its functioning and that cannot be removed for the purpose of transport. An inner packaging shall not be an article.

2.0.5.2 Such articles may in addition contain cells or batteries. Lithium cells and batteries that are integral to the article shall be of a type proven to meet the testing requirements of the *Manual of Tests and Criteria*, part III, sub-section 38.3. For articles containing pre-production prototype lithium cells or batteries transported for testing, or for articles containing lithium cells or batteries manufactured in production runs of not more than 100 cells or batteries, the requirements of special provision 310 of chapter 3.3 shall apply.

2.0.5.3 This section does not apply to articles for which a more specific proper shipping name already exists in the Dangerous Goods List of chapter 3.2.

2.0.5.4 This section does not apply to dangerous goods of Class 1, Division 6.2, Class 7 or radioactive material contained in articles. However, this section applies to articles containing explosives which are excluded from Class 1 in accordance with 2.1.3.6.4.

2.0.5.5 Articles containing dangerous goods shall be assigned to the appropriate Class or Division determined by the hazards present using, where applicable, the Precedence of Hazards table in 2.0.3.3 for each of the dangerous goods contained in the article. If dangerous goods classified as Class 9 are contained within the article, all other dangerous goods present in the article shall be considered to present a higher hazard.

2.0.5.6 Subsidiary hazards shall be representative of the primary hazard posed by the other dangerous goods contained within the article. When only one item of dangerous goods is present in the article, the subsidiary hazard(s), if any, shall be the subsidiary hazard(s) identified in column 4 of the Dangerous Goods List. If the article contains more than one item of dangerous goods and these could react dangerously with one another during transport, each of the dangerous goods shall be enclosed separately (see 4.1.1.6).

CHAPTER 2.1

CLASS 1 - EXPLOSIVES

Introductory notes

NOTE 1: *Class 1 is a restricted class, that is, only those explosive substances and articles that are listed in the Dangerous Goods List in chapter 3.2 may be accepted for transport. However, competent authorities retain the right by mutual agreement to approve transport of explosive substances and articles for special purposes under special conditions. Therefore, entries have been included in the Dangerous Goods List for "Substances, explosive, not otherwise specified" and "Articles, explosive, not otherwise specified". It is intended that these entries shall be used only when no other method of operation is possible.*

NOTE 2: *General entries such as "Explosive, blasting, Type A" are used to allow for the transport of new substances. In preparing these requirements, military ammunition and explosives have been taken into consideration to the extent that they are likely to be transported by commercial carriers.*

NOTE 3: *A number of substances and articles in Class 1 are described in appendix B. These descriptions are given because a term may not be well-known or may be at variance with its usage for regulatory purposes.*

NOTE 4: *Class 1 is unique in that the type of packaging frequently has a decisive effect on the hazard and therefore on the assignment to a particular division. The correct division is determined by use of the procedures provided in this chapter.*

2.1.1 Definitions and general provisions

2.1.1.1 Class 1 comprises:

(a) Explosive substances (a substance which is not itself an explosive but which can form an explosive atmosphere of gas, vapour or dust is not included in Class 1), except those that are too dangerous to transport or those where the predominant hazard is appropriate to another class;

(b) Explosive articles, except devices containing explosive substances in such quantity or of such a character that their inadvertent or accidental ignition or initiation during transport shall not cause any effect external to the device either by projection, fire, smoke, heat or loud noise (see 2.1.3.6); and

(c) Substances and articles not mentioned under (a) and (b) which are manufactured with a view to producing a practical explosive or pyrotechnic effect.

2.1.1.2 Transport of explosive substances which are unduly sensitive or so reactive as to be subject to spontaneous reaction is prohibited.

2.1.1.3 *Definitions*

For the purposes of these Regulations, the following definitions apply:

(a) *Explosive substance* is a solid or liquid substance (or a mixture of substances) which is in itself capable by chemical reaction of producing gas at such a temperature and pressure and at such a speed as to cause damage to the surroundings. Pyrotechnic substances are included even when they do not evolve gases;

(b) *Pyrotechnic substance* is an explosive substance designed to produce an effect by heat, light, sound, gas or smoke or a combination of these as the result of non-detonative self-sustaining exothermic chemical reactions;

(c) *Explosive article* is an article containing one or more explosive substances;

(d) *Phlegmatized* means that a substance (or "phlegmatizer") has been added to an explosive to enhance its safety in handling and transport. The phlegmatizer renders the explosive insensitive, or less sensitive, to the following actions: heat, shock, impact, percussion or friction. Typical phlegmatizing agents include, but are not limited to: wax, paper, water, polymers (such as chlorofluoropolymers), alcohol and oils (such as petroleum jelly and paraffin);

(e) *Explosive or pyrotechnic effect* means, in the context of 2.1.1.1 (c), an effect produced by self-sustaining exothermic chemical reactions including shock, blast, fragmentation, projection, heat, light, sound, gas and smoke.

2.1.1.4 *Divisions*

Class 1 is divided into six divisions as follows:

(a) Division 1.1: Substances and articles which have a mass explosion hazard (a mass explosion is one which affects almost the entire load virtually instantaneously);

(b) Division 1.2: Substances and articles which have a projection hazard but not a mass explosion hazard;

(c) Division 1.3: Substances and articles which have a fire hazard and either a minor blast hazard or a minor projection hazard or both, but not a mass explosion hazard.

This division comprises substances and articles:

(i) which give rise to considerable radiant heat; or

(ii) which burn one after another, producing minor blast or projection effects or both;

(d) Division 1.4: Substances and articles which present no significant hazard

This division comprises substances and articles which present only a small hazard in the event of ignition or initiation during transport. The effects are largely confined to the package and no projection of fragments of appreciable size or range is to be expected. An external fire shall not cause virtually instantaneous explosion of almost the entire contents of the package;

NOTE: *Substances and articles of this division are in Compatibility Group S if they are so packaged or designed that any hazardous effects arising from accidental functioning are confined within the package unless the package has been degraded by fire, in which case all blast or projection effects are limited to the extent that they do not significantly hinder fire-fighting or other emergency response efforts in the immediate vicinity of the package.*

(e) Division 1.5: Very insensitive substances which have a mass explosion hazard

This division comprises substances which have a mass explosion hazard but are so insensitive that there is very little probability of initiation or of transition from burning to detonation under normal conditions of transport;

NOTE: *The probability of transition from burning to detonation is greater when large quantities are carried in a ship.*

(f) Division 1.6: Extremely insensitive articles which do not have a mass explosion hazard

This division comprises articles which predominantly contain extremely insensitive substances and which demonstrate a negligible probability of accidental initiation or propagation.

NOTE: *The hazard from articles of Division 1.6 is limited to the explosion of a single article.*

2.1.1.5　　Any substance or article having or suspected of having explosive characteristics shall first be considered for classification in Class 1 in accordance with the procedures in 2.1.3. Goods are not classified in Class 1 when:

(a) Unless specially authorized, the transport of an explosive substance is prohibited because sensitivity of the substance is excessive;

(b) The substance or article comes within the scope of those explosive substances and articles which are specifically excluded from Class 1 by the definition of this class; or

(c) The substance or article has no explosive properties.

2.1.2　　Compatibility groups

2.1.2.1　　Goods of Class 1 are assigned to one of six divisions, depending on the type of hazard they present (see 2.1.1.4) and to one of thirteen compatibility groups which identify the kinds of explosive substances and articles that are deemed to be compatible. The tables in 2.1.2.1.1 and 2.1.2.1.2 show the scheme of classification into compatibility groups, the possible hazard divisions associated with each group and the consequential classification codes.

2.1.2.1.1   *Classification codes*

Description of substance or article to be classified	Compatibility Group	Classification Code
Primary explosive substance	A	1.1A
Article containing a primary explosive substance and not containing two or more effective protective features. Some articles, such as detonators for blasting, detonator assemblies for blasting and primers, cap-type, are included, even though they do not contain primary explosives	B	1.1B 1.2B 1.4B
Propellant explosive substance or other deflagrating explosive substance or article containing such explosive substance	C	1.1C 1.2C 1.3C 1.4C
Secondary detonating explosive substance or black powder or article containing a secondary detonating explosive substance, in each case without means of initiation and without a propelling charge, or article containing a primary explosive substance and containing two or more effective protective features	D	1.1D 1.2D 1.4D 1.5D
Article containing a secondary detonating explosive substance, without means of initiation, with a propelling charge (other than one containing a flammable liquid or gel or hypergolic liquids)	E	1.1E 1.2E 1.4E
Article containing a secondary detonating explosive substance with its own means of initiation, with a propelling charge (other than one containing a flammable liquid or gel or hypergolic liquids) or without a propelling charge	F	1.1F 1.2F 1.3F 1.4F
Pyrotechnic substance, or article containing a pyrotechnic substance, or article containing both an explosive substance and an illuminating, incendiary, tear- or smoke-producing substance (other than a water-activated article or one containing white phosphorus, phosphides, a pyrophoric substance, a flammable liquid or gel, or hypergolic liquids)	G	1.1G 1.2G 1.3G 1.4G
Article containing both an explosive substance and white phosphorus	H	1.2H 1.3H
Article containing both an explosive substance and a flammable liquid or gel	J	1.1J 1.2J 1.3J
Article containing both an explosive substance and a toxic chemical agent	K	1.2K 1.3K
Explosive substance or article containing an explosive substance and presenting a special hazard (e.g. due to water-activation or presence of hypergolic liquids, phosphides or a pyrophoric substance) and needing isolation of each type (see 7.1.3.1.5)	L	1.1L 1.2L 1.3L
Articles predominantly containing extremely insensitive substances	N	1.6N
Substance or article so packed or designed that any hazardous effects arising from accidental functioning are confined within the package unless the package has been degraded by fire, in which case all blast or projection effects are limited to the extent that they do not significantly hinder or prohibit fire fighting or other emergency response efforts in the immediate vicinity of the package	S	1.4S

NOTE 1: *Articles of compatibility groups D and E may be fitted or packed together with their own means of initiation provided that such means have at least two effective protective features designed to prevent an explosion in the event of accidental functioning of the means of initiation. Such articles and packages shall be assigned to compatibility groups D or E.*

NOTE 2: *Articles of compatibility groups D and E may be packed together with their own means of initiation, which do not have two effective protective features when, in the opinion of the competent authority of the country of origin, the accidental functioning of the means of initiation does not cause the explosion of an article under normal conditions of transport. Such packages shall be assigned to compatibility groups D or E.*

2.1.2.1.2 *Scheme of classification of explosives, combination of hazard division with compatibility group*

Hazard Division	Compatibility Group												
	A	B	C	D	E	F	G	H	J	K	L	N	S	A-S Σ
1.1	1.1A	1.1B	1.1C	1.1D	1.1E	1.1F	1.1G		1.1J		1.1L			9
1.2		1.2B	1.2C	1.2D	1.2E	1.2F	1.2G	1.2H	1.2J	1.2K	1.2L			10
1.3			1.3C			1.3F	1.3G	1.3H	1.3J	1.3K	1.3L			7
1.4		1.4B	1.4C	1.4D	1.4E	1.4F	1.4G						1.4S	7
1.5				1.5D										1
1.6												1.6N		1
1.1-1.6 Σ	1	3	4	4	3	4	4	2	3	2	3	1	1	35

2.1.2.2 The definitions of compatibility groups in 2.1.2.1.1 are intended to be mutually exclusive, except for a substance or article which qualifies for Compatibility Group S. Since the criterion of Compatibility Group S is an empirical one, assignment to this group is necessarily linked to the tests for assignment to Division 1.4.

2.1.3 **Classification procedure**

2.1.3.1 *General*

2.1.3.1.1 Any substance or article having or suspected of having explosives characteristics shall be considered for classification in Class 1. Substances and articles classified in Class 1 shall be assigned to the appropriate division and compatibility group.

2.1.3.1.2 Except for substances which are listed by their proper shipping name in the Dangerous Goods List in chapter 3.2, goods shall not be offered for transport as Class 1 until they have been subjected to the classification procedure prescribed in this section. In addition, the classification procedure shall be undertaken before a new product is offered for transport. In this context a new product is one which, in the opinion of the competent authority, involves any of the following:

(a) A new explosive substance or a combination or a mixture of explosive substances which is considered to be significantly different from other combinations or mixtures already classified;

(b) A new design of article or an article containing a new explosive substance or a new combination or mixture of explosive substances;

(c) A new design of package for an explosive substance or article including a new type of inner packaging;

> ***NOTE:*** *The importance of this can be overlooked unless it is realized that a relatively minor change in an inner or outer packaging can be critical and can convert a lesser hazard into a mass explosion hazard.*

2.1.3.1.3　　The producer or other applicant for classification of a product shall provide adequate information concerning the names and characteristics of all explosive substances in the product and shall furnish the results of all relevant tests which have been done. It is assumed that all the explosive substances in a new article have been properly tested and then approved.

2.1.3.1.4　　A report on the series of tests shall be drawn up in accordance with the requirements of the competent authority. It shall in particular contain information on:

　　(a)　　The composition of the substance or the structure of the article;

　　(b)　　The quantity of substance or number of articles per test;

　　(c)　　The type and construction of the packaging;

　　(d)　　The test assembly, including in particular the nature, quantity and arrangement of the means of initiation or ignition used;

　　(e)　　The course of the test, including in particular the time elapsing until the occurrence of the first noteworthy reaction of the substance or article, the duration and characteristics of the reaction, and an estimate of the latter's completeness;

　　(f)　　The effect of the reaction on the immediate surroundings (up to 25 m from the site of the test);

　　(g)　　The effect of the reaction on the more remote surroundings (more than 25 m from the site of the test); and

　　(h)　　The atmospheric conditions during the test.

2.1.3.1.5　　Verification of the classification shall be undertaken if the substance or article or its packaging is degraded and the degradation might affect the behaviour of the item in the tests.

2.1.3.2　　*Procedure*

2.1.3.2.1　　Figure 2.1.1 indicates the general scheme for classifying a substance or article which is to be considered for inclusion in Class 1. The assessment is in two stages. First, the potential of a substance or article to explode must be ascertained and its stability and sensitivity, both chemical and physical, must be shown to be acceptable. In order to promote uniform assessments by competent authorities, it is recommended that data from suitable tests be analyzed systematically with respect to the appropriate test criteria using the flow chart of figure 10.2 in part I of the *Manual of Tests and Criteria*. If the substance or article is acceptable for Class 1 it is then necessary to proceed to the second stage, to assign the correct hazard division by the flow chart of figure 10.3 in the same publication.

2.1.3.2.2　　The tests for acceptance and the further tests to determine the correct division in Class 1 are conveniently grouped into seven series as listed in part I of the *Manual of Tests and Criteria*. The numbering of these series relates to the sequence of assessing results rather than the order in which the tests are conducted.

2.1.3.2.3　　*Scheme of procedure for classifying a substance or article*

NOTE 1: *The competent authority which prescribes the definitive test method corresponding to each of the Test Types should specify the appropriate test criteria. Where there is international agreement on test criteria, the details are given in the publication referred to above describing the seven series of tests.*

NOTE 2: *The scheme of assessment is only designed for the classification of packaged substances and articles and for individual unpacked articles. Transport in freight containers, road vehicles and rail wagons* *may require special tests which take into consideration the quantity (self-confinement) and kind of substance and the container for the substance. Such tests may be specified by the competent authorities.*

NOTE 3: *Since there will be borderline cases with any scheme of testing there should be an ultimate authority who will make the final decision. Such a decision may not receive international acceptance and may therefore be valid only in the country where it is made. The United Nations Committee of Experts on the Transport of Dangerous Goods provides a forum for the discussion of borderline cases. Where international recognition is sought for a classification, the competent authority should submit full details of all tests made including the nature of any variations introduced.*

Figure 2.1.1: Scheme of procedure for classifying a substance or article

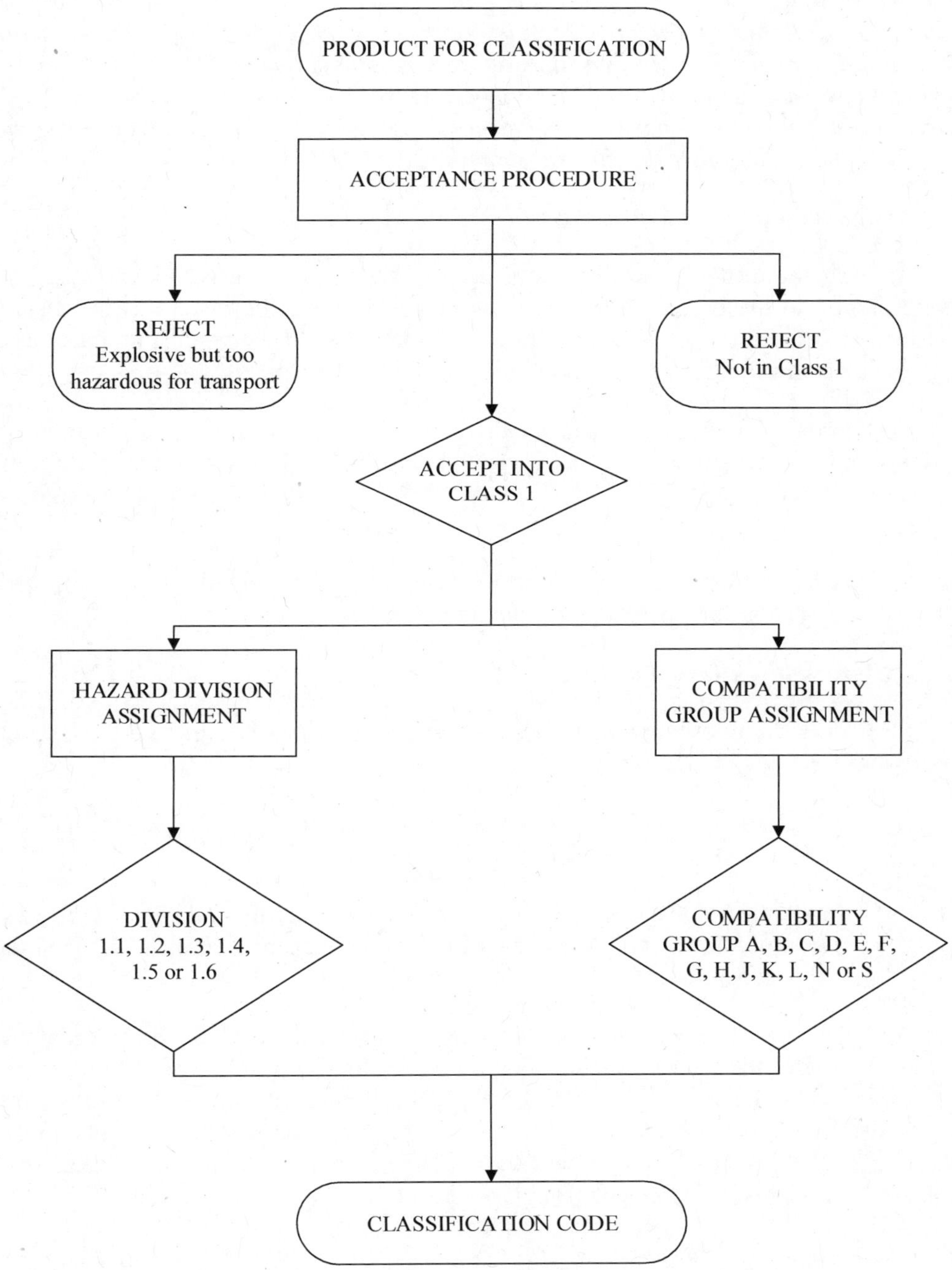

```
           PRODUCT FOR CLASSIFICATION
                      │
                      ▼
            ACCEPTANCE PROCEDURE
                      │
        ┌─────────────┼─────────────┐
        ▼             ▼             ▼
     REJECT       ACCEPT INTO     REJECT
  Explosive but    CLASS 1      Not in Class 1
  too hazardous
  for transport
                      │
        ┌─────────────┴─────────────┐
        ▼                           ▼
   HAZARD DIVISION            COMPATIBILITY
    ASSIGNMENT              GROUP ASSIGNMENT
        │                           │
        ▼                           ▼
     DIVISION                  COMPATIBILITY
  1.1, 1.2, 1.3, 1.4,         GROUP A, B, C, D, E, F,
     1.5 or 1.6                G, H, J, K, L, N or S
        │                           │
        └─────────────┬─────────────┘
                      ▼
             CLASSIFICATION CODE
```

2.1.3.3 *Acceptance procedure*

2.1.3.3.1   The results from preliminary tests and those from test series 1 to 4 are used to determine whether or not the product is acceptable for Class 1. If the substance is manufactured with a view to producing a practical explosive or pyrotechnic effect, it is unnecessary to conduct test series 1 and 2. If an article, a packaged article or a packaged substance is rejected by test series 3 and/or 4 it may be practicable to redesign the article or the packaging to render it acceptable.

NOTE: Some devices may function accidentally during transport. Theoretical analysis, test data or other evidence of safety should be provided to establish that such an event is very unlikely or that the consequences would not be significant. The assessment should take account of vibration related to the proposed modes of transport, static electricity, electromagnetic radiation at all relevant frequencies (maximum intensity 100 $W·m^{-2}$), adverse climatic conditions and compatibility of explosive substances with glues, paints and packaging materials with which they may come in contact. All articles containing primary explosive substances should be assessed to evaluate the risk and consequences of accidental functioning during transport. The reliability of fuzes should be assessed taking account of the number of independent safety features. All articles and packaged substances should be assessed to ensure they have been designed in a good workmanlike manner (e.g. there is no possibility of formation of voids or thin films of explosive substance, and no possibility of grinding or nipping explosive substances between hard surfaces).

2.1.3.4 *Assignment to hazard divisions*

2.1.3.4.1   Assessment of the hazard division is usually made on the basis of test results. A substance or article shall be assigned to the hazard division which corresponds to the results of the tests to which the substance or article, as offered for transport, has been subjected. Other test results, and data assembled from accidents which have occurred, may also be taken into account.

2.1.3.4.2   Test series 5, 6 and 7 are used for the determination of the hazard division. Test series 5 is used to determine whether a substance can be assigned to Division 1.5. Test series 6 is used for the assignment of substances and articles to Divisions 1.1, 1.2, 1.3 and 1.4. Test series 7 is used for the assignment of articles to Division 1.6.

2.1.3.4.3   In the case of Compatibility Group S the tests may be waived by the competent authority if classification by analogy is possible using test results for a comparable article.

2.1.3.5 *Assignment of fireworks to hazard divisions*

2.1.3.5.1   Fireworks shall normally be assigned to hazard divisions 1.1, 1.2, 1.3, and 1.4 on the basis of test data derived from test series 6. However:

(a) waterfalls containing flash composition (see note 2 of 2.1.3.5.5) shall be classified as 1.1G regardless of the results of test series 6;

(b) since the range of fireworks is very extensive and the availability of test facilities may be limited, assignment to hazard divisions may also be made in accordance with the procedure in 2.1.3.5.2.

2.1.3.5.2   Assignment of fireworks to UN Nos. 0333, 0334, 0335 or 0336, and assignment of articles to UN 0431 for those used for theatrical effects meeting the definition for article type and the 1.4G specification in the default fireworks classification table in 2.1.3.5.5 may be made on the basis of analogy, without the need for test series 6 testing, in accordance with the default fireworks classification table in 2.1.3.5.5. Such assignment shall be made with the agreement of the competent authority. Items not specified in the table shall be classified on the basis of test data derived from test series 6.

NOTE 1:   The addition of other types of fireworks to Column 1 of the table in 2.1.3.5.5 should only be made on the basis of full test data submitted to the UN Sub-Committee on the Transport of Dangerous Goods for consideration.

NOTE 2: Test data derived by competent authorities which validates, or contradicts the assignment of fireworks specified in Column 4 of the table in 2.1.3.5.5 to hazard divisions in Column 5 should be submitted to the UN Sub-Committee on the Transport of Dangerous Goods for information (see also note 3 in 2.1.3.2.3).

2.1.3.5.3 Where fireworks of more than one hazard division are packed in the same package they shall be classified on the basis of the highest hazard division unless test data derived from test series 6 indicate otherwise.

2.1.3.5.4 The classification shown in the table in 2.1.3.5.5 applies only for articles packed in fibreboard boxes (4G).

2.1.3.5.5 *Default fireworks classification table[1]*

NOTE 1: *References to percentages in the table, unless otherwise stated, are to the mass of all pyrotechnic substances (e.g. rocket motors, lifting charge, bursting charge and effect charge).*

NOTE 2: *"Flash composition" in this table refers to pyrotechnic substances in powder form or as pyrotechnic units as presented in the fireworks that are used in waterfalls, or to produce an aural effect or used as a bursting charge, or propellant charge unless:*

(a) *The time taken for the pressure rise in the HSL Flash Composition Test in appendix 7 of the "Manual of Tests and Criteria" is demonstrated to be more than 6 ms for 0.5 g of pyrotechnic substance; or*

(b) *The pyrotechnic substance gives a negative "-" result in the US Flash Composition Test in appendix 7 of the "Manual of Tests and Criteria".*

NOTE 3: *Dimensions in mm refer to:*

(a) *for spherical and peanut shells, the diameter of the sphere of the shell;*

(b) *for cylinder shells, the length of the shell;*

(c) *for a shell in mortar, Roman candle, shot tube firework or mine, the inside diameter of the tube comprising or containing the firework;*

(d) *for a bag mine or cylinder mine, the inside diameter of the mortar intended to contain the mine.*

---

[1] *This table contains a list of firework classifications that may be used in the absence of test series 6 data (see 2.1.3.5.2).*

Type	Includes: / Synonym:	Definition	Specification	Classification
Shell, spherical or cylindrical	spherical display shell: aerial shell, colour shell, dye shell, multi-break shell, multi-effect shell, nautical shell, parachute shell, smoke shell, star shell; report shell: maroon, salute, sound shell, thunderclap, aerial shell kit	device with or without propellant charge, with delay fuse and bursting charge, pyrotechnic unit(s) or loose pyrotechnic substance and designed to be projected from a mortar	all report shells	1.1G
			colour shell: ≥ 180 mm	1.1G
			colour shell: < 180 mm with > 25 % flash composition, as loose powder and/ or report effects	1.1G
			colour shell: < 180 mm with ≤ 25 % flash composition, as loose powder and/ or report effects	1.3G
			colour shell: ≤ 50 mm, or ≤ 60 g pyrotechnic substance, with ≤ 2 % flash composition as loose powder and/ or report effects	1.4G
	peanut shell	device with two or more spherical aerial shells in a common wrapper propelled by the same propellant charge with separate external delay fuses	the most hazardous spherical aerial shell determines the classification	
	preloaded mortar, shell in mortar	assembly comprising a spherical or cylindrical shell inside a mortar from which the shell is designed to be projected	all report shells	1.1G
			colour shell: ≥ 180 mm	1.1G
			colour shell: > 25 % flash composition as loose powder and/ or report effects	1.1G
			colour shell: > 50 mm and < 180 mm	1.2G
			Colour shell: ≤ 50 mm, or ≤ 60 g pyrotechnic substance, with ≤ 25 % flash composition as loose powder and/ or report effects	1.3G

Type	Includes: / Synonym:	Definition	Specification	Classification
Shell, spherical or cylindrical *(cont'd)*	shell of shells (spherical) (Reference to percentages for shell of shells are to the gross mass of the fireworks article)	device without propellant charge, with delay fuse and bursting charge, containing report shells and inert materials and designed to be projected from a mortar	> 120 mm	1.1G
		device without propellant charge, with delay fuse and bursting charge, containing report shells ≤ 25g flash composition per report unit, with ≤ 33 % flash composition and ≥ 60 % inert materials and designed to be projected from a mortar	≤ 120 mm	1.3G
		device without propellant charge, with delay fuse and bursting charge, containing colour shells and/or pyrotechnic units and designed to be projected from a mortar	> 300 mm	1.1G
		device without propellant charge, with delay fuse and bursting charge, containing colour shells ≤ 70mm and/or pyrotechnic units, with ≤ 25 % flash composition and ≤ 60 % pyrotechnic substance and designed to be projected from a mortar	> 200 mm and ≤ 300 mm	1.3G
		device with propellant charge, with delay fuse and bursting charge, containing colour shells ≤ 70 mm and/or pyrotechnic units, with ≤ 25 % flash composition and ≤ 60 % pyrotechnic substance and designed to be projected from a mortar	≤ 200 mm	1.3G
Battery/ combination	barrage, bombardos, cakes, finale box, flowerbed, hybrid, multiple tubes, shell cakes, banger batteries, flash banger batteries	assembly including several elements either containing the same type or several types each corresponding to one of the types of fireworks listed in this table, with one or two points of ignition	the most hazardous firework type determines the classification	

Type	Includes: / Synonym:	Definition	Specification	Classification
Roman candle	exhibition candle, candle, bombettes	tube containing a series of pyrotechnic units consisting of alternate pyrotechnic substance, propellant charge, and transmitting fuse	≥ 50 mm inner diameter, containing flash composition, or < 50 mm with >25 % flash composition	1.1G
			≥ 50 mm inner diameter, containing no flash composition	1.2G
			< 50 mm inner diameter and ≤ 25 % flash composition	1.3G
			≤ 30 mm. inner diameter, each pyrotechnic unit ≤ 25 g and ≤ 5 % flash composition	1.4G
Shot tube	single shot Roman candle, small preloaded mortar	tube containing a pyrotechnic unit consisting of pyrotechnic substance, propellant charge with or without transmitting fuse	≤ 30 mm inner diameter and pyrotechnic unit > 25 g, or > 5 % and ≤ 25 % flash composition	1.3G
			≤ 30 mm inner diameter, pyrotechnic unit ≤ 25 g and ≤ 5 % flash composition	1.4G
Rocket	avalanche rocket, signal rocket, whistling rocket, bottle rocket, sky rocket, missile type rocket, table rocket	tube containing pyrotechnic substance and/or pyrotechnic units, equipped with stick(s) or other means for stabilization of flight, and designed to be propelled into the air	Flash composition effects only	1.1G
			Flash composition > 25 % of the pyrotechnic substance	1.1G
			> 20 g pyrotechnic substance and flash composition ≤ 25 %	1.3G
			≤ 20 g pyrotechnic substance, black powder bursting charge and ≤ 0.13 g flash composition per report and ≤ 1 g in total	1.4G
Mine	pot-a-feu, ground mine, bag mine, cylinder mine	tube containing propellant charge and pyrotechnic units and designed to be placed on the ground or to be fixed in the ground. The principal effect is ejection of all the pyrotechnic units in a single burst producing a widely dispersed visual and/or aural effect in the air; or cloth or paper bag or cloth or paper cylinder containing propellant charge and pyrotechnic units, designed to be placed in a mortar and to function as a mine	> 25 % flash composition, as loose powder and/ or report effects	1.1G
			≥ 180mm and ≤ 25 % flash composition, as loose powder and/ or report effects	1.1G
			< 180mm and ≤ 25 % flash composition, as loose powder and/ or report effects	1.3G
			≤ 150g pyrotechnic substance, containing ≤ 5 % flash composition as loose powder and/ or report effects. Each pyrotechnic unit ≤ 25 g, each report effect < 2g ; each whistle, if any, ≤ 3 g	1.4G

Type	Includes: / Synonym:	Definition	Specification	Classification
Fountain	volcanos, gerbs, lances, Bengal fire, flitter sparkle, cylindrical fountains, cone fountains, illuminating torch	non-metallic case containing pressed or consolidated sparks and flame producing pyrotechnic substance **NOTE:** *Fountains intended to produce a vertical cascade or curtain of sparks are considered to be waterfalls (see row below).*	≥ 1 kg pyrotechnic substance	1.3G
			< 1 kg pyrotechnic substance	1.4G
Waterfall	cascades, showers	pyrotechnic fountain intended to produce a vertical cascade or curtain of sparks	containing flash composition regardless of the results of test series 6 (see 2.1.3.5.1 (a))	1.1G
			not containing flash composition	1.3G
Sparkler	handheld sparklers, non-handheld sparklers, wire sparklers	rigid wire partially coated (along one end) with slow burning pyrotechnic substance with or without an ignition tip	perchlorate based sparklers: > 5 g per item or > 10 items per pack	1.3G
			perchlorate based sparklers: ≤ 5 g per item and ≤ 10 items per pack; nitrate based sparklers: ≤ 30 g per item	1.4G
Bengal stick	Dipped stick	non-metallic stick partially coated (along one end) with slow-burning pyrotechnic substance and designed to be held in the hand	perchlorate based items: > 5 g per item or > 10 items per pack	1.3 G
			perchlorate based items: ≤ 5 g per item and ≤ 10 items per pack; nitrate based items: ≤ 30 g per item	1.4G
Low hazard fireworks and novelties	table bombs, throwdowns, crackling granules, smokes, fog, snakes, glow worm, serpents, snaps, party poppers	device designed to produce very limited visible and/ or audible effect which contains small amounts of pyrotechnic and/or explosive substance	Throwdowns and snaps may contain up to 1.6 mg of silver fulminate; snaps and party poppers may contain up to 16 mg of potassium chlorate/ red phosphorous mixture; other articles may contain up to 5 g of pyrotechnic substance, but no flash composition	1.4G
Spinner	aerial spinner, helicopter, chaser, ground spinner	non-metallic tube or tubes containing gas- or spark-producing pyrotechnic substance, with or without noise producing composition, with or without aerofoils attached	pyrotechnic substance per item > 20 g, containing ≤ 3 % flash composition as report effects, or whistle composition ≤ 5 g	1.3G
			pyrotechnic substance per item ≤ 20 g, containing ≤ 3 % flash composition as report effects, or whistle composition ≤ 5 g	1.4G

Type	Includes: / Synonym:	Definition	Specification	Classification
Wheels	Catherine wheels, Saxon	assembly including drivers containing pyrotechnic substance and provided with a means of attaching it to a support so that it can rotate	≥ 1 kg total pyrotechnic substance, no report effect, each whistle (if any) ≤ 25 g and ≤ 50 g whistle composition per wheel	1.3G
			< 1 kg total pyrotechnic substance, no report effect, each whistle (if any) ≤ 5 g and ≤ 10 g whistle composition per wheel	1.4G
Aerial wheel	flying Saxon, UFO's, rising crown	tubes containing propellant charges and sparks- flame- and/ or noise producing pyrotechnic substances, the tubes being fixed to a supporting ring	> 200 g total pyrotechnic substance or > 60 g pyrotechnic substance per driver, ≤ 3 % flash composition as report effects, each whistle (if any) ≤ 25 g and ≤ 50 g whistle composition per wheel	1.3G
			≤ 200 g total pyrotechnic substance and ≤ 60 g pyrotechnic substance per driver, ≤ 3 % flash composition as report effects, each whistle (if any) ≤ 5 g and ≤ 10 g whistle composition per wheel	1.4G
Selection pack	display selection box, display selection pack, garden selection box, indoor selection box; assortment	A pack of more than one type each corresponding to one of the types of fireworks listed in this table	The most hazardous firework type determines the classification	
Firecracker	Celebration cracker, celebration roll, string cracker	Assembly of tubes (paper or cardboard) linked by a pyrotechnic fuse, each tube intended to produce an aural effect	each tube ≤ 140 mg of flash composition or ≤ 1 g black powder	1.4G
Banger	Salute, flash banger, lady cracker	Non-metallic tube containing report composition intended to produce an aural effect	> 2 g flash composition per item	1.1G
			≤ 2 g flash composition per item and ≤ 10 g per inner packaging	1.3G
			≤ 1 g flash composition per item and ≤ 10 g per inner packaging or ≤ 10 g black powder per item	1.4G

2.1.3.6 *Exclusion from Class 1*

2.1.3.6.1   The competent authority may exclude an article or substance from Class 1 by virtue of test results and the Class 1 definition.

2.1.3.6.2   Where a substance provisionally accepted into Class 1 is excluded from Class 1 by performing test series 6 on a specific type and size of package, this substance, when meeting the classification criteria or definition for another class or division, should be listed in the Dangerous Goods List of chapter 3.2 in that class or division with a special provision restricting it to the type and size of package tested.

2.1.3.6.3   Where a substance is assigned to Class 1 but is diluted to be excluded from Class 1 by test series 6, this diluted substance (hereafter referred to as desensitized explosive) shall be listed in the Dangerous Goods List of chapter 3.2 with an indication of the highest concentration which excluded it from Class 1 (see 2.3.1.4 and 2.4.2.4.1) and if applicable, the concentration below which it is no longer deemed subject to these Regulations. New solid desensitized explosives subject to these Regulations shall be listed in Division 4.1 and new liquid desensitized explosives shall be listed in Class 3. When the desensitized explosive meets the criteria or definition for another class or division, the corresponding subsidiary hazard(s) shall be assigned to it.

2.1.3.6.4   An article may be excluded from Class 1 when three unpackaged articles, each individually activated by its own means of initiation or ignition or external means to function in the designed mode, meet the following test criteria:

(a) No external surface shall have a temperature of more than 65° C. A momentary spike in temperature up to 200 °C is acceptable;

(b) No rupture or fragmentation of the external casing or movement of the article or detached parts thereof of more than one metre in any direction;

NOTE: Where the integrity of the article may be affected in the event of an external fire these criteria shall be examined by a fire test. One such method is described in ISO 14451-2 using a heating rate of 80 K/min.

(c) No audible report exceeding 135 dB(C) peak at a distance of one metre;

(d) No flash or flame capable of igniting a material such as a sheet of 80 ± 10 g/m² paper in contact with the article; and

(e) No production of smoke, fumes or dust in such quantities that the visibility in a one cubic metre chamber equipped with appropriately sized blow out panels is reduced more than 50 % as measured by a calibrated light (lux) meter or radiometer located one metre from a constant light source located at the midpoint on opposite walls. The general guidance on Optical Density Testing in ISO 5659-1 and the general guidance on the Photometric System described in section 7.5 in ISO 5659-2 may be used or similar optical density measurement methods designed to accomplish the same purpose may also be employed. A suitable hood cover surrounding the back and sides of the light meter shall be used to minimize effects of scattered or leaking light not emitted directly from the source.

NOTE 1:   *If during the tests addressing criteria (a), (b), (c) and (d) no or very little smoke is observed the test described in (e) may be waived.*

NOTE 2:   *The competent authority may require testing in packaged form if it is determined that, as packaged for transport, the article may pose a greater hazard.*

2.1.3.7 *Classification documentation*

2.1.3.7.1   A competent authority assigning an article or substance into Class 1 should confirm with the applicant that classification in writing.

2.1.3.7.2　　A competent authority classification document may be in any form and may consist of more than one page, provided pages are numbered consecutively. The document should have a unique reference.

2.1.3.7.3　　The information provided shall be easy to identify, legible and durable.

2.1.3.7.4　　Examples of the information that may be provided in the classification documents are as follows:

(a) The name of the competent authority and the provisions in national legislation under which it is granted its authority;

(b) The modal or national regulations for which the classification document is applicable;

(c) Confirmation that the classification has been approved, made or agreed in accordance with the United Nations Recommendations on the Transport of Dangerous Goods or the relevant modal regulations;

(d) The name and address of the person in law to which the classification has been assigned and any company registration which uniquely identifies a company or other body corporate under national legislation;

(e) The name under which the explosives will be placed onto the market or otherwise supplied for transport;

(f) The Proper Shipping Name, UN number, Class, Hazard Division and corresponding compatibility group of the explosives;

(g) Where appropriate, the maximum net explosive mass of the package or article;

(h) The name, signature, stamp, seal or other identification of the person authorised by the competent authority to issue the classification document is clearly visible;

(i) Where safety in transport or the hazard division is assessed as being dependent upon the packaging, the packaging mark or a description of the permitted:

- Inner packagings

- Intermediate packagings

- Outer packagings

(j) The classification document states the part number, stock number or other identifying reference under which the explosives will be placed onto the market or otherwise supplied for transport;

(k) The name and address of the person in law who manufactured the explosives and any company registration which uniquely identifies a company or other body corporate under national legislation;

(l) Any additional information regarding the applicable packing instruction and special packing provisions where appropriate;

(m) The basis for assigning the classification, i.e. whether on the basis of test results, default for fireworks, analogy with classified explosive, by definition from the Dangerous Goods List etc.;

(n) Any special conditions or limitations that the competent authority has identified as relevant to the safety for transport of the explosives, the communication of the hazard and international transport;

(o) The expiry date of the classification document is given where the competent authority considers one to be appropriate.

CHAPTER 2.2

CLASS 2 - GASES

2.2.1 **Definitions and general provisions**

2.2.1.1 A gas is a substance which:

(a) At 50 °C has a vapour pressure greater than 300 kPa; or

Is completely gaseous at 20 °C at a standard pressure of 101.3 kPa.

2.2.1.2 The transport condition of a gas is described according to its physical state as:

(a) *Compressed gas* – a gas which when packaged under pressure for transport is entirely gaseous at -50 °C; this category includes all gases with a critical temperature less than or equal to -50 °C;

(b) *Liquefied gas* – a gas which when packaged under pressure for transport is partially liquid at temperatures above -50 °C. A distinction is made between:

(i) *High pressure liquefied gas* – a gas with a critical temperature between -50 °C and +65 °C, and

(ii) *Low pressure liquefied gas* – a gas with a critical temperature above +65 °C;

(c) *Refrigerated liquefied gas* – a gas which when packaged for transport is made partially liquid because of its low temperature;

(d) *Dissolved gas* – a gas which when packaged under pressure for transport is dissolved in a liquid phase solvent;

(e) *Adsorbed gas* – a gas which when packaged for transport is adsorbed onto a solid porous material resulting in an internal receptacle pressure of less than 101.3 kPa at 20 °C and less than 300 kPa at 50 °C.

2.2.1.3 The class comprises compressed gases, liquefied gases, dissolved gases, refrigerated liquefied gases, adsorbed gases, mixtures of one or more gases with one or more vapours of substances of other classes, articles charged with a gas, aerosols and chemicals under pressure.

2.2.2 **Divisions**

2.2.2.1 Substances of Class 2 are assigned to one of three divisions based on the primary hazard of the gas during transport.

NOTE: *For UN 1950 AEROSOLS, see also the criteria in special provision 63. For chemicals under pressure of UN Nos. 3500 to 3505, see also special provision 362. For UN 2037 RECEPTACLES, SMALL, CONTAINING GAS (GAS CARTRIDGES) see also special provision 303.*

(a) Division 2.1 - *Flammable gases*

Gases which at 20 °C and a standard pressure of 101.3 kPa:

(i) are ignitable when in a mixture of 13 per cent or less by volume with air; or

(ii) have a flammable range with air of at least 12 percentage points regardless of the lower flammability limit. Flammability shall be determined by tests or by calculation in accordance with methods adopted by ISO (see ISO 10156:2017). Where insufficient data are available to use these methods, tests by a comparable method recognized by a national competent authority may be used;

    (b)   Division 2.2 - *Non-flammable, non-toxic gases*

Gases which:

    (i)   are asphyxiant - gases which dilute or replace the oxygen normally in the atmosphere; or

    (ii)   are oxidizing - gases which may, generally by providing oxygen, cause or contribute to the combustion of other material more than air does; or

    (iii)   do not come under the other divisions;

NOTE: *In 2.2.2.1 (b) (ii), "gases which cause or contribute to the combustion of other material more than air does" means pure gases or gas mixtures with an oxidizing power greater than 23.5 % as determined by a method specified in ISO 10156:2017.*

    (c)   Division 2.3 - *Toxic gases*

Gases which:

    (i)   are known to be so toxic or corrosive to humans as to pose a hazard to health; or

    (ii)   are presumed to be toxic or corrosive to humans because they have an LC_{50} value (as defined in 2.6.2.1) equal to or less than 5 000 ml/m³ (ppm).

NOTE: *Gases meeting the above criteria owing to their corrosivity are to be classified as toxic with a subsidiary corrosive hazard.*

2.2.2.2   Gases and gas mixtures with hazards associated with more than one division take the following precedence:

    (a)   Division 2.3 takes precedence over all other divisions;

    (b)   Division 2.1 takes precedence over Division 2.2.

2.2.2.3   Gases of Division 2.2 are not subject to these Regulations if they are transported at a pressure of less than 200 kPa at 20 °C and are not liquefied or refrigerated liquefied gases.

2.2.2.4   Gases of Division 2.2 are not subject to these Regulations when contained in the following:

    (a)   Foodstuffs, including carbonated beverages (except UN 1950);

    (b)   Balls intended for use in sports; or

    (c)   Tyres (except for air transport).

NOTE: *This exemption does not apply to lamps. For lamps see 1.1.1.9.*

2.2.3   Mixtures of gases

Gas mixtures are to be classified in one of the three divisions (including vapours of substances from other classes) by applying the following procedures:

    (a)   Flammability shall be determined by tests or by calculation in accordance with methods adopted by ISO (see ISO 10156:2017). Where insufficient data are available to use these methods, tests by a comparable method recognized by a national competent authority may be used;

(b) The level of toxicity is determined either by tests to measure the LC_{50} value (as defined in 2.6.2.1) or by a calculation method using the following formula:

$$LC_{50} \text{ Toxic (mixture)} = \frac{1}{\sum_{i=1}^{n} \frac{f_i}{T_i}}$$

where: f_i = mole fraction of the ith component substance of the mixture

T_i = Toxicity index of the ith component substance of the mixture (the T_i equals the LC_{50} value when available).

When LC_{50} values are unknown the toxicity index is determined by using the lowest LC_{50} value of substances of similar physiological and chemical effects, or through testing if this is the only practical possibility;

(c) A gas mixture has a subsidiary hazard of corrosivity when the mixture is known by human experience to be destructive to the skin, eyes or mucous membranes or when the LC_{50} value of the corrosive components of the mixture is equal to or less than 5 000 ml/m³ (ppm) when the LC_{50} is calculated by the formula:

$$LC_{50} \text{ Corrosive (mixture)} = \frac{1}{\sum_{i=1}^{n} \frac{f_{ci}}{T_{ci}}}$$

where: f_{ci} = mole fraction of the ith corrosive component substance of the mixture

T_{ci} = Toxicity index of the ith corrosive component substance of the mixture (the T_{ci} equals the LC_{50} value when available);

(d) Oxidizing ability is determined either by tests or by calculation methods adopted by ISO (see the note in 2.2.2.1 (b) and ISO 10156:2017).

2.2.4 Gases not accepted for transport

Chemically unstable gases of Class 2 shall not be accepted for transport unless the necessary precautions have been taken to prevent the possibility of a dangerous decomposition or polymerization under normal conditions of transport or unless transported in accordance with special packing provision "r" of packing instruction P200 (5) of 4.1.4.1, as applicable. For the precautions necessary to prevent polymerization, see special provision 386 of chapter 3.3. To this end particular care shall be taken to ensure that receptacles and tanks do not contain any substances liable to promote these reactions.

CHAPTER 2.3

CLASS 3 - FLAMMABLE LIQUIDS

Introductory notes

NOTE 1: *The word "flammable" has the same meaning as "inflammable".*

NOTE 2: *The flash point of a flammable liquid may be altered by the presence of an impurity. The substances listed in Class 3 in the Dangerous Goods List in chapter 3.2 shall generally be regarded as chemically pure. Since commercial products may contain added substances or impurities, flash points may vary, and this may have an effect on classification or determination of the packing group for the product. In the event of doubt regarding the classification or packing group of a substance, the flash point of the substance shall be determined experimentally.*

2.3.1 Definition and general provisions

2.3.1.1 Class 3 includes the following substances:

    (a) Flammable liquids (see 2.3.1.2 and 2.3.1.3);

    (b) Liquid desensitized explosives (see 2.3.1.4).

2.3.1.2 *Flammable liquids* are liquids, or mixtures of liquids, or liquids containing solids in solution or suspension (for example, paints, varnishes, lacquers, etc., but not including substances otherwise classified on account of their dangerous characteristics) which give off a flammable vapour at temperatures of not more than 60 °C, closed-cup test, or not more than 65.6 °C, open-cup test, normally referred to as the flash point. This class also includes:

    (a) Liquids offered for transport at temperatures at or above their flash point; and

    (b) Substances that are transported or offered for transport at elevated temperatures in a liquid state and which give off a flammable vapour at a temperature at or below the maximum transport temperature.

NOTE: *Since the results of open-cup tests and of closed-cup tests are not strictly comparable and even individual results by the same test are often variable, regulations varying from the above figures to make allowance for such differences would be within the spirit of this definition.*

2.3.1.3 Liquids meeting the definition in 2.3.1.2 with a flash point of more than 35 °C which do not sustain combustion need not be considered as flammable liquids for the purposes of these Regulations. Liquids are considered to be unable to sustain combustion for the purposes of these Regulations (i.e. they do not sustain combustion under defined test conditions) if:

    (a) They have passed a suitable combustibility test (see SUSTAINED COMBUSTIBILITY TEST prescribed in the *Manual of Tests and Criteria*, part III, sub-section 32.5.2);

    (b) Their fire point according to ISO 2592:2000 is greater than 100 °C; or

    (c) They are water miscible solutions with a water content of more than 90 % by mass.

2.3.1.4 Liquid desensitized explosives are explosive substances which are dissolved or suspended in water or other liquid substances, to form a homogeneous liquid mixture to suppress their explosive properties (see 2.1.3.6.3). Entries in the Dangerous Goods List for liquid desensitized explosives are UN Nos. 1204, 2059, 3064, 3343, 3357, 3379 and 3555.

2.3.2 Assignment of packing groups

2.3.2.1 The criteria in 2.3.2.6 are used to determine the hazard grouping of a liquid that presents a hazard due to flammability.

2.3.2.1.1 For liquids whose only hazard is flammability, the packing group for the substance is the hazard grouping shown in 2.3.2.6.

2.3.2.1.2 For a liquid with additional hazard(s), the hazard group determined from 2.3.2.6 and the hazard group based on the severity of the additional hazard(s) shall be considered, and the classification and packing group determined in accordance with the provisions in chapter 2.0.

2.3.2.2 Viscous flammable liquids such as paints, enamels, lacquers, varnishes, adhesives and polishes having a flash-point of less than 23 °C may be placed in packing group III in conformity with the procedures prescribed in the *Manual of Tests and Criteria*, part III, sub-section 32.3, provided that:

(a) The viscosity[1] and flash-point are in accordance with the following table:

Kinematic viscosity (extrapolated) v (at near-zero shear rate) mm^2/s at 23 °C	Flow-time t in seconds	Jet diameter (mm)	Flash-point, closed-cup (°C)
$20 < v \leq 80$	$20 < t \leq 60$	4	above 17
$80 < v \leq 135$	$60 < t \leq 100$	4	above 10
$135 < v \leq 220$	$20 < t \leq 32$	6	above 5
$220 < v \leq 300$	$32 < t \leq 44$	6	above -1
$300 < v \leq 700$	$44 < t \leq 100$	6	above -5
$700 < v$	$100 < t$	6	No limit

(b) Less than 3 % of the clear solvent layer separates in the solvent separation test;

(c) The mixture or any separated solvent does not meet the criteria for Division 6.1 or Class 8;

(d) The substances are packed in receptacles of not more than 450 litres capacity.

2.3.2.3 *Reserved.*

2.3.2.4 Substances classified as flammable liquids due to their being transported or offered for transport at elevated temperatures are included in packing group III.

2.3.2.5 *Viscous liquids*

2.3.2.5.1 Except as provided for in 2.3.2.5.2, viscous liquids which:

- have a flash point of 23 °C or above and less than or equal to 60 °C;

- are not toxic, corrosive or environmentally hazardous;

---

[1] *Viscosity determination: Where the substance concerned is non-Newtonian, or where a flow cup method of viscosity determination is otherwise unsuitable, a variable shear-rate viscometer shall be used to determine the dynamic viscosity coefficient of the substance, at 23 °C, at a number of shear rates. The values obtained are plotted against shear rate and then extrapolated to zero shear rate. The dynamic viscosity thus obtained, divided by the density, gives the apparent kinematic viscosity at near-zero shear rate.*

- contain not more than 20 % nitrocellulose provided the nitrocellulose contains not more than 12.6 % nitrogen by dry mass; and

- are packed in receptacles of not more than 450 litre capacity;

are not subject to these Regulations, if:

(a) in the solvent separation test (see *Manual of Tests and Criteria*, part III, sub-section 32.5.1), the height of the separated layer of solvent is less than 3 % of the total height; and

(b) the flowtime in the viscosity test (see *Manual of Tests and Criteria*, part III, sub-section 32.4.3), with a jet diameter of 6 mm is equal to or greater than:

   (i) 60 seconds; or

   (ii) 40 seconds if the viscous liquid contains not more than 60 % of Class 3 substances.

2.3.2.5.2 Viscous liquids which are also environmentally hazardous, but meet all other criteria in 2.3.2.5.1, are not subject to any other provisions of these Regulations when they are transported in single or combination packagings containing a net quantity per single or inner packaging of 5 litres or less, provided the packagings meet the general provisions of 4.1.1.1, 4.1.1.2 and 4.1.1.4 to 4.1.1.8.

2.3.2.6 *Hazard grouping based on flammability*

Packing group	Flash point (closed-cup)	Initial boiling point
I	--	≤ 35 °C
II	< 23 °C	> 35 °C
III	≥ 23 °C ≤ 60 °C	> 35 °C

2.3.3 **Determination of flash point**

The following methods for determining the flash point of flammable liquids may be used:

<u>International standards:</u>

   ISO 1516
   ISO 1523
   ISO 2719
   ISO 13736
   ISO 3679
   ISO 3680

<u>National standards:</u>

American Society for Testing Materials International, 100 Barr Harbor Drive, PO Box C700, West Conshohocken, Pennsylvania, USA 19428-2959:

   ASTM D3828-07a, Standard Test Methods for Flash Point by Small Scale Closed Cup Tester
   ASTM D56-05, Standard Test Method for Flash Point by Tag Closed Cup Tester
   ASTM D3278-96(2004)e1, Standard Test Methods for Flash Point of Liquids by Small Scale Closed-Cup Apparatus
   ASTM D93-08, Standard Test Methods for Flash Point by Pensky-Martens Closed Cup Tester

Association française de normalisation, AFNOR, 11, rue de Pressensé, 93571 La Plaine Saint-Denis Cedex:

    French Standard NF M 07 - 019
    French Standards NF M 07 - 011 / NF T 30 - 050 / NF T 66 - 009
    French Standard NF M 07 - 036

Deutsches Institut für Normung, Burggrafenstr. 6, D-10787 Berlin:

    Standard DIN 51755 (flash points below 65 °C)

State Committee of the Council of Ministers for Standardization, 113813, GSP, Moscow, M-49 Leninsky Prospect, 9:

    GOST 12.1.044-84.

2.3.4   **Determination of initial boiling point**

The following methods for determining the initial boiling point of flammable liquids may be used:

International standards:

    ISO 3924
    ISO 4626
    ISO 3405

National standards:

American Society for Testing Materials International, 100 Barr Harbor Drive, PO Box C700, West Conshohocken, Pennsylvania, USA 19428-2959:

    ASTM D86-07a, Standard Test Method for Distillation of Petroleum Products at Atmospheric Pressure
    ASTM D1078-05, Standard Test Method for Distillation Range of Volatile Organic Liquids

Further acceptable methods:

    Method A.2 as described in part A of the annex to Commission Regulation (EC) No 440/2008[2].

2.3.5   **Substances not accepted for transport**

Chemically unstable substances of Class 3 shall not be accepted for transport unless the necessary precautions have been taken to prevent the possibility of a dangerous decomposition or polymerization under normal conditions of transport. For the precautions necessary to prevent polymerization, see special provision 386 of chapter 3.3. To this end particular care shall be taken to ensure that receptacles and tanks do not contain any substances liable to promote these reactions.

---

[2] *Commission Regulation (EC) No 440/2008 of 30 May 2008 laying down test methods pursuant to Regulation (EC) No 1907/2006 of the European Parliament and of the Council on the Registration, Evaluation, Authorisation and Restriction of Chemicals (REACH) (Official Journal of the European Union, No. L 142 of 31.05.2008, p.1-739 and No. L 143 of 03.06.2008, p.55).*

CHAPTER 2.4

CLASS 4 - FLAMMABLE SOLIDS; SUBSTANCES LIABLE TO SPONTANEOUS COMBUSTION; SUBSTANCES WHICH, IN CONTACT WITH WATER, EMIT FLAMMABLE GASES

Introductory notes

NOTE 1:   *Where the term "water-reactive" is used in these Regulations, it refers to a substance which in contact with water emits flammable gas.*

NOTE 2:   *Because of the different properties exhibited by dangerous goods within Divisions 4.1 and 4.2, it is impracticable to establish a single criterion for classification in either of these divisions. Tests and criteria for assignment to the three divisions of Class 4 are addressed in this chapter (and in the "Manual of Tests and Criteria", part III, section 33).*

NOTE 3:   *Since organometallic substances can be classified in divisions 4.2 or 4.3 with additional subsidiary hazards, depending on their properties, a specific classification flow chart for these substances is given in 2.4.5.*

2.4.1 Definitions and general provisions

2.4.1.1   Class 4 is divided into three divisions as follows:

    (a)   Division 4.1 – *Flammable solids*

    Solids which, under conditions encountered in transport, are readily combustible or may cause or contribute to fire through friction; self-reactive substances and polymerizing substances which are liable to undergo a strongly exothermic reaction; solid desensitized explosives which may explode if not diluted sufficiently;

    (b)   Division 4.2 – *Substances liable to spontaneous combustion*

    Substances which are liable to spontaneous heating under normal conditions encountered in transport, or to heating up in contact with air, and being then liable to catch fire;

    (c)   Division 4.3 – *Substances which in contact with water emit flammable gases*

    Substances which, by interaction with water, are liable to become spontaneously flammable or to give off flammable gases in dangerous quantities.

2.4.1.2   As referenced in this chapter, test methods and criteria, with advice on application of the tests, are given in the *Manual of Tests and Criteria*, for the classification of the following types of substances of Class 4:

    (a)   Flammable solids (Division 4.1);

    (b)   Self-reactive substances (Division 4.1);

    (c)   Polymerizing substances (Division 4.1);

    (d)   Pyrophoric solids (Division 4.2);

    (e)   Pyrophoric liquids (Division 4.2);

    (f)   Self-heating substances (Division 4.2); and

(g) Substances which, in contact with water, emit flammable gases (Division 4.3).

Test methods and criteria for self-reactive substances and polymerizing substances are given in part II of the *Manual of Tests and Criteria*, and test methods and criteria for the other types of substances of Class 4 are given in the *Manual of Tests and Criteria*, part III, section 33.

2.4.2 Division 4.1 – Flammable solids, self-reactive substances, solid desensitized explosives and polymerizing substances

2.4.2.1 *General*

Division 4.1 includes the following types of substances:

(a) Flammable solids (see 2.4.2.2);

(b) Self-reactive substances (see 2.4.2.3);

(c) Solid desensitized explosives (see 2.4.2.4); and

(d) Polymerizing substances (see 2.4.2.5).

2.4.2.2 *Division 4.1 - Flammable solids*

2.4.2.2.1 *Definitions and properties*

2.4.2.2.1.1 *Flammable solids* are readily combustible solids and solids which may cause fire through friction.

2.4.2.2.1.2 *Readily combustible solids* are powdered, granular, or pasty substances which are dangerous if they can be easily ignited by brief contact with an ignition source, such as a burning match, and if the flame spreads rapidly. The danger may come not only from the fire but also from toxic combustion products. Metal powders are especially dangerous because of the difficulty of extinguishing a fire since normal extinguishing agents such as carbon dioxide or water can increase the hazard.

2.4.2.2.1.3 *Metal powders* are powders of metals or metal alloys.

2.4.2.2.2 *Classification of flammable solids*

2.4.2.2.2.1 Powdered, granular or pasty substances shall be classified as readily combustible solids of Division 4.1 when the time of burning of one or more of the test runs, performed in accordance with the test method described in the *Manual of Tests and Criteria*, part III, sub-section 33.2, is less than 45 s or the rate of burning is more than 2.2 mm/s. Metal powders shall be classified in Division 4.1 when they can be ignited and the reaction spreads over the whole length of the sample in 10 minutes or less.

2.4.2.2.2.2 Solids which may cause fire through friction shall be classified in Division 4.1 by analogy with existing entries (e.g. matches) until definitive criteria are established.

2.4.2.2.3 *Assignment of packing groups*

2.4.2.2.3.1 Packing groups are assigned on the basis of the test methods referred to in 2.4.2.2.2.1. For readily combustible solids (other than metal powders), Packing group II shall be assigned if the burning time is less than 45 s and the flame passes the wetted zone. Packing group II shall be assigned to metal powders if the zone of reaction spreads over the whole length of the sample in five minutes or less.

2.4.2.2.3.2 Packing groups are assigned on the basis of the test methods referred to in 2.4.2.2.2.1. For readily combustible solids (other than metal powders), Packing group III shall be assigned if the burning time is less than 45 s and the wetted zone stops the flame propagation for at least four minutes. Packing group III shall be assigned to metal powders if the reaction spreads over the whole length of the sample in more than five minutes but not more than ten minutes.

2.4.2.2.3.3 For solids which may cause fire through friction, the packing group shall be assigned by analogy with existing entries or in accordance with any appropriate special provision.

2.4.2.3 ***Division 4.1 - Self-reactive substances***

2.4.2.3.1 *Definitions and properties*

2.4.2.3.1.1 Definitions

For the purposes of these Regulations:

Self-reactive substances are thermally unstable substances liable to undergo a strongly exothermic decomposition even without participation of oxygen (air). Substances are not considered to be self-reactive substances of Division 4.1, if:

(a) They are explosives according to the criteria of Class 1;

(b) They are oxidizing substances according to the classification procedure for Division 5.1 (see 2.5.2.1.1) except that mixtures of oxidizing substances which contain 5.0 % or more of combustible organic substances shall be subjected to the classification procedure defined in note 3;

(c) They are organic peroxides according to the criteria of Division 5.2;

(d) Their heat of decomposition is less than 300 J/g; or

(e) Their self-accelerating decomposition temperature (SADT) (see 2.4.2.3.4) is greater than 75 °C for a 50 kg package.

NOTE 1: *The heat of decomposition can be determined using any internationally recognised method e.g. differential scanning calorimetry and adiabatic calorimetry.*

NOTE 2: *Any substance which shows the properties of a self-reactive substance shall be classified as such, even if this substance gives a positive test result according to 2.4.3.2 for inclusion in Division 4.2.*

NOTE 3: *Mixtures of oxidizing substances meeting the criteria of Division 5.1 which contain 5.0 % or more of combustible organic substances, which do not meet the criteria mentioned in (a), (c), (d) or (e) above, shall be subjected to the self-reactive substance classification procedure.*

A mixture showing the properties of a self-reactive substance, type B to F, shall be classified as a self-reactive substance of Division 4.1.

A mixture showing the properties of a self-reactive substance, type G, according to the principle of 2.4.2.3.3.2 (g) shall be considered for classification as a substance of Division 5.1 (see 2.5.2.1.1).

2.4.2.3.1.2 Properties

The decomposition of self-reactive substances can be initiated by heat, contact with catalytic impurities (e.g. acids, heavy-metal compounds, bases), friction or impact. The rate of decomposition increases with temperature and varies with the substance. Decomposition, particularly if no ignition occurs, may result in the evolution of toxic gases or vapours. For certain self-reactive substances, the temperature shall be controlled. Some self-reactive substances may decompose explosively, particularly if confined. This characteristic may be modified by the addition of diluents or by the use of appropriate packagings. Some self-reactive substances burn vigorously. Self-reactive substances are, for example, some compounds of the types listed below:

(a) Aliphatic azo compounds (-C-N=N-C-);

(b) Organic azides (-C-N$_3$);

(c) Diazonium salts ($-CN_2^+Z^-$);

(d) N-nitroso compounds (-N-N=O); and

(e) Aromatic sulphonylhydrazides ($-SO_2-NH-NH_2$).

This list is not exhaustive and substances with other reactive groups and some mixtures of substances may have similar properties.

2.4.2.3.2 *Classification of self-reactive substances*

2.4.2.3.2.1 Self-reactive substances are classified into seven types according to the degree of danger they present. The types of self-reactive substance range from type A, which may not be accepted for transport in the packaging in which it is tested, to type G, which is not subject to the provisions for self-reactive substances of Division 4.1. The classification of types B to F is directly related to the maximum quantity allowed in one packaging.

2.4.2.3.2.2 Self-reactive substances permitted for transport in packagings are listed in 2.4.2.3.2.3, those permitted for transport in IBCs are listed in packing instruction IBC520 and those permitted for transport in portable tanks are listed in portable tank instruction T23. For each permitted substance listed, the appropriate generic entry of the Dangerous Goods List (UN Nos. 3221 to 3240) is assigned, and appropriate subsidiary hazards and remarks providing relevant transport information are given. The generic entries specify:

(a) Self-reactive substance type (B to F);

(b) Physical state (liquid or solid); and

(c) Temperature control, when required (see 2.4.2.3.4).

2.4.2.3.2.3 List of currently assigned self-reactive substances in packagings

In the column "Packing Method", codes "OP1" to "OP8" refer to packing methods in packing instruction P520. Self-reactive substances to be transported shall fulfil the classification and the control and emergency temperatures (derived from the SADT) as listed. For substances permitted in IBCs, see packing instruction IBC520, and for those permitted in tanks, see portable tank instruction T23. The formulations not listed in this sub-section but listed in packing instruction IBC520 of 4.1.4.2 and in portable tank instruction T23 of 4.2.5.2.6 may also be transported packed in accordance with packing method OP8 of packing instruction P520 of 4.1.4.1, with the same control and emergency temperatures, if applicable.

NOTE: *The classification given in this table is based on the technically pure substance (except where a concentration of less than 100 % is specified). For other concentrations, the substances may be classified differently following the procedures in 2.4.2.3.3 and 2.4.2.3.4.*

SELF-REACTIVE SUBSTANCE	Concentration (%)	Packing method	Control temperature (°C)	Emergency temperature (°C)	UN generic entry	Remarks
ACETONE-PYROGALLOL COPOLYMER 2-DIAZO-1-NAPHTHOL-5-SULPHONATE	100	OP8			3228	
AZODICARBONAMIDE FORMULATION TYPE B, TEMPERATURE CONTROLLED	< 100	OP5			3232	(1) (2)
AZODICARBONAMIDE FORMULATION TYPE C	< 100	OP6			3224	(3)
AZODICARBONAMIDE FORMULATION TYPE C, TEMPERATURE CONTROLLED	< 100	OP6			3234	(4)
AZODICARBONAMIDE FORMULATION TYPE D	< 100	OP7			3226	(5)
AZODICARBONAMIDE FORMULATION TYPE D, TEMPERATURE CONTROLLED	< 100	OP7			3236	(6)
2,2'-AZODI(2,4-DIMETHYL- 4-METHOXY VALERONITRILE)	100	OP7	-5	+5	3236	
2,2'-AZODI(2,4-DIMETHYL- VALERONITRILE)	100	OP7	+10	+15	3236	
2,2'-AZODI(ETHYL-2-METHYLPROPIONATE)	100	OP7	+20	+25	3235	
1,1-AZODI(HEXAHYDROBENZONITRILE)	100	OP7			3226	
2,2'-AZODI(ISOBUTYRONITRILE)	100	OP6	+40	+45	3234	
2,2'-AZODI(ISOBUTYRONITRILE) as a water based paste	≤ 50	OP6			3224	
2,2'-AZODI(2-METHYLBUTYRONITRILE)	100	OP7	+35	+40	3236	
BENZENE-1,3-DISULPHONYL HYDRAZIDE, as a paste	52	OP7			3226	
BENZENESULPHONYL HYDRAZIDE	100	OP7			3226	
4-(BENZYL(ETHYL)AMINO)-3-ETHOXY-BENZENEDIAZONIUM ZINC CHLORIDE	100	OP7			3226	
4-(BENZYL(METHYL)AMINO)-3-ETHOXY BENZENEDIAZONIUM ZINC CHLORIDE	100	OP7	+40	+45	3236	
3-CHLORO-4-DIETHYLAMINOBENZENE-DIAZONIUM ZINC CHLORIDE	100	OP7			3226	
2-DIAZO-1-NAPHTHOL-4- SULPHONYL-CHLORIDE	100	OP5			3222	(2)
2-DIAZO-1-NAPHTHOL-5- SULPHONYL CHLORIDE	100	OP5			3222	(2)
2-DIAZO-1-NAPHTHOL SULPHONIC ACID ESTER MIXTURE, TYPE D	<100	OP7			3226	(9)
2,5-DIBUTOXY-4-(4-MORPHOLINYL) BENZENEDIAZONIUM, TETRACHLOROZINCATE (2:1)	100	OP8			3228	
2,5-DIETHOXY-4-MORPHOLINO- BENZENEDIAZONIUM ZINC CHLORIDE	67-100	OP7	+35	+40	3236	
2,5-DIETHOXY-4-MORPHOLINO- BENZENEDIAZONIUM ZINC CHLORIDE	66	OP7	+40	+45	3236	
2,5-DIETHOXY-4-MORPHOLINO- BENZENEDIAZONIUM TETRAFLUOROBORATE	100	OP7	+30	+35	3236	

SELF-REACTIVE SUBSTANCE	Concen-tration (%)	Packing method	Control temperature (°C)	Emergency temperature (°C)	UN generic entry	Remarks
2,5-DIETHOXY-4-(4-MORPHOLINYL)- BENZENEDIAZONIUM SULPHATE	100	OP7			3226	
2,5- DIETHOXY-4-(PHENYLSULPHONYL)-BENZENEDIAZONIUM ZINC CHLORIDE	67	OP7	+40	+45	3236	
DIETHYLENEGLYCOL BIS (ALLYL CARBONATE) + DI ISOPROPYLPEROXYDICARBONATE	≥ 88 + ≤ 12	OP8	-10	0	3237	
2,5-DIMETHOXY-4-(4-METHYL-PHENYLSULPHONYL)BENZENE- DIAZONIUM ZINC CHLORIDE	79	OP7	+40	+45	3236	
4-(DIMETHYLAMINO)-BENZENE-DIAZONIUM TRICHLOROZINCATE (-1)	100	OP8			3228	
4-DIMETHYLAMINO-6-(2-DIMETHYL-AMINOETHOXY) TOLUENE- 2-DIAZONIUM ZINC CHLORIDE	100	OP7	+40	+45	3236	
N,N'-DINITROSO-N,N'-DIMETHYL TEREPHTHALAMIDE, as a paste	72	OP6			3224	
N,N'-DINITROSOPENTAMETHYLENE-TETRAMINE	82	OP6			3224	(7)
DIPHENYLOXIDE-4,4'-DISULPHONYL HYDRAZIDE	100	OP7			3226	
4-DIPROPYLAMINOBENZENE-DIAZONIUM ZINC CHLORIDE	100	OP7			3226	
2-(N,N-ETHOXYCARBONYL-PHENYLAMINO)-3-METHOXY-4- (N-METHYL-N-CYCLOHEXYLAMINO BENZENEDIAZONIUM ZINC CHLORIDE	63-92	OP7	+40	+45	3236	
2-(N,N-ETHOXYCARBONYL- PHENYLAMINO)-3-METHOXY-4- (N-METHYL-N- CYCLOHEXYLAMINO) BENZENEDIAZONIUM ZINC CHLORIDE	62	OP7	+35	+40	3236	
N-FORMYL-2-(NITROMETHYLENE) -1,3-PERHYDROTHIAZINE	100	OP7	+45	+50	3236	
2-(2-HYDROXYETHOXY)-1- (PYRROLIDIN-1-YL)BENZENE-4- DIAZONIUM ZINC CHLORIDE	100	OP7	+ 45	+ 50	3236	
3-(2-HYDROXYETHOXY)-4- (PYRROLIDIN-1-YL)BENZENE DIAZONIUM ZINC CHLORIDE	100	OP7	+40	+45	3236	
(7-METHOXY-5-METHYL-BENZOTHIOPHEN-2-YL) BORONIC ACID	88-100	OP7			3230	(11)
2-(N,N-METHYLAMINOETHYL- CARBONYL)-4-(3,4-DIMETHYL- PHENYLSULPHONYL)BENZENE- DIAZONIUM HYDROGEN SULPHATE	96	OP7	+45	+50	3236	
4-METHYLBENZENESULPHONYL- HYDRAZIDE	100	OP7			3226	
3-METHYL-4-(PYRROLIDIN-1-YL) BENZENEDIAZONIUM TETRAFLUOROBORATE	95	OP6	+45	+50	3234	

SELF-REACTIVE SUBSTANCE	Concen-tration (%)	Packing method	Control tempera-ture (°C)	Emergency tempera-ture (°C)	UN generic entry	Remarks
4-NITROSOPHENOL	100	OP7	+35	+40	3236	
PHOSPHOROTHIOIC ACID, O-[(CYANOPHENYL METHYLENE) AZANYL] O,O-DIETHYL ESTER	82-91 (Z isomer)	OP8			3227	(10)
SELF-REACTIVE LIQUID, SAMPLE		OP2			3223	(8)
SELF-REACTIVE LIQUID, SAMPLE, TEMPERATURE CONTROLLED		OP2			3233	(8)
SELF-REACTIVE SOLID, SAMPLE		OP2			3224	(8)
SELF-REACTIVE SOLID, SAMPLE, TEMPERATURE CONTROLLED		OP2			3234	(8)
SODIUM 2-DIAZO-1-NAPHTHOL- 4-SULPHONATE	100	OP7			3226	
SODIUM 2-DIAZO-1-NAPHTHOL- 5-SULPHONATE	100	OP7			3226	
TETRAMINE PALLADIUM (II) NITRATE	100	OP6	+30	+35	3234	

Remarks

(1) Azodicarbonamide formulations which fulfil the criteria of 2.4.2.3.3.2 (b). The control and emergency temperatures shall be determined by the procedure given in 7.1.5.3 to 7.1.5.3.6.

(2) "EXPLOSIVE" subsidiary hazard label (Model No 1, see 5.2.2.2.2) required.

(3) Azodicarbonamide formulations which fulfil the criteria of 2.4.2.3.3.2 (c).

(4) Azodicarbonamide formulations which fulfil the criteria of 2.4.2.3.3.2 (c). The control and emergency temperatures shall be determined by the procedure given in 7.1.5.3 to 7.1.5.3.6.

(5) Azodicarbonamide formulations which fulfil the criteria of 2.4.2.3.3.2 (d).

(6) Azodicarbonamide formulations which fulfil the criteria of 2.4.2.3.3.2 (d). The control and emergency temperatures shall be determined by the procedure given in 7.1.5.3 to 7.1.5.3.6.

(7) With a compatible diluent having a boiling point of not less than 150 °C.

(8) See 2.4.2.3.2.4 (b).

(9) This entry applies to mixtures of esters of 2-diazo-1-naphthol-4-sulphonic acid and 2-diazo-1-naphthol-5-sulphonic acid meeting the criteria of 2.4.2.3.3.2 (d).

(10) This entry applies to the technical mixture in n-butanol within the specified concentration limits of the (Z) isomer.

(11) The technical compound with the specified concentration limits may contain up to 12 % water and up to 1 % organic impurities.

2.4.2.3.2.4   Classification of self-reactive substances not listed in 2.4.2.3.2.3, packing instruction IBC520 or portable tank instruction T23 and assignment to a generic entry shall be made by the competent authority of the country of origin on the basis of a test report. Principles applying to the classification of such substances are provided in 2.4.2.3.3. The applicable classification procedures, test methods and criteria, and an example of a suitable test report, are given in the *Manual of Tests and Criteria*, part II. The statement of approval shall contain the classification and the relevant transport conditions.

(a) Activators, such as zinc compounds, may be added to some self-reactive substances to change their reactivity. Depending on both the type and the concentration of the activator, this may result in a decrease in thermal stability and a change in explosive properties. If either of these properties is altered, the new formulation shall be assessed in accordance with this classification procedure;

(b) Samples of self-reactive substances or formulations of self-reactive substances not listed in 2.4.2.3.2.3, for which a complete set of test results is not available and which are to be transported for further testing or evaluation, may be assigned to one of the appropriate entries for self-reactive substances type C provided the following conditions are met:

(i) The available data indicate that the sample would be no more dangerous than self-reactive substances type B;

(ii) The sample is packaged in accordance with packing method OP2 (see applicable packing instruction) and the quantity per cargo transport unit is limited to 10 kg; and

(iii) The available data indicate that the control temperature, if any, is sufficiently low to prevent any dangerous decomposition and sufficiently high to prevent any dangerous phase separation.

2.4.2.3.3 *Principles for classification of self-reactive substances*

NOTE: *This section refers only to those properties of self-reactive substances which are decisive for their classification. A flow chart, presenting the classification principles in the form of a graphically arranged scheme of questions concerning the decisive properties together with the possible answers, is given in figure 2.4.1. These properties shall be determined experimentally using the test methods and criteria given in the "Manual of Tests and Criteria", part II.*

2.4.2.3.3.1 A self-reactive substance is regarded as possessing explosive properties when in laboratory testing the formulation is liable to detonate, to deflagrate rapidly or to show a violent effect when heated under confinement.

2.4.2.3.3.2 The following principles apply to the classification of self-reactive substances not listed in 2.4.2.3.2.3.

(a) Any substance which can detonate or deflagrate rapidly, as packaged for transport, is prohibited from transport under the provisions for self-reactive substances of Division 4.1 in that packaging (defined as self-reactive substance type A, exit box A of figure 2.4.1);

(b) Any substance possessing explosive properties and which, as packaged for transport, neither detonates nor deflagrates rapidly, but is liable to undergo a thermal explosion in that package, shall also bear an "EXPLOSIVE" subsidiary hazard label (Model No. 1, see 5.2.2.2.2). Such a substance may be packaged in amounts of up to 25 kg unless the maximum quantity has to be limited to a lower amount to preclude detonation or rapid deflagration in the package (defined as self-reactive substance type B, exit box B of figure 2.4.1);

(c) Any substance possessing explosive properties may be transported without an "EXPLOSIVE" subsidiary hazard label when the substance as packaged (maximum 50 kg) for transport cannot detonate or deflagrate rapidly or undergo a thermal explosion (defined as self-reactive substance type C, exit box C of figure 2.4.1);

(d) Any substance which in laboratory testing:

(i) detonates partially, does not deflagrate rapidly and shows no violent effect when heated under confinement; or

(ii) does not detonate at all, deflagrates slowly and shows no violent effect when heated under confinement; or

(iii) does not detonate or deflagrate at all and shows a medium effect when heated under confinement;

may be accepted for transport in packages of not more than 50 kg net mass (defined as self-reactive substance type D, exit box D of figure 2.4.1);

(e) Any substance which, in laboratory testing, neither detonates nor deflagrates at all and shows low or no effect when heated under confinement may be accepted for transport in packages of not more than 400 kg/450 litres (defined as self-reactive substance type E, exit box E of figure 2.4.1);

(f) Any substance which, in laboratory testing, neither detonates in the cavitated state nor deflagrates at all and shows only a low or no effect when heated under confinement as well as low or no explosive power may be considered for transport in IBCs or tanks (defined as self-reactive substance type F, exit box F of figure 2.4.1); (for additional provisions see 4.1.7.2.2 and 4.2.1.13);

(g) Any substance which, in laboratory testing, neither detonates in the cavitated state nor deflagrates at all and shows no effect when heated under confinement nor any explosive power shall be exempted from classification as a self-reactive substance of Division 4.1 provided that the formulation is thermally stable (self-accelerating decomposition temperature 60 °C to 75 °C for a 50 kg package) and any diluent meets the requirements of 2.4.2.3.5 (defined as self-reactive substance type G, exit box G of figure 2.4.1). If the formulation is not thermally stable or a compatible diluent having a boiling point less than 150 °C is used for desensitization, the formulation shall be defined as SELF-REACTIVE LIQUID/SOLID TYPE F.

Figure 2.4.1: Flow chart scheme for self-reactive substances

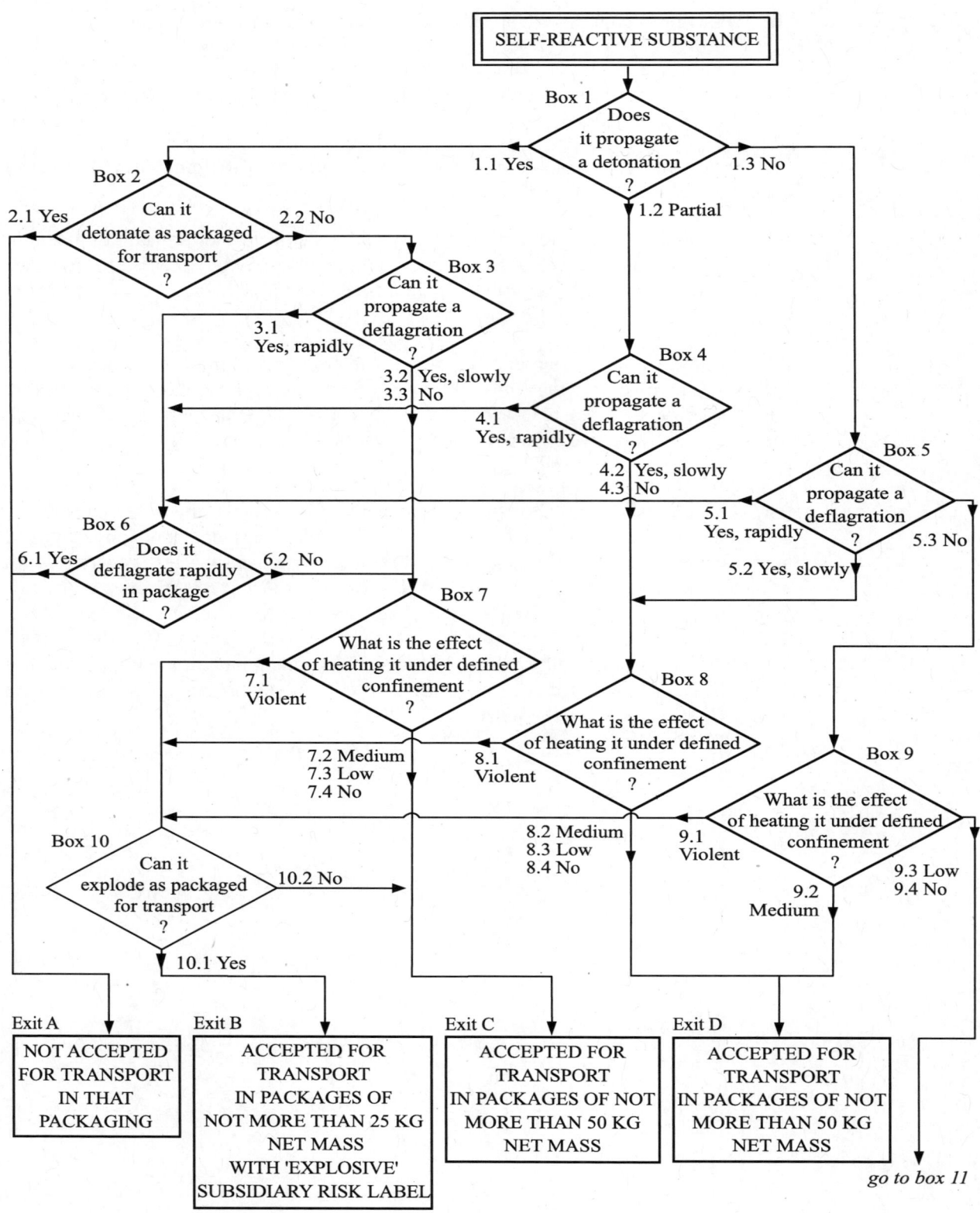

Figure 2.4.1: Flow chart scheme for self-reactive substances (cont'd)

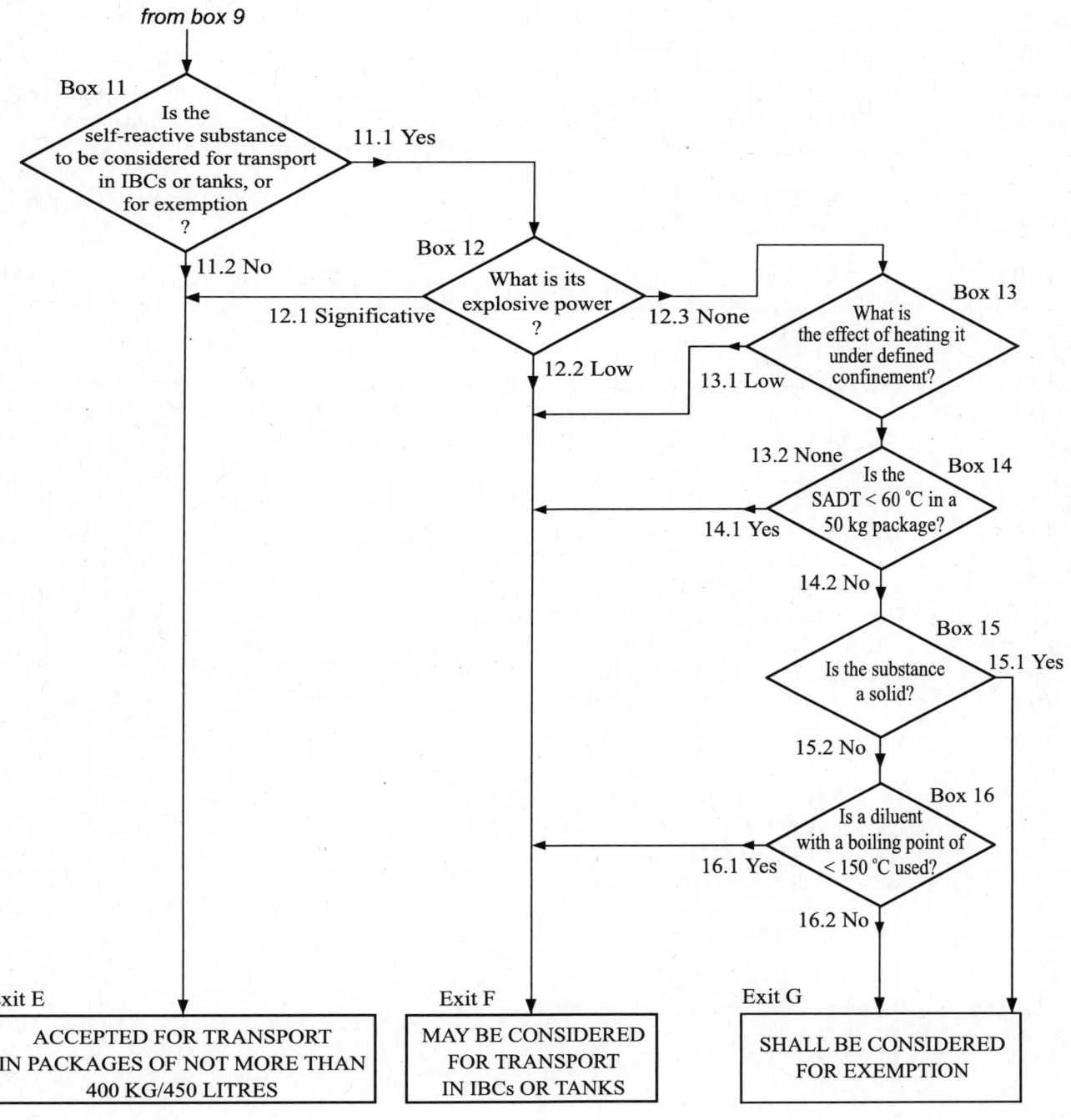

2.4.2.3.4   *Temperature control requirements*

Self-reactive substances are subject to temperature control in transport if their self-accelerating decomposition temperature (SADT) is less than or equal to 55 °C. Test methods for determining the SADT are given in the *Manual of Tests and Criteria*, part II, section 28. The test selected shall be conducted in a manner which is representative, both in size and material, of the package to be transported.

2.4.2.3.5   *Desensitization of self-reactive substances*

2.4.2.3.5.1   In order to ensure safety during transport, self-reactive substances may be desensitized through the use of a diluent. If a diluent is used, the self-reactive substance shall be tested with the diluent present in the concentration and form used in transport.

2.4.2.3.5.2   Diluents which may allow a self-reactive substance to concentrate to a dangerous extent in the event of leakage from a package shall not be used.

2.4.2.3.5.3   The diluent shall be compatible with the self-reactive substance. In this regard, compatible diluents are those solids or liquids which have no detrimental influence on the thermal stability and hazard type of the self-reactive substance.

2.4.2.3.5.4   Liquid diluents in liquid formulations requiring temperature control shall have a boiling point of at least 60 °C and a flash point not less than 5 °C. The boiling point of the liquid shall be at least 50 °C higher than the control temperature of the self-reactive substance (see 7.1.5.3).

2.4.2.4   *Division 4.1 - Solid desensitized explosives*

2.4.2.4.1   *Definition*

Solid desensitized explosives are explosive substances which are wetted with water or alcohols or are diluted with other substances, to form a homogeneous solid mixture to suppress their explosive properties (see 2.1.3.6.3). Entries in the Dangerous Goods List for solid desensitized explosives are UN Nos. 1310, 1320, 1321, 1322, 1336, 1337, 1344, 1347, 1348, 1349, 1354, 1355, 1356, 1357, 1517, 1571, 2555, 2556, 2557, 2852, 2907, 3317, 3319, 3344, 3364, 3365, 3366, 3367, 3368, 3369, 3370, 3376, 3380 and 3474.

2.4.2.4.2   Substances that:

(a)   have been provisionally accepted into Class 1 according to test series 1 and 2 but exempted from Class 1 by test series 6;

(b)   are not self-reactive substances of Division 4.1;

(c)   are not substances of Class 5;

are also assigned to Division 4.1. Though not desensitized explosives, UN Nos. 2956, 3241, 3242 and 3251 are such entries that are assigned to Division 4.1.

2.4.2.5   *Division 4.1 - Polymerizing substances and mixtures (stabilized)*

2.4.2.5.1   *Definitions and properties*

Polymerizing substances are substances which, without stabilization, are liable to undergo a strongly exothermic reaction resulting in the formation of larger molecules or resulting in the formation of polymers under conditions normally encountered in transport. Such substances are considered to be polymerizing substances of Division 4.1 when:

(a)   Their self-accelerating polymerization temperature (SAPT) is 75 °C or less under the conditions (with or without chemical stabilization as offered for transport) and in the packaging, IBC or portable tank in which the substance or mixture is to be transported;

(b)   They exhibit a heat of reaction of more than 300 J/g; and

(c) They do not meet any other criteria for inclusion in Classes 1-8.

A mixture meeting the criteria of a polymerizing substance shall be classified as a polymerizing substance of Division 4.1.

2.4.2.5.2 Polymerizing substances are subject to temperature control in transport if their self-accelerating polymerization temperature (SAPT) is:

(a) When offered for transport in a packaging or IBC, 50 °C or less in the packaging or IBC in which the substance is to be transported; or

(b) When offered for transport in a portable tank, 45 °C or less in the portable tank in which the substance is to be transported.

NOTE: *Substances meeting the criteria of a polymerizing substance and also for inclusion in Classes 1 to 8 are subject to the requirements of special provision 386 of chapter 3.3.*

2.4.3 Division 4.2 – Substances liable to spontaneous combustion

2.4.3.1 *Definitions and properties*

2.4.3.1.1 Division 4.2 includes:

(a) Pyrophoric substances, which are substances, including mixtures and solutions (liquid or solid), which even in small quantities ignite within five minutes of coming in contact with air. These are the Division 4.2 substances the most liable to spontaneous combustion; and

(b) Self-heating substances, which are substances, other than pyrophoric substances, which in contact with air without energy supply are liable to self-heating. These substances will ignite only when in large amounts (kilograms) and after long periods of time (hours or days).

2.4.3.1.2 Self-heating of a substance is a process where the gradual reaction of that substance with oxygen (in air) generates heat. If the rate of heat production exceeds the rate of heat loss, then the temperature of the substance will rise which, after an induction time, may lead to self-ignition and combustion.

2.4.3.2 *Classification in Division 4.2*

2.4.3.2.1 Solids are considered pyrophoric solids which shall be classified in Division 4.2 if, in tests performed in accordance with the test method given in the *Manual of Tests and Criteria*, part III, sub-section 33.4.4, the sample ignites in one of the tests.

2.4.3.2.2 Liquids are considered pyrophoric liquids which shall be classified in Division 4.2 if, in tests performed in accordance with the test method given in the *Manual of Tests and Criteria*, part III, sub-section 33.4.5, the liquid ignites in the first part of the test, or if it ignites or chars the filter paper.

2.4.3.2.3 *Self-heating substances*

2.4.3.2.3.1 A substance shall be classified as a self-heating substance of Division 4.2 if, in tests performed in accordance with the test method given in the *Manual of Tests and Criteria*, part III, sub-section 33.4.6:

(a) A positive result is obtained using a 25 mm cube sample at 140 °C;

(b) A positive result is obtained in a test using a 100 mm sample cube at 140 °C and a negative result is obtained in a test using a 100 mm cube sample at 120 °C <u>and</u> the substance is to be transported in packages with a volume of more than 3 m^3;

(c) A positive result is obtained in a test using a 100 mm sample cube at 140 °C and a negative result is obtained in a test using a 100 mm cube sample at 100 °C <u>and</u> the substance is to be transported in packages with a volume of more than 450 litres;

(d) A positive result is obtained in a test using a 100 mm sample cube at 140 °C <u>and</u> a positive result is obtained using a 100 mm cube sample at 100 °C.

NOTE: *Self-reactive substances giving also a positive result with this test method, shall not be classified in Division 4.2 but in Division 4.1 (see 2.4.2.3.1.1).*

2.4.3.2.3.2 A substance shall not be classified in Division 4.2 if:

(a) A negative result is obtained in a test using a 100 mm cube sample at 140 °C;

(b) A positive result is obtained in a test using a 100 mm sample cube at 140 °C and a negative result is obtained in a test using a 25 mm cube sample at 140 °C, a negative result is obtained in a test using a 100 mm cube sample at 120 °C <u>and</u> the substance is to be transported in packages with a volume not more than 3 m^3;

(c) A positive result is obtained in a test using a 100 mm sample cube at 140 °C and a negative result is obtained in a test using a 25 mm cube sample at 140 °C, a negative result is obtained in a test using a 100 mm cube sample at 100 °C <u>and</u> the substance is to be transported in packages with a volume not more than 450 litres.

2.4.3.3 *Assignment of packing groups*

2.4.3.3.1 Packing group I shall be assigned to all pyrophoric solids and liquids.

2.4.3.3.2 Packing group II shall be assigned to self-heating substances which give a positive result in a test using a 25 mm sample cube at 140 °C.

2.4.3.3.3 Packing group III shall be assigned to self-heating substances if:

(a) A positive result is obtained in a test using a 100 mm sample cube at 140 °C and a negative result is obtained in a test using a 25 mm cube sample at 140 °C <u>and</u> the substance is to be transported in packages with a volume of more than 3 m^3;

(b) A positive result is obtained in a test using a 100 mm sample cube at 140 °C and a negative result is obtained in a test using a 25 mm cube sample at 140 °C, a positive result is obtained in a test using a 100 mm cube sample at 120 °C <u>and</u> the substance is to be transported in packages with a volume of more than 450 litres;

(c) A positive result is obtained in a test using a 100 mm sample cube at 140 °C and a negative result is obtained in a test using a 25 mm cube sample at 140 °C <u>and</u> a positive result is obtained in a test using a 100 mm cube sample at 100 °C.

2.4.4 Division 4.3 – Substances which in contact with water emit flammable gases

2.4.4.1 *Definitions and properties*

Certain substances in contact with water may emit flammable gases that can form explosive mixtures with air. Such mixtures are easily ignited by all ordinary sources of ignition, for example naked lights, sparking handtools or unprotected lamps. The resulting blast wave and flames may endanger people and the environment. The test method referred to in 2.4.4.2 is used to determine whether the reaction of a substance with water leads to the development of a dangerous amount of gases which may be flammable. This test method shall not be applied to pyrophoric substances.

2.4.4.2 *Classification in Division 4.3*

Substances which in contact with water emit flammable gases shall be classified in Division 4.3 if, in tests performed in accordance with the test method given in the *Manual of Tests and Criteria*, part III, sub-section 33.5:

(a) Spontaneous ignition takes place in any step of the test procedure; or

(b) There is an evolution of a flammable gas at a rate greater than 1 litre per kilogram of the substance per hour.

2.4.4.3 *Assignment of packing groups*

2.4.4.3.1 Packing group I shall be assigned to any substance which reacts vigorously with water at ambient temperatures and demonstrates generally a tendency for the gas produced to ignite spontaneously, or which reacts readily with water at ambient temperatures such that the rate of evolution of flammable gas is equal to or greater than 10 litres per kilogram of substance over any one minute.

2.4.4.3.2 Packing group II shall be assigned to any substance which reacts readily with water at ambient temperatures such that the maximum rate of evolution of flammable gas is equal to or greater than 20 litres per kilogram of substance per hour, and which does not meet the criteria for packing group I.

2.4.4.3.3 Packing group III shall be assigned to any substance which reacts slowly with water at ambient temperatures such that the maximum rate of evolution of flammable gas is greater than 1 litre per kilogram of substance per hour, and which does not meet the criteria for packing groups I or II.

2.4.5 **Classification of organometallic substances**

Depending on their properties, organometallic substances may be classified in divisions 4.2 or 4.3, as appropriate, in accordance with the flowchart scheme given in figure 2.4.2.

Figure 2.4.2: Flowchart scheme for organometallic substances[b]

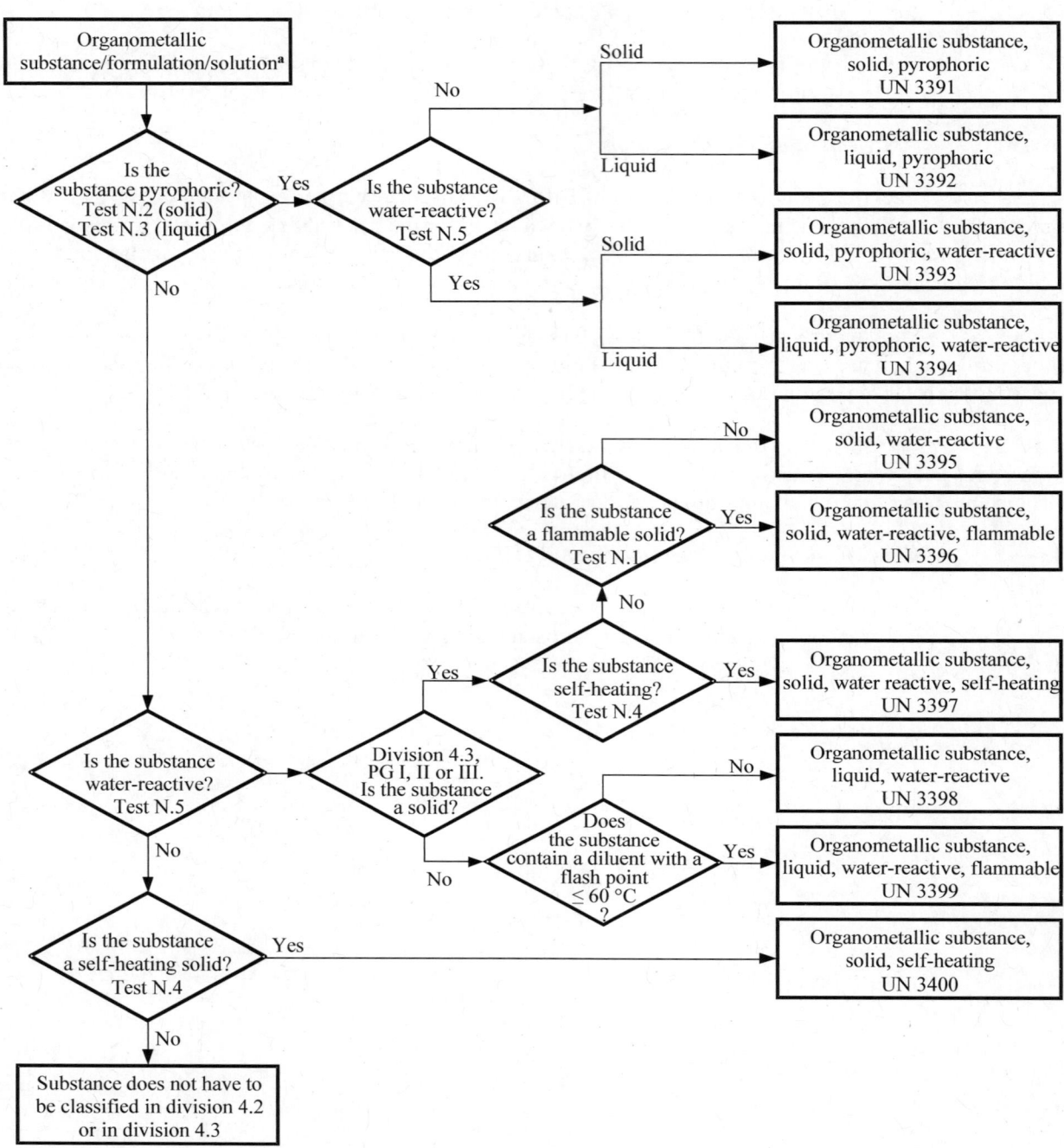

---
[a]   *If applicable and testing is relevant, taking into account reactivity properties, class 6.1 and 8 properties should be considered according to the precedence of hazard table 2.0.3.3.*
[b]   *Test methods N.1 to N.5 can be found in the Manual of tests and Criteria, part III, section 33.*

CHAPTER 2.5

CLASS 5 - OXIDIZING SUBSTANCES AND ORGANIC PEROXIDES

Introductory note

NOTE: *Because of the different properties exhibited by dangerous goods within Divisions 5.1 and 5.2, it is impracticable to establish a single criterion for classification in either division. Tests and criteria for assignment to the two divisions of Class 5 are addressed in this chapter.*

2.5.1 Definitions and general provisions

Class 5 is divided into two divisions as follows:

(a) Division 5.1 – *Oxidizing substances*

Substances which, while in themselves not necessarily combustible, may, generally by yielding oxygen, cause, or contribute to, the combustion of other material. Such substances may be contained in an article;

(b) Division 5.2 – *Organic peroxides*

Organic substances which contain the bivalent -O-O- structure and may be considered derivatives of hydrogen peroxide, where one or both of the hydrogen atoms have been replaced by organic radicals. Organic peroxides are thermally unstable substances, which may undergo exothermic self-accelerating decomposition. In addition, they may have one or more of the following properties:

(i) be liable to explosive decomposition;

(ii) burn rapidly;

(iii) be sensitive to impact or friction;

(iv) react dangerously with other substances;

(v) cause damage to the eyes.

2.5.2 Division 5.1 – Oxidizing substances

2.5.2.1 *Classification in Division 5.1*

2.5.2.1.1 Oxidizing substances are classified in Division 5.1 in accordance with the test methods, procedures and criteria in 2.5.2.2, 2.5.2.3 and the *Manual of Tests and Criteria*, part III, section 34. In the event of divergence between test results and known experience, judgement based on known experience shall take precedence over test results.

NOTE: *Where substances of this Division are listed in the Dangerous Goods List in chapter 3.2, reclassification of those substances in accordance with this criteria shall be undertaken only when this is necessary for safety.*

2.5.2.1.2 By exception, solid ammonium nitrate based fertilizers shall be classified in accordance with the procedure as set out in the *Manual of Tests and Criteria*, part III, section 39.

2.5.2.1.3 For substances having other hazards, e.g. toxicity or corrosivity, the requirements of chapter 2.0 shall be met.

2.5.2.2 *Oxidizing solids*

2.5.2.2.1 *Criteria for classification in Division 5.1*

2.5.2.2.1.1 Tests are performed to measure the potential for the solid substance to increase the burning rate or burning intensity of a combustible substance when the two are thoroughly mixed. The procedure is given in the *Manual of Tests and Criteria,* part III, sub-section 34.4.1 (test O.1) or alternatively, in sub-section 34.4.3 (test O.3). Tests are conducted on the substance to be evaluated mixed with dry fibrous cellulose in mixing ratios of 1:1 and 4:1, by mass, of sample to cellulose. The burning characteristics of the mixtures are compared:

(a) In the test O.1, with the standard 3:7 mixture, by mass, of potassium bromate to cellulose. If the burning time is equal to or less than this standard mixture, the burning times shall be compared with those from the packing group I or II reference standards, 3:2 and 2:3 ratios, by mass, of potassium bromate to cellulose respectively; or

(b) In the test O.3, with the standard 1:2 mixture, by mass, of calcium peroxide to cellulose. If the burning rate is equal to or greater than this standard mixture, the burning rates shall be compared with those from the packing group I or II reference standards 3:1 and 1:1 ratios, by mass, of calcium peroxide to cellulose, respectively.

2.5.2.2.1.2 The classification test results are assessed on the basis of:

(a) The comparison of the mean burning time (for the test O.1) or burning rate (for the test O.3) with those of the reference mixtures; and

(b) Whether the mixture of substance and cellulose ignites and burns.

2.5.2.2.1.3 A solid substance is classified in Division 5.1 if the 4:1 or 1:1 sample-to-cellulose ratio (by mass) tested, exhibits:

(a) In the test O.1, a mean burning time equal to or less than the mean burning time of a 3:7 mixture (by mass) of potassium bromate and cellulose; or

(b) In the test O.3, a mean burning rate equal to or greater than the mean burning rate of a 1:2 mixture (by mass) of calcium peroxide and cellulose.

2.5.2.2.2 *Assignment of packing groups*

Solid oxidizing substances are assigned to a packing group according to the test procedure in the *Manual of Tests and Criteria*, part III, section 34.4.1 (test O.1) or alternatively, in sub-section 34.4.3 (test O.3), in accordance with the following criteria:

(a) Test O.1:

(i) Packing group I: any substance which, in the 4:1 or 1:1 sample-to-cellulose ratio (by mass) tested, exhibits a mean burning time less than the mean burning time of a 3:2 mixture, by mass, of potassium bromate and cellulose;

(ii) Packing group II: any substance which, in the 4:1 or 1:1 sample-to-cellulose ratio (by mass) tested, exhibits a mean burning time equal to or less than the mean burning time of a 2:3 mixture (by mass) of potassium bromate and cellulose and the criteria for packing group I are not met;

(iii) Packing group III: any substance which, in the 4:1 or 1:1 sample-to-cellulose ratio (by mass) tested, exhibits a mean burning time equal to or less than the mean burning time of a 3:7 mixture (by mass) of potassium bromate and cellulose and the criteria for packing groups I and II are not met;

(iv) Not Division 5.1: any substance which, in both the 4:1 and 1:1 sample-to-cellulose ratio (by mass) tested, does not ignite and burn, or exhibits mean burning times greater than that of a 3:7 mixture (by mass) of potassium bromate and cellulose.

(b) Test O.3:

(i) Packing group I: any substance which, in the 4:1 or 1:1 sample-to-cellulose ratio (by mass) tested, exhibits a mean burning rate greater than the mean burning rate of a 3:1 mixture (by mass) of calcium peroxide and cellulose;

(ii) Packing group II: any substance which, in the 4:1 or 1:1 sample-to-cellulose ratio (by mass) tested, exhibits a mean burning rate equal to or greater than the mean burning rate of a 1:1 mixture (by mass) of calcium peroxide and cellulose, and the criteria for packing group I are not met;

(iii) Packing group III: any substance which, in the 4:1 or 1:1 sample-to-cellulose ratio (by mass) tested, exhibits a mean burning rate equal to or greater than the mean burning rate of a 1:2 mixture (by mass) of calcium peroxide and cellulose, and the criteria for packing groups I and II are not met;

(iv) Not Division 5.1: any substance which, in both the 4:1 and 1:1 sample-to-cellulose ratio (by mass) tested, does not ignite and burn, or exhibits a mean burning rate less than the mean burning rate of a 1:2 mixture (by mass) of calcium peroxide and cellulose.

2.5.2.3 *Oxidizing liquids*

2.5.2.3.1 *Criteria for classification in Division 5.1*

2.5.2.3.1.1 A test is performed to determine the potential for a liquid substance to increase the burning rate or burning intensity of a combustible substance or for spontaneous ignition to occur when the two are thoroughly mixed. The procedure is given in the *Manual of Tests and Criteria*, part III, sub-section 34.4.2 (Test O.2). It measures the pressure rise time during combustion. Whether a liquid is an oxidizing substance of Division 5.1 and, if so, whether packing groups I, II or III shall be assigned, is decided on the basis of the test result (see also precedence of hazards characteristics in 2.0.3).

2.5.2.3.1.2 The classification test results are assessed on the basis of:

(a) Whether the mixture of substance and cellulose spontaneously ignites;

(b) The comparison of the mean time taken for the pressure to rise from 690 kPa to 2070 kPa gauge with those of the reference substances.

2.5.2.3.1.3 A liquid substance is classified in Division 5.1 if the 1:1 mixture, by mass, of substance and cellulose tested, exhibits a mean pressure rise time less than or equal to the mean pressure rise time of a 1:1 mixture, by mass, of 65 % aqueous nitric acid and cellulose.

2.5.2.3.2 *Assignment of packing groups*

Liquid oxidizing substances are assigned to a packing group according to the test procedure in the *Manual of Tests and Criteria*, part III, section 34.4.2, in accordance with the following criteria:

(a) Packing group I: any substance which, in the 1:1 mixture, by mass, of substance and cellulose tested, spontaneously ignites; or the mean pressure rise time of a 1:1 mixture, by mass, of substance and cellulose is less than that of a 1:1 mixture, by mass, of 50 % perchloric acid and cellulose;

(b) Packing group II: any substance which, in the 1:1 mixture, by mass, of substance and cellulose tested, exhibits a mean pressure rise time less than or equal to the mean pressure rise time of a 1:1 mixture, by mass, of 40 % aqueous sodium chlorate solution and cellulose; and the criteria for packing group I are not met;

(c) Packing group III: any substance which, in the 1:1 mixture, by mass, of substance and cellulose tested, exhibits a mean pressure rise time less than or equal to the mean pressure rise time of a 1:1 mixture, by mass, of 65 % aqueous nitric acid and cellulose; and the criteria for packing groups I and II are not met;

(d) Not Division 5.1: any substance which, in the 1:1 mixture, by mass, of substance and cellulose tested, exhibits a pressure rise of less than 2 070 kPa gauge; or exhibits a mean pressure rise time greater than the mean pressure rise time of a 1:1 mixture, by mass, of 65 % aqueous nitric acid and cellulose.

2.5.3 Division 5.2 – Organic peroxides

2.5.3.1 *Properties*

2.5.3.1.1 Organic peroxides are liable to exothermic decomposition at normal or elevated temperatures. The decomposition can be initiated by heat, contact with impurities (e.g. acids, heavy-metal compounds, amines), friction or impact. The rate of decomposition increases with temperature and varies with the organic peroxide formulation. Decomposition may result in the evolution of harmful, or flammable, gases or vapours. For certain organic peroxides the temperature shall be controlled during transport. Some organic peroxides may decompose explosively, particularly if confined. This characteristic may be modified by the addition of diluents or by the use of appropriate packagings. Many organic peroxides burn vigorously.

2.5.3.1.2 Contact of organic peroxides with the eyes is to be avoided. Some organic peroxides will cause serious injury to the cornea, even after brief contact, or will be corrosive to the skin.

2.5.3.2 *Classification of organic peroxides*

2.5.3.2.1 Any organic peroxide shall be considered for classification in Division 5.2, unless the organic peroxide formulation contains:

(a) Not more than 1.0 % available oxygen from the organic peroxides when containing not more than 1.0 % hydrogen peroxide; or

(b) Not more than 0.5 % available oxygen from the organic peroxides when containing more than 1.0 % but not more than 7.0 % hydrogen peroxide.

NOTE: *The available oxygen content (%) of an organic peroxide formulation is given by the formula:*

$$16 \times \sum (n_i \times c_i / m_i)$$

where: n_i = *number of peroxygen groups per molecule of organic peroxide i;*

c_i = *concentration (mass %) of organic peroxide i;*

m_i = *molecular mass of organic peroxide i.*

2.5.3.2.2 Organic peroxides are classified into seven types according to the degree of danger they present. The types of organic peroxide range from type A, which may not be accepted for transport in the packaging in which it is tested, to type G, which is not subject to the provisions for organic peroxides of Division 5.2. The classification of types B to F is directly related to the maximum quantity allowed in one packaging.

2.5.3.2.3 Organic peroxides permitted for transport in packagings are listed in 2.5.3.2.4, those permitted for transport in IBCs are listed in packing instruction IBC520 and those permitted for transport in portable tanks are listed in portable tank instruction T23. For each permitted substance listed, the generic entry of the Dangerous Goods List (UN Nos. 3101 to 3120) is assigned, appropriate subsidiary hazards and remarks providing relevant transport information are given. The generic entries specify:

    (a)   Organic peroxide type (B to F);

    (b)   Physical state (liquid or solid); and

    (c)   Temperature control, when required (see 2.5.3.4).

2.5.3.2.3.1   Mixtures of the listed formulations may be classified as the same type of organic peroxide as that of the most dangerous component and be transported under the conditions of transport given for this type. However, as two stable components can form a thermally less stable mixture, the self-accelerating decomposition temperature (SADT) of the mixture shall be determined and, if necessary, temperature control applied as required by 2.5.3.4.

2.5.3.2.4   *List of currently assigned organic peroxides in packagings*

"Packing Method" codes "OP1" to "OP8" refer to packing methods in packing instruction P520. Peroxides to be transported should fulfil the classification and the control and emergency temperatures (derived from the SADT) as listed. For substances permitted in IBCs see packing instruction IBC520, and for those permitted in tanks, see portable tank instruction T23. The formulations not listed in this sub-section but listed in packing instruction IBC520 of 4.1.4.2 and in portable tank instruction T23 of 4.2.5.2.6 may also be transported packed in accordance with packing method OP8 of packing instruction P520 of 4.1.4.1, with the same control and emergency temperatures, if applicable.

ORGANIC PEROXIDE	Concentration (%)	Diluent type A (%)	Diluent type B¹ (%)	Inert solid (%)	Water (%)	Packing Method	Control temperature (°C)	Emergency temperature (°C)	Number (Generic entry)	Subsidiary hazards and remarks
ACETYL ACETONE PEROXIDE	≤42	≥48			≥8	OP7			3105	2)
"	≤35	≥57			≥8	OP8			3107	32)
"	≤32 as a paste					OP7			3106	20)
ACETYL CYCLOHEXANESULPHONYL PEROXIDE	≤82				≥12	OP4	-10	0	3112	3)
"	≤32		≥68			OP7	-10	0	3115	
tert-AMYL HYDROPEROXIDE	≤88	≥6			≥6	OP8			3107	
tert-AMYL PEROXYACETATE	≤62	≥38				OP7			3105	
tert-AMYL PEROXYBENZOATE	≤100					OP5			3103	
tert-AMYL PEROXY-2-ETHYLHEXANOATE	≤100					OP7	+20	+25	3115	
tert-AMYL PEROXY-2-ETHYLHEXYL CARBONATE	≤100					OP7			3105	
tert-AMYL PEROXY ISOPROPYL CARBONATE	≤77	≥23				OP5			3103	
tert-AMYL PEROXYNEODECANOATE	≤77		≥23			OP7	0	+10	3115	
"	≤47	≥53				OP8	0	+10	3119	
tert-AMYL PEROXYPIVALATE	≤77		≥23			OP5	+10	+15	3113	
tert-AMYLPEROXY-3,5,5-TRIMETHYLHEXANOATE	≤100					OP7			3105	
tert-BUTYL CUMYL PEROXIDE	>42 - 100			≥48		OP8			3109	
"	≤52					OP8			3108	
n-BUTYL-4,4-DI-(tert-BUTYLPEROXY)VALERATE	>52 - 100					OP5			3103	
"	≤52			≥48		OP8			3108	
tert-BUTYL HYDROPEROXIDE	>79 - 90				≥10	OP5			3103	13)
"	≤80	≥20				OP7			3105	4) 13)
"	≤79				>14	OP8			3107	13) 23)
"	≤72				≥28	OP8			3109	13)
tert-BUTYL HYDROPEROXIDE + DI-tert-BUTYLPEROXIDE	<82 + >9				≥7	OP5			3103	13)

ORGANIC PEROXIDE	Concentration (%)	Diluent type A (%)	Diluent type B¹ (%)	Inert solid (%)	Water (%)	Packing Method	Control temperature (°C)	Emergency temperature (°C)	Number (Generic entry)	Subsidiary hazards and remarks
tert-BUTYL MONOPEROXYMALEATE	> 52 - 100					OP5			3102	3)
"	≤ 52	≥ 48				OP6			3103	
"	≤ 52			≥ 48		OP8			3108	
"	≤ 52 as a paste					OP8			3108	
tert-BUTYL PEROXYACETATE	> 52 - 77	≥ 23				OP5			3101	3)
"	> 32 - 52	≥ 48				OP6			3103	
"	≤ 32		≥ 68			OP8			3109	
tert-BUTYL PEROXYBENZOATE	> 77 - 100					OP5			3103	
"	> 52 - 77	≥ 23				OP7			3105	
"	≤ 52			≥ 48		OP7			3106	
tert-BUTYL PEROXYBUTYL FUMARATE	≤ 52	≥ 48				OP7			3105	
tert-BUTYL PEROXYCROTONATE	≤ 77	≥ 23				OP7			3105	
tert-BUTYL PEROXYDIETHYLACETATE	≤ 100					OP5	+20	+25	3113	
tert-BUTYL PEROXY-2-ETHYLHEXANOATE	> 52 – 100					OP6	+20	+25	3113	
"	> 32 - 52		≥ 48			OP8	+30	+35	3117	
"	≤ 52			≥ 48		OP8	+20	+25	3118	
"	≤ 32		≥ 68			OP8	+40	+45	3119	
tert-BUTYL PEROXY-2-ETHYLHEXANOATE + 2,2-DI-(tert-BUTYLPEROXY)BUTANE	≤ 12 + ≤ 14	≥ 14		≥ 60		OP7			3106	
"	≤ 31 + ≤ 36		≥ 33			OP7	+35	+40	3115	
tert-BUTYL PEROXY-2-ETHYLHEXYLCARBONATE	≤ 100					OP5			3105	
tert-BUTYL PEROXYISOBUTYRATE	> 52 - 77		≥ 23			OP5	+15	+20	3111	3)
"	≤ 52		≥ 48			OP7	+15	+20	3115	
tert-BUTYLPEROXY ISOPROPYLCARBONATE	≤ 77	≥ 23				OP5			3103	
"	≤ 62		≥ 38			OP7			3105	
1-(2-tert-BUTYLPEROXY ISOPROPYL)-3-ISOPROPENYLBENZENE	≤ 77	≥ 23				OP7			3105	
"	≤ 42			≥ 58		OP8			3108	
tert-BUTYL PEROXY-2-METHYLBENZOATE	≤ 100					OP5			3103	

ORGANIC PEROXIDE	Concentration (%)	Diluent type A (%)	Diluent type B¹ (%)	Inert solid (%)	Water (%)	Packing Method	Control temperature (°C)	Emergency temperature (°C)	Number (Generic entry)	Subsidiary hazards and remarks
tert-BUTYL PEROXYNEODECANOATE	> 77 - 100					OP7	-5	+5	3115	
"	≤ 77		≥ 23			OP7	0	+10	3115	
"	≤ 52 as a stable dispersion in water					OP8	0	+10	3119	
"	≤ 42 as a stable dispersion in water (frozen)					OP8	0	+10	3118	
"	≤ 32	≥ 68				OP8	0	+10	3119	
tert-BUTYL PEROXYNEOHEPTANOATE	≤ 77	≥ 23				OP7	0	+10	3115	
"	≤ 42 as a stable dispersion in water					OP8	0	+10	3117	
tert-BUTYL PEROXYPIVALATE	> 67 - 77	≥ 23				OP5	0	+10	3113	
"	> 27 - 67		≥ 33			OP7	0	+10	3115	
"	≤ 27		≥ 73			OP8	+30	+35	3119	
tert-BUTYLPEROXY STEARYLCARBONATE	≤ 100					OP7			3106	
tert-BUTYL PEROXY-3,5,5-TRIMETHYLHEXANOATE	> 37 - 100					OP7			3105	
"	≤ 42			≥ 58		OP7			3106	
"	≤ 37		≥ 63			OP8			3109	
3-CHLOROPEROXYBENZOIC ACID	> 57 - 86			≥ 14		OP1			3102	3)
"	≤ 57			≥ 3	≥ 40	OP7			3106	
"	≤ 77			≥ 6	≥ 17	OP7			3106	
CUMYL HYDROPEROXIDE	> 90 - 98	≤ 10				OP8			3107	13)
"	≤ 90	≥ 10				OP8			3109	13) 18)
CUMYL PEROXYNEODECANOATE	≤ 87	≥ 13				OP7	- 10	0	3115	
"	≤ 77		≥ 23			OP7	-10	0	3115	
"	≤ 52 as a stable dispersion in water					OP8	-10	0	3119	
CUMYL PEROXYNEOHEPTANOATE	≤ 77	≥ 23				OP7	0	0	3115	

ORGANIC PEROXIDE	Concentration (%)	Diluent type A (%)	Diluent type B¹ (%)	Inert solid (%)	Water (%)	Packing Method	Control temperature (°C)	Emergency temperature (°C)	Number (Generic entry)	Subsidiary hazards and remarks
CUMYL PEROXYPIVALATE	≤77		≥23			OP7	-5	+5	3115	
CYCLOHEXANONE PEROXIDE(S)	≤91				≥9	OP6			3104	13)
"	≤72	≥28				OP7			3105	5)
"	≤72 as a paste					OP7			3106	5) 20)
"	≤32			≥68					Exempt	29)
([3R-(3R,5aS,6S,8aS,9R,10R,12S,12aR**)]-DECAHYDRO-10-METHOXY-3,6,9-TRIMETHYL-3,12-EPOXY-12H-PYRANO[4,3-j]-1,2-BENZODIOXEPIN)	≤100					OP7			3106	
DIACETONE ALCOHOL PEROXIDES	≤57		≥26		≥8	OP7	+40	+45	3115	6)
DIACETYL PEROXIDE	≤27		≥73			OP7	+20	+25	3115	7) 13)
DI-tert-AMYL PEROXIDE	≤100					OP8			3107	
2,2-DI-(tert-AMYLPEROXY)BUTANE	≤57	≥43				OP7			3105	
1,1-DI-(tert-AMYLPEROXY)CYCLOHEXANE	≤82	≥18				OP6			3103	
DIBENZOYL PEROXIDE	>52 – 100			≤48		OP2			3102	3)
"	>77 - 94				≥6	OP4			3102	3)
"	≤77				≥23	OP6			3104	
"	≤62			≥28	≥10	OP7			3106	
"	>52 – 62 as a paste					OP7			3106	20)
"	>35 – 52			≥48		OP7			3106	
"	>36 - 42	≥18			≤40	OP8			3107	
"	≤56.5 as a paste				≥15	OP8			3108	20)
"	≤52 as a paste					OP8			3108	
"	≤42	≥38			≥13	OP8			3109	
"	≤42 as a stable dispersion in water								3109	
"	≤35			≥65					Exempt	29)
DI-(4-tert-BUTYLCYCLOHEXYL) PEROXYDICARBONATE	≤100					OP6	+30	+35	3114	
"	≤42 as a stable dispersion in water					OP8	+30	+35	3119	

ORGANIC PEROXIDE	Concentration (%)	Diluent type A (%)	Diluent type B[1] (%)	Inert solid (%)	Water (%)	Packing Method	Control temperature (°C)	Emergency temperature (°C)	Number (Generic entry)	Subsidiary hazards and remarks
DI-(4-tert-BUTYLCYCLOHEXYL) PEROXYDICARBONATE	≤42 (as a paste)					OP8	+35	+40	3118	
DI-(tert-BUTYL PEROXIDE	>52 - 100					OP8			3107	
"	≤52		≥48			OP8			3109	25)
DI-tert-BUTYL PEROXYAZELATE	≤52	≥48				OP7			3105	
2,2-DI-(tert-BUTYLPEROXY)BUTANE	≤52	≥48				OP6			3103	
1,6-DI-(tert-BUTYLPEROXYCARBONYLOXY) HEXANE	≤72	≥28				OP5			3103	
1,1-DI-(tert-BUTYLPEROXY) CYCLOHEXANE	>80 - 100					OP5			3101	3)
"	≤72		≥28			OP5			3103	30)
"	>52 - 80	≥20				OP5			3103	
"	>42 - 52	≥48				OP7			3105	
"	≤42	≥13		≥45		OP7			3106	
"	≤42	≥58				OP8			3109	
"	≤27	≥25				OP8			3107	21)
"	≤13	≥13	≥74			OP8			3109	
1,1-DI-(tert-BUTYLPEROXY)CYCLOHEXANE + tert-BUTYL PEROXY-2-ETHYLHEXANOATE	≤43 + ≤16	≥41				OP 7			3105	
DI-n-BUTYL PEROXYDICARBONATE	>27 - 52		≥48			OP7	-15	-5	3115	
"	≤42 as a stable dispersion in water (frozen)					OP8	-15	-5	3118	
"	≤27		≥73			OP8	-10	0	3117	
DI-sec-BUTYL PEROXYDICARBONATE	>52 - 100					OP4	-20	-10	3113	
"	≤52		≥48			OP7	-15	-5	3115	
DI-(tert-BUTYLPEROXYISOPROPYL)BENZENE(S)	>42 - 100			≤57		OP7			3106	
"	≤42			≥58		OP7			Exempt	29)
DI-(tert-BUTYLPEROXY) PHTHALATE	>42 - 52	≥48				OP7			3105	
"	≤52 as a paste					OP7			3106	20)
"	≤42	≥58				OP8			3107	

ORGANIC PEROXIDE	Concentration (%)	Diluent type A (%)	Diluent type B¹ (%)	Inert solid (%)	Water (%)	Packing Method	Control temperature (°C)	Emergency temperature (°C)	Number (Generic entry)	Subsidiary hazards and remarks
2,2-DI-(tert-BUTYLPEROXY)PROPANE	≤ 52	≥ 48				OP7			3105	
"	≤ 42	≥ 13		≥ 45		OP7			3106	
1,1-DI-(tert-BUTYLPEROXY)-3,3,5-TRIMETHYLCYCLOHEXANE	> 90 - 100					OP5			3101	3)
"	≤ 90		≥ 10			OP5			3103	30)
"	> 57 - 90	≥ 10				OP5			3103	
"	≤ 77		≥ 23			OP5			3103	
"	≤ 57			≥ 43		OP8			3110	
"	≤ 57	≥ 43				OP8			3107	
"	≤ 32	≥ 26	≥ 42			OP8			3107	
DICETYL PEROXYDICARBONATE	≤ 100					OP8	+30	+35	3120	
"	≤ 42 as a stable dispersion in water					OP8	+30	+35	3119	
DI-4-CHLOROBENZOYL PEROXIDE	≤ 77				≥ 23	OP5			3102	3)
"	≤ 52 as a paste					OP7			3106	20)
"	≤ 32			≥ 68					Exempt	29)
DICUMYL PEROXIDE	> 52 - 100					OP8			3110	12)
"	≤ 52			≥ 48					Exempt	29)
DICYCLOHEXYL PEROXYDICARBONATE	> 91 - 100					OP3	+10	+15	3112	3)
"	≤ 91				≥ 9	OP5	+10	+15	3114	
"	≤ 42 as a stable dispersion in water					OP8	+15	+20	3119	
DIDECANOYL PEROXIDE	≤ 100					OP6	+30	+35	3114	
2,2-DI-(4,4-DI (tert-BUTYLPEROXY)CYCLOHEXYL) PROPANE	≤ 42			≥ 58		OP7			3106	
"	≤ 22		≥ 78			OP8			3107	
DI-2,4-DICHLOROBENZOYL PEROXIDE	≤ 77				≥ 23	OP5			3102	3)
"	≤ 52 as a paste					OP8	+ 20	+ 25	3118	
"	≤ 52 as a paste with silicon oil					OP5			3104	

ORGANIC PEROXIDE	Concentration (%)	Diluent type A (%)	Diluent type B[1] (%)	Inert solid (%)	Water (%)	Packing Method	Control temperature (°C)	Emergency temperature (°C)	Number (Generic entry)	Subsidiary hazards and remarks
DI-(2-ETHOXYETHYL) PEROXYDICARBONATE	≤ 52		≥ 48			OP7	-10	0	3115	
DI-(2-ETHYLHEXYL) PEROXYDICARBONATE	> 77 - 100					OP5	-20	-10	3113	
"	≤ 77		≥ 23			OP7	-15	-5	3115	
"	≤ 62 as a stable dispersion in water					OP8	-15	-5	3119	
"	≤ 52 as a stable dispersion in water (frozen)					OP8	-15	-5	3120	
2,2-DIHYDROPEROXYPROPANE	≤ 27			≥ 73		OP5			3102	3)
DI-(1-HYDROXYCYCLOHEXYL) PEROXIDE	≤ 100					OP7			3106	
DIISOBUTYRYL PEROXIDE	> 32 - 52		≥ 48			OP5	-20	-10	3111	3)
"	≤ 42 (as a stable dispersion in water)					OP8	-20	-10	3119	
"	≤ 32		≥ 68			OP7	-20	-10	3115	
DIISOPROPYLBENZENE DIHYDROPEROXIDE	≤ 82	≥ 5			≥ 5	OP7	-15	-5	3106	24)
DIISOPROPYL PEROXYDICARBONATE	> 52-100					OP2	-15	-5	3112	3)
"	≤ 52		≥ 48			OP7	-20	-10	3115	
"	≤ 32	≥ 68				OP7	-15	-5	3115	
DILAUROYL PEROXIDE	≤ 100					OP7			3106	
"	≤ 42 as a stable dispersion in water					OP8			3109	
DI-(3-METHOXYBUTYL) PEROXYDICARBONATE	≤ 52		≥ 48			OP7	-5	+5	3115	
DI-(2-METHYLBENZOYL) PEROXIDE	≤ 87			≥ 18	≥ 13	OP5	+30	+35	3112	3)
DI-(3-METHYLBENZOYL) PEROXIDE + BENZOYL (3-METHYLBENZOYL) PEROXIDE + DIBENZOYL PEROXIDE	≤ 20 + ≤ 18 + ≤ 4		≥ 58			OP7	+35	+40	3115	
DI-(4-METHYLBENZOYL) PEROXIDE	≤ 52 as a paste with silicon oil					OP7			3106	
2,5-DIMETHYL-2,5-DI-(BENZOYLPEROXY)HEXANE	> 82-100					OP5			3102	3)
"	≤ 82					OP7			3106	
"	≤ 82				≥ 18	OP5			3104	

ORGANIC PEROXIDE	Concentration (%)	Diluent type A (%)	Diluent type B¹ (%)	Inert solid (%)	Water (%)	Packing Method	Control temperature (°C)	Emergency temperature (°C)	Number (Generic entry)	Subsidiary hazards and remarks
2,5-DIMETHYL-2,5-DI-(tert-BUTYLPEROXY)HEXANE	> 90 - 100					OP5			3103	
"	> 52 - 90	≥ 10				OP7			3105	
"	≤ 77			≥ 23		OP8			3108	
"	≤ 52	≥ 48				OP8			3109	
"	≤ 47 as a paste					OP8			3108	
"	≤ 22			≥ 78					Exempt	29)
2,5-DIMETHYL-2,5-DI-(tert-BUTYLPEROXY)HEXYNE-3	> 86-100					OP5			3101	3)
"	> 52-86	≥ 14				OP5			3103	26)
"	≤ 52			≥ 48		OP7			3106	
2,5-DIMETHYL-2,5-DI-(2-ETHYLHEXANOYLPEROXY) HEXANE	≤ 100					OP5	+20	+25	3113	
2,5-DIMETHYL-2,5-DIHYDROPEROXYHEXANE	≤ 82				≥ 18	OP6			3104	
2,5-DIMETHYL-2,5-DI-(3,5,5-TRIMETHYLHEXANOYL-PEROXY)HEXANE	≤ 77	≥ 23				OP7			3105	
1,1-DIMETHYL-3-HYDROXYBUTYL PEROXYNEOHEPTANOATE	≤ 52	≥ 48				OP8	0	+10	3117	
DIMYRISTYL PEROXYDICARBONATE	≤ 100					OP7	+20	+25	3116	
"	≤ 42 as a stable dispersion in water					OP8	+20	+25	3119	
DI-(2-NEODECANOYLPEROXYISOPROPYL) BENZENE	≤ 52	≥ 48				OP7	-10	0	3115	
DI-n-NONANOYL PEROXIDE	≤ 100					OP7	0	+10	3116	
DI-n-OCTANOYL PEROXIDE	≤ 100					OP5	+10	+15	3114	
DI-(2-PHENOXYETHYL) PEROXYDICARBONATE	>85-100					OP5			3102	3)
"	≤ 85				≥ 15	OP7			3106	
DIPROPIONYL PEROXIDE	≤ 27		≥ 73			OP8	+15	+20	3117	
DI-n-PROPYL PEROXYDICARBONATE	≤ 100					OP3	-25	-15	3113	
"	≤ 77		≥ 23			OP5	-20	-10	3113	
DISUCCINIC ACID PEROXIDE	> 72-100					OP4	+10	+15	3102	3) 17)
"	≤ 72				≥ 28	OP7			3116	

ORGANIC PEROXIDE	Concentration (%)	Diluent type A (%)	Diluent type B¹ (%)	Inert solid (%)	Water (%)	Packing Method	Control temperature (°C)	Emergency temperature (°C)	Number (Generic entry)	Subsidiary hazards and remarks
DI-(3,5,5-TRIMETHYLHEXANOYL) PEROXIDE	> 52-82	≥ 18				OP7	0	+10	3115	
"	≤ 52 as a stable dispersion in water					OP8	+10	+15	3119	
"	> 38-52	≥ 48				OP8	+10	+15	3119	
"	≤ 38	≥ 62				OP8	+20	+25	3119	
ETHYL 3,3-DI-(tert-AMYLPEROXY)BUTYRATE	≤ 67	≥ 33				OP7			3105	
ETHYL 3,3-DI-(tert-BUTYLPEROXY)BUTYRATE	> 77 - 100					OP5			3103	
"	≤ 77	≥ 23				OP7			3105	
"	≤ 52			≥ 48		OP7			3106	
1-(2-ETHYLHEXANOYLPEROXY)-1,3-DIMETHYLBUTYL PEROXYPIVALATE	≤ 52	≥ 45	≥ 10			OP7	-20	-10	3115	
tert-HEXYL PEROXYNEODECANOATE	≤ 71	≥ 29				OP7	0	+10	3115	
tert-HEXYL PEROXYPIVALATE	≤ 72		≥ 28			OP7	+10	+15	3115	
"	≤ 52 as a stable dispersion in water					OP8	+15	+20	3117	
3-HYDROXY-1,1-DIMETHYLBUTYL PEROXYNEODECANOATE	≤ 77	≥ 23				OP 7	- 5	+ 5	3115	
"	≤ 52	≥ 48				OP 8	- 5	+ 5	3117	
"	≤ 52 as a stable dispersion in water					OP 8	- 5	+ 5	3119	
ISOPROPYL sec-BUTYL PEROXYDICARBONATE + DI-sec-BUTYL PEROXYDICARBONATE+DI-ISOPROPYL PEROXYDICARBONATE	≤ 32 + ≤ 15 – 18 + ≤ 12 - 15	≥ 38				OP7	-20	-10	3115	
"	≤ 52 + ≤ 28 + ≤ 22					OP5	-20	-10	3111	3)
ISOPROPYLCUMYL HYDROPEROXIDE	≤ 72	≥ 28				OP8			3109	13)
p-MENTHYL HYDROPEROXIDE	> 72 - 100					OP7			3105	13)
"	≤ 72	≥ 28				OP8			3109	27)
METHYLCYCLOHEXANONE PEROXIDE(S)	≤ 67		≥ 33			OP7	+35	+40	3115	

ORGANIC PEROXIDE	Concentration (%)	Diluent type A (%)	Diluent type B¹ (%)	Inert solid (%)	Water (%)	Packing Method	Control temperature (°C)	Emergency temperature (°C)	Number (Generic entry)	Subsidiary hazards and remarks
METHYL ETHYL KETONE PEROXIDE(S)	See remark 33	≥ 41			≥ 9	OP8			3105	33) 34)
"	See remark 8	≥ 48				OP5			3101	3) 8) 13)
"	See remark 9	≥ 55				OP7			3105	9)
"	See remark 10	≥ 60				OP8			3107	10)
METHYL ISOBUTYL KETONE PEROXIDE(S)	≤ 62	≥ 19				OP7			3105	22)
METHYL ISOPROPYL KETONE PEROXIDE(S)	See remark 31)	≥ 70				OP8			3109	31)
ORGANIC PEROXIDE, LIQUID, SAMPLE						OP2			3103	11)
ORGANIC PEROXIDE, LIQUID, SAMPLE, TEMPERATURE CONTROLLED						OP2			3113	11)
ORGANIC PEROXIDE, SOLID, SAMPLE						OP2			3104	11)
ORGANIC PEROXIDE, SOLID, SAMPLE, TEMPERATURE CONTROLLED						OP2			3114	11)
3,3,5,7,7-PENTAMETHYL-1,2,4-TRIOXEPANE	≤ 100					OP8			3107	
PEROXYACETIC ACID, TYPE D, stabilized	≤ 43					OP7			3105	13) 14) 19)
PEROXYACETIC ACID, TYPE E, stabilized	≤ 43					OP8			3107	13) 15) 19)
PEROXYACETIC ACID, TYPE F, stabilized	≤ 43					OP8			3109	13) 16) 19)
PEROXYLAURIC ACID	≤ 100					OP8	+35	+40	3118	
1-PHENYLETHYL HYDROPEROXIDE	≤ 38		≥ 62			OP8			3109	
PINANYL HYDROPEROXIDE	> 56 - 100					OP7			3105	13)
"	≤ 56	≥ 44				OP8			3109	
POLYETHER POLY-tert-BUTYLPEROXYCARBONATE	≤ 52		≥ 48			OP8			3107	
1,1,3,3-TETRAMETHYLBUTYL HYDROPEROXIDE	≤ 100					OP7			3105	
1,1,3,3-TETRAMETHYLBUTYL PEROXY-2 ETHYL-HEXANOATE	≤ 100					OP7	+15	+20	3115	
1,1,3,3- TETRAMETHYLBUTYL PEROXYNEODECANOATE	≤ 72		≥ 28			OP7	-5	+5	3115	
"	≤ 52 as a stable dispersion in water					OP8	-5	+5	3119	
1,1,3,3-TETRAMETHYLBUTYL PEROXYPIVALATE	≤ 77	≥ 23				OP7	0	+10	3115	
3,6,9-TRIETHYL-3,6,9-TRIMETHYL-1,4,7 TRIPEROXONANE	≤ 42	≥ 58				OP7			3105	28)
"	≤ 17	≥ 18		≥ 65		OP8			3110	

Notes on 2.5.3.2.4:

1) Diluent type B may always be replaced by diluent type A. The boiling point of diluent type B should be at least 60 °C higher than the SADT of the organic peroxide.

2) Available oxygen ≤ 4.7 %.

3) "EXPLOSIVE" subsidiary hazard label required (Model No.1, see 5.2.2.2.2).

4) Diluent may be replaced by di-tert-butyl peroxide.

5) Available oxygen ≤ 9 %.

6) With ≤ 9 % hydrogen peroxide; available oxygen ≤ 10 %.

7) Only non-metallic packagings allowed.

8) Available oxygen > 10 % and ≤ 10.7 %, with or without water.

9) Available oxygen ≤ 10 %, with or without water.

10) Available oxygen ≤ 8.2 %, with or without water.

11) See 2.5.3.2.5.1.

12) Up to 2 000 kg per receptacle assigned to ORGANIC PEROXIDE TYPE F on the basis of large scale trials.

13) "CORROSIVE" subsidiary hazard label required (Model No 8, see 5.2.2.2.2).

14) Peroxyacetic acid formulations which fulfil the criteria of 2.5.3.3.2 (d).

15) Peroxyacetic acid formulations which fulfil the criteria of 2.5.3.3.2 (e).

16) Peroxyacetic acid formulations which fulfil the criteria of 2.5.3.3.2 (f).

17) Addition of water to this organic peroxide will decrease its thermal stability.

18) No "CORROSIVE" subsidiary hazard label required for concentrations below 80 %.

19) Mixtures with hydrogen peroxide, water and acid(s).

20) With diluent type A, with or without water.

21) With ≥ 25 % diluent type A by mass, and in addition ethylbenzene.

22) With ≥ 19 % diluent type A by mass, and in addition methyl isobutyl ketone.

23) With < 6 % di-tert-butyl peroxide.

24) With ≤ 8 % 1-isopropylhydroperoxy-4-isopropylhydroxybenzene.

25) Diluent type B with boiling point > 110 °C.

26) With < 0.5 % hydroperoxides content.

27) For concentrations more than 56 %, "CORROSIVE" subsidiary hazard label (Model No 8, see 5.2.2.2.2) required.

28) Available active oxygen ≤ 7.6 % in diluent Type A having a 95 % boil-off point in the range of 200 - 260 °C.

29) Not subject to the requirements of these Model Regulations for Division 5.2.

30) Diluent type B with boiling point > 130 °C.

31) Active oxygen ≤ 6.7 %.

32) Active oxygen ≤ 4.15 %.

33) Available oxygen ≤ 10 %.

34) Sum of diluent type A and water ≥ 55 %, and in addition methyl ethyl ketone.

2.5.3.2.5   Classification of organic peroxides not listed in 2.5.3.2.4, packing instruction IBC520 or portable tank instruction T23 and assignment to a generic entry shall be made by the competent authority of the country of origin on the basis of a test report. Principles applying to the classification of such substances are provided in 2.5.3.3. The applicable classification procedures, test methods and criteria, and an example of a suitable test report, are given in the current edition of the *Manual of Tests and Criteria*, part II. The statement of approval shall contain the classification and the relevant transport conditions.

2.5.3.2.5.1   Samples of new organic peroxides or new formulations of organic peroxides not listed in 2.5.3.2.4, for which complete test data are not available and which are to be transported for further testing or evaluation, may be assigned to one of the appropriate entries for ORGANIC PEROXIDE TYPE C provided the following conditions are met:

(a) The available data indicate that the sample would be no more dangerous than ORGANIC PEROXIDE TYPE B;

(b) The sample is packaged in accordance with packing method OP2 (see applicable packing instruction) and the quantity per cargo transport unit is limited to 10 kg;

(c) The available data indicate that the control temperature, if any, is sufficiently low to prevent any dangerous decomposition and sufficiently high to prevent any dangerous phase separation.

2.5.3.3   *Principles for classification of organic peroxides*

NOTE: *This section refers only to those properties of organic peroxides which are decisive for their classification. A flow chart, presenting the classification principles in the form of a graphically arranged scheme of questions concerning the decisive properties together with the possible answers, is given in figure 2.5.1. These properties shall be determined experimentally. Suitable test methods with pertinent evaluation criteria are given in the "Manual of Tests and Criteria", part II.*

2.5.3.3.1   An organic peroxide formulation shall be regarded as possessing explosive properties when in laboratory testing the formulation is liable to detonate, to deflagrate rapidly or to show a violent effect when heated under confinement.

2.5.3.3.2   The following principles apply to the classification of organic peroxide formulations not listed in 2.5.3.2.4:

(a) Any organic peroxide formulation which can detonate or deflagrate rapidly, as packaged for transport, is prohibited from transport in that packaging under Division 5.2 (defined as ORGANIC PEROXIDE TYPE A, exit box A of figure 2.5.1);

(b) Any organic peroxide formulation possessing explosive properties and which, as packaged for transport, neither detonates nor deflagrates rapidly, but is liable to undergo a thermal explosion in that package, shall bear an "EXPLOSIVE" subsidiary hazard label (Model No 1, see 5.2.2.2.2). Such an organic peroxide may be packaged in amounts of up to 25 kg unless the maximum quantity has to be limited to a lower amount to preclude detonation or rapid deflagration in the package (defined as ORGANIC PEROXIDE TYPE B, exit box B of figure 2.5.1);

(c) Any organic peroxide formulation possessing explosive properties may be transported without an "EXPLOSIVE" subsidiary hazard label when the substance as packaged (maximum 50 kg) for transport cannot detonate or deflagrate rapidly or undergo a thermal explosion (defined as ORGANIC PEROXIDE TYPE C, exit box C of figure 2.5.1);

(d) Any organic peroxide formulation which in laboratory testing:

(i) detonates partially, does not deflagrate rapidly and shows no violent effect when heated under confinement; or

        (ii)   does not detonate at all, deflagrates slowly and shows no violent effect when heated under confinement; or

        (iii)   does not detonate or deflagrate at all and shows a medium effect when heated under confinement;

    is acceptable for transport in packages of not more than 50 kg net mass (defined as ORGANIC PEROXIDE TYPE D, exit box D of figure 2.5.1);

(e)   Any organic peroxide formulation which, in laboratory testing, neither detonates nor deflagrates at all and shows low or no effect when heated under confinement is acceptable for transport in packages of not more than 400 kg/450 litres (defined as ORGANIC PEROXIDE TYPE E, exit box E of figure 2.5.1);

(f)   Any organic peroxide formulation which, in laboratory testing, neither detonates in the cavitated state nor deflagrates at all and shows only a low or no effect when heated under confinement as well as low or no explosive power may be considered for transport in IBCs or tanks (defined as ORGANIC PEROXIDE TYPE F, exit box F of figure 2.5.1); for additional requirements see 4.1.7 and 4.2.1.13;

(g)   Any organic peroxide formulation which, in laboratory testing, neither detonates in the cavitated state nor deflagrates at all and shows no effect when heated under confinement nor any explosive power shall be exempted from Division 5.2, provided that the formulation is thermally stable (self-accelerating decomposition temperature is 60 °C or higher for a 50 kg package) and for liquid formulations diluent type A is used for desensitization (defined as ORGANIC PEROXIDE TYPE G, exit box G of figure 2.5.1). If the formulation is not thermally stable or a diluent other than type A is used for desensitization, the formulation shall be defined as ORGANIC PEROXIDE TYPE F.

Figure 2.5.1: Flow chart scheme for organic peroxides

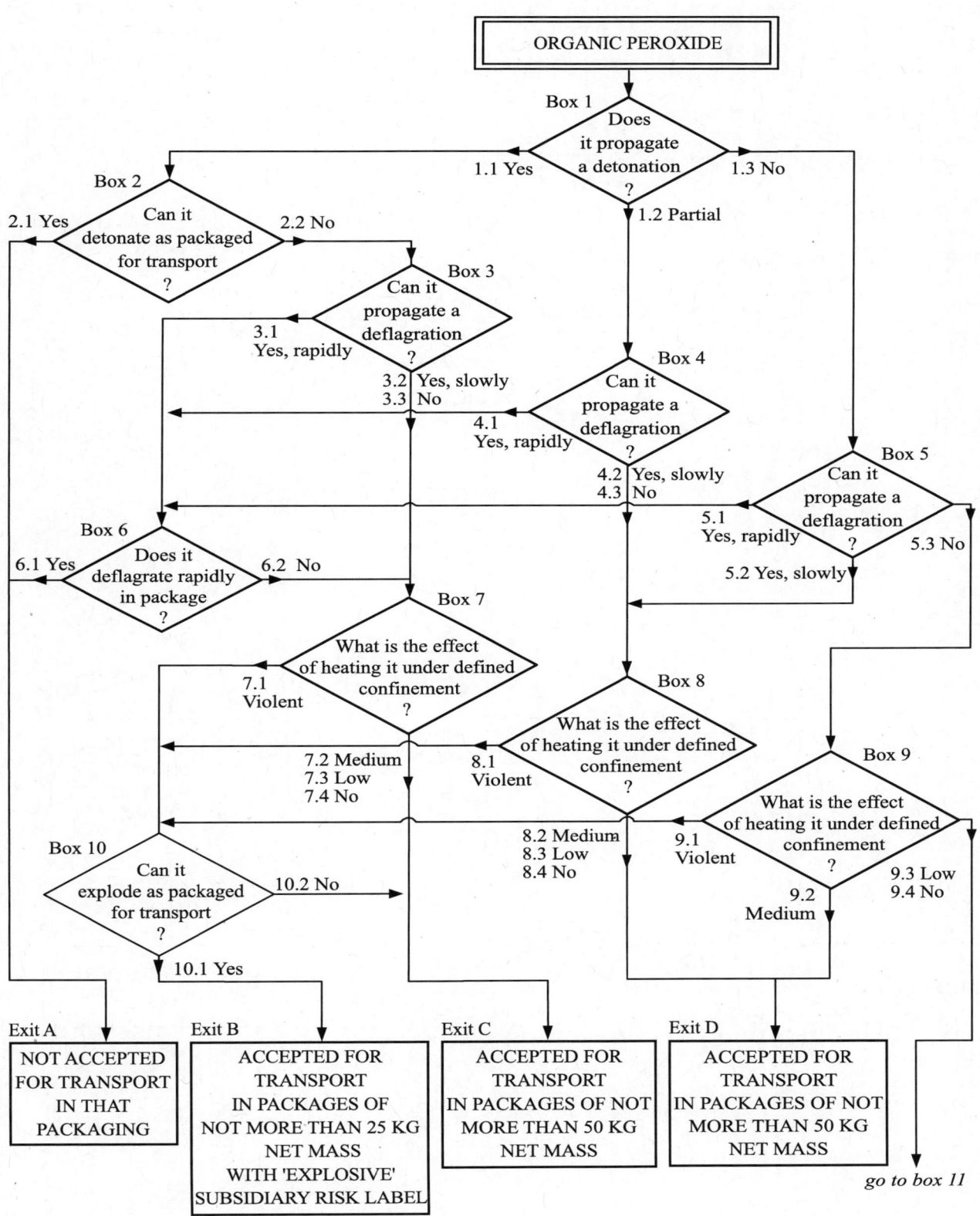

Figure 2.5.1: Flow chart scheme for organic peroxides (cont'd)

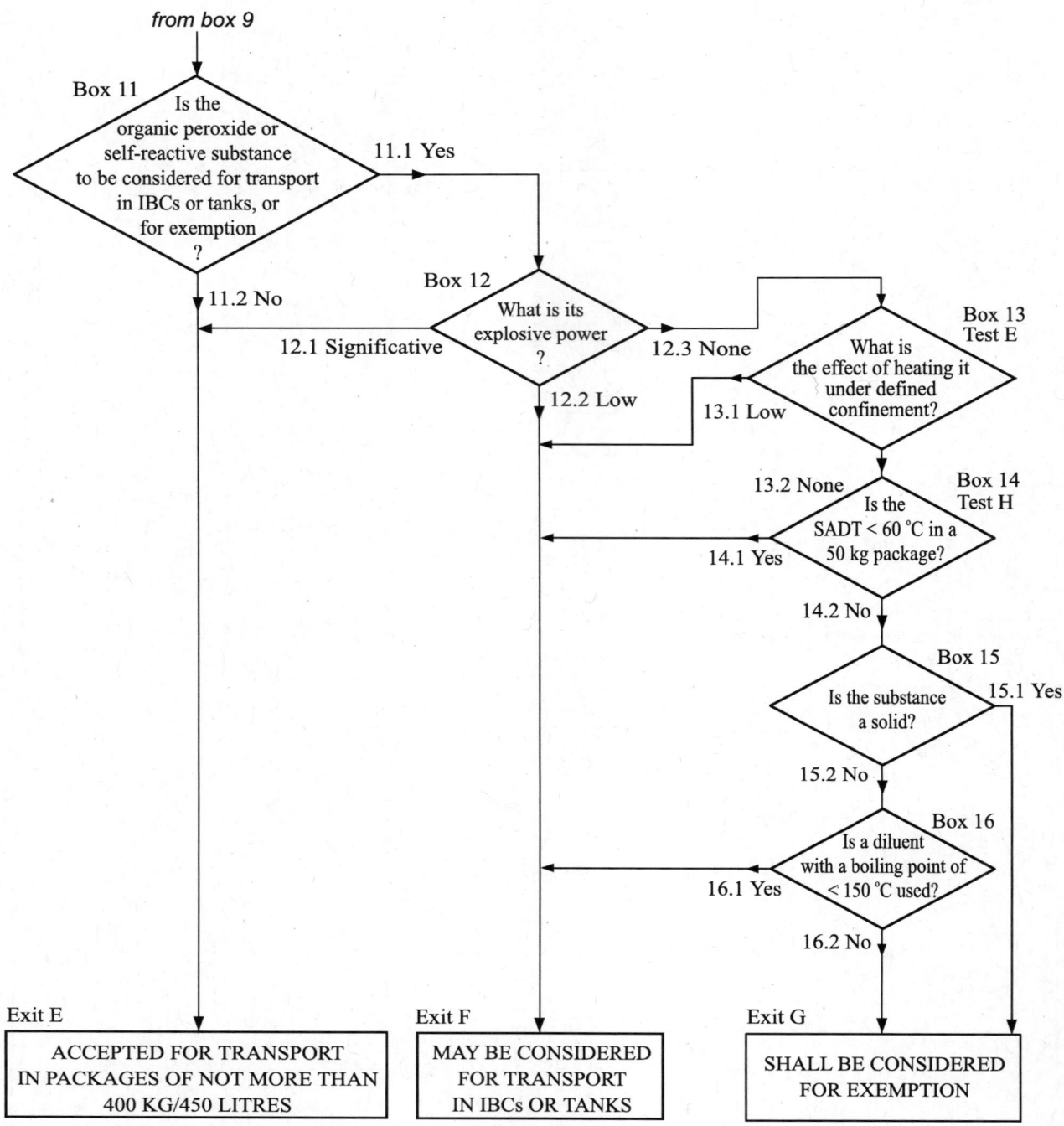

2.5.3.4 *Temperature control requirements*

2.5.3.4.1 The following organic peroxides shall be subjected to temperature control during transport:

    (a) Organic peroxides type B and C with an SADT ≤ 50 °C;

    (b) Organic peroxides type D showing a medium effect when heated under confinement[1] with an SADT ≤ 50 °C or showing a low or no effect when heated under confinement with an SADT ≤ 45 °C; and

    (c) Organic peroxides types E and F with an SADT ≤ 45 °C.

2.5.3.4.2 Test methods for determining the SADT are given in the *Manual of Tests and Criteria*, part II, section 28. The test selected shall be conducted in a manner which is representative, both in size and material, of the package to be transported.

2.5.3.4.3 Test methods for determining the flammability are given in the *Manual of Tests and Criteria*, part III, sub-section 32.4. Because organic peroxides may react vigorously when heated it is recommended to determine their flash point using small sample sizes such as described in ISO 3679.

2.5.3.5 *Desensitization of organic peroxides*

2.5.3.5.1 In order to ensure safety during transport, organic peroxides are in many cases desensitized by organic liquids or solids, inorganic solids or water. Where a percentage of a substance is stipulated, this refers to the percentage by mass, rounded to the nearest whole number. In general, desensitization shall be such that, in case of spillage or fire, the organic peroxide will not concentrate to a dangerous extent.

2.5.3.5.2 Unless otherwise stated for the individual organic peroxide formulation, the following definitions apply for diluents used for desensitization:

    (a) *Diluents type A* are organic liquids which are compatible with the organic peroxide and which have a boiling point of not less than 150 °C. Type A diluents may be used for desensitizing all organic peroxides;

    (b) *Diluents type B* are organic liquids which are compatible with the organic peroxide and which have a boiling point of less than 150 °C but not less than 60 °C and a flash point of not less than 5 °C. Type B diluents may be used for desensitization of all organic peroxides provided that the boiling point is at least 60 °C higher than the SADT in a 50 kg package.

2.5.3.5.3 Diluents, other than type A or type B, may be added to organic peroxide formulations as listed in 2.5.3.2.4 provided that they are compatible. However, replacement of all or part of a type A or type B diluent by another diluent with differing properties requires that the organic peroxide formulation be re-assessed in accordance with the normal acceptance procedure for Division 5.2.

2.5.3.5.4 Water may only be used for the desensitization of organic peroxides which are shown in 2.5.3.2.4 or in the statement of approval according to 2.5.3.2.5 as being with water or as a stable dispersion in water.

2.5.3.5.5 Organic and inorganic solids may be used for desensitization of organic peroxides provided that they are compatible.

2.5.3.5.6 Compatible liquids and solids are those which have no detrimental influence on the thermal stability and hazard type of the organic peroxide formulation.

---

[1] *As determined by test series E as prescribed in the "Manual of Tests and Criteria", part II.*

CHAPTER 2.6

CLASS 6 - TOXIC SUBSTANCES AND INFECTIOUS SUBSTANCES

Introductory notes

NOTE 1: *Genetically modified microorganisms and organisms which do not meet the definition of a toxic or an infectious substance shall be considered for classification in Class 9 and assignment to UN 3245.*

NOTE 2: *Toxins from plant, animal or bacterial sources which do not contain any infectious substances, or toxins that are contained in substances which are not infectious substances, shall be considered for classification in Division 6.1 and assignment to UN Nos. 3172 or 3462.*

2.6.1 Definitions

Class 6 is divided into two divisions as follows:

(a) Division 6.1 – *Toxic substances*

These are substances liable either to cause death or serious injury or to harm human health swallowed or inhaled or by skin contact;

(b) Division 6.2 – *Infectious substances*

These are substances known or reasonably expected to contain pathogens. Pathogens are defined as microorganisms (including bacteria, viruses, parasites, fungi) and other agents such as prions, which can cause disease in humans or animals.

2.6.2 Division 6.1 – Toxic substances

2.6.2.1 *Definitions*

For the purposes of these Regulations:

2.6.2.1.1 *LD_{50} (median lethal dose) for acute oral toxicity* is the statistically derived single dose of a substance that can be expected to cause death within 14 days in 50 per cent of young adult albino rats when administered by the oral route. The LD_{50} value is expressed in terms of mass of test substance per mass of test animal (mg/kg).

2.6.2.1.2 *LD_{50} for acute dermal toxicity* is that dose of the substance which, administered by continuous contact for 24 hours with the bare skin of albino rabbits, is most likely to cause death within 14 days in one half of the animals tested. The number of animals tested shall be sufficient to give a statistically significant result and be in conformity with good pharmacological practice. The result is expressed in milligrams per kg body mass.

2.6.2.1.3 *LC_{50} for acute toxicity on inhalation* is that concentration of vapour, mist or dust which, administered by continuous inhalation to both male and female young adult albino rats for one hour, is most likely to cause death within 14 days in one half of the animals tested. A solid substance shall be tested if at least 10 % (by mass) of its total mass is likely to be dust in a respirable range, e.g. the aerodynamic diameter of that particle-fraction is 10 microns or less. A liquid substance shall be tested if a mist is likely to be generated in a leakage of the transport containment. Both for solid and liquid substances more than 90 % (by mass) of a specimen prepared for inhalation toxicity shall be in the respirable range as defined above. The result is expressed in milligrams per litre of air for dusts and mists or in millilitres per cubic metre of air (parts per million) for vapours.

2.6.2.2 *Assignment of packing groups*

2.6.2.2.1   Substances of Division 6.1, including pesticides, are allocated among the three packing groups according to their degree of toxic hazard in transport as follows:

(a) *Packing group I*: Substances and preparations presenting a very severe toxicity hazard;

(b) *Packing group II*: Substances and preparations presenting a serious toxicity hazard;

(c) *Packing group III*: Substances and preparations presenting a relatively low toxicity hazard.

2.6.2.2.2   In making this grouping, account shall be taken of human experience in instances of accidental poisoning and of special properties possessed by any individual substance, such as liquid state, high volatility, any special likelihood of penetration, and special biological effects.

2.6.2.2.3   In the absence of human experience the grouping shall be based on data obtained from animal experiments. Three possible routes of administration shall be examined. These routes are exposure through:

(a) Oral ingestion;

(b) Dermal contact; and

(c) Inhalation of dusts, mists, or vapours.

2.6.2.2.3.1   Appropriate animal tests for the various routes of exposure are described in 2.6.2.1. When a substance exhibits a different order of toxicity by two or more of these routes of administration, the highest degree of danger indicated by the tests shall be assigned.

2.6.2.2.4   The criteria to be applied for grouping a substance according to the toxicity it exhibits by all three routes of administration are presented in the following paragraphs.

2.6.2.2.4.1   The grouping criteria for the oral and dermal routes as well as for inhalation of dusts and mists are as shown in the following table.

GROUPING CRITERIA FOR ADMINISTRATION THROUGH ORAL INGESTION, DERMAL CONTACT AND INHALATION OF DUSTS AND MISTS

Packing group	Oral toxicity LD_{50} (mg/kg)	Dermal toxicity LD_{50} (mg/kg)	Inhalation toxicity by dusts and mists LC_{50} (mg/l)
I	≤ 5.0	≤ 50	≤ 0.2
II	> 5.0 and ≤ 50	> 50 and ≤ 200	> 0.2 and ≤ 2.0
III[a]	> 50 and ≤ 300	> 200 and $\leq 1\,000$	> 2.0 and ≤ 4.0

[a]   Tear gas substances shall be included in packing group II even if their toxicity data correspond to packing group III values.

NOTE: *Substances meeting the criteria of Class 8 and with an inhalation toxicity of dusts and mists (LC_{50}) leading to packing group I are only accepted for an allocation to Division 6.1 if the toxicity through oral ingestion or dermal contact is at least in the range of packing group I or II. Otherwise an allocation to Class 8 is made when appropriate (see 2.8.2.4).*

2.6.2.2.4.2   The criteria for inhalation toxicity of dusts and mists in 2.6.2.2.4.1 are based on LC_{50} data relating to 1 hour exposures and where such information is available it shall be used. However, where only LC_{50} data relating to 4 hours exposures to dusts and mists are available, such figures can be multiplied by four and the product substituted in the above criteria, i.e. LC_{50} (4 hours) × 4 is considered the equivalent of LC_{50} (1 hour).

2.6.2.2.4.3   Liquids having toxic vapours shall be assigned to the following packing groups, where "V" is the saturated vapour concentration in millilitres per cubic metre of air (volatility) at 20 °C and standard atmospheric pressure:

(a) Packing group I: If $V \geq 10\ LC_{50}$ and $LC_{50} \leq 1\ 000\ ml/m^3$;

(b) Packing group II: If $V \geq LC_{50}$ and $LC_{50} \leq 3\ 000\ ml/m^3$, and not meeting the criteria for packing group I;

(c) Packing group III[1]: If $V \geq 1/5\ LC_{50}$ and $LC_{50} \leq 5\ 000\ ml/m^3$, and not meeting the criteria for packing groups I or II.

2.6.2.2.4.4   In figure 2.6.1, the criteria according to 2.6.2.2.4.3 are expressed in graphical form, as an aid to easy classification. However, because of approximations inherent in the use of graphs, substances on or near packing group borderlines shall be checked using numerical criteria.

---

[1] *Tear gas substances are included in Packing group II even if their toxicity data correspond to packing group III values.*

Figure 2.6.1: Inhalation toxicity: packing group borderlines

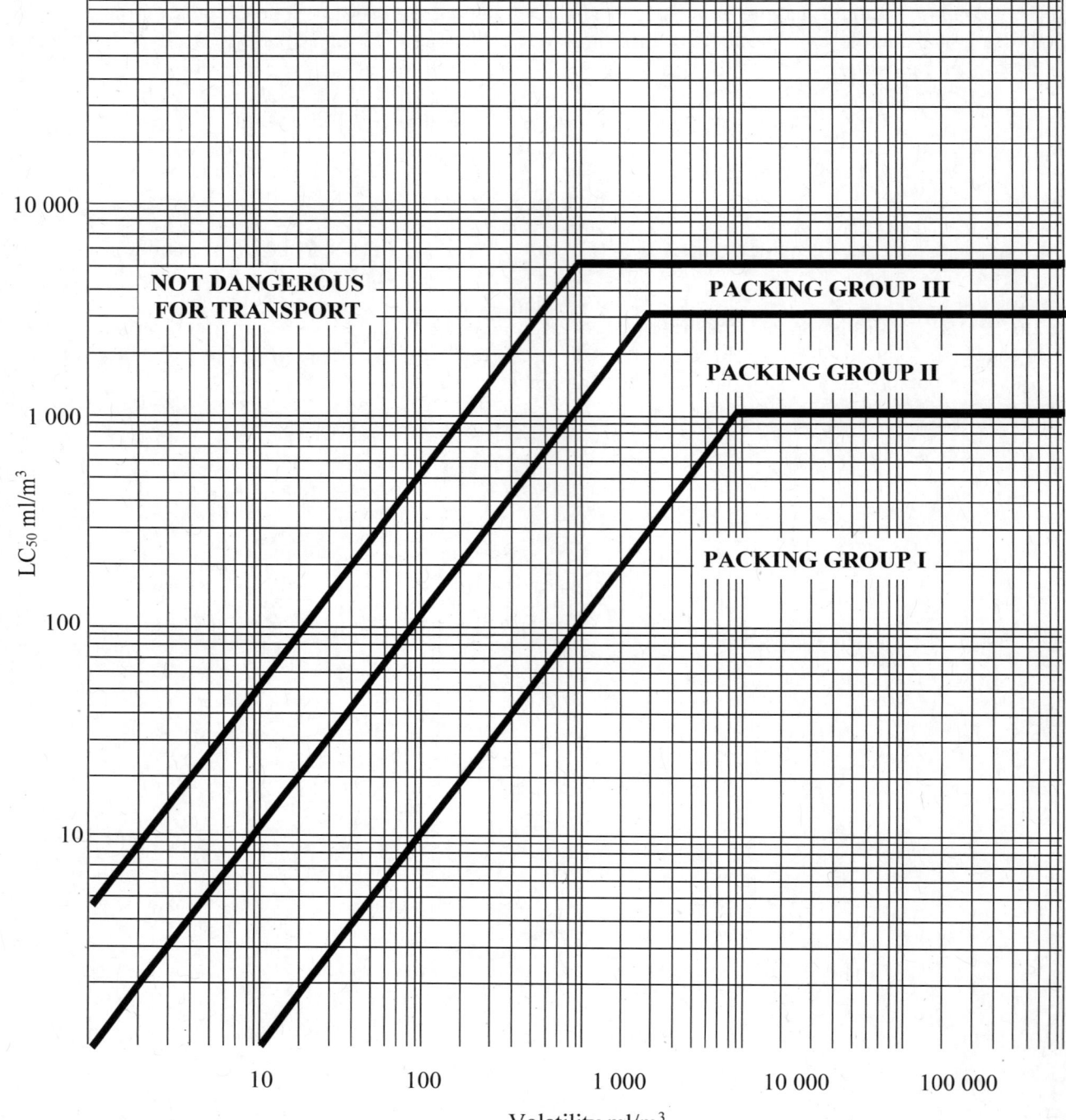

2.6.2.2.4.5   The criteria for inhalation toxicity of vapours in 2.6.2.2.4.3 are based on LC_{50} data relating to 1 hour exposure, and where such information is available it shall be used. However, where only LC_{50} data relating to 4 hours exposures to the vapours are available, such figures can be multiplied by two and the product substituted in the above criteria, i.e. LC_{50} (4 hours) × 2 is considered to be the equivalent of LC_{50} (1 hour).

2.6.2.2.4.6   Mixtures of liquids that are toxic by inhalation shall be assigned to packing groups according to 2.6.2.2.4.7 or 2.6.2.2.4.8.

2.6.2.2.4.7   If LC_{50} data are available for each of the toxic substances comprising a mixture, the packing group may be determined as follows:

(a) Estimate the LC_{50} of the mixture using the formula:

$$LC_{50}(\text{mixture}) = \frac{1}{\sum_{i=1}^{n}\left(\frac{f_i}{LC_{50i}}\right)}$$

where: f_i = mole fraction of the ith component substance of the mixture;
LC_{50i} = mean lethal concentration of the ith component substance in ml/m³;

(b) Estimate the volatility of each component substance comprising the mixture using the formula:

$$V_i = \left(\frac{P_i \times 10^6}{101.3}\right) \text{ml}/\text{m}^3$$

where: P_i = partial pressure of the ith component substance in kPa at 20 °C and one atmosphere pressure;

(c) Calculate the ratio of the volatility to the LC_{50} using the formula:

$$R = \sum_{i=1}^{n}\left(\frac{V_i}{LC_{50i}}\right);$$

(d) Using the calculated values LC_{50}(mixture) and R, the packing group for the mixture is determined:

  (i) *Packing group I*: $R \geq 10$ and LC_{50}(mixture) $\leq 1\,000$ ml/m³;

  (ii) *Packing group II*: $R \geq 1$ and LC_{50}(mixture) $\leq 3\,000$ ml/m³ and not meeting criteria for packing group I;

  (iii) *Packing group III*: $R \geq 1/5$ and LC_{50}(mixture) $\leq 5\,000$ ml/m³ and not meeting criteria for packing groups I or II.

2.6.2.2.4.8 In the absence of LC_{50} data on the toxic constituent substances, the mixture may be assigned a packing group based on the following simplified threshold toxicity tests. When these threshold tests are used, the most restrictive packing group determined is used for transporting the mixture.

(a) A mixture is assigned to packing group I only if it meets both of the following criteria:

  (i) A sample of the liquid mixture is vaporized and diluted with air to create a test atmosphere of 1 000 ml/m³ vaporized mixture in air. Ten albino rats (five male and five female) are exposed to the test atmosphere for one hour and observed for fourteen days. If five or more of the animals die within the fourteen day observation period, the mixture is presumed to have an LC_{50} equal to or less than 1 000 ml/m³;

  (ii) A sample of the vapour in equilibrium with the liquid mixture at 20 °C is diluted with 9 equal volumes of air to form a test atmosphere. Ten albino rats (five male and five female) are exposed to the test atmosphere for one hour and observed for fourteen days. If five or more of the animals die within the fourteen day observation period, the mixture is presumed to have a volatility equal to or greater than 10 times the mixture LC_{50};

(b) A mixture is assigned to packing group II only if it meets both of the following criteria, and the mixture does not meet the criteria for packing group I:

    (i) A sample of the liquid mixture is vaporized and diluted with air to create a test atmosphere of 3 000 ml/m³ vaporized mixture in air. Ten albino rats (five male and five female) are exposed to the test atmosphere for one hour and observed for fourteen days. If five or more of the animals die within the fourteen day observation period, the mixture is presumed to have an LC_{50} equal to or less than 3 000 ml/m³;

    (ii) A sample of the vapour in equilibrium with the liquid mixture at 20 °C is used to form a test atmosphere. Ten albino rats (five male and five female) are exposed to the test atmosphere for one hour and observed for fourteen days. If five or more of the animals die within the fourteen day observation period, the mixture is presumed to have a volatility equal to or greater than the mixture LC_{50};

(c) A mixture is assigned to packing group III only if it meets both of the following criteria, and the mixture does not meet the criteria for packing groups I or II:

    (i) A sample of the liquid mixture is vaporized and diluted with air to create a test atmosphere of 5 000 ml/m³ vaporized mixture in air. Ten albino rats (five male and five female) are exposed to the test atmosphere for one hour and observed for fourteen days. If five or more of the animals die within the fourteen day observation period, the mixture is presumed to have an LC_{50} equal to or less than 5 000 ml/m³;

    (ii) The vapour pressure of the liquid mixture is measured and if the vapour concentration is equal to or greater than 1 000 ml/m³, the mixture is presumed to have a volatility equal to or greater than 1/5 the mixture LC_{50}.

2.6.2.3 *Methods for determining oral and dermal toxicity of mixtures*

2.6.2.3.1 When classifying and assigning the appropriate packing group to mixtures in Division 6.1, in accordance with the oral and dermal toxicity criteria in 2.6.2.2, it is necessary to determine the acute LD_{50} of the mixture.

2.6.2.3.2 If a mixture contains only one active substance, and the LD_{50} of that constituent is known, in the absence of reliable acute oral and dermal toxicity data on the actual mixture to be transported, the oral or dermal LD_{50} may be obtained by the following method:

$$LD_{50} \text{ value of preparation} = \frac{LD_{50} \text{ value of active substance} \times 100}{\text{percentage of active substance by mass}}$$

2.6.2.3.3 If a mixture contains more than one active constituent, there are three possible approaches that may be used to determine the oral or dermal LD_{50} of the mixture. The preferred method is to obtain reliable acute oral and dermal toxicity data on the actual mixture to be transported. If reliable, accurate data are not available, then either of the following methods may be performed:

(a) Classify the formulation according to the most hazardous constituent of the mixture as if that constituent were present in the same concentration as the total concentration of all active constituents; or

(b) Apply the formula: $\dfrac{C_A}{T_A} + \dfrac{C_B}{T_B} + ... + \dfrac{C_Z}{T_Z} = \dfrac{100}{T_M}$

where: C = the % concentration of constituent A, B ... Z in the mixture;
T = the oral LD_{50} values of constituent A, B ... Z;
T_M = the oral LD_{50} value of the mixture.

NOTE: *This formula can also be used for dermal toxicities provided that this information is available on the same species for all constituents. The use of this formula does not take into account any potentiation or protective phenomena.*

2.6.2.4   *Classification of pesticides*

2.6.2.4.1   All active pesticide substances and their preparations for which the LC_{50} and/or LD_{50} values are known and which are classified in Division 6.1 shall be classified under appropriate packing groups in accordance with the criteria given in 2.6.2.2. Substances and preparations which are characterized by subsidiary hazards shall be classified according to the precedence of hazard table in chapter 2.0 with the assignment of appropriate packing groups.

2.6.2.4.2   If the oral or dermal LD_{50} value for a pesticide preparation is not known, but the LD_{50} value of its active substance(s) is known, the LD_{50} value for the preparation may be obtained by applying the procedures in 2.6.2.3.

NOTE: *LD_{50} toxicity data for a number of common pesticides may be obtained from the most current edition of the document "The WHO Recommended Classification of Pesticides by Hazard and Guidelines to Classification" available from the International Programme on Chemical Safety, World Health Organisation (WHO), 1211 Geneva 27, Switzerland. While that document may be used as a source of LD_{50} data for pesticides, its classification system shall not be used for purposes of transport classification of, or assignment of packing groups to, pesticides, which shall be in accordance with these regulations.*

2.6.2.4.3   The proper shipping name used in the transport of the pesticide shall be selected on the basis of the active ingredient, of the physical state of the pesticide and any subsidiary hazards it may exhibit.

2.6.2.5   *Substances not accepted for transport*

Chemically unstable substances of Division 6.1 shall not be accepted for transport unless the necessary precautions have been taken to prevent the possibility of a dangerous decomposition or polymerization under normal conditions of transport. For the precautions necessary to prevent polymerization, see special provision 386 of chapter 3.3. To this end particular care shall be taken to ensure that receptacles and tanks do not contain any substances liable to promote these reactions.

2.6.3   Division 6.2 – Infectious substances

2.6.3.1   *Definitions*

For the purposes of these Regulations:

2.6.3.1.1   *Infectious substances* are substances which are known or are reasonably expected to contain pathogens. Pathogens are defined as microorganisms (including bacteria, viruses, parasites, fungi) and other agents such as prions, which can cause disease in humans or animals.

2.6.3.1.2   *Biological products* are those products derived from living organisms which are manufactured and distributed in accordance with the requirements of appropriate national authorities, which may have special licensing requirements, and are used either for prevention, treatment, or diagnosis of disease in humans or animals, or for development, experimental or investigational purposes related thereto. They include, but are not limited to, finished or unfinished products such as vaccines.

2.6.3.1.3   *Cultures* are the result of a process by which pathogens are intentionally propagated. This definition does not include human or animal patient specimens as defined in 2.6.3.1.4.

2.6.3.1.4   *Patient specimens* are those, collected directly from humans or animals, including, but not limited to, excreta, secreta, blood and its components, tissue and tissue fluid swabs, and body parts being transported for purposes such as research, diagnosis, investigational activities, disease treatment and prevention.

2.6.3.1.5   *Deleted.*

2.6.3.1.6   *Medical or clinical wastes* are wastes derived from the veterinary treatment of animals, the medical treatment of humans or from bio-research.

2.6.3.2   ***Classification of infectious substances***

2.6.3.2.1   Infectious substances shall be classified in Division 6.2 and assigned to UN Nos. 2814, 2900, 3291, 3373 or 3549, as appropriate.

2.6.3.2.2   Infectious substances are divided into the following categories:

2.6.3.2.2.1   Category A: An infectious substance which is transported in a form that, when exposure to it occurs, is capable of causing permanent disability, life-threatening or fatal disease in otherwise healthy humans or animals. Indicative examples of substances that meet these criteria are given in the table in this paragraph.

NOTE: *An exposure occurs when an infectious substance is released outside of the protective packaging, resulting in physical contact with humans or animals.*

(a)   Infectious substances meeting these criteria which cause disease in humans or both in humans and animals shall be assigned to UN 2814. Infectious substances which cause disease only in animals shall be assigned to UN 2900.

(b)   Assignment to UN Nos. 2814 or 2900 shall be based on the known medical history and symptoms of the source human or animal, endemic local conditions, or professional judgement concerning individual circumstances of the source human or animal.

NOTE 1:   *The proper shipping name for UN 2814 is INFECTIOUS SUBSTANCE, AFFECTING HUMANS. The proper shipping name for UN 2900 is INFECTIOUS SUBSTANCE, AFFECTING ANIMALS only.*

NOTE 2:   *The following table is not exhaustive. Infectious substances, including new or emerging pathogens, which do not appear in the table but which meet the same criteria shall be assigned to Category A. In addition, if there is doubt as to whether or not a substance meets the criteria it shall be included in Category A.*

NOTE 3:   *In the following table, the microorganisms written in italics are bacteria or fungi.*

INDICATIVE EXAMPLES OF INFECTIOUS SUBSTANCES INCLUDED IN CATEGORY A IN ANY FORM UNLESS OTHERWISE INDICATED (2.6.3.2.2.1 (a))	
UN Number and Proper Shipping Name	**Microorganism**
UN 2814 Infectious substances affecting humans	*Bacillus anthracis* (cultures only) *Brucella abortus* (cultures only) *Brucella melitensis* (cultures only) *Brucella suis* (cultures only) *Burkholderia mallei* - *Pseudomonas mallei* – Glanders (cultures only) *Burkholderia pseudomallei* – *Pseudomonas pseudomallei* (cultures only) *Chlamydia psittaci* - avian strains (cultures only) *Clostridium botulinum* (cultures only) *Coccidioides immitis* (cultures only) *Coxiella burnetii* (cultures only) Crimean-Congo haemorrhagic fever virus Dengue virus (cultures only) Eastern equine encephalitis virus (cultures only) *Escherichia coli*, verotoxigenic (cultures only) Ebola virus Flexal virus *Francisella tularensis* (cultures only) Guanarito virus Hantaan virus Hantaviruses causing haemorrhagic fever with renal syndrome Hendra virus Hepatitis B virus (cultures only) Herpes B virus (cultures only) Human immunodeficiency virus (cultures only) Highly pathogenic avian influenza virus (cultures only) Japanese Encephalitis virus (cultures only) Junin virus Kyasanur Forest disease virus Lassa virus Machupo virus Marburg virus Monkeypox virus (cultures only) *Mycobacterium tuberculosis* (cultures only) Nipah virus Omsk haemorrhagic fever virus Poliovirus (cultures only) Rabies virus (cultures only) *Rickettsia prowazekii* (cultures only) *Rickettsia rickettsii* (cultures only) Rift Valley fever virus (cultures only) Russian spring-summer encephalitis virus (cultures only) Sabia virus *Shigella dysenteriae* type 1 (cultures only) Tick-borne encephalitis virus (cultures only) Variola virus Venezuelan equine encephalitis virus (cultures only) West Nile virus (cultures only) Yellow fever virus (cultures only) *Yersinia pestis* (cultures only)

INDICATIVE EXAMPLES OF INFECTIOUS SUBSTANCES INCLUDED IN CATEGORY A IN ANY FORM UNLESS OTHERWISE INDICATED (2.6.3.2.2.1 (a))	
UN Number and Proper Shipping Name	**Microorganism**
UN 2900 Infectious substances affecting animals only	African swine fever virus (cultures only) Avian paramyxovirus Type 1 - Velogenic Newcastle disease virus (cultures only) Classical swine fever virus (cultures only) Foot and mouth disease virus (cultures only) Lumpy skin disease virus (cultures only) *Mycoplasma mycoides* - Contagious bovine pleuropneumonia (cultures only) Peste des petits ruminants virus (cultures only) Rinderpest virus (cultures only) Sheep-pox virus (cultures only) Goatpox virus (cultures only) Swine vesicular disease virus (cultures only) Vesicular stomatitis virus (cultures only)

2.6.3.2.2.2   Category B: An infectious substance which does not meet the criteria for inclusion in Category A. Infectious substances in Category B shall be assigned to UN 3373.

NOTE: *The proper shipping name of UN 3373 is "BIOLOGICAL SUBSTANCE, CATEGORY B".*

2.6.3.2.3   *Exemptions*

2.6.3.2.3.1   Substances which do not contain infectious substances or substances which are unlikely to cause disease in humans or animals are not subject to these Regulations unless they meet the criteria for inclusion in another class.

2.6.3.2.3.2   Substances containing microorganisms which are non-pathogenic to humans or animals are not subject to these Regulations unless they meet the criteria for inclusion in another class.

2.6.3.2.3.3   Substances in a form that any present pathogens have been neutralized or inactivated such that they no longer pose a health risk are not subject to these Regulations unless they meet the criteria for inclusion in another class.

NOTE: *Medical equipment which has been drained of free liquid is deemed to meet the requirements of this paragraph and is not subject to these Regulations.*

2.6.3.2.3.4   Environmental samples (including food and water samples) which are not considered to pose a significant risk of infection are not subject to these Regulations unless they meet the criteria for inclusion in another class.

2.6.3.2.3.5   Dried blood spots, collected by applying a drop of blood onto absorbent material, are not subject to these Regulations.

2.6.3.2.3.6   Faecal occult blood screening samples are not subject to these Regulations.

2.6.3.2.3.7   Blood or blood components which have been collected for the purposes of transfusion or for the preparation of blood products to be used for transfusion or transplantation and any tissues or organs intended for use in transplantation as well as samples drawn in connection with such purposes are not subject to these Regulations.

2.6.3.2.3.8   Human or animal specimens for which there is minimal likelihood that pathogens are present are not subject to these Regulations if the specimen is transported in a packaging which will prevent any leakage and which is marked with the words "Exempt human specimen" or "Exempt animal specimen", as appropriate. The packaging should meet the following conditions:

(a) The packaging should consist of three components:

    (i) a leak-proof primary receptacle(s);

    (ii) a leak-proof secondary packaging; and

    (iii) an outer packaging of adequate strength for its capacity, mass and intended use, and with at least one surface having minimum dimensions of 100 mm × 100 mm;

(b) For liquids, absorbent material in sufficient quantity to absorb the entire contents should be placed between the primary receptacle(s) and the secondary packaging so that, during transport, any release or leak of a liquid substance will not reach the outer packaging and will not compromise the integrity of the cushioning material;

(c) When multiple fragile primary receptacles are placed in a single secondary packaging, they should be either individually wrapped or separated to prevent contact between them.

NOTE 1: *An element of professional judgment is required to determine if a substance is exempt under this paragraph. That judgment should be based on the known medical history, symptoms and individual circumstances of the source, human or animal, and endemic local conditions. Examples of specimens which may be transported under this paragraph include the blood or urine tests to monitor cholesterol levels, blood glucose levels, hormone levels, or prostate specific antibodies (PSA); those required to monitor organ function such as heart, liver or kidney function for humans or animals with non-infectious diseases, or for therapeutic drug monitoring; those conducted for insurance or employment purposes and are intended to determine the presence of drugs or alcohol; pregnancy test; biopsies to detect cancer; and antibody detection in humans or animals in the absence of any concern for infection (e.g. evaluation of vaccine induced immunity, diagnosis of autoimmune disease, etc.).*

NOTE 2: *For air transport, packagings for specimens exempted under this paragraph shall meet the conditions in (a) to (c).*

2.6.3.2.3.9 Except for:

(a) Medical waste (UN Nos. 3291 and 3549);

(b) Medical devices or equipment contaminated with or containing infectious substances in Category A (UN Nos. 2814 or 2900); and

(c) Medical devices or equipment contaminated with or containing other dangerous goods that meet the definition of another hazard class,

medical devices or equipment potentially contaminated with or containing infectious substances which are being transported for disinfection, cleaning, sterilization, repair, or equipment evaluation are not subject to the provisions of these Regulations if packed in packagings designed and constructed in such a way that, under normal conditions of transport, they cannot break, be punctured or leak their contents. Packagings shall be designed to meet the construction requirements listed in 6.1.4 or 6.6.5.

These packagings shall meet the general packing requirements of 4.1.1.1 and 4.1.1.2 and be capable of retaining the medical devices and equipment when dropped from a height of 1.2 m. For air transport, additional requirements may apply.

The packagings *shall be marked "USED MEDICAL DEVICE" or "USED MEDICAL EQUIPMENT". When using overpacks, these shall be marked in the same way, except when the inscription remains visible.*

2.6.3.3 *Biological products*

2.6.3.3.1 For the purposes of these Regulations, biological products are divided into the following groups:

(a) those which are manufactured and packaged in accordance with the requirements of appropriate national authorities and transported for the purposes of final packaging or distribution, and use for personal health care by medical professionals or individuals. Substances in this group are not subject to these Regulations;

(b) those which do not fall under paragraph (a) and are known or reasonably believed to contain infectious substances and which meet the criteria for inclusion in Category A or Category B. Substances in this group shall be assigned to UN Nos. 2814, 2900 or 3373, as appropriate.

NOTE: *Some licensed biological products may present a biohazard only in certain parts of the world. In that case, competent authorities may require these biological products to be in compliance with local requirements for infectious substances or may impose other restrictions.*

2.6.3.4 *Genetically modified microorganisms and organisms*

2.6.3.4.1 Genetically modified microorganisms not meeting the definition of infectious substance shall be classified according to chapter 2.9.

2.6.3.5 *Medical or clinical wastes*

2.6.3.5.1 Medical or clinical wastes containing:

(a) Category A infectious substances shall be assigned to UN Nos. 2814, 2900 or 3549, as appropriate. Solid medical waste containing Category A infectious substances generated from the medical treatment of humans or veterinary treatment of animals may be assigned to UN 3549. The UN 3549 entry shall not be used for waste from bio-research or liquid waste;

(b) Category B infectious substances shall be assigned to UN 3291.

2.6.3.5.2 Medical or clinical wastes which are reasonably believed to have a low probability of containing infectious substances shall be assigned to UN 3291.

For the assignment, international, regional or national waste catalogues may be taken into account.

NOTE: *The proper shipping name for UN 3291 is "CLINICAL WASTE, UNSPECIFIED, N.O.S." or "(BIO) MEDICAL WASTE, N.O.S" or "REGULATED MEDICAL WASTE, N.O.S.".*

2.6.3.5.3 Decontaminated medical or clinical wastes which previously contained infectious substances are not subject to these Regulations unless they meet the criteria for inclusion in another class.

2.6.3.6 *Infected animals*

2.6.3.6.1 Unless an infectious substance cannot be consigned by any other means, live animals shall not be used to consign such a substance. A live animal which has been intentionally infected and is known or suspected to contain an infectious substance shall only be transported under terms and conditions approved by the competent authority.

2.6.3.6.2 *Deleted.*

CHAPTER 2.7

CLASS 7 - RADIOACTIVE MATERIAL

NOTE: *For Class 7, the type of packaging may have a decisive effect on classification.*

2.7.1 Definitions

2.7.1.1 *Radioactive material* means any material containing radionuclides where both the activity concentration and the total activity in the consignment exceed the values specified in 2.7.2.2.1 to 2.7.2.2.6.

2.7.1.2 *Contamination*

Contamination means the presence of a radioactive substance on a surface in quantities in excess of 0.4 Bq/cm² for beta and gamma emitters and low toxicity alpha emitters, or 0.04 Bq/cm² for all other alpha emitters.

Non-fixed contamination means contamination that can be removed from a surface during routine conditions of transport.

Fixed contamination means contamination other than non-fixed contamination.

2.7.1.3 *Definitions of specific terms*

A_1 and A_2

A_1 means the activity value of special form radioactive material which is listed in the table 2.7.2.2.1 or derived in 2.7.2.2.2 and is used to determine the activity limits for the requirements of these Regulations.

A_2 means the activity value of radioactive material, other than special form radioactive material, which is listed in the table 2.7.2.2.1 or derived in 2.7.2.2.2 and is used to determine the activity limits for the requirements of these Regulations.

Fissile nuclides means uranium-233, uranium-235, plutonium-239 and plutonium-241. *Fissile material* means a material containing any of the fissile nuclides. Excluded from the definition of fissile material are the following:

    (a)   Natural uranium or depleted uranium which is unirradiated;

    (b)   Natural uranium or depleted uranium which has been irradiated in thermal reactors only;

    (c)   material with fissile nuclides less than a total of 0.25 g;

    (d)   any combination of (a), (b) and/or (c).

These exclusions are only valid if there is no other material with fissile nuclides in the package or in the consignment if shipped unpackaged.

Low dispersible radioactive material means either a solid radioactive material or a solid radioactive material in a sealed capsule, that has limited dispersibility and is not in powder form.

Low specific activity (LSA) material means radioactive material which by its nature has a limited specific activity, or radioactive material for which limits of estimated average specific activity apply. External shielding materials surrounding the LSA material shall not be considered in determining the estimated average specific activity.

Low toxicity alpha emitters are: natural uranium; depleted uranium; natural thorium; uranium-235 or uranium-238; thorium-232; thorium-228 and thorium-230 when contained in ores or physical and chemical concentrates; or alpha emitters with a half-life of less than 10 days.

Special form radioactive material means either:

    (a)   An indispersible solid radioactive material; or

    (b)   A sealed capsule containing radioactive material.

Specific activity of a radionuclide means the activity per unit mass of that nuclide. The specific activity of a material shall mean the activity per unit mass of the material in which the radionuclides are essentially uniformly distributed.

NOTE: The terms "activity concentration" and "specific activity" are synonymous for the purpose of these Regulations.

Surface contaminated object (SCO) means a solid object which is not itself radioactive but which has radioactive material distributed on its surface.

Unirradiated thorium means thorium containing not more than 10^{-7} g of uranium-233 per gram of thorium-232.

Unirradiated uranium means uranium containing not more than 2×10^3 Bq of plutonium per gram of uranium-235, not more than 9×10^6 Bq of fission products per gram of uranium-235 and not more than 5×10^{-3} g of uranium-236 per gram of uranium-235.

Uranium - natural, depleted, enriched means the following:

Natural uranium means uranium (which may be chemically separated) containing the naturally occurring distribution of uranium isotopes (approximately 99.28 % uranium-238, and 0.72 % uranium-235 by mass).

Depleted uranium means uranium containing a lesser mass percentage of uranium-235 than in natural uranium.

Enriched uranium means uranium containing a greater mass percentage of uranium-235 than 0.72 %.

In all cases, a very small mass percentage of uranium-234 is present.

2.7.2   **Classification**

2.7.2.1   *General provisions*

2.7.2.1.1   Radioactive material shall be assigned to one of the UN numbers specified in table 2.7.2.1.1, in accordance with 2.7.2.4 to 2.7.2.5, taking into account the material characteristics determined in 2.7.2.3.

Table 2.7.2.1.1: Assignment of UN numbers

UN No.	Proper shipping name and description[a]
Excepted packages (1.5.1.5)	
2908	RADIOACTIVE MATERIAL, EXCEPTED PACKAGE - EMPTY PACKAGING
2909	RADIOACTIVE MATERIAL, EXCEPTED PACKAGE - ARTICLES MANUFACTURED FROM NATURAL URANIUM or DEPLETED URANIUM or NATURAL THORIUM
2910	RADIOACTIVE MATERIAL, EXCEPTED PACKAGE - LIMITED QUANTITY OF MATERIAL
2911	RADIOACTIVE MATERIAL, EXCEPTED PACKAGE - INSTRUMENTS or ARTICLES
3507	URANIUM HEXAFLUORIDE, RADIOACTIVE MATERIAL, EXCEPTED PACKAGE less than 0.1 kg per package, non-fissile or fissile-excepted[b,c]
Low specific activity radioactive material (2.7.2.3.1)	
2912	RADIOACTIVE MATERIAL, LOW SPECIFIC ACTIVITY (LSA-I), non-fissile or fissile-excepted[b]
3321	RADIOACTIVE MATERIAL, LOW SPECIFIC ACTIVITY (LSA-II), non fissile or fissile-excepted[b]
3322	RADIOACTIVE MATERIAL, LOW SPECIFIC ACTIVITY (LSA-III), non fissile or fissile-excepted[b]
3324	RADIOACTIVE MATERIAL, LOW SPECIFIC ACTIVITY (LSA-II), FISSILE
3325	RADIOACTIVE MATERIAL, LOW SPECIFIC ACTIVITY, (LSA-III), FISSILE
Surface contaminated objects (2.7.2.3.2)	
2913	RADIOACTIVE MATERIAL, SURFACE CONTAMINATED OBJECTS (SCO-I, SCO-II or SCO-III), non-fissile or fissile-excepted[b]
3326	RADIOACTIVE MATERIAL, SURFACE CONTAMINATED OBJECTS (SCO-I or SCO-II), FISSILE
Type A packages (2.7.2.4.4)	
2915	RADIOACTIVE MATERIAL, TYPE A PACKAGE, non-special form, non-fissile or fissile-excepted[b]
3327	RADIOACTIVE MATERIAL, TYPE A PACKAGE, FISSILE, non-special form
3332	RADIOACTIVE MATERIAL, TYPE A PACKAGE, SPECIAL FORM, non fissile or fissile-excepted[b]
3333	RADIOACTIVE MATERIAL, TYPE A PACKAGE, SPECIAL FORM, FISSILE
Type B(U) packages (2.7.2.4.6)	
2916	RADIOACTIVE MATERIAL, TYPE B(U) PACKAGE, non-fissile or fissile-excepted[b]
3328	RADIOACTIVE MATERIAL, TYPE B(U) PACKAGE, FISSILE
Type B(M) packages (2.7.2.4.6)	
2917	RADIOACTIVE MATERIAL, TYPE B(M) PACKAGE, non-fissile or fissile-excepted[b]
3329	RADIOACTIVE MATERIAL, TYPE B(M) PACKAGE, FISSILE
Type C packages (2.7.2.4.6)	
3323	RADIOACTIVE MATERIAL, TYPE C PACKAGE, non fissile or fissile-excepted[b]
3330	RADIOACTIVE MATERIAL, TYPE C PACKAGE, FISSILE
Special arrangement (2.7.2.5)	
2919	RADIOACTIVE MATERIAL, TRANSPORTED UNDER SPECIAL ARRANGEMENT, non-fissile or fissile-excepted[b]
3331	RADIOACTIVE MATERIAL, TRANSPORTED UNDER SPECIAL ARRANGEMENT, FISSILE
Uranium hexafluoride (2.7.2.4.5)	
2977	RADIOACTIVE MATERIAL, URANIUM HEXAFLUORIDE, FISSILE
2978	RADIOACTIVE MATERIAL, URANIUM HEXAFLUORIDE, non-fissile or fissile-excepted[b]
3507	URANIUM HEXAFLUORIDE, RADIOACTIVE MATERIAL, EXCEPTED PACKAGE less than 0.1 kg per package, non-fissile or fissile-excepted[b,c]

[a] The proper shipping name is found in the column "proper shipping name and description" and is restricted to that part shown in capital letters. In the cases of UN Nos. 2909, 2911, 2913 and 3326, where alternative proper shipping names are separated by the word "or" only the relevant proper shipping name shall be used;

[b] The term "fissile-excepted" refers only to material excepted under 2.7.2.3.5.

[c] For UN 3507, see also special provision 369 in chapter 3.3.

2.7.2.2 *Determination of basic radionuclide values*

2.7.2.2.1 The following basic values for individual radionuclides are given in table 2.7.2.2.1:

(a) A_1 and A_2 in TBq;

(b) Activity concentration limits for exempt material in Bq/g; and

(c) Activity limits for exempt consignments in Bq.

Table 2.7.2.2.1: Basic radionuclides values for individual radionuclides

Radionuclide (atomic number)	A_1 (TBq)	A_2 (TBq)	Activity concentration limit for exempt material (Bq/g)	Activity limit for an exempt consignment (Bq)
Actinium (89)				
Ac-225 (a)	8×10^{-1}	6×10^{-3}	1×10^{1}	1×10^{4}
Ac-227 (a)	9×10^{-1}	9×10^{-5}	1×10^{-1}	1×10^{3}
Ac-228	6×10^{-1}	5×10^{-1}	1×10^{1}	1×10^{6}
Silver (47)				
Ag-105	2×10^{0}	2×10^{0}	1×10^{2}	1×10^{6}
Ag-108m (a)	7×10^{-1}	7×10^{-1}	1×10^{1} (b)	1×10^{6} (b)
Ag-110m (a)	4×10^{-1}	4×10^{-1}	1×10^{1}	1×10^{6}
Ag-111	2×10^{0}	6×10^{-1}	1×10^{3}	1×10^{6}
Aluminium (13)				
Al-26	1×10^{-1}	1×10^{-1}	1×10^{1}	1×10^{5}
Americium (95)				
Am-241	1×10^{1}	1×10^{-3}	1×10^{0}	1×10^{4}
Am-242m (a)	1×10^{1}	1×10^{-3}	1×10^{0} (b)	1×10^{4} (b)
Am-243 (a)	5×10^{0}	1×10^{-3}	1×10^{0} (b)	1×10^{3} (b)
Argon (18)				
Ar-37	4×10^{1}	4×10^{1}	1×10^{6}	1×10^{8}
Ar-39	4×10^{1}	2×10^{1}	1×10^{7}	1×10^{4}
Ar-41	3×10^{-1}	3×10^{-1}	1×10^{2}	1×10^{9}
Arsenic (33)				
As-72	3×10^{-1}	3×10^{-1}	1×10^{1}	1×10^{5}
As-73	4×10^{1}	4×10^{1}	1×10^{3}	1×10^{7}
As-74	1×10^{0}	9×10^{-1}	1×10^{1}	1×10^{6}
As-76	3×10^{-1}	3×10^{-1}	1×10^{2}	1×10^{5}
As-77	2×10^{1}	7×10^{-1}	1×10^{3}	1×10^{6}
Astatine (85)				
At-211 (a)	2×10^{1}	5×10^{-1}	1×10^{3}	1×10^{7}
Gold (79)				
Au-193	7×10^{0}	2×10^{0}	1×10^{2}	1×10^{7}
Au-194	1×10^{0}	1×10^{0}	1×10^{1}	1×10^{6}
Au-195	1×10^{1}	6×10^{0}	1×10^{2}	1×10^{7}
Au-198	1×10^{0}	6×10^{-1}	1×10^{2}	1×10^{6}
Au-199	1×10^{1}	6×10^{-1}	1×10^{2}	1×10^{6}
Barium (56)				
Ba-131 (a)	2×10^{0}	2×10^{0}	1×10^{2}	1×10^{6}
Ba-133	3×10^{0}	3×10^{0}	1×10^{2}	1×10^{6}
Ba-133m	2×10^{1}	6×10^{-1}	1×10^{2}	1×10^{6}
Ba-135m	2×10^{1}	6×10^{-1}	1×10^{2}	1×10^{6}
Ba-140 (a)	5×10^{-1}	3×10^{-1}	1×10^{1} (b)	1×10^{5} (b)
Beryllium (4)				
Be-7	2×10^{1}	2×10^{1}	1×10^{3}	1×10^{7}
Be-10	4×10^{1}	6×10^{-1}	1×10^{4}	1×10^{6}

Radionuclide (atomic number)	A_1 (TBq)	A_2 (TBq)	Activity concentration limit for exempt material (Bq/g)	Activity limit for an exempt consignment (Bq)
Bismuth (83)				
Bi-205	7×10^{-1}	7×10^{-1}	1×10^1	1×10^6
Bi-206	3×10^{-1}	3×10^{-1}	1×10^1	1×10^5
Bi-207	7×10^{-1}	7×10^{-1}	1×10^1	1×10^6
Bi-210	1×10^0	6×10^{-1}	1×10^3	1×10^6
Bi-210m (a)	6×10^{-1}	2×10^{-2}	1×10^1	1×10^5
Bi-212 (a)	7×10^{-1}	6×10^{-1}	1×10^1 (b)	1×10^5 (b)
Berkelium (97)				
Bk-247	8×10^0	8×10^{-4}	1×10^0	1×10^4
Bk-249 (a)	4×10^1	3×10^{-1}	1×10^3	1×10^6
Bromine (35)				
Br-76	4×10^{-1}	4×10^{-1}	1×10^1	1×10^5
Br-77	3×10^0	3×10^0	1×10^2	1×10^6
Br-82	4×10^{-1}	4×10^{-1}	1×10^1	1×10^6
Carbon (6)				
C-11	1×10^0	6×10^{-1}	1×10^1	1×10^6
C-14	4×10^1	3×10^0	1×10^4	1×10^7
Calcium (20)				
Ca-41	Unlimited	Unlimited	1×10^5	1×10^7
Ca-45	4×10^1	1×10^0	1×10^4	1×10^7
Ca-47 (a)	3×10^0	3×10^{-1}	1×10^1	1×10^6
Cadmium (48)				
Cd-109	3×10^1	2×10^0	1×10^4	1×10^6
Cd-113m	4×10^1	5×10^{-1}	1×10^3	1×10^6
Cd-115 (a)	3×10^0	4×10^{-1}	1×10^2	1×10^6
Cd-115m	5×10^{-1}	5×10^{-1}	1×10^3	1×10^6
Cerium (58)				
Ce-139	7×10^0	2×10^0	1×10^2	1×10^6
Ce-141	2×10^1	6×10^{-1}	1×10^2	1×10^7
Ce-143	9×10^{-1}	6×10^{-1}	1×10^2	1×10^6
Ce-144 (a)	2×10^{-1}	2×10^{-1}	1×10^2 (b)	1×10^5 (b)
Californium (98)				
Cf-248	4×10^1	6×10^{-3}	1×10^1	1×10^4
Cf-249	3×10^0	8×10^{-4}	1×10^0	1×10^3
Cf-250	2×10^1	2×10^{-3}	1×10^1	1×10^4
Cf-251	7×10^0	7×10^{-4}	1×10^0	1×10^3
Cf-252	1×10^{-1}	3×10^{-3}	1×10^1	1×10^4
Cf-253 (a)	4×10^1	4×10^{-2}	1×10^2	1×10^5
Cf-254	1×10^{-3}	1×10^{-3}	1×10^0	1×10^3
Chlorine (17)				
Cl-36	1×10^1	6×10^{-1}	1×10^4	1×10^6
Cl-38	2×10^{-1}	2×10^{-1}	1×10^1	1×10^5
Curium (96)				
Cm-240	4×10^1	2×10^{-2}	1×10^2	1×10^5
Cm-241	2×10^0	1×10^0	1×10^2	1×10^6
Cm-242	4×10^1	1×10^{-2}	1×10^2	1×10^5
Cm-243	9×10^0	1×10^{-3}	1×10^0	1×10^4
Cm-244	2×10^1	2×10^{-3}	1×10^1	1×10^4
Cm-245	9×10^0	9×10^{-4}	1×10^0	1×10^3
Cm-246	9×10^0	9×10^{-4}	1×10^0	1×10^3
Cm-247 (a)	3×10^0	1×10^{-3}	1×10^0	1×10^4
Cm-248	2×10^{-2}	3×10^{-4}	1×10^0	1×10^3

Radionuclide (atomic number)	A_1 (TBq)	A_2 (TBq)	Activity concentration limit for exempt material (Bq/g)	Activity limit for an exempt consignment (Bq)
Cobalt (27)				
Co-55	5×10^{-1}	5×10^{-1}	1×10^1	1×10^6
Co-56	3×10^{-1}	3×10^{-1}	1×10^1	1×10^5
Co-57	1×10^1	1×10^1	1×10^2	1×10^6
Co-58	1×10^0	1×10^0	1×10^1	1×10^6
Co-58m	4×10^1	4×10^1	1×10^4	1×10^7
Co-60	4×10^{-1}	4×10^{-1}	1×10^1	1×10^5
Chromium (24)				
Cr-51	3×10^1	3×10^1	1×10^3	1×10^7
Caesium (55)				
Cs-129	4×10^0	4×10^0	1×10^2	1×10^5
Cs-131	3×10^1	3×10^1	1×10^3	1×10^6
Cs-132	1×10^0	1×10^0	1×10^1	1×10^5
Cs-134	7×10^{-1}	7×10^{-1}	1×10^1	1×10^4
Cs-134m	4×10^1	6×10^{-1}	1×10^3	1×10^5
Cs-135	4×10^1	1×10^0	1×10^4	1×10^7
Cs-136	5×10^{-1}	5×10^{-1}	1×10^1	1×10^5
Cs-137 (a)	2×10^0	6×10^{-1}	1×10^1 (b)	1×10^4 (b)
Copper (29)				
Cu-64	6×10^0	1×10^0	1×10^2	1×10^6
Cu-67	1×10^1	7×10^{-1}	1×10^2	1×10^6
Dysprosium (66)				
Dy-159	2×10^1	2×10^1	1×10^3	1×10^7
Dy-165	9×10^{-1}	6×10^{-1}	1×10^3	1×10^6
Dy-166 (a)	9×10^{-1}	3×10^{-1}	1×10^3	1×10^6
Erbium (68)				
Er-169	4×10^1	1×10^0	1×10^4	1×10^7
Er-171	8×10^{-1}	5×10^{-1}	1×10^2	1×10^6
Europium (63)				
Eu-147	2×10^0	2×10^0	1×10^2	1×10^6
Eu-148	5×10^{-1}	5×10^{-1}	1×10^1	1×10^6
Eu-149	2×10^1	2×10^1	1×10^2	1×10^7
Eu-150 (short lived)	2×10^0	7×10^{-1}	1×10^3	1×10^6
Eu-150 (long lived)	7×10^{-1}	7×10^{-1}	1×10^1	1×10^6
Eu-152	1×10^0	1×10^0	1×10^1	1×10^6
Eu-152m	8×10^{-1}	8×10^{-1}	1×10^2	1×10^6
Eu-154	9×10^{-1}	6×10^{-1}	1×10^1	1×10^6
Eu-155	2×10^1	3×10^0	1×10^2	1×10^7
Eu-156	7×10^{-1}	7×10^{-1}	1×10^1	1×10^6
Fluorine (9)				
F-18	1×10^0	6×10^{-1}	1×10^1	1×10^6
Iron (26)				
Fe-52 (a)	3×10^{-1}	3×10^{-1}	1×10^1	1×10^6
Fe-55	4×10^1	4×10^1	1×10^4	1×10^6
Fe-59	9×10^{-1}	9×10^{-1}	1×10^1	1×10^6
Fe-60 (a)	4×10^1	2×10^{-1}	1×10^2	1×10^5
Gallium (31)				
Ga-67	7×10^0	3×10^0	1×10^2	1×10^6
Ga-68	5×10^{-1}	5×10^{-1}	1×10^1	1×10^5
Ga-72	4×10^{-1}	4×10^{-1}	1×10^1	1×10^5
Gadolinium (64)				
Gd-146 (a)	5×10^{-1}	5×10^{-1}	1×10^1	1×10^6
Gd-148	2×10^1	2×10^{-3}	1×10^1	1×10^4
Gd-153	1×10^1	9×10^0	1×10^2	1×10^7
Gd-159	3×10^0	6×10^{-1}	1×10^3	1×10^6

Radionuclide (atomic number)	A_1 (TBq)	A_2 (TBq)	Activity concentration limit for exempt material (Bq/g)	Activity limit for an exempt consignment (Bq)
Germanium (32)				
Ge-68 (a)	5×10^{-1}	5×10^{-1}	1×10^1	1×10^5
Ge-69	1×10^0	1×10^0	1×10^1	1×10^6
Ge-71	4×10^1	4×10^1	1×10^4	1×10^8
Ge-77	3×10^{-1}	3×10^{-1}	1×10^1	1×10^5
Hafnium (72)				
Hf-172 (a)	6×10^{-1}	6×10^{-1}	1×10^1	1×10^6
Hf-175	3×10^0	3×10^0	1×10^2	1×10^6
Hf-181	2×10^0	5×10^{-1}	1×10^1	1×10^6
Hf-182	Unlimited	Unlimited	1×10^2	1×10^6
Mercury (80)				
Hg-194 (a)	1×10^0	1×10^0	1×10^1	1×10^6
Hg-195m (a)	3×10^0	7×10^{-1}	1×10^2	1×10^6
Hg-197	2×10^1	1×10^1	1×10^2	1×10^7
Hg-197m	1×10^1	4×10^{-1}	1×10^2	1×10^6
Hg-203	5×10^0	1×10^0	1×10^2	1×10^5
Holmium (67)				
Ho-166	4×10^{-1}	4×10^{-1}	1×10^3	1×10^5
Ho-166m	6×10^{-1}	5×10^{-1}	1×10^1	1×10^6
Iodine (53)				
I-123	6×10^0	3×10^0	1×10^2	1×10^7
I-124	1×10^0	1×10^0	1×10^1	1×10^6
I-125	2×10^1	3×10^0	1×10^3	1×10^6
I-126	2×10^0	1×10^0	1×10^2	1×10^6
I-129	Unlimited	Unlimited	1×10^2	1×10^5
I-131	3×10^0	7×10^{-1}	1×10^2	1×10^6
I-132	4×10^{-1}	4×10^{-1}	1×10^1	1×10^5
I-133	7×10^{-1}	6×10^{-1}	1×10^1	1×10^6
I-134	3×10^{-1}	3×10^{-1}	1×10^1	1×10^5
I-135 (a)	6×10^{-1}	6×10^{-1}	1×10^1	1×10^6
Indium (49)				
In-111	3×10^0	3×10^0	1×10^2	1×10^6
In-113m	4×10^0	2×10^0	1×10^2	1×10^6
In-114m (a)	1×10^1	5×10^{-1}	1×10^2	1×10^6
In-115m	7×10^0	1×10^0	1×10^2	1×10^6
Iridium (77)				
Ir-189 (a)	1×10^1	1×10^1	1×10^2	1×10^7
Ir-190	7×10^{-1}	7×10^{-1}	1×10^1	1×10^6
Ir-192	1×10^0(c)	6×10^{-1}	1×10^1	1×10^4
Ir-193m	4×10^1	4×10^0	1×10^4	1×10^7
Ir-194	3×10^{-1}	3×10^{-1}	1×10^2	1×10^5
Potassium (19)				
K-40	9×10^{-1}	9×10^{-1}	1×10^2	1×10^6
K-42	2×10^{-1}	2×10^{-1}	1×10^2	1×10^6
K-43	7×10^{-1}	6×10^{-1}	1×10^1	1×10^6
Krypton (36)				
Kr-79	4×10^0	2×10^0	1×10^3	1×10^5
Kr-81	4×10^1	4×10^1	1×10^4	1×10^7
Kr-85	1×10^1	1×10^1	1×10^5	1×10^4
Kr-85m	8×10^0	3×10^0	1×10^3	1×10^{10}
Kr-87	2×10^{-1}	2×10^{-1}	1×10^2	1×10^9
Lanthanum (57)				
La-137	3×10^1	6×10^0	1×10^3	1×10^7
La-140	4×10^{-1}	4×10^{-1}	1×10^1	1×10^5

Radionuclide (atomic number)	A_1 (TBq)	A_2 (TBq)	Activity concentration limit for exempt material (Bq/g)	Activity limit for an exempt consignment (Bq)
Lutetium (71)				
Lu-172	6×10^{-1}	6×10^{-1}	1×10^1	1×10^6
Lu-173	8×10^0	8×10^0	1×10^2	1×10^7
Lu-174	9×10^0	9×10^0	1×10^2	1×10^7
Lu-174m	2×10^1	1×10^1	1×10^2	1×10^7
Lu-177	3×10^1	7×10^{-1}	1×10^3	1×10^7
Magnesium (12)				
Mg-28 (a)	3×10^{-1}	3×10^{-1}	1×10^1	1×10^5
Manganese (25)				
Mn-52	3×10^{-1}	3×10^{-1}	1×10^1	1×10^5
Mn-53	Unlimited	Unlimited	1×10^4	1×10^9
Mn-54	1×10^0	1×10^0	1×10^1	1×10^6
Mn-56	3×10^{-1}	3×10^{-1}	1×10^1	1×10^5
Molybdenum (42)				
Mo-93	4×10^1	2×10^1	1×10^3	1×10^8
Mo-99 (a)	1×10^0	6×10^{-1}	1×10^2	1×10^6
Nitrogen (7)				
N-13	9×10^{-1}	6×10^{-1}	1×10^2	1×10^9
Sodium (11)				
Na-22	5×10^{-1}	5×10^{-1}	1×10^1	1×10^6
Na-24	2×10^{-1}	2×10^{-1}	1×10^1	1×10^5
Niobium (41)				
Nb-93m	4×10^1	3×10^1	1×10^4	1×10^7
Nb-94	7×10^{-1}	7×10^{-1}	1×10^1	1×10^6
Nb-95	1×10^0	1×10^0	1×10^1	1×10^6
Nb-97	9×10^{-1}	6×10^{-1}	1×10^1	1×10^6
Neodymium (60)				
Nd-147	6×10^0	6×10^{-1}	1×10^2	1×10^6
Nd-149	6×10^{-1}	5×10^{-1}	1×10^2	1×10^6
Nickel (28)				
Ni-57	6×10^{-1}	6×10^{-1}	1×10^1	1×10^6
Ni-59	Unlimited	Unlimited	1×10^4	1×10^8
Ni-63	4×10^1	3×10^1	1×10^5	1×10^8
Ni-65	4×10^{-1}	4×10^{-1}	1×10^1	1×10^6
Neptunium (93)				
Np-235	4×10^1	4×10^1	1×10^3	1×10^7
Np-236 (short-lived)	2×10^1	2×10^0	1×10^3	1×10^7
Np-236 (long-lived)	9×10^0	2×10^{-2}	1×10^2	1×10^5
Np-237	2×10^1	2×10^{-3}	1×10^0 (b)	1×10^3 (b)
Np-239	7×10^0	4×10^{-1}	1×10^2	1×10^7
Osmium (76)				
Os-185	1×10^0	1×10^0	1×10^1	1×10^6
Os-191	1×10^1	2×10^0	1×10^2	1×10^7
Os-191m	4×10^1	3×10^1	1×10^3	1×10^7
Os-193	2×10^0	6×10^{-1}	1×10^2	1×10^6
Os-194 (a)	3×10^{-1}	3×10^{-1}	1×10^2	1×10^5
Phosphorus (15)				
P-32	5×10^{-1}	5×10^{-1}	1×10^3	1×10^5
P-33	4×10^1	1×10^0	1×10^5	1×10^8
Protactinium (91)				
Pa-230 (a)	2×10^0	7×10^{-2}	1×10^1	1×10^6
Pa-231	4×10^0	4×10^{-4}	1×10^0	1×10^3
Pa-233	5×10^0	7×10^{-1}	1×10^2	1×10^7

Radionuclide (atomic number)	A_1 (TBq)	A_2 (TBq)	Activity concentration limit for exempt material (Bq/g)	Activity limit for an exempt consignment (Bq)
Lead (82)				
Pb-201	1×10^0	1×10^0	1×10^1	1×10^6
Pb-202	4×10^1	2×10^1	1×10^3	1×10^6
Pb-203	4×10^0	3×10^0	1×10^2	1×10^6
Pb-205	Unlimited	Unlimited	1×10^4	1×10^7
Pb-210 (a)	1×10^0	5×10^{-2}	1×10^1 (b)	1×10^4 (b)
Pb-212 (a)	7×10^{-1}	2×10^{-1}	1×10^1 (b)	1×10^5 (b)
Palladium (46)				
Pd-103 (a)	4×10^1	4×10^1	1×10^3	1×10^8
Pd-107	Unlimited	Unlimited	1×10^5	1×10^8
Pd-109	2×10^0	5×10^{-1}	1×10^3	1×10^6
Promethium (61)				
Pm-143	3×10^0	3×10^0	1×10^2	1×10^6
Pm-144	7×10^{-1}	7×10^{-1}	1×10^1	1×10^6
Pm-145	3×10^1	1×10^1	1×10^3	1×10^7
Pm-147	4×10^1	2×10^0	1×10^4	1×10^7
Pm-148m (a)	8×10^{-1}	7×10^{-1}	1×10^1	1×10^6
Pm-149	2×10^0	6×10^{-1}	1×10^3	1×10^6
Pm-151	2×10^0	6×10^{-1}	1×10^2	1×10^6
Polonium (84)				
Po-210	4×10^1	2×10^{-2}	1×10^1	1×10^4
Praseodymium (59)				
Pr-142	4×10^{-1}	4×10^{-1}	1×10^2	1×10^5
Pr-143	3×10^0	6×10^{-1}	1×10^4	1×10^6
Platinum (78)				
Pt-188 (a)	1×10^0	8×10^{-1}	1×10^1	1×10^6
Pt-191	4×10^0	3×10^0	1×10^2	1×10^6
Pt-193	4×10^1	4×10^1	1×10^4	1×10^7
Pt-193m	4×10^1	5×10^{-1}	1×10^3	1×10^7
Pt-195m	1×10^1	5×10^{-1}	1×10^2	1×10^6
Pt-197	2×10^1	6×10^{-1}	1×10^3	1×10^6
Pt-197m	1×10^1	6×10^{-1}	1×10^2	1×10^6
Plutonium (94)				
Pu-236	3×10^1	3×10^{-3}	1×10^1	1×10^4
Pu-237	2×10^1	2×10^1	1×10^3	1×10^7
Pu-238	1×10^1	1×10^{-3}	1×10^0	1×10^4
Pu-239	1×10^1	1×10^{-3}	1×10^0	1×10^4
Pu-240	1×10^1	1×10^{-3}	1×10^0	1×10^3
Pu-241 (a)	4×10^1	6×10^{-2}	1×10^2	1×10^5
Pu-242	1×10^1	1×10^{-3}	1×10^0	1×10^4
Pu-244 (a)	4×10^{-1}	1×10^{-3}	1×10^0	1×10^4
Radium (88)				
Ra-223 (a)	4×10^{-1}	7×10^{-3}	1×10^2 (b)	1×10^5 (b)
Ra-224 (a)	4×10^{-1}	2×10^{-2}	1×10^1 (b)	1×10^5 (b)
Ra-225 (a)	2×10^{-1}	4×10^{-3}	1×10^2	1×10^5
Ra-226 (a)	2×10^{-1}	3×10^{-3}	1×10^1 (b)	1×10^4 (b)
Ra-228 (a)	6×10^{-1}	2×10^{-2}	1×10^1 (b)	1×10^5 (b)
Rubidium (37)				
Rb-81	2×10^0	8×10^{-1}	1×10^1	1×10^6
Rb-83 (a)	2×10^0	2×10^0	1×10^2	1×10^6
Rb-84	1×10^0	1×10^0	1×10^1	1×10^6
Rb-86	5×10^{-1}	5×10^{-1}	1×10^2	1×10^5
Rb-87	Unlimited	Unlimited	1×10^4	1×10^7
Rb (natural)	Unlimited	Unlimited	1×10^4	1×10^7

Radionuclide (atomic number)	A_1 (TBq)	A_2 (TBq)	Activity concentration limit for exempt material (Bq/g)	Activity limit for an exempt consignment (Bq)
Rhenium (75)				
Re-184	1×10^0	1×10^0	1×10^1	1×10^6
Re-184m	3×10^0	1×10^0	1×10^2	1×10^6
Re-186	2×10^0	6×10^{-1}	1×10^3	1×10^6
Re-187	Unlimited	Unlimited	1×10^6	1×10^9
Re-188	4×10^{-1}	4×10^{-1}	1×10^2	1×10^5
Re-189 (a)	3×10^0	6×10^{-1}	1×10^2	1×10^6
Re (natural)	Unlimited	Unlimited	1×10^6	1×10^9
Rhodium (45)				
Rh-99	2×10^0	2×10^0	1×10^1	1×10^6
Rh-101	4×10^0	3×10^0	1×10^2	1×10^7
Rh-102	5×10^{-1}	5×10^{-1}	1×10^1	1×10^6
Rh-102m	2×10^0	2×10^0	1×10^2	1×10^6
Rh-103m	4×10^1	4×10^1	1×10^4	1×10^8
Rh-105	1×10^1	8×10^{-1}	1×10^2	1×10^7
Radon (86)				
Rn-222 (a)	3×10^{-1}	4×10^{-3}	1×10^1 (b)	1×10^8 (b)
Ruthenium (44)				
Ru-97	5×10^0	5×10^0	1×10^2	1×10^7
Ru-103 (a)	2×10^0	2×10^0	1×10^2	1×10^6
Ru-105	1×10^0	6×10^{-1}	1×10^1	1×10^6
Ru-106 (a)	2×10^{-1}	2×10^{-1}	1×10^2 (b)	1×10^5 (b)
Sulphur (16)				
S-35	4×10^1	3×10^0	1×10^5	1×10^8
Antimony (51)				
Sb-122	4×10^{-1}	4×10^{-1}	1×10^2	1×10^4
Sb-124	6×10^{-1}	6×10^{-1}	1×10^1	1×10^6
Sb-125	2×10^0	1×10^0	1×10^2	1×10^6
Sb-126	4×10^{-1}	4×10^{-1}	1×10^1	1×10^5
Scandium (21)				
Sc-44	5×10^{-1}	5×10^{-1}	1×10^1	1×10^5
Sc-46	5×10^{-1}	5×10^{-1}	1×10^1	1×10^6
Sc-47	1×10^1	7×10^{-1}	1×10^2	1×10^6
Sc-48	3×10^{-1}	3×10^{-1}	1×10^1	1×10^5
Selenium (34)				
Se-75	3×10^0	3×10^0	1×10^2	1×10^6
Se-79	4×10^1	2×10^0	1×10^4	1×10^7
Silicon (14)				
Si-31	6×10^{-1}	6×10^{-1}	1×10^3	1×10^6
Si-32	4×10^1	5×10^{-1}	1×10^3	1×10^6
Samarium (62)				
Sm-145	1×10^1	1×10^1	1×10^2	1×10^7
Sm-147	Unlimited	Unlimited	1×10^1	1×10^4
Sm-151	4×10^1	1×10^1	1×10^4	1×10^8
Sm-153	9×10^0	6×10^{-1}	1×10^2	1×10^6
Tin (50)				
Sn-113 (a)	4×10^0	2×10^0	1×10^3	1×10^7
Sn-117m	7×10^0	4×10^{-1}	1×10^2	1×10^6
Sn-119m	4×10^1	3×10^1	1×10^3	1×10^7
Sn-121m (a)	4×10^1	9×10^{-1}	1×10^3	1×10^7
Sn-123	8×10^{-1}	6×10^{-1}	1×10^3	1×10^6
Sn-125	4×10^{-1}	4×10^{-1}	1×10^2	1×10^5
Sn-126 (a)	6×10^{-1}	4×10^{-1}	1×10^1	1×10^5

Radionuclide (atomic number)	A_1 (TBq)	A_2 (TBq)	Activity concentration limit for exempt material (Bq/g)	Activity limit for an exempt consignment (Bq)
Strontium (38)				
Sr-82 (a)	2×10^{-1}	2×10^{-1}	1×10^1	1×10^5
Sr-83	1×10^0	1×10^0	1×10^1	1×10^6
Sr-85	2×10^0	2×10^0	1×10^2	1×10^6
Sr-85m	5×10^0	5×10^0	1×10^2	1×10^7
Sr-87m	3×10^0	3×10^0	1×10^2	1×10^6
Sr-89	6×10^{-1}	6×10^{-1}	1×10^3	1×10^6
Sr-90 (a)	3×10^{-1}	3×10^{-1}	1×10^2 (b)	1×10^4 (b)
Sr-91 (a)	3×10^{-1}	3×10^{-1}	1×10^1	1×10^5
Sr-92 (a)	1×10^0	3×10^{-1}	1×10^1	1×10^6
Tritium (1)				
T(H-3)	4×10^1	4×10^1	1×10^6	1×10^9
Tantalum (73)				
Ta-178 (long-lived)	1×10^0	8×10^{-1}	1×10^1	1×10^6
Ta-179	3×10^1	3×10^1	1×10^3	1×10^7
Ta-182	9×10^{-1}	5×10^{-1}	1×10^1	1×10^4
Terbium (65)				
Tb-149	8×10^{-1}	8×10^{-1}	1×10^1	1×10^6
Tb-157	4×10^1	4×10^1	1×10^4	1×10^7
Tb-158	1×10^0	1×10^0	1×10^1	1×10^6
Tb-160	1×10^0	6×10^{-1}	1×10^1	1×10^6
Tb-161	3×10^1	7×10^{-1}	1×10^3	1×10^6
Technetium (43)				
Tc-95m (a)	2×10^0	2×10^0	1×10^1	1×10^6
Tc-96	4×10^{-1}	4×10^{-1}	1×10^1	1×10^6
Tc-96m (a)	4×10^{-1}	4×10^{-1}	1×10^3	1×10^7
Tc-97	Unlimited	Unlimited	1×10^3	1×10^8
Tc-97m	4×10^1	1×10^0	1×10^3	1×10^7
Tc-98	8×10^{-1}	7×10^{-1}	1×10^1	1×10^6
Tc-99	4×10^1	9×10^{-1}	1×10^4	1×10^7
Tc-99m	1×10^1	4×10^0	1×10^2	1×10^7
Tellurium (52)				
Te-121	2×10^0	2×10^0	1×10^1	1×10^6
Te-121m	5×10^0	3×10^0	1×10^2	1×10^6
Te-123m	8×10^0	1×10^0	1×10^2	1×10^7
Te-125m	2×10^1	9×10^{-1}	1×10^3	1×10^7
Te-127	2×10^1	7×10^{-1}	1×10^3	1×10^6
Te-127m (a)	2×10^1	5×10^{-1}	1×10^3	1×10^7
Te-129	7×10^{-1}	6×10^{-1}	1×10^2	1×10^6
Te-129m (a)	8×10^{-1}	4×10^{-1}	1×10^3	1×10^6
Te-131m (a)	7×10^{-1}	5×10^{-1}	1×10^1	1×10^6
Te-132 (a)	5×10^{-1}	4×10^{-1}	1×10^2	1×10^7
Thorium (90)				
Th-227	1×10^1	5×10^{-3}	1×10^1	1×10^4
Th-228 (a)	5×10^{-1}	1×10^{-3}	1×10^0 (b)	1×10^4 (b)
Th-229	5×10^0	5×10^{-4}	1×10^0 (b)	1×10^3 (b)
Th-230	1×10^1	1×10^{-3}	1×10^0	1×10^4
Th-231	4×10^1	2×10^{-2}	1×10^3	1×10^7
Th-232	Unlimited	Unlimited	1×10^1	1×10^4
Th-234 (a)	3×10^{-1}	3×10^{-1}	1×10^3 (b)	1×10^5 (b)
Th (natural)	Unlimited	Unlimited	1×10^0 (b)	1×10^3 (b)
Titanium (22)				
Ti-44 (a)	5×10^{-1}	4×10^{-1}	1×10^1	1×10^5

Radionuclide (atomic number)	A_1 (TBq)	A_2 (TBq)	Activity concentration limit for exempt material (Bq/g)	Activity limit for an exempt consignment (Bq)
Thallium (81)				
Tl-200	9×10^{-1}	9×10^{-1}	1×10^1	1×10^6
Tl-201	1×10^1	4×10^0	1×10^2	1×10^6
Tl-202	2×10^0	2×10^0	1×10^2	1×10^6
Tl-204	1×10^1	7×10^{-1}	1×10^4	1×10^4
Thulium (69)				
Tm-167	7×10^0	8×10^{-1}	1×10^2	1×10^6
Tm-170	3×10^0	6×10^{-1}	1×10^3	1×10^6
Tm-171	4×10^1	4×10^1	1×10^4	1×10^8
Uranium (92)				
U-230 (fast lung absorption) (a)(d)	4×10^1	1×10^{-1}	1×10^1 (b)	1×10^5 (b)
U-230 (medium lung absorption) (a)(e)	4×10^1	4×10^{-3}	1×10^1	1×10^4
U-230 (slow lung absorption) (a)(f)	3×10^1	3×10^{-3}	1×10^1	1×10^4
U-232 (fast lung absorption) (d)	4×10^1	1×10^{-2}	1×10^0 (b)	1×10^3 (b)
U-232 (medium lung absorption) (e)	4×10^1	7×10^{-3}	1×10^1	1×10^4
U-232 (slow lung absorption) (f)	1×10^1	1×10^{-3}	1×10^1	1×10^4
U-233 (fast lung absorption) (d)	4×10^1	9×10^{-2}	1×10^1	1×10^4
U-233 (medium lung absorption) (e)	4×10^1	2×10^{-2}	1×10^2	1×10^5
U-233 (slow lung absorption) (f)	4×10^1	6×10^{-3}	1×10^1	1×10^5
U-234 (fast lung absorption) (d)	4×10^1	9×10^{-2}	1×10^1	1×10^4
U-234 (medium lung absorption) (e)	4×10^1	2×10^{-2}	1×10^2	1×10^5
U-234 (slow lung absorption) (f)	4×10^1	6×10^{-3}	1×10^1	1×10^5
U-235 (all lung absorption types) (a)(d)(e)(f)	Unlimited	Unlimited	1×10^1 (b)	1×10^4 (b)
U-236 (fast lung absorption) (d)	Unlimited	Unlimited	1×10^1	1×10^4
U-236 (medium lung absorption) (e)	4×10^1	2×10^{-2}	1×10^2	1×10^5
U-236 (slow lung absorption) (f)	4×10^1	6×10^{-3}	1×10^1	1×10^4
U-238 (all lung absorption types) (d)(e)(f)	Unlimited	Unlimited	1×10^1 (b)	1×10^4 (b)
U (natural)	Unlimited	Unlimited	1×10^0 (b)	1×10^3 (b)
U (enriched to 20 % or less) (g)	Unlimited	Unlimited	1×10^0	1×10^3
U (depleted)	Unlimited	Unlimited	1×10^0	1×10^3
Vanadium (23)				
V-48	4×10^{-1}	4×10^{-1}	1×10^1	1×10^5
V-49	4×10^1	4×10^1	1×10^4	1×10^7
Tungsten (74)				
W-178 (a)	9×10^0	5×10^0	1×10^1	1×10^6
W-181	3×10^1	3×10^1	1×10^3	1×10^7
W-185	4×10^1	8×10^{-1}	1×10^4	1×10^7
W-187	2×10^0	6×10^{-1}	1×10^2	1×10^6
W-188 (a)	4×10^{-1}	3×10^{-1}	1×10^2	1×10^5
Xenon (54)				
Xe-122 (a)	4×10^{-1}	4×10^{-1}	1×10^2	1×10^9
Xe-123	2×10^0	7×10^{-1}	1×10^2	1×10^9
Xe-127	4×10^0	2×10^0	1×10^3	1×10^5
Xe-131m	4×10^1	4×10^1	1×10^4	1×10^4
Xe-133	2×10^1	1×10^1	1×10^3	1×10^4
Xe-135	3×10^0	2×10^0	1×10^3	1×10^{10}

Radionuclide (atomic number)	A_1 (TBq)	A_2 (TBq)	Activity concentration limit for exempt material (Bq/g)	Activity limit for an exempt consignment (Bq)
Yttrium (39)				
Y-87 (a)	1×10^0	1×10^0	1×10^1	1×10^6
Y-88	4×10^{-1}	4×10^{-1}	1×10^1	1×10^6
Y-90	3×10^{-1}	3×10^{-1}	1×10^3	1×10^5
Y-91	6×10^{-1}	6×10^{-1}	1×10^3	1×10^6
Y-91m	2×10^0	2×10^0	1×10^2	1×10^6
Y-92	2×10^{-1}	2×10^{-1}	1×10^2	1×10^5
Y-93	3×10^{-1}	3×10^{-1}	1×10^2	1×10^5
Ytterbium (70)				
Yb-169	4×10^0	1×10^0	1×10^2	1×10^7
Yb-175	3×10^1	9×10^{-1}	1×10^3	1×10^7
Zinc (30)				
Zn-65	2×10^0	2×10^0	1×10^1	1×10^6
Zn-69	3×10^0	6×10^{-1}	1×10^4	1×10^6
Zn-69m (a)	3×10^0	6×10^{-1}	1×10^2	1×10^6
Zirconium (40)				
Zr-88	3×10^0	3×10^0	1×10^2	1×10^6
Zr-93	Unlimited	Unlimited	1×10^3 (b)	1×10^7 (b)
Zr-95 (a)	2×10^0	8×10^{-1}	1×10^1	1×10^6
Zr-97 (a)	4×10^{-1}	4×10^{-1}	1×10^1 (b)	1×10^5 (b)

(a) A_1 and/or A_2 values for these parent radionuclides include contributions from their progeny with half-lives less than 10 days, as listed in the following:

Mg-28	Al-28
Ar-42	K-42
Ca-47	Sc-47
Ti-44	Sc-44
Fe-52	Mn-52m
Fe-60	Co-60m
Zn-69m	Zn-69
Ge-68	Ga-68
Rb-83	Kr-83m
Sr-82	Rb-82
Sr-90	Y-90
Sr-91	Y-91m
Sr-92	Y-92
Y-87	Sr-87m
Zr-95	Nb-95m
Zr-97	Nb-97m, Nb-97
Mo-99	Tc-99m
Tc-95m	Tc-95
Tc-96m	Tc-96
Ru-103	Rh-103m
Ru-106	Rh-106
Pd-103	Rh-103m
Ag-108m	Ag-108
Ag-110m	Ag-110
Cd-115	In-115m
In-114m	In-114
Sn-113	In-113m
Sn-121m	Sn-121
Sn-126	Sb-126m
Te-118	Sb-118

Te-127m	Te-127
Te-129m	Te-129
Te-131m	Te-131
Te-132	I-132
I-135	Xe-135m
Xe-122	I-122
Cs-137	Ba-137m
Ba-131	Cs-131
Ba-140	La-140
Ce-144	Pr-144m, Pr-144
Pm-148m	Pm-148
Gd-146	Eu-146
Dy-166	Ho-166
Hf-172	Lu-172
W-178	Ta-178
W-188	Re-188
Re-189	Os-189m
Os-194	Ir-194
Ir-189	Os-189m
Pt-188	Ir-188
Hg-194	Au-194
Hg-195m	Hg-195
Pb-210	Bi-210
Pb-212	Bi-212, Tl-208, Po-212
Bi-210m	Tl-206
Bi-212	Tl-208, Po-212
At-211	Po-211
Rn-222	Po-218, Pb-214, At-218, Bi-214, Po-214
Ra-223	Rn-219, Po-215, Pb-211, Bi-211, Po-211, Tl-207
Ra-224	Rn-220, Po-216, Pb-212, Bi-212, Tl-208, Po-212
Ra-225	Ac-225, Fr-221, At-217, Bi-213, Tl-209, Po-213, Pb-209
Ra-226	Rn-222, Po-218, Pb-214, At-218, Bi-214, Po-214
Ra-228	Ac-228
Ac-225	Fr-221, At-217, Bi-213, Tl-209, Po-213, Pb-209
Ac-227	Fr-223
Th-228	Ra-224, Rn-220, Po-216, Pb-212, Bi-212, Tl-208, Po-212
Th-234	Pa-234m, Pa-234
Pa-230	Ac-226, Th-226, Fr-222, Ra-222, Rn-218, Po-214
U-230	Th-226, Ra-222, Rn-218, Po-214
U-235	Th-231
Pu-241	U-237
Pu-244	U-240, Np-240m
Am-242m	Am-242, Np-238
Am-243	Np-239
Cm-247	Pu-243
Bk-249	Am-245
Cf-253	Cm-249;

(b) Parent nuclides and their progeny included in secular equilibrium are listed in the following (the activity to be taken into account is that of the parent nuclide only):

Sr-90	Y-90
Zr-93	Nb-93m
Zr-97	Nb-97
Ru-106	Rh-106
Ag-108m	Ag-108
Cs-137	Ba-137m

Ce-144	Pr-144
Ba-140	La-140
Bi-212	Tl-208 (0.36), Po-212 (0.64)
Pb-210	Bi-210, Po-210
Pb-212	Bi-212, Tl-208 (0.36), Po-212 (0.64)
Rn-222	Po-218, Pb-214, Bi-214, Po-214
Ra-223	Rn-219, Po-215, Pb-211, Bi-211, Tl-207
Ra-224	Rn-220, Po-216, Pb-212, Bi-212, Tl-208 (0.36), Po-212 (0.64)
Ra-226	Rn-222, Po-218, Pb-214, Bi-214, Po-214, Pb-210, Bi-210, Po-210
Ra-228	Ac-228
Th-228	Ra-224, Rn-220, Po-216, Pb212, Bi-212, Tl208 (0.36), Po-212 (0.64)
Th-229	Ra-225, Ac-225, Fr-221, At-217, Bi-213, Po-213, Pb-209
Th-nat[1]	Ra-228, Ac-228, Th-228, Ra-224, Rn-220, Po-216, Pb-212, Bi-212, Tl-208 (0.36), Po-212 (0.64)
Th-234	Pa-234m
U-230	Th-226, Ra-222, Rn-218, Po-214
U-232	Th-228, Ra-224, Rn-220, Po-216, Pb-212, Bi-212, Tl-208 (0.36), Po-212 (0.64)
U-235	Th-231
U-238	Th-234, Pa-234m
U-nat[1]	Th-234, Pa-234m, U-234, Th-230, Ra-226, Rn-222, Po-218, Pb-214, Bi-214, Po-214, Pb-210, Bi-210, Po-210
Np-237	Pa-233
Am-242m	Am-242
Am-243	Np-239;

(c) The quantity may be determined from a measurement of the rate of decay or a measurement of the dose rate at a prescribed distance from the source;

(d) These values apply only to compounds of uranium that take the chemical form of UF_6, UO_2F_2 and $UO_2(NO_3)_2$ in both normal and accident conditions of transport;

(e) These values apply only to compounds of uranium that take the chemical form of UO_3, UF_4, UCl_4 and hexavalent compounds in both normal and accident conditions of transport;

(f) These values apply to all compounds of uranium other than those specified in (d) and (e) above;

(g) These values apply to unirradiated uranium only.

2.7.2.2.2 For individual radionuclides:

(a) Which are not listed in table 2.7.2.2.1 the determination of the basic radionuclide values referred to in 2.7.2.2.1 shall require multilateral approval. For these radionuclides, activity concentration limits for exempt material and activity limits for exempt consignments shall be calculated in accordance with the principles established in "Radiation Protection and Safety of Radiation Sources: International Basic Safety Standards", IAEA Safety Standards Series No. GSR Part 3, IAEA, Vienna (2014). It is permissible to use an A_2 value calculated using a dose coefficient for the appropriate lung absorption type as recommended by the International Commission on Radiological Protection, if the chemical forms of each radionuclide under both normal and accident conditions of transport are taken into consideration. Alternatively, the radionuclide values in table 2.7.2.2.2 may be used without obtaining competent authority approval;

---

[1] *In the case of Th-natural, the parent nuclide is Th-232, in the case of U-natural the parent nuclide is U-238.*

(b) In instruments or articles in which the radioactive material is enclosed or is included as a component part of the instrument or other manufactured article and which meet 2.7.2.4.1.3 (c), alternative basic radionuclide values to those in table 2.7.2.2.1 for the activity limit for an exempt consignment are permitted and shall require multilateral approval. Such alternative activity limits for an exempt consignment shall be calculated in accordance with the principles set out in GSR Part 3.

Table 2.7.2.2.2: Basic radionuclide values for unknown radionuclides or mixtures

Radioactive contents	A_1 (TBq)	A_2 (TBq)	Activity concentration limit for exempt material (Bq/g)	Activity limit for exempt consignments (Bq)
Only beta or gamma emitting nuclides are known to be present	0.1	0.02	1×10^1	1×10^4
Alpha emitting nuclides but no neutron emitters are known to be present	0.2	9×10^{-5}	1×10^{-1}	1×10^3
Neutron emitting nuclides are known to be present or no relevant data are available	0.001	9×10^{-5}	1×10^{-1}	1×10^3

2.7.2.2.3 In the calculations of A_1 and A_2 for a radionuclide not in table 2.7.2.2.1, a single radioactive decay chain in which the radionuclides are present in their naturally occurring proportions, and in which no progeny nuclide has a half-life either longer than 10 days or longer than that of the parent nuclide, shall be considered as a single radionuclide; and the activity to be taken into account and the A_1 or A_2 value to be applied shall be those corresponding to the parent nuclide of that chain. In the case of radioactive decay chains in which any progeny nuclide has a half-life either longer than 10 days or greater than that of the parent nuclide, the parent and such progeny nuclides shall be considered as mixtures of different nuclides.

2.7.2.2.4 For mixtures of radionuclides, the basic radionuclide values referred to in 2.7.2.2.1 may be determined as follows:

$$X_m = \frac{1}{\sum_i \frac{f(i)}{X(i)}}$$

where,

f(i) is the fraction of activity or activity concentration of radionuclide i in the mixture;

X(i) is the appropriate value of A_1 or A_2, or the activity concentration limit for exempt material or the activity limit for an exempt consignment as appropriate for the radionuclide i; and

X_m is the derived value of A_1 or A_2, or the activity concentration limit for exempt material or the activity limit for an exempt consignment in the case of a mixture.

2.7.2.2.5 When the identity of each radionuclide is known but the individual activities of some of the radionuclides are not known, the radionuclides may be grouped and the lowest radionuclide value, as appropriate, for the radionuclides in each group may be used in applying the formulas in 2.7.2.2.4 and 2.7.2.4.4. Groups may be based on the total alpha activity and the total beta/gamma activity when these are known, using the lowest radionuclide values for the alpha emitters or beta/gamma emitters, respectively.

2.7.2.2.6   For individual radionuclides or for mixtures of radionuclides for which relevant data are not available, the values shown in table 2.7.2.2.2 shall be used.

2.7.2.3   *Determination of other material characteristics*

2.7.2.3.1   *Low specific activity (LSA) material*

2.7.2.3.1.1   Reserved.

2.7.2.3.1.2   LSA material shall be in one of three groups:

(a)   LSA-I

   (i)   uranium and thorium ores and concentrates of such ores, and other ores containing naturally occurring radionuclides;

   (ii)   Natural uranium, depleted uranium, natural thorium or their compounds or mixtures, that are unirradiated and in solid or liquid form;

   (iii)   radioactive material for which the A_2 value is unlimited. Fissile material may be included only if excepted under 2.7.2.3.5;

   (iv)   other radioactive material in which the activity is distributed throughout and the estimated average specific activity does not exceed 30 times the values for activity concentration specified in 2.7.2.2.1 to 2.7.2.2.6. Fissile material may be included only if excepted under 2.7.2.3.5;

(b)   LSA-II

   (i)   water with tritium concentration up to 0.8 TBq/l;

   (ii)   other material in which the activity is distributed throughout and the estimated average specific activity does not exceed 10^{-4} A_2/g for solids and gases, and 10^{-5} A_2/g for liquids;

(c)   LSA-III - Solids (e.g. consolidated wastes, activated materials), excluding powders, in which:

   (i)   the radioactive material is distributed throughout a solid or a collection of solid objects, or is essentially uniformly distributed in a solid compact binding agent (such as concrete, bitumen and ceramic);

   (ii)   the estimated average specific activity of the solid, excluding any shielding material, does not exceed 2×10^{-3} A_2/g.

2.7.2.3.1.3 to 2.7.2.3.1.5   Deleted.

2.7.2.3.2   *Surface contaminated object (SCO)*

SCO is classified in one of three groups:

(a)   SCO-I: A solid object on which:

   (i)   the non-fixed contamination on the accessible surface averaged over 300 cm^2 (or the area of the surface if less than 300 cm^2) does not exceed 4 Bq/cm^2 for beta and gamma emitters and low toxicity alpha emitters, or 0.4 Bq/cm^2 for all other alpha emitters;

   (ii)   the fixed contamination on the accessible surface averaged over 300 cm^2 (or the area of the surface if less than 300 cm^2) does not exceed 4×10^4 Bq/cm^2 for beta and gamma emitters and low toxicity alpha emitters, or 4×10^3 Bq/cm² for all other alpha emitters; and

(iii) the non-fixed contamination plus the fixed contamination on the inaccessible surface averaged over 300 cm² (or the area of the surface if less than 300 cm²) does not exceed 4×10^4 Bq/cm² for beta and gamma emitters and low toxicity alpha emitters, or 4×10^3 Bq/cm² for all other alpha emitters;

(b) SCO-II: A solid object on which either the fixed or non-fixed contamination on the surface exceeds the applicable limits specified for SCO-I in (a) above and on which:

(i) the non-fixed contamination on the accessible surface averaged over 300 cm² (or the area of the surface if less than 300 cm²) does not exceed 400 Bq/cm² for beta and gamma emitters and low toxicity alpha emitters, or 40 Bq/cm² for all other alpha emitters;

(ii) the fixed contamination on the accessible surface, averaged over 300 cm² (or the area of the surface if less than 300 cm²) does not exceed 8×10^5 Bq/cm² for beta and gamma emitters and low toxicity alpha emitters, or 8×10^4 Bq/cm² for all other alpha emitters; and

(iii) the non-fixed contamination plus the fixed contamination on the inaccessible surface averaged over 300 cm² (or the area of the surface if less than 300 cm²) does not exceed 8×10^5 Bq/cm² for beta and gamma emitters and low toxicity alpha emitters, or 8×10^4 Bq/cm² for all other alpha emitters.

(c) SCO-III: A large solid object which, because of its size, cannot be transported in a type of package described in these Regulations and for which:

(i) All openings are sealed to prevent release of radioactive material during conditions defined in 4.1.9.2.4 (e);

(ii) The inside of the object is as dry as practicable;

(iii) The non-fixed contamination on the external surfaces does not exceed the limits specified in 4.1.9.1.2.

(iv) The non-fixed contamination plus the fixed contamination on the inaccessible surface averaged over 300 cm² does not exceed 8×105 Bq/cm² for beta and gamma emitters and low toxicity alpha emitters, or 8×104 Bq/cm² for all other alpha emitters.

2.7.2.3.3 *Special form radioactive material*

2.7.2.3.3.1 Special form radioactive material shall have at least one dimension not less than 5 mm. When a sealed capsule constitutes part of the special form radioactive material, the capsule shall be so manufactured that it can be opened only by destroying it. The design for special form radioactive material requires unilateral approval.

2.7.2.3.3.2 Special form radioactive material shall be of such a nature or shall be so designed that if it is subjected to the tests specified in 2.7.2.3.3.4 to 2.7.2.3.3.8, it shall meet the following requirements:

(a) It would not break or shatter under the impact, percussion and bending tests 2.7.2.3.3.5 (a), (b), (c) and 2.7.2.3.3.6 (a) as applicable;

(b) It would not melt or disperse in the applicable heat test 2.7.2.3.3.5 (d) or 2.7.2.3.3.6 (b) as applicable; and

(c) The activity in the water from the leaching tests specified in 2.7.2.3.3.7 and 2.7.2.3.3.8 would not exceed 2 kBq; or alternatively for sealed sources, the leakage rate for the volumetric leakage assessment test specified in ISO 9978:1992 "Radiation Protection – Sealed Radioactive Sources – Leakage Test Methods", would not exceed the applicable acceptance threshold acceptable to the competent authority.

2.7.2.3.3.3 Demonstration of compliance with the performance standards in 2.7.2.3.3.2 shall be in accordance with 6.4.12.1 and 6.4.12.2.

2.7.2.3.3.4 Specimens that comprise or simulate special form radioactive material shall be subjected to the impact test, the percussion test, the bending test, and the heat test specified in 2.7.2.3.3.5 or alternative tests as authorized in 2.7.2.3.3.6. A different specimen may be used for each of the tests. Following each test, a leaching assessment or volumetric leakage test shall be performed on the specimen by a method no less sensitive than the methods given in 2.7.2.3.3.7 for indispersible solid material or 2.7.2.3.3.8 for encapsulated material.

2.7.2.3.3.5 The relevant test methods are:

(a) Impact test: The specimen shall drop onto the target from a height of 9 m. The target shall be as defined in 6.4.14;

(b) Percussion test: The specimen shall be placed on a sheet of lead which is supported by a smooth solid surface and struck by the flat face of a mild steel bar so as to cause an impact equivalent to that resulting from a free drop of 1.4 kg from a height of 1 m. The lower part of the bar shall be 25 mm in diameter with the edges rounded off to a radius of (3.0 ± 0.3) mm. The lead, of hardness number 3.5 to 4.5 on the Vickers scale and not more than 25 mm thick, shall cover an area greater than that covered by the specimen. A fresh surface of lead shall be used for each impact. The bar shall strike the specimen so as to cause maximum damage;

(c) Bending test: The test shall apply only to long, slender sources with both a minimum length of 10 cm and a length to minimum width ratio of not less than 10. The specimen shall be rigidly clamped in a horizontal position so that one half of its length protrudes from the face of the clamp. The orientation of the specimen shall be such that the specimen will suffer maximum damage when its free end is struck by the flat face of a steel bar. The bar shall strike the specimen so as to cause an impact equivalent to that resulting from a free vertical drop of 1.4 kg from a height of 1 m. The lower part of the bar shall be 25 mm in diameter with the edges rounded off to a radius of (3.0 ± 0.3) mm;

(d) Heat test: The specimen shall be heated in air to a temperature of 800 °C and held at that temperature for a period of 10 minutes and shall then be allowed to cool.

2.7.2.3.3.6 Specimens that comprise or simulate radioactive material enclosed in a sealed capsule may be excepted from:

(a) The tests prescribed in 2.7.2.3.3.5 (a) and (b) provided that the specimens are alternatively subjected to the impact test prescribed in ISO 2919:2012: "Radiation Protection - Sealed Radioactive Sources - General requirements and classification":

(i) The Class 4 impact test if the mass of the special form radioactive material is less than 200 g;

(ii) The Class 5 impact test if the mass of the special form radioactive material is equal to or more than 200 g but is less than 500 g;

(b) The test prescribed in 2.7.2.3.3.5 (d) provided they are alternatively subjected to the Class 6 temperature test specified in ISO 2919:2012 "Radiation protection – Sealed radioactive sources – General requirements and classification".

2.7.2.3.3.7   For specimens which comprise or simulate indispersible solid material, a leaching assessment shall be performed as follows:

- (a) The specimen shall be immersed for 7 days in water at ambient temperature. The volume of water to be used in the test shall be sufficient to ensure that at the end of the 7 day test period the free volume of the unabsorbed and unreacted water remaining shall be at least 10 % of the volume of the solid test sample itself. The water shall have an initial pH of 6-8 and a maximum conductivity of 1 mS/m at 20 °C;

- (b) The water and the specimen shall then be heated to a temperature of (50 ± 5) °C and maintained at this temperature for 4 hours;

- (c) The activity of the water shall then be determined;

- (d) The specimen shall then be kept for at least 7 days in still air at not less than 30 °C and relative humidity not less than 90 %;

- (e) The specimen shall then be immersed in water of the same specification as in (a) above and the water and the specimen heated to (50 ± 5) °C and maintained at this temperature for 4 hours;

- (f) The activity of the water shall then be determined.

2.7.2.3.3.8   For specimens which comprise or simulate radioactive material enclosed in a sealed capsule, either a leaching assessment or a volumetric leakage assessment shall be performed as follows:

- (a) The leaching assessment shall consist of the following steps:

    - (i) the specimen shall be immersed in water at ambient temperature. The water shall have an initial pH of 6-8 with a maximum conductivity of 1 mS/m at 20 °C;

    - (ii) the water and specimen shall then be heated to a temperature of (50 ± 5) °C and maintained at this temperature for 4 hours;

    - (iii) the activity of the water shall then be determined;

    - (iv) the specimen shall then be kept for at least 7 days in still air at not less than 30 °C and relative humidity of not less than 90 %;

    - (v) the process in (i), (ii) and (iii) shall be repeated;

- (b) The alternative volumetric leakage assessment shall comprise any of the tests prescribed in ISO 9978:1992 "Radiation Protection – Sealed radioactive sources – Leakage test methods", provided that they are acceptable to the competent authority.

2.7.2.3.4   *Low dispersible radioactive material*

2.7.2.3.4.1   The design for low dispersible radioactive material shall require multilateral approval. Low dispersible radioactive material shall be such that the total amount of this radioactive material in a package, taking into account the provisions of 6.4.8.14, shall meet the following requirements:

- (a) The dose rate at 3 m from the unshielded radioactive material does not exceed 10 mSv/h;

- (b) If subjected to the tests specified in 6.4.20.3 and 6.4.20.4, the airborne release in gaseous and particulate forms of up to 100 μm aerodynamic equivalent diameter would not exceed 100 A_2. A separate specimen may be used for each test; and

(c) If subjected to the test specified in 2.7.2.3.4.3 the activity in the water would not exceed 100 A_2. In the application of this test, the damaging effects of the tests specified in (b) above shall be taken into account.

2.7.2.3.4.2 Low dispersible material shall be tested as follows:

A specimen that comprises or simulates low dispersible radioactive material shall be subjected to the enhanced thermal test specified in 6.4.20.3 and the impact test specified in 6.4.20.4. A different specimen may be used for each of the tests. Following each test, the specimen shall be subjected to the leach test specified in 2.7.2.3.1.4. After each test it shall be determined if the applicable requirements of 2.7.2.3.4.1 have been met.

2.7.2.3.4.3 A solid material sample representing the entire contents of the package shall be immersed for 7 days in water at ambient temperature. The volume of water to be used in the test shall be sufficient to ensure that at the end of the 7-day test period the free volume of the unabsorbed and unreacted water remaining shall be at least 10 % of the volume of the solid test sample itself. The water shall have an initial pH of 6-8 and a maximum conductivity of 1 mS/m at 20 °C. The total activity of the free volume of water shall be measured following the 7-day immersion of the test sample.

2.7.2.3.4.4 Demonstration of compliance with the performance standards in 2.7.2.3.4.1, 2.7.2.3.4.2 and 2.7.2.3.4.3 shall be in accordance with 6.4.12.1 and 6.4.12.2.

2.7.2.3.5 *Fissile material*

Fissile material and packages containing fissile material shall be classified under the relevant entry as "FISSILE" in accordance with table 2.7.2.1.1 unless excepted by one of the provisions of sub-paragraphs (a) to (f) below and transported subject to the requirements of 7.1.8.4.3. All provisions apply only to material in packages that meets the requirements of 6.4.7.2 unless unpackaged material is specifically allowed in the provision.

(a) Uranium enriched in uranium-235 to a maximum of 1 % by mass, and with a total plutonium and uranium-233 content not exceeding 1 % of the mass of uranium-235, provided that the fissile nuclides are distributed essentially homogeneously throughout the material. In addition, if uranium-235 is present in metallic, oxide or carbide forms, it shall not form a lattice arrangement;

(b) Liquid solutions of uranyl nitrate enriched in uranium-235 to a maximum of 2 % by mass, with a total plutonium and uranium-233 content not exceeding 0.002 % of the mass of uranium, and with a minimum nitrogen to uranium atomic ratio (N/U) of 2;

(c) Uranium with a maximum uranium enrichment of 5 % by mass uranium-235 provided:

(i) there is no more than 3.5 g of uranium-235 per package;

(ii) the total plutonium and uranium-233 content does not exceed 1 % of the mass of uranium-235 per package;

(iii) Transport of the package is subject to the consignment limit provided in 7.1.8.4.3 (c);

(d) Fissile nuclides with a total mass not greater than 2.0 g per package provided the package is transported subject to the consignment limit provided in 7.1.8.4.3 (d);

(e) Fissile nuclides with a total mass not greater than 45 g either packaged or unpackaged subject to the requirements of 7.1.8.4.3 (e);

(f) A fissile material that meets the requirements of 7.1.8.4.3 (b), 2.7.2.3.6 and 5.1.5.2.1.

2.7.2.3.6　　　Fissile material excepted from classification as "FISSILE" under 2.7.2.3.5 (f) shall be subcritical without the need for accumulation control under the following conditions:

(a)　　The conditions of 6.4.11.1 (a);

(b)　　The conditions consistent with the assessment provisions stated in 6.4.11.12 (b) and 6.4.11.13 (b) for packages;

(c)　　The conditions specified in 6.4.11.11 (a), if transported by air.

2.7.2.4　　*Classification of packages or unpacked material*

The quantity of radioactive material in a package shall not exceed the relevant limits for the package type as specified below.

2.7.2.4.1　　*Classification as excepted package*

2.7.2.4.1.1　　A package may be classified as an excepted package if it meets one of the following conditions:

(a)　　It is an empty package having contained radioactive material;

(b)　　It contains instruments or articles not exceeding the activity limits specified in columns (2) and (3) of table 2.7.2.4.1.2;

(c)　　It contains articles manufactured of natural uranium, depleted uranium or natural thorium;

(d)　　It contains radioactive material not exceeding the activity limits specified in column (4) of table 2.7.2.4.1.2; or

(e)　　It contains less than 0.1 kg of uranium hexafluoride not exceeding the activity limits specified in column (4) of table 2.7.2.4.1.2.

2.7.2.4.1.2　　A package containing radioactive material may be classified as an excepted package provided that the dose rate at any point on its external surface does not exceed 5 µSv/h.

Table 2.7.2.4.1.2: Activity limits for excepted packages

Physical state of contents	Instruments or article		Materials
	Item limits [a]	Package limits [a]	Package limits [a]
(1)	(2)	(3)	(4)
Solids			
special form	$10^{-2}\ A_1$	A_1	$10^{-3}\ A_1$
other form	$10^{-2}\ A_2$	A_2	$10^{-3}\ A_2$
Liquids	$10^{-3}\ A_2$	$10^{-1}\ A_2$	$10^{-4}\ A_2$
Gases			
tritium	$2 \times 10^{-2}\ A_2$	$2 \times 10^{-1}\ A_2$	$2 \times 10^{-2}\ A_2$
special form	$10^{-3}\ A_1$	$10^{-2}\ A_1$	$10^{-3}\ A_1$
other forms	$10^{-3}\ A_2$	$10^{-2}\ A_2$	$10^{-3}\ A_2$

[a]　　*For mixtures of radionuclides, see 2.7.2.2.4 to 2.7.2.2.6.*

2.7.2.4.1.3　　Radioactive material which is enclosed in or is included as a component part of an instrument or other manufactured article may be classified under UN 2911 RADIOACTIVE MATERIAL, EXCEPTED PACKAGE - INSTRUMENTS or ARTICLES provided that:

(a) The dose rate at 10 cm from any point on the external surface of any unpackaged instrument or article is not greater than 0.1 mSv/h; and

(b) Each instrument or manufactured article bears the mark "RADIOACTIVE" on its external surface except for the following:

  (i) radioluminescent time-pieces or devices;

  (ii) consumer products that either have received regulatory approval in accordance with 1.5.1.4 (e) or do not individually exceed the activity limit for an exempt consignment in table 2.7.2.2.1 (fifth column), provided such products are transported in a package that bears the mark "RADIOACTIVE" on its internal surface in such a manner that a warning of the presence of radioactive material is visible on opening the package; and

  (iii) Other instruments or articles too small to bear the mark "RADIOACTIVE", provided that they are transported in a package that bears the mark "RADIOACTIVE" on its internal surface in such a manner that a warning of the presence of radioactive material is visible on opening the package;

(c) The active material is completely enclosed by non-active components (a device performing the sole function of containing radioactive material shall not be considered to be an instrument or manufactured article);

(d) The limits specified in columns 2 and 3 of table 2.7.2.4.1.2 are met for each individual item and each package, respectively;

(e) Reserved;

(f) If the package contains fissile material, one of the provisions of 2.7.2.3.5 (a) to (f) applies.

2.7.2.4.1.4 Radioactive material in forms other than as specified in 2.7.2.4.1.3 and with an activity not exceeding the limits specified in column 4 of table 2.7.2.4.1.2, may be classified under UN 2910 RADIOACTIVE MATERIAL, EXCEPTED PACKAGE - LIMITED QUANTITY OF MATERIAL provided that:

(a) The package retains its radioactive contents under routine conditions of transport;

(b) The package bears the mark "RADIOACTIVE" on either:

  (i) An internal surface in such a manner that a warning of the presence of radioactive material is visible on opening the package; or

  (ii) The outside of the package, where it is impractical to mark an internal surface; and

(c) If the package contains fissile material, one of the provisions of 2.7.2.3.5 (a) to (f) applies.

2.7.2.4.1.5 Uranium hexafluoride not exceeding the limits specified in Column 4 of table 2.7.2.4.1.2 may be classified under UN 3507 URANIUM HEXAFLUORIDE, RADIOACTIVE MATERIAL, EXCEPTED PACKAGE, less than 0.1 kg per package, non-fissile or fissile-excepted provided that:

(a) The mass of uranium hexafluoride in the package is less than 0.1 kg;

(b) The conditions of 2.7.2.4.5.1 and 2.7.2.4.1.4 (a) and (b) are met.

2.7.2.4.1.6　　Articles manufactured of natural uranium, depleted uranium or natural thorium and articles in which the sole radioactive material is unirradiated natural uranium, unirradiated depleted uranium or unirradiated natural thorium may be classified under UN 2909 RADIOACTIVE MATERIAL, EXCEPTED PACKAGE - ARTICLES MANUFACTURED FROM NATURAL URANIUM or DEPLETED URANIUM or NATURAL THORIUM, provided that the outer surface of the uranium or thorium is enclosed in an inactive sheath made of metal or some other substantial material.

2.7.2.4.1.7　　An empty packaging which had previously contained radioactive material may be classified under UN 2908 RADIOACTIVE MATERIAL, EXCEPTED PACKAGE - EMPTY PACKAGING, provided that:

(a) It is in a well-maintained condition and securely closed;

(b) The outer surface of any uranium or thorium in its structure is covered with an inactive sheath made of metal or some other substantial material;

(c) The level of internal non-fixed contamination, when averaged over any 300 cm^2, does not exceed:

(i) 400 Bq/cm^2 for beta and gamma emitters and low toxicity alpha emitters; and

(ii) 40 Bq/cm^2 for all other alpha emitters;

(d) Any labels which may have been displayed on it in conformity with 5.2.2.1.12.1 are no longer visible; and

(e) If the packaging has contained fissile material, one of the provisions of 2.7.2.3.5 (a) to (f) or one of the provisions for exclusion in 2.7.1.3 applies.

2.7.2.4.2　　*Classification as Low specific activity (LSA) material*

Radioactive material may only be classified as LSA material if the definition of LSA in 2.7.1.3 and the conditions of 2.7.2.3.1, 4.1.9.2 and 7.1.8.2 are met.

2.7.2.4.3　　*Classification as Surface contaminated object (SCO)*

Radioactive material may be classified as SCO if the definition of SCO in 2.7.1.3 and the conditions of 2.7.2.3.2, 4.1.9.2 and 7.1.8.2 are met.

2.7.2.4.4　　*Classification as Type A package*

Packages containing radioactive material may be classified as Type A packages provided that the following conditions are met:

Type A packages shall not contain activities greater than either of the following:

(a) For special form radioactive material - A_1;

(b) For all other radioactive material - A_2.

For mixtures of radionuclides whose identities and respective activities are known, the following condition shall apply to the radioactive contents of a Type A package:

$$\sum_i \frac{B(i)}{A_1(i)} + \sum_j \frac{C(j)}{A_2(j)} \leq 1$$

where　　$B(i)$　　is the activity of radionuclide i as special form radioactive material;

$A_1(i)$　　is the A_1 value for radionuclide i;

        C (j)   is the activity of radionuclide j as other than special form radioactive material;

        A_2 (j)   is the A_2 value for radionuclide j.

2.7.2.4.5 *Classification of Uranium hexafluoride*

2.7.2.4.5.1   Uranium hexafluoride shall only be assigned to:

(a) UN 2977, RADIOACTIVE MATERIAL, URANIUM HEXAFLUORIDE, FISSILE;

(b) UN 2978, RADIOACTIVE MATERIAL, URANIUM HEXAFLUORIDE, non-fissile or fissile-excepted; or

(c) UN 3507, URANIUM HEXAFLUORIDE, RADIOACTIVE MATERIAL, EXCEPTED PACKAGE less than 0.1 kg per package, non-fissile or fissile-excepted.

2.7.2.4.5.2   The contents of a package containing uranium hexafluoride shall comply with the following requirements:

(a) For UN Nos. 2977 and 2978, the mass of uranium hexafluoride shall not be different from that allowed for the package design, and for UN 3507, the mass of uranium hexafluoride shall be less than 0.1 kg;

(b) The mass of uranium hexafluoride shall not be greater than a value that would lead to an ullage smaller than 5 % at the maximum temperature of the package as specified for the plant systems where the package shall be used; and

(c) The uranium hexafluoride shall be in solid form and the internal pressure shall not be above atmospheric pressure when presented for transport.

2.7.2.4.6 *Classification as Type B(U), Type B(M) or Type C packages*

2.7.2.4.6.1   Packages not otherwise classified in 2.7.2.4 (2.7.2.4.1 to 2.7.2.4.5) shall be classified in accordance with the competent authority certificate of approval for the package issued by the country of origin of design.

2.7.2.4.6.2   The contents of a Type B(U), Type B(M) or Type C package shall be as specified in the certificate of approval.

2.7.2.4.6.3 and 2.7.2.4.6.4   *Deleted.*

2.7.2.5 **Special arrangements**

Radioactive material shall be classified as transported under special arrangement when it is intended to be transported in accordance with 1.5.4.

CHAPTER 2.8

CLASS 8 - CORROSIVE SUBSTANCES

2.8.1 Definition and general provisions

2.8.1.1 *Corrosive substances* are substances which, by chemical action, will cause irreversible damage to the skin, or, in the case of leakage, will materially damage, or even destroy, other goods or the means of transport.

2.8.1.2 For substances and mixtures that are corrosive to skin, general classification provisions are provided in section 2.8.2. Skin corrosion refers to the production of irreversible damage to the skin, namely, visible necrosis through the epidermis and into the dermis occurring after exposure to a substance or mixture.

2.8.1.3 Liquids and solids which may become liquid during transport, which are judged not to be skin corrosive shall still be considered for their potential to cause corrosion to certain metal surfaces in accordance with the criteria in 2.8.3.3 (c) (ii).

2.8.2 General classification provisions

2.8.2.1 Substances and mixtures of Class 8 are divided among the three packing groups according to their degree of danger in transport:

    (a) Packing group I: very dangerous substances and mixtures;

    (b) Packing group II: substances and mixtures presenting medium danger;

    (c) Packing group III: substances and mixtures that present minor danger.

2.8.2.2 Allocation of substances listed in the Dangerous Goods List in chapter 3.2 to the packing groups in Class 8 has been made on the basis of experience taking into account such additional factors as inhalation risk (see 2.8.2.4) and reactivity with water (including the formation of dangerous decomposition products).

2.8.2.3 New substances and mixtures can be assigned to packing groups on the basis of the length of time of contact necessary to produce irreversible damage of intact skin tissue in accordance with the criteria in 2.8.3. Alternatively, for mixtures, the criteria in 2.8.4 can be used.

2.8.2.4 A substance or mixture meeting the criteria of Class 8 having an inhalation toxicity of dusts and mists (LC_{50}) in the range of packing group I, but toxicity through oral ingestion or dermal contact only in the range of packing group III or less, shall be allocated to Class 8 (see note under 2.6.2.2.4.1).

2.8.3 Packing group assignment for substances and mixtures

2.8.3.1 Existing human and animal data including information from single or repeated exposure shall be the first line of evaluation, as they give information directly relevant to effects on the skin.

2.8.3.2 In assigning the packing group in accordance with 2.8.2.3, account shall be taken of human experience in instances of accidental exposure. In the absence of human experience, classification shall be based on data obtained from experiments in accordance with OECD Test Guidelines Nos. 404[1], 435[2], 431[3] or

---

[1] *OECD Guideline for the testing of chemicals No. 404 "Acute Dermal Irritation/Corrosion" 2015.*
[2] *OECD Guideline for the testing of chemicals No. 435 "In Vitro Membrane Barrier Test Method for Skin Corrosion" 2015.*
[3] *OECD Guideline for the testing of chemicals No. 431 "In vitro skin corrosion: reconstructed human epidermis (RHE) test method" 2016.*

430[4]. A substance or mixture which is determined not to be corrosive in accordance with one of these or non-classified in accordance with OECD Test Guideline No. 439[5] may be considered not to be corrosive to skin for the purposes of these Regulations without further testing. If the test results indicate that the substance or mixture is corrosive and not assigned to packing group I, but the test method does not allow discrimination between packing groups II and III, it shall be considered to be packing group II. If the test results indicate that the substance or mixture is corrosive, but the test method does not allow discrimination between packing groups, it shall be assigned to packing group I if no other test results indicate a different packing group.

2.8.3.3   Packing groups are assigned to corrosive substances in accordance with the following criteria (see table 2.8.3.4):

(a) Packing group I is assigned to substances that cause irreversible damage of intact skin tissue within an observation period up to 60 minutes starting after the exposure time of three minutes or less;

(b) Packing group II is assigned to substances that cause irreversible damage of intact skin tissue within an observation period up to 14 days starting after the exposure time of more than three minutes but not more than 60 minutes;

(c) Packing group III is assigned to substances that:

(i) Cause irreversible damage of intact skin tissue within an observation period up to 14 days starting after the exposure time of more than 60 minutes but not more than 4 hours; or

(ii) Are judged not to cause irreversible damage of intact skin tissue but which exhibit a corrosion rate on either steel or aluminium surfaces exceeding 6.25 mm a year at a test temperature of 55 °C when tested on both materials. For the purposes of testing steel, type S235JR+CR (1.0037 resp. St 37-2), S275J2G3+CR (1.0144 resp. St 44-3), ISO 3574, Unified Numbering System (UNS) G10200 or SAE 1020, and for testing aluminium, non-clad, types 7075–T6 or AZ5GU-T6 shall be used. An acceptable test is prescribed in the *Manual of Tests and Criteria*, part III, section 37.

NOTE: *Where an initial test on either steel or aluminium indicates the substance being tested is corrosive the follow up test on the other metal is not required.*

Table 2.8.3.4: Table summarizing the criteria in 2.8.3.3

Packing Group	Exposure Time	Observation Period	Effect
I	≤ 3 min	≤ 60 min	Irreversible damage of intact skin
II	> 3 min, ≤ 1 h	≤ 14 d	Irreversible damage of intact skin
III	> 1 h, ≤ 4 h	≤ 14 d	Irreversible damage of intact skin
III	-	-	Corrosion rate on either steel or aluminium surfaces exceeding 6.25 mm a year at a test temperature of 55 °C when tested on both materials

---

[4] *OECD Guideline for the testing of chemicals No. 430 "In Vitro Skin Corrosion: Transcutaneous Electrical Resistance Test Method (TER)" 2015.*
[5] *OECD Guideline for the testing of chemicals No. 439 "In Vitro Skin Irritation: Reconstructed Human Epidermis Test Method" 2015.*

2.8.4 Alternative packing group assignment methods for mixtures: Step-wise approach

2.8.4.1 *General provisions*

2.8.4.1.1 For mixtures it is necessary to obtain or derive information that allows the criteria to be applied to the mixture for the purpose of classification and assignment of packing groups. The approach to classification and assignment of packing groups is tiered, and is dependent upon the amount of information available for the mixture itself, for similar mixtures and/or for its ingredients. The flow chart of figure 2.8.4.1 below outlines the process to be followed:

Figure 2.8.4.1: Step-wise approach to classify and assign packing group of corrosive mixtures

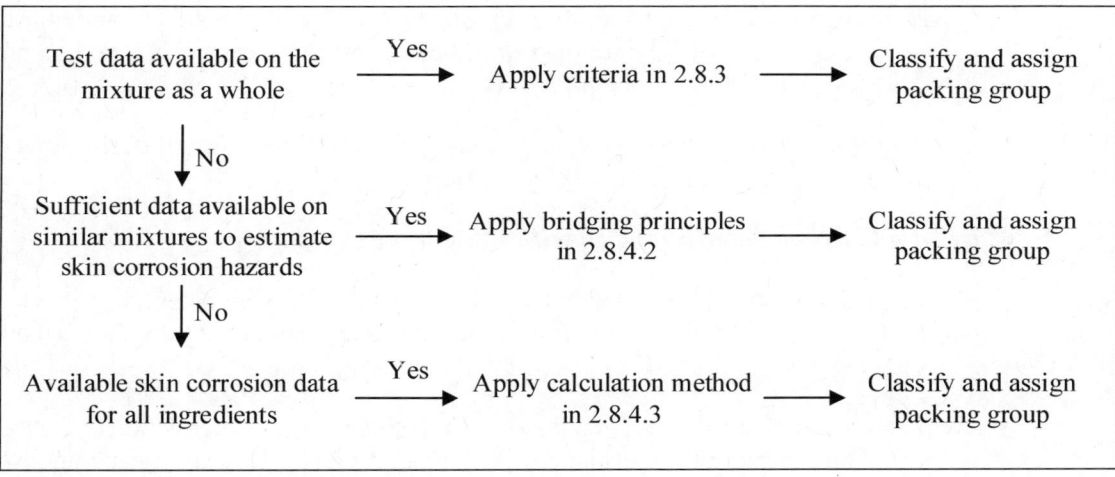

2.8.4.2 *Bridging principles*

2.8.4.2.1 Where a mixture has not been tested to determine its skin corrosion potential, but there are sufficient data on both the individual ingredients and similar tested mixtures to adequately classify and assign a packing group for the mixture, these data will be used in accordance with the following bridging principles. This ensures that the classification process uses the available data to the greatest extent possible in characterizing the hazards of the mixture.

(a) **Dilution:** If a tested mixture is diluted with a diluent which does not meet the criteria for Class 8 and does not affect the packing group of other ingredients, then the new diluted mixture may be assigned to the same packing group as the original tested mixture.

NOTE: in certain cases, diluting a mixture or substance may lead to an increase in the corrosive properties. If this is the case, this bridging principle cannot be used.

(b) **Batching:** The skin corrosion potential of a tested production batch of a mixture can be assumed to be substantially equivalent to that of another untested production batch of the same commercial product when produced by or under the control of the same manufacturer, unless there is reason to believe there is significant variation such that the skin corrosion potential of the untested batch has changed. If the latter occurs, a new classification is necessary.

(c) **Concentration of mixtures of packing group I:** If a tested mixture meeting the criteria for inclusion in packing group I is concentrated, the more concentrated untested mixture may be assigned to packing group I without additional testing.

(d) **Interpolation within one packing group:** For three mixtures (A, B and C) with identical ingredients, where mixtures A and B have been tested and are in the same skin corrosion packing group, and where untested mixture C has the same Class 8 ingredients as mixtures A and B but has concentrations of Class 8 ingredients intermediate to the concentrations in mixtures A and B, then mixture C is assumed to be in the same skin corrosion packing group as A and B.

(e) **Substantially similar mixtures:** Given the following:

(i) Two mixtures: (A+B) and (C+B);

(ii) The concentration of ingredient B is the same in both mixtures;

(iii) The concentration of ingredient A in mixture (A+B) equals the concentration of ingredient C in mixture (C+B);

(iv) Data on skin corrosion for ingredients A and C are available and substantially equivalent, i.e. they are the same skin corrosion packing group and do not affect the skin corrosion potential of B.

If mixture (A+B) or (C+B) is already classified based on test data, then the other mixture may be assigned to the same packing group.

2.8.4.3 *Calculation method based on the classification of the substances*

2.8.4.3.1   Where a mixture has not been tested to determine its skin corrosion potential, nor is sufficient data available on similar mixtures, the corrosive properties of the substances in the mixture shall be considered to classify and assign a packing group.

Applying the calculation method is only allowed if there are no synergistic effects that make the mixture more corrosive than the sum of its substances. This restriction applies only if packing group II or III would be assigned to the mixture.

2.8.4.3.2   When using the calculation method, all Class 8 ingredients present at a concentration of $\geq 1\%$ shall be taken into account, or $< 1\%$ if these ingredients are still relevant for classifying the mixture to be corrosive to skin.

2.8.4.3.3   To determine whether a mixture containing corrosive substances shall be considered a corrosive mixture and to assign a packing group, the calculation method in the flow chart in figure 2.8.4.3 shall be applied. For this calculation method, generic concentration limits apply where 1 % is used in the first step for the assessment of the packing group I substances, and where 5 % is used for the other steps respectively.

2.8.4.3.4   When a specific concentration limit (SCL) is assigned to a substance following its entry in the Dangerous Goods List or in a Special Provision, this limit shall be used instead of the generic concentration limits (GCL).

2.8.4.3.5   For this purpose, the summation formula for each step of the calculation method shall be adapted. This means that, where applicable, the generic concentration limit shall be substituted by the specific concentration limit assigned to the substance(s) (SCLi), and the adapted formula is a weighted average of the different concentration limits assigned to the different substances in the mixture:

$$\frac{PGx_1}{GCL} + \frac{PGx_2}{SCL_2} + \cdots + \frac{PGx_i}{SCL_i} \geq 1$$

Where:

PGx_i = concentration of substance 1, 2, ..., i in the mixture, assigned to packing group x (I, II or III)

GCL = generic concentration limit

SCL_i = specific concentration limit assigned to substance i

The criterion for a packing group is fulfilled when the result of the calculation is ≥ 1. The generic concentration limits to be used for the evaluation in each step of the calculation method are those found in figure 2.8.4.3.

Examples for the application of the above formula can be found in the note below.

NOTE: *Examples for the application of the above formula*

Example 1: A mixture contains one corrosive substance in a concentration of 5 % assigned to packing group I without a specific concentration limit:

Calculation for packing group I:

$$\frac{5}{5\ (GCL)} = 1 \rightarrow \text{assign to class 8, packing group I.}$$

Example 2: A mixture contains three substances corrosive to skin; two of them (A and B) have specific concentration limits; for the third one (C) the generic concentration limits applies. The rest of the mixture needs not to be taken into consideration:

Substance X in the mixture and its packing group assignment within Class 8	Concentration (conc) in the mixture in %	Specific concentration limit (SCL) for packing group I	Specific concentration limit (SCL) for packing group II	Specific concentration limit (SCL) for packing group III
A, assigned to packing group I	3	30 %	none	none
B, assigned to packing group I	2	20 %	10 %	none
C, assigned to packing group III	10	none	none	none

Calculation for packing group I:

$$\frac{3\ (conc\ A)}{30\ (SCL\ PGI)} + \frac{2\ (conc\ B)}{20\ (SCL\ PGI)} = 0.2 < 1$$

The criterion for packing group I is not fulfilled.

Calculation for packing group II:

$$\frac{3\ (conc\ A)}{5\ (GCL\ PGII)} + \frac{2\ (conc\ B)}{10\ (SCL\ PGII)} = 0.8 < 1$$

The criterion for packing group II is not fulfilled.

Calculation for packing group III:

$$\frac{3\ (conc\ A)}{5\ (GCL\ PGIII)} + \frac{2\ (conc\ B)}{5\ (GCL\ PGIII)} + \frac{10\ (conc\ C)}{5\ (GCL\ PGIII)} = 3 \geq 1$$

The criterion for packing group III is fulfilled, the mixture shall be assigned to class 8, packing group III.

Figure 2.8.4.3: Calculation method

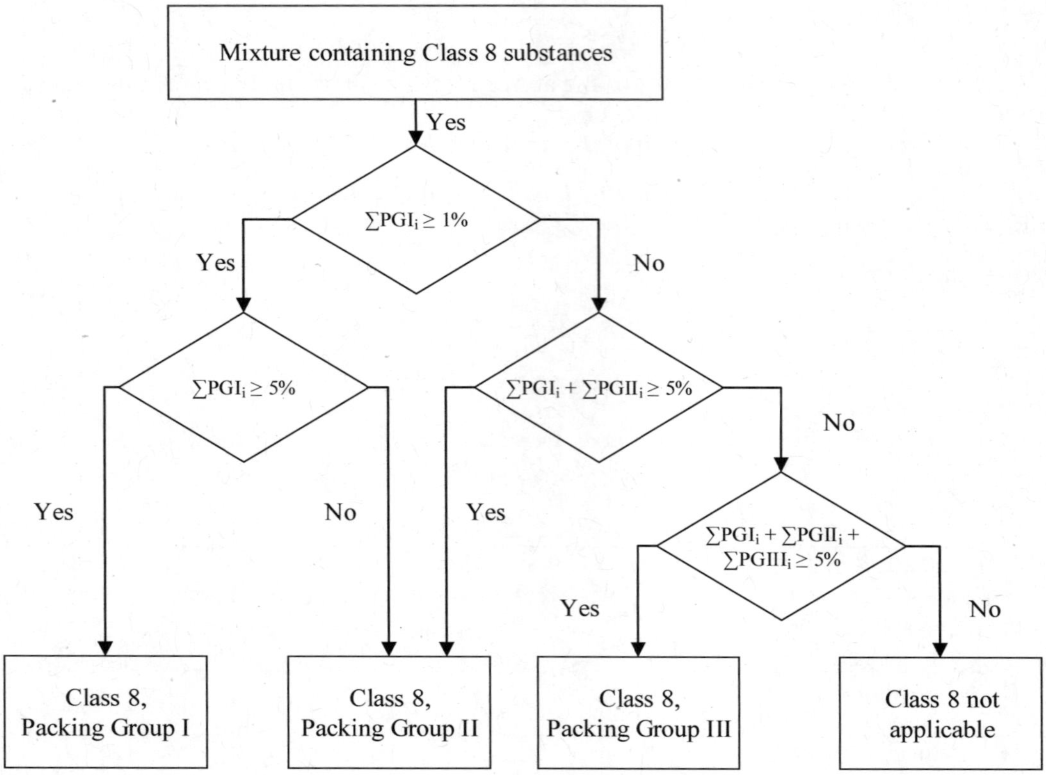

```
                    Mixture containing Class 8 substances
                                    │
                                   Yes
                                    ▼
                            ┌───────────────┐
                            │  ∑PGIᵢ ≥ 1%   │
                            └───────────────┘
                   Yes                          No
                    │                            │
                    ▼                            ▼
           ┌───────────────┐          ┌───────────────────────┐
           │  ∑PGIᵢ ≥ 5%   │          │ ∑PGIᵢ + ∑PGIIᵢ ≥ 5%   │
           └───────────────┘          └───────────────────────┘
          Yes          No              Yes              No
           │            │                │                │
           │            │                │                ▼
           │            │                │    ┌───────────────────────┐
           │            │                │    │ ∑PGIᵢ + ∑PGIIᵢ +     │
           │            │                │    │ ∑PGIIIᵢ ≥ 5%          │
           │            │                │    └───────────────────────┘
           │            │                │       Yes           No
           ▼            ▼                ▼         ▼            ▼
      ┌─────────┐  ┌─────────┐    ┌─────────┐  ┌─────────┐
      │ Class 8,│  │ Class 8,│    │ Class 8,│  │ Class 8 │
      │ Packing │  │ Packing │    │ Packing │  │   not   │
      │ Group I │  │Group II │    │Group III│  │applicable│
      └─────────┘  └─────────┘    └─────────┘  └─────────┘
```

2.8.5 Substances not accepted for transport

Chemically unstable substances of Class 8 shall not be accepted for transport unless the necessary precautions have been taken to prevent the possibility of a dangerous decomposition or polymerization under normal conditions of transport. For the precautions necessary to prevent polymerization, see special provision 386 of chapter 3.3. To this end particular care shall be taken to ensure that receptacles and tanks do not contain any substances liable to promote these reactions.

CHAPTER 2.9

CLASS 9 – MISCELLANEOUS DANGEROUS SUBSTANCES AND ARTICLES, INCLUDING ENVIRONMENTALLY HAZARDOUS SUBSTANCES

2.9.1 Definitions

2.9.1.1 *Class 9 substances and articles (miscellaneous dangerous substances and articles)* are substances and articles which, during transport present a danger not covered by other classes.

2.9.1.2 *Deleted.*

2.9.2 Assignment to Class 9

The substances and articles of Class 9 are subdivided as follows:

Substances which, on inhalation as fine dust, may endanger health

- 2212 ASBESTOS, AMPHIBOLE (amosite, tremolite, actinolite, anthophyllite, crocidolite)
- 2590 ASBESTOS, CHRYSOTILE

Substances evolving flammable vapour

- 2211 POLYMERIC BEADS, EXPANDABLE, evolving flammable vapour
- 3314 PLASTICS MOULDING COMPOUND in dough, sheet or extruded rope form evolving flammable vapour

Lithium batteries

- 3090 LITHIUM METAL BATTERIES (including lithium alloy batteries)
- 3091 LITHIUM METAL BATTERIES CONTAINED IN EQUIPMENT (including lithium alloy batteries) or
- 3091 LITHIUM METAL BATTERIES PACKED WITH EQUIPMENT (including lithium alloy batteries)
- 3480 LITHIUM ION BATTERIES (including lithium ion polymer batteries)
- 3481 LITHIUM ION BATTERIES CONTAINED IN EQUIPMENT (including lithium ion polymer batteries) or
- 3481 LITHIUM ION BATTERIES PACKED WITH EQUIPMENT (including lithium ion polymer batteries)
- 3536 LITHIUM BATTERIES INSTALLED IN CARGO TRANSPORT UNIT

NOTE: *See 2.9.4.*

Sodium ion batteries

- 3551 SODIUM ION BATTERIES with organic electrolyte
- 3552 SODIUM ION BATTERIES CONTAINED IN EQUIPMENT or SODIUM ION BATTERIES PACKED WITH EQUIPMENT, with organic electrolyte

Capacitors

- 3499 CAPACITOR, ELECTRIC DOUBLE LAYER (with an energy storage capacity greater than 0.3Wh)
- 3508 CAPACITOR, ASYMMETRIC (with an energy storage capacity greater than 0.3Wh))

Life-saving appliances

- 2990 LIFE-SAVING APPLIANCES, SELF-INFLATING
- 3072 LIFE-SAVING APPLIANCES NOT SELF-INFLATING containing dangerous goods as equipment
- 3268 SAFETY DEVICES, electrically initiated
- 3559 FIRE SUPPRESSANT DISPERSING DEVICES

Substances and articles which, in the event of fire, may form dioxins

This group of substances includes:

- 2315 POLYCHLORINATED BIPHENYLS, LIQUID
- 3432 POLYCHLORINATED BIPHENYLS, SOLID
- 3151 POLYHALOGENATED BIPHENYLS, LIQUID or
- 3151 HALOGENATED MONOMETHYLDIPHENYLMETHANES, LIQUID or
- 3151 POLYHALOGENATED TERPHENYLS, LIQUID
- 3152 POLYHALOGENATED BIPHENYLS, SOLID or
- 3152 HALOGENATED MONOMETHYLDIPHENYLMETHANES, SOLID or
- 3152 POLYHALOGENATED TERPHENYLS, SOLID

Examples of articles are transformers, condensers and apparatus containing those substances.

Substances transported or offered for transport at elevated temperatures (liquid)

- 3257 ELEVATED TEMPERATURE LIQUID, N.O.S., at or above 100 °C and below its flash-point (including molten metal, molten salts, etc.)

Substances transported or offered for transport at elevated temperatures (solid)

- 3258 ELEVATED TEMPERATURE SOLID, N.O.S., at or above 240 °C

Environmentally hazardous substances (solid)

- 3077 ENVIRONMENTALLY HAZARDOUS SUBSTANCE, SOLID, N.O.S.

Environmentally hazardous substances (liquid)

- 3082 ENVIRONMENTALLY HAZARDOUS SUBSTANCE, LIQUID, N.O.S.

These designations are used for substances and mixtures which are dangerous to the aquatic environment that do not meet the classification criteria of any other class or another substance within Class 9. These designations may also be used for wastes not otherwise subject to these Regulations but which are covered under the *Basel Convention on the Control of Transboundary Movements of Hazardous Wastes and their Disposal* and for substances designated to be environmentally hazardous substances by the competent authority of the country of origin, transit or destination which do not meet the criteria for an environmentally hazardous substance according to these Regulations or for any other hazard Class. The criteria for substances which are hazardous to the aquatic environment are given in section 2.9.3.

Genetically modified micro-organisms (GMMOs) and genetically modified organisms (GMOs)

- 3245 GENETICALLY MODIFIED MICRO-ORGANISMS or
- 3245 GENETICALLY MODIFIED ORGANISMS

GMMOs and GMOs which do not meet the definition of toxic substances (see 2.6.2) or infectious substances (see 2.6.3) shall be assigned to UN 3245.

GMMOs or GMOs are not subject to these Regulations when authorized for use by the competent authorities of the countries of origin, transit and destination.

Pharmaceutical products (such as vaccines) that are packed in a form ready to be administered, including those in clinical trials, and that contain GMMOs or GMOs are not subject to these Regulations.

Genetically modified live animals shall be transported under terms and conditions of the competent authorities of the countries of origin and destination.

Ammonium nitrate based fertilizers

    2071   AMMONIUM NITRATE BASED FERTILIZERS

Solid ammonium nitrate based fertilizers shall be classified in accordance with the procedure as set out in the *Manual of Tests and Criteria*, part III, section 39.

Other substances or articles presenting a danger during transport, but not meeting the definitions of another class

1841	ACETALDEHYDE AMMONIA
1845	CARBON DIOXIDE, SOLID (DRY ICE)
1931	ZINC DITHIONITE (ZINC HYDROSULPHITE)
1941	DIBROMODIFLUOROMETHANE
1990	BENZALDEHYDE
2216	FISH MEAL (FISH SCRAP), STABILIZED
2807	MAGNETIZED MATERIAL
2969	CASTOR BEANS or
2969	CASTOR MEAL or
2969	CASTOR POMACE or
2969	CASTOR FLAKE
3166	VEHICLE, FLAMMABLE GAS POWERED or
3166	VEHICLE, FLAMMABLE LIQUID POWERED or
3166	VEHICLE, FUEL CELL, FLAMMABLE GAS POWERED or
3166	VEHICLE, FUEL CELL, FLAMMABLE LIQUID POWERED
3171	BATTERY-POWERED VEHICLE or
3171	BATTERY-POWERED EQUIPMENT
3316	CHEMICAL KIT or
3316	FIRST AID KIT
3334	AVIATION REGULATED LIQUID, N.O.S.
3335	AVIATION REGULATED SOLID, N.O.S.
3359	FUMIGATED CARGO TRANSPORT UNIT
3363	DANGEROUS GOODS IN ARTICLES or
3363	DANGEROUS GOODS IN MACHINERY or
3363	DANGEROUS GOODS IN APPARATUS
3509	PACKAGINGS, DISCARDED, EMPTY, UNCLEANED
3530	ENGINE, INTERNAL COMBUSTION or
3530	MACHINERY, INTERNAL COMBUSTION
3548	ARTICLES CONTAINING MISCELLANEOUS DANGEROUS GOODS N.O.S.
3556	VEHICLE, LITHIUM ION BATTERY POWERED
3557	VEHICLE, LITHIUM METAL BATTERY POWERED
3558	VEHICLE, SODIUM ION BATTERY POWERED

2.9.3   Environmentally hazardous substances (aquatic environment)

2.9.3.1   *General definitions*

2.9.3.1.1   Environmentally hazardous substances include, inter alia, liquid or solid substances pollutant to the aquatic environment and solutions and mixtures of such substances (such as preparations and wastes).

For the purposes of this section,

Substance means chemical elements and their compounds in the natural state or obtained by any production process, including any additive necessary to preserve the stability of the product and any impurities deriving from the process used, but excluding any solvent which may be separated without affecting the stability of the substance or changing its composition.

2.9.3.1.2　　The aquatic environment may be considered in terms of the aquatic organisms that live in the water, and the aquatic ecosystem of which they are part[1]. The basis, therefore, of the identification of hazard is the aquatic toxicity of the substance or mixture, although this may be modified by further information on the degradation and bioaccumulation behaviour.

2.9.3.1.3　　While the following classification procedure is intended to apply to all substances and mixtures, it is recognised that in some cases, e.g. metals or poorly soluble inorganic compounds, special guidance will be necessary[2].

2.9.3.1.4　　The following definitions apply for acronyms or terms used in this section:

- BCF: Bioconcentration Factor;

- BOD: Biochemical Oxygen Demand;

- COD: Chemical Oxygen Demand;

- GLP: Good Laboratory Practices;

- EC_x: the concentration associated with x % response;

- EC_{50}: the effective concentration of substance that causes 50 % of the maximum response;

- ErC_{50}: EC_{50} in terms of reduction of growth;

- K_{ow}: octanol/water partition coefficient;

- LC_{50} (50 % lethal concentration): the concentration of a substance in water which causes the death of 50 % (one half) in a group of test animals;

- $L(E)C_{50}$: LC_{50} or EC_{50};

- NOEC (No Observed Effect Concentration): the test concentration immediately below the lowest tested concentration with statistically significant adverse effect. The NOEC has no statistically significant adverse effect compared to the control;

- OECD Test Guidelines: Test guidelines published by the Organization for Economic Cooperation and Development (OECD);

2.9.3.2　　*Definitions and data requirements*

2.9.3.2.1　　The basic elements for classification of environmentally hazardous substances (aquatic environment) are:

  (a)　　Acute aquatic toxicity;

  (b)　　Chronic aquatic toxicity;

  (c)　　Potential for or actual bioaccumulation; and

---

[1]　*This does not address aquatic pollutants for which there may be a need to consider effects beyond the aquatic environment such as the impacts on human health etc.*

[2]　*This can be found in annex 10 of the GHS.*

(d) Degradation (biotic or abiotic) for organic chemicals.

2.9.3.2.2 While data from internationally harmonised test methods are preferred, in practice, data from national methods may also be used where they are considered as equivalent. In general, it has been agreed that freshwater and marine species toxicity data can be considered as equivalent data and are preferably to be derived using OECD Test Guidelines or equivalent according to the principles of Good Laboratory Practices (GLP). Where such data are not available, classification shall be based on the best available data.

2.9.3.2.3 *Acute aquatic toxicity* means the intrinsic property of a substance to be injurious to an organism in a short-term aquatic exposure to that substance.

Acute (short-term) hazard, for classification purposes, means the hazard of a chemical caused by its acute toxicity to an organism during short-term aquatic exposure to that chemical.

Acute aquatic toxicity shall normally be determined using a fish 96 hour LC_{50} (OECD Test Guideline 203 or equivalent), a crustacea species 48 hour EC_{50} (OECD Test Guideline 202 or equivalent) and/or an algal species 72 or 96 hour EC_{50} (OECD Test Guideline 201 or equivalent). These species are considered as surrogate for all aquatic organisms and data on other species such as Lemna may also be considered if the test methodology is suitable.

2.9.3.2.4 *Chronic aquatic toxicity* means the intrinsic property of a substance to cause adverse effects to aquatic organisms during aquatic exposures which are determined in relation to the life-cycle of the organism.

Long-term hazard, for classification purposes, means the hazard of a chemical caused by its chronic toxicity following long-term exposure in the aquatic environment.

Chronic toxicity data are less available than acute data and the range of testing procedures less standardised. Data generated according to the OECD Test Guidelines 210 (Fish Early Life Stage) or 211 (Daphnia Reproduction) and 201 (Algal Growth Inhibition) may be accepted. Other validated and internationally accepted tests may also be used. The NOECs or other equivalent EC_x shall be used.

2.9.3.2.5 *Bioaccumulation* means net result of uptake, transformation and elimination of a substance in an organism due to all routes of exposure (i.e. air, water, sediment/soil and food).

The potential for bioaccumulation shall normally be determined by using the octanol/water partition coefficient, usually reported as a log K_{ow} determined according to OECD Test Guidelines 107, 117 or 123. While this represents a potential to bioaccumulate, an experimentally determined Bioconcentration Factor (BCF) provides a better measure and shall be used in preference when available. A BCF shall be determined according to OECD Test Guideline 305.

2.9.3.2.6 *Degradation* means the decomposition of organic molecules to smaller molecules and eventually to carbon dioxide, water and salts.

Environmental degradation may be biotic or abiotic (eg. hydrolysis) and the criteria used reflect this fact. Ready biodegradation is most easily defined using the biodegradability tests (A-F) of OECD Test Guideline 301. A pass level in these tests may be considered as indicative of rapid degradation in most environments. These are freshwater tests and thus the use of the results from OECD Test Guideline 306, which is more suitable for marine environments, has also been included. Where such data are not available, a BOD(5 days)/COD ratio ≥ 0.5 is considered as indicative of rapid degradation. Abiotic degradation such as hydrolysis, primary degradation, both abiotic and biotic, degradation in non-aquatic media and proven rapid degradation in the environment may all be considered in defining rapid degradability[3].

Substances are considered rapidly degradable in the environment if the following criteria are met:

---

[3] *Special guidance on data interpretation is provided in chapter 4.1 and annex 9 of the GHS.*

(a) In 28-day ready biodegradation studies, the following levels of degradation are achieved:

(i) Tests based on dissolved organic carbon: 70 %;

(ii) Tests based on oxygen depletion or carbon dioxide generation: 60 % of theoretical maxima;

These levels of biodegradation shall be achieved within 10 days of the start of degradation which point is taken as the time when 10 % of the substance has been degraded, unless the substance is identified as a complex, multi-component substance with structurally similar constituents. In this case, and where there is sufficient justification, the 10-day window condition may be waived and the pass level applied at 28 days[4];

(b) In those cases where only BOD and COD data are available, when the ratio of BOD_5/COD is ≥ 0.5; or

(c) If other convincing scientific evidence is available to demonstrate that the substance or mixture can be degraded (biotically and/or abiotically) in the aquatic environment to a level above 70 % within a 28-day period.

2.9.3.3 *Substance classification categories and criteria*

2.9.3.3.1 Substances shall be classified as "environmentally hazardous substances (aquatic environment)", if they satisfy the criteria for Acute 1, Chronic 1 or Chronic 2, according to table 2.9.1. These criteria describe in detail the classification categories. They are diagrammatically summarized in table 2.9.2.

Table 2.9.1: Categories for substances hazardous to the aquatic environment *(see note 1)*

(a) **Acute (short-term) aquatic hazard**

Category Acute 1: *(see note 2)*	
96 h LC_{50} (for fish)	≤ 1 mg/l and/or
48 h EC_{50} (for crustacea)	≤ 1 mg/l and/or
72 or 96 h ErC_{50} (for algae or other aquatic plants)	≤ 1 mg/l *(see note 3)*

(b) **Long-term aquatic hazard** *(see also figure 2.9.1)*

(i) **Non-rapidly degradable substances (see note 4) for which there are adequate chronic toxicity data available**

Category Chronic 1: (see *note 2*)	
Chronic NOEC or EC_x (for fish)	≤ 0.1 mg/l and/or
Chronic NOEC or EC_x (for crustacea)	≤ 0.1 mg/l and/or
Chronic NOEC or EC_x (for algae or other aquatic plants)	≤ 0.1 mg/l
Category Chronic 2:	
Chronic NOEC or EC_x (for fish)	≤ 1 mg/l and/or
Chronic NOEC or EC_x (for crustacea)	≤ 1 mg/l and/or
Chronic NOEC or EC_x (for algae or other aquatic plants)	≤ 1 mg/l

---

[4] *See chapter 4.1 and annex 9, paragraph A9.4.2.2.3 of the GHS.*

(ii) Rapidly degradable substances for which there are adequate chronic toxicity data available

Category Chronic 1: *(see note 2)*	
Chronic NOEC or EC_x (for fish)	≤ 0.01 mg/l and/or
Chronic NOEC or EC_x (for crustacea)	≤ 0.01 mg/l and/or
Chronic NOEC or EC_x (for algae or other aquatic plants)	≤ 0.01 mg/l
Category Chronic 2:	
Chronic NOEC or EC_x (for fish)	≤ 0.1 mg/l and/or
Chronic NOEC or EC_x (for crustacea)	≤ 0.1 mg/l and/or
Chronic NOEC or EC_x (for algae or other aquatic plants)	≤ 0.1 mg/l

(iii) Substances for which adequate chronic toxicity data are not available

Category Chronic 1: *(see note 2)*	
96 h LC_{50} (for fish)	≤ 1 mg/l and/or
48 h EC_{50} (for crustacea)	≤ 1 mg/l and/or
72 or 96 h ErC_{50} (for algae or other aquatic plants)	≤ 1 mg/l *(see note 3)*
and the substance is not rapidly degradable and/or the experimentally determined BCF is ≥ 500 (or, if absent the log $K_{ow} \geq 4$) *(see notes 4 and 5)*.	
Category Chronic 2:	
96 h LC_{50} (for fish)	>1 but ≤ 10 mg/l and/or
48 h EC_{50} (for crustacea)	>1 but ≤ 10 mg/l and/or
72 or 96 h ErC_{50} (for algae or other aquatic plants)	>1 but ≤ 10 mg/l *(see note 3)*
and the substance is not rapidly degradable and/or the experimentally determined BCF is ≥ 500 (or, if absent the log $K_{ow} \geq 4$ *(see notes 4 and 5)*.	

NOTE 1: *The organisms fish, crustacea and algae are tested as surrogate species covering a range of trophic levels and taxa, and the test methods are highly standardized. Data on other organisms may also be considered, however, provided they represent equivalent species and test endpoints.*

NOTE 2: *When classifying substances as Acute 1 and/or Chronic 1 it is necessary at the same time to indicate an appropriate M factor (see 2.9.3.4.6.4) to apply the summation method.*

NOTE 3: *Where the algal toxicity ErC_{50} (= EC_{50} (growth rate)) falls more than 100 times below the next most sensitive species and results in a classification based solely on this effect, consideration shall be given to whether this toxicity is representative of the toxicity to aquatic plants. Where it can be shown that this is not the case, professional judgment shall be used in deciding if classification shall be applied. Classification shall be based on the ErC_{50}. In circumstances where the basis of the EC_{50} is not specified and no ErC_{50} is recorded, classification shall be based on the lowest EC_{50} available.*

NOTE 4: *Lack of rapid degradability is based on either a lack of ready biodegradability or other evidence of lack of rapid degradation. When no useful data on degradability are available, either experimentally determined or estimated data, the substance shall be regarded as not rapidly degradable.*

NOTE 5: *Potential to bioaccumulate, based on an experimentally derived BCF ≥ 500 or, if absent, a log $K_{ow} \geq 4$ provided log K_{ow} is an appropriate descriptor for the bioaccumulation potential of the substance. Measured log K_{ow} values take precedence over estimated values and measured BCF values take precedence over log K_{ow} values.*

Figure 2.9.1: Categories for substances long-term hazardous to the aquatic environment

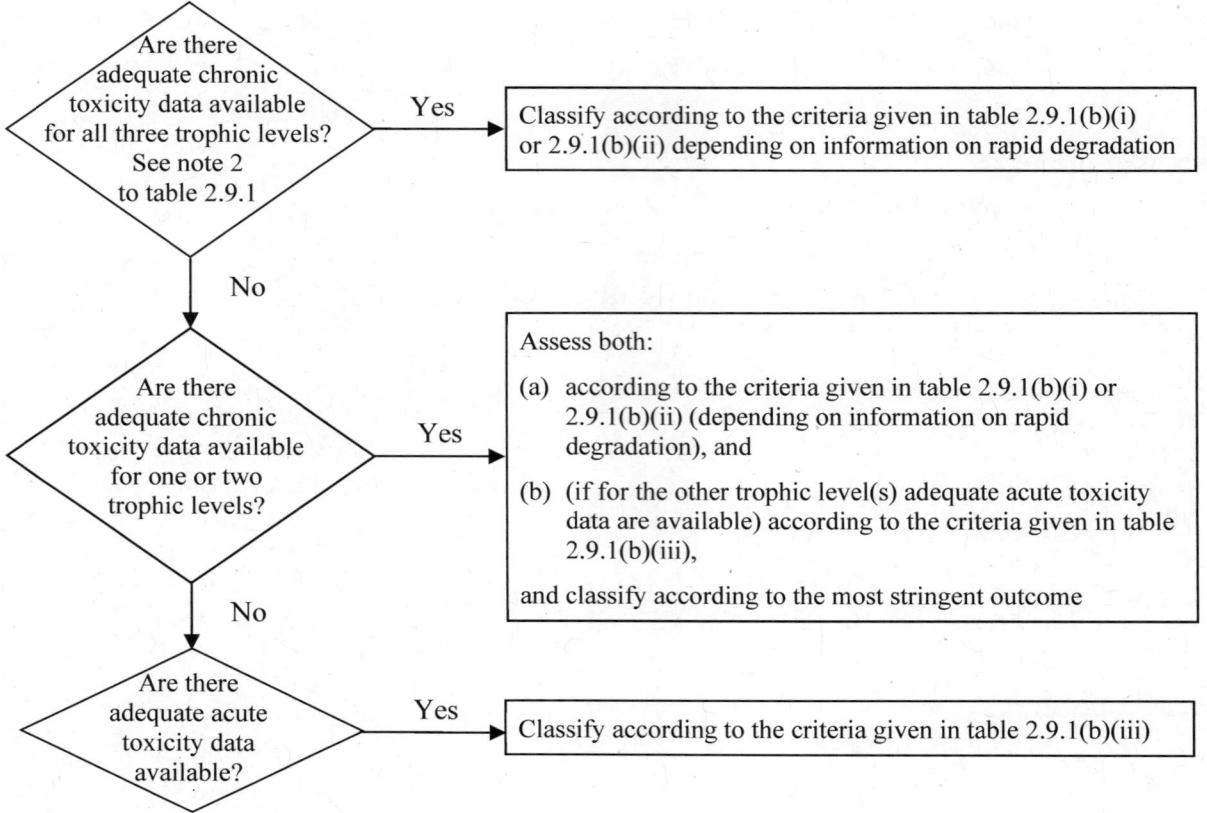

2.9.3.3.2   The classification scheme in table 2.9.2 below summarizes the classification criteria for substances.

Table 2.9.2: Classification scheme for substances hazardous to the aquatic environment

	Classification categories			
Acute hazard (*see note 1*)	**Long-term hazard** (*see note 2*)			
	Adequate chronic toxicity data available		Adequate chronic toxicity data not available (*see note 1*)
	Non-rapidly degradable substances (*see note 3*)	**Rapidly degradable substances** (*see note 3*)	
Category: Acute 1 $L(E)C_{50} \leq 1.00$	**Category: Chronic 1** NOEC or $EC_x \leq 0.1$	**Category: Chronic 1** NOEC or $EC_x \leq 0.01$	**Category: Chronic 1** $L(E)C_{50} \leq 1.00$ and lack of rapid degradability and/or BCF $\geq$ 500 or, if absent log $K_{ow} \geq 4$
	Category: Chronic 2 $0.1 <$ NOEC or $EC_x \leq 1$	**Category: Chronic 2** $0.01 <$ NOEC or $EC_x \leq 0.1$	**Category: Chronic 2** $1.00 < L(E)C_{50} \leq 10.0$ and lack of rapid degradability and/or BCF $\geq$ 500 or, if absent log $K_{ow} \geq 4$

NOTE 1: *Acute toxicity band based on $L(E)C_{50}$ values in mg/l for fish, crustacea and/or algae or other aquatic plants (or Quantitative Structure Activity Relationships (QSAR) estimation if no experimental data[5]).*

NOTE 2: *Substances are classified in the various chronic categories unless there are adequate chronic toxicity data available for all three trophic levels above the water solubility or above 1 mg/l. ("Adequate" means that the data sufficiently cover the endpoint of concern. Generally this would mean measured test data, but in order to avoid unnecessary testing it can on a case by case basis also be estimated data, e.g. (Q)SAR, or for obvious cases expert judgment).*

NOTE 3: *Chronic toxicity band based on NOEC or equivalent EC_x values in mg/l for fish or crustacea or other recognized measures for chronic toxicity.*

2.9.3.4 *Mixture classification categories and criteria*

2.9.3.4.1   The classification system for mixtures covers the classification categories which are used for substances, meaning categories Acute 1 and Chronic 1 and 2. In order to make use of all available data for purposes of classifying the aquatic environmental hazards of the mixture, the following assumption is made and is applied where appropriate:

> The "relevant ingredients" of a mixture are those which are present in a concentration equal to or greater than 0.1 % (by mass) for ingredients classified as Acute and/or Chronic 1 and equal to or greater than 1 % for other ingredients, unless there is a presumption (e.g. in the case of highly toxic ingredients) that an ingredient present at less than 0.1 % can still be relevant for classifying the mixture for aquatic environmental hazards.

2.9.3.4.2   The approach for classification of aquatic environmental hazards is tiered, and is dependent upon the type of information available for the mixture itself and for its ingredients. Elements of the tiered approach include:

(a)   Classification based on tested mixtures;

(b)   Classification based on bridging principles;

(c)   The use of "summation of classified ingredients" and /or an "additivity formula".

Figure 2.9.2 below outlines the process to be followed.

---

[5]   *Special guidance is provided in chapter 4.1, paragraph 4.1.2.13 and annex 9, section A9.6 of the GHS.*

Figure 2.9.2: Tiered approach to classification of mixtures for acute and long-term aquatic environmental hazards

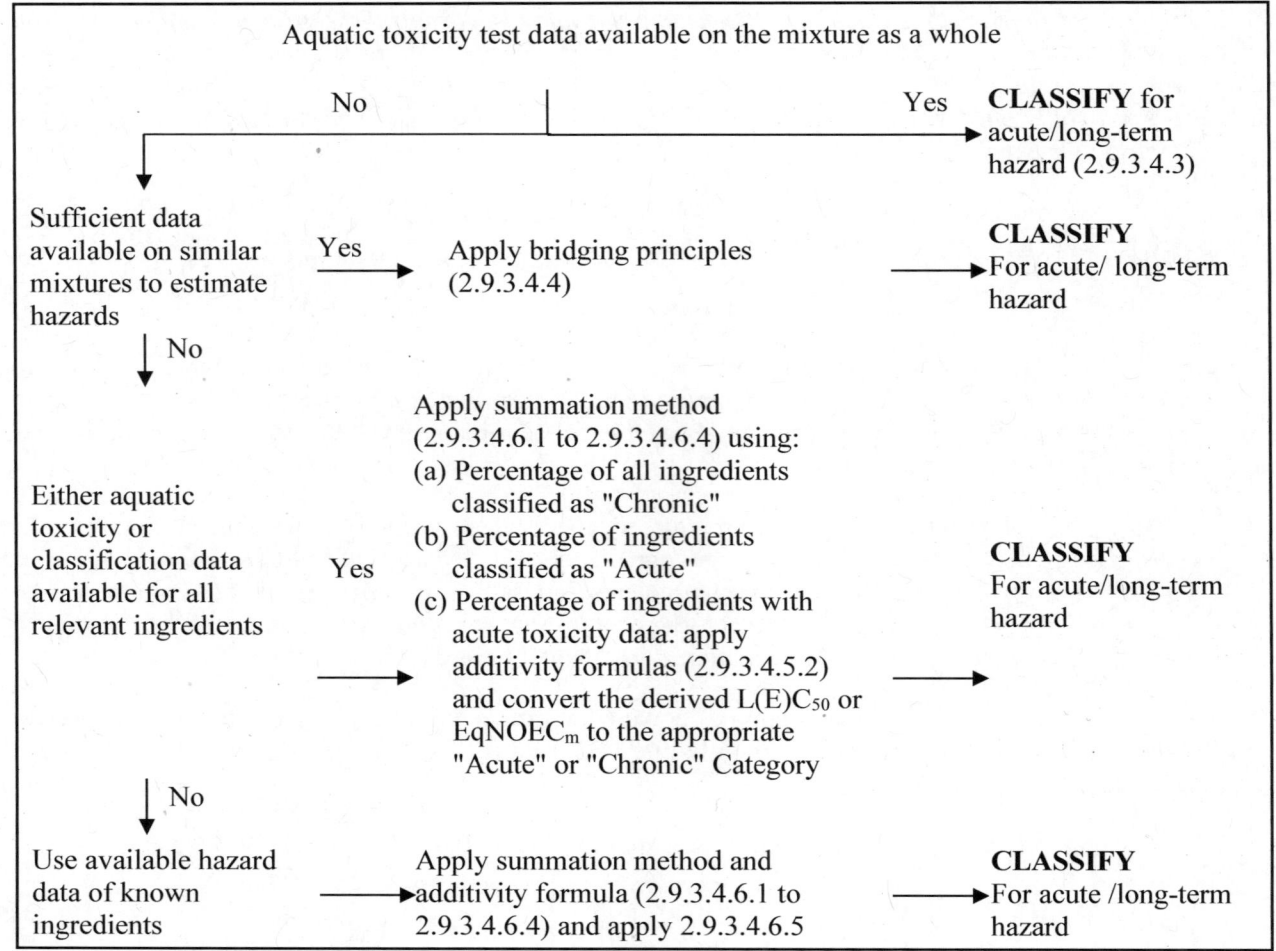

2.9.3.4.3   *Classification of mixtures when toxicity data are available for the complete mixture*

2.9.3.4.3.1   When the mixture as a whole has been tested to determine its aquatic toxicity, this information shall be used for classifying the mixture according to the criteria that have been agreed for substances. The classification is normally based on the data for fish, crustacea and algae/plants (see 2.9.3.2.3 and 2.9.3.2.4). When adequate acute or chronic data for the mixture as a whole are lacking, "bridging principles" or "summation method" shall be applied (see 2.9.3.4.4 to 2.9.3.4.6).

2.9.3.4.3.2   The long-term hazard classification of mixtures requires additional information on degradability and in certain cases bioaccumulation. There are no degradability and bioaccumulation data for mixtures as a whole. Degradability and bioaccumulation tests for mixtures are not used as they are usually difficult to interpret, and such tests may be meaningful only for single substances.

2.9.3.4.3.3   Classification for category Acute 1

(a)   When there are adequate acute toxicity test data (LC_{50} or EC_{50}) available for the mixture as a whole showing $L(E)C_{50} \leq 1$ mg/l:

Classify the mixture as Acute 1 in accordance with table 2.9.1 (a);

(b)   When there are acute toxicity test data ($LC_{50}(s)$ or $EC_{50}(s)$) available for the mixture as a whole showing $L(E)C_{50}(s) > 1$ mg/l, or above the water solubility:

No need to classify for acute hazard under these Regulations.

2.9.3.4.3.4 Classification for categories Chronic 1 and 2

    (a) When there are adequate chronic toxicity data (EC_x or NOEC) available for the mixture as a whole showing EC_x or NOEC of the tested mixture ≤ 1 mg/l:

        (i) classify the mixture as Chronic 1 or 2 in accordance with table 2.9.1 (b) (ii) (rapidly degradable) if the available information allows the conclusion that all relevant ingredients of the mixture are rapidly degradable;

        NOTE: *In this situation, when ECx or NOEC of the tested mixture > 0.1 mg/l, there is no need to classify for long-term hazard under these Regulations.*

        (ii) classify the mixture as Chronic 1 or 2 in all other cases in accordance with table 2.9.1 (b) (i) (non-rapidly degradable);

    (b) When there are adequate chronic toxicity data (EC_x or NOEC) available for the mixture as a whole showing $EC_x(s)$ or NOEC(s) of the tested mixture > 1 mg/l or above the water solubility:

    No need to classify for long-term hazard under these Regulations.

2.9.3.4.4 *Classification of mixtures when toxicity data are not available for the complete mixture: bridging principles*

2.9.3.4.4.1 Where the mixture itself has not been tested to determine its aquatic environmental hazard, but there are sufficient data on the individual ingredients and similar tested mixtures to adequately characterize the hazards of the mixture, these data shall be used in accordance with the following agreed bridging rules. This ensures that the classification process uses the available data to the greatest extent possible in characterizing the hazards of the mixture without the necessity for additional testing in animals.

2.9.3.4.4.2 Dilution

2.9.3.4.4.2.1 Where a new mixture is formed by diluting a tested mixture or a substance with a diluent which has an equivalent or lower aquatic hazard classification than the least toxic original ingredient and which is not expected to affect the aquatic hazards of other ingredients, then the resulting mixture shall be classified as equivalent to the original tested mixture or substance. Alternatively, the method explained in 2.9.3.4.5 may be applied.

2.9.3.4.4.2.2 If a mixture is formed by diluting another classified mixture or a substance with water or other totally non-toxic material, the toxicity of the mixture shall be calculated from the original mixture or substance.

2.9.3.4.4.3 Batching

2.9.3.4.4.3.1 The aquatic hazard classification of a tested production batch of a mixture shall be assumed to be substantially equivalent to that of another untested production batch of the same commercial product when produced by or under the control of the same manufacturer, unless there is reason to believe there is significant variation such that the aquatic hazard classification of the untested batch has changed. If the latter occurs, new classification is necessary.

2.9.3.4.4.4 Concentration of mixtures which are classified with the most severe classification categories (Chronic 1 and Acute 1)

2.9.3.4.4.4.1 If a tested mixture is classified as Chronic 1 and/or Acute 1, and the ingredients of the mixture which are classified as Chronic 1 and/or Acute 1 are further concentrated, the more concentrated untested mixture shall be classified with the same classification category as the original tested mixture without additional testing.

2.9.3.4.4.5 Interpolation within one toxicity category

2.9.3.4.4.5.1 For three mixtures (A, B and C) with identical ingredients, where mixtures A and B have been tested and are in the same toxicity category, and where untested mixture C has the same toxicologically active ingredients as mixtures A and B but has concentrations of toxicologically active ingredients intermediate to the concentrations in mixtures A and B, then mixture C is assumed to be in the same category as A and B.

2.9.3.4.4.6 Substantially similar mixtures

2.9.3.4.4.6.1 Given the following:

(a) Two mixtures:

(i) A + B

(ii) C + B;

(b) The concentration of ingredient B is essentially the same in both mixtures;

(c) The concentration of ingredient A in mixture (i) equals that of ingredient C in mixture (ii);

(d) Data on aquatic hazards for A and C are available and are substantially equivalent, i.e. they are in the same hazard category and are not expected to affect the aquatic toxicity of B.

If mixture (i) or (ii) is already classified based on test data, then the other mixture can be assigned the same hazard category.

2.9.3.4.5 *Classification of mixtures when toxicity data are available for all ingredients or only for some ingredients of the mixture*

2.9.3.4.5.1 The classification of a mixture shall be based on summation of the concentrations of its classified ingredients. The percentage of ingredients classified as "Acute" or "Chronic" will feed straight into the summation method. Details of the summation method are described in 2.9.3.4.6.1 to 2.9.3.4.6.4.1.

2.9.3.4.5.2 Mixtures may be made of a combination of both ingredients that are classified (as Acute 1 and/or Chronic 1, 2) and those for which adequate toxicity test data are available. When adequate toxicity data are available for more than one ingredient in the mixture, the combined toxicity of those ingredients shall be calculated using the following additivity formulas (a) or (b), depending on the nature of the toxicity data:

(a) Based on acute aquatic toxicity:

$$\frac{\sum C_i}{L(E)C_{50m}} = \sum_n \frac{C_i}{L(E)C_{50i}}$$

where:

C_i = concentration of ingredient i (mass percentage);
$L(E)C_{50i}$ = LC_{50} or EC_{50} for ingredient i (mg/l);
n = number of ingredients, and i is running from 1 to n;
$L(E)C_{50m}$ = $L(E)C_{50}$ of the part of the mixture with test data

The calculated toxicity shall be used to assign that portion of the mixture an acute hazard category which is then subsequently used in applying the summation method;

(b) Based on chronic aquatic toxicity:

$$\frac{\sum C_i + \sum C_j}{EqNOEC_m} = \sum_n \frac{C_i}{NOEC_i} + \sum_n \frac{C_j}{0.1 \times NOEC_j}$$

where:

C_i = concentration of ingredient i (mass percentage) covering the rapidly degradable ingredients;

C_j = concentration of ingredient j (mass percentage) covering the non-rapidly degradable ingredients;

$NOEC_i$ = NOEC (or other recognized measures for chronic toxicity) for ingredient i covering the rapidly degradable ingredients, in mg/l;

$NOEC_j$ = NOEC (or other recognized measures for chronic toxicity) for ingredient j covering the non-rapidly degradable ingredients, in mg/l;

n = number of ingredients, and i and j are running from 1 to n;

$EqNOEC_m$ = equivalent NOEC of the part of the mixture with test data;

The equivalent toxicity thus reflects the fact that non-rapidly degrading substances are classified one hazard category level more "severe" than rapidly degrading substances.

The calculated equivalent toxicity shall be used to assign that portion of the mixture a long-term hazard category, in accordance with the criteria for rapidly degradable substances (table 2.9.1 (b) (ii)), which is then subsequently used in applying the summation method.

2.9.3.4.5.3   When applying the additivity formula for part of the mixture, it is preferable to calculate the toxicity of this part of the mixture using for each ingredient toxicity values that relate to the same taxonomic group (i.e. fish, crustacea or algae) and then to use the highest toxicity (lowest value) obtained (i.e. use the most sensitive of the three groups). However, when toxicity data for each ingredient are not available in the same taxonomic group, the toxicity value of each ingredient shall be selected in the same manner that toxicity values are selected for the classification of substances, i.e. the higher toxicity (from the most sensitive test organism) is used. The calculated acute and chronic toxicity shall then be used to classify this part of the mixture as Acute 1 and/or Chronic 1 or 2 using the same criteria described for substances.

2.9.3.4.5.4   If a mixture is classified in more than one way, the method yielding the more conservative result shall be used.

2.9.3.4.6   *Summation method*

2.9.3.4.6.1   Classification procedure

2.9.3.4.6.1.1   In general a more severe classification for mixtures overrides a less severe classification, e.g. a classification with Chronic 1 overrides a classification with Chronic 2. As a consequence the classification procedure is already completed if the results of the classification is Chronic 1. A more severe classification than Chronic 1 is not possible; therefore, it is not necessary to pursue the classification procedure further.

2.9.3.4.6.2   Classification for category Acute 1

2.9.3.4.6.2.1   First, all ingredients classified as Acute 1 are considered. If the sum of the concentrations (in %) of these ingredients is greater than or equal to 25 % the whole mixture shall be classified as Acute 1. If the result of the calculation is a classification of the mixture as Acute 1, the classification process is completed.

2.9.3.4.6.2.2   The classification of mixtures for acute hazards based on this summation of the concentrations of classified ingredients is summarized in table 2.9.3 below.

Table 2.9.3: Classification of a mixture for acute hazards based on summation of the concentrations of classified ingredients

Sum of the concentrations (in %) of ingredients classified as:		Mixture classified as:
Acute 1 × M [a]	≥ 25 %	Acute 1

[a] For explanation of the M factor, see 2.9.3.4.6.4.

2.9.3.4.6.3   Classification for categories Chronic 1 and 2

2.9.3.4.6.3.1   First, all ingredients classified as Chronic 1 are considered. If the sum of the concentrations (in %) of these ingredients is greater than or equal to 25 % the mixture shall be classified as Chronic 1. If the result of the calculation is a classification of the mixture as Chronic 1 the classification procedure is completed.

2.9.3.4.6.3.2   In cases where the mixture is not classified as Chronic 1, classification of the mixture as Chronic 2 is considered. A mixture shall be classified as Chronic 2 if 10 times the sum of the concentrations (in %) of all ingredients classified as Chronic 1 plus the sum of the concentrations (in %) of all ingredients classified as Chronic 2 is greater than or equal to 25 %. If the result of the calculation is classification of the mixture as Chronic 2, the classification process is completed.

2.9.3.4.6.3.3   The classification of mixtures for long-term hazards based on this summation of the concentrations of classified ingredients is summarized in table 2.9.4 below.

Table 2.9.4: Classification of a mixture for long-term hazards based on summation of the concentrations of classified ingredients

Sum of the concentrations (in %) of ingredients classified as:		Mixture classified as:
Chronic 1 × M [a]	≥ 25 %	Chronic 1
(M × 10 × Chronic 1) + Chronic 2	≥ 25 %	Chronic 2

[a] For explanation of the M factor, see 2.9.3.4.6.4.

2.9.3.4.6.4   Mixtures with highly toxic ingredients

2.9.3.4.6.4.1   Acute 1 or Chronic 1 ingredients with acute toxicities well below 1 mg/l and/or chronic toxicities well below 0.1 mg/l (if non-rapidly degradable) and 0.01 mg/l (if rapidly degradable) may influence the toxicity of the mixture and are given increased weight in applying the summation method. When a mixture contains ingredients classified as Acute 1 or Chronic 1, the tiered approach described in 2.9.3.4.6.2 and 2.9.3.4.6.3 shall be applied using a weighted sum by multiplying the concentrations of Acute 1 and Chronic 1 ingredients by a factor, instead of merely adding up the percentages. This means that the concentration of "Acute 1" in the left column of table 2.9.3 and the concentration of "Chronic 1" in the left column of table 2.9.4 are multiplied by the appropriate multiplying factor. The multiplying factors to be applied to these ingredients are defined using the toxicity value, as summarized in table 2.9.5 below. Therefore, in order to classify a mixture containing Acute 1 and/or Chronic 1 ingredients, the classifier needs to be informed of the value of the M factor in order to apply the summation method. Alternatively, the additivity formula (2.9.3.4.5.2) may be used when toxicity data are available for all highly toxic ingredients in the mixture and there is convincing evidence that all other ingredients, including those for which specific acute and/or chronic toxicity data are not available, are of low or no toxicity and do not significantly contribute to the environmental hazard of the mixture.

Table 2.9.5: Multiplying factors for highly toxic ingredients of mixtures

Acute toxicity	M factor	Chronic toxicity	M factor	
$L(E)C_{50}$ value		NOEC value	NRD^a ingredients	RD^b ingredients
$0.1 < L(E)C_{50} \leq 1$	1	$0.01 < NOEC \leq 0.1$	1	-
$0.01 < L(E)C_{50} \leq 0.1$	10	$0.001 < NOEC \leq 0.01$	10	1
$0.001 < L(E)C_{50} \leq 0.01$	100	$0.0001 < NOEC \leq 0.001$	100	10
$0.0001 < L(E)C_{50} \leq 0.001$	1 000	$0.00001 < NOEC \leq 0.0001$	1 000	100
$0.00001 < L(E)C_{50} \leq 0.0001$	10 000	$0.000001 < NOEC \leq 0.00001$	10 000	1 000
(continue in factor 10 intervals)		(continue in factor 10 intervals)		

[a] *Non-rapidly degradable.*
[b] *Rapidly degradable.*

2.9.3.4.6.5   Classification of mixtures with ingredients without any useable information

2.9.3.4.6.5.1   In the event that no useable information on acute and/or chronic aquatic toxicity is available for one or more relevant ingredients, it is concluded that the mixture cannot be attributed (a) definitive hazard category(ies). In this situation the mixture shall be classified based on the known ingredients only.

2.9.4 Lithium batteries

Cells and batteries, cells and batteries contained in equipment, or cells and batteries packed with equipment, containing lithium in any form shall be assigned to UN Nos. 3090, 3091, 3480 or 3481 as appropriate. They may be transported under these entries if they meet the following provisions:

(a) Each cell or battery is of the type proved to meet the requirements of each test of the *Manual of Tests and Criteria*, part III, sub-section 38.3;

Cells and batteries manufactured according to a type meeting the requirements of sub-section 38.3 of the *Manual of Tests and Criteria*, Revision 3, Amendment 1 or any subsequent revision and amendment applicable at the date of the type testing may continue to be transported, unless otherwise provided in these Regulations.

Cell and battery types only meeting the requirements of the *Manual of Tests and Criteria*, Revision 3, are no longer valid. However, cells and batteries manufactured in conformity with such types before 1 July 2003 may continue to be transported if all other applicable requirements are fulfilled.

NOTE: *Batteries shall be of a type proved to meet the testing requirements of the "Manual of Tests and Criteria", part III, sub-section 38.3, irrespective of whether the cells of which they are composed are of a tested type.*

(b) Each cell and battery incorporates a safety venting device or is designed to preclude a violent rupture under conditions normally incident to transport;

(c) Each cell and battery is equipped with an effective means of preventing external short circuits;

(d) Each battery containing cells or series of cells connected in parallel is equipped with effective means as necessary to prevent dangerous reverse current flow (e.g., diodes, fuses, etc.);

(e) Cells and batteries shall be manufactured under a quality management programme that includes:

   (i) A description of the organizational structure and responsibilities of personnel with regard to design and product quality;

   (ii) The relevant inspection and test, quality control, quality assurance, and process operation instructions that will be used;

   (iii) Process controls that should include relevant activities to prevent and detect internal short circuit failure during manufacture of cells;

   (iv) Quality records, such as inspection reports, test data, calibration data and certificates. Test data shall be kept and made available to the competent authority upon request;

   (v) Management reviews to ensure the effective operation of the quality management programme;

   (vi) A process for control of documents and their revision;

   (vii) A means for control of cells or batteries that are not conforming to the type tested as mentioned in (a) above;

   (viii) Training programmes and qualification procedures for relevant personnel; and

   (ix) Procedures to ensure that there is no damage to the final product.

   NOTE: *In house quality management programmes may be accepted. Third party certification is not required, but the procedures listed in (i) to (ix) above shall be properly recorded and traceable. A copy of the quality management programme shall be made available to the competent authority upon request.*

(f) Lithium batteries, containing both primary lithium metal cells and rechargeable lithium ion cells, that are not designed to be externally charged (see special provision 387 of chapter 3.3) shall meet the following conditions:

   (i) The rechargeable lithium ion cells can only be charged from the primary lithium metal cells;

   (ii) Overcharge of the rechargeable lithium ion cells is precluded by design;

   (iii) The battery has been tested as a lithium primary battery;

   (iv) Component cells of the battery shall be of a type proved to meet the respective testing requirements of the *Manual of Tests and Criteria*, part III, sub-section 38.3.

(g) Except for button cells installed in equipment (including circuit boards), manufacturers and subsequent distributors of cells or batteries manufactured after 30 June 2003 shall make available the test summary as specified in the *Manual of Tests and Criteria*, part III, sub-section 38.3, paragraph 38.3.5.

   NOTE: *The term "make available" means that manufacturers and subsequent distributors ensure that the test summary for lithium cells or batteries or equipment with installed lithium cells or batteries is accessible so that the consignor or other persons in the supply chain can confirm compliance.*

2.9.5 Sodium ion batteries

Cells and batteries, cells and batteries contained in equipment, or cells and batteries packed with equipment containing sodium ion, which are a rechargeable electrochemical system where the positive and negative electrode are both intercalation or insertion compounds, constructed with no metallic sodium (or sodium alloy) in either electrode and with an organic non aqueous compound as electrolyte, shall be assigned to UN Nos. 3551 or 3552 as appropriate.

NOTE: *Intercalated sodium exists in an ionic or quasi-atomic form in the lattice of the electrode material.*

They may be transported under these entries if they meet the following provisions:

(a) Each cell or battery is of the type proved to meet the requirements of applicable tests of the *Manual of Tests and Criteria*, part III, sub-section 38.3.

(b) Each cell and battery incorporates a safety venting device or is designed to preclude a violent rupture under conditions normally encountered during transport;

(c) Each cell and battery is equipped with an effective means of preventing external short circuits;

(d) Each battery containing cells or a series of cells connected in parallel is equipped with effective means as necessary to prevent dangerous reverse current flow (e.g., diodes, fuses, etc.);

(e) Cells and batteries shall be manufactured under a quality management program as prescribed under 2.9.4 (e) (i) to (ix);

(f) Manufacturers and subsequent distributors of cells or batteries shall make available the test summary as specified in the *Manual of Tests and Criteria*, part III, sub-section 38.3, paragraph 38.3.5.

PART 3

DANGEROUS GOODS LIST, SPECIAL PROVISIONS AND EXCEPTIONS

CHAPTER 3.1

GENERAL

3.1.1 Scope and general provisions

3.1.1.1 The Dangerous Goods List in this chapter lists the dangerous goods most commonly carried but is not exhaustive. It is intended that the list cover, as far as practicable, all dangerous substances of commercial importance.

3.1.1.2 Where a substance or article is specifically listed by name in the Dangerous Goods List, it shall be transported in accordance with the provisions in the List which are appropriate for that substance or article. A "generic" or "not otherwise specified" entry may be used to permit the transport of substances or articles which do not appear specifically by name in the Dangerous Goods List. Such a substance or article may be transported only after its dangerous properties have been determined. The substance or article shall then be classified according to the class definitions and test criteria and the name in the Dangerous Goods List which most appropriately describes the substance or article shall be used. The classification shall be made by the appropriate competent authority when so required or may otherwise be made by the consignor. Once the class of the substance or article has been so established, all conditions for dispatch and transport, as provided in these Regulations shall be met. Any substance or article having or suspected of having explosive characteristics shall first be considered for inclusion in Class 1. Some collective entries may be of the "generic" or "not otherwise specified" type provided that the regulations contain provisions ensuring safety, both by excluding extremely dangerous goods from normal transport and by covering all subsidiary hazards inherent in some goods.

3.1.1.3 The Dangerous Goods List does not include goods which are so dangerous that their transport, except with special authorization, is prohibited. Such goods are not listed because the transport of some goods may be prohibited for some modes of transport and allowed in others and, in addition, because it would be impossible to draw up an exhaustive list. Moreover, any such list would soon cease to be exhaustive because of the frequent introduction of new substances; and the absence of a substance from such a list might give the mistaken impression that that substance could be carried without special restrictions. Inherent instability in goods may take different dangerous forms, for example, explosion, polymerization, with intense evolution of heat, or emission of toxic gases. In respect of most substances, such tendencies can be controlled by correct packing, dilution, stabilization, addition of an inhibitor, refrigeration or other precautions.

3.1.1.4 Where precautionary measures are laid down in the Dangerous Goods List in respect of a given substance or article (e.g. that it shall be "stabilized" or "with x % water or phlegmatizer") such substance or article may not normally be carried when these measures have not been taken, unless the item in question is listed elsewhere (e.g. Class 1) without any indication of, or with different, precautionary measures.

3.1.2 Proper shipping name

NOTE: For proper shipping names to be used for the transport of samples, see 2.0.4.

3.1.2.1 The proper shipping name is that portion of the entry most accurately describing the goods in the Dangerous Goods List, which is shown in upper case characters (plus any numbers, Greek letters, "sec", "tert", and the letters m, n, o, p, which form an integral part of the name). An alternative proper shipping name may be shown in brackets following the main proper shipping name [e.g., ETHANOL (ETHYL ALCOHOL)]. Portions of an entry appearing in lower case need not be considered as part of the proper shipping name but may be used.

3.1.2.2 When a combination of several distinct proper shipping names are listed under a single UN number, and these are separated by "or" in lower case or are punctuated by commas, only the most appropriate shall be shown in the transport document and package marks. Examples illustrating the selection of the proper shipping name for such entries are:

(a) UN 1057 LIGHTERS or LIGHTER REFILLS - The proper shipping name is the most appropriate of the following possible combinations:

LIGHTERS
LIGHTER REFILLS;

(b) UN 2793 FERROUS METAL BORINGS, SHAVINGS, TURNINGS or CUTTINGS in a form liable to self-heating. The proper shipping name is the most appropriate of the following combinations:

FERROUS METAL BORINGS
FERROUS METAL SHAVINGS
FERROUS METAL TURNINGS
FERROUS METAL CUTTINGS

3.1.2.3 Proper shipping names may be used in the singular or plural as appropriate. In addition, when qualifying words are used as part of the proper shipping name, their sequence on documentation or package marks is optional. For instance, "DIMETHYLAMINE AQUEOUS SOLUTION" may alternatively be shown "AQUEOUS SOLUTION OF DIMETHYLAMINE". Commercial or military names for goods of Class 1 which contain the proper shipping name supplemented by additional descriptive text may be used.

3.1.2.4 Many substances have an entry for both the liquid and solid state (see definitions for liquid and solid in 1.2.1), or for the solid and solution. These are allocated separate UN numbers which are not necessarily adjacent to each other. Details are provided in the alphabetical index, e.g.:

NITROXYLENES, LIQUID   6.1   1665
NITROXYLENES, SOLID   6.1   3447

3.1.2.5 Unless it is already included in capital letters in the name indicated in the Dangerous Goods List, the qualifying word "MOLTEN" shall be added as part of the proper shipping name when a substance, which is a solid in accordance with the definition in 1.2.1, is offered for transport in the molten state (e.g. ALKYLPHENOL, SOLID, N.O.S., MOLTEN).

3.1.2.6 Except for self-reactive substances and organic peroxides and unless it is already included in capital letters in the name indicated in the Dangerous Goods List, the word STABILIZED shall be added as part of the proper shipping name of a substance which, without stabilization, would be forbidden from transport in accordance with 1.1.2 due to it being liable to dangerously react under conditions normally encountered in transport (e.g.: "TOXIC LIQUID, ORGANIC, N.O.S., STABILIZED").

When temperature control is used to stabilize such substances to prevent the development of any dangerous excess pressure or the evolution of excessive heat, or when chemical stabilization is used in combination with temperature control, then:

(a) For liquids and solids where the SAPT (measured without or with inhibitor, when chemical stabilization is applied) is less than or equal to that prescribed in 2.4.2.5.2, special provision 386 of chapter 3.3 and the provisions of 7.1.5 apply;

(b) Unless it is already included in capital letters in the name indicated in the Dangerous Goods List, the words "TEMPERATURE CONTROLLED" shall be added as part of the proper shipping name;

(c) For gases: the conditions of transport shall be approved by the competent authority.

3.1.2.7 Hydrates may be transported under the proper shipping name for the anhydrous substance.

3.1.2.8 *Generic or "not otherwise specified" (N.O.S.) names*

3.1.2.8.1 Generic and "not otherwise specified" proper shipping names that are assigned to special provision 274 or 318 in Column 6 of the Dangerous Goods List shall be supplemented with the technical or chemical group names unless a national law or international convention prohibits its disclosure if it is a controlled substance. For explosives of Class 1, the dangerous goods description may be supplemented by additional descriptive text to indicate commercial or military names. Technical and chemical group names shall be entered in brackets immediately following the proper shipping name. An appropriate modifier, such as "contains" or "containing" or other qualifying words such as "mixture", "solution", etc. and the percentage of the technical constituent may also be used. For example: "UN 1993 Flammable liquid, n.o.s. (contains xylene and benzene), 3, PG II".

3.1.2.8.1.1   The technical name shall be a recognized chemical or biological name, or other name currently used in scientific and technical handbooks, journals and texts. Trade names shall not be used for this purpose. In the case of pesticides, only ISO common name(s), other name(s) in the World Health Organisation (WHO) Recommended Classification of Pesticides by Hazard and Guidelines to Classification, or the name(s) of the active substance(s) may be used.

3.1.2.8.1.2   When a mixture of dangerous goods or articles containing dangerous goods are described by one of the "N.O.S." or "generic" entries to which special provision 274 has been allocated in the Dangerous Goods List, not more than the two constituents which most predominantly contribute to the hazard or hazards of the mixture or of the articles need to be shown, excluding controlled substances when their disclosure is prohibited by national law or international convention. If a package containing a mixture is labelled with any subsidiary hazard label, one of the two technical names shown in brackets shall be the name of the constituent which compels the use of the subsidiary hazard label.

3.1.2.8.1.3   Examples illustrating the selection of the proper shipping name supplemented with the technical name of goods for such N.O.S. entries are:

>   UN 2902   PESTICIDE, LIQUID, TOXIC, N.O.S. (drazoxolon).
>   UN 3394   ORGANOMETALLIC SUBSTANCE, LIQUID, PYROPHORIC, WATER-REACTIVE (trimethylgallium)
>   UN 3540   ARTICLES CONTAINING FLAMMABLE LIQUIDS N.O.S. (pyrrolidine)

3.1.3   Mixtures or solutions

NOTE: Where a substance is specifically listed by name in the Dangerous Goods List, it shall be identified in transport by the proper shipping name in the Dangerous Goods List. Such substances may contain technical impurities (for example those deriving from the production process) or additives for stability or other purposes that do not affect its classification. However, a substance listed by name containing technical impurities or additives for stability or other purposes affecting its classification shall be considered a mixture or solution (see 2.0.2.2 and 2.0.2.5).

3.1.3.1   A mixture or solution is not subject to these Regulations if the characteristics, properties, form or physical state of the mixture or solution are such that it does not meet the criteria, including human experience criteria, for inclusion in any class.

3.1.3.2   A mixture or solution meeting the classification criteria of these Regulations composed of a single predominant substance identified by name in the Dangerous Goods List and one or more substances not subject to these Regulations and/or traces of one or more substances identified by name in the Dangerous Goods List, shall be assigned the UN number and proper shipping name of the predominant substance named in the Dangerous Goods List unless:

> (a)   The mixture or solution is identified by name in the Dangerous Goods List;
>
> (b)   The name and description of the substance named in the Dangerous Goods List specifically indicate that they apply only to the pure substance;
>
> (c)   The hazard class or division, subsidiary hazard(s), packing group, or physical state of the mixture or solution is different from that of the substance named in the Dangerous Goods List; or

(d) The hazard characteristics and properties of the mixture or solution necessitate emergency response measures that are different from those required for the substance identified by name in the Dangerous Goods List.

3.1.3.2.1 Qualifying words such as "MIXTURE" or "SOLUTION", as appropriate, shall be added as part of the proper shipping name, for example, "ACETONE SOLUTION". In addition, the concentration of the mixture or solution may also be indicated after the basic description of the mixture or solution, for example, "ACETONE 75 % SOLUTION".

3.1.3.3 A mixture or solution meeting the classification criteria of these Regulations that is not identified by name in the Dangerous Goods List and that is composed of two or more dangerous goods shall be assigned to an entry that has the proper shipping name, description, hazard class or division, subsidiary hazard(s) and packing group that most precisely describe the mixture or solution.

CHAPTER 3.2

DANGEROUS GOODS LIST

3.2.1 Structure of the dangerous goods list

The Dangerous Goods List is divided into 11 columns as follows:

Column 1   "UN No." - this column contains the serial number assigned to the article or substance under the United Nations system.

Column 2   "Name and description" - this column contains the proper shipping names in uppercase characters, which may be followed by additional descriptive text presented in lowercase characters (see 3.1.2). An explanation of some of the terms used appears in appendix B. Proper shipping names may be shown in the plural where isomers of similar classification exist. Hydrates may be included under the proper shipping name for the anhydrous substance, as appropriate.

Unless otherwise indicated for an entry in the dangerous goods list, the word "solution" in a proper shipping name means one or more named dangerous goods dissolved in a liquid that is not otherwise subject to these Regulations.

Column 3   "Class or division" - this column contains the class or division and in the case of Class 1, the compatibility group assigned to the article or substance according to the classification system described in chapter 2.1.

Column 4   "Subsidiary hazard" - this column contains the class or division number of any important subsidiary hazards which have been identified by applying the classification system described in part 2.

Column 5   "UN packing group" - this column contains the UN packing group number (i.e. I, II or III) assigned to the substance. If more than one packing group is indicated for the entry, the packing group of the substance or formulation to be transported shall be determined, based on its properties, through application of the hazard grouping criteria as provided in part 2.

Column 6   "Special provisions" - this column contains a number referring to any special provision(s) indicated in 3.3.1 that are relevant to the article or substance. Special provisions apply to all the packing groups permitted for a particular substance or article unless the wording makes it otherwise apparent.

Column 7a   "Limited Quantities" - this column provides the maximum quantity per inner packaging or article for transporting dangerous goods as limited quantities in accordance with chapter 3.4.

Column 7b   "Excepted Quantities" - this column provides an alphanumeric code described in sub-section 3.5.1.2 which indicates the maximum quantity per inner and outer packaging for transporting dangerous goods as excepted quantities in accordance with chapter 3.5.

Column 8   "Packing instruction" - This column contains alphanumeric codes which refer to the relevant packing instructions specified in section 4.1.4. The packing instructions indicate the packaging (including IBCs and large packagings), which may be used for the transport of substances and articles.

A code including the letter "P" refers to packing instructions for the use of packagings described in chapters 6.1, 6.2 or 6.3.

A code including the letters "IBC" refers to packing instructions for the use of IBCs described in chapter 6.5.

A code including the letters "LP" refers to packing instructions for the use of large packagings described in chapter 6.6.

When a particular code is not provided, it means the substance is not authorized in the type of packaging that may be used according to the packing instructions bearing that code.

When N/A is included in the column it means that the substance or article need not be packaged.

The packing instructions are listed in numerical order in section 4.1.4 as follows:

>Sub-section 4.1.4.1: Packing instructions concerning the use of packagings (except IBCs and large packagings) (P);

>Sub-section 4.1.4.2: Packing instructions concerning the use of IBCs (IBC);

>Sub-section 4.1.4.3: Packing instructions concerning the use of large packagings (LP).

Column 9 "Special packing provisions" - this column contains alphanumeric codes which refer to the relevant special packing provisions specified in section 4.1.4. The special packing provisions indicate the special provisions for packaging (including IBCs and large packagings).

A special packing provision including the letters "PP" refers to special packing provision applicable to the use of packing instructions bearing the Code "P" in 4.1.4.1.

A special packing provision including the letter "B" refers to special packing provision applicable to the use of packing instructions bearing the code "IBC" in 4.1.4.2.

A special provision including the letter "L" refers to special packing provision applicable to packing instructions bearing the code "LP" in 4.1.4.3.

Column 10 "Portable tank and bulk containers/Instructions" - this column contains a number preceded by the letter "T" which refers to the relevant instruction in 4.2.5 specifying the tank type(s) required for the transport of the substance in portable tanks.

A code including the letters "BK" refers to types of bulk containers used for the transport of bulk goods described in chapter 6.8.

The gases authorized for transport in MEGCs are indicated in the column "MEGC" in tables 1 and 2 of packing instruction P200 in 4.1.4.1.

Column 11 "Portable tank and bulk containers/Special provisions" - this column contains a number preceded by the letters "TP" referring to any special provisions indicated in 4.2.5.3 that apply to the transport of the substance in portable tanks.

3.2.2 **Abbreviations and symbols**

The following abbreviations or symbols are used in the Dangerous Goods List and have the meanings shown:

Abbreviation	Column	Meaning
N.O.S.	2	Not otherwise specified.
†	2	Entry for which there is an explanation in appendix B.

UN No.	Name and description	Class or division	Subsidiary hazard	UN packing group	Special provisions	Limited and excepted quantities		Packagings and IBCs		Portable tanks and bulk containers	
								Packing instruction	Special packing provisions	Instructions	Special provisions
(1)	(2)	(3)	(4)	(5)	(6)	(7a)	(7b)	(8)	(9)	(10)	(11)
-	3.1.2	2.0	2.0	2.0.1.3	3.3	3.4	3.5	4.1.4	4.1.4	4.2.5 / 4.3.2	4.2.5
0004	AMMONIUM PICRATE dry or wetted with less than 10 % water, by mass†	1.1D				0	E0	P112(a) P112(b) P112(c)	PP26		
0005	CARTRIDGES FOR WEAPONS with bursting charge†	1.1F				0	E0	P130 LP101			
0006	CARTRIDGES FOR WEAPONS with bursting charge†	1.1E				0	E0	P130 LP101	PP67 L1		
0007	CARTRIDGES FOR WEAPONS with bursting charge†	1.2F				0	E0	P130 LP101			
0009	AMMUNITION, INCENDIARY with or without burster, expelling charge or propelling charge†	1.2G				0	E0	P130 LP101	PP67 L1		
0010	AMMUNITION, INCENDIARY with or without burster, expelling charge or propelling charge†	1.3G				0	E0	P130 LP101	PP67 L1		
0012	CARTRIDGES FOR WEAPONS, INERT PROJECTILE or CARTRIDGES, SMALL ARMS†	1.4S			364	5 kg	E0	P130 LP101			
0014	CARTRIDGES FOR WEAPONS, BLANK or CARTRIDGES, SMALL ARMS, BLANK or CARTRIDGES FOR TOOLS, BLANK†	1.4S			364	5 kg	E0	P130 LP101			
0015	AMMUNITION, SMOKE with or without burster, expelling charge or propelling charge†	1.2G			204	0	E0	P130 LP101	PP67 L1		
0016	AMMUNITION, SMOKE with or without burster, expelling charge or propelling charge†	1.3G			204	0	E0	P130 LP101	PP67 L1		
0018	AMMUNITION, TEAR-PRODUCING with burster, expelling charge or propelling charge†	1.2G	6.1 8			0	E0	P130 LP101	PP67 L1		
0019	AMMUNITION, TEAR-PRODUCING with burster, expelling charge or propelling charge†	1.3G	6.1 8			0	E0	P130 LP101	PP67 L1		
0020	AMMUNITION, TOXIC with burster, expelling charge or propelling charge†	1.2K	6.1		274	0	E0	P101			
0021	AMMUNITION, TOXIC with burster, expelling charge or propelling charge†	1.3K	6.1		274	0	E0	P101			
0027	BLACK POWDER (GUNPOWDER), granular or as a meal†	1.1D				0	E0	P113	PP50		
0028	BLACK POWDER (GUNPOWDER), COMPRESSED or BLACK POWDER (GUNPOWDER), IN PELLETS†	1.1D				0	E0	P113	PP51		
0029	DETONATORS, NON-ELECTRIC for blasting†	1.1B				0	E0	P131	PP68		
0030	DETONATORS, ELECTRIC for blasting†	1.1B			399	0	E0	P131			
0033	BOMBS with bursting charge†	1.1F				0	E0	P130 LP101			
0034	BOMBS with bursting charge†	1.1D				0	E0	P130 LP101	PP67 L1		
0035	BOMBS with bursting charge†	1.2D				0	E0	P130 LP101	PP67 L1		

UN No.	Name and description	Class or division	Subsidiary hazard	UN packing group	Special provisions	Limited and excepted quantities		Packagings and IBCs		Portable tanks and bulk containers	
								Packing instruction	Special packing provisions	Instructions	Special provisions
(1)	(2)	(3)	(4)	(5)	(6)	(7a)	(7b)	(8)	(9)	(10)	(11)
-	3.1.2	2.0	2.0	2.0.1.3	3.3	3.4	3.5	4.1.4	4.1.4	4.2.5 / 4.3.2	4.2.5
0037	BOMBS, PHOTO-FLASH†	1.1F				0	E0	P130 LP101			
0038	BOMBS, PHOTO-FLASH†	1.1D				0	E0	P130 LP101	PP67 L1		
0039	BOMBS, PHOTO-FLASH†	1.2G				0	E0	P130 LP101	PP67 L1		
0042	BOOSTERS without detonator†	1.1D				0	E0	P132(a) P132(b)			
0043	BURSTERS, explosive†	1.1D				0	E0	P133	PP69		
0044	PRIMERS, CAP TYPE†	1.4S				0	E0	P133			
0048	CHARGES, DEMOLITION†	1.1D				0	E0	P130 LP101	PP67 L1		
0049	CARTRIDGES, FLASH†	1.1G				0	E0	P135			
0050	CARTRIDGES, FLASH†	1.3G				0	E0	P135			
0054	CARTRIDGES, SIGNAL†	1.3G				0	E0	P135			
0055	CASES, CARTRIDGE, EMPTY, WITH PRIMER†	1.4S			364	5 kg	E0	P136			
0056	CHARGES, DEPTH†	1.1D				0	E0	P130 LP101	PP67 L1		
0059	CHARGES, SHAPED without detonator†	1.1D				0	E0	P137	PP70		
0060	CHARGES, SUPPLEMENTARY, EXPLOSIVE†	1.1D				0	E0	P132(a) P132(b)			
0065	CORD, DETONATING, flexible†	1.1D				0	E0	P139	PP71 PP72		
0066	CORD, IGNITER†	1.4G				0	E0	P140			
0070	CUTTERS, CABLE, EXPLOSIVE†	1.4S				0	E0	P134 LP102			
0072	CYCLOTRIMETHYLENE-TRINITRAMINE (CYCLONITE; HEXOGEN; RDX), WETTED with not less than 15 % water, by mass†	1.1D			266	0	E0	P112(a)	PP45		
0073	DETONATORS FOR AMMUNITION†	1.1B				0	E0	P133			
0074	DIAZODINITROPHENOL, WETTED with not less than 40 % water, or mixture of alcohol and water, by mass†	1.1A			266	0	E0	P110(a) P110(b)	PP42		
0075	DIETHYLENEGLYCOL DINITRATE, DESENSITIZED with not less than 25 % non-volatile, water-insoluble phlegmatizer, by mass†	1.1D			266	0	E0	P115	PP53 PP54 PP57 PP58		
0076	DINITROPHENOL, dry or wetted with less than 15 % water, by mass†	1.1D	6.1			0	E0	P112(a) P112(b) P112(c)	PP26		
0077	DINITROPHENOLATES, alkali metals, dry or wetted with less than 15 % water, by mass†	1.3C	6.1			0	E0	P114(a) P114(b)	PP26		
0078	DINITRORESORCINOL, dry or wetted with less than 15 % water, by mass†	1.1D				0	E0	P112(a) P112(b) P112(c)	PP26		
0079	HEXANITRODIPHENYLAMINE (DIPICRYLAMINE; HEXYL)†	1.1D				0	E0	P112(b) P112(c)			
0081	EXPLOSIVE, BLASTING, TYPE A†	1.1D				0	E0	P116	PP63 PP66		

UN No.	Name and description	Class or division	Subsidiary hazard	UN packing group	Special provisions	Limited and excepted quantities		Packagings and IBCs		Portable tanks and bulk containers	
								Packing instruction	Special packing provisions	Instructions	Special provisions
(1)	(2)	(3)	(4)	(5)	(6)	(7a)	(7b)	(8)	(9)	(10)	(11)
-	3.1.2	2.0	2.0	2.0.1.3	3.3	3.4	3.5	4.1.4	4.1.4	4.2.5 / 4.3.2	4.2.5
0082	EXPLOSIVE, BLASTING, TYPE B†	1.1D				0	E0	P116 IBC100	PP61 PP62 B9		
0083	EXPLOSIVE, BLASTING, TYPE C†	1.1D			267	0	E0	P116			
0084	EXPLOSIVE, BLASTING, TYPE D†	1.1D				0	E0	P116			
0092	FLARES, SURFACE†	1.3G				0	E0	P135			
0093	FLARES, AERIAL†	1.3G				0	E0	P135			
0094	FLASH POWDER†	1.1G				0	E0	P113	PP49		
0099	FRACTURING DEVICES, EXPLOSIVE without detonator, for oil wells	1.1D				0	E0	P134 LP102			
0101	FUSE, NON-DETONATING†	1.3G				0	E0	P140	PP74 PP75		
0102	CORD (FUSE), DETONATING, metal clad†	1.2D				0	E0	P139	PP71		
0103	FUSE, IGNITER, tubular, metal clad†	1.4G				0	E0	P140			
0104	CORD (FUSE), DETONATING, MILD EFFECT, metal clad†	1.4D				0	E0	P139	PP71		
0105	FUSE, SAFETY†	1.4S				0	E0	P140	PP73		
0106	FUZES, DETONATING†	1.1B				0	E0	P141			
0107	FUZES, DETONATING†	1.2B				0	E0	P141			
0110	GRENADES, PRACTICE, hand or rifle†	1.4S				0	E0	P141			
0113	GUANYL NITROSAMINO-GUANYLIDENE HYDRAZINE, WETTED with not less than 30 % water, by mass†	1.1A			266	0	E0	P110(a) P110(b)	PP42		
0114	GUANYL NITROSAMINO-GUANYLTETRAZENE (TETRAZENE), WETTED with not less than 30 % water, or mixture of alcohol and water, by mass†	1.1A			266	0	E0	P110(a) P110(b)	PP42		
0118	HEXOLITE (HEXOTOL), dry or wetted with less than 15 % water, by mass†	1.1D				0	E0	P112(a) P112(b) P112(c)			
0121	IGNITERS†	1.1G				0	E0	P142			
0124	JET PERFORATING GUNS, CHARGED, oil well, without detonator†	1.1D				0	E0	P101			
0129	LEAD AZIDE, WETTED with not less than 20 % water, or mixture of alcohol and water, by mass†	1.1A			266	0	E0	P110(a) P110(b)	PP42		
0130	LEAD STYPHNATE (LEAD TRINITRORESORCINATE), WETTED with not less than 20 % water, or mixture of alcohol and water, by mass†	1.1A			266	0	E0	P110(a) P110(b)	PP42		
0131	LIGHTERS, FUSE†	1.4S				0	E0	P142			
0132	DEFLAGRATING METAL SALTS OF AROMATIC NITRODERIVATIVES, N.O.S.†	1.3C				0	E0	P114(a) P114(b)	PP26		
0133	MANNITOL HEXANITRATE (NITROMANNITE), WETTED with not less than 40 % water, or mixture of alcohol and water, by mass†	1.1D			266	0	E0	P112(a)			

UN No.	Name and description	Class or division	Subsidiary hazard	UN packing group	Special provisions	Limited and excepted quantities		Packagings and IBCs		Portable tanks and bulk containers	
								Packing instruction	Special packing provisions	Instructions	Special provisions
(1)	(2)	(3)	(4)	(5)	(6)	(7a)	(7b)	(8)	(9)	(10)	(11)
-	3.1.2	2.0	2.0	2.0.1.3	3.3	3.4	3.5	4.1.4	4.1.4	4.2.5 / 4.3.2	4.2.5
0135	MERCURY FULMINATE, WETTED with not less than 20 % water, or mixture of alcohol and water, by mass†	1.1A			266	0	E0	P110(a) P110(b)	PP42		
0136	MINES with bursting charge†	1.1F				0	E0	P130 LP101			
0137	MINES with bursting charge†	1.1D				0	E0	P130 LP101	PP67 L1		
0138	MINES with bursting charge†	1.2D				0	E0	P130 LP101	PP67 L1		
0143	NITROGLYCERIN, DESENSITIZED with not less than 40 % non-volatile water-insoluble phlegmatizer, by mass†	1.1D	6.1		266 271	0	E0	P115	PP53 PP54 PP57 PP58		
0144	NITROGLYCERIN SOLUTION IN ALCOHOL with more than 1 % but not more than 10 % nitroglycerin†	1.1D			358	0	E0	P115	PP45 PP55 PP56 PP59 PP60		
0146	NITROSTARCH, dry or wetted with less than 20 % water, by mass†	1.1D				0	E0	P112(a) P112(b) P112(c)			
0147	NITRO UREA†	1.1D				0	E0	P112(b)			
0150	PENTAERYTHRITE TETRANITRATE (PENTAERYTHRITOL TETRANITRATE; PETN), WETTED with not less than 25 % water, by mass, or PENTAERYTHRITE TETRANITRATE (PENTAERYTHRITOL TETRANITRATE; PETN), DESENSITIZED with not less than 15 % phlegmatizer, by mass†	1.1D			266	0	E0	P112(a) P112(b)			
0151	PENTOLITE, dry or wetted with less than 15 % water, by mass†	1.1D				0	E0	P112(a) P112(b) P112(c)			
0153	TRINITROANILINE (PICRAMIDE)†	1.1D				0	E0	P112(b) P112(c)			
0154	TRINITROPHENOL (PICRIC ACID), dry or wetted with less than 30 % water, by mass†	1.1D				0	E0	P112(a) P112(b) P112(c)	PP26		
0155	TRINITROCHLOROBENZENE (PICRYL CHLORIDE)†	1.1D				0	E0	P112(b) P112(c)			
0159	POWDER CAKE (POWDER PASTE), WETTED with not less than 25 % water, by mass†	1.3C			266	0	E0	P111	PP43		
0160	POWDER, SMOKELESS†	1.1C				0	E0	P114(b)	PP50 PP52		
0161	POWDER, SMOKELESS†	1.3C				0	E0	P114(b)	PP50 PP52		
0167	PROJECTILES with bursting charge†	1.1F				0	E0	P130 LP101			
0168	PROJECTILES with bursting charge†	1.1D				0	E0	P130 LP101	PP67 L1		
0169	PROJECTILES with bursting charge†	1.2D				0	E0	P130 LP101	PP67 L1		
0171	AMMUNITION, ILLUMINATING with or without burster, expelling charge or propelling charge†	1.2G				0	E0	P130 LP101	PP67 L1		

UN No.	Name and description	Class or division	Subsidiary hazard	UN packing group	Special provisions	Limited and excepted quantities		Packagings and IBCs		Portable tanks and bulk containers	
								Packing instruction	Special packing provisions	Instructions	Special provisions
(1)	(2)	(3)	(4)	(5)	(6)	(7a)	(7b)	(8)	(9)	(10)	(11)
-	3.1.2	2.0	2.0	2.0.1.3	3.3	3.4	3.5	4.1.4	4.1.4	4.2.5 / 4.3.2	4.2.5
0173	RELEASE DEVICES, EXPLOSIVE†	1.4S				0	E0	P134 LP102			
0174	RIVETS, EXPLOSIVE	1.4S				0	E0	P134 LP102			
0180	ROCKETS with bursting charge†	1.1F				0	E0	P130 LP101			
0181	ROCKETS with bursting charge†	1.1E				0	E0	P130 LP101	PP67 L1		
0182	ROCKETS with bursting charge†	1.2E				0	E0	P130 LP101	PP67 L1		
0183	ROCKETS with inert head†	1.3C				0	E0	P130 LP101	PP67 L1		
0186	ROCKET MOTORS†	1.3C				0	E0	P130 LP101	PP67 L1		
0190	SAMPLES, EXPLOSIVE, other than initiating explosive†				16 274		E0	P101			
0191	SIGNAL DEVICES, HAND†	1.4G				0	E0	P135			
0192	SIGNALS, RAILWAY TRACK, EXPLOSIVE†	1.1G				0	E0	P135			
0193	SIGNALS, RAILWAY TRACK, EXPLOSIVE†	1.4S				0	E0	P135			
0194	SIGNALS, DISTRESS, ship†	1.1G				0	E0	P135			
0195	SIGNALS, DISTRESS, ship†	1.3G				0	E0	P135			
0196	SIGNALS, SMOKE†	1.1G				0	E0	P135			
0197	SIGNALS, SMOKE†	1.4G				0	E0	P135			
0204	SOUNDING DEVICES, EXPLOSIVE†	1.2F				0	E0	P134 LP102			
0207	TETRANITROANILINE†	1.1D				0	E0	P112(b) P112(c)			
0208	TRINITROPHENYLMETHYL-NITRAMINE (TETRYL)†	1.1D				0	E0	P112(b) P112(c)			
0209	TRINITROTOLUENE (TNT), dry or wetted with less than 30 % water, by mass†	1.1D				0	E0	P112(b) P112(c)	PP46		
0212	TRACERS FOR AMMUNITION†	1.3G				0	E0	P133	PP69		
0213	TRINITROANISOLE†	1.1D				0	E0	P112(b) P112(c)			
0214	TRINITROBENZENE, dry or wetted with less than 30 % water, by mass†	1.1D				0	E0	P112(a) P112(b) P112(c)			
0215	TRINITROBENZOIC ACID, dry or wetted with less than 30 % water, by mass†	1.1D				0	E0	P112(a) P112(b) P112(c)			
0216	TRINITRO-m-CRESOL†	1.1D				0	E0	P112(b) P112(c)	PP26		
0217	TRINITRONAPHTHALENE†	1.1D				0	E0	P112(b) P112(c)			
0218	TRINITROPHENETOLE†	1.1D				0	E0	P112(b) P112(c)			
0219	TRINITRORESORCINOL (STYPHNIC ACID), dry or wetted with less than 20 % water, or mixture of alcohol and water, by mass†	1.1D				0	E0	P112(a) P112(b) P112(c)	PP26		
0220	UREA NITRATE, dry or wetted with less than 20 % water, by mass†	1.1D				0	E0	P112(a) P112(b) P112(c)			

UN No.	Name and description	Class or division	Subsidiary hazard	UN packing group	Special provisions	Limited and excepted quantities		Packagings and IBCs		Portable tanks and bulk containers	
								Packing instruction	Special packing provisions	Instructions	Special provisions
(1)	(2)	(3)	(4)	(5)	(6)	(7a)	(7b)	(8)	(9)	(10)	(11)
-	3.1.2	2.0	2.0	2.0.1.3	3.3	3.4	3.5	4.1.4	4.1.4	4.2.5 / 4.3.2	4.2.5
0221	WARHEADS, TORPEDO with bursting charge†	1.1D				0	E0	P130 LP101	PP67 L1		
0222	AMMONIUM NITRATE	1.1D			370	0	E0	P112(b) P112(c) IBC100	PP47 B2, B3, B17		
0224	BARIUM AZIDE, dry or wetted with less than 50 % water, by mass†	1.1A	6.1			0	E0	P110(a) P110(b)	PP42		
0225	BOOSTERS WITH DETONATOR†	1.1B				0	E0	P133	PP69		
0226	CYCLOTETRAMETHYLENE-TETRANITRAMINE (HMX; OCTOGEN), WETTED with not less than 15 % water, by mass†	1.1D			266	0	E0	P112(a)	PP45		
0234	SODIUM DINITRO-o-CRESOLATE, dry or wetted with less than 15 % water, by mass†	1.3C				0	E0	P114(a) P114(b)	PP26		
0235	SODIUM PICRAMATE, dry or wetted with less than 20 % water, by mass†	1.3C				0	E0	P114(a) P114(b)	PP26		
0236	ZIRCONIUM PICRAMATE, dry or wetted with less than 20 % water, by mass†	1.3C				0	E0	P114(a) P114(b)	PP26		
0237	CHARGES, SHAPED, FLEXIBLE, LINEAR†	1.4D				0		P138			
0238	ROCKETS, LINE-THROWING†	1.2G				0	E0	P130 LP101			
0240	ROCKETS, LINE-THROWING†	1.3G				0	E0	P130 LP101			
0241	EXPLOSIVE, BLASTING, TYPE E†	1.1D				0	E0	P116 IBC100	PP61 PP62 B10		
0242	CHARGES, PROPELLING, FOR CANNON†	1.3C				0	E0	P130 LP101			
0243	AMMUNITION, INCENDIARY, WHITE PHOSPHORUS with burster, expelling charge or propelling charge†	1.2H				0	E0	P130 LP101	PP67 L1		
0244	AMMUNITION, INCENDIARY, WHITE PHOSPHORUS with burster, expelling charge or propelling charge†	1.3H				0	E0	P130 LP101	PP67 L1		
0245	AMMUNITION, SMOKE, WHITE PHOSPHORUS with burster, expelling charge or propelling charge†	1.2H				0	E0	P130 LP101	PP67 L1		
0246	AMMUNITION, SMOKE, WHITE PHOSPHORUS with burster, expelling charge or propelling charge†	1.3H				0	E0	P130 LP101	PP67 L1		
0247	AMMUNITION, INCENDIARY, liquid or gel, with burster, expelling charge or propelling charge†	1.3J				0	E0	P101			
0248	CONTRIVANCES, WATER-ACTIVATED with burster, expelling charge or propelling charge†	1.2L			274	0	E0	P144	PP77		
0249	CONTRIVANCES, WATER-ACTIVATED with burster, expelling charge or propelling charge†	1.3L			274	0	E0	P144	PP77		

UN No.	Name and description	Class or division	Subsidiary hazard	UN packing group	Special provisions	Limited and excepted quantities		Packagings and IBCs		Portable tanks and bulk containers	
								Packing instruction	Special packing provisions	Instructions	Special provisions
(1)	(2)	(3)	(4)	(5)	(6)	(7a)	(7b)	(8)	(9)	(10)	(11)
-	3.1.2	2.0	2.0	2.0.1.3	3.3	3.4	3.5	4.1.4	4.1.4	4.2.5 / 4.3.2	4.2.5
0250	ROCKET MOTORS WITH HYPERGOLIC LIQUIDS with or without expelling charge†	1.3L				0	E0	P101			
0254	AMMUNITION, ILLUMINATING with or without burster, expelling charge or propelling charge†	1.3G				0	E0	P130 LP101	PP67 L1		
0255	DETONATORS, ELECTRIC for blasting†	1.4B			399	0	E0	P131			
0257	FUZES, DETONATING†	1.4B				0	E0	P141			
0266	OCTOLITE (OCTOL), dry or wetted with less than 15 % water, by mass†	1.1D				0	E0	P112(a) P112(b) P112(c)			
0267	DETONATORS, NON-ELECTRIC for blasting†	1.4B				0	E0	P131	PP68		
0268	BOOSTERS WITH DETONATOR†	1.2B				0	E0	P133	PP69		
0271	CHARGES, PROPELLING†	1.1C				0	E0	P143	PP76		
0272	CHARGES, PROPELLING†	1.3C				0	E0	P143	PP76		
0275	CARTRIDGES, POWER DEVICE†	1.3C				0	E0	P134 LP102			
0276	CARTRIDGES, POWER DEVICE†	1.4C				0	E0	P134 LP102			
0277	CARTRIDGES, OIL WELL†	1.3C				0	E0	P134 LP102			
0278	CARTRIDGES, OIL WELL†	1.4C				0	E0	P134 LP102			
0279	CHARGES, PROPELLING, FOR CANNON†	1.1C				0	E0	P130 LP101			
0280	ROCKET MOTORS†	1.1C				0	E0	P130 LP101	PP67 L1		
0281	ROCKET MOTORS†	1.2C				0	E0	P130 LP101	PP67 L1		
0282	NITROGUANIDINE (PICRITE), dry or wetted with less than 20 % water, by mass†	1.1D				0	E0	P112(a) P112(b) P112(c)			
0283	BOOSTERS without detonator†	1.2D				0	E0	P132(a) P132(b)			
0284	GRENADES, hand or rifle, with bursting charge†	1.1D				0	E0	P141			
0285	GRENADES, hand or rifle, with bursting charge†	1.2D				0	E0	P141			
0286	WARHEADS, ROCKET with bursting charge†	1.1D				0	E0	P130 LP101	PP67 L1		
0287	WARHEADS, ROCKET with bursting charge†	1.2D				0	E0	P130 LP101	PP67 L1		
0288	CHARGES, SHAPED, FLEXIBLE, LINEAR†	1.1D				0	E0	P138			
0289	CORD, DETONATING, flexible†	1.4D				0	E0	P139	PP71 PP72		
0290	CORD (FUSE), DETONATING, metal clad†	1.1D				0	E0	P139	PP71		
0291	BOMBS with bursting charge†	1.2F				0	E0	P130 LP101			
0292	GRENADES, hand or rifle, with bursting charge†	1.1F				0	E0	P141			
0293	GRENADES, hand or rifle, with bursting charge†	1.2F				0	E0	P141			
0294	MINES with bursting charge†	1.2F				0	E0	P130 LP101			

UN No.	Name and description	Class or division	Subsidiary hazard	UN packing group	Special provisions	Limited and excepted quantities		Packagings and IBCs		Portable tanks and bulk containers	
						(7a)	(7b)	Packing instruction	Special packing provisions	Instructions	Special provisions
(1)	(2)	(3)	(4)	(5)	(6)	(7a)	(7b)	(8)	(9)	(10)	(11)
-	3.1.2	2.0	2.0	2.0.1.3	3.3	3.4	3.5	4.1.4	4.1.4	4.2.5 / 4.3.2	4.2.5
0295	ROCKETS with bursting charge†	1.2F				0	E0	P130 LP101			
0296	SOUNDING DEVICES, EXPLOSIVE†	1.1F				0	E0	P134 LP102			
0297	AMMUNITION, ILLUMINATING with or without burster, expelling charge or propelling charge†	1.4G				0	E0	P130 LP101	PP67 L1		
0299	BOMBS, PHOTO-FLASH†	1.3G				0	E0	P130 LP101	PP67 L1		
0300	AMMUNITION, INCENDIARY with or without burster, expelling charge or propelling charge†	1.4G				0	E0	P130 LP101	PP67 L1		
0301	AMMUNITION, TEAR-PRODUCING with burster, expelling charge or propelling charge†	1.4G	6.1 8			0	E0	P130 LP101	PP67 L1		
0303	AMMUNITION, SMOKE with or without burster, expelling charge or propelling charge†	1.4G			204	0	E0	P130 LP101	PP67 L1		
0305	FLASH POWDER†	1.3G				0	E0	P113	PP49		
0306	TRACERS FOR AMMUNITION†	1.4G				0	E0	P133	PP69		
0312	CARTRIDGES, SIGNAL†	1.4G				0	E0	P135			
0313	SIGNALS, SMOKE†	1.2G				0	E0	P135			
0314	IGNITERS†	1.2G				0	E0	P142			
0315	IGNITERS†	1.3G				0	E0	P142			
0316	FUZES, IGNITING†	1.3G				0	E0	P141			
0317	FUZES, IGNITING†	1.4G				0	E0	P141			
0318	GRENADES, PRACTICE, hand or rifle†	1.3G				0	E0	P141			
0319	PRIMERS, TUBULAR†	1.3G				0	E0	P133			
0320	PRIMERS, TUBULAR†	1.4G				0	E0	P133			
0321	CARTRIDGES FOR WEAPONS with bursting charge†	1.2E				0	E0	P130 LP101	PP67 L1		
0322	ROCKET MOTORS WITH HYPERGOLIC LIQUIDS with or without expelling charge†	1.2L				0	E0	P101			
0323	CARTRIDGES, POWER DEVICE†	1.4S			347	0	E0	P134 LP102			
0324	PROJECTILES with bursting charge†	1.2F				0	E0	P130 LP101			
0325	IGNITERS†	1.4G				0	E0	P142			
0326	CARTRIDGES FOR WEAPONS, BLANK†	1.1C				0	E0	P130 LP101			
0327	CARTRIDGES FOR WEAPONS, BLANK or CARTRIDGES, SMALL ARMS, BLANK†	1.3C				0	E0	P130 LP101			
0328	CARTRIDGES FOR WEAPONS, INERT PROJECTILE†	1.2C				0	E0	P130 LP101	PP67 L1		
0329	TORPEDOES with bursting charge†	1.1E				0	E0	P130 LP101	PP67 L1		
0330	TORPEDOES with bursting charge†	1.1F				0	E0	P130 LP101			
0331	EXPLOSIVE, BLASTING, TYPE B† (AGENT, BLASTING, TYPE B)	1.5D				0	E0	P116 IBC100	PP61 PP62 PP64	T1	TP17 TP32

UN No.	Name and description	Class or division	Subsi-diary hazard	UN packing group	Special provisions	Limited and excepted quantities		Packagings and IBCs		Portable tanks and bulk containers	
								Packing instruction	Special packing provisions	Instruc-tions	Special provisions
(1)	(2)	(3)	(4)	(5)	(6)	(7a)	(7b)	(8)	(9)	(10)	(11)
-	3.1.2	2.0	2.0	2.0.1.3	3.3	3.4	3.5	4.1.4	4.1.4	4.2.5 / 4.3.2	4.2.5
0332	EXPLOSIVE, BLASTING, TYPE E† (AGENT, BLASTING, TYPE E)	1.5D				0	E0	P116 IBC100	PP61 PP62	T1	TP1 TP17 TP32
0333	FIREWORKS†	1.1G				0	E0	P135			
0334	FIREWORKS†	1.2G				0	E0	P135			
0335	FIREWORKS†	1.3G				0	E0	P135			
0336	FIREWORKS†	1.4G				0	E0	P135			
0337	FIREWORKS†	1.4S				0	E0	P135			
0338	CARTRIDGES FOR WEAPONS, BLANK or CARTRIDGES, SMALL ARMS, BLANK†	1.4C				0	E0	P130 LP101			
0339	CARTRIDGES FOR WEAPONS, INERT PROJECTILE or CARTRIDGES, SMALL ARMS†	1.4C				0	E0	P130 LP101			
0340	NITROCELLULOSE, dry or wetted with less than 25 % water (or alcohol), by mass†	1.1D			393	0	E0	P112(a) P112(b)			
0341	NITROCELLULOSE, unmodified or plasticized with less than 18 % plasticizing substance, by mass†	1.1D			393	0	E0	P112(b)			
0342	NITROCELLULOSE, WETTED with not less than 25 % alcohol, by mass†	1.3C			105 393	0	E0	P114(a)	PP43		
0343	NITROCELLULOSE, PLASTICIZED with not less than 18 % plasticizing substance, by mass†	1.3C			105 393	0	E0	P111			
0344	PROJECTILES with bursting charge†	1.4D				0	E0	P130 LP101	PP67 L1		
0345	PROJECTILES, inert with tracer†	1.4S				0	E0	P130 LP101	PP67 L1		
0346	PROJECTILES with burster or expelling charge†	1.2D				0	E0	P130 LP101	PP67 L1		
0347	PROJECTILES with burster or expelling charge†	1.4D				0	E0	P130 LP101	PP67 L1		
0348	CARTRIDGES FOR WEAPONS with bursting charge†	1.4F				0	E0	P130 LP101			
0349	ARTICLES, EXPLOSIVE, N.O.S.	1.4S			178 274 347	0	E0	P101			
0350	ARTICLES, EXPLOSIVE, N.O.S.	1.4B			178 274	0	E0	P101			
0351	ARTICLES, EXPLOSIVE, N.O.S.	1.4C			178 274	0	E0	P101			
0352	ARTICLES, EXPLOSIVE, N.O.S.	1.4D			178 274	0	E0	P101			
0353	ARTICLES, EXPLOSIVE, N.O.S.	1.4G			178 274	0	E0	P101			
0354	ARTICLES, EXPLOSIVE, N.O.S.	1.1L			178 274	0	E0	P101			
0355	ARTICLES, EXPLOSIVE, N.O.S.	1.2L			178 274	0	E0	P101			
0356	ARTICLES, EXPLOSIVE, N.O.S.	1.3L			178 274	0	E0	P101			
0357	SUBSTANCES, EXPLOSIVE, N.O.S.	1.1L			178 274	0	E0	P101			
0358	SUBSTANCES, EXPLOSIVE, N.O.S.	1.2L			178 274	0	E0	P101			

UN No.	Name and description	Class or division	Subsidiary hazard	UN packing group	Special provisions	Limited and excepted quantities		Packagings and IBCs		Portable tanks and bulk containers	
								Packing instruction	Special packing provisions	Instructions	Special provisions
(1)	(2)	(3)	(4)	(5)	(6)	(7a)	(7b)	(8)	(9)	(10)	(11)
-	3.1.2	2.0	2.0	2.0.1.3	3.3	3.4	3.5	4.1.4	4.1.4	4.2.5 / 4.3.2	4.2.5
0359	SUBSTANCES, EXPLOSIVE, N.O.S.	1.3L			178 274	0	E0	P101			
0360	DETONATOR ASSEMBLIES, NON-ELECTRIC for blasting†	1.1B				0	E0	P131			
0361	DETONATOR ASSEMBLIES, NON-ELECTRIC for blasting†	1.4B				0	E0	P131			
0362	AMMUNITION, PRACTICE†	1.4G				0	E0	P130 LP101	PP67 L1		
0363	AMMUNITION, PROOF†	1.4G				0	E0	P130 LP101	PP67 L1		
0364	DETONATORS FOR AMMUNITION†	1.2B				0	E0	P133			
0365	DETONATORS FOR AMMUNITION†	1.4B				0	E0	P133			
0366	DETONATORS FOR AMMUNITION†	1.4S			347	0	E0	P133			
0367	FUZES, DETONATING†	1.4S			347	0	E0	P141			
0368	FUZES, IGNITING†	1.4S				0	E0	P141			
0369	WARHEADS, ROCKET with bursting charge†	1.1F				0	E0	P130 LP101			
0370	WARHEADS, ROCKET with burster or expelling charge†	1.4D				0	E0	P130 LP101	PP67 L1		
0371	WARHEADS, ROCKET with burster or expelling charge†	1.4F				0	E0	P130 LP101			
0372	GRENADES, PRACTICE, hand or rifle†	1.2G				0	E0	P141			
0373	SIGNAL DEVICES, HAND†	1.4S				0	E0	P135			
0374	SOUNDING DEVICES, EXPLOSIVE†	1.1D				0	E0	P134 LP102			
0375	SOUNDING DEVICES, EXPLOSIVE†	1.2D				0	E0	P134 LP102			
0376	PRIMERS, TUBULAR†	1.4S				0	E0	P133			
0377	PRIMERS, CAP TYPE†	1.1B				0	E0	P133			
0378	PRIMERS, CAP TYPE†	1.4B				0	E0	P133			
0379	CASES, CARTRIDGE, EMPTY, WITH PRIMER†	1.4C				0	E0	P136			
0380	ARTICLES, PYROPHORIC†	1.2L				0	E0	P101			
0381	CARTRIDGES, POWER DEVICE†	1.2C				0	E0	P134 LP102			
0382	COMPONENTS, EXPLOSIVE TRAIN, N.O.S.†	1.2B			178 274	0	E0	P101			
0383	COMPONENTS, EXPLOSIVE TRAIN, N.O.S.†	1.4B			178 274	0	E0	P101			
0384	COMPONENTS, EXPLOSIVE TRAIN, N.O.S.†	1.4S			178 274 347	0	E0	P101			
0385	5-NITROBENZOTRIAZOL†	1.1D				0	E0	P112(b) P112(c)			
0386	TRINITROBENZENE-SULPHONIC ACID†	1.1D				0	E0	P112(b) P112(c)	PP26		
0387	TRINITROFLUORENONE†	1.1D				0	E0	P112(b) P112(c)			
0388	TRINITROTOLUENE (TNT) AND TRINITROBENZENE MIXTURE or TRINITROTOLUENE (TNT) AND HEXANITROSTILBENE MIXTURE†	1.1D				0	E0	P112(b) P112(c)			

UN No.	Name and description	Class or division	Subsidiary hazard	UN packing group	Special provisions	Limited and excepted quantities		Packagings and IBCs		Portable tanks and bulk containers	
								Packing instruction	Special packing provisions	Instructions	Special provisions
(1)	(2)	(3)	(4)	(5)	(6)	(7a)	(7b)	(8)	(9)	(10)	(11)
-	3.1.2	2.0	2.0	2.0.1.3	3.3	3.4	3.5	4.1.4	4.1.4	4.2.5 / 4.3.2	4.2.5
0389	TRINITROTOLUENE (TNT) MIXTURE CONTAINING TRINITROBENZENE AND HEXANITROSTILBENE†	1.1D				0	E0	P112(b) P112(c)			
0390	TRITONAL†	1.1D				0	E0	P112(b) P112(c)			
0391	CYCLOTRIMETHYLENE-TRINITRAMINE (CYCLONITE; HEXOGEN; RDX) AND CYCLOTETRAMETHYLENE-TETRANITRAMINE (HMX; OCTOGEN) MIXTURE, WETTED with not less than 15 % water, by mass or CYCLOTRIMETHYLENE-TRINITRAMINE (CYCLONITE; HEXOGEN; RDX) AND CYCLOTETRAMETHYLENE-TETRANITRAMINE (HMX; OCTOGEN) MIXTURE, DESENSITIZED with not less than 10 % phlegmatizer, by mass†	1.1D			266	0	E0	P112(a) P112(b)			
0392	HEXANITROSTILBENE†	1.1D				0	E0	P112(b) P112(c)			
0393	HEXOTONAL†	1.1D				0	E0	P112(b)			
0394	TRINITRORESORCINOL (STYPHNIC ACID), WETTED with not less than 20 % water, or mixture of alcohol and water, by mass†	1.1D				0	E0	P112(a)	PP26		
0395	ROCKET MOTORS, LIQUID FUELLED†	1.2J				0	E0	P101			
0396	ROCKET MOTORS, LIQUID FUELLED†	1.3J				0	E0	P101			
0397	ROCKETS, LIQUID FUELLED with bursting charge†	1.1J				0	E0	P101			
0398	ROCKETS, LIQUID FUELLED with bursting charge†	1.2J				0	E0	P101			
0399	BOMBS WITH FLAMMABLE LIQUID with bursting charge†	1.1J				0	E0	P101			
0400	BOMBS WITH FLAMMABLE LIQUID with bursting charge†	1.2J				0	E0	P101			
0401	DIPICRYL SULPHIDE, dry or wetted with less than 10 % water, by mass†	1.1D				0	E0	P112(a) P112(b) P112(c)			
0402	AMMONIUM PERCHLORATE†	1.1D			152	0	E0	P112(b) P112(c)			
0403	FLARES, AERIAL†	1.4G				0	E0	P135			
0404	FLARES, AERIAL†	1.4S				0	E0	P135			
0405	CARTRIDGES, SIGNAL†	1.4S				0	E0	P135			
0406	DINITROSOBENZENE†	1.3C				0	E0	P114(b)			
0407	TETRAZOL-1-ACETIC ACID†	1.4C				0	E0	P114(b)			
0408	FUZES, DETONATING with protective features†	1.1D				0	E0	P141			
0409	FUZES, DETONATING with protective features†	1.2D				0	E0	P141			
0410	FUZES, DETONATING with protective features†	1.4D				0	E0	P141			

UN No.	Name and description	Class or division	Subsidiary hazard	UN packing group	Special provisions	Limited and excepted quantities		Packagings and IBCs		Portable tanks and bulk containers	
								Packing instruction	Special packing provisions	Instructions	Special provisions
(1)	(2)	(3)	(4)	(5)	(6)	(7a)	(7b)	(8)	(9)	(10)	(11)
-	3.1.2	2.0	2.0	2.0.1.3	3.3	3.4	3.5	4.1.4	4.1.4	4.2.5 / 4.3.2	4.2.5
0411	PENTAERYTHRITE TETRANITRATE (PENTAERYTHRITOL TETRANITRATE; PETN) with not less than 7 % wax, by mass†	1.1D			131	0	E0	P112(b) P112(c)			
0412	CARTRIDGES FOR WEAPONS with bursting charge†	1.4E				0	E0	P130 LP101	PP67 L1		
0413	CARTRIDGES FOR WEAPONS, BLANK†	1.2C				0	E0	P130 LP101			
0414	CHARGES, PROPELLING, FOR CANNON†	1.2C				0	E0	P130 LP101			
0415	CHARGES, PROPELLING†	1.2C				0	E0	P143	PP76		
0417	CARTRIDGES FOR WEAPONS, INERT PROJECTILE or CARTRIDGES, SMALL ARMS†	1.3C				0	E0	P130 LP101			
0418	FLARES, SURFACE†	1.1G				0	E0	P135			
0419	FLARES, SURFACE†	1.2G				0	E0	P135			
0420	FLARES, AERIAL†	1.1G				0	E0	P135			
0421	FLARES, AERIAL†	1.2G				0	E0	P135			
0424	PROJECTILES, inert with tracer†	1.3G				0	E0	P130 LP101	PP67 L1		
0425	PROJECTILES, inert with tracer†	1.4G				0	E0	P130 LP101	PP67 L1		
0426	PROJECTILES with burster or expelling charge†	1.2F				0	E0	P130 LP101			
0427	PROJECTILES with burster or expelling charge†	1.4F				0	E0	P130 LP101			
0428	ARTICLES, PYROTECHNIC for technical purposes†	1.1G				0	E0	P135			
0429	ARTICLES, PYROTECHNIC for technical purposes†	1.2G				0	E0	P135			
0430	ARTICLES, PYROTECHNIC for technical purposes†	1.3G				0	E0	P135			
0431	ARTICLES, PYROTECHNIC for technical purposes†	1.4G				0	E0	P135			
0432	ARTICLES, PYROTECHNIC for technical purposes†	1.4S				0	E0	P135			
0433	POWDER CAKE (POWDER PASTE), WETTED with not less than 17 % alcohol, by mass†	1.1C			266	0	E0	P111			
0434	PROJECTILES with burster or expelling charge†	1.2G				0	E0	P130 LP101	PP67 L1		
0435	PROJECTILES with burster or expelling charge†	1.4G				0	E0	P130 LP101	PP67 L1		
0436	ROCKETS with expelling charge†	1.2C				0	E0	P130 LP101	PP67 L1		
0437	ROCKETS with expelling charge†	1.3C				0	E0	P130 LP101	PP67 L1		
0438	ROCKETS with expelling charge†	1.4C				0	E0	P130 LP101	PP67 L1		
0439	CHARGES, SHAPED, without detonator†	1.2D				0	E0	P137	PP70		
0440	CHARGES, SHAPED, without detonator†	1.4D				0	E0	P137	PP70		
0441	CHARGES, SHAPED, without detonator†	1.4S			347	0	E0	P137	PP70		
0442	CHARGES, EXPLOSIVE, COMMERCIAL without detonator†	1.1D				0	E0	P137			

UN No.	Name and description	Class or division	Subsidiary hazard	UN packing group	Special provisions	Limited and excepted quantities		Packagings and IBCs		Portable tanks and bulk containers	
								Packing instruction	Special packing provisions	Instructions	Special provisions
(1)	(2)	(3)	(4)	(5)	(6)	(7a)	(7b)	(8)	(9)	(10)	(11)
-	3.1.2	2.0	2.0	2.0.1.3	3.3	3.4	3.5	4.1.4	4.1.4	4.2.5 / 4.3.2	4.2.5
0443	CHARGES, EXPLOSIVE, COMMERCIAL without detonator†	1.2D				0	E0	P137			
0444	CHARGES, EXPLOSIVE, COMMERCIAL without detonator†	1.4D				0	E0	P137			
0445	CHARGES, EXPLOSIVE, COMMERCIAL without detonator†	1.4S			347	0	E0	P137			
0446	CASES, COMBUSTIBLE, EMPTY, WITHOUT PRIMER†	1.4C				0	E0	P136			
0447	CASES, COMBUSTIBLE, EMPTY, WITHOUT PRIMER†	1.3C				0	E0	P136			
0448	5-MERCAPTOTETRAZOL-1-ACETIC ACID†	1.4C				0	E0	P114(b)			
0449	TORPEDOES, LIQUID FUELLED with or without bursting charge†	1.1J				0	E0	P101			
0450	TORPEDOES, LIQUID FUELLED with inert head†	1.3J				0	E0	P101			
0451	TORPEDOES with bursting charge†	1.1D				0	E0	P130 LP101	PP67 L1		
0452	GRENADES, PRACTICE, hand or rifle†	1.4G				0	E0	P141			
0453	ROCKETS, LINE-THROWING†	1.4G				0	E0	P130 LP101			
0454	IGNITERS†	1.4S				0	E0	P142			
0455	DETONATORS, NON-ELECTRIC for blasting†	1.4S			347	0	E0	P131	PP68		
0456	DETONATORS, ELECTRIC for blasting†	1.4S			347 399	0	E0	P131			
0457	CHARGES, BURSTING, PLASTICS BONDED	1.1D				0	E0	P130 LP101			
0458	CHARGES, BURSTING, PLASTICS BONDED	1.2D				0	E0	P130 LP101			
0459	CHARGES, BURSTING, PLASTICS BONDED	1.4D				0	E0	P130 LP101			
0460	CHARGES, BURSTING, PLASTICS BONDED	1.4S			347	0	E0	P130 LP101			
0461	COMPONENTS, EXPLOSIVE TRAIN, N.O.S.†	1.1B			178 274	0	E0	P101			
0462	ARTICLES, EXPLOSIVE, N.O.S.	1.1C			178 274	0	E0	P101			
0463	ARTICLES, EXPLOSIVE, N.O.S.	1.1D			178 274	0	E0	P101			
0464	ARTICLES, EXPLOSIVE, N.O.S.	1.1E			178 274	0	E0	P101			
0465	ARTICLES, EXPLOSIVE, N.O.S.	1.1F			178 274	0	E0	P101			
0466	ARTICLES, EXPLOSIVE, N.O.S.	1.2C			178 274	0	E0	P101			
0467	ARTICLES, EXPLOSIVE, N.O.S.	1.2D			178 274	0	E0	P101			
0468	ARTICLES, EXPLOSIVE, N.O.S.	1.2E			178 274	0	E0	P101			
0469	ARTICLES, EXPLOSIVE, N.O.S.	1.2F			178 274	0	E0	P101			
0470	ARTICLES, EXPLOSIVE, N.O.S.	1.3C			178 274	0	E0	P101			
0471	ARTICLES, EXPLOSIVE, N.O.S.	1.4E			178 274	0	E0	P101			

UN No.	Name and description	Class or division	Subsidiary hazard	UN packing group	Special provisions	Limited and excepted quantities		Packagings and IBCs		Portable tanks and bulk containers	
						Packing instruction	Special packing provisions	Instructions	Special provisions
(1)	(2)	(3)	(4)	(5)	(6)	(7a)	(7b)	(8)	(9)	(10)	(11)
-	3.1.2	2.0	2.0	2.0.1.3	3.3	3.4	3.5	4.1.4	4.1.4	4.2.5 / 4.3.2	4.2.5
0472	ARTICLES, EXPLOSIVE, N.O.S.	1.4F			178 274	0	E0	P101			
0473	SUBSTANCES, EXPLOSIVE, N.O.S.	1.1A			178 274	0	E0	P101			
0474	SUBSTANCES, EXPLOSIVE, N.O.S.	1.1C			178 274	0	E0	P101			
0475	SUBSTANCES, EXPLOSIVE, N.O.S.	1.1D			178 274	0	E0	P101			
0476	SUBSTANCES, EXPLOSIVE, N.O.S.	1.1G			178 274	0	E0	P101			
0477	SUBSTANCES, EXPLOSIVE, N.O.S.	1.3C			178 274	0	E0	P101			
0478	SUBSTANCES, EXPLOSIVE, N.O.S.	1.3G			178 274	0	E0	P101			
0479	SUBSTANCES, EXPLOSIVE, N.O.S.	1.4C			178 274	0	E0	P101			
0480	SUBSTANCES, EXPLOSIVE, N.O.S.	1.4D			178 274	0	E0	P101			
0481	SUBSTANCES, EXPLOSIVE, N.O.S.	1.4S			178 274 347	0	E0	P101			
0482	SUBSTANCES, EXPLOSIVE, VERY INSENSITIVE (SUBSTANCES, EVI), N.O.S.†	1.5D			178 274	0	E0	P101			
0483	CYCLOTRIMETHYLENE-TRINITRAMINE (CYCLONITE; HEXOGEN; RDX), DESENSITIZED	1.1D				0	E0	P112(b) P112(c)			
0484	CYCLOTETRAMETHYLENE-TETRANITRAMINE (HMX; OCTOGEN), DESENSITIZED	1.1D				0	E0	P112(b) P112(c)			
0485	SUBSTANCES, EXPLOSIVE, N.O.S.	1.4G			178 274	0	E0	P101			
0486	ARTICLES, EXPLOSIVE, EXTREMELY INSENSITIVE (ARTICLES, EEI)†	1.6N				0	E0	P101			
0487	SIGNALS, SMOKE†	1.3G				0	E0	P135			
0488	AMMUNITION, PRACTICE†	1.3G				0	E0	P130 LP101	PP67 L1		
0489	DINITROGLYCOLURIL (DINGU)†	1.1D				0	E0	P112(b) P112(c)			
0490	NITROTRIAZOLONE (NTO)†	1.1D				0	E0	P112(b) P112(c)			
0491	CHARGES, PROPELLING†	1.4C				0	E0	P143	PP76		
0492	SIGNALS, RAILWAY TRACK, EXPLOSIVE†	1.3G				0	E0	P135			
0493	SIGNALS, RAILWAY TRACK, EXPLOSIVE†	1.4G				0	E0	P135			
0494	JET PERFORATING GUNS, CHARGED, oil well, without detonator†	1.4D				0	E0	P101			
0495	PROPELLANT, LIQUID†	1.3C			224	0	E0	P115	PP53 PP54 PP57 PP58		
0496	OCTONAL	1.1D				0	E0	P112(b) P112(c)			

UN No.	Name and description	Class or division	Subsidiary hazard	UN packing group	Special provisions	Limited and excepted quantities		Packagings and IBCs		Portable tanks and bulk containers	
						Packing instruction	Special packing provisions	Instructions	Special provisions
(1)	(2)	(3)	(4)	(5)	(6)	(7a)	(7b)	(8)	(9)	(10)	(11)
-	3.1.2	2.0	2.0	2.0.1.3	3.3	3.4	3.5	4.1.4	4.1.4	4.2.5 / 4.3.2	4.2.5
0497	PROPELLANT, LIQUID†	1.1C			224	0	E0	P115	PP53 PP54 PP57 PP58		
0498	PROPELLANT, SOLID†	1.1C				0	E0	P114(b)			
0499	PROPELLANT, SOLID†	1.3C				0	E0	P114(b)			
0500	DETONATOR ASSEMBLIES, NON-ELECTRIC for blasting†	1.4S			347	0	E0	P131			
0501	PROPELLANT, SOLID†	1.4C				0	E0	P114(b)			
0502	ROCKETS with inert head†	1.2C				0	E0	P130 LP101	PP67 L1		
0503	SAFETY DEVICES, PYROTECHNIC†	1.4G			235 289	0	E0	P135			
0504	1H-TETRAZOLE	1.1D				0	E0	P112(c)	PP48		
0505	SIGNALS, DISTRESS, ship†	1.4G				0	E0	P135			
0506	SIGNALS, DISTRESS, ship†	1.4S				0	E0	P135			
0507	SIGNALS, SMOKE†	1.4S				0	E0	P135			
0508	1-HYDROXYBENZOTRIAZOLE, ANHYDROUS, dry or wetted with less than 20 % water, by mass	1.3C				0	E0	P114(b)	PP48 PP50		
0509	POWDER, SMOKELESS†	1.4C				0	E0	P114(b)	PP48		
0510	ROCKET MOTORS†	1.4C				0	E0	P130 LP101	PP67 L1		
0511	DETONATORS, ELECTRONIC programmable for blasting†	1.1B			399	0	E0	P131			
0512	DETONATORS, ELECTRONIC programmable for blasting†	1.4B			399	0	E0	P131			
0513	DETONATORS, ELECTRONIC programmable for blasting†	1.4S			347 399	0	E0	P131			
0514	FIRE SUPPRESSANT DISPERSING DEVICES†	1.4S			407	0	E0	P135			
1001	ACETYLENE, DISSOLVED	2.1				0	E0	P200			
1002	AIR, COMPRESSED	2.2			392 397	120 ml	E1	P200			
1003	AIR, REFRIGERATED LIQUID	2.2	5.1			0	E0	P203		T75	TP5 TP22
1005	AMMONIA, ANHYDROUS	2.3	8		23 379	0	E0	P200		T50	
1006	ARGON, COMPRESSED	2.2			378 392 406	120 ml	E1	P200			
1008	BORON TRIFLUORIDE	2.3	8		373	0	E0	P200			
1009	BROMOTRIFLUOROMETHANE (REFRIGERANT GAS R 13B1)	2.2				120 ml	E1	P200		T50	
1010	BUTADIENES, STABILIZED or BUTADIENES AND HYDROCARBON MIXTURE, STABILIZED, containing more than 20 % butadienes	2.1			386 402	0	E0	P200		T50	
1011	BUTANE	2.1			392	0	E0	P200		T50	
1012	BUTYLENE	2.1			398	0	E0	P200		T50	
1013	CARBON DIOXIDE	2.2			378 392 406	120 ml	E1	P200			
1016	CARBON MONOXIDE, COMPRESSED	2.3	2.1			0	E0	P200			

UN No.	Name and description	Class or division	Subsidiary hazard	UN packing group	Special provisions	Limited and excepted quantities		Packagings and IBCs		Portable tanks and bulk containers	
								Packing instruction	Special packing provisions	Instructions	Special provisions
(1)	(2)	(3)	(4)	(5)	(6)	(7a)	(7b)	(8)	(9)	(10)	(11)
-	3.1.2	2.0	2.0	2.0.1.3	3.3	3.4	3.5	4.1.4	4.1.4	4.2.5 / 4.3.2	4.2.5
1017	CHLORINE	2.3	5.1 8			0	E0	P200		T50	TP19
1018	CHLORODIFLUOROMETHANE (REFRIGERANT GAS R 22)	2.2				120 ml	E1	P200		T50	
1020	CHLOROPENTAFLUORO-ETHANE (REFRIGERANT GAS R 115)	2.2				120 ml	E1	P200		T50	
1021	1-CHLORO-1,2,2,2-TETRAFLUOROETHANE (REFRIGERANT GAS R 124)	2.2				120 ml	E1	P200		T50	
1022	CHLOROTRIFLUORO-METHANE (REFRIGERANT GAS R 13)	2.2				120 ml	E1	P200			
1023	COAL GAS, COMPRESSED	2.3	2.1			0	E0	P200			
1026	CYANOGEN	2.3	2.1			0	E0	P200			
1027	CYCLOPROPANE	2.1				0	E0	P200		T50	
1028	DICHLORODIFLUORO-METHANE (REFRIGERANT GAS R 12)	2.2				120 ml	E1	P200		T50	
1029	DICHLOROFLUOROMETHANE (REFRIGERANT GAS R 21)	2.2				120 ml	E1	P200		T50	
1030	1,1-DIFLUOROETHANE (REFRIGERANT GAS R 152a)	2.1				0	E0	P200		T50	
1032	DIMETHYLAMINE, ANHYDROUS	2.1				0	E0	P200		T50	
1033	DIMETHYL ETHER	2.1				0	E0	P200		T50	
1035	ETHANE	2.1				0	E0	P200			
1036	ETHYLAMINE	2.1				0	E0	P200		T50	
1037	ETHYL CHLORIDE	2.1				0	E0	P200		T50	
1038	ETHYLENE, REFRIGERATED LIQUID	2.1				0	E0	P203		T75	TP5
1039	ETHYL METHYL ETHER	2.1				0	E0	P200			
1040	ETHYLENE OXIDE, or ETHYLENE OXIDE WITH NITROGEN up to a total pressure of 1 MPa (10 bar) at 50 °C	2.3	2.1		342	0	E0	P200		T50	TP20
1041	ETHYLENE OXIDE AND CARBON DIOXIDE MIXTURE with more than 9 % but not more than 87 % ethylene oxide	2.1				0	E0	P200		T50	
1043	FERTILIZER AMMONIATING SOLUTION with free ammonia	2.2				120 ml	E0	P200			
1044	FIRE EXTINGUISHERS with compressed or liquefied gas	2.2			225	120 ml	E0	P003	PP91		
1045	FLUORINE, COMPRESSED	2.3	5.1 8			0	E0	P200			
1046	HELIUM, COMPRESSED	2.2			378 392 406	120 ml	E1	P200			
1048	HYDROGEN BROMIDE, ANHYDROUS	2.3	8			0	E0	P200			
1049	HYDROGEN, COMPRESSED	2.1			392	0	E0	P200			
1050	HYDROGEN CHLORIDE, ANHYDROUS	2.3	8			0	E0	P200			
1051	HYDROGEN CYANIDE, STABILIZED containing less than 3 % water	6.1	3	I	386	0	E0	P200			

UN No.	Name and description	Class or division	Subsidiary hazard	UN packing group	Special provisions	Limited and excepted quantities		Packagings and IBCs		Portable tanks and bulk containers	
								Packing instruction	Special packing provisions	Instructions	Special provisions
(1)	(2)	(3)	(4)	(5)	(6)	(7a)	(7b)	(8)	(9)	(10)	(11)
-	3.1.2	2.0	2.0	2.0.1.3	3.3	3.4	3.5	4.1.4	4.1.4	4.2.5 / 4.3.2	4.2.5
1052	HYDROGEN FLUORIDE, ANHYDROUS	8	6.1	I		0	E0	P200		T10	TP2
1053	HYDROGEN SULPHIDE	2.3	2.1			0	E0	P200			
1055	ISOBUTYLENE	2.1				0	E0	P200		T50	
1056	KRYPTON, COMPRESSED	2.2			378 392	120 ml	E1	P200			
1057	LIGHTERS or LIGHTER REFILLS containing flammable gas	2.1			201	0	E0	P002	PP84		
1058	LIQUEFIED GASES, non-flammable, charged with nitrogen, carbon dioxide or air	2.2			392	120 ml	E1	P200			
1060	METHYLACETYLENE AND PROPADIENE MIXTURE, STABILIZED	2.1			386	0	E0	P200		T50	
1061	METHYLAMINE, ANHYDROUS	2.1				0	E0	P200		T50	
1062	METHYL BROMIDE with not more than 2 % chloropicrin	2.3			23	0	E0	P200		T50	
1063	METHYL CHLORIDE (REFRIGERANT GAS R 40)	2.1				0	E0	P200		T50	
1064	METHYL MERCAPTAN	2.3	2.1			0	E0	P200		T50	
1065	NEON, COMPRESSED	2.2			378 392	120 ml	E1	P200			
1066	NITROGEN, COMPRESSED	2.2			378 392 406	120 ml	E1	P200			
1067	DINITROGEN TETROXIDE (NITROGEN DIOXIDE)	2.3	5.1 8			0	E0	P200		T50	TP21
1069	NITROSYL CHLORIDE	2.3	8			0	E0	P200			
1070	NITROUS OXIDE	2.2	5.1			0	E0	P200			
1071	OIL GAS, COMPRESSED	2.3	2.1			0	E0	P200			
1072	OXYGEN, COMPRESSED	2.2	5.1		355	0	E0	P200			
1073	OXYGEN, REFRIGERATED LIQUID	2.2	5.1			0	E0	P203		T75	TP5 TP22
1075	PETROLEUM GASES, LIQUEFIED	2.1			392	0	E0	P200		T50	
1076	PHOSGENE	2.3	8			0	E0	P200			
1077	PROPYLENE	2.1				0	E0	P200		T50	
1078	REFRIGERANT GAS, N.O.S.	2.2			274	120 ml	E1	P200		T50	
1079	SULPHUR DIOXIDE	2.3	8			0	E0	P200		T50	TP19
1080	SULPHUR HEXAFLUORIDE	2.2			392	120 ml	E1	P200			
1081	TETRAFLUOROETHYLENE, STABILIZED	2.1			386	0	E0	P200			
1082	TRIFLUOROCHLORO-ETHYLENE, STABILIZED (REFRIGERANT GAS R 1113)	2.3	2.1		386	0	E0	P200		T50	
1083	TRIMETHYLAMINE, ANHYDROUS	2.1				0	E0	P200		T50	
1085	VINYL BROMIDE, STABILIZED	2.1			386	0	E0	P200		T50	
1086	VINYL CHLORIDE, STABILIZED	2.1			386	0	E0	P200		T50	
1087	VINYL METHYL ETHER, STABILIZED	2.1			386	0	E0	P200		T50	
1088	ACETAL	3		II		1 L	E2	P001 IBC02		T4	TP1
1089	ACETALDEHYDE	3		I		0	E0	P001		T11	TP2 TP7

UN No.	Name and description	Class or division	Subsidiary hazard	UN packing group	Special provisions	Limited and excepted quantities		Packagings and IBCs		Portable tanks and bulk containers	
								Packing instruction	Special packing provisions	Instructions	Special provisions
(1)	(2)	(3)	(4)	(5)	(6)	(7a)	(7b)	(8)	(9)	(10)	(11)
-	3.1.2	2.0	2.0	2.0.1.3	3.3	3.4	3.5	4.1.4	4.1.4	4.2.5 / 4.3.2	4.2.5
1090	ACETONE	3		II		1 L	E2	P001 IBC02		T4	TP1
1091	ACETONE OILS	3		II		1 L	E2	P001 IBC02		T4	TP1 TP8
1092	ACROLEIN, STABILIZED	6.1	3	I	354 386	0	E0	P601		T22	TP2 TP7 TP13
1093	ACRYLONITRILE, STABILIZED	3	6.1	I	386	0	E0	P001		T14	TP2 TP13
1098	ALLYL ALCOHOL	6.1	3	I	354	0	E0	P602		T20	TP2 TP13
1099	ALLYL BROMIDE	3	6.1	I		0	E0	P001		T14	TP2 TP13
1100	ALLYL CHLORIDE	3	6.1	I		0	E0	P001		T14	TP2 TP13
1104	AMYL ACETATES	3		III		5 L	E1	P001 IBC03 LP01		T2	TP1
1105	PENTANOLS	3		II		1 L	E2	P001 IBC02		T4	TP1 TP29
1105	PENTANOLS	3		III	223	5 L	E1	P001 IBC03 LP01		T2	TP1
1106	AMYLAMINE	3	8	II		1 L	E2	P001 IBC02		T7	TP1
1106	AMYLAMINE	3	8	III	223	5 L	E1	P001 IBC03		T4	TP1
1107	AMYL CHLORIDE	3		II		1 L	E2	P001 IBC02		T4	TP1
1108	1-PENTENE (n-AMYLENE)	3		I		0	E3	P001		T11	TP2
1109	AMYL FORMATES	3		III		5 L	E1	P001 IBC03 LP01		T2	TP1
1110	n-AMYL METHYL KETONE	3		III		5 L	E1	P001 IBC03 LP01		T2	TP1
1111	AMYL MERCAPTAN	3		II		1 L	E2	P001 IBC02		T4	TP1
1112	AMYL NITRATE	3		III		5 L	E1	P001 IBC03 LP01		T2	TP1
1113	AMYL NITRITE	3		II		1 L	E2	P001 IBC02		T4	TP1
1114	BENZENE	3		II		1 L	E2	P001 IBC02		T4	TP1
1120	BUTANOLS	3		II		1 L	E2	P001 IBC02		T4	TP1 TP29
1120	BUTANOLS	3		III	223	5 L	E1	P001 IBC03 LP01		T2	TP1
1123	BUTYL ACETATES	3		II		1 L	E2	P001 IBC02		T4	TP1
1123	BUTYL ACETATES	3		III	223	5 L	E1	P001 IBC03 LP01		T2	TP1
1125	n-BUTYLAMINE	3	8	II		1 L	E2	P001 IBC02		T7	TP1
1126	1-BROMOBUTANE	3		II		1 L	E2	P001 IBC02		T4	TP1

UN No.	Name and description	Class or division	Subsi-diary hazard	UN packing group	Special provi-sions	Limited and excepted quantities		Packagings and IBCs		Portable tanks and bulk containers	
								Packing instruction	Special packing provisions	Instruc-tions	Special provisions
(1)	(2)	(3)	(4)	(5)	(6)	(7a)	(7b)	(8)	(9)	(10)	(11)
-	3.1.2	2.0	2.0	2.0.1.3	3.3	3.4	3.5	4.1.4	4.1.4	4.2.5 / 4.3.2	4.2.5
1127	CHLOROBUTANES	3		II		1 L	E2	P001 IBC02		T4	TP1
1128	n-BUTYL FORMATE	3		II		1 L	E2	P001 IBC02		T4	TP1
1129	BUTYRALDEHYDE	3		II		1 L	E2	P001 IBC02		T4	TP1
1130	CAMPHOR OIL	3		III		5 L	E1	P001 IBC03 LP01		T2	TP1
1131	CARBON DISULPHIDE	3	6.1	I		0	E0	P001	PP31	T14	TP2 TP7 TP13
1133	ADHESIVES containing flammable liquid	3		I		500 ml	E3	P001		T11	TP1 TP8 TP27
1133	ADHESIVES containing flammable liquid	3		II		5 L	E2	P001 IBC02	PP1	T4	TP1 TP8
1133	ADHESIVES containing flammable liquid	3		III	223	5 L	E1	P001 IBC03 LP01	PP1	T2	TP1
1134	CHLOROBENZENE	3		III		5 L	E1	P001 IBC03 LP01		T2	TP1
1135	ETHYLENE CHLOROHYDRIN	6.1	3	I	354	0	E0	P602		T20	TP2 TP13
1136	COAL TAR DISTILLATES, FLAMMABLE	3		II		1 L	E2	P001 IBC02		T4	TP1
1136	COAL TAR DISTILLATES, FLAMMABLE	3		III	223	5 L	E1	P001 IBC03 LP01		T4	TP1 TP29
1139	COATING SOLUTION (includes surface treatments or coatings used for industrial or other purposes such as vehicle undercoating, drum or barrel lining)	3		I		500 ml	E3	P001		T11	TP1 TP8 TP27
1139	COATING SOLUTION (includes surface treatments or coatings used for industrial or other purposes such as vehicle undercoating, drum or barrel lining)	3		II		5 L	E2	P001 IBC02		T4	TP1 TP8
1139	COATING SOLUTION (includes surface treatments or coatings used for industrial or other purposes such as vehicle undercoating, drum or barrel lining)	3		III	223	5 L	E1	P001 IBC03 LP01		T2	TP1
1143	CROTONALDEHYDE or CROTONALDEHYDE, STABILIZED	6.1	3	I	324 354 386	0	E0	P602		T20	TP2 TP13
1144	CROTONYLENE	3		I		0	E3	P001		T11	TP2
1145	CYCLOHEXANE	3		II		1 L	E2	P001 IBC02		T4	TP1
1146	CYCLOPENTANE	3		II		1 L	E2	P001 IBC02		T7	TP1
1147	DECAHYDRONAPHTHALENE	3		III		5 L	E1	P001 IBC03 LP01		T2	TP1
1148	DIACETONE ALCOHOL	3		II		1 L	E2	P001 IBC02		T4	TP1
1148	DIACETONE ALCOHOL	3		III	223	5 L	E1	P001 IBC03 LP01		T2	TP1

UN No.	Name and description	Class or division	Subsidiary hazard	UN packing group	Special provisions	Limited and excepted quantities		Packagings and IBCs		Portable tanks and bulk containers	
								Packing instruction	Special packing provisions	Instructions	Special provisions
(1)	(2)	(3)	(4)	(5)	(6)	(7a)	(7b)	(8)	(9)	(10)	(11)
-	3.1.2	2.0	2.0	2.0.1.3	3.3	3.4	3.5	4.1.4	4.1.4	4.2.5 / 4.3.2	4.2.5
1149	DIBUTYL ETHERS	3		III		5 L	E1	P001 IBC03 LP01		T2	TP1
1150	1,2-DICHLOROETHYLENE	3		II		1 L	E2	P001 IBC02		T7	TP2
1152	DICHLOROPENTANES	3		III		5 L	E1	P001 IBC03 LP01		T2	TP1
1153	ETHYLENE GLYCOL DIETHYL ETHER	3		II		1 L	E2	P001 IBC02		T4	TP1
1153	ETHYLENE GLYCOL DIETHYL ETHER	3		III		5 L	E1	P001 IBC03 LP01		T2	TP1
1154	DIETHYLAMINE	3	8	II		1 L	E2	P001 IBC02		T7	TP1
1155	DIETHYL ETHER (ETHYL ETHER)	3		I		0	E3	P001		T11	TP2
1156	DIETHYL KETONE	3		II		1 L	E2	P001 IBC02		T4	TP1
1157	DIISOBUTYL KETONE	3		III		5 L	E1	P001 IBC03 LP01		T2	TP1
1158	DIISOPROPYLAMINE	3	8	II		1 L	E2	P001 IBC02		T7	TP1
1159	DIISOPROPYL ETHER	3		II		1 L	E2	P001 IBC02		T4	TP1
1160	DIMETHYLAMINE AQUEOUS SOLUTION	3	8	II		1 L	E2	P001 IBC02		T7	TP1
1161	DIMETHYL CARBONATE	3		II		1 L	E2	P001 IBC02		T4	TP1
1162	DIMETHYLDICHLOROSILANE	3	8	II		0	E0	P010		T10	TP2 TP7 TP13
1163	DIMETHYLHYDRAZINE, UNSYMMETRICAL	6.1	3 8	I	354	0	E0	P602		T20	TP2 TP13
1164	DIMETHYL SULPHIDE	3		II		1 L	E2	P001 IBC02	B8	T7	TP2
1165	DIOXANE	3		II		1 L	E2	P001 IBC02		T4	TP1
1166	DIOXOLANE	3		II		1 L	E2	P001 IBC02		T4	TP1
1167	DIVINYL ETHER, STABILIZED	3		I	386	0	E3	P001		T11	TP2
1170	ETHANOL (ETHYL ALCOHOL) or ETHANOL SOLUTION (ETHYL ALCOHOL SOLUTION)	3		II	144	1 L	E2	P001 IBC02		T4	TP1
1170	ETHANOL (ETHYL ALCOHOL) or ETHANOL SOLUTION (ETHYL ALCOHOL SOLUTION)	3		III	144 223	5 L	E1	P001 IBC03 LP01		T2	TP1
1171	ETHYLENE GLYCOL MONOETHYL ETHER	3		III		5 L	E1	P001 IBC03 LP01		T2	TP1
1172	ETHYLENE GLYCOL MONOETHYL ETHER ACETATE	3		III		5 L	E1	P001 IBC03 LP01		T2	TP1
1173	ETHYL ACETATE	3		II		1 L	E2	P001 IBC02		T4	TP1
1175	ETHYLBENZENE	3		II		1 L	E2	P001 IBC02		T4	TP1

UN No.	Name and description	Class or division	Subsidiary hazard	UN packing group	Special provisions	Limited and excepted quantities		Packagings and IBCs		Portable tanks and bulk containers	
						Packing instruction	Special packing provisions	Instructions	Special provisions
(1)	(2)	(3)	(4)	(5)	(6)	(7a)	(7b)	(8)	(9)	(10)	(11)
-	3.1.2	2.0	2.0	2.0.1.3	3.3	3.4	3.5	4.1.4	4.1.4	4.2.5 / 4.3.2	4.2.5
1176	ETHYL BORATE	3		II		1 L	E2	P001 IBC02		T4	TP1
1177	2-ETHYLBUTYL ACETATE	3		III		5 L	E1	P001 IBC03 LP01		T2	TP1
1178	2-ETHYLBUTYRALDEHYDE	3		II		1 L	E2	P001 IBC02		T4	TP1
1179	ETHYL BUTYL ETHER	3		II		1 L	E2	P001 IBC02		T4	TP1
1180	ETHYL BUTYRATE	3		III		5 L	E1	P001 IBC03 LP01		T2	TP1
1181	ETHYL CHLOROACETATE	6.1	3	II		100 ml	E4	P001 IBC02		T7	TP2
1182	ETHYL CHLOROFORMATE	6.1	3 8	I	354	0	E0	P602		T20	TP2 TP13
1183	ETHYLDICHLOROSILANE	4.3	3 8	I		0	E0	P401		T14	TP2 TP7 TP13
1184	ETHYLENE DICHLORIDE	3	6.1	II		1 L	E2	P001 IBC02		T7	TP1
1185	ETHYLENEIMINE, STABILIZED	6.1	3	I	354 386	0	E0	P601		T22	TP2 TP13
1188	ETHYLENE GLYCOL MONOMETHYL ETHER	3		III		5 L	E1	P001 IBC03 LP01		T2	TP1
1189	ETHYLENE GLYCOL MONOMETHYL ETHER ACETATE	3		III		5 L	E1	P001 IBC03 LP01		T2	TP1
1190	ETHYL FORMATE	3		II		1 L	E2	P001 IBC02		T4	TP1
1191	OCTYL ALDEHYDES	3		III		5 L	E1	P001 IBC03 LP01		T2	TP1
1192	ETHYL LACTATE	3		III		5 L	E1	P001 IBC03 LP01		T2	TP1
1193	ETHYL METHYL KETONE (METHYL ETHYL KETONE)	3		II		1 L	E2	P001 IBC02		T4	TP1
1194	ETHYL NITRITE SOLUTION	3	6.1	I		0	E0	P001			
1195	ETHYL PROPIONATE	3		II		1 L	E2	P001 IBC02		T4	TP1
1196	ETHYLTRICHLOROSILANE	3	8	II		0	E0	P010		T10	TP2 TP7 TP13
1197	EXTRACTS, LIQUID, for flavour or aroma	3		II		5 L	E2	P001 IBC02		T4	TP1 TP8
1197	EXTRACTS, LIQUID, for flavour or aroma	3		III	223	5 L	E1	P001 IBC03 LP01		T2	TP1
1198	FORMALDEHYDE SOLUTION, FLAMMABLE	3	8	III		5 L	E1	P001 IBC03		T4	TP1
1199	FURALDEHYDES	6.1	3	II		100 ml	E4	P001 IBC02		T7	TP2
1201	FUSEL OIL	3		II		1 L	E2	P001 IBC02		T4	TP1
1201	FUSEL OIL	3		III	223	5 L	E1	P001 IBC03 LP01		T2	TP1

UN No.	Name and description	Class or division	Subsidiary hazard	UN packing group	Special provisions	Limited and excepted quantities		Packagings and IBCs		Portable tanks and bulk containers	
								Packing instruction	Special packing provisions	Instructions	Special provisions
(1)	(2)	(3)	(4)	(5)	(6)	(7a)	(7b)	(8)	(9)	(10)	(11)
-	3.1.2	2.0	2.0	2.0.1.3	3.3	3.4	3.5	4.1.4	4.1.4	4.2.5 / 4.3.2	4.2.5
1202	GAS OIL or DIESEL FUEL or HEATING OIL, LIGHT	3		III		5 L	E1	P001 IBC03 LP01		T2	TP1
1203	MOTOR SPIRIT or GASOLINE or PETROL	3		II	243	1 L	E2	P001 IBC02		T4	TP1
1204	NITROGLYCERIN SOLUTION IN ALCOHOL with not more than 1 % nitroglycerin	3		II	28	1 L	E0	P001 IBC02	PP5		
1206	HEPTANES	3		II		1 L	E2	P001 IBC02		T4	TP1
1207	HEXALDEHYDE	3		III		5 L	E1	P001 IBC03 LP01		T2	TP1
1208	HEXANES	3		II		1 L	E2	P001 IBC02		T4	TP1
1210	PRINTING INK, flammable or PRINTING INK RELATED MATERIAL (including printing ink thinning or reducing compound), flammable	3		I	163 367	500 ml	E3	P001		T11	TP1 TP8
1210	PRINTING INK, flammable or PRINTING INK RELATED MATERIAL (including printing ink thinning or reducing compound), flammable	3		II	163 367	5 L	E2	P001 IBC02	PP1	T4	TP1 TP8
1210	PRINTING INK, flammable or PRINTING INK RELATED MATERIAL (including printing ink thinning or reducing compound), flammable	3		III	163 223 367	5 L	E1	P001 IBC03 LP01	PP1	T2	TP1
1212	ISOBUTANOL (ISOBUTYL ALCOHOL)	3		III		5 L	E1	P001 IBC03 LP01		T2	TP1
1213	ISOBUTYL ACETATE	3		II		1 L	E2	P001 IBC02		T4	TP1
1214	ISOBUTYLAMINE	3	8	II		1 L	E2	P001 IBC02		T7	TP1
1216	ISOOCTENES	3		II		1 L	E2	P001 IBC02		T4	TP1
1218	ISOPRENE, STABILIZED	3		I	386	0	E3	P001		T11	TP2
1219	ISOPROPANOL (ISOPROPYL ALCOHOL)	3		II		1 L	E2	P001 IBC02		T4	TP1
1220	ISOPROPYL ACETATE	3		II		1 L	E2	P001 IBC02		T4	TP1
1221	ISOPROPYLAMINE	3	8	I		0	E0	P001		T11	TP2
1222	ISOPROPYL NITRATE	3		II	26	1 L	E2	P001 IBC02	B7		
1223	KEROSENE	3		III		5 L	E1	P001 IBC03 LP01		T2	TP2
1224	KETONES, LIQUID, N.O.S.	3		II	274	1 L	E2	P001 IBC02		T7	TP1 TP8 TP28
1224	KETONES, LIQUID, N.O.S.	3		III	223 274	5 L	E1	P001 IBC03 LP01		T4	TP1 TP29
1228	MERCAPTANS, LIQUID, FLAMMABLE, TOXIC, N.O.S. or MERCAPTAN MIXTURE, LIQUID, FLAMMABLE, TOXIC, N.O.S.	3	6.1	II	274	1 L	E0	P001 IBC02		T11	TP2 TP27

UN No.	Name and description	Class or division	Subsidiary hazard	UN packing group	Special provisions	Limited and excepted quantities		Packagings and IBCs		Portable tanks and bulk containers	
								Packing instruction	Special packing provisions	Instructions	Special provisions
(1)	(2)	(3)	(4)	(5)	(6)	(7a)	(7b)	(8)	(9)	(10)	(11)
-	3.1.2	2.0	2.0	2.0.1.3	3.3	3.4	3.5	4.1.4	4.1.4	4.2.5 / 4.3.2	4.2.5
1228	MERCAPTANS, LIQUID, FLAMMABLE, TOXIC, N.O.S. or MERCAPTAN MIXTURE, LIQUID, FLAMMABLE, TOXIC, N.O.S.	3	6.1	III	223 274	5 L	E1	P001 IBC03		T7	TP1 TP28
1229	MESITYL OXIDE	3		III		5 L	E1	P001 IBC03 LP01		T2	TP1
1230	METHANOL	3	6.1	II	279	1 L	E2	P001 IBC02		T7	TP2
1231	METHYL ACETATE	3		II		1 L	E2	P001 IBC02		T4	TP1
1233	METHYLAMYL ACETATE	3		III		5 L	E1	P001 IBC03 LP01		T2	TP1
1234	METHYLAL	3		II		1 L	E2	P001 IBC02	B8	T7	TP2
1235	METHYLAMINE, AQUEOUS SOLUTION	3	8	II		1 L	E2	P001 IBC02		T7	TP1
1237	METHYL BUTYRATE	3		II		1 L	E2	P001 IBC02		T4	TP1
1238	METHYL CHLOROFORMATE	6.1	3 8	I	354	0	E0	P602		T22	TP2 TP13
1239	METHYL CHLOROMETHYL ETHER	6.1	3	I	354	0	E0	P602		T22	TP2 TP13
1242	METHYLDICHLOROSILANE	4.3	3 8	I		0	E0	P401		T14	TP2 TP7 TP13
1243	METHYL FORMATE	3		I		0	E3	P001		T11	TP2
1244	METHYLHYDRAZINE	6.1	3 8	I	354	0	E0	P602		T22	TP2 TP13
1245	METHYL ISOBUTYL KETONE	3		II		1 L	E2	P001 IBC02		T4	TP1
1246	METHYL ISOPROPENYL KETONE, STABILIZED	3		II	386	1 L	E2	P001 IBC02		T4	TP1
1247	METHYL METHACRYLATE MONOMER, STABILIZED	3		II	386	1 L	E2	P001 IBC02		T4	TP1
1248	METHYL PROPIONATE	3		II		1 L	E2	P001 IBC02		T4	TP1
1249	METHYL PROPYL KETONE	3		II		1 L	E2	P001 IBC02		T4	TP1
1250	METHYLTRICHLOROSILANE	3	8	II		0	E0	P010		T10	TP2 TP7 TP13
1251	METHYL VINYL KETONE, STABILIZED	6.1	3 8	I	354 386	0	E0	P601		T22	TP2 TP13
1259	NICKEL CARBONYL	6.1	3	I		0	E0	P601			
1261	NITROMETHANE	3		II	26	1 L	E0	P001			
1262	OCTANES	3		II		1 L	E2	P001 IBC02		T4	TP1
1263	PAINT (including paint, lacquer, enamel, stain, shellac, varnish, polish, liquid filler and liquid lacquer base) or PAINT RELATED MATERIAL (including paint thinning or reducing compound)	3		I	163 367	500 ml	E3	P001		T11	TP1 TP8 TP27

UN No.	Name and description	Class or division	Subsidiary hazard	UN packing group	Special provisions	Limited and excepted quantities		Packagings and IBCs		Portable tanks and bulk containers	
								Packing instruction	Special packing provisions	Instructions	Special provisions
(1)	(2)	(3)	(4)	(5)	(6)	(7a)	(7b)	(8)	(9)	(10)	(11)
-	3.1.2	2.0	2.0	2.0.1.3	3.3	3.4	3.5	4.1.4	4.1.4	4.2.5 / 4.3.2	4.2.5
1263	PAINT (including paint, lacquer, enamel, stain, shellac, varnish, polish, liquid filler and liquid lacquer base) or PAINT RELATED MATERIAL (including paint thinning or reducing compound)	3		II	163 367	5 L	E2	P001 IBC02	PP1	T4	TP1 TP8 TP28
1263	PAINT (including paint, lacquer, enamel, stain, shellac, varnish, polish, liquid filler and liquid lacquer base) or PAINT RELATED MATERIAL (including paint thinning or reducing compound)	3		III	163 223 367	5 L	E1	P001 IBC03 LP01	PP1	T2	TP1 TP29
1264	PARALDEHYDE	3		III		5 L	E1	P001 IBC03 LP01		T2	TP1
1265	PENTANES, liquid	3		I		0	E3	P001		T11	TP2
1265	PENTANES, liquid	3		II		1 L	E2	P001 IBC02	B8	T4	TP1
1266	PERFUMERY PRODUCTS with flammable solvents	3		II	163	5 L	E2	P001 IBC02		T4	TP1 TP8
1266	PERFUMERY PRODUCTS with flammable solvents	3		III	163 223	5 L	E1	P001 IBC03 LP01		T2	TP1
1267	PETROLEUM CRUDE OIL	3		I	357	500 ml	E3	P001		T11	TP1 TP8
1267	PETROLEUM CRUDE OIL	3		II	357	1 L	E2	P001 IBC02		T4	TP1 TP8
1267	PETROLEUM CRUDE OIL	3		III	223 357	5 L	E1	P001 IBC03 LP01		T2	TP1
1268	PETROLEUM DISTILLATES, N.O.S. or PETROLEUM PRODUCTS, N.O.S.	3		I		500 ml	E3	P001		T11	TP1 TP8
1268	PETROLEUM DISTILLATES, N.O.S. or PETROLEUM PRODUCTS, N.O.S.	3		II		1 L	E2	P001 IBC02		T7	TP1 TP8 TP28
1268	PETROLEUM DISTILLATES, N.O.S. or PETROLEUM PRODUCTS, N.O.S.	3		III	223	5 L	E1	P001 IBC03 LP01		T4	TP1 TP29
1272	PINE OIL	3		III		5 L	E1	P001 IBC03 LP01		T2	TP1
1274	n-PROPANOL (PROPYL ALCOHOL, NORMAL)	3		II		1 L	E2	P001 IBC02		T4	TP1
1274	n-PROPANOL (PROPYL ALCOHOL, NORMAL)	3		III	223	5 L	E1	P001 IBC03 LP01		T2	TP1
1275	PROPIONALDEHYDE	3		II		1 L	E2	P001 IBC02		T7	TP1
1276	n-PROPYL ACETATE	3		II		1 L	E2	P001 IBC02		T4	TP1
1277	PROPYLAMINE	3	8	II		1 L	E2	P001 IBC02		T7	TP1
1278	1-CHLOROPROPANE	3		II		1 L	E0	P001 IBC02	B8	T7	TP2
1279	1,2-DICHLOROPROPANE	3		II		1 L	E2	P001 IBC02		T4	TP1
1280	PROPYLENE OXIDE	3		I		0	E3	P001		T11	TP2 TP7

UN No.	Name and description	Class or division	Subsidiary hazard	UN packing group	Special provisions	Limited and excepted quantities		Packagings and IBCs		Portable tanks and bulk containers	
								Packing instruction	Special packing provisions	Instructions	Special provisions
(1)	(2)	(3)	(4)	(5)	(6)	(7a)	(7b)	(8)	(9)	(10)	(11)
-	3.1.2	2.0	2.0	2.0.1.3	3.3	3.4	3.5	4.1.4	4.1.4	4.2.5 / 4.3.2	4.2.5
1281	PROPYL FORMATES	3		II		1 L	E2	P001 IBC02		T4	TP1
1282	PYRIDINE	3		II		1 L	E2	P001 IBC02		T4	TP2
1286	ROSIN OIL	3		II		5 L	E2	P001 IBC02		T4	TP1
1286	ROSIN OIL	3		III	223	5 L	E1	P001 IBC03 LP01		T2	TP1
1287	RUBBER SOLUTION	3		II		5 L	E2	P001 IBC02		T4	TP1 TP8
1287	RUBBER SOLUTION	3		III	223	5 L	E1	P001 IBC03 LP01		T2	TP1
1288	SHALE OIL	3		II		1 L	E2	P001 IBC02		T4	TP1 TP8
1288	SHALE OIL	3		III	223	5 L	E1	P001 IBC03 LP01		T2	TP1
1289	SODIUM METHYLATE SOLUTION in alcohol	3	8	II		1 L	E2	P001 IBC02		T7	TP1 TP8
1289	SODIUM METHYLATE SOLUTION in alcohol	3	8	III	223	5 L	E1	P001 IBC03		T4	TP1
1292	TETRAETHYL SILICATE	3		III		5 L	E1	P001 IBC03 LP01		T2	TP1
1293	TINCTURES, MEDICINAL	3		II		1 L	E2	P001 IBC02		T4	TP1 TP8
1293	TINCTURES, MEDICINAL	3		III	223	5 L	E1	P001 IBC03 LP01		T2	TP1
1294	TOLUENE	3		II		1 L	E2	P001 IBC02		T4	TP1
1295	TRICHLOROSILANE	4.3	3 8	I		0	E0	P401		T14	TP2 TP7 TP13
1296	TRIETHYLAMINE	3	8	II		1 L	E2	P001 IBC02		T7	TP1
1297	TRIMETHYLAMINE, AQUEOUS SOLUTION, not more than 50 % trimethylamine, by mass	3	8	I		0	E0	P001		T11	TP1
1297	TRIMETHYLAMINE, AQUEOUS SOLUTION, not more than 50 % trimethylamine, by mass	3	8	II		1 L	E2	P001 IBC02		T7	TP1
1297	TRIMETHYLAMINE, AQUEOUS SOLUTION, not more than 50 % trimethylamine, by mass	3	8	III	223	5 L	E1	P001 IBC03		T7	TP1
1298	TRIMETHYLCHLOROSILANE	3	8	II		0	E0	P010		T10	TP2 TP7 TP13
1299	TURPENTINE	3		III		5 L	E1	P001 IBC03 LP01		T2	TP1
1300	TURPENTINE SUBSTITUTE	3		II		1 L	E2	P001 IBC02		T4	TP1
1300	TURPENTINE SUBSTITUTE	3		III	223	5 L	E1	P001 IBC03 LP01		T2	TP1
1301	VINYL ACETATE, STABILIZED	3		II	386	1 L	E2	P001 IBC02		T4	TP1

UN No.	Name and description	Class or division	Subsidiary hazard	UN packing group	Special provisions	Limited and excepted quantities		Packagings and IBCs		Portable tanks and bulk containers	
								Packing instruction	Special packing provisions	Instructions	Special provisions
(1)	(2)	(3)	(4)	(5)	(6)	(7a)	(7b)	(8)	(9)	(10)	(11)
-	3.1.2	2.0	2.0	2.0.1.3	3.3	3.4	3.5	4.1.4	4.1.4	4.2.5 / 4.3.2	4.2.5
1302	VINYL ETHYL ETHER, STABILIZED	3		I	386	0	E3	P001		T11	TP2
1303	VINYLIDENE CHLORIDE, STABILIZED	3		I	386	0	E3	P001		T12	TP2 TP7
1304	VINYL ISOBUTYL ETHER, STABILIZED	3		II	386	1 L	E2	P001 IBC02		T4	TP1
1305	VINYLTRICHLOROSILANE	3	8	II		0	E0	P010		T10	TP2 TP7 TP13
1306	WOOD PRESERVATIVES, LIQUID	3		II		5 L	E2	P001 IBC02		T4	TP1 TP8
1306	WOOD PRESERVATIVES, LIQUID	3		III	223	5 L	E1	P001 IBC03 LP01		T2	TP1
1307	XYLENES	3		II		1 L	E2	P001 IBC02		T4	TP1
1307	XYLENES	3		III	223	5 L	E1	P001 IBC03 LP01		T2	TP1
1308	ZIRCONIUM SUSPENDED IN A FLAMMABLE LIQUID	3		I		0	E0	P001	PP33		
1308	ZIRCONIUM SUSPENDED IN A FLAMMABLE LIQUID	3		II		1 L	E2	P001	PP33		
1308	ZIRCONIUM SUSPENDED IN A FLAMMABLE LIQUID	3		III	223	5 L	E1	P001			
1309	ALUMINIUM POWDER, COATED	4.1		II		1 kg	E2	P002 IBC08	PP38 B2, B4	T3	TP33
1309	ALUMINIUM POWDER, COATED	4.1		III	223	5 kg	E1	P002 IBC08 LP02	PP11 B3	T1	TP33
1310	AMMONIUM PICRATE, WETTED with not less than 10 % water, by mass	4.1		I	28	0	E0	P406	PP26		
1312	BORNEOL	4.1		III		5 kg	E1	P002 IBC08 LP02	B3	T1	TP33
1313	CALCIUM RESINATE	4.1		III		5 kg	E1	P002 IBC06		T1	TP33
1314	CALCIUM RESINATE, FUSED	4.1		III		5 kg	E1	P002 IBC04		T1	TP33
1318	COBALT RESINATE, PRECIPITATED	4.1		III		5 kg	E1	P002 IBC06		T1	TP33
1320	DINITROPHENOL, WETTED with not less than 15 % water, by mass	4.1	6.1	I	28	0	E0	P406	PP26		
1321	DINITROPHENOLATES, WETTED with not less than 15 % water, by mass	4.1	6.1	I	28	0	E0	P406	PP26		
1322	DINITRORESORCINOL, WETTED with not less than 15 % water, by mass	4.1		I	28	0	E0	P406	PP26		
1323	FERROCERIUM	4.1		II	249	1 kg	E2	P002 IBC08	B2, B4	T3	TP33
1324	FILMS, NITROCELLULOSE BASE, gelatin coated, except scrap	4.1		III		5 kg	E1	P002	PP15		
1325	FLAMMABLE SOLID, ORGANIC, N.O.S.	4.1		II	274	1 kg	E2	P002 IBC08	B2, B4	T3	TP33
1325	FLAMMABLE SOLID, ORGANIC, N.O.S.	4.1		III	223 274	5 kg	E1	P002 IBC08 LP02	B3	T1	TP33

UN No.	Name and description	Class or division	Subsidiary hazard	UN packing group	Special provisions	Limited and excepted quantities		Packagings and IBCs		Portable tanks and bulk containers	
								Packing instruction	Special packing provisions	Instructions	Special provisions
(1)	(2)	(3)	(4)	(5)	(6)	(7a)	(7b)	(8)	(9)	(10)	(11)
-	3.1.2	2.0	2.0	2.0.1.3	3.3	3.4	3.5	4.1.4	4.1.4	4.2.5 / 4.3.2	4.2.5
1326	HAFNIUM POWDER, WETTED with not less than 25 % water (a visible excess of water must be present) (a) mechanically produced, particle size less than 53 microns; (b) chemically produced, particle size less than 840 microns	4.1		II		1 kg	E2	P410 IBC06	PP40 B2	T3	TP33
1327	HAY, STRAW or BHUSA	4.1			281	3 kg	E0	P003 IBC08	PP19 B6		
1328	HEXAMETHYLENE-TETRAMINE	4.1		III		5 kg	E1	P002 IBC08	B3	T1	TP33
1330	MANGANESE RESINATE	4.1		III		5 kg	E1	P002 IBC08		T1	TP33
1331	MATCHES, 'STRIKE ANYWHERE'	4.1		III	293	5 kg	E0	P407	PP27		
1332	METALDEHYDE	4.1		III		5 kg	E1	P002 IBC08 LP02	B3	T1	TP33
1333	CERIUM, slabs, ingots or rods	4.1		II		1 kg	E2	P002 IBC08	B2, B4		
1334	NAPHTHALENE, CRUDE or NAPHTHALENE, REFINED	4.1		III		5 kg	E1	P002 IBC08 LP02	B3	T1 BK1 BK2 BK3	TP33
1336	NITROGUANIDINE (PICRITE), WETTED with not less than 20 % water, by mass	4.1		I	28	0	E0	P406			
1337	NITROSTARCH, WETTED with not less than 20 % water, by mass	4.1		I	28	0	E0	P406			
1338	PHOSPHORUS, AMORPHOUS	4.1		III		5 kg	E1	P410 IBC08	B3	T1	TP33
1339	PHOSPHORUS HEPTASULPHIDE, free from yellow and white phosphorus	4.1		II		1 kg	E2	P410 IBC04		T3	TP33
1340	PHOSPHORUS PENTASULPHIDE, free from yellow and white phosphorus	4.3	4.1	II		500 g	E2	P410 IBC04		T3	TP33
1341	PHOSPHORUS SESQUISULPHIDE, free from yellow and white phosphorus	4.1		II		1 kg	E2	P410 IBC04		T3	TP33
1343	PHOSPHORUS TRISULPHIDE, free from yellow and white phosphorus	4.1		II		1 kg	E2	P410 IBC04		T3	TP33
1344	TRINITROPHENOL (PICRIC ACID), WETTED with not less than 30 % water, by mass	4.1		I	28	0	E0	P406	PP26		
1345	RUBBER SCRAP or RUBBER SHODDY, powdered or granulated, not exceeding 840 microns and rubber content exceeding 45 %	4.1		II	223	1 kg	E2	P002 IBC08	B2, B4	T3	TP33
1346	SILICON POWDER, AMORPHOUS	4.1		III	32	5 kg	E1	P002 IBC08 LP02	B3	T1	TP33
1347	SILVER PICRATE, WETTED with not less than 30 % water, by mass	4.1		I	28	0	E0	P406	PP25 PP26		
1348	SODIUM DINITRO-o-CRESOLATE, WETTED with not less than 15 % water, by mass	4.1	6.1	I	28	0	E0	P406	PP26		
1349	SODIUM PICRAMATE, WETTED with not less than 20 % water, by mass	4.1		I	28	0	E0	P406	PP26		

UN No.	Name and description	Class or division	Subsidiary hazard	UN packing group	Special provisions	Limited and excepted quantities		Packagings and IBCs		Portable tanks and bulk containers	
								Packing instruction	Special packing provisions	Instructions	Special provisions
(1)	(2)	(3)	(4)	(5)	(6)	(7a)	(7b)	(8)	(9)	(10)	(11)
-	3.1.2	2.0	2.0	2.0.1.3	3.3	3.4	3.5	4.1.4	4.1.4	4.2.5 / 4.3.2	4.2.5
1350	SULPHUR	4.1		III	242	5 kg	E1	P002 IBC08 LP02	B3	T1 BK1 BK2 BK3	TP33
1352	TITANIUM POWDER, WETTED with not less than 25 % water (a visible excess of water must be present) (a) mechanically produced, particle size less than 53 microns; (b) chemically produced particle size less than 840 microns	4.1		II		1 kg	E2	P410 IBC06	PP40 B2	T3	TP33
1353	FIBRES or FABRICS IMPREGNATED WITH WEAKLY NITRATED NITROCELLULOSE, N.O.S.	4.1		III		5 kg	E1	P410 IBC08	B3		
1354	TRINITROBENZENE, WETTED with not less than 30 % water, by mass	4.1		I	28	0	E0	P406			
1355	TRINITROBENZOIC ACID, WETTED with not less than 30 % water, by mass	4.1		I	28	0	E0	P406			
1356	TRINITROTOLUENE (TNT), WETTED with not less than 30 % water, by mass	4.1		I	28	0	E0	P406			
1357	UREA NITRATE, WETTED with not less than 20 % water, by mass	4.1		I	28 227	0	E0	P406			
1358	ZIRCONIUM POWDER, WETTED with not less than 25 % water (a visible excess of water must be present) (a) mechanically produced, particle size less than 53 microns; (b) chemically produced particle size less than 840 microns	4.1		II		1 kg	E2	P410 IBC06	PP40 B2	T3	TP33
1360	CALCIUM PHOSPHIDE	4.3	6.1	I		0	E0	P403			
1361	CARBON, animal or vegetable origin	4.2		II		0	E0	P002 IBC06	PP12	T3	TP33
1361	CARBON, animal or vegetable origin	4.2		III	223	0	E0	P002 IBC08 LP02	PP12 B3	T1	TP33
1362	CARBON, ACTIVATED	4.2		III	223	0	E1	P002 IBC08 LP02	PP11 B3	T1	TP33
1363	COPRA	4.2		III	29	0	E0	P003 IBC08 LP02	PP20 B3, B6	BK2	
1364	COTTON WASTE, OILY	4.2		III		0	E0	P003 IBC08 LP02	PP19 B3, B6		
1365	COTTON, WET	4.2		III	29	0	E0	P003 IBC08 LP02	PP19 B3, B6		
1369	p-NITROSODIMETHYLANILINE	4.2		II		0	E2	P410 IBC06	B2	T3	TP33
1372	FIBRES, ANIMAL or FIBRES, VEGETABLE burnt, wet or damp	4.2		III	123	0	E1	P410			
1373	FIBRES or FABRICS, ANIMAL or VEGETABLE or SYNTHETIC, N.O.S. with oil	4.2		III		0	E0	P410 IBC08	B3	T1	TP33
1374	FISH MEAL (FISH SCRAP), UNSTABILIZED	4.2		II	300	0	E2	P410 IBC08	B2, B4	T3	TP33

UN No.	Name and description	Class or division	Subsidiary hazard	UN packing group	Special provisions	Limited and excepted quantities		Packagings and IBCs		Portable tanks and bulk containers	
								Packing instruction	Special packing provisions	Instructions	Special provisions
(1)	(2)	(3)	(4)	(5)	(6)	(7a)	(7b)	(8)	(9)	(10)	(11)
-	3.1.2	2.0	2.0	2.0.1.3	3.3	3.4	3.5	4.1.4	4.1.4	4.2.5 / 4.3.2	4.2.5
1376	IRON OXIDE, SPENT or IRON SPONGE, SPENT obtained from coal gas purification	4.2		III	223	0	E0	P002 IBC08 LP02	B3	T1 BK2	TP33
1378	METAL CATALYST, WETTED with a visible excess of liquid	4.2		II	274	0	E0	P410 IBC01	PP39	T3	TP33
1379	PAPER, UNSATURATED OIL TREATED, incompletely dried (including carbon paper)	4.2		III		0	E0	P410 IBC08	B3		
1380	PENTABORANE	4.2	6.1	I		0	E0	P601			
1381	PHOSPHORUS, WHITE or YELLOW, DRY or UNDER WATER or IN SOLUTION	4.2	6.1	I		0	E0	P405		T9	TP3 TP31
1382	POTASSIUM SULPHIDE, ANHYDROUS or POTASSIUM SULPHIDE with less than 30 % water of crystallization	4.2		II		0	E2	P410 IBC06	B2	T3	TP33
1383	PYROPHORIC METAL, N.O.S. or PYROPHORIC ALLOY, N.O.S.	4.2		I	274	0	E0	P404		T21	TP7 TP33
1384	SODIUM DITHIONITE (SODIUM HYDROSULPHITE)	4.2		II		0	E2	P410 IBC06	B2	T3	TP33
1385	SODIUM SULPHIDE, ANHYDROUS or SODIUM SULPHIDE with less than 30 % water of crystallization	4.2		II		0	E2	P410 IBC06	B2	T3	TP33
1386	SEED CAKE with more than 1.5 % oil and not more than 11 % moisture	4.2		III	29	0	E0	P003 IBC08 LP02	PP20 B3, B6	BK2	
1387	WOOL WASTE, WET	4.2		III	123	0	E1	P410			
1389	ALKALI METAL AMALGAM, LIQUID	4.3		I	182	0	E0	P402			
1390	ALKALI METAL AMIDES	4.3		II	182	500 g	E2	P410 IBC07	B2	T3	TP33
1391	ALKALI METAL DISPERSION or ALKALINE EARTH METAL DISPERSION	4.3		I	182 183	0	E0	P402		T13	TP2 TP7 TP42
1392	ALKALINE EARTH METAL AMALGAM, LIQUID	4.3		I	183	0	E0	P402			
1393	ALKALINE EARTH METAL ALLOY, N.O.S.	4.3		II		500 g	E2	P410 IBC07	B2	T3	TP33
1394	ALUMINIUM CARBIDE	4.3		II		500 g	E2	P410 IBC07	B2	T3	TP33
1395	ALUMINIUM FERROSILICON POWDER	4.3	6.1	II		500 g	E2	P410 IBC05	B2	T3	TP33
1396	ALUMINIUM POWDER, UNCOATED	4.3		II		500 g	E2	P410 IBC07	B2	T3	TP33
1396	ALUMINIUM POWDER, UNCOATED	4.3		III	223	1 kg	E1	P410 IBC08	B4	T1	TP33
1397	ALUMINIUM PHOSPHIDE	4.3	6.1	I		0	E0	P403			
1398	ALUMINIUM SILICON POWDER, UNCOATED	4.3		III	37 223	1 kg	E1	P410 IBC08	B4	T1 BK2	TP33
1400	BARIUM	4.3		II		500 g	E2	P410 IBC07	B2	T3	TP33
1401	CALCIUM	4.3		II		500 g	E2	P410 IBC07	B2	T3	TP33
1402	CALCIUM CARBIDE	4.3		I		0	E0	P403 IBC04	B1	T9	TP7 TP33
1402	CALCIUM CARBIDE	4.3		II		500 g	E2	P410 IBC07	B2	T3	TP33

UN No.	Name and description	Class or division	Subsidiary hazard	UN packing group	Special provisions	Limited and excepted quantities		Packagings and IBCs		Portable tanks and bulk containers	
								Packing instruction	Special packing provisions	Instructions	Special provisions
(1)	(2)	(3)	(4)	(5)	(6)	(7a)	(7b)	(8)	(9)	(10)	(11)
-	3.1.2	2.0	2.0	2.0.1.3	3.3	3.4	3.5	4.1.4	4.1.4	4.2.5 / 4.3.2	4.2.5
1403	CALCIUM CYANAMIDE with more than 0.1 % calcium carbide	4.3		III	38	1 kg	E1	P410 IBC08	B4	T1	TP33
1404	CALCIUM HYDRIDE	4.3		I		0	E0	P403			
1405	CALCIUM SILICIDE	4.3		II		500 g	E2	P410 IBC07	B2	T3	TP33
1405	CALCIUM SILICIDE	4.3		III	223	1 kg	E1	P410 IBC08	B4	T1	TP33
1407	CAESIUM	4.3		I		0	E0	P403 IBC04	B1		
1408	FERROSILICON with 30 % or more but less than 90 % silicon	4.3	6.1	III	39 223	1 kg	E1	P003 IBC08	PP20 B4, B6	T1 BK2	TP33
1409	METAL HYDRIDES, WATER-REACTIVE, N.O.S.	4.3		I	274	0	E0	P403			
1409	METAL HYDRIDES, WATER-REACTIVE, N.O.S.	4.3		II	274	500 g	E2	P410 IBC04		T3	TP33
1410	LITHIUM ALUMINIUM HYDRIDE	4.3		I		0	E0	P403			
1411	LITHIUM ALUMINIUM HYDRIDE, ETHEREAL	4.3	3	I		0	E0	P402			
1413	LITHIUM BOROHYDRIDE	4.3		I		0	E0	P403			
1414	LITHIUM HYDRIDE	4.3		I		0	E0	P403			
1415	LITHIUM	4.3		I		0	E0	P403 IBC04	B1	T9	TP7 TP33
1417	LITHIUM SILICON	4.3		II		500 g	E2	P410 IBC07	B2	T3	TP33
1418	MAGNESIUM POWDER or MAGNESIUM ALLOYS POWDER	4.3	4.2	I		0	E0	P403			
1418	MAGNESIUM POWDER or MAGNESIUM ALLOYS POWDER	4.3	4.2	II		0	E2	P410 IBC05	B2	T3	TP33
1418	MAGNESIUM POWDER or MAGNESIUM ALLOYS POWDER	4.3	4.2	III	223	0	E1	P410 IBC08	B4	T1	TP33
1419	MAGNESIUM ALUMINIUM PHOSPHIDE	4.3	6.1	I		0	E0	P403			
1420	POTASSIUM METAL ALLOYS, LIQUID	4.3		I		0	E0	P402			
1421	ALKALI METAL ALLOY, LIQUID, N.O.S.	4.3		I	182	0	E0	P402			
1422	POTASSIUM SODIUM ALLOYS, LIQUID	4.3		I		0	E0	P402		T9	TP3 TP7 TP31
1423	RUBIDIUM	4.3		I		0	E0	P403 IBC04	B1		
1426	SODIUM BOROHYDRIDE	4.3		I		0	E0	P403			
1427	SODIUM HYDRIDE	4.3		I		0	E0	P403			
1428	SODIUM	4.3		I		0	E0	P403 IBC04	B1	T9	TP7 TP33
1431	SODIUM METHYLATE	4.2	8	II		0	E2	P410 IBC05	B2	T3	TP33
1432	SODIUM PHOSPHIDE	4.3	6.1	I		0	E0	P403			
1433	STANNIC PHOSPHIDES	4.3	6.1	I		0	E0	P403			
1435	ZINC ASHES	4.3		III	223	1 kg	E1	P002 IBC08	B4	T1 BK2	TP33
1436	ZINC POWDER or ZINC DUST	4.3	4.2	I		0	E0	P403			
1436	ZINC POWDER or ZINC DUST	4.3	4.2	II		0	E2	P410 IBC07	B2	T3	TP33

UN No.	Name and description	Class or division	Subsidiary hazard	UN packing group	Special provisions	Limited and excepted quantities		Packagings and IBCs		Portable tanks and bulk containers	
								Packing instruction	Special packing provisions	Instructions	Special provisions
(1)	(2)	(3)	(4)	(5)	(6)	(7a)	(7b)	(8)	(9)	(10)	(11)
-	3.1.2	2.0	2.0	2.0.1.3	3.3	3.4	3.5	4.1.4	4.1.4	4.2.5 / 4.3.2	4.2.5
1436	ZINC POWDER or ZINC DUST	4.3	4.2	III	223	0	E1	P410 IBC08	B4	T1	TP33
1437	ZIRCONIUM HYDRIDE	4.1		II		1 kg	E2	P410 IBC04	PP40	T3	TP33
1438	ALUMINIUM NITRATE	5.1		III		5 kg	E1	P002 IBC08 LP02	B3	T1 BK1 BK2	TP33
1439	AMMONIUM DICHROMATE	5.1		II		1 kg	E2	P002 IBC08	B2, B4	T3	TP33
1442	AMMONIUM PERCHLORATE	5.1		II	152	1 kg	E2	P002 IBC06	B2	T3	TP33
1444	AMMONIUM PERSULPHATE	5.1		III		5 kg	E1	P002 IBC08 LP02	B3	T1	TP33
1445	BARIUM CHLORATE, SOLID	5.1	6.1	II		1 kg	E2	P002 IBC06	B2	T3	TP33
1446	BARIUM NITRATE	5.1	6.1	II		1 kg	E2	P002 IBC08	B2, B4	T3	TP33
1447	BARIUM PERCHLORATE, SOLID	5.1	6.1	II		1 kg	E2	P002 IBC06	B2	T3	TP33
1448	BARIUM PERMANGANATE	5.1	6.1	II		1 kg	E2	P002 IBC06	B2	T3	TP33
1449	BARIUM PEROXIDE	5.1	6.1	II		1 kg	E2	P002 IBC06	B2	T3	TP33
1450	BROMATES, INORGANIC, N.O.S.	5.1		II	274 350	1 kg	E2	P002 IBC08	B2, B4	T3	TP33
1451	CAESIUM NITRATE	5.1		III		5 kg	E1	P002 IBC08 LP02	B3	T1	TP33
1452	CALCIUM CHLORATE	5.1		II		1 kg	E2	P002 IBC08	B2, B4	T3	TP33
1453	CALCIUM CHLORITE	5.1		II		1 kg	E2	P002 IBC08	B2, B4	T3	TP33
1454	CALCIUM NITRATE	5.1		III	208	5 kg	E1	P002 IBC08 LP02	B3	T1 BK1 BK2 BK3	TP33
1455	CALCIUM PERCHLORATE	5.1		II		1 kg	E2	P002 IBC06	B2	T3	TP33
1456	CALCIUM PERMANGANATE	5.1		II		1 kg	E2	P002 IBC06	B2	T3	TP33
1457	CALCIUM PEROXIDE	5.1		II		1 kg	E2	P002 IBC06	B2	T3	TP33
1458	CHLORATE AND BORATE MIXTURE	5.1		II		1 kg	E2	P002 IBC08	B2, B4	T3	TP33
1458	CHLORATE AND BORATE MIXTURE	5.1		III	223	5 kg	E1	P002 IBC08 LP02	B3	T1	TP33
1459	CHLORATE AND MAGNESIUM CHLORIDE MIXTURE, SOLID	5.1		II		1 kg	E2	P002 IBC08	B2, B4	T3	TP33
1459	CHLORATE AND MAGNESIUM CHLORIDE MIXTURE, SOLID	5.1		III	223	5 kg	E1	P002 IBC08 LP02	B3	T1	TP33
1461	CHLORATES, INORGANIC, N.O.S.	5.1		II	274 351	1 kg	E2	P002 IBC06	B2	T3	TP33
1462	CHLORITES, INORGANIC, N.O.S.	5.1		II	274 352	1 kg	E2	P002 IBC06	B2	T3	TP33
1463	CHROMIUM TRIOXIDE, ANHYDROUS	5.1	6.1 8	II		1 kg	E2	P002 IBC08	B2, B4	T3	TP33

UN No.	Name and description	Class or division	Subsidiary hazard	UN packing group	Special provisions	Limited and excepted quantities		Packagings and IBCs		Portable tanks and bulk containers	
								Packing instruction	Special packing provisions	Instructions	Special provisions
(1)	(2)	(3)	(4)	(5)	(6)	(7a)	(7b)	(8)	(9)	(10)	(11)
-	3.1.2	2.0	2.0	2.0.1.3	3.3	3.4	3.5	4.1.4	4.1.4	4.2.5 / 4.3.2	4.2.5
1465	DIDYMIUM NITRATE	5.1		III		5 kg	E1	P002 IBC08 LP02	B3	T1	TP33
1466	FERRIC NITRATE	5.1		III		5 kg	E1	P002 IBC08 LP02	B3	T1	TP33
1467	GUANIDINE NITRATE	5.1		III		5 kg	E1	P002 IBC08 LP02	B3	T1	TP33
1469	LEAD NITRATE	5.1	6.1	II		1 kg	E2	P002 IBC08	B2, B4	T3	TP33
1470	LEAD PERCHLORATE, SOLID	5.1	6.1	II		1 kg	E2	P002 IBC06	B2	T3	TP33
1471	LITHIUM HYPOCHLORITE, DRY or LITHIUM HYPOCHLORITE MIXTURE	5.1		II		1 kg	E2	P002 IBC08	B2, B4		
1471	LITHIUM HYPOCHLORITE, DRY or LITHIUM HYPOCHLORITE MIXTURE	5.1		III	223	5 kg	E1	P002 IBC08 LP02	B3	T1	TP33
1472	LITHIUM PEROXIDE	5.1		II		1 kg	E2	P002 IBC06	B2	T3	TP33
1473	MAGNESIUM BROMATE	5.1		II		1 kg	E2	P002 IBC08	B2, B4	T3	TP33
1474	MAGNESIUM NITRATE	5.1		III	332	5 kg	E1	P002 IBC08 LP02	B3	T1 BK1 BK2 BK3	TP33
1475	MAGNESIUM PERCHLORATE	5.1		II		1 kg	E2	P002 IBC06	B2	T3	TP33
1476	MAGNESIUM PEROXIDE	5.1		II		1 kg	E2	P002 IBC06	B2	T3	TP33
1477	NITRATES, INORGANIC, N.O.S.	5.1		II		1 kg	E2	P002 IBC08	B2, B4	T3	TP33
1477	NITRATES, INORGANIC, N.O.S.	5.1		III	223	5 kg	E1	P002 IBC08 LP02	B3	T1	TP33
1479	OXIDIZING SOLID, N.O.S.	5.1		I	274	0	E0	P503 IBC05	B1		
1479	OXIDIZING SOLID, N.O.S.	5.1		II	274	1 kg	E2	P002 IBC08	B2, B4	T3	TP33
1479	OXIDIZING SOLID, N.O.S.	5.1		III	223 274	5 kg	E1	P002 IBC08 LP02	B3	T1	TP33
1481	PERCHLORATES, INORGANIC, N.O.S.	5.1		II		1 kg	E2	P002 IBC06	B2	T3	TP33
1481	PERCHLORATES, INORGANIC, N.O.S.	5.1		III	223	5 kg	E1	P002 IBC08 LP02	B3	T1	TP33
1482	PERMANGANATES, INORGANIC, N.O.S.	5.1		II	206 274 353	1 kg	E2	P002 IBC06	B2	T3	TP33
1482	PERMANGANATES, INORGANIC, N.O.S.	5.1		III	206 223 274 353	5 kg	E1	P002 IBC08 LP02	B3	T1	TP33
1483	PEROXIDES, INORGANIC, N.O.S.	5.1		II		1 kg	E2	P002 IBC06	B2	T3	TP33
1483	PEROXIDES, INORGANIC, N.O.S.	5.1		III	223	5 kg	E1	P002 IBC08 LP02	B3	T1	TP33

UN No.	Name and description	Class or division	Subsidiary hazard	UN packing group	Special provisions	Limited and excepted quantities		Packagings and IBCs		Portable tanks and bulk containers	
								Packing instruction	Special packing provisions	Instructions	Special provisions
(1)	(2)	(3)	(4)	(5)	(6)	(7a)	(7b)	(8)	(9)	(10)	(11)
-	3.1.2	2.0	2.0	2.0.1.3	3.3	3.4	3.5	4.1.4	4.1.4	4.2.5 / 4.3.2	4.2.5
1484	POTASSIUM BROMATE	5.1		II		1 kg	E2	P002 IBC08	B2, B4	T3	TP33
1485	POTASSIUM CHLORATE	5.1		II		1 kg	E2	P002 IBC08	B2, B4	T3	TP33
1486	POTASSIUM NITRATE	5.1		III		5 kg	E1	P002 IBC08 LP02	B3	T1 BK1 BK2 BK3	TP33
1487	POTASSIUM NITRATE AND SODIUM NITRITE MIXTURE	5.1		II		1 kg	E2	P002 IBC08	B2, B4	T3	TP33
1488	POTASSIUM NITRITE	5.1		II		1 kg	E2	P002 IBC08	B2, B4	T3	TP33
1489	POTASSIUM PERCHLORATE	5.1		II		1 kg	E2	P002 IBC06	B2	T3	TP33
1490	POTASSIUM PERMANGANATE	5.1		II		1 kg	E2	P002 IBC08	B2, B4	T3	TP33
1491	POTASSIUM PEROXIDE	5.1		I		0	E0	P503 IBC06	B1		
1492	POTASSIUM PERSULPHATE	5.1		III		5 kg	E1	P002 IBC08 LP02	B3	T1	TP33
1493	SILVER NITRATE	5.1		II		1 kg	E2	P002 IBC08	B2, B4	T3	TP33
1494	SODIUM BROMATE	5.1		II		1 kg	E2	P002 IBC08	B2, B4	T3	TP33
1495	SODIUM CHLORATE	5.1		II		1 kg	E2	P002 IBC08	B2, B4	T3 BK1 BK2	TP33
1496	SODIUM CHLORITE	5.1		II		1 kg	E2	P002 IBC08	B2, B4	T3	TP33
1498	SODIUM NITRATE	5.1		III		5 kg	E1	P002 IBC08 LP02	B3	T1 BK1 BK2 BK3	TP33
1499	SODIUM NITRATE AND POTASSIUM NITRATE MIXTURE	5.1		III		5 kg	E1	P002 IBC08 LP02	B3	T1 BK1 BK2 BK3	TP33
1500	SODIUM NITRITE	5.1	6.1	III		5 kg	E1	P002 IBC08	B3	T1	TP33
1502	SODIUM PERCHLORATE	5.1		II		1 kg	E2	P002 IBC06	B2	T3	TP33
1503	SODIUM PERMANGANATE	5.1		II		1 kg	E2	P002 IBC06	B2	T3	TP33
1504	SODIUM PEROXIDE	5.1		I		0	E0	P503 IBC05	B1		
1505	SODIUM PERSULPHATE	5.1		III		5 kg	E1	P002 IBC08 LP02	B3	T1	TP33
1506	STRONTIUM CHLORATE	5.1		II		1 kg	E2	P002 IBC08	B2, B4	T3	TP33
1507	STRONTIUM NITRATE	5.1		III		5 kg	E1	P002 IBC08 LP02	B3	T1	TP33
1508	STRONTIUM PERCHLORATE	5.1		II		1 kg	E2	P002 IBC06	B2	T3	TP33
1509	STRONTIUM PEROXIDE	5.1		II		1 kg	E2	P002 IBC06	B2	T3	TP33
1510	TETRANITROMETHANE	6.1	5.1	I	354	0	E0	P602			

UN No.	Name and description	Class or division	Subsidiary hazard	UN packing group	Special provisions	Limited and excepted quantities		Packagings and IBCs		Portable tanks and bulk containers	
						(7a)	(7b)	Packing instruction	Special packing provisions	Instructions	Special provisions
(1)	(2)	(3)	(4)	(5)	(6)	(7a)	(7b)	(8)	(9)	(10)	(11)
-	3.1.2	2.0	2.0	2.0.1.3	3.3	3.4	3.5	4.1.4	4.1.4	4.2.5 / 4.3.2	4.2.5
1511	UREA HYDROGEN PEROXIDE	5.1	8	III		5 kg	E1	P002 IBC08	B3	T1	TP33
1512	ZINC AMMONIUM NITRITE	5.1		II		1 kg	E2	P002 IBC08	B2, B4	T3	TP33
1513	ZINC CHLORATE	5.1		II		1 kg	E2	P002 IBC08	B2, B4	T3	TP33
1514	ZINC NITRATE	5.1		II		1 kg	E2	P002 IBC08	B2, B4	T3	TP33
1515	ZINC PERMANGANATE	5.1		II		1 kg	E2	P002 IBC06	B2	T3	TP33
1516	ZINC PEROXIDE	5.1		II		1 kg	E2	P002 IBC06	B2	T3	TP33
1517	ZIRCONIUM PICRAMATE, WETTED with not less than 20 % water, by mass	4.1		I	28	0	E0	P406	PP26		
1541	ACETONE CYANOHYDRIN, STABILIZED	6.1		I	354	0	E0	P602		T20	TP2 TP13
1544	ALKALOIDS, SOLID, N.O.S. or ALKALOID SALTS, SOLID, N.O.S.	6.1		I	43 274	0	E5	P002 IBC07	B1	T6	TP33
1544	ALKALOIDS, SOLID, N.O.S. or ALKALOID SALTS, SOLID, N.O.S.	6.1		II	43 274	500 g	E4	P002 IBC08	B2, B4	T3	TP33
1544	ALKALOIDS, SOLID, N.O.S. or ALKALOID SALTS, SOLID, N.O.S.	6.1		III	43 223 274	5 kg	E1	P002 IBC08 LP02	B3	T1	TP33
1545	ALLYL ISOTHIOCYANATE, STABILIZED	6.1	3	II	386	100 ml	E0	P001 IBC02		T7	TP2
1546	AMMONIUM ARSENATE	6.1		II		500 g	E4	P002 IBC08	B2, B4	T3	TP33
1547	ANILINE	6.1		II	279	100 ml	E4	P001 IBC02		T7	TP2
1548	ANILINE HYDROCHLORIDE	6.1		III		5 kg	E1	P002 IBC08 LP02	B3	T1	TP33
1549	ANTIMONY COMPOUND, INORGANIC, SOLID, N.O.S.	6.1		III	45 274	5 kg	E1	P002 IBC08 LP02	B3	T1	TP33
1550	ANTIMONY LACTATE	6.1		III		5 kg	E1	P002 IBC08 LP02	B3	T1	TP33
1551	ANTIMONY POTASSIUM TARTRATE	6.1		III		5 kg	E1	P002 IBC08 LP02	B3	T1	TP33
1553	ARSENIC ACID, LIQUID	6.1		I		0	E5	P001		T20	TP2 TP7 TP13
1554	ARSENIC ACID, SOLID	6.1		II		500 g	E4	P002 IBC08	B2, B4	T3	TP33
1555	ARSENIC BROMIDE	6.1		II		500 g	E4	P002 IBC08	B2, B4	T3	TP33
1556	ARSENIC COMPOUND, LIQUID, N.O.S., inorganic, including: Arsenates, n.o.s., Arsenites, n.o.s.; and Arsenic sulphides, n.o.s.	6.1		I	43 274	0	E5	P001		T14	TP2 TP13 TP27
1556	ARSENIC COMPOUND, LIQUID, N.O.S., inorganic, including: Arsenates, n.o.s., Arsenites, n.o.s.; and Arsenic sulphides, n.o.s.	6.1		II	43 274	100 ml	E4	P001 IBC02		T11	TP2 TP13 TP27

UN No.	Name and description	Class or division	Subsidiary hazard	UN packing group	Special provisions	Limited and excepted quantities		Packagings and IBCs		Portable tanks and bulk containers	
								Packing instruction	Special packing provisions	Instructions	Special provisions
(1)	(2)	(3)	(4)	(5)	(6)	(7a)	(7b)	(8)	(9)	(10)	(11)
-	3.1.2	2.0	2.0	2.0.1.3	3.3	3.4	3.5	4.1.4	4.1.4	4.2.5 / 4.3.2	4.2.5
1556	ARSENIC COMPOUND, LIQUID, N.O.S., inorganic, including: Arsenates, n.o.s., Arsenites, n.o.s.; and Arsenic sulphides, n.o.s.	6.1		III	43 223 274	5 L	E1	P001 IBC03 LP01		T7	TP2 TP28
1557	ARSENIC COMPOUND, SOLID, N.O.S., inorganic, including: Arsenates, n.o.s.; Arsenites, n.o.s.; and Arsenic sulphides, n.o.s.	6.1		I	43 274	0	E5	P002 IBC07	B1	T6	TP33
1557	ARSENIC COMPOUND, SOLID, N.O.S., inorganic, including: Arsenates, n.o.s.; Arsenites, n.o.s.; and Arsenic sulphides, n.o.s.	6.1		II	43 274	500 g	E4	P002 IBC08	B2, B4	T3	TP33
1557	ARSENIC COMPOUND, SOLID, N.O.S., inorganic, including: Arsenates, n.o.s.; Arsenites, n.o.s.; and Arsenic sulphides, n.o.s.	6.1		III	43 223 274	5 kg	E1	P002 IBC08 LP02	B3	T1	TP33
1558	ARSENIC	6.1		II		500 g	E4	P002 IBC08	B2, B4	T3	TP33
1559	ARSENIC PENTOXIDE	6.1		II		500 g	E4	P002 IBC08	B2, B4	T3	TP33
1560	ARSENIC TRICHLORIDE	6.1		I		0	E0	P602		T14	TP2 TP13
1561	ARSENIC TRIOXIDE	6.1		II		500 g	E4	P002 IBC08	B2, B4	T3	TP33
1562	ARSENICAL DUST	6.1		II		500 g	E4	P002 IBC08	B2, B4	T3	TP33
1564	BARIUM COMPOUND, N.O.S.	6.1		II	177 274	500 g	E4	P002 IBC08	B2, B4	T3	TP33
1564	BARIUM COMPOUND, N.O.S.	6.1		III	177 223 274	5 kg	E1	P002 IBC08 LP02	B3	T1	TP33
1565	BARIUM CYANIDE	6.1		I		0	E5	P002 IBC07	B1	T6	TP33
1566	BERYLLIUM COMPOUND, N.O.S.	6.1		II	274	500 g	E4	P002 IBC08	B2, B4	T3	TP33
1566	BERYLLIUM COMPOUND, N.O.S.	6.1		III	223 274	5 kg	E1	P002 IBC08 LP02	B3	T1	TP33
1567	BERYLLIUM POWDER	6.1	4.1	II		500 g	E4	P002 IBC08	B2, B4	T3	TP33
1569	BROMOACETONE	6.1	3	II		0	E0	P602		T20	TP2 TP13
1570	BRUCINE	6.1		I	43	0	E5	P002 IBC07	B1	T6	TP33
1571	BARIUM AZIDE, WETTED with not less than 50 % water, by mass	4.1	6.1	I	28	0	E0	P406			
1572	CACODYLIC ACID	6.1		II		500 g	E4	P002 IBC08	B2, B4	T3	TP33
1573	CALCIUM ARSENATE	6.1		II		500 g	E4	P002 IBC08	B2, B4	T3	TP33
1574	CALCIUM ARSENATE AND CALCIUM ARSENITE MIXTURE, SOLID	6.1		II		500 g	E4	P002 IBC08	B2, B4	T3	TP33
1575	CALCIUM CYANIDE	6.1		I		0	E5	P002 IBC07	B1	T6	TP33
1577	CHLORODINITROBENZENES, LIQUID	6.1		II	279	100 ml	E4	P001 IBC02		T7	TP2
1578	CHLORONITROBENZENES, SOLID	6.1		II	279	500 g	E4	P002 IBC08	B2, B4	T3	TP33

UN No.	Name and description	Class or division	Subsidiary hazard	UN packing group	Special provisions	Limited and excepted quantities		Packagings and IBCs		Portable tanks and bulk containers	
								Packing instruction	Special packing provisions	Instructions	Special provisions
(1)	(2)	(3)	(4)	(5)	(6)	(7a)	(7b)	(8)	(9)	(10)	(11)
-	3.1.2	2.0	2.0	2.0.1.3	3.3	3.4	3.5	4.1.4	4.1.4	4.2.5 / 4.3.2	4.2.5
1579	4-CHLORO-o-TOLUIDINE HYDROCHLORIDE, SOLID	6.1		III		5 kg	E1	P002 IBC08 LP02	B3	T1	TP33
1580	CHLOROPICRIN	6.1		I	354	0	E0	P601		T22	TP2 TP13
1581	CHLOROPICRIN AND METHYL BROMIDE MIXTURE with more than 2 % chloropicrin	2.3				0	E0	P200		T50	
1582	CHLOROPICRIN AND METHYL CHLORIDE MIXTURE	2.3				0	E0	P200		T50	
1583	CHLOROPICRIN MIXTURE, N.O.S.	6.1		I	274 315	0	E0	P602			
1583	CHLOROPICRIN MIXTURE, N.O.S.	6.1		II	274	100 ml	E0	P001 IBC02			
1583	CHLOROPICRIN MIXTURE, N.O.S.	6.1		III	223 274	5 L	E0	P001 IBC03 LP01			
1585	COPPER ACETOARSENITE	6.1		II		500 g	E4	P002 IBC08	B2, B4	T3	TP33
1586	COPPER ARSENITE	6.1		II		500 g	E4	P002 IBC08	B2, B4	T3	TP33
1587	COPPER CYANIDE	6.1		II		500 g	E4	P002 IBC08	B2, B4	T3	TP33
1588	CYANIDES, INORGANIC, SOLID, N.O.S.	6.1		I	47 274	0	E5	P002 IBC07	B1	T6	TP33
1588	CYANIDES, INORGANIC, SOLID, N.O.S.	6.1		II	47 274	500 g	E4	P002 IBC08	B2, B4	T3	TP33
1588	CYANIDES, INORGANIC, SOLID, N.O.S.	6.1		III	47 223 274	5 kg	E1	P002 IBC08 LP02	B3	T1	TP33
1589	CYANOGEN CHLORIDE, STABILIZED	2.3	8		386	0	E0	P200			
1590	DICHLOROANILINES, LIQUID	6.1		II	279	100 ml	E4	P001 IBC02		T7	TP2
1591	o-DICHLOROBENZENE	6.1		III	279	5 L	E1	P001 IBC03 LP01		T4	TP1
1593	DICHLOROMETHANE	6.1		III		5 L	E1	P001 IBC03 LP01	B8	T7	TP2
1594	DIETHYL SULPHATE	6.1		II		100 ml	E4	P001 IBC02		T7	TP2
1595	DIMETHYL SULPHATE	6.1	8	I	354	0	E0	P602		T20	TP2 TP13
1596	DINITROANILINES	6.1		II		500 g	E4	P002 IBC08	B2, B4	T3	TP33
1597	DINITROBENZENES, LIQUID	6.1		II		100 ml	E4	P001 IBC02		T7	TP2
1597	DINITROBENZENES, LIQUID	6.1		III	223	5 L	E1	P001 IBC03 LP01		T7	TP2
1598	DINITRO-o-CRESOL	6.1		II	43	500 g	E4	P002 IBC08	B2, B4	T3	TP33
1599	DINITROPHENOL SOLUTION	6.1		II		100 ml	E4	P001 IBC02		T7	TP2
1599	DINITROPHENOL SOLUTION	6.1		III	223	5 L	E1	P001 IBC03 LP01		T4	TP1
1600	DINITROTOLUENES, MOLTEN	6.1		II		0	E0	NONE		T7	TP3

UN No.	Name and description	Class or division	Subsidiary hazard	UN packing group	Special provisions	Limited and excepted quantities		Packagings and IBCs		Portable tanks and bulk containers	
								Packing instruction	Special packing provisions	Instructions	Special provisions
(1)	(2)	(3)	(4)	(5)	(6)	(7a)	(7b)	(8)	(9)	(10)	(11)
-	3.1.2	2.0	2.0	2.0.1.3	3.3	3.4	3.5	4.1.4	4.1.4	4.2.5 / 4.3.2	4.2.5
1601	DISINFECTANT, SOLID, TOXIC, N.O.S.	6.1		I	274	0	E5	P002 IBC07	B1	T6	TP33
1601	DISINFECTANT, SOLID, TOXIC, N.O.S.	6.1		II	274	500 g	E4	P002 IBC08	B2, B4	T3	TP33
1601	DISINFECTANT, SOLID, TOXIC, N.O.S.	6.1		III	274	5 kg	E1	P002 IBC08 LP02	B3	T1	TP33
1602	DYE, LIQUID, TOXIC, N.O.S. or DYE INTERMEDIATE, LIQUID, TOXIC, N.O.S.	6.1		I	274	0	E5	P001			
1602	DYE, LIQUID, TOXIC, N.O.S. or DYE INTERMEDIATE, LIQUID, TOXIC, N.O.S.	6.1		II	274	100 ml	E4	P001 IBC02			
1602	DYE, LIQUID, TOXIC, N.O.S. or DYE INTERMEDIATE, LIQUID, TOXIC, N.O.S.	6.1		III	223 274	5 L	E1	P001 IBC03 LP01			
1603	ETHYL BROMOACETATE	6.1	3	II		100 ml	E0	P001 IBC02		T7	TP2
1604	ETHYLENEDIAMINE	8	3	II		1 L	E2	P001 IBC02		T7	TP2
1605	ETHYLENE DIBROMIDE	6.1		I	354	0	E0	P602		T20	TP2 TP13
1606	FERRIC ARSENATE	6.1		II		500 g	E4	P002 IBC08	B2, B4	T3	TP33
1607	FERRIC ARSENITE	6.1		II		500 g	E4	P002 IBC08	B2, B4	T3	TP33
1608	FERROUS ARSENATE	6.1		II		500 g	E4	P002 IBC08	B2, B4	T3	TP33
1611	HEXAETHYL TETRAPHOSPHATE	6.1		II		100 ml	E4	P001 IBC02		T7	TP2
1612	HEXAETHYL TETRAPHOSPHATE AND COMPRESSED GAS MIXTURE	2.3				0	E0	P200			
1613	HYDROCYANIC ACID, AQUEOUS SOLUTION (HYDROGEN CYANIDE, AQUEOUS SOLUTION) with not more than 20 % hydrogen cyanide	6.1		I	48	0	E0	P601		T14	TP2 TP13
1614	HYDROGEN CYANIDE, STABILIZED, containing less than 3 % water and absorbed in a porous inert material	6.1		I	386	0	E0	P099			
1616	LEAD ACETATE	6.1		III		5 kg	E1	P002 IBC08 LP02	B3	T1	TP33
1617	LEAD ARSENATES	6.1		II		500 g	E4	P002 IBC08	B2, B4	T3	TP33
1618	LEAD ARSENITES	6.1		II		500 g	E4	P002 IBC08	B2, B4	T3	TP33
1620	LEAD CYANIDE	6.1		II		500 g	E4	P002 IBC08	B2, B4	T3	TP33
1621	LONDON PURPLE	6.1		II	43	500 g	E4	P002 IBC08	B2, B4	T3	TP33
1622	MAGNESIUM ARSENATE	6.1		II		500 g	E4	P002 IBC08	B2, B4	T3	TP33
1623	MERCURIC ARSENATE	6.1		II		500 g	E4	P002 IBC08	B2, B4	T3	TP33
1624	MERCURIC CHLORIDE	6.1		II		500 g	E4	P002 IBC08	B2, B4	T3	TP33

UN No.	Name and description	Class or division	Subsidiary hazard	UN packing group	Special provisions	Limited and excepted quantities		Packagings and IBCs		Portable tanks and bulk containers	
								Packing instruction	Special packing provisions	Instructions	Special provisions
(1)	(2)	(3)	(4)	(5)	(6)	(7a)	(7b)	(8)	(9)	(10)	(11)
-	3.1.2	2.0	2.0	2.0.1.3	3.3	3.4	3.5	4.1.4	4.1.4	4.2.5 / 4.3.2	4.2.5
1625	MERCURIC NITRATE	6.1		II		500 g	E4	P002 IBC08	B2, B4	T3	TP33
1626	MERCURIC POTASSIUM CYANIDE	6.1		I		0	E5	P002 IBC07	B1	T6	TP33
1627	MERCUROUS NITRATE	6.1		II		500 g	E4	P002 IBC08	B2, B4	T3	TP33
1629	MERCURY ACETATE	6.1		II		500 g	E4	P002 IBC08	B2, B4	T3	TP33
1630	MERCURY AMMONIUM CHLORIDE	6.1		II		500 g	E4	P002 IBC08	B2, B4	T3	TP33
1631	MERCURY BENZOATE	6.1		II		500 g	E4	P002 IBC08	B2, B4	T3	TP33
1634	MERCURY BROMIDES	6.1		II		500 g	E4	P002 IBC08	B2, B4	T3	TP33
1636	MERCURY CYANIDE	6.1		II		500 g	E4	P002 IBC08	B2, B4	T3	TP33
1637	MERCURY GLUCONATE	6.1		II		500 g	E4	P002 IBC08	B2, B4	T3	TP33
1638	MERCURY IODIDE	6.1		II		500 g	E4	P002 IBC08	B2, B4	T3	TP33
1639	MERCURY NUCLEATE	6.1		II		500 g	E4	P002 IBC08	B2, B4	T3	TP33
1640	MERCURY OLEATE	6.1		II		500 g	E4	P002 IBC08	B2, B4	T3	TP33
1641	MERCURY OXIDE	6.1		II		500 g	E4	P002 IBC08	B2, B4	T3	TP33
1642	MERCURY OXYCYANIDE, DESENSITIZED	6.1		II		500 g	E4	P002 IBC08	B2, B4	T3	TP33
1643	MERCURY POTASSIUM IODIDE	6.1		II		500 g	E4	P002 IBC08	B2, B4	T3	TP33
1644	MERCURY SALICYLATE	6.1		II		500 g	E4	P002 IBC08	B2, B4	T3	TP33
1645	MERCURY SULPHATE	6.1		II		500 g	E4	P002 IBC08	B2, B4	T3	TP33
1646	MERCURY THIOCYANATE	6.1		II		500 g	E4	P002 IBC08	B2, B4	T3	TP33
1647	METHYL BROMIDE AND ETHYLENE DIBROMIDE MIXTURE, LIQUID	6.1		I	354	0	E0	P602		T20	TP2 TP13
1648	ACETONITRILE	3		II		1 L	E2	P001 IBC02		T7	TP2
1649	MOTOR FUEL ANTI-KNOCK MIXTURE	6.1		I		0	E0	P602		T14	TP2 TP13
1650	beta-NAPHTHYLAMINE, SOLID	6.1		II		500 g	E4	P002 IBC08	B2, B4	T3	TP33
1651	NAPHTHYLTHIOUREA	6.1		II	43	500 g	E4	P002 IBC08	B2, B4	T3	TP33
1652	NAPHTHYLUREA	6.1		II		500 g	E4	P002 IBC08	B2, B4	T3	TP33
1653	NICKEL CYANIDE	6.1		II		500 g	E4	P002 IBC08	B2, B4	T3	TP33
1654	NICOTINE	6.1		II		100 ml	E4	P001 IBC02			
1655	NICOTINE COMPOUND, SOLID, N.O.S. or NICOTINE PREPARATION, SOLID, N.O.S.	6.1		I	43 274	0	E5	P002 IBC07	B1	T6	TP33

UN No.	Name and description	Class or division	Subsidiary hazard	UN packing group	Special provisions	Limited and excepted quantities		Packagings and IBCs		Portable tanks and bulk containers	
								Packing instruction	Special packing provisions	Instructions	Special provisions
(1)	(2)	(3)	(4)	(5)	(6)	(7a)	(7b)	(8)	(9)	(10)	(11)
-	3.1.2	2.0	2.0	2.0.1.3	3.3	3.4	3.5	4.1.4	4.1.4	4.2.5 / 4.3.2	4.2.5
1655	NICOTINE COMPOUND, SOLID, N.O.S. or NICOTINE PREPARATION, SOLID, N.O.S.	6.1		II	43 274	500 g	E4	P002 IBC08	B2, B4	T3	TP33
1655	NICOTINE COMPOUND, SOLID, N.O.S. or NICOTINE PREPARATION, SOLID, N.O.S.	6.1		III	43 223 274	5 kg	E1	P002 IBC08 LP02	B3	T1	TP33
1656	NICOTINE HYDROCHLORIDE, LIQUID or SOLUTION	6.1		II	43	100 ml	E4	P001 IBC02			
1656	NICOTINE HYDROCHLORIDE, LIQUID or SOLUTION	6.1		III	43 223	5 L	E1	P001 IBC03 LP01			
1657	NICOTINE SALICYLATE	6.1		II		500 g	E4	P002 IBC08	B2, B4	T3	TP33
1658	NICOTINE SULPHATE SOLUTION	6.1		II		100 ml	E4	P001 IBC02		T7	TP2
1658	NICOTINE SULPHATE SOLUTION	6.1		III	223	5 L	E1	P001 IBC03 LP01		T7	TP2
1659	NICOTINE TARTRATE	6.1		II		500 g	E4	P002 IBC08	B2, B4	T3	TP33
1660	NITRIC OXIDE, COMPRESSED	2.3	5.1 8			0	E0	P200			
1661	NITROANILINES (o-, m-, p-)	6.1		II	279	500 g	E4	P002 IBC08	B2, B4	T3	TP33
1662	NITROBENZENE	6.1		II	279	100 ml	E4	P001 IBC02		T7	TP2
1663	NITROPHENOLS (o-, m-, p-)	6.1		III	279	5 kg	E1	P002 IBC08 LP02	B3	T1	TP33
1664	NITROTOLUENES, LIQUID	6.1		II		100 ml	E4	P001 IBC02		T7	TP2
1665	NITROXYLENES, LIQUID	6.1		II		100 ml	E4	P001 IBC02		T7	TP2
1669	PENTACHLOROETHANE	6.1		II		100 ml	E4	P001 IBC02		T7	TP2
1670	PERCHLOROMETHYL MERCAPTAN	6.1		I	354	0	E0	P602		T20	TP2 TP13
1671	PHENOL, SOLID	6.1		II	279	500 g	E4	P002 IBC08	B2, B4	T3	TP33
1672	PHENYLCARBYLAMINE CHLORIDE	6.1		I		0	E0	P602		T14	TP2 TP13
1673	PHENYLENEDIAMINES (o-, m-, p-)	6.1		III	279	5 kg	E1	P002 IBC08 LP02	B3	T1	TP33
1674	PHENYLMERCURIC ACETATE	6.1		II	43	500 g	E4	P002 IBC08	B2, B4	T3	TP33
1677	POTASSIUM ARSENATE	6.1		II		500 g	E4	P002 IBC08	B2, B4	T3	TP33
1678	POTASSIUM ARSENITE	6.1		II		500 g	E4	P002 IBC08	B2, B4	T3	TP33
1679	POTASSIUM CUPROCYANIDE	6.1		II		500 g	E4	P002 IBC08	B2, B4	T3	TP33
1680	POTASSIUM CYANIDE, SOLID	6.1		I		0	E5	P002 IBC07	B1	T6	TP33
1683	SILVER ARSENITE	6.1		II		500 g	E4	P002 IBC08	B2, B4	T3	TP33
1684	SILVER CYANIDE	6.1		II		500 g	E4	P002 IBC08	B2, B4	T3	TP33

UN No.	Name and description	Class or division	Subsidiary hazard	UN packing group	Special provisions	Limited and excepted quantities		Packagings and IBCs		Portable tanks and bulk containers	
								Packing instruction	Special packing provisions	Instructions	Special provisions
(1)	(2)	(3)	(4)	(5)	(6)	(7a)	(7b)	(8)	(9)	(10)	(11)
-	3.1.2	2.0	2.0	2.0.1.3	3.3	3.4	3.5	4.1.4	4.1.4	4.2.5 / 4.3.2	4.2.5
1685	SODIUM ARSENATE	6.1		II		500 g	E4	P002 IBC08	B2, B4	T3	TP33
1686	SODIUM ARSENITE, AQUEOUS SOLUTION	6.1		II	43	100 ml	E4	P001 IBC02		T7	TP2
1686	SODIUM ARSENITE, AQUEOUS SOLUTION	6.1		III	43 223	5 L	E1	P001 IBC03 LP01		T4	TP2
1687	SODIUM AZIDE	6.1		II		500 g	E4	P002 IBC08	B2, B4		
1688	SODIUM CACODYLATE	6.1		II		500 g	E4	P002 IBC08	B2, B4	T3	TP33
1689	SODIUM CYANIDE, SOLID	6.1		I		0	E5	P002 IBC07	B1	T6	TP33
1690	SODIUM FLUORIDE, SOLID	6.1		III		5 kg	E1	P002 IBC08 LP02	B3	T1	TP33
1691	STRONTIUM ARSENITE	6.1		II		500 g	E4	P002 IBC08	B2, B4	T3	TP33
1692	STRYCHNINE or STRYCHNINE SALTS	6.1		I		0	E5	P002 IBC07	B1	T6	TP33
1693	TEAR GAS SUBSTANCE, LIQUID, N.O.S.	6.1		I	274	0	E0	P001			
1693	TEAR GAS SUBSTANCE, LIQUID, N.O.S.	6.1		II	274	0	E0	P001 IBC02			
1694	BROMOBENZYL CYANIDES, LIQUID	6.1		I	138	0	E0	P001		T14	TP2 TP13
1695	CHLOROACETONE, STABILIZED	6.1	3 8	I	354	0	E0	P602		T20	TP2 TP13
1697	CHLOROACETOPHENONE, SOLID	6.1		II		0	E0	P002 IBC08	B2, B4	T3	TP33
1698	DIPHENYLAMINE CHLOROARSINE	6.1		I		0	E0	P002		T6	TP33
1699	DIPHENYLCHLOROARSINE, LIQUID	6.1		I		0	E0	P001			
1700	TEAR GAS CANDLES	6.1	4.1			0	E0	P600			
1701	XYLYL BROMIDE, LIQUID	6.1		II		0	E0	P001 IBC02		T7	TP2 TP13
1702	1,1,2,2-TETRACHLORO-ETHANE	6.1		II		100 ml	E4	P001 IBC02		T7	TP2
1704	TETRAETHYL DITHIOPYROPHOSPHATE	6.1		II	43	100 ml	E4	P001 IBC02		T7	TP2
1707	THALLIUM COMPOUND, N.O.S.	6.1		II	43 274	500 g	E4	P002 IBC08	B2, B4	T3	TP33
1708	TOLUIDINES, LIQUID	6.1		II	279	100 ml	E4	P001 IBC02		T7	TP2
1709	2,4-TOLUYLENEDIAMINE, SOLID	6.1		III		5 kg	E1	P002 IBC08 LP02	B3	T1	TP33
1710	TRICHLOROETHYLENE	6.1		III		5 L	E1	P001 IBC03 LP01		T4	TP1
1711	XYLIDINES, LIQUID	6.1		II		100 ml	E4	P001 IBC02		T7	TP2
1712	ZINC ARSENATE, ZINC ARSENITE or ZINC ARSENATE AND ZINC ARSENITE MIXTURE	6.1		II		500 g	E4	P002 IBC08	B2, B4	T3	TP33
1713	ZINC CYANIDE	6.1		I		0	E5	P002 IBC07	B1	T6	TP33

UN No.	Name and description	Class or division	Subsidiary hazard	UN packing group	Special provisions	Limited and excepted quantities		Packagings and IBCs		Portable tanks and bulk containers	
								Packing instruction	Special packing provisions	Instructions	Special provisions
(1)	(2)	(3)	(4)	(5)	(6)	(7a)	(7b)	(8)	(9)	(10)	(11)
-	3.1.2	2.0	2.0	2.0.1.3	3.3	3.4	3.5	4.1.4	4.1.4	4.2.5 / 4.3.2	4.2.5
1714	ZINC PHOSPHIDE	4.3	6.1	I		0	E0	P403			
1715	ACETIC ANHYDRIDE	8	3	II		1 L	E2	P001 IBC02		T7	TP2
1716	ACETYL BROMIDE	8		II		1 L	E2	P001 IBC02		T8	TP2
1717	ACETYL CHLORIDE	3	8	II		1 L	E2	P001 IBC02		T8	TP2
1718	BUTYL ACID PHOSPHATE	8		III		5 L	E1	P001 IBC03 LP01		T4	TP1
1719	CAUSTIC ALKALI LIQUID, N.O.S.	8		II	274	1 L	E2	P001 IBC02		T11	TP2 TP27
1719	CAUSTIC ALKALI LIQUID, N.O.S.	8		III	223 274	5 L	E1	P001 IBC03		T7	TP1 TP28
1722	ALLYL CHLOROFORMATE	6.1	3 8	I		0	E0	P001		T14	TP2 TP13
1723	ALLYL IODIDE	3	8	II		1 L	E2	P001 IBC02		T7	TP2 TP13
1724	ALLYLTRICHLOROSILANE, STABILIZED	8	3	II	386	0	E0	P010		T10	TP2 TP7 TP13
1725	ALUMINIUM BROMIDE, ANHYDROUS	8		II		1 kg	E2	P002 IBC08	B2, B4	T3	TP33
1726	ALUMINIUM CHLORIDE, ANHYDROUS	8		II		1 kg	E2	P002 IBC08	B2, B4	T3	TP33
1727	AMMONIUM HYDROGENDIFLUORIDE, SOLID	8		II		1 kg	E2	P002 IBC08	B2, B4	T3	TP33
1728	AMYLTRICHLOROSILANE	8		II		0	E0	P010		T10	TP2 TP7 TP13
1729	ANISOYL CHLORIDE	8		II		1 kg	E2	P002 IBC08	B2, B4	T3	TP33
1730	ANTIMONY PENTACHLORIDE, LIQUID	8		II		1 L	E2	P001 IBC02		T7	TP2
1731	ANTIMONY PENTACHLORIDE SOLUTION	8		II		1 L	E2	P001 IBC02		T7	TP2
1731	ANTIMONY PENTACHLORIDE SOLUTION	8		III	223	5 L	E1	P001 IBC03 LP01		T4	TP1
1732	ANTIMONY PENTAFLUORIDE	8	6.1	II		1 L	E0	P001 IBC02		T7	TP2
1733	ANTIMONY TRICHLORIDE	8		II		1 kg	E2	P002 IBC08	B2, B4	T3	TP33
1736	BENZOYL CHLORIDE	8		II		1 L	E2	P001 IBC02		T8	TP2 TP13
1737	BENZYL BROMIDE	6.1	8	II		0	E4	P001 IBC02		T8	TP2 TP13
1738	BENZYL CHLORIDE	6.1	8	II		0	E4	P001 IBC02		T8	TP2 TP13
1739	BENZYL CHLOROFORMATE	8		I		0	E0	P001		T10	TP2 TP13
1740	HYDROGENDIFLUORIDES, SOLID, N.O.S.	8		II		1 kg	E2	P002 IBC08	B2, B4	T3	TP33
1740	HYDROGENDIFLUORIDES, SOLID, N.O.S.	8		III	223	5 kg	E1	P002 IBC08 LP02	B3	T1	TP33
1741	BORON TRICHLORIDE	2.3	8			0	E0	P200			

UN No.	Name and description	Class or division	Subsidiary hazard	UN packing group	Special provisions	Limited and excepted quantities		Packagings and IBCs		Portable tanks and bulk containers	
						Packing instruction	Special packing provisions	Instructions	Special provisions
						(7a)	(7b)				
(1)	(2)	(3)	(4)	(5)	(6)	(7a)	(7b)	(8)	(9)	(10)	(11)
-	3.1.2	2.0	2.0	2.0.1.3	3.3	3.4	3.5	4.1.4	4.1.4	4.2.5 / 4.3.2	4.2.5
1742	BORON TRIFLUORIDE ACETIC ACID COMPLEX, LIQUID	8		II		1 L	E2	P001 IBC02		T8	TP2
1743	BORON TRIFLUORIDE PROPIONIC ACID COMPLEX, LIQUID	8		II		1 L	E2	P001 IBC02		T8	TP2
1744	BROMINE or BROMINE SOLUTION	8	6.1	I		0	E0	P804		T22	TP2 TP10 TP13
1745	BROMINE PENTAFLUORIDE	5.1	6.1 8	I		0	E0	P200		T22	TP2 TP13
1746	BROMINE TRIFLUORIDE	5.1	6.1 8	I		0	E0	P200		T22	TP2 TP13
1747	BUTYLTRICHLOROSILANE	8	3	II		0	E0	P010		T10	TP2 TP7 TP13
1748	CALCIUM HYPOCHLORITE, DRY or CALCIUM HYPOCHLORITE MIXTURE, DRY with more than 39 % available chlorine (8.8 % available oxygen)	5.1		II	314	1 kg	E2	P002 IBC08	PP85 B2, B4, B13		
1748	CALCIUM HYPOCHLORITE, DRY or CALCIUM HYPOCHLORITE MIXTURE, DRY with more than 39 % available chlorine (8.8 % available oxygen)	5.1		III	316	5 kg	E1	P002 IBC08	PP85 B4, B13		
1749	CHLORINE TRIFLUORIDE	2.3	5.1 8			0	E0	P200			
1750	CHLOROACETIC ACID SOLUTION	6.1	8	II		100 ml	E4	P001 IBC02		T7	TP2
1751	CHLOROACETIC ACID, SOLID	6.1	8	II		500 g	E4	P002 IBC08	B2, B4	T3	TP33
1752	CHLOROACETYL CHLORIDE	6.1	8	I	354	0	E0	P602		T20	TP2 TP13
1753	CHLOROPHENYL-TRICHLOROSILANE	8		II		0	E0	P010		T10	TP2 TP7
1754	CHLOROSULPHONIC ACID (with or without sulphur trioxide)	8		I		0	E0	P001		T20	TP2
1755	CHROMIC ACID SOLUTION	8		II		1 L	E2	P001 IBC02		T8	TP2
1755	CHROMIC ACID SOLUTION	8		III	223	5 L	E1	P001 IBC03 LP01		T4	TP1
1756	CHROMIC FLUORIDE, SOLID	8		II		1 kg	E2	P002 IBC08	B2, B4	T3	TP33
1757	CHROMIC FLUORIDE SOLUTION	8		II		1 L	E2	P001 IBC02		T7	TP2
1757	CHROMIC FLUORIDE SOLUTION	8		III	223	5 L	E1	P001 IBC03 LP01		T4	TP1
1758	CHROMIUM OXYCHLORIDE	8		I		0	E0	P001		T10	TP2
1759	CORROSIVE SOLID, N.O.S.	8		I	274	0	E0	P002 IBC07	B1	T6	TP33
1759	CORROSIVE SOLID, N.O.S.	8		II	274	1 kg	E2	P002 IBC08	B2, B4	T3	TP33
1759	CORROSIVE SOLID, N.O.S.	8		III	223 274	5 kg	E1	P002 IBC08 LP02	B3	T1	TP33
1760	CORROSIVE LIQUID, N.O.S.	8		I	274	0	E0	P001		T14	TP2 TP27

UN No.	Name and description	Class or division	Subsidiary hazard	UN packing group	Special provisions	Limited and excepted quantities		Packagings and IBCs		Portable tanks and bulk containers	
								Packing instruction	Special packing provisions	Instructions	Special provisions
(1)	(2)	(3)	(4)	(5)	(6)	(7a)	(7b)	(8)	(9)	(10)	(11)
-	3.1.2	2.0	2.0	2.0.1.3	3.3	3.4	3.5	4.1.4	4.1.4	4.2.5 / 4.3.2	4.2.5
1760	CORROSIVE LIQUID, N.O.S.	8		II	274	1 L	E2	P001 IBC02		T11	TP2 TP27
1760	CORROSIVE LIQUID, N.O.S.	8		III	223 274	5 L	E1	P001 IBC03 LP01		T7	TP1 TP28
1761	CUPRIETHYLENEDIAMINE SOLUTION	8	6.1	II		1 L	E2	P001 IBC02		T7	TP2
1761	CUPRIETHYLENEDIAMINE SOLUTION	8	6.1	III	223	5 L	E1	P001 IBC03		T7	TP1 TP28
1762	CYCLOHEXENYL-TRICHLOROSILANE	8		II		0	E0	P010		T10	TP2 TP7 TP13
1763	CYCLOHEXYL-TRICHLOROSILANE	8		II		0	E0	P010		T10	TP2 TP7 TP13
1764	DICHLOROACETIC ACID	8		II		1 L	E2	P001 IBC02		T8	TP2
1765	DICHLOROACETYL CHLORIDE	8		II		1 L	E2	P001 IBC02		T7	TP2
1766	DICHLOROPHENYL-TRICHLOROSILANE	8		II		0	E0	P010		T10	TP2 TP7 TP13
1767	DIETHYLDICHLOROSILANE	8	3	II		0	E0	P010		T10	TP2 TP7 TP13
1768	DIFLUOROPHOSPHORIC ACID, ANHYDROUS	8		II		1 L	E2	P001 IBC02		T8	TP2
1769	DIPHENYLDICHLOROSILANE	8		II		0	E0	P010		T10	TP2 TP7 TP13
1770	DIPHENYLMETHYL BROMIDE	8		II		1 kg	E2	P002 IBC08	B2, B4	T3	TP33
1771	DODECYLTRICHLOROSILANE	8		II		0	E0	P010		T10	TP2 TP7 TP13
1773	FERRIC CHLORIDE, ANHYDROUS	8		III		5 kg	E1	P002 IBC08 LP02	B3	T1	TP33
1774	FIRE EXTINGUISHER CHARGES, corrosive liquid	8		II		1 L	E0	P001	PP4		
1775	FLUOROBORIC ACID	8		II		1 L	E2	P001 IBC02		T7	TP2
1776	FLUOROPHOSPHORIC ACID, ANHYDROUS	8		II		1 L	E2	P001 IBC02		T8	TP2
1777	FLUOROSULPHONIC ACID	8		I		0	E0	P001		T10	TP2
1778	FLUOROSILICIC ACID	8		II		1 L	E2	P001 IBC02		T8	TP2
1779	FORMIC ACID with more than 85 % acid by mass	8	3	II		1 L	E2	P001 IBC02		T7	TP2
1780	FUMARYL CHLORIDE	8		II		1 L	E2	P001 IBC02		T7	TP2
1781	HEXADECYL-TRICHLOROSILANE	8		II		0	E0	P010		T10	TP2 TP7 TP13
1782	HEXAFLUOROPHOSPHORIC ACID	8		II		1 L	E2	P001 IBC02		T8	TP2
1783	HEXAMETHYLENEDIAMINE SOLUTION	8		II		1 L	E2	P001 IBC02		T7	TP2

UN No.	Name and description	Class or division	Subsidiary hazard	UN packing group	Special provisions	Limited and excepted quantities		Packagings and IBCs		Portable tanks and bulk containers	
								Packing instruction	Special packing provisions	Instructions	Special provisions
(1)	(2)	(3)	(4)	(5)	(6)	(7a)	(7b)	(8)	(9)	(10)	(11)
-	3.1.2	2.0	2.0	2.0.1.3	3.3	3.4	3.5	4.1.4	4.1.4	4.2.5 / 4.3.2	4.2.5
1783	HEXAMETHYLENEDIAMINE SOLUTION	8		III	223	5 L	E1	P001 IBC03 LP01		T4	TP1
1784	HEXYLTRICHLOROSILANE	8		II		0	E0	P010		T10	TP2 TP7 TP13
1786	HYDROFLUORIC ACID AND SULPHURIC ACID MIXTURE	8	6.1	I		0	E0	P001		T10	TP2 TP13
1787	HYDRIODIC ACID	8		II		1 L	E2	P001 IBC02		T7	TP2
1787	HYDRIODIC ACID	8		III	223	5 L	E1	P001 IBC03 LP01		T4	TP1
1788	HYDROBROMIC ACID	8		II		1 L	E2	P001 IBC02		T7	TP2
1788	HYDROBROMIC ACID	8		III	223	5 L	E1	P001 IBC03 LP01		T4	TP1
1789	HYDROCHLORIC ACID	8		II		1 L	E2	P001 IBC02		T8	TP2
1789	HYDROCHLORIC ACID	8		III	223	5 L	E1	P001 IBC03 LP01		T4	TP1
1790	HYDROFLUORIC ACID, with more than 60 % hydrogen fluoride	8	6.1	I		0	E0	P802	PP79 PP81	T10	TP2 TP13
1790	HYDROFLUORIC ACID, with not more than 60 % hydrogen fluoride	8	6.1	II		1 L	E2	P001 IBC02		T8	TP2
1791	HYPOCHLORITE SOLUTION	8		II		1 L	E2	P001 IBC02	PP10 B5	T7	TP2 TP24
1791	HYPOCHLORITE SOLUTION	8		III	223	5 L	E1	P001 IBC03 LP01		T4	TP2 TP24
1792	IODINE MONOCHLORIDE, SOLID	8		II		1 kg	E0	P002 IBC08	B2, B4	T7	TP2
1793	ISOPROPYL ACID PHOSPHATE	8		III		5 L	E1	P001 IBC02 LP01		T4	TP1
1794	LEAD SULPHATE with more than 3 % free acid	8		II		1 kg	E2	P002 IBC08	B2, B4	T3	TP33
1796	NITRATING ACID MIXTURE with more than 50 % nitric acid	8	5.1	I		0	E0	P001		T10	TP2 TP13
1796	NITRATING ACID MIXTURE with not more than 50 % nitric acid	8		II		1 L	E0	P001 IBC02		T8	TP2 TP13
1798	NITROHYDROCHLORIC ACID	8		I		0	E0	P802		T10	TP2 TP13
1799	NONYLTRICHLOROSILANE	8		II		0	E0	P010		T10	TP2 TP7 TP13
1800	OCTADECYL-TRICHLOROSILANE	8		II		0	E0	P010		T10	TP2 TP7 TP13
1801	OCTYLTRICHLOROSILANE	8		II		0	E0	P010		T10	TP2 TP7 TP13
1802	PERCHLORIC ACID with not more than 50 % acid, by mass	8	5.1	II		1 L	E0	P001 IBC02		T7	TP2
1803	PHENOLSULPHONIC ACID, LIQUID	8		II		1 L	E2	P001 IBC02		T7	TP2

UN No.	Name and description	Class or division	Subsidiary hazard	UN packing group	Special provisions	Limited and excepted quantities		Packagings and IBCs		Portable tanks and bulk containers	
								Packing instruction	Special packing provisions	Instructions	Special provisions
(1)	(2)	(3)	(4)	(5)	(6)	(7a)	(7b)	(8)	(9)	(10)	(11)
-	3.1.2	2.0	2.0	2.0.1.3	3.3	3.4	3.5	4.1.4	4.1.4	4.2.5 / 4.3.2	4.2.5
1804	PHENYLTRICHLOROSILANE	8		II		0	E0	P010		T10	TP2 TP7 TP13
1805	PHOSPHORIC ACID, SOLUTION	8		III	223	5 L	E1	P001 IBC03 LP01		T4	TP1
1806	PHOSPHORUS PENTACHLORIDE	8		II		1 kg	E0	P002 IBC08	B2, B4	T3	TP33
1807	PHOSPHORUS PENTOXIDE	8		II		1 kg	E2	P002 IBC08	B2, B4	T3	TP33
1808	PHOSPHORUS TRIBROMIDE	8		II		1 L	E0	P001 IBC02		T7	TP2
1809	PHOSPHORUS TRICHLORIDE	6.1	8	I	354	0	E0	P602		T20	TP2 TP13
1810	PHOSPHORUS OXYCHLORIDE	6.1	8	I	354	0	E0	P602		T20	TP2 TP13
1811	POTASSIUM HYDROGEN DIFLUORIDE SOLID	8	6.1	II		1 kg	E2	P002 IBC08	B2, B4	T3	TP33
1812	POTASSIUM FLUORIDE, SOLID	6.1		III		5 kg	E1	P002 IBC08 LP02	B3	T1	TP33
1813	POTASSIUM HYDROXIDE, SOLID	8		II		1 kg	E2	P002 IBC08	B2, B4	T3	TP33
1814	POTASSIUM HYDROXIDE SOLUTION	8		II		1 L	E2	P001 IBC02		T7	TP2
1814	POTASSIUM HYDROXIDE SOLUTION	8		III	223	5 L	E1	P001 IBC03 LP01		T4	TP1
1815	PROPIONYL CHLORIDE	3	8	II		1 L	E2	P001 IBC02		T7	TP1
1816	PROPYLTRICHLOROSILANE	8	3	II	-	0	E0	P010		T10	TP2 TP7 TP13
1817	PYROSULPHURYL CHLORIDE	8		II		1 L	E2	P001 IBC02		T8	TP2
1818	SILICON TETRACHLORIDE	8		II		0	E0	P010		T10	TP2 TP7 TP13
1819	SODIUM ALUMINATE SOLUTION	8		II		1 L	E2	P001 IBC02		T7	TP2
1819	SODIUM ALUMINATE SOLUTION	8		III	223	5 L	E1	P001 IBC03 LP01		T4	TP1
1823	SODIUM HYDROXIDE, SOLID	8		II		1 kg	E2	P002 IBC08	B2, B4	T3	TP33
1824	SODIUM HYDROXIDE SOLUTION	8		II		1 L	E2	P001 IBC02		T7	TP2
1824	SODIUM HYDROXIDE SOLUTION	8		III	223	5 L	E1	P001 IBC03 LP01		T4	TP1
1825	SODIUM MONOXIDE	8		II		1 kg	E2	P002 IBC08	B2, B4	T3	TP33
1826	NITRATING ACID MIXTURE, SPENT, with more than 50 % nitric acid	8	5.1	I	113	0	E0	P001		T10	TP2 TP13
1826	NITRATING ACID MIXTURE, SPENT, with not more than 50 % nitric acid	8		II	113	1 L	E0	P001 IBC02		T8	TP2
1827	STANNIC CHLORIDE, ANHYDROUS	8		II		1 L	E2	P001 IBC02		T7	TP2

UN No.	Name and description	Class or division	Subsidiary hazard	UN packing group	Special provisions	Limited and excepted quantities		Packagings and IBCs		Portable tanks and bulk containers	
								Packing instruction	Special packing provisions	Instructions	Special provisions
(1)	(2)	(3)	(4)	(5)	(6)	(7a)	(7b)	(8)	(9)	(10)	(11)
-	3.1.2	2.0	2.0	2.0.1.3	3.3	3.4	3.5	4.1.4	4.1.4	4.2.5 / 4.3.2	4.2.5
1828	SULPHUR CHLORIDES	8		I		0	E0	P602		T20	TP2
1829	SULPHUR TRIOXIDE, STABILIZED	8		I	386	0	E0	P001		T20	TP4 TP13 TP25 TP26
1830	SULPHURIC ACID with more than 51 % acid	8		II		1 L	E2	P001 IBC02		T8	TP2
1831	SULPHURIC ACID, FUMING	8	6.1	I		0	E0	P602		T20	TP2 TP13
1832	SULPHURIC ACID, SPENT	8		II	113	1 L	E0	P001 IBC02		T8	TP2
1833	SULPHUROUS ACID	8		II		1 L	E2	P001 IBC02		T7	TP2
1834	SULPHURYL CHLORIDE	6.1	8	I	354	0	E0	P602		T20	TP2 TP13
1835	TETRAMETHYLAMMONIUM HYDROXIDE AQUEOUS SOLUTION with more than 2.5 % but less than 25 % tetramethylammonium hydroxide	8	6.1	II	279 408 409	1 L	E2	P001 IBC02		T7	TP2
1835	TETRAMETHYLAMMONIUM HYDROXIDE AQUEOUS SOLUTION with not more than 2.5 % tetramethylammonium hydroxide	8		III	223 408 409	5 L	E1	P001 IBC03 LP01		T7	TP2
1836	THIONYL CHLORIDE	8		I		0	E0	P802		T10	TP2 TP13
1837	THIOPHOSPHORYL CHLORIDE	8		II		1 L	E0	P001 IBC02		T7	TP2
1838	TITANIUM TETRACHLORIDE	6.1	8	I	354	0	E0	P602		T20	TP2 TP13
1839	TRICHLOROACETIC ACID	8		II		1 kg	E2	P002 IBC08	B2, B4	T3	TP33
1840	ZINC CHLORIDE SOLUTION	8		III	223	5 L	E1	P001 IBC03 LP01		T4	TP1
1841	ACETALDEHYDE AMMONIA	9		III		5 kg	E1	P002 IBC08 LP02	B3, B6	T1	TP33
1843	AMMONIUM DINITRO-o-CRESOLATE, SOLID	6.1		II		500 g	E4	P002 IBC08	B2, B4	T3	TP33
1845	CARBON DIOXIDE, SOLID (DRY ICE)	9				0	E0	P003	PP18		
1846	CARBON TETRACHLORIDE	6.1		II		100 ml	E4	P001 IBC02		T7	TP2
1847	POTASSIUM SULPHIDE, HYDRATED with not less than 30 % water of crystallization	8		II		1 kg	E2	P002 IBC08	B2, B4	T3	TP33
1848	PROPIONIC ACID with not less than 10 % and less than 90 % acid by mass	8		III		5 L	E1	P001 IBC03 LP01		T4	TP1
1849	SODIUM SULPHIDE, HYDRATED with not less than 30 % water	8		II		1 kg	E2	P002 IBC08	B2, B4	T3	TP33
1851	MEDICINE, LIQUID, TOXIC, N.O.S.	6.1		II	221	100 ml	E4	P001			
1851	MEDICINE, LIQUID, TOXIC, N.O.S.	6.1		III	221 223	5 L	E1	P001			
1854	BARIUM ALLOYS, PYROPHORIC	4.2		I		0	E0	P404		T21	TP7 TP33

UN No.	Name and description	Class or division	Subsidiary hazard	UN packing group	Special provisions	Limited and excepted quantities		Packagings and IBCs		Portable tanks and bulk containers	
						(7a)	(7b)	Packing instruction	Special packing provisions	Instructions	Special provisions
(1)	(2)	(3)	(4)	(5)	(6)	(7a)	(7b)	(8)	(9)	(10)	(11)
-	3.1.2	2.0	2.0	2.0.1.3	3.3	3.4	3.5	4.1.4	4.1.4	4.2.5 / 4.3.2	4.2.5
1855	CALCIUM, PYROPHORIC or CALCIUM ALLOYS, PYROPHORIC	4.2		I		0	E0	P404			
1856	RAGS, OILY	4.2			29 123	0	E0	P003 IBC08	PP19 B6		
1857	TEXTILE WASTE, WET	4.2		III	123	0	E1	P410			
1858	HEXAFLUOROPROPYLENE (REFRIGERANT GAS R 1216)	2.2				120 ml	E1	P200		T50	
1859	SILICON TETRAFLUORIDE	2.3	8			0	E0	P200			
1860	VINYL FLUORIDE, STABILIZED	2.1			386	0	E0	P200			
1862	ETHYL CROTONATE	3		II		1 L	E2	P001 IBC02		T4	TP2
1863	FUEL, AVIATION, TURBINE ENGINE	3		I		500 ml	E3	P001		T11	TP1 TP8 TP28
1863	FUEL, AVIATION, TURBINE ENGINE	3		II		1 L	E2	P001 IBC02		T4	TP1 TP8
1863	FUEL, AVIATION, TURBINE ENGINE	3		III	223	5 L	E1	P001 IBC03 LP01		T2	TP1
1865	n-PROPYL NITRATE	3		II	26	1 L	E2	P001 IBC02	B7		
1866	RESIN SOLUTION, flammable	3		I		500 ml	E3	P001		T11	TP1 TP8 TP28
1866	RESIN SOLUTION, flammable	3		II		5 L	E2	P001 IBC02	PP1	T4	TP1 TP8
1866	RESIN SOLUTION, flammable	3		III	223	5 L	E1	P001 IBC03 LP01	PP1	T2	TP1
1868	DECABORANE	4.1	6.1	II		1 kg	E0	P002 IBC06	B2	T3	TP33
1869	MAGNESIUM or MAGNESIUM ALLOYS with more than 50 % magnesium in pellets, turnings or ribbons	4.1		III	59	5 kg	E1	P002 IBC08 LP02	B3	T1	TP33
1870	POTASSIUM BOROHYDRIDE	4.3		I		0	E0	P403			
1871	TITANIUM HYDRIDE	4.1		II		1 kg	E2	P410 IBC04	PP40	T3	TP33
1872	LEAD DIOXIDE	5.1		III		5 kg	E1	P002 IBC08 LP02	B3	T1	TP33
1873	PERCHLORIC ACID with more than 50 % but not more than 72 % acid, by mass	5.1	8	I	60	0	E0	P502	PP28	T10	TP1
1884	BARIUM OXIDE	6.1		III		5 kg	E1	P002 IBC08 LP02	B3	T1	TP33
1885	BENZIDINE	6.1		II		500 g	E4	P002 IBC08	B2, B4	T3	TP33
1886	BENZYLIDENE CHLORIDE	6.1		II		100 ml	E4	P001 IBC02		T7	TP2
1887	BROMOCHLOROMETHANE	6.1		III		5 L	E1	P001 IBC03 LP01		T4	TP1
1888	CHLOROFORM	6.1		III		5 L	E1	P001 IBC03 LP01		T7	TP2
1889	CYANOGEN BROMIDE	6.1	8	I		0	E0	P002		T6	TP33

UN No.	Name and description	Class or division	Subsidiary hazard	UN packing group	Special provisions	Limited and excepted quantities		Packagings and IBCs		Portable tanks and bulk containers	
						Packing instruction	Special packing provisions	Instructions	Special provisions
						(7a)	(7b)				
(1)	(2)	(3)	(4)	(5)	(6)	(7a)	(7b)	(8)	(9)	(10)	(11)
-	3.1.2	2.0	2.0	2.0.1.3	3.3	3.4	3.5	4.1.4	4.1.4	4.2.5 / 4.3.2	4.2.5
1891	ETHYL BROMIDE	3	6.1	II		1 L	E2	P001 IBC02	B8	T7	TP2 TP13
1892	ETHYLDICHLOROARSINE	6.1		I	354	0	E0	P602		T20	TP2 TP13
1894	PHENYLMERCURIC HYDROXIDE	6.1		II		500 g	E4	P002 IBC08	B2, B4	T3	TP33
1895	PHENYLMERCURIC NITRATE	6.1		II		500 g	E4	P002 IBC08	B2, B4	T3	TP33
1897	TETRACHLOROETHYLENE	6.1		III		5 L	E1	P001 IBC03 LP01		T4	TP1
1898	ACETYL IODIDE	8		II		1 L	E2	P001 IBC02		T7	TP2 TP13
1902	DIISOOCTYL ACID PHOSPHATE	8		III		5 L	E1	P001 IBC03 LP01		T4	TP1
1903	DISINFECTANT, LIQUID, CORROSIVE, N.O.S.	8		I	274	0	E0	P001			
1903	DISINFECTANT, LIQUID, CORROSIVE, N.O.S.	8		II	274	1 L	E2	P001 IBC02			
1903	DISINFECTANT, LIQUID, CORROSIVE, N.O.S.	8		III	223 274	5 L	E1	P001 IBC03 LP01			
1905	SELENIC ACID	8		I		0	E0	P002 IBC07	B1	T6	TP33
1906	SLUDGE ACID	8		II		1 L	E0	P001 IBC02		T8	TP2 TP28
1907	SODA LIME with more than 4 % sodium hydroxide	8		III	62	5 kg	E1	P002 IBC08 LP02	B3	T1	TP33
1908	CHLORITE SOLUTION	8		II		1 L	E2	P001 IBC02		T7	TP2 TP24
1908	CHLORITE SOLUTION	8		III	223	5 L	E1	P001 IBC03 LP01		T4	TP2 TP24
1910	CALCIUM OXIDE	8		III	106	5 kg	E1	P002 IBC08 LP02	B3	T1	TP33
1911	DIBORANE	2.3	2.1			0	E0	P200			
1912	METHYL CHLORIDE AND METHYLENE CHLORIDE MIXTURE	2.1			228	0	E0	P200		T50	
1913	NEON, REFRIGERATED LIQUID	2.2				120 ml	E1	P203		T75	TP5
1914	BUTYL PROPIONATES	3		III		5 L	E1	P001 IBC03 LP01		T2	TP1
1915	CYCLOHEXANONE	3		III		5 L	E1	P001 IBC03 LP01		T2	TP1
1916	2,2'-DICHLORODIETHYL ETHER	6.1	3	II		100 ml	E4	P001 IBC02		T7	TP2
1917	ETHYL ACRYLATE, STABILIZED	3		II	386	1 L	E2	P001 IBC02		T4	TP1 TP13
1918	ISOPROPYLBENZENE	3		III		5 L	E1	P001 IBC03 LP01		T2	TP1
1919	METHYL ACRYLATE, STABILIZED	3		II	386	1 L	E2	P001 IBC02		T4	TP1 TP13

UN No.	Name and description	Class or division	Subsidiary hazard	UN packing group	Special provisions	Limited and excepted quantities		Packagings and IBCs		Portable tanks and bulk containers	
						Packing instruction	Special packing provisions	Instructions	Special provisions
(1)	(2)	(3)	(4)	(5)	(6)	(7a)	(7b)	(8)	(9)	(10)	(11)
-	3.1.2	2.0	2.0	2.0.1.3	3.3	3.4	3.5	4.1.4	4.1.4	4.2.5 / 4.3.2	4.2.5
1920	NONANES	3		III		5 L	E1	P001 IBC03 LP01		T2	TP1
1921	PROPYLENEIMINE, STABILIZED	3	6.1	I	386	0	E0	P001		T14	TP2 TP13
1922	PYRROLIDINE	3	8	II		1 L	E2	P001 IBC02		T7	TP1
1923	CALCIUM DITHIONITE (CALCIUM HYDROSULPHITE)	4.2		II		0	E2	P410 IBC06	B2	T3	TP33
1928	METHYL MAGNESIUM BROMIDE IN ETHYL ETHER	4.3	3	I		0	E0	P402			
1929	POTASSIUM DITHIONITE (POTASSIUM HYDROSULPHITE)	4.2		II		0	E2	P410 IBC06	B2	T3	TP33
1931	ZINC DITHIONITE (ZINC HYDROSULPHITE)	9		III		5 kg	E1	P002 IBC08 LP02	B3	T1	TP33
1932	ZIRCONIUM SCRAP	4.2		III	223	0	E0	P002 IBC08 LP02	B3	T1	TP33
1935	CYANIDE SOLUTION, N.O.S.	6.1		I	274	0	E5	P001		T14	TP2 TP13 TP27
1935	CYANIDE SOLUTION, N.O.S.	6.1		II	274	100 ml	E4	P001 IBC02		T11	TP2 TP13 TP27
1935	CYANIDE SOLUTION, N.O.S.	6.1		III	223 274	5 L	E1	P001 IBC03 LP01		T7	TP2 TP13 TP28
1938	BROMOACETIC ACID SOLUTION	8		II		1 L	E2	P001 IBC02		T7	TP2
1938	BROMOACETIC ACID SOLUTION	8		III	223	5 L	E1	P001 IBC03 LP01		T7	TP2
1939	PHOSPHORUS OXYBROMIDE	8		II		1 kg	E0	P002 IBC08	B2, B4	T3	TP33
1940	THIOGLYCOLIC ACID	8		II		1 L	E2	P001 IBC02		T7	TP2
1941	DIBROMODIFLUOROMETHANE	9		III		5 L	E1	P001 LP01		T11	TP2
1942	AMMONIUM NITRATE with not more than 0.2 % combustible substances, including any organic substance calculated as carbon, to the exclusion of any other added substance	5.1		III	306	5 kg	E1	P002 IBC08 LP02	B3	T1 BK1 BK2 BK3	TP33
1944	MATCHES, SAFETY (book, card or strike on box)	4.1		III	293 294	5 kg	E1	P407			
1945	MATCHES, WAX 'VESTA'	4.1		III	293 294	5 kg	E1	P407			
1950	AEROSOLS	2			63 190 277 327 344 381	See SP 277	E0	P207 LP200	PP87 L2		
1951	ARGON, REFRIGERATED LIQUID	2.2				120 ml	E1	P203		T75	TP5

UN No.	Name and description	Class or division	Subsidiary hazard	UN packing group	Special provisions	Limited and excepted quantities		Packagings and IBCs		Portable tanks and bulk containers	
								Packing instruction	Special packing provisions	Instructions	Special provisions
(1)	(2)	(3)	(4)	(5)	(6)	(7a)	(7b)	(8)	(9)	(10)	(11)
-	3.1.2	2.0	2.0	2.0.1.3	3.3	3.4	3.5	4.1.4	4.1.4	4.2.5 / 4.3.2	4.2.5
1952	ETHYLENE OXIDE AND CARBON DIOXIDE MIXTURE with not more than 9 % ethylene oxide	2.2			392	120 ml	E1	P200			
1953	COMPRESSED GAS, TOXIC, FLAMMABLE, N.O.S.	2.3	2.1		274	0	E0	P200			
1954	COMPRESSED GAS, FLAMMABLE, N.O.S.	2.1			274 392	0	E0	P200			
1955	COMPRESSED GAS, TOXIC, N.O.S.	2.3			274	0	E0	P200			
1956	COMPRESSED GAS, N.O.S.	2.2			274 378 392	120 ml	E1	P200			
1957	DEUTERIUM, COMPRESSED	2.1				0	E0	P200			
1958	1,2-DICHLORO-1,1,2,2-TETRAFLUOROETHANE (REFRIGERANT GAS R 114)	2.2				120 ml	E1	P200		T50	
1959	1,1-DIFLUOROETHYLENE (REFRIGERANT GAS R 1132a)	2.1				0	E0	P200			
1961	ETHANE, REFRIGERATED LIQUID	2.1				0	E0	P203		T75	TP5
1962	ETHYLENE	2.1				0	E0	P200			
1963	HELIUM, REFRIGERATED LIQUID	2.2				120 ml	E1	P203		T75	TP5 TP34
1964	HYDROCARBON GAS MIXTURE, COMPRESSED, N.O.S.	2.1			274	0	E0	P200			
1965	HYDROCARBON GAS MIXTURE, LIQUEFIED, N.O.S.	2.1			274 392	0	E0	P200		T50	
1966	HYDROGEN, REFRIGERATED LIQUID	2.1				0	E0	P203		T75	TP5 TP34
1967	INSECTICIDE GAS, TOXIC, N.O.S.	2.3			274	0	E0	P200			
1968	INSECTICIDE GAS, N.O.S.	2.2			274	120 ml	E1	P200			
1969	ISOBUTANE	2.1			392	0	E0	P200		T50	
1970	KRYPTON, REFRIGERATED LIQUID	2.2				120 ml	E1	P203		T75	TP5
1971	METHANE, COMPRESSED or NATURAL GAS, COMPRESSED with high methane content	2.1			392	0	E0	P200			
1972	METHANE, REFRIGERATED LIQUID or NATURAL GAS, REFRIGERATED LIQUID with high methane content	2.1				0	E0	P203		T75	TP5
1973	CHLORODIFLUOROMETHANE AND CHLOROPENTAFLUORO-ETHANE MIXTURE with fixed boiling point, with approximately 49 % chlorodifluoromethane (REFRIGERANT GAS R 502)	2.2				120 ml	E1	P200		T50	
1974	CHLORODIFLUORO-BROMOMETHANE (REFRIGERANT GAS R 12B1)	2.2				120 ml	E1	P200		T50	
1975	NITRIC OXIDE AND DINITROGEN TETROXIDE MIXTURE (NITRIC OXIDE AND NITROGEN DIOXIDE MIXTURE)	2.3	5.1 8			0	E0	P200			
1976	OCTAFLUOROCYCLOBUTANE (REFRIGERANT GAS RC 318)	2.2				120 ml	E1	P200		T50	

UN No.	Name and description	Class or division	Subsidiary hazard	UN packing group	Special provisions	Limited and excepted quantities		Packagings and IBCs		Portable tanks and bulk containers	
								Packing instruction	Special packing provisions	Instructions	Special provisions
(1)	(2)	(3)	(4)	(5)	(6)	(7a)	(7b)	(8)	(9)	(10)	(11)
-	3.1.2	2.0	2.0	2.0.1.3	3.3	3.4	3.5	4.1.4	4.1.4	4.2.5 / 4.3.2	4.2.5
1977	NITROGEN, REFRIGERATED LIQUID	2.2			345 346	120 ml	E1	P203		T75	TP5
1978	PROPANE	2.1			392	0	E0	P200		T50	
1982	TETRAFLUOROMETHANE (REFRIGERANT GAS R 14)	2.2				120 ml	E1	P200			
1983	1-CHLORO-2,2,2-TRIFLUOROETHANE (REFRIGERANT GAS R 133a)	2.2				120 ml	E1	P200		T50	
1984	TRIFLUOROMETHANE (REFRIGERANT GAS R 23)	2.2				120 ml	E1	P200			
1986	ALCOHOLS, FLAMMABLE, TOXIC, N.O.S.	3	6.1	I	274	0	E0	P001		T14	TP2 TP13 TP27
1986	ALCOHOLS, FLAMMABLE, TOXIC, N.O.S.	3	6.1	II	274	1 L	E2	P001 IBC02		T11	TP2 TP27
1986	ALCOHOLS, FLAMMABLE, TOXIC, N.O.S.	3	6.1	III	223 274	5 L	E1	P001 IBC03		T7	TP1 TP28
1987	ALCOHOLS, N.O.S.	3		II	274	1 L	E2	P001 IBC02		T7	TP1 TP8 TP28
1987	ALCOHOLS, N.O.S.	3		III	223 274	5 L	E1	P001 IBC03 LP01		T4	TP1 TP29
1988	ALDEHYDES, FLAMMABLE, TOXIC, N.O.S.	3	6.1	I	274	0	E0	P001		T14	TP2 TP13 TP27
1988	ALDEHYDES, FLAMMABLE, TOXIC, N.O.S.	3	6.1	II	274	1 L	E2	P001 IBC02		T11	TP2 TP27
1988	ALDEHYDES, FLAMMABLE, TOXIC, N.O.S.	3	6.1	III	223 274	5 L	E1	P001 IBC03		T7	TP1 TP28
1989	ALDEHYDES, N.O.S.	3		I	274	0	E3	P001		T11	TP1 TP27
1989	ALDEHYDES, N.O.S.	3		II	274	1 L	E2	P001 IBC02		T7	TP1 TP8 TP28
1989	ALDEHYDES, N.O.S.	3		III	223 274	5 L	E1	P001 IBC03 LP01		T4	TP1 TP29
1990	BENZALDEHYDE	9		III		5 L	E1	P001 IBC03 LP01		T2	TP1
1991	CHLOROPRENE, STABILIZED	3	6.1	I	386	0	E0	P001		T14	TP2 TP6 TP13
1992	FLAMMABLE LIQUID, TOXIC, N.O.S.	3	6.1	I	274	0	E0	P001		T14	TP2 TP13 TP27
1992	FLAMMABLE LIQUID, TOXIC, N.O.S.	3	6.1	II	274	1 L	E2	P001 IBC02		T7	TP2 TP13
1992	FLAMMABLE LIQUID, TOXIC, N.O.S.	3	6.1	III	223 274	5 L	E1	P001 IBC03		T7	TP1 TP28
1993	FLAMMABLE LIQUID, N.O.S.	3		I	274	0	E3	P001		T11	TP1 TP27
1993	FLAMMABLE LIQUID, N.O.S.	3		II	274	1 L	E2	P001 IBC02		T7	TP1 TP8 TP28
1993	FLAMMABLE LIQUID, N.O.S.	3		III	223 274	5 L	E1	P001 IBC03 LP01		T4	TP1 TP29

UN No.	Name and description	Class or division	Subsidiary hazard	UN packing group	Special provisions	Limited and excepted quantities		Packagings and IBCs		Portable tanks and bulk containers	
						(7a)	(7b)	Packing instruction	Special packing provisions	Instructions	Special provisions
(1)	(2)	(3)	(4)	(5)	(6)	(7a)	(7b)	(8)	(9)	(10)	(11)
-	3.1.2	2.0	2.0	2.0.1.3	3.3	3.4	3.5	4.1.4	4.1.4	4.2.5 / 4.3.2	4.2.5
1994	IRON PENTACARBONYL	6.1	3	I	354	0	E0	P601		T22	TP2 TP13
1999	TARS, LIQUID, including road oils, and cutback bitumens	3		II		5 L	E2	P001 IBC02		T3	TP3 TP29
1999	TARS, LIQUID, including road oils, and cutback bitumens	3		III	223	5 L	E1	P001 IBC03 LP01		T1	TP3
2000	CELLULOID in block, rods, rolls, sheets, tubes, etc., except scrap	4.1		III	223 383	5 kg	E1	P002 LP02	PP7		
2001	COBALT NAPHTHENATES, POWDER	4.1		III		5 kg	E1	P002 IBC08 LP02	B3	T1	TP33
2002	CELLULOID, SCRAP	4.2		III	223	0	E0	P002 IBC08 LP02	PP8 B3		
2004	MAGNESIUM DIAMIDE	4.2		II		0	E2	P410 IBC06		T3	TP33
2006	PLASTICS, NITROCELLULOSE-BASED, SELF-HEATING, N.O.S.	4.2		III	274	0	E0	P002			
2008	ZIRCONIUM POWDER, DRY	4.2		I		0	E0	P404		T21	TP7 TP33
2008	ZIRCONIUM POWDER, DRY	4.2		II		0	E2	P410 IBC06	B2	T3	TP33
2008	ZIRCONIUM POWDER, DRY	4.2		III	223	0	E1	P002 IBC08 LP02	B3	T1	TP33
2009	ZIRCONIUM, DRY, finished sheets, strip or coiled wire	4.2		III	223	0	E1	P002 LP02			
2010	MAGNESIUM HYDRIDE	4.3		I		0	E0	P403			
2011	MAGNESIUM PHOSPHIDE	4.3	6.1	I		0	E0	P403			
2012	POTASSIUM PHOSPHIDE	4.3	6.1	I		0	E0	P403			
2013	STRONTIUM PHOSPHIDE	4.3	6.1	I		0	E0	P403			
2014	HYDROGEN PEROXIDE, AQUEOUS SOLUTION with not less than 20 % but not more than 60 % hydrogen peroxide (stabilized as necessary)	5.1	8	II		1 L	E2	P504 IBC02	PP10 B5	T7	TP2 TP6 TP24
2015	HYDROGEN PEROXIDE, STABILIZED or HYDROGEN PEROXIDE, AQUEOUS SOLUTION, STABILIZED with more than 60 % hydrogen peroxide	5.1	8	I		0	E0	P501		T9	TP2 TP6 TP24
2016	AMMUNITION, TOXIC, NON-EXPLOSIVE without burster or expelling charge, non-fuzed	6.1				0	E0	P600			
2017	AMMUNITION, TEAR-PRODUCING, NON-EXPLOSIVE without burster or expelling charge, non-fuzed	6.1	8			0	E0	P600			
2018	CHLOROANILINES, SOLID	6.1		II		500 g	E4	P002 IBC08	B2, B4	T3	TP33
2019	CHLOROANILINES, LIQUID	6.1		II		100 ml	E4	P001 IBC02		T7	TP2
2020	CHLOROPHENOLS, SOLID	6.1		III	205	5 kg	E1	P002 IBC08 LP02	B3	T1	TP33
2021	CHLOROPHENOLS, LIQUID	6.1		III		5 L	E1	P001 IBC03 LP01		T4	TP1

UN No.	Name and description	Class or division	Subsidiary hazard	UN packing group	Special provisions	Limited and excepted quantities		Packagings and IBCs		Portable tanks and bulk containers	
								Packing instruction	Special packing provisions	Instructions	Special provisions
(1)	(2)	(3)	(4)	(5)	(6)	(7a)	(7b)	(8)	(9)	(10)	(11)
-	3.1.2	2.0	2.0	2.0.1.3	3.3	3.4	3.5	4.1.4	4.1.4	4.2.5 / 4.3.2	4.2.5
2022	CRESYLIC ACID	6.1	8	II		100 ml	E4	P001 IBC02		T7	TP2 TP13
2023	EPICHLOROHYDRIN	6.1	3	II	279	100 ml	E4	P001 IBC02		T7	TP2 TP13
2024	MERCURY COMPOUND, LIQUID, N.O.S.	6.1		I	43 66 274	0	E5	P001			
2024	MERCURY COMPOUND, LIQUID, N.O.S.	6.1		II	43 66 274	100 ml	E4	P001 IBC02			
2024	MERCURY COMPOUND, LIQUID, N.O.S.	6.1		III	43 66 223 274	5 L	E1	P001 IBC03 LP01			
2025	MERCURY COMPOUND, SOLID, N.O.S.	6.1		I	43 66 274	0	E5	P002 IBC07	B1	T6	TP33
2025	MERCURY COMPOUND, SOLID, N.O.S.	6.1		II	43 66 274	500 g	E4	P002 IBC08	B2, B4	T3	TP33
2025	MERCURY COMPOUND, SOLID, N.O.S.	6.1		III	43 66 223 274	5 kg	E1	P002 IBC08 LP02	B3	T1	TP33
2026	PHENYLMERCURIC COMPOUND, N.O.S.	6.1		I	43 274	0	E5	P002 IBC07	B1	T6	TP33
2026	PHENYLMERCURIC COMPOUND, N.O.S.	6.1		II	43 274	500 g	E4	P002 IBC08	B2, B4	T3	TP33
2026	PHENYLMERCURIC COMPOUND, N.O.S.	6.1		III	43 223 274	5 kg	E1	P002 IBC08 LP02	B3	T1	TP33
2027	SODIUM ARSENITE, SOLID	6.1		II	43	500 g	E4	P002 IBC08	B2, B4	T3	TP33
2028	BOMBS, SMOKE, NON-EXPLOSIVE with corrosive liquid, without initiating device	8				0	E0	P803			
2029	HYDRAZINE, ANHYDROUS	8	3 6.1	I		0	E0	P001			
2030	HYDRAZINE AQUEOUS SOLUTION with more than 37 % hydrazine, by mass	8	6.1	I		0	E0	P001		T10	TP2 TP13
2030	HYDRAZINE AQUEOUS SOLUTION with more than 37 % hydrazine, by mass	8	6.1	II		1 L	E0	P001 IBC02		T7	TP2 TP13
2030	HYDRAZINE AQUEOUS SOLUTION with more than 37 % hydrazine, by mass	8	6.1	III		5 L	E1	P001 IBC03 LP01		T4	TP1
2031	NITRIC ACID, other than red fuming, with more than 70 % nitric acid	8	5.1	I		0	E0	P001	PP81	T10	TP2 TP13
2031	NITRIC ACID, other than red fuming, with at least 65 %, but not more than 70 % nitric acid	8	5.1	II		1 L	E2	P001 IBC02	PP81 B15	T8	TP2
2031	NITRIC ACID, other than red fuming, with less than 65 % nitric acid	8		II		1 L	E2	P001 IBC02	PP81 B15	T8	TP2
2032	NITRIC ACID, RED FUMING	8	5.1 6.1	I		0	E0	P602	PP81	T20	TP2 TP13
2033	POTASSIUM MONOXIDE	8		II		1 kg	E2	P002 IBC08	B2, B4	T3	TP33

UN No.	Name and description	Class or division	Subsidiary hazard	UN packing group	Special provisions	Limited and excepted quantities		Packagings and IBCs		Portable tanks and bulk containers	
								Packing instruction	Special packing provisions	Instructions	Special provisions
(1)	(2)	(3)	(4)	(5)	(6)	(7a)	(7b)	(8)	(9)	(10)	(11)
-	3.1.2	2.0	2.0	2.0.1.3	3.3	3.4	3.5	4.1.4	4.1.4	4.2.5 / 4.3.2	4.2.5
2034	HYDROGEN AND METHANE MIXTURE, COMPRESSED	2.1				0	E0	P200			
2035	1,1,1-TRIFLUOROETHANE (REFRIGERANT GAS R 143a)	2.1				0	E0	P200		T50	
2036	XENON	2.2			378 392	120 ml	E1	P200			
2037	RECEPTACLES, SMALL, CONTAINING GAS (GAS CARTRIDGES) without a release device, non-refillable	2			191 277 303 327 344	See SP 277	E0	P003 LP200	PP17, PP96 L2		
2038	DINITROTOLUENES, LIQUID	6.1		II		100 ml	E4	P001 IBC02		T7	TP2
2044	2,2-DIMETHYLPROPANE	2.1				0	E0	P200			
2045	ISOBUTYRALDEHYDE (ISOBUTYL ALDEHYDE)	3		II		1 L	E2	P001 IBC02		T4	TP1
2046	CYMENES	3		III		5 L	E1	P001 IBC03 LP01		T2	TP1
2047	DICHLOROPROPENES	3		II		1 L	E2	P001 IBC02		T4	TP1
2047	DICHLOROPROPENES	3		III	223	5 L	E1	P001 IBC03 LP01		T2	TP1
2048	DICYCLOPENTADIENE	3		III		5 L	E1	P001 IBC03 LP01		T2	TP1
2049	DIETHYLBENZENE	3		III		5 L	E1	P001 IBC03 LP01		T2	TP1
2050	DIISOBUTYLENE, ISOMERIC COMPOUNDS	3		II		1 L	E2	P001 IBC02		T4	TP1
2051	2-DIMETHYLAMINOETHANOL	8	3	II		1 L	E2	P001 IBC02		T7	TP2
2052	DIPENTENE	3		III		5 L	E1	P001 IBC03 LP01		T2	TP1
2053	METHYL ISOBUTYL CARBINOL	3		III		5 L	E1	P001 IBC03 LP01		T2	TP1
2054	MORPHOLINE	8	3	I		0	E0	P001		T10	TP2
2055	STYRENE MONOMER, STABILIZED	3		III	386	5 L	E1	P001 IBC03 LP01		T2	TP1
2056	TETRAHYDROFURAN	3		II		1 L	E2	P001 IBC02		T4	TP1
2057	TRIPROPYLENE	3		II		1 L	E2	P001 IBC02		T4	TP1
2057	TRIPROPYLENE	3		III	223	5 L	E1	P001 IBC03 LP01		T2	TP1
2058	VALERALDEHYDE	3		II		1 L	E2	P001 IBC02		T4	TP1
2059	NITROCELLULOSE SOLUTION, FLAMMABLE with not more than 12.6 % nitrogen, by dry mass, and not more than 55 % nitrocellulose	3		I	28 198	0	E0	P001		T11	TP1 TP8 TP27

UN No.	Name and description	Class or division	Subsidiary hazard	UN packing group	Special provisions	Limited and excepted quantities		Packagings and IBCs		Portable tanks and bulk containers	
								Packing instruction	Special packing provisions	Instructions	Special provisions
(1)	(2)	(3)	(4)	(5)	(6)	(7a)	(7b)	(8)	(9)	(10)	(11)
-	3.1.2	2.0	2.0	2.0.1.3	3.3	3.4	3.5	4.1.4	4.1.4	4.2.5 / 4.3.2	4.2.5
2059	NITROCELLULOSE SOLUTION, FLAMMABLE with not more than 12.6 % nitrogen, by dry mass, and not more than 55 % nitrocellulose	3		II	28 198	1 L	E0	P001 IBC02		T4	TP1 TP8
2059	NITROCELLULOSE SOLUTION, FLAMMABLE with not more than 12.6 % nitrogen, by dry mass, and not more than 55 % nitrocellulose	3		III	28 198 223	5 L	E0	P001 IBC03 LP01		T2	TP1
2067	AMMONIUM NITRATE BASED FERTILIZER	5.1		III	306 307	5 kg	E1	P002 IBC08 LP02	B3	T1 BK1 BK2 BK3	TP33
2071	AMMONIUM NITRATE BASED FERTILIZER	9		III	193	5 kg	E1	P002 IBC08 LP02	B3	BK2	
2073	AMMONIA SOLUTION, relative density less than 0.880 at 15 °C in water, with more than 35 % but not more than 50 % ammonia	2.2				120 ml	E0	P200			
2074	ACRYLAMIDE, SOLID	6.1		III		5 kg	E1	P002 IBC08 LP02	B3	T1	TP33
2075	CHLORAL, ANHYDROUS, STABILIZED	6.1		II		100 ml	E4	P001 IBC02		T7	TP2
2076	CRESOLS, LIQUID	6.1	8	II		100 ml	E4	P001 IBC02		T7	TP2
2077	alpha-NAPHTHYLAMINE	6.1		III		5 kg	E1	P002 IBC08 LP02	B3	T1	TP33
2078	TOLUENE DIISOCYANATE	6.1		II	279	100 ml	E4	P001 IBC02		T7	TP2 TP13
2079	DIETHYLENETRIAMINE	8		II		1 L	E2	P001 IBC02		T7	TP2
2186	HYDROGEN CHLORIDE, REFRIGERATED LIQUID	2.3	8			0	E0	P099			
2187	CARBON DIOXIDE, REFRIGERATED LIQUID	2.2				120 ml	E1	P203		T75	TP5
2188	ARSINE	2.3	2.1			0	E0	P200			
2189	DICHLOROSILANE	2.3	2.1 8			0	E0	P200			
2190	OXYGEN DIFLUORIDE, COMPRESSED	2.3	5.1 8			0	E0	P200			
2191	SULPHURYL FLUORIDE	2.3				0	E0	P200			
2192	GERMANE	2.3	2.1			0	E0	P200			
2193	HEXAFLUOROETHANE (REFRIGERANT GAS R 116)	2.2				120 ml	E1	P200			
2194	SELENIUM HEXAFLUORIDE	2.3	8			0	E0	P200			
2195	TELLURIUM HEXAFLUORIDE	2.3	8			0	E0	P200			
2196	TUNGSTEN HEXAFLUORIDE	2.3	8			0	E0	P200			
2197	HYDROGEN IODIDE, ANHYDROUS	2.3	8			0	E0	P200			
2198	PHOSPHORUS PENTAFLUORIDE	2.3	8			0	E0	P200			
2199	PHOSPHINE	2.3	2.1			0	E0	P200			
2200	PROPADIENE, STABILIZED	2.1			386	0	E0	P200			
2201	NITROUS OXIDE, REFRIGERATED LIQUID	2.2	5.1			0	E0	P203		T75	TP5 TP22

UN No.	Name and description	Class or division	Subsidiary hazard	UN packing group	Special provisions	Limited and excepted quantities		Packagings and IBCs		Portable tanks and bulk containers	
								Packing instruction	Special packing provisions	Instructions	Special provisions
(1)	(2)	(3)	(4)	(5)	(6)	(7a)	(7b)	(8)	(9)	(10)	(11)
-	3.1.2	2.0	2.0	2.0.1.3	3.3	3.4	3.5	4.1.4	4.1.4	4.2.5 / 4.3.2	4.2.5
2202	HYDROGEN SELENIDE, ANHYDROUS	2.3	2.1			0	E0	P200			
2203	SILANE	2.1				0	E0	P200			
2204	CARBONYL SULPHIDE	2.3	2.1			0	E0	P200			
2205	ADIPONITRILE	6.1		III		5 L	E1	P001 IBC03 LP01		T3	TP1
2206	ISOCYANATES, TOXIC, N.O.S. or ISOCYANATE SOLUTION, TOXIC, N.O.S.	6.1		II	274	100 ml	E4	P001 IBC02		T11	TP2 TP13 TP27
2206	ISOCYANATES, TOXIC, N.O.S. or ISOCYANATE SOLUTION, TOXIC, N.O.S.	6.1		III	223 274	5 L	E1	P001 IBC03 LP01		T7	TP1 TP13 TP28
2208	CALCIUM HYPOCHLORITE MIXTURE, DRY with more than 10 % but not more than 39 % available chlorine	5.1		III	314	5 kg	E1	P002 IBC08 LP02	PP85 B3, B13 L3		
2209	FORMALDEHYDE SOLUTION with not less than 25 % formaldehyde	8		III		5 L	E1	P001 IBC03 LP01		T4	TP1
2210	MANEB or MANEB PREPARATION with not less than 60 % maneb	4.2	4.3	III	273	0	E1	P002 IBC06		T1	TP33
2211	POLYMERIC BEADS, EXPANDABLE, evolving flammable vapour	9		III	382	5 kg	E1	P002 IBC08	PP14 B3, B6	T1	TP33
2212	ASBESTOS, AMPHIBOLE (amosite, tremolite, actinolite, anthophyllite, crocidolite)	9		II	168 274	1 kg	E0	P002 IBC08	PP37 B2, B4	T3	TP33
2213	PARAFORMALDEHYDE	4.1		III	223	5 kg	E1	P002 IBC08 LP02	PP12 B3	T1 BK1 BK2 BK3	TP33
2214	PHTHALIC ANHYDRIDE with more than 0.05 % of maleic anhydride	8		III	169	5 kg	E1	P002 IBC08 LP02	B3	T1	TP33
2215	MALEIC ANHYDRIDE	8		III		5 kg	E1	P002 IBC08	B3	T1	TP33
2215	MALEIC ANHYDRIDE, MOLTEN	8		III		0	E0	NONE		T4	TP3
2216	FISH MEAL (FISH SCRAP), STABILIZED	9		III	29 117 300 308	0	E1	P900 IBC08	B3	T1 BK2	TP33
2217	SEED CAKE with not more than 1.5 % oil and not more than 11 % moisture	4.2		III	29 142	0	E0	P002 IBC08 LP02	PP20 B3, B6	BK2	
2218	ACRYLIC ACID, STABILIZED	8	3	II	386	1 L	E2	P001 IBC02		T7	TP2
2219	ALLYL GLYCIDYL ETHER	3		III		5 L	E1	P001 IBC03 LP01		T2	TP1
2222	ANISOLE	3		III		5 L	E1	P001 IBC03 LP01		T2	TP1
2224	BENZONITRILE	6.1		II		100 ml	E4	P001 IBC02		T7	TP2
2225	BENZENESULPHONYL CHLORIDE	8		III		5 L	E1	P001 IBC03 LP01		T4	TP1

UN No.	Name and description	Class or division	Subsi-diary hazard	UN packing group	Special provi-sions	Limited and excepted quantities		Packagings and IBCs		Portable tanks and bulk containers	
								Packing instruction	Special packing provisions	Instruc-tions	Special provisions
(1)	(2)	(3)	(4)	(5)	(6)	(7a)	(7b)	(8)	(9)	(10)	(11)
-	3.1.2	2.0	2.0	2.0.1.3	3.3	3.4	3.5	4.1.4	4.1.4	4.2.5 / 4.3.2	4.2.5
2226	BENZOTRICHLORIDE	8		II		1 L	E2	P001 IBC02		T7	TP2
2227	n-BUTYL METHACRYLATE, STABILIZED	3		III	386	5 L	E1	P001 IBC03 LP01		T2	TP1
2232	2-CHLOROETHANAL	6.1		I	354	0	E0	P602		T20	TP2 TP13
2233	CHLOROANISIDINES	6.1		III		5 kg	E1	P002 IBC08 LP02	B3	T1	TP33
2234	CHLOROBENZOTRIFLUORIDES	3		III		5 L	E1	P001 IBC03 LP01		T2	TP1
2235	CHLOROBENZYL CHLORIDES, LIQUID	6.1		III		5 L	E1	P001 IBC03 LP01		T4	TP1
2236	3-CHLORO-4-METHYLPHENYL ISOCYANATE, LIQUID	6.1		II		100 ml	E4	P001 IBC02			
2237	CHLORONITROANILINES	6.1		III		5 kg	E1	P002 IBC08 LP02	B3	T1	TP33
2238	CHLOROTOLUENES	3		III		5 L	E1	P001 IBC03 LP01		T2	TP1
2239	CHLOROTOLUIDINES, SOLID	6.1		III		5 kg	E1	P002 IBC08 LP02	B3	T1	TP33
2240	CHROMOSULPHURIC ACID	8		I		0	E0	P001		T10	TP2 TP13
2241	CYCLOHEPTANE	3		II		1 L	E2	P001 IBC02		T4	TP1
2242	CYCLOHEPTENE	3		II		1 L	E2	P001 IBC02		T4	TP1
2243	CYCLOHEXYL ACETATE	3		III		5 L	E1	P001 IBC03 LP01		T2	TP1
2244	CYCLOPENTANOL	3		III		5 L	E1	P001 IBC03 LP01		T2	TP1
2245	CYCLOPENTANONE	3		III		5 L	E1	P001 IBC03 LP01		T2	TP1
2246	CYCLOPENTENE	3		II		1 L	E2	P001 IBC02	B8	T7	TP2
2247	n-DECANE	3		III		5 L	E1	P001 IBC03 LP01		T2	TP1
2248	DI-n-BUTYLAMINE	8	3	II		1 L	E2	P001 IBC02		T7	TP2
2249	DICHLORODIMETHYL ETHER, SYMMETRICAL	6.1	3	I		0	E0	P099			
2250	DICHLOROPHENYL ISOCYANATES	6.1		II		500 g	E4	P002 IBC08	B2, B4	T3	TP33
2251	BICYCLO[2.2.1]-HEPTA-2,5-DIENE, STABILIZED (2,5-NORBORNADIENE, STABILIZED)	3		II	386	1 L	E2	P001 IBC02		T7	TP2
2252	1,2-DIMETHOXYETHANE	3		II		1 L	E2	P001 IBC02		T4	TP1

UN No.	Name and description	Class or division	Subsidiary hazard	UN packing group	Special provisions	Limited and excepted quantities		Packagings and IBCs		Portable tanks and bulk containers	
								Packing instruction	Special packing provisions	Instructions	Special provisions
(1)	(2)	(3)	(4)	(5)	(6)	(7a)	(7b)	(8)	(9)	(10)	(11)
-	3.1.2	2.0	2.0	2.0.1.3	3.3	3.4	3.5	4.1.4	4.1.4	4.2.5 / 4.3.2	4.2.5
2253	N,N-DIMETHYLANILINE	6.1		II		100 ml	E4	P001 IBC02		T7	TP2
2254	MATCHES, FUSEE	4.1		III	293	5 kg	E0	P407			
2256	CYCLOHEXENE	3		II		1 L	E2	P001 IBC02		T4	TP1
2257	POTASSIUM	4.3		I		0	E0	P403 IBC04	B1	T9	TP7 TP33
2258	1,2-PROPYLENEDIAMINE	8	3	II		1 L	E2	P001 IBC02		T7	TP2
2259	TRIETHYLENETETRAMINE	8		II		1 L	E2	P001 IBC02		T7	TP2
2260	TRIPROPYLAMINE	3	8	III		5 L	E1	P001 IBC03		T4	TP1
2261	XYLENOLS, SOLID	6.1		II		500 g	E4	P002 IBC08	B2, B4	T3	TP33
2262	DIMETHYLCARBAMOYL CHLORIDE	8		II		1 L	E2	P001 IBC02		T7	TP2
2263	DIMETHYLCYCLOHEXANES	3		II		1 L	E2	P001 IBC02		T4	TP1
2264	N,N-DIMETHYL-CYCLOHEXYLAMINE	8	3	II		1 L	E2	P001 IBC02		T7	TP2
2265	N,N-DIMETHYLFORMAMIDE	3		III		5 L	E1	P001 IBC03 LP01		T2	TP2
2266	DIMETHYL-N-PROPYLAMINE	3	8	II		1 L	E2	P001 IBC02		T7	TP2 TP13
2267	DIMETHYL THIOPHOSPHORYL CHLORIDE	6.1	8	II		100 ml	E4	P001 IBC02		T7	TP2
2269	3,3'-IMINODIPROPYLAMINE	8		III		5 L	E1	P001 IBC03 LP01		T4	TP2
2270	ETHYLAMINE, AQUEOUS SOLUTION with not less than 50 % but not more than 70 % ethylamine	3	8	II		1 L	E2	P001 IBC02		T7	TP1
2271	ETHYL AMYL KETONE	3		III		5 L	E1	P001 IBC03 LP01		T2	TP1
2272	N-ETHYLANILINE	6.1		III		5 L	E1	P001 IBC03 LP01		T4	TP1
2273	2-ETHYLANILINE	6.1		III		5 L	E1	P001 IBC03 LP01		T4	TP1
2274	N-ETHYL-N-BENZYLANILINE	6.1		III		5 L	E1	P001 IBC03 LP01		T4	TP1
2275	2-ETHYLBUTANOL	3		III		5 L	E1	P001 IBC03 LP01		T2	TP1
2276	2-ETHYLHEXYLAMINE	3	8	III		5 L	E1	P001 IBC03		T4	TP1
2277	ETHYL METHACRYLATE, STABILIZED	3		II	386	1 L	E2	P001 IBC02		T4	TP1
2278	n-HEPTENE	3		II		1 L	E2	P001 IBC02		T4	TP1
2279	HEXACHLOROBUTADIENE	6.1		III		5 L	E1	P001 IBC03 LP01		T4	TP1

UN No.	Name and description	Class or division	Subsidiary hazard	UN packing group	Special provisions	Limited and excepted quantities		Packagings and IBCs		Portable tanks and bulk containers	
								Packing instruction	Special packing provisions	Instructions	Special provisions
(1)	(2)	(3)	(4)	(5)	(6)	(7a)	(7b)	(8)	(9)	(10)	(11)
-	3.1.2	2.0	2.0	2.0.1.3	3.3	3.4	3.5	4.1.4	4.1.4	4.2.5 / 4.3.2	4.2.5
2280	HEXAMETHYLENEDIAMINE, SOLID	8		III		5 kg	E1	P002 IBC08 LP02	B3	T1	TP33
2281	HEXAMETHYLENE-DIISOCYANATE	6.1		II		100 ml	E4	P001 IBC02		T7	TP2 TP13
2282	HEXANOLS	3		III		5 L	E1	P001 IBC03 LP01		T2	TP1
2283	ISOBUTYL METHACRYLATE, STABILIZED	3		III	386	5 L	E1	P001 IBC03 LP01		T2	TP1
2284	ISOBUTYRONITRILE	3	6.1	II		1 L	E2	P001 IBC02		T7	TP2 TP13
2285	ISOCYANATOBENZO-TRIFLUORIDES	6.1	3	II		100 ml	E4	P001 IBC02		T7	TP2
2286	PENTAMETHYLHEPTANE	3		III		5 L	E1	P001 IBC03 LP01		T2	TP1
2287	ISOHEPTENES	3		II		1 L	E2	P001 IBC02		T4	TP1
2288	ISOHEXENES	3		II		1 L	E2	P001 IBC02	B8	T11	TP1
2289	ISOPHORONEDIAMINE	8		III		5 L	E1	P001 IBC03 LP01		T4	TP1
2290	ISOPHORONE DIISOCYANATE	6.1		III		5 L	E1	P001 IBC03 LP01		T4	TP2
2291	LEAD COMPOUND, SOLUBLE, N.O.S.	6.1		III	199 274	5 kg	E1	P002 IBC08 LP02	B3	T1	TP33
2293	4-METHOXY-4-METHYLPENTAN-2-ONE	3		III		5 L	E1	P001 IBC03 LP01		T2	TP1
2294	N-METHYLANILINE	6.1		III		5 L	E1	P001 IBC03 LP01		T4	TP1
2295	METHYL CHLOROACETATE	6.1	3	I		0	E0	P001		T14	TP2 TP13
2296	METHYLCYCLOHEXANE	3		II		1 L	E2	P001 IBC02		T4	TP1
2297	METHYLCYCLOHEXANONE	3		III		5 L	E1	P001 IBC03 LP01		T2	TP1
2298	METHYLCYCLOPENTANE	3		II		1 L	E2	P001 IBC02		T4	TP1
2299	METHYL DICHLOROACETATE	6.1		III		5 L	E1	P001 IBC03 LP01		T4	TP1
2300	2-METHYL-5-ETHYLPYRIDINE	6.1		III		5 L	E1	P001 IBC03 LP01		T4	TP1
2301	2-METHYLFURAN	3		II		1 L	E2	P001 IBC02		T4	TP1
2302	5-METHYLHEXAN-2-ONE	3		III		5 L	E1	P001 IBC03 LP01		T2	TP1
2303	ISOPROPENYLBENZENE	3		III		5 L	E1	P001 IBC03 LP01		T2	TP1

UN No.	Name and description	Class or division	Subsidiary hazard	UN packing group	Special provisions	Limited and excepted quantities		Packagings and IBCs		Portable tanks and bulk containers	
								Packing instruction	Special packing provisions	Instructions	Special provisions
(1)	(2)	(3)	(4)	(5)	(6)	(7a)	(7b)	(8)	(9)	(10)	(11)
-	3.1.2	2.0	2.0	2.0.1.3	3.3	3.4	3.5	4.1.4	4.1.4	4.2.5 / 4.3.2	4.2.5
2304	NAPHTHALENE, MOLTEN	4.1		III		0	E0	NONE		T1	TP3
2305	NITROBENZENESULPHONIC ACID	8		II		1 kg	E2	P002 IBC08	B2, B4	T3	TP33
2306	NITROBENZOTRIFLUORIDES, LIQUID	6.1		II		100 ml	E4	P001 IBC02		T7	TP2
2307	3-NITRO-4-CHLOROBENZOTRIFLUORIDE	6.1		II		100 ml	E4	P001 IBC02		T7	TP2
2308	NITROSYLSULPHURIC ACID, LIQUID	8		II		1 L	E2	P001 IBC02		T8	TP2
2309	OCTADIENE	3		II		1 L	E2	P001 IBC02		T4	TP1
2310	PENTANE-2,4-DIONE	3	6.1	III		5 L	E1	P001 IBC03		T4	TP1
2311	PHENETIDINES	6.1		III	279	5 L	E1	P001 IBC03 LP01		T4	TP1
2312	PHENOL, MOLTEN	6.1		II		0	E0	NONE		T7	TP3
2313	PICOLINES	3		III		5 L	E1	P001 IBC03 LP01		T4	TP1
2315	POLYCHLORINATED BIPHENYLS, LIQUID	9		II	305	1 L	E2	P906 IBC02		T4	TP1
2316	SODIUM CUPROCYANIDE, SOLID	6.1		I		0	E5	P002 IBC07	B1	T6	TP33
2317	SODIUM CUPROCYANIDE SOLUTION	6.1		I		0	E5	P001		T14	TP2 TP13
2318	SODIUM HYDROSULPHIDE with less than 25 % water of crystallization	4.2		II		0	E2	P410 IBC06	B2	T3	TP33
2319	TERPENE HYDROCARBONS, N.O.S.	3		III		5 L	E1	P001 IBC03 LP01		T4	TP1 TP29
2320	TETRAETHYLENEPENTAMINE	8		III		5 L	E1	P001 IBC03 LP01		T4	TP1
2321	TRICHLOROBENZENES, LIQUID	6.1		III		5 L	E1	P001 IBC03 LP01		T4	TP1
2322	TRICHLOROBUTENE	6.1		II		100 ml	E4	P001 IBC02		T7	TP2
2323	TRIETHYL PHOSPHITE	3		III		5 L	E1	P001 IBC03 LP01		T2	TP1
2324	TRIISOBUTYLENE	3		III		5 L	E1	P001 IBC03 LP01		T4	TP1
2325	1,3,5-TRIMETHYLBENZENE	3		III		5 L	E1	P001 IBC03 LP01		T2	TP1
2326	TRIMETHYL-CYCLOHEXYLAMINE	8		III		5 L	E1	P001 IBC03 LP01		T4	TP1
2327	TRIMETHYL-HEXAMETHYLENEDIAMINES	8		III		5 L	E1	P001 IBC03 LP01		T4	TP1
2328	TRIMETHYLHEXAMETHYLENE DIISOCYANATE	6.1		III		5 L	E1	P001 IBC03 LP01		T4	TP2 TP13

UN No.	Name and description	Class or division	Subsidiary hazard	UN packing group	Special provisions	Limited and excepted quantities		Packagings and IBCs		Portable tanks and bulk containers	
								Packing instruction	Special packing provisions	Instructions	Special provisions
(1)	(2)	(3)	(4)	(5)	(6)	(7a)	(7b)	(8)	(9)	(10)	(11)
-	3.1.2	2.0	2.0	2.0.1.3	3.3	3.4	3.5	4.1.4	4.1.4	4.2.5 / 4.3.2	4.2.5
2329	TRIMETHYL PHOSPHITE	3		III		5 L	E1	P001 IBC03 LP01		T2	TP1
2330	UNDECANE	3		III		5 L	E1	P001 IBC03 LP01		T2	TP1
2331	ZINC CHLORIDE, ANHYDROUS	8		III		5 kg	E1	P002 IBC08 LP02	B3	T1	TP33
2332	ACETALDEHYDE OXIME	3		III		5 L	E1	P001 IBC03 LP01		T4	TP1
2333	ALLYL ACETATE	3	6.1	II		1 L	E2	P001 IBC02		T7	TP1 TP13
2334	ALLYLAMINE	6.1	3	I	354	0	E0	P602		T20	TP2 TP13
2335	ALLYL ETHYL ETHER	3	6.1	II		1 L	E2	P001 IBC02		T7	TP1 TP13
2336	ALLYL FORMATE	3	6.1	I		0	E0	P001		T14	TP2 TP13
2337	PHENYL MERCAPTAN	6.1	3	I	354	0	E0	P602		T20	TP2 TP13
2338	BENZOTRIFLUORIDE	3		II		1 L	E2	P001 IBC02		T4	TP1
2339	2-BROMOBUTANE	3		II		1 L	E2	P001 IBC02		T4	TP1
2340	2-BROMOETHYL ETHYL ETHER	3		II		1 L	E2	P001 IBC02		T4	TP1
2341	1-BROMO-3-METHYLBUTANE	3		III		5 L	E1	P001 IBC03 LP01		T2	TP1
2342	BROMOMETHYLPROPANES	3		II		1 L	E2	P001 IBC02		T4	TP1
2343	2-BROMOPENTANE	3		II		1 L	E2	P001 IBC02		T4	TP1
2344	BROMOPROPANES	3		II		1 L	E2	P001 IBC02		T4	TP1
2344	BROMOPROPANES	3		III	223	5 L	E1	P001 IBC03 LP01		T2	TP1
2345	3-BROMOPROPYNE	3		II		1 L	E2	P001 IBC02		T4	TP1
2346	BUTANEDIONE	3		II		1 L	E2	P001 IBC02		T4	TP1
2347	BUTYL MERCAPTAN	3		II		1 L	E2	P001 IBC02		T4	TP1
2348	BUTYL ACRYLATES, STABILIZED	3		III	386	5 L	E1	P001 IBC03 LP01		T2	TP1
2350	BUTYL METHYL ETHER	3		II		1 L	E2	P001 IBC02		T4	TP1
2351	BUTYL NITRITES	3		II		1 L	E2	P001 IBC02		T4	TP1
2351	BUTYL NITRITES	3		III	223	5 L	E1	P001 IBC03 LP01		T2	TP1
2352	BUTYL VINYL ETHER, STABILIZED	3		II	386	1 L	E2	P001 IBC02		T4	TP1

UN No.	Name and description	Class or division	Subsi-diary hazard	UN packing group	Special provi-sions	Limited and excepted quantities		Packagings and IBCs		Portable tanks and bulk containers	
								Packing instruction	Special packing provisions	Instruc-tions	Special provisions
(1)	(2)	(3)	(4)	(5)	(6)	(7a)	(7b)	(8)	(9)	(10)	(11)
-	3.1.2	2.0	2.0	2.0.1.3	3.3	3.4	3.5	4.1.4	4.1.4	4.2.5 / 4.3.2	4.2.5
2353	BUTYRYL CHLORIDE	3	8	II		1 L	E2	P001 IBC02		T8	TP2 TP13
2354	CHLOROMETHYL ETHYL ETHER	3	6.1	II		1 L	E2	P001 IBC02		T7	TP1 TP13
2356	2-CHLOROPROPANE	3		I		0	E3	P001		T11	TP2 TP13
2357	CYCLOHEXYLAMINE	8	3	II		1 L	E2	P001 IBC02		T7	TP2
2358	CYCLOOCTATETRAENE	3		II		1 L	E2	P001 IBC02		T4	TP1
2359	DIALLYLAMINE	3	6.1 8	II		1 L	E2	P001 IBC99		T7	TP1
2360	DIALLYL ETHER	3	6.1	II		1 L	E2	P001 IBC02		T7	TP1 TP13
2361	DIISOBUTYLAMINE	3	8	III		5 L	E1	P001 IBC03		T4	TP1
2362	1,1-DICHLOROETHANE	3		II		1 L	E2	P001 IBC02		T4	TP1
2363	ETHYL MERCAPTAN	3		I		0	E0	P001		T11	TP2 TP13
2364	n-PROPYLBENZENE	3		III		5 L	E1	P001 IBC03 LP01		T2	TP1
2366	DIETHYL CARBONATE	3		III		5 L	E1	P001 IBC03 LP01		T2	TP1
2367	alpha-METHYL-VALERALDEHYDE	3		II		1 L	E2	P001 IBC02		T4	TP1
2368	alpha-PINENE	3		III		5 L	E1	P001 IBC03 LP01		T2	TP1
2370	1-HEXENE	3		II		1 L	E2	P001 IBC02		T4	TP1
2371	ISOPENTENES	3		I		0	E3	P001		T11	TP2
2372	1,2-DI-(DIMETHYLAMINO) ETHANE	3		II		1 L	E2	P001 IBC02		T4	TP1
2373	DIETHOXYMETHANE	3		II		1 L	E2	P001 IBC02		T4	TP1
2374	3,3-DIETHOXYPROPENE	3		II		1 L	E2	P001 IBC02		T4	TP1
2375	DIETHYL SULPHIDE	3		II		1 L	E2	P001 IBC02		T7	TP1 TP13
2376	2,3-DIHYDROPYRAN	3		II		1 L	E2	P001 IBC02		T4	TP1
2377	1,1-DIMETHOXYETHANE	3		II		1 L	E2	P001 IBC02		T7	TP1
2378	2-DIMETHYL-AMINOACETONITRILE	3	6.1	II		1 L	E2	P001 IBC02		T7	TP1
2379	1,3-DIMETHYLBUTYLAMINE	3	8	II		1 L	E2	P001 IBC02		T7	TP1
2380	DIMETHYLDIETHOXYSILANE	3		II		1 L	E2	P001 IBC02		T4	TP1
2381	DIMETHYL DISULPHIDE	3	6.1	II		1 L	E0	P001 IBC02		T7	TP2 TP13
2382	DIMETHYLHYDRAZINE, SYMMETRICAL	6.1	3	I	354	0	E0	P602		T20	TP2 TP13
2383	DIPROPYLAMINE	3	8	II		1 L	E2	P001 IBC02		T7	TP1

UN No.	Name and description	Class or division	Subsidiary hazard	UN packing group	Special provisions	Limited and excepted quantities		Packagings and IBCs		Portable tanks and bulk containers	
								Packing instruction	Special packing provisions	Instructions	Special provisions
(1)	(2)	(3)	(4)	(5)	(6)	(7a)	(7b)	(8)	(9)	(10)	(11)
-	3.1.2	2.0	2.0	2.0.1.3	3.3	3.4	3.5	4.1.4	4.1.4	4.2.5 / 4.3.2	4.2.5
2384	DI-n-PROPYL ETHER	3		II		1 L	E2	P001 IBC02		T4	TP1
2385	ETHYL ISOBUTYRATE	3		II		1 L	E2	P001 IBC02		T4	TP1
2386	1-ETHYLPIPERIDINE	3	8	II		1 L	E2	P001 IBC02		T7	TP1
2387	FLUOROBENZENE	3		II		1 L	E2	P001 IBC02		T4	TP1
2388	FLUOROTOLUENES	3		II		1 L	E2	P001 IBC02		T4	TP1
2389	FURAN	3		I		0	E3	P001		T12	TP2 TP13
2390	2-IODOBUTANE	3		II		1 L	E2	P001 IBC02		T4	TP1
2391	IODOMETHYLPROPANES	3		II		1 L	E2	P001 IBC02		T4	TP1
2392	IODOPROPANES	3		III		5 L	E1	P001 IBC03 LP01		T2	TP1
2393	ISOBUTYL FORMATE	3		II		1 L	E2	P001 IBC02		T4	TP1
2394	ISOBUTYL PROPIONATE	3		III		5 L	E1	P001 IBC03 LP01		T2	TP1
2395	ISOBUTYRYL CHLORIDE	3	8	II		1 L	E2	P001 IBC02		T7	TP2
2396	METHACRYLALDEHYDE, STABILIZED	3	6.1	II	386	1 L	E2	P001 IBC02		T7	TP1 TP13
2397	3-METHYLBUTAN-2-ONE	3		II		1 L	E2	P001 IBC02		T4	TP1
2398	METHYL tert-BUTYL ETHER	3		II		1 L	E2	P001 IBC02		T7	TP1
2399	1-METHYLPIPERIDINE	3	8	II		1 L	E2	P001 IBC02		T7	TP1
2400	METHYL ISOVALERATE	3		II		1 L	E2	P001 IBC02		T4	TP1
2401	PIPERIDINE	8	3	I		0	E0	P001		T10	TP2
2402	PROPANETHIOLS	3		II		1 L	E2	P001 IBC02		T4	TP1 TP13
2403	ISOPROPENYL ACETATE	3		II		1 L	E2	P001 IBC02		T4	TP1
2404	PROPIONITRILE	3	6.1	II		1 L	E0	P001 IBC02		T7	TP1 TP13
2405	ISOPROPYL BUTYRATE	3		III		5 L	E1	P001 IBC03 LP01		T2	TP1
2406	ISOPROPYL ISOBUTYRATE	3		II		1 L	E2	P001 IBC02		T4	TP1
2407	ISOPROPYL CHLOROFORMATE	6.1	3 8	I	354	0	E0	P602			
2409	ISOPROPYL PROPIONATE	3		II		1 L	E2	P001 IBC02		T4	TP1
2410	1,2,3,6-TETRAHYDROPYRIDINE	3		II		1 L	E2	P001 IBC02		T4	TP1
2411	BUTYRONITRILE	3	6.1	II		1 L	E2	P001 IBC02		T7	TP1 TP13
2412	TETRAHYDROTHIOPHENE	3		II		1 L	E2	P001 IBC02		T4	TP1

UN No.	Name and description	Class or division	Subsidiary hazard	UN packing group	Special provisions	Limited and excepted quantities		Packagings and IBCs		Portable tanks and bulk containers	
								Packing instruction	Special packing provisions	Instructions	Special provisions
(1)	(2)	(3)	(4)	(5)	(6)	(7a)	(7b)	(8)	(9)	(10)	(11)
-	3.1.2	2.0	2.0	2.0.1.3	3.3	3.4	3.5	4.1.4	4.1.4	4.2.5 / 4.3.2	4.2.5
2413	TETRAPROPYL ORTHOTITANATE	3		III		5 L	E1	P001 IBC03 LP01		T4	TP1
2414	THIOPHENE	3		II		1 L	E2	P001 IBC02		T4	TP1
2416	TRIMETHYL BORATE	3		II		1 L	E2	P001 IBC02		T7	TP1
2417	CARBONYL FLUORIDE	2.3	8			0	E0	P200			
2418	SULPHUR TETRAFLUORIDE	2.3	8			0	E0	P200			
2419	BROMOTRIFLUOROETHYLENE	2.1				0	E0	P200			
2420	HEXAFLUOROACETONE	2.3	8			0	E0	P200			
2421	NITROGEN TRIOXIDE	2.3	5.1 8			0	E0	P200			
2422	OCTAFLUOROBUT-2-ENE (REFRIGERANT GAS R 1318)	2.2				120 ml	E1	P200			
2424	OCTAFLUOROPROPANE (REFRIGERANT GAS R 218)	2.2				120 ml	E1	P200		T50	
2426	AMMONIUM NITRATE, LIQUID (hot concentrated solution)	5.1			252	0	E0	NONE		T7	TP1 TP16 TP17
2427	POTASSIUM CHLORATE, AQUEOUS SOLUTION	5.1		II		1 L	E2	P504 IBC02		T4	TP1
2427	POTASSIUM CHLORATE, AQUEOUS SOLUTION	5.1		III	223	5 L	E1	P504 IBC02		T4	TP1
2428	SODIUM CHLORATE, AQUEOUS SOLUTION	5.1		II		1 L	E2	P504 IBC02		T4	TP1
2428	SODIUM CHLORATE, AQUEOUS SOLUTION	5.1		III	223	5 L	E1	P504 IBC02		T4	TP1
2429	CALCIUM CHLORATE, AQUEOUS SOLUTION	5.1		II		1 L	E2	P504 IBC02		T4	TP1
2429	CALCIUM CHLORATE, AQUEOUS SOLUTION	5.1		III	223	5 L	E1	P504 IBC02		T4	TP1
2430	ALKYLPHENOLS, SOLID, N.O.S. (including C2-C12 homologues)	8		I		0	E0	P002 IBC07	B1	T6	TP33
2430	ALKYLPHENOLS, SOLID, N.O.S. (including C2-C12 homologues)	8		II		1 kg	E2	P002 IBC08	B2, B4	T3	TP33
2430	ALKYLPHENOLS, SOLID, N.O.S. (including C2-C12 homologues)	8		III	223	5 kg	E1	P002 IBC08 LP02	B3	T1	TP33
2431	ANISIDINES	6.1		III		5 L	E1	P001 IBC03 LP01		T4	TP1
2432	N,N-DIETHYLANILINE	6.1		III	279	5 L	E1	P001 IBC03 LP01		T4	TP1
2433	CHLORONITROTOLUENES, LIQUID	6.1		III		5 L	E1	P001 IBC03 LP01		T4	TP1
2434	DIBENZYLDICHLOROSILANE	8		II		0	E0	P010		T10	TP2 TP7 TP13
2435	ETHYLPHENYL-DICHLOROSILANE	8		II		0	E0	P010		T10	TP2 TP7 TP13
2436	THIOACETIC ACID	3		II		1 L	E2	P001 IBC02		T4	TP1
2437	METHYLPHENYL-DICHLOROSILANE	8		II		0	E0	P010		T10	TP2 TP7 TP13

UN No.	Name and description	Class or division	Subsidiary hazard	UN packing group	Special provisions	Limited and excepted quantities		Packagings and IBCs		Portable tanks and bulk containers	
								Packing instruction	Special packing provisions	Instructions	Special provisions
(1)	(2)	(3)	(4)	(5)	(6)	(7a)	(7b)	(8)	(9)	(10)	(11)
-	3.1.2	2.0	2.0	2.0.1.3	3.3	3.4	3.5	4.1.4	4.1.4	4.2.5 / 4.3.2	4.2.5
2438	TRIMETHYLACETYL CHLORIDE	6.1	3 8	I		0	E0	P001		T14	TP2 TP13
2439	SODIUM HYDROGENDIFLUORIDE	8		II		1 kg	E2	P002 IBC08	B2, B4	T3	TP33
2440	STANNIC CHLORIDE PENTAHYDRATE	8		III		5 kg	E1	P002 IBC08 LP02	B3	T1	TP33
2441	TITANIUM TRICHLORIDE, PYROPHORIC or TITANIUM TRICHLORIDE MIXTURE, PYROPHORIC	4.2	8	I		0	E0	P404			
2442	TRICHLOROACETYL CHLORIDE	8		II		0	E0	P001		T7	TP2
2443	VANADIUM OXYTRICHLORIDE	8		II		1 L	E0	P001 IBC02		T7	TP2
2444	VANADIUM TETRACHLORIDE	8		I		0	E0	P802		T10	TP2
2446	NITROCRESOLS, SOLID	6.1		III		5 kg	E1	P002 IBC08 LP02	B3	T1	TP33
2447	PHOSPHORUS, WHITE, MOLTEN	4.2	6.1	I		0	E0	NONE		T21	TP3 TP7 TP26
2448	SULPHUR, MOLTEN	4.1		III		0	E0	IBC01		T1	TP3
2451	NITROGEN TRIFLUORIDE	2.2	5.1			0	E0	P200			
2452	ETHYLACETYLENE, STABILIZED	2.1			386	0	E0	P200			
2453	ETHYL FLUORIDE (REFRIGERANT GAS R 161)	2.1				0	E0	P200			
2454	METHYL FLUORIDE (REFRIGERANT GAS R 41)	2.1				0	E0	P200			
2455	METHYL NITRITE	2.2				120 ml	E1	P200			
2456	2-CHLOROPROPENE	3		I		0	E3	P001		T11	TP2
2457	2,3-DIMETHYLBUTANE	3		II		1 L	E2	P001 IBC02		T7	TP1
2458	HEXADIENE	3		II		1 L	E2	P001 IBC02		T4	TP1
2459	2-METHYL-1-BUTENE	3		I		0	E3	P001		T11	TP2
2460	2-METHYL-2-BUTENE	3		II		1 L	E2	P001 IBC02	B8	T7	TP1
2461	METHYLPENTADIENE	3		II		1 L	E2	P001 IBC02		T4	TP1
2463	ALUMINIUM HYDRIDE	4.3		I		0	E0	P403			
2464	BERYLLIUM NITRATE	5.1	6.1	II		1 kg	E2	P002 IBC08	B2, B4	T3	TP33
2465	DICHLOROISOCYANURIC ACID, DRY or DICHLOROISOCYANURIC ACID SALTS	5.1		II	135	1 kg	E2	P002 IBC08	B2, B4	T3	TP33
2466	POTASSIUM SUPEROXIDE	5.1		I		0	E0	P503 IBC06	B1		
2468	TRICHLOROISOCYANURIC ACID, DRY	5.1		II		1 kg	E2	P002 IBC08	B2, B4	T3	TP33
2469	ZINC BROMATE	5.1		III		5 kg	E1	P002 IBC08 LP02	B3	T1	TP33
2470	PHENYLACETONITRILE, LIQUID	6.1		III		5 L	E1	P001 IBC03 LP01		T4	TP1

UN No.	Name and description	Class or division	Subsidiary hazard	UN packing group	Special provisions	Limited and excepted quantities		Packagings and IBCs		Portable tanks and bulk containers	
								Packing instruction	Special packing provisions	Instructions	Special provisions
(1)	(2)	(3)	(4)	(5)	(6)	(7a)	(7b)	(8)	(9)	(10)	(11)
-	3.1.2	2.0	2.0	2.0.1.3	3.3	3.4	3.5	4.1.4	4.1.4	4.2.5 / 4.3.2	4.2.5
2471	OSMIUM TETROXIDE	6.1		I		0	E5	P002 IBC07	PP30 B1	T6	TP33
2473	SODIUM ARSANILATE	6.1		III		5 kg	E1	P002 IBC08 LP02	B3	T1	TP33
2474	THIOPHOSGENE	6.1		I	279 354	0	E0	P602		T20	TP2 TP13
2475	VANADIUM TRICHLORIDE	8		III		5 kg	E1	P002 IBC08 LP02	B3	T1	TP33
2477	METHYL ISOTHIOCYANATE	6.1	3	I	354	0	E0	P602		T20	TP2 TP13
2478	ISOCYANATES, FLAMMABLE, TOXIC, N.O.S. or ISOCYANATE SOLUTION, FLAMMABLE, TOXIC, N.O.S.	3	6.1	II	274	1 L	E2	P001 IBC02		T11	TP2 TP13 TP27
2478	ISOCYANATES, FLAMMABLE, TOXIC, N.O.S. or ISOCYANATE SOLUTION, FLAMMABLE, TOXIC, N.O.S.	3	6.1	III	223 274	5 L	E1	P001 IBC03		T7	TP1 TP13 TP28
2480	METHYL ISOCYANATE	6.1	3	I	354	0	E0	P601		T22	TP2 TP13
2481	ETHYL ISOCYANATE	6.1	3	I	354	0	E0	P602		T20	TP2 TP13
2482	n-PROPYL ISOCYANATE	6.1	3	I	354	0	E0	P602		T20	TP2 TP13
2483	ISOPROPYL ISOCYANATE	6.1	3	I	354	0	E0	P602		T20	TP2 TP13
2484	tert-BUTYL ISOCYANATE	6.1	3	I	354	0	E0	P602		T20	TP2 TP13
2485	n-BUTYL ISOCYANATE	6.1	3	I	354	0	E0	P602		T20	TP2 TP13
2486	ISOBUTYL ISOCYANATE	6.1	3	I	354	0	E0	P602		T20	TP2 TP13
2487	PHENYL ISOCYANATE	6.1	3	I	354	0	E0	P602		T20	TP2 TP13
2488	CYCLOHEXYL ISOCYANATE	6.1	3	I	354	0	E0	P602		T20	TP2 TP13
2490	DICHLOROISOPROPYL ETHER	6.1		II		100 ml	E4	P001 IBC02		T7	TP2
2491	ETHANOLAMINE or ETHANOLAMINE SOLUTION	8		III	223	5 L	E1	P001 IBC03 LP01		T4	TP1
2493	HEXAMETHYLENEIMINE	3	8	II		1 L	E2	P001 IBC02		T7	TP1
2495	IODINE PENTAFLUORIDE	5.1	6.1 8	I		0	E0	P200			
2496	PROPIONIC ANHYDRIDE	8		III		5 L	E1	P001 IBC03 LP01		T4	TP1
2498	1,2,3,6-TETRAHYDRO-BENZALDEHYDE	3		III		5 L	E1	P001 IBC03 LP01		T2	TP1
2501	TRIS-(1-AZIRIDINYL) PHOSPHINE OXIDE SOLUTION	6.1		II		100 ml	E4	P001 IBC02		T7	TP2
2501	TRIS-(1-AZIRIDINYL) PHOSPHINE OXIDE SOLUTION	6.1		III	223	5 L	E1	P001 IBC03 LP01		T4	TP1
2502	VALERYL CHLORIDE	8	3	II		1 L	E2	P001 IBC02		T7	TP2

UN No.	Name and description	Class or division	Subsidiary hazard	UN packing group	Special provisions	Limited and excepted quantities		Packagings and IBCs		Portable tanks and bulk containers	
								Packing instruction	Special packing provisions	Instructions	Special provisions
(1)	(2)	(3)	(4)	(5)	(6)	(7a)	(7b)	(8)	(9)	(10)	(11)
-	3.1.2	2.0	2.0	2.0.1.3	3.3	3.4	3.5	4.1.4	4.1.4	4.2.5 / 4.3.2	4.2.5
2503	ZIRCONIUM TETRACHLORIDE	8		III		5 kg	E1	P002 IBC08 LP02	B3	T1	TP33
2504	TETRABROMOETHANE	6.1		III		5 L	E1	P001 IBC03 LP01		T4	TP1
2505	AMMONIUM FLUORIDE	6.1		III		5 kg	E1	P002 IBC08 LP02	B3	T1	TP33
2506	AMMONIUM HYDROGEN SULPHATE	8		II		1 kg	E2	P002 IBC08	B2, B4	T3	TP33
2507	CHLOROPLATINIC ACID, SOLID	8		III		5 kg	E1	P002 IBC08 LP02	B3	T1	TP33
2508	MOLYBDENUM PENTACHLORIDE	8		III		5 kg	E1	P002 IBC08 LP02	B3	T1	TP33
2509	POTASSIUM HYDROGEN SULPHATE	8		II		1 kg	E2	P002 IBC08	B2, B4	T3	TP33
2511	2-CHLOROPROPIONIC ACID	8		III	223	5 L	E1	P001 IBC03 LP01		T4	TP2
2512	AMINOPHENOLS (o-, m-, p-)	6.1		III	279	5 kg	E1	P002 IBC08 LP02	B3	T1	TP33
2513	BROMOACETYL BROMIDE	8		II		1 L	E2	P001 IBC02		T8	TP2
2514	BROMOBENZENE	3		III		5 L	E1	P001 IBC03 LP01		T2	TP1
2515	BROMOFORM	6.1		III		5 L	E1	P001 IBC03 LP01		T4	TP1
2516	CARBON TETRABROMIDE	6.1		III		5 kg	E1	P002 IBC08 LP02	B3	T1	TP33
2517	1-CHLORO-1,1-DIFLUOROETHANE (REFRIGERANT GAS R 142b)	2.1				0	E0	P200		T50	
2518	1,5,9-CYCLODODECATRIENE	6.1		III		5 L	E1	P001 IBC03 LP01		T4	TP1
2520	CYCLOOCTADIENES	3		III		5 L	E1	P001 IBC03 LP01		T2	TP1
2521	DIKETENE, STABILIZED	6.1	3	I	354 386	0	E0	P602		T20	TP2 TP13
2522	2-DIMETHYLAMINOETHYL METHACRYLATE, STABILIZED	6.1		II	386	100 ml	E4	P001 IBC02		T7	TP2
2524	ETHYL ORTHOFORMATE	3		III		5 L	E1	P001 IBC03 LP01		T2	TP1
2525	ETHYL OXALATE	6.1		III		5 L	E1	P001 IBC03 LP01		T4	TP1
2526	FURFURYLAMINE	3	8	III		5 L	E1	P001 IBC03		T4	TP1
2527	ISOBUTYL ACRYLATE, STABILIZED	3		III	386	5 L	E1	P001 IBC03 LP01		T2	TP1

UN No.	Name and description	Class or division	Subsidiary hazard	UN packing group	Special provisions	Limited and excepted quantities		Packagings and IBCs		Portable tanks and bulk containers	
								Packing instruction	Special packing provisions	Instructions	Special provisions
(1)	(2)	(3)	(4)	(5)	(6)	(7a)	(7b)	(8)	(9)	(10)	(11)
-	3.1.2	2.0	2.0	2.0.1.3	3.3	3.4	3.5	4.1.4	4.1.4	4.2.5 / 4.3.2	4.2.5
2528	ISOBUTYL ISOBUTYRATE	3		III		5 L	E1	P001 IBC03 LP01		T2	TP1
2529	ISOBUTYRIC ACID	3	8	III		5 L	E1	P001 IBC03		T4	TP1
2531	METHACRYLIC ACID, STABILIZED	8		II	386	1 L	E2	P001 IBC02 LP01		T7	TP2 TP18 TP30
2533	METHYL TRICHLOROACETATE	6.1		III		5 L	E1	P001 IBC03 LP01		T4	TP1
2534	METHYLCHLOROSILANE	2.3	2.1 8			0	E0	P200			
2535	4-METHYLMORPHOLINE (N-METHYLMORPHOLINE)	3	8	II		1 L	E2	P001 IBC02		T7	TP1
2536	METHYLTETRAHYDROFURAN	3		II		1 L	E2	P001 IBC02		T4	TP1
2538	NITRONAPHTHALENE	4.1		III		5 kg	E1	P002 IBC08 LP02	B3	T1	TP33
2541	TERPINOLENE	3		III		5 L	E1	P001 IBC03 LP01		T2	TP1
2542	TRIBUTYLAMINE	6.1		II		100 ml	E4	P001 IBC02		T7	TP2
2545	HAFNIUM POWDER, DRY	4.2		I		0	E0	P404			
2545	HAFNIUM POWDER, DRY	4.2		II		0	E2	P410 IBC06	B2	T3	TP33
2545	HAFNIUM POWDER, DRY	4.2		III	223	0	E1	P002 IBC08 LP02	B3	T1	TP33
2546	TITANIUM POWDER, DRY	4.2		I		0	E0	P404			
2546	TITANIUM POWDER, DRY	4.2		II		0	E2	P410 IBC06	B2	T3	TP33
2546	TITANIUM POWDER, DRY	4.2		III	223	0	E1	P002 IBC08 LP02	B3	T1	TP33
2547	SODIUM SUPEROXIDE	5.1		I		0	E0	P503 IBC06	B1		
2548	CHLORINE PENTAFLUORIDE	2.3	5.1 8			0	E0	P200			
2552	HEXAFLUOROACETONE HYDRATE, LIQUID	6.1		II		100 ml	E4	P001 IBC02		T7	TP2
2554	METHYLALLYL CHLORIDE	3		II		1 L	E2	P001 IBC02		T4	TP1 TP13
2555	NITROCELLULOSE WITH WATER (not less than 25 % water, by mass)	4.1		II	28 394	0	E0	P406			
2556	NITROCELLULOSE WITH ALCOHOL (not less than 25 % alcohol, by mass, and not more than 12.6 % nitrogen, by dry mass)	4.1		II	28 394	0	E0	P406			
2557	NITROCELLULOSE, with not more than 12.6 % nitrogen, by dry mass, MIXTURE WITH or WITHOUT PLASTICIZER, WITH or WITHOUT PIGMENT	4.1		II	241 394	0	E0	P406			
2558	EPIBROMOHYDRIN	6.1	3	I		0	E0	P001		T14	TP2 TP13

UN No.	Name and description	Class or division	Subsidiary hazard	UN packing group	Special provisions	Limited and excepted quantities		Packagings and IBCs		Portable tanks and bulk containers	
						Packing instruction	Special packing provisions	Instructions	Special provisions
(1)	(2)	(3)	(4)	(5)	(6)	(7a)	(7b)	(8)	(9)	(10)	(11)
-	3.1.2	2.0	2.0	2.0.1.3	3.3	3.4	3.5	4.1.4	4.1.4	4.2.5 / 4.3.2	4.2.5
2560	2-METHYLPENTAN-2-OL	3		III		5 L	E1	P001 IBC03 LP01		T2	TP1
2561	3-METHYL-1-BUTENE	3		I		0	E3	P001		T11	TP2
2564	TRICHLOROACETIC ACID SOLUTION	8		II		1 L	E2	P001 IBC02		T7	TP2
2564	TRICHLOROACETIC ACID SOLUTION	8		III	223	5 L	E1	P001 IBC03 LP01		T4	TP1
2565	DICYCLOHEXYLAMINE	8		III		5 L	E1	P001 IBC03 LP01		T4	TP1
2567	SODIUM PENTACHLOROPHENATE	6.1		II		500 g	E4	P002 IBC08	B2, B4	T3	TP33
2570	CADMIUM COMPOUND	6.1		I	274	0	E5	P002 IBC07	B1	T6	TP33
2570	CADMIUM COMPOUND	6.1		II	274	500 g	E4	P002 IBC08	B2, B4	T3	TP33
2570	CADMIUM COMPOUND	6.1		III	223 274	5 kg	E1	P002 IBC08 LP02	B3	T1	TP33
2571	ALKYLSULPHURIC ACIDS	8		II		1 L	E2	P001 IBC02		T8	TP2 TP13 TP28
2572	PHENYLHYDRAZINE	6.1		II		100 ml	E4	P001 IBC02		T7	TP2
2573	THALLIUM CHLORATE	5.1	6.1	II		1 kg	E2	P002 IBC06	B2	T3	TP33
2574	TRICRESYL PHOSPHATE with more than 3 % ortho isomer	6.1		II		100 ml	E4	P001 IBC02		T7	TP2
2576	PHOSPHORUS OXYBROMIDE, MOLTEN	8		II		0	E0	NONE		T7	TP3 TP13
2577	PHENYLACETYL CHLORIDE	8		II		1 L	E2	P001 IBC02		T7	TP2
2578	PHOSPHORUS TRIOXIDE	8		III		5 kg	E1	P002 IBC08 LP02	B3	T1	TP33
2579	PIPERAZINE	8		III		5 kg	E1	P002 IBC08 LP02	B3	T1	TP33
2580	ALUMINIUM BROMIDE SOLUTION	8		III	223	5 L	E1	P001 IBC03 LP01		T4	TP1
2581	ALUMINIUM CHLORIDE SOLUTION	8		III	223	5 L	E1	P001 IBC03 LP01		T4	TP1
2582	FERRIC CHLORIDE SOLUTION	8		III	223	5 L	E1	P001 IBC03 LP01		T4	TP1
2583	ALKYLSULPHONIC ACIDS, SOLID or ARYLSULPHONIC ACIDS, SOLID with more than 5 % free sulphuric acid	8		II		1 kg	E2	P002 IBC08	B2, B4	T3	TP33
2584	ALKYSULPHONIC ACIDS, LIQUID or ARYLSULPHONIC ACIDS, LIQUID with more than 5 % free sulphuric acid	8		II		1 L	E2	P001 IBC02		T8	TP2 TP13

UN No.	Name and description	Class or division	Subsidiary hazard	UN packing group	Special provisions	Limited and excepted quantities		Packagings and IBCs		Portable tanks and bulk containers	
								Packing instruction	Special packing provisions	Instructions	Special provisions
(1)	(2)	(3)	(4)	(5)	(6)	(7a)	(7b)	(8)	(9)	(10)	(11)
-	3.1.2	2.0	2.0	2.0.1.3	3.3	3.4	3.5	4.1.4	4.1.4	4.2.5 / 4.3.2	4.2.5
2585	ALKYLSULPHONIC ACIDS, SOLID or ARYLSULPHONIC ACIDS, SOLID with not more than 5 % free sulphuric acid	8		III		5 kg	E1	P002 IBC08 LP02	B3	T1	TP33
2586	ALKYLSULPHONIC ACIDS, LIQUID or ARYLSULPHONIC ACIDS, LIQUID with not more than 5 % free sulphuric acid	8		III		5 L	E1	P001 IBC03 LP01		T4	TP1
2587	BENZOQUINONE	6.1		II		500 g	E4	P002 IBC08	B2, B4	T3	TP33
2588	PESTICIDE, SOLID, TOXIC, N.O.S.	6.1		I	61 274	0	E5	P002 IBC99		T6	TP33
2588	PESTICIDE, SOLID, TOXIC, N.O.S.	6.1		II	61 274	500 g	E4	P002 IBC08	B2, B4	T3	TP33
2588	PESTICIDE, SOLID, TOXIC, N.O.S.	6.1		III	61 223 274	5 kg	E1	P002 IBC08 LP02	B3	T1	TP33
2589	VINYL CHLOROACETATE	6.1	3	II		100 ml	E4	P001 IBC02		T7	TP2
2590	ASBESTOS, CHRYSOTILE	9		III	168	5 kg	E1	P002 IBC08	PP37 B2, B3	T1	TP33
2591	XENON, REFRIGERATED LIQUID	2.2				120 ml	E1	P203		T75	TP5
2599	CHLOROTRIFLUOROMETHANE AND TRIFLUOROMETHANE AZEOTROPIC MIXTURE with approximately 60 % chlorotrifluoromethane (REFRIGERANT GAS R 503)	2.2				120 ml	E1	P200			
2601	CYCLOBUTANE	2.1				0	E0	P200			
2602	DICHLORODIFLUORO-METHANE AND DIFLUOROETHANE AZEOTROPIC MIXTURE with approximately 74 % dichlorodifluoromethane (REFRIGERANT GAS R 500)	2.2				120 ml	E1	P200		T50	
2603	CYCLOHEPTATRIENE	3	6.1	II		1 L	E2	P001 IBC02		T7	TP1 TP13
2604	BORON TRIFLUORIDE DIETHYL ETHERATE	8	3	I		0	E0	P001		T10	TP2
2605	METHOXYMETHYL ISOCYANATE	6.1	3	I	354	0	E0	P602		T20	TP2 TP13
2606	METHYL ORTHOSILICATE	6.1	3	I	354	0	E0	P602		T20	TP2 TP13
2607	ACROLEIN DIMER, STABILIZED	3		III	386	5 L	E1	P001 IBC03 LP01		T2	TP1
2608	NITROPROPANES	3		III		5 L	E1	P001 IBC03 LP01		T2	TP1
2609	TRIALLYL BORATE	6.1		III		5 L	E1	P001 IBC03 LP01			
2610	TRIALLYLAMINE	3	8	III		5 L	E1	P001 IBC03		T4	TP1
2611	PROPYLENE CHLOROHYDRIN	6.1	3	II		100 ml	E4	P001 IBC02		T7	TP2 TP13
2612	METHYL PROPYL ETHER	3		II		1 L	E2	P001 IBC02	B8	T7	TP2

UN No.	Name and description	Class or division	Subsidiary hazard	UN packing group	Special provisions	Limited and excepted quantities		Packagings and IBCs		Portable tanks and bulk containers	
						Packing instruction	Special packing provisions	Instructions	Special provisions
(1)	(2)	(3)	(4)	(5)	(6)	(7a)	(7b)	(8)	(9)	(10)	(11)
-	3.1.2	2.0	2.0	2.0.1.3	3.3	3.4	3.5	4.1.4	4.1.4	4.2.5 / 4.3.2	4.2.5
2614	METHALLYL ALCOHOL	3		III		5 L	E1	P001 IBC03 LP01		T2	TP1
2615	ETHYL PROPYL ETHER	3		II		1 L	E2	P001 IBC02		T4	TP1
2616	TRIISOPROPYL BORATE	3		II		1 L	E2	P001 IBC02		T4	TP1
2616	TRIISOPROPYL BORATE	3		III	223	5 L	E1	P001 IBC03 LP01		T2	TP1
2617	METHYLCYCLOHEXANOLS, flammable	3		III		5 L	E1	P001 IBC03 LP01		T2	TP1
2618	VINYLTOLUENES, STABILIZED	3		III	386	5 L	E1	P001 IBC03 LP01		T2	TP1
2619	BENZYLDIMETHYLAMINE	8	3	II		1 L	E2	P001 IBC02		T7	TP2
2620	AMYL BUTYRATES	3		III		5 L	E1	P001 IBC03 LP01		T2	TP1
2621	ACETYL METHYL CARBINOL	3		III		5 L	E1	P001 IBC03 LP01		T2	TP1
2622	GLYCIDALDEHYDE	3	6.1	II		1 L	E2	P001 IBC02	B8	T7	TP1
2623	FIRELIGHTERS, SOLID with flammable liquid	4.1		III		5 kg	E1	P002 LP02	PP15		
2624	MAGNESIUM SILICIDE	4.3		II		500 g	E2	P410 IBC07	B2	T3	TP33
2626	CHLORIC ACID, AQUEOUS SOLUTION with not more than 10 % chloric acid	5.1		II		1 L	E0	P504 IBC02		T4	TP1
2627	NITRITES, INORGANIC, N.O.S.	5.1		II	103 274	1 kg	E2	P002 IBC08	B2, B4	T3	TP33
2628	POTASSIUM FLUOROACETATE	6.1		I		0	E5	P002 IBC07	B1	T6	TP33
2629	SODIUM FLUOROACETATE	6.1		I		0	E5	P002 IBC07	B1	T6	TP33
2630	SELENATES or SELENITES	6.1		I	274	0	E5	P002 IBC07	B1	T6	TP33
2642	FLUOROACETIC ACID	6.1		I		0	E5	P002 IBC07	B1	T6	TP33
2643	METHYL BROMOACETATE	6.1		II		100 ml	E4	P001 IBC02		T7	TP2
2644	METHYL IODIDE	6.1		I	354	0	E0	P602		T20	TP2 TP13
2645	PHENACYL BROMIDE	6.1		II		500 g	E4	P002 IBC08	B2, B4	T3	TP33
2646	HEXACHLOROCYCLO-PENTADIENE	6.1		I	354	0	E0	P602		T20	TP2 TP13
2647	MALONONITRILE	6.1		II		500 g	E4	P002 IBC08	B2, B4	T3	TP33
2648	1,2-DIBROMOBUTAN-3-ONE	6.1		II		100 ml	E4	P001 IBC02			
2649	1,3-DICHLOROACETONE	6.1		II		500 g	E4	P002 IBC08	B2, B4	T3	TP33
2650	1,1-DICHLORO-1-NITROETHANE	6.1		II		100 ml	E4	P001 IBC02		T7	TP2

UN No.	Name and description	Class or division	Subsidiary hazard	UN packing group	Special provisions	Limited and excepted quantities		Packagings and IBCs		Portable tanks and bulk containers	
								Packing instruction	Special packing provisions	Instructions	Special provisions
(1)	(2)	(3)	(4)	(5)	(6)	(7a)	(7b)	(8)	(9)	(10)	(11)
-	3.1.2	2.0	2.0	2.0.1.3	3.3	3.4	3.5	4.1.4	4.1.4	4.2.5 / 4.3.2	4.2.5
2651	4,4'-DIAMINODIPHENYL-METHANE	6.1		III		5 kg	E1	P002 IBC08 LP02	B3	T1	TP33
2653	BENZYL IODIDE	6.1		II		100 ml	E4	P001 IBC02		T7	TP2
2655	POTASSIUM FLUOROSILICATE	6.1		III		5 kg	E1	P002 IBC08 LP02	B3	T1	TP33
2656	QUINOLINE	6.1		III		5 L	E1	P001 IBC03 LP01		T4	TP1
2657	SELENIUM DISULPHIDE	6.1		II		500 g	E4	P002 IBC08	B2, B4	T3	TP33
2659	SODIUM CHLOROACETATE	6.1		III		5 kg	E1	P002 IBC08 LP02	B3	T1	TP33
2660	NITROTOLUIDINES (MONO)	6.1		III		5 kg	E1	P002 IBC08 LP02	B3	T1	TP33
2661	HEXACHLOROACETONE	6.1		III		5 L	E1	P001 IBC03 LP01		T4	TP1
2664	DIBROMOMETHANE	6.1		III		5 L	E1	P001 IBC03 LP01		T4	TP1
2667	BUTYLTOLUENES	6.1		III		5 L	E1	P001 IBC03 LP01		T4	TP1
2668	CHLOROACETONITRILE	6.1	3	I	354	0	E0	P602		T20	TP2 TP13
2669	CHLOROCRESOLS SOLUTION	6.1		II		100 ml	E4	P001 IBC02		T7	TP2
2669	CHLOROCRESOLS SOLUTION	6.1		III	223	5 L	E1	P001 IBC03 LP01		T7	TP2
2670	CYANURIC CHLORIDE	8		II		1 kg	E2	P002 IBC08	B2, B4	T3	TP33
2671	AMINOPYRIDINES (o-, m-, p,)	6.1		II		500 g	E4	P002 IBC08	B2, B4	T3	TP33
2672	AMMONIA SOLUTION, relative density between 0.880 and 0.957 at 15 °C in water, with more than 10 % but not more than 35 % ammonia	8		III		5 L	E1	P001 IBC03 LP01	B11	T7	TP1
2673	2-AMINO-4-CHLOROPHENOL	6.1		II		500 g	E4	P002 IBC08	B2, B4	T3	TP33
2674	SODIUM FLUOROSILICATE	6.1		III		5 kg	E1	P002 IBC08 LP02	B3	T1	TP33
2676	STIBINE	2.3	2.1			0	E0	P200			
2677	RUBIDIUM HYDROXIDE SOLUTION	8		II		1 L	E2	P001 IBC02		T7	TP2
2677	RUBIDIUM HYDROXIDE SOLUTION	8		III	223	5 L	E1	P001 IBC03 LP01		T4	TP1
2678	RUBIDIUM HYDROXIDE	8		II		1 kg	E2	P002 IBC08	B2, B4	T3	TP33
2679	LITHIUM HYDROXIDE SOLUTION	8		II		1 L	E2	P001 IBC02		T7	TP2

UN No.	Name and description	Class or division	Subsidiary hazard	UN packing group	Special provisions	Limited and excepted quantities		Packagings and IBCs		Portable tanks and bulk containers	
								Packing instruction	Special packing provisions	Instructions	Special provisions
(1)	(2)	(3)	(4)	(5)	(6)	(7a)	(7b)	(8)	(9)	(10)	(11)
-	3.1.2	2.0	2.0	2.0.1.3	3.3	3.4	3.5	4.1.4	4.1.4	4.2.5 / 4.3.2	4.2.5
2679	LITHIUM HYDROXIDE SOLUTION	8		III	223	5 L	E1	P001 IBC03 LP01		T4	TP2
2680	LITHIUM HYDROXIDE	8		II		1 kg	E2	P002 IBC08	B2, B4	T3	TP33
2681	CAESIUM HYDROXIDE SOLUTION	8		II		1 L	E2	P001 IBC02		T7	TP2
2681	CAESIUM HYDROXIDE SOLUTION	8		III	223	5 L	E1	P001 IBC03 LP01		T4	TP1
2682	CAESIUM HYDROXIDE	8		II		1 kg	E2	P002 IBC08	B2, B4	T3	TP33
2683	AMMONIUM SULPHIDE SOLUTION	8	3 6.1	II		1 L	E2	P001 IBC01		T7	TP2 TP13
2684	3-DIETHYLAMINOPROPYL-AMINE	3	8	III		5 L	E1	P001 IBC03		T4	TP1
2685	N,N-DIETHYLETHYLENE-DIAMINE	8	3	II		1 L	E2	P001 IBC02		T7	TP2
2686	2-DIETHYLAMINOETHANOL	8	3	II		1 L	E2	P001 IBC02		T7	TP2
2687	DICYCLOHEXYLAMMONIUM NITRITE	4.1		III		5 kg	E1	P002 IBC08 LP02	B3	T1	TP33
2688	1-BROMO-3-CHLOROPROPANE	6.1		III		5 L	E1	P001 IBC03 LP01		T4	TP1
2689	GLYCEROL alpha-MONOCHLOROHYDRIN	6.1		III		5 L	E1	P001 IBC03 LP01		T4	TP1
2690	N,n-BUTYLIMIDAZOLE	6.1		II		100 ml	E4	P001 IBC02		T7	TP2
2691	PHOSPHORUS PENTABROMIDE	8		II		1 kg	E0	P002 IBC08	B2, B4	T3	TP33
2692	BORON TRIBROMIDE	8		I		0	E0	P602		T20	TP2 TP13
2693	BISULPHITES, AQUEOUS SOLUTION, N.O.S.	8		III	274	5 L	E1	P001 IBC03 LP01		T7	TP1 TP28
2698	TETRAHYDROPHTHALIC ANHYDRIDES with more than 0.05 % of maleic anhydride	8		III	29 169	5 kg	E1	P002 IBC08 LP02	PP14 B3	T1	TP33
2699	TRIFLUOROACETIC ACID	8		I		0	E0	P001		T10	TP2
2705	1-PENTOL	8		II		1 L	E2	P001 IBC02		T7	TP2
2707	DIMETHYLDIOXANES	3		II		1 L	E2	P001 IBC02		T4	TP1
2707	DIMETHYLDIOXANES	3		III	223	5 L	E1	P001 IBC03 LP01		T2	TP1
2709	BUTYLBENZENES	3		III		5 L	E1	P001 IBC03 LP01		T2	TP1
2710	DIPROPYL KETONE	3		III		5 L	E1	P001 IBC03 LP01		T2	TP1
2713	ACRIDINE	6.1		III		5 kg	E1	P002 IBC08 LP02	B3	T1	TP33
2714	ZINC RESINATE	4.1		III		5 kg	E1	P002 IBC06		T1	TP33

UN No.	Name and description	Class or division	Subsidiary hazard	UN packing group	Special provisions	Limited and excepted quantities		Packagings and IBCs		Portable tanks and bulk containers	
								Packing instruction	Special packing provisions	Instructions	Special provisions
(1)	(2)	(3)	(4)	(5)	(6)	(7a)	(7b)	(8)	(9)	(10)	(11)
-	3.1.2	2.0	2.0	2.0.1.3	3.3	3.4	3.5	4.1.4	4.1.4	4.2.5 / 4.3.2	4.2.5
2715	ALUMINIUM RESINATE	4.1		III		5 kg	E1	P002 IBC06		T1	TP33
2716	1,4-BUTYNEDIOL	6.1		III		5 kg	E1	P002 IBC08 LP02	B3	T1	TP33
2717	CAMPHOR, synthetic	4.1		III		5 kg	E1	P002 IBC08 LP02	B3	T1	TP33
2719	BARIUM BROMATE	5.1	6.1	II		1 kg	E2	P002 IBC08	B2, B4	T3	TP33
2720	CHROMIUM NITRATE	5.1		III		5 kg	E1	P002 IBC08 LP02	B3	T1	TP33
2721	COPPER CHLORATE	5.1		II		1 kg	E2	P002 IBC08	B2, B4	T3	TP33
2722	LITHIUM NITRATE	5.1		III		5 kg	E1	P002 IBC08 LP02	B3	T1	TP33
2723	MAGNESIUM CHLORATE	5.1		II		1 kg	E2	P002 IBC08	B2, B4	T3	TP33
2724	MANGANESE NITRATE	5.1		III		5 kg	E1	P002 IBC08 LP02	B3	T1	TP33
2725	NICKEL NITRATE	5.1		III		5 kg	E1	P002 IBC08 LP02	B3	T1	TP33
2726	NICKEL NITRITE	5.1		III		5 kg	E1	P002 IBC08 LP02	B3	T1	TP33
2727	THALLIUM NITRATE	6.1	5.1	II		500 g	E4	P002 IBC06	B2	T3	TP33
2728	ZIRCONIUM NITRATE	5.1		III		5 kg	E1	P002 IBC08 LP02	B3	T1	TP33
2729	HEXACHLOROBENZENE	6.1		III		5 kg	E1	P002 IBC08 LP02	B3	T1	TP33
2730	NITROANISOLES, LIQUID	6.1		III		5 L	E1	P001 IBC03 LP01		T4	TP1
2732	NITROBROMOBENZENES, LIQUID	6.1		III		5 L	E1	P001 IBC03 LP01		T4	TP1
2733	AMINES, FLAMMABLE, CORROSIVE, N.O.S. or POLYAMINES, FLAMMABLE, CORROSIVE, N.O.S.	3	8	I	274	0	E0	P001		T14	TP1 TP27
2733	AMINES, FLAMMABLE, CORROSIVE, N.O.S. or POLYAMINES, FLAMMABLE, CORROSIVE, N.O.S.	3	8	II	274	1 L	E2	P001 IBC02		T11	TP1 TP27
2733	AMINES, FLAMMABLE, CORROSIVE, N.O.S. or POLYAMINES, FLAMMABLE, CORROSIVE, N.O.S.	3	8	III	223 274	5 L	E1	P001 IBC03		T7	TP1 TP28
2734	AMINES, LIQUID, CORROSIVE, FLAMMABLE, N.O.S. or POLYAMINES, LIQUID, CORROSIVE, FLAMMABLE, N.O.S.	8	3	I	274	0	E0	P001		T14	TP2 TP27

UN No.	Name and description	Class or division	Subsidiary hazard	UN packing group	Special provisions	Limited and excepted quantities		Packagings and IBCs		Portable tanks and bulk containers	
								Packing instruction	Special packing provisions	Instructions	Special provisions
(1)	(2)	(3)	(4)	(5)	(6)	(7a)	(7b)	(8)	(9)	(10)	(11)
-	3.1.2	2.0	2.0	2.0.1.3	3.3	3.4	3.5	4.1.4	4.1.4	4.2.5 / 4.3.2	4.2.5
2734	AMINES, LIQUID, CORROSIVE, FLAMMABLE, N.O.S. or POLYAMINES, LIQUID, CORROSIVE, FLAMMABLE, N.O.S.	8	3	II	274	1 L	E2	P001 IBC02		T11	TP2 TP27
2735	AMINES, LIQUID, CORROSIVE, N.O.S. or POLYAMINES, LIQUID, CORROSIVE, N.O.S.	8		I	274	0	E0	P001		T14	TP2 TP27
2735	AMINES, LIQUID, CORROSIVE, N.O.S. or POLYAMINES, LIQUID, CORROSIVE, N.O.S.	8		II	274	1 L	E2	P001 IBC02		T11	TP1 TP27
2735	AMINES, LIQUID, CORROSIVE, N.O.S. or POLYAMINES, LIQUID, CORROSIVE, N.O.S.	8		III	223 274	5 L	E1	P001 IBC03 LP01		T7	TP1 TP28
2738	N-BUTYLANILINE	6.1		II		100 ml	E4	P001 IBC02		T7	TP2
2739	BUTYRIC ANHYDRIDE	8		III		5 L	E1	P001 IBC03 LP01		T4	TP1
2740	n-PROPYL CHLOROFORMATE	6.1	3 8	I		0	E0	P602		T20	TP2 TP13
2741	BARIUM HYPOCHLORITE with more than 22 % available chlorine	5.1	6.1	II		1 kg	E2	P002 IBC08	B2, B4	T3	TP33
2742	CHLOROFORMATES, TOXIC, CORROSIVE, FLAMMABLE, N.O.S.	6.1	3 8	II	274	100 ml	E4	P001 IBC01			
2743	n-BUTYL CHLOROFORMATE	6.1	3 8	II		100 ml	E0	P001		T20	TP2 TP13
2744	CYCLOBUTYL CHLOROFORMATE	6.1	3 8	II		100 ml	E4	P001 IBC01		T7	TP2 TP13
2745	CHLOROMETHYL CHLOROFORMATE	6.1	8	II		100 ml	E4	P001 IBC02		T7	TP2 TP13
2746	PHENYL CHLOROFORMATE	6.1	8	II		100 ml	E4	P001 IBC02		T7	TP2 TP13
2747	tert-BUTYLCYCLOHEXYL CHLOROFORMATE	6.1		III		5 L	E1	P001 IBC03 LP01		T4	TP1
2748	2-ETHYLHEXYL CHLOROFORMATE	6.1	8	II		100 ml	E4	P001 IBC02		T7	TP2 TP13
2749	TETRAMETHYLSILANE	3		I		0	E0	P001		T14	TP2
2750	1,3-DICHLOROPROPANOL-2	6.1		II		100 ml	E4	P001 IBC02		T7	TP2
2751	DIETHYLTHIOPHOSPHORYL CHLORIDE	8		II		1 L	E2	P001 IBC02		T7	TP2
2752	1,2-EPOXY-3-ETHOXYPROPANE	3		III		5 L	E1	P001 IBC03 LP01		T2	TP1
2753	N-ETHYLBENZYLTOLUIDINES, LIQUID	6.1		III		5 L	E1	P001 IBC03 LP01		T7	TP1
2754	N-ETHYLTOLUIDINES	6.1		II		100 ml	E4	P001 IBC02		T7	TP2
2757	CARBAMATE PESTICIDE, SOLID, TOXIC	6.1		I	61 274	0	E5	P002 IBC07	B1	T6	TP33
2757	CARBAMATE PESTICIDE, SOLID, TOXIC	6.1		II	61 274	500 g	E4	P002 IBC08	B2, B4	T3	TP33
2757	CARBAMATE PESTICIDE, SOLID, TOXIC	6.1		III	61 223 274	5 kg	E1	P002 IBC08 LP02	B3	T1	TP33

UN No.	Name and description	Class or division	Subsidiary hazard	UN packing group	Special provisions	Limited and excepted quantities		Packagings and IBCs		Portable tanks and bulk containers	
								Packing instruction	Special packing provisions	Instructions	Special provisions
(1)	(2)	(3)	(4)	(5)	(6)	(7a)	(7b)	(8)	(9)	(10)	(11)
-	3.1.2	2.0	2.0	2.0.1.3	3.3	3.4	3.5	4.1.4	4.1.4	4.2.5 / 4.3.2	4.2.5
2758	CARBAMATE PESTICIDE, LIQUID, FLAMMABLE, TOXIC, flash point less than 23 °C	3	6.1	I	61 274	0	E0	P001		T14	TP2 TP13 TP27
2758	CARBAMATE PESTICIDE, LIQUID, FLAMMABLE, TOXIC, flash point less than 23 °C	3	6.1	II	61 274	1 L	E2	P001 IBC02		T11	TP2 TP13 TP27
2759	ARSENICAL PESTICIDE, SOLID, TOXIC	6.1		I	61 274	0	E5	P002 IBC07	B1	T6	TP33
2759	ARSENICAL PESTICIDE, SOLID, TOXIC	6.1		II	61 274	500 g	E4	P002 IBC08	B2, B4	T3	TP33
2759	ARSENICAL PESTICIDE, SOLID, TOXIC	6.1		III	61 223 274	5 kg	E1	P002 IBC08 LP02	B3	T1	TP33
2760	ARSENICAL PESTICIDE, LIQUID, FLAMMABLE, TOXIC, flash point less than 23 °C	3	6.1	I	61 274	0	E0	P001		T14	TP2 TP13 TP27
2760	ARSENICAL PESTICIDE, LIQUID, FLAMMABLE, TOXIC, flash point less than 23 °C	3	6.1	II	61 274	1 L	E2	P001 IBC02		T11	TP2 TP13 TP27
2761	ORGANOCHLORINE PESTICIDE, SOLID, TOXIC	6.1		I	61 274	0	E5	P002 IBC07	B1	T6	TP33
2761	ORGANOCHLORINE PESTICIDE, SOLID, TOXIC	6.1		II	61 274	500 g	E4	P002 IBC08	B2, B4	T3	TP33
2761	ORGANOCHLORINE PESTICIDE, SOLID, TOXIC	6.1		III	61 223 274	5 kg	E1	P002 IBC08 LP02	B3	T1	TP33
2762	ORGANOCHLORINE PESTICIDE, LIQUID, FLAMMABLE, TOXIC, flash point less than 23 °C	3	6.1	I	61 274	0	E0	P001		T14	TP2 TP13 TP27
2762	ORGANOCHLORINE PESTICIDE, LIQUID, FLAMMABLE, TOXIC, flash point less than 23 °C	3	6.1	II	61 274	1 L	E2	P001 IBC02		T11	TP2 TP13 TP27
2763	TRIAZINE PESTICIDE, SOLID, TOXIC	6.1		I	61 274	0	E5	P002 IBC07	B1	T6	TP33
2763	TRIAZINE PESTICIDE, SOLID, TOXIC	6.1		II	61 274	500 g	E4	P002 IBC08	B2, B4	T3	TP33
2763	TRIAZINE PESTICIDE, SOLID, TOXIC	6.1		III	61 223 274	5 kg	E1	P002 IBC08	B3	T1	TP33
2764	TRIAZINE PESTICIDE, LIQUID, FLAMMABLE, TOXIC, flash point less than 23 °C	3	6.1	I	61 274	0	E0	P001		T14	TP2 TP13 TP27
2764	TRIAZINE PESTICIDE, LIQUID, FLAMMABLE, TOXIC, flash point less than 23 °C	3	6.1	II	61 274	1 L	E2	P001 IBC02		T11	TP2 TP13 TP27
2771	THIOCARBAMATE PESTICIDE, SOLID, TOXIC	6.1		I	61 274	0	E5	P002 IBC07	B1	T6	TP33
2771	THIOCARBAMATE PESTICIDE, SOLID, TOXIC	6.1		II	61 274	500 g	E4	P002 IBC08	B2, B4	T3	TP33
2771	THIOCARBAMATE PESTICIDE, SOLID, TOXIC	6.1		III	61 223 274	5 kg	E1	P002 IBC08 LP02	B3	T1	TP33
2772	THIOCARBAMATE PESTICIDE, LIQUID, FLAMMABLE, TOXIC, flash point less than 23 °C	3	6.1	I	61 274	0	E0	P001		T14	TP2 TP13 TP27
2772	THIOCARBAMATE PESTICIDE, LIQUID, FLAMMABLE, TOXIC, flash point less than 23 °C	3	6.1	II	61 274	1 L	E2	P001 IBC02		T11	TP2 TP13 TP27
2775	COPPER BASED PESTICIDE, SOLID, TOXIC	6.1		I	61 274	0	E5	P002 IBC07	B1	T6	TP33

UN No.	Name and description	Class or division	Subsidiary hazard	UN packing group	Special provisions	Limited and excepted quantities		Packagings and IBCs		Portable tanks and bulk containers	
								Packing instruction	Special packing provisions	Instructions	Special provisions
(1)	(2)	(3)	(4)	(5)	(6)	(7a)	(7b)	(8)	(9)	(10)	(11)
-	3.1.2	2.0	2.0	2.0.1.3	3.3	3.4	3.5	4.1.4	4.1.4	4.2.5 / 4.3.2	4.2.5
2775	COPPER BASED PESTICIDE, SOLID, TOXIC	6.1		II	61 274	500 g	E4	P002 IBC08	B2, B4	T3	TP33
2775	COPPER BASED PESTICIDE, SOLID, TOXIC	6.1		III	61 223 274	5 kg	E1	P002 IBC08 LP02	B3	T1	TP33
2776	COPPER BASED PESTICIDE, LIQUID, FLAMMABLE, TOXIC, flash point less than 23 °C	3	6.1	I	61 274	0	E0	P001		T14	TP2 TP13 TP27
2776	COPPER BASED PESTICIDE, LIQUID, FLAMMABLE, TOXIC, flash point less than 23 °C	3	6.1	II	61 274	1 L	E2	P001 IBC02		T11	TP2 TP13 TP27
2777	MERCURY BASED PESTICIDE, SOLID, TOXIC	6.1		I	61 274	0	E5	P002 IBC07	B1	T6	TP33
2777	MERCURY BASED PESTICIDE, SOLID, TOXIC	6.1		II	61 274	500 g	E4	P002 IBC08	B2, B4	T3	TP33
2777	MERCURY BASED PESTICIDE, SOLID, TOXIC	6.1		III	61 223 274	5 kg	E1	P002 IBC08 LP02	B3	T1	TP33
2778	MERCURY BASED PESTICIDE, LIQUID, FLAMMABLE, TOXIC, flash point less than 23 °C	3	6.1	I	61 274	0	E0	P001		T14	TP2 TP13 TP27
2778	MERCURY BASED PESTICIDE, LIQUID, FLAMMABLE, TOXIC, flash point less than 23 °C	3	6.1	II	61 274	1 L	E2	P001 IBC02		T11	TP2 TP13 TP27
2779	SUBSTITUTED NITROPHENOL PESTICIDE, SOLID, TOXIC	6.1		I	61 274	0	E5	P002 IBC07	B1	T6	TP33
2779	SUBSTITUTED NITROPHENOL PESTICIDE, SOLID, TOXIC	6.1		II	61 274	500 g	E4	P002 IBC08	B2, B4	T3	TP33
2779	SUBSTITUTED NITROPHENOL PESTICIDE, SOLID, TOXIC	6.1		III	61 223 274	5 kg	E1	P002 IBC08 LP02	B3	T1	TP33
2780	SUBSTITUTED NITROPHENOL PESTICIDE, LIQUID, FLAMMABLE, TOXIC, flash point less than 23 °C	3	6.1	I	61 274	0	E0	P001		T14	TP2 TP13 TP27
2780	SUBSTITUTED NITROPHENOL PESTICIDE, LIQUID, FLAMMABLE, TOXIC, flash point less than 23 °C	3	6.1	II	61 274	1 L	E2	P001 IBC02		T11	TP2 TP13 TP27
2781	BIPYRIDILIUM PESTICIDE, SOLID, TOXIC	6.1		I	61 274	0	E5	P002 IBC07	B1	T6	TP33
2781	BIPYRIDILIUM PESTICIDE, SOLID, TOXIC	6.1		II	61 274	500 g	E4	P002 IBC08	B2, B4	T3	TP33
2781	BIPYRIDILIUM PESTICIDE, SOLID, TOXIC	6.1		III	61 223 274	5 kg	E1	P002 IBC08 LP02	B3	T1	TP33
2782	BIPYRIDILIUM PESTICIDE, LIQUID, FLAMMABLE, TOXIC, flash point less than 23 °C	3	6.1	I	61 274	0	E0	P001		T14	TP2 TP13 TP27
2782	BIPYRIDILIUM PESTICIDE, LIQUID, FLAMMABLE, TOXIC, flash point less than 23 °C	3	6.1	II	61 274	1 L	E2	P001 IBC02		T11	TP2 TP13 TP27
2783	ORGANOPHOSPHORUS PESTICIDE, SOLID, TOXIC	6.1		I	61 274	0	E5	P002 IBC07	B1	T6	TP33
2783	ORGANOPHOSPHORUS PESTICIDE, SOLID, TOXIC	6.1		II	61 274	500 g	E4	P002 IBC08	B2, B4	T3	TP33
2783	ORGANOPHOSPHORUS PESTICIDE, SOLID, TOXIC	6.1		III	61 223 274	5 kg	E1	P002 IBC08 LP02	B3	T1	TP33

UN No.	Name and description	Class or division	Subsidiary hazard	UN packing group	Special provisions	Limited and excepted quantities		Packagings and IBCs		Portable tanks and bulk containers	
								Packing instruction	Special packing provisions	Instructions	Special provisions
(1)	(2)	(3)	(4)	(5)	(6)	(7a)	(7b)	(8)	(9)	(10)	(11)
-	3.1.2	2.0	2.0	2.0.1.3	3.3	3.4	3.5	4.1.4	4.1.4	4.2.5 / 4.3.2	4.2.5
2784	ORGANOPHOSPHORUS PESTICIDE, LIQUID, FLAMMABLE, TOXIC, flash point less than 23 °C	3	6.1	I	61 274	0	E0	P001		T14	TP2 TP13 TP27
2784	ORGANOPHOSPHORUS PESTICIDE, LIQUID, FLAMMABLE, TOXIC, flash point less than 23 °C	3	6.1	II	61 274	1 L	E2	P001 IBC02		T11	TP2 TP13 TP27
2785	4-THIAPENTANAL	6.1		III		5 L	E1	P001 IBC03 LP01		T4	TP1
2786	ORGANOTIN PESTICIDE, SOLID, TOXIC	6.1		I	61 274	0	E5	P002 IBC07	B1	T6	TP33
2786	ORGANOTIN PESTICIDE, SOLID, TOXIC	6.1		II	61 274	500 g	E4	P002 IBC08	B2, B4	T3	TP33
2786	ORGANOTIN PESTICIDE, SOLID, TOXIC	6.1		III	61 223 274	5 kg	E1	P002 IBC08 LP02	B3	T1	TP33
2787	ORGANOTIN PESTICIDE, LIQUID, FLAMMABLE, TOXIC, flash point less than 23 °C	3	6.1	I	61 274	0	E0	P001		T14	TP2 TP13 TP27
2787	ORGANOTIN PESTICIDE, LIQUID, FLAMMABLE, TOXIC, flash point less than 23 °C	3	6.1	II	61 274	1 L	E2	P001 IBC02		T11	TP2 TP13 TP27
2788	ORGANOTIN COMPOUND, LIQUID, N.O.S.	6.1		I	43 274	0	E5	P001		T14	TP2 TP13 TP27
2788	ORGANOTIN COMPOUND, LIQUID, N.O.S.	6.1		II	43 274	100 ml	E4	P001 IBC02		T11	TP2 TP13 TP27
2788	ORGANOTIN COMPOUND, LIQUID, N.O.S.	6.1		III	43 223 274	5 L	E1	P001 IBC03 LP01		T7	TP2 TP28
2789	ACETIC ACID, GLACIAL or ACETIC ACID SOLUTION, more than 80 % acid, by mass	8	3	II		1 L	E2	P001 IBC02		T7	TP2
2790	ACETIC ACID SOLUTION, not less than 50 % but not more than 80 % acid, by mass	8		II		1 L	E2	P001 IBC02		T7	TP2
2790	ACETIC ACID SOLUTION, more than 10 % and less than 50 % acid, by mass	8		III		5 L	E1	P001 IBC03 LP01		T4	TP1
2793	FERROUS METAL BORINGS, SHAVINGS, TURNINGS or CUTTINGS in a form liable to self-heating	4.2		III	223	0	E1	P003 IBC08 LP02	PP20 B3, B6	BK2	
2794	BATTERIES, WET, FILLED WITH ACID, electric storage	8			295	1 L	E0	P801			
2795	BATTERIES, WET, FILLED WITH ALKALI, electric storage	8			295 401	1 L	E0	P801			
2796	SULPHURIC ACID with not more than 51 % acid or BATTERY FLUID, ACID	8		II		1 L	E2	P001 IBC02		T8	TP2
2797	BATTERY FLUID, ALKALI	8		II		1 L	E2	P001 IBC02		T7	TP2 TP28
2798	PHENYLPHOSPHORUS DICHLORIDE	8		II		1 L	E0	P001 IBC02		T7	TP2 TP28
2799	PHENYLPHOSPHORUS THIODICHLORIDE	8		II		1 L	E0	P001 IBC02		T7	TP2
2800	BATTERIES, WET, NON-SPILLABLE, electric storage	8			238	1 L	E0	P003	PP16		

UN No.	Name and description	Class or division	Subsidiary hazard	UN packing group	Special provisions	Limited and excepted quantities		Packagings and IBCs		Portable tanks and bulk containers	
								Packing instruction	Special packing provisions	Instructions	Special provisions
(1)	(2)	(3)	(4)	(5)	(6)	(7a)	(7b)	(8)	(9)	(10)	(11)
-	3.1.2	2.0	2.0	2.0.1.3	3.3	3.4	3.5	4.1.4	4.1.4	4.2.5 / 4.3.2	4.2.5
2801	DYE, LIQUID, CORROSIVE, N.O.S. or DYE INTERMEDIATE, LIQUID, CORROSIVE, N.O.S.	8		I	274	0	E0	P001		T14	TP2 TP27
2801	DYE, LIQUID, CORROSIVE, N.O.S. or DYE INTERMEDIATE, LIQUID, CORROSIVE, N.O.S.	8		II	274	1 L	E2	P001 IBC02		T11	TP2 TP27
2801	DYE, LIQUID, CORROSIVE, N.O.S. or DYE INTERMEDIATE, LIQUID, CORROSIVE, N.O.S.	8		III	223 274	5 L	E1	P001 IBC03 LP01		T7	TP1 TP28
2802	COPPER CHLORIDE	8		III		5 kg	E1	P002 IBC08 LP02	B3	T1	TP33
2803	GALLIUM	8		III	365	5 kg	E0	P800	PP41	T1	TP33
2805	LITHIUM HYDRIDE, FUSED SOLID	4.3		II		500 g	E2	P410 IBC04		T3	TP33
2806	LITHIUM NITRIDE	4.3		I		0	E0	P403 IBC04	B1		
2807	MAGNETIZED MATERIAL	9			106		E0				
2809	MERCURY	8	6.1	III	365	5 kg	E0	P800			
2810	TOXIC LIQUID, ORGANIC, N.O.S.	6.1		I	274 315	0	E5	P001		T14	TP2 TP13 TP27
2810	TOXIC LIQUID, ORGANIC, N.O.S.	6.1		II	274	100 ml	E4	P001 IBC02		T11	TP2 TP13 TP27
2810	TOXIC LIQUID, ORGANIC, N.O.S.	6.1		III	223 274	5 L	E1	P001 IBC03 LP01		T7	TP1 TP28
2811	TOXIC SOLID, ORGANIC, N.O.S.	6.1		I	274	0	E5	P002 IBC99		T6	TP33
2811	TOXIC SOLID, ORGANIC, N.O.S.	6.1		II	274	500 g	E4	P002 IBC08	B2, B4	T3	TP33
2811	TOXIC SOLID, ORGANIC, N.O.S.	6.1		III	223 274	5 kg	E1	P002 IBC08 LP02	B3	T1	TP33
2812	SODIUM ALUMINATE, SOLID	8		III	106	5 kg	E1	P002 IBC08 LP02	B3	T1	TP33
2813	WATER-REACTIVE SOLID, N.O.S.	4.3		I	274	0	E0	P403 IBC99		T9	TP7 TP33
2813	WATER-REACTIVE SOLID, N.O.S.	4.3		II	274	500 g	E2	P410 IBC07	B2	T3	TP33
2813	WATER-REACTIVE SOLID, N.O.S.	4.3		III	223 274	1 kg	E1	P410 IBC08	B4	T1	TP33
2814	INFECTIOUS SUBSTANCE, AFFECTING HUMANS	6.2			318 341	0	E0	P620		BK1 BK2	
2815	N-AMINOETHYLPIPERAZINE	8	6.1	III		5 L	E1	P001 IBC03 LP01		T4	TP1
2817	AMMONIUM HYDROGEN-DIFLUORIDE SOLUTION	8	6.1	II		1 L	E2	P001 IBC02		T8	TP2 TP13
2817	AMMONIUM HYDROGEN-DIFLUORIDE SOLUTION	8	6.1	III	223	5 L	E1	P001 IBC03		T4	TP1 TP13
2818	AMMONIUM POLYSULPHIDE SOLUTION	8	6.1	II		1 L	E2	P001 IBC02		T7	TP2 TP13
2818	AMMONIUM POLYSULPHIDE SOLUTION	8	6.1	III	223	5 L	E1	P001 IBC03		T4	TP1 TP13

UN No.	Name and description	Class or division	Subsidiary hazard	UN packing group	Special provisions	Limited and excepted quantities		Packagings and IBCs		Portable tanks and bulk containers	
						Packing instruction	Special packing provisions	Instructions	Special provisions
						(7a)	(7b)	(8)	(9)	(10)	(11)
(1)	(2)	(3)	(4)	(5)	(6)	(7a)	(7b)	(8)	(9)	(10)	(11)
-	3.1.2	2.0	2.0	2.0.1.3	3.3	3.4	3.5	4.1.4	4.1.4	4.2.5 / 4.3.2	4.2.5
2819	AMYL ACID PHOSPHATE	8		III		5 L	E1	P001 IBC03 LP01		T4	TP1
2820	BUTYRIC ACID	8		III		5 L	E1	P001 IBC03 LP01		T4	TP1
2821	PHENOL SOLUTION	6.1		II		100 ml	E4	P001 IBC02		T7	TP2
2821	PHENOL SOLUTION	6.1		III	223	5 L	E1	P001 IBC03 LP01		T4	TP1
2822	2-CHLOROPYRIDINE	6.1		II		100 ml	E4	P001 IBC02		T7	TP2
2823	CROTONIC ACID, SOLID	8		III		5 kg	E1	P002 IBC08 LP02	B3	T1	TP33
2826	ETHYL CHLOROTHIOFORMATE	8	3	II		0	E0	P001		T7	TP2
2829	CAPROIC ACID	8		III		5 L	E1	P001 IBC03 LP01		T4	TP1
2830	LITHIUM FERROSILICON	4.3		II		500 g	E2	P410 IBC07	B2	T3	TP33
2831	1,1,1-TRICHLOROETHANE	6.1		III		5 L	E1	P001 IBC03 LP01		T4	TP1
2834	PHOSPHOROUS ACID	8		III		5 kg	E1	P002 IBC08 LP02	B3	T1	TP33
2835	SODIUM ALUMINIUM HYDRIDE	4.3		II		500 g	E0	P410 IBC04		T3	TP33
2837	BISULPHATES, AQUEOUS SOLUTION	8		II		1 L	E2	P001 IBC02		T7	TP2
2837	BISULPHATES, AQUEOUS SOLUTION	8		III	223	5 L	E1	P001 IBC03 LP01		T4	TP1
2838	VINYL BUTYRATE, STABILIZED	3		II	386	1 L	E2	P001 IBC02		T4	TP1
2839	ALDOL	6.1		II		100 ml	E4	P001 IBC02		T7	TP2
2840	BUTYRALDOXIME	3		III		5 L	E1	P001 IBC03 LP01		T2	TP1
2841	DI-n-AMYLAMINE	3	6.1	III		5 L	E1	P001 IBC03		T4	TP1
2842	NITROETHANE	3		III		5 L	E1	P001 IBC03 LP01		T2	TP1
2844	CALCIUM MANGANESE SILICON	4.3		III		1 kg	E1	P410 IBC08	B4	T1	TP33
2845	PYROPHORIC LIQUID, ORGANIC, N.O.S.	4.2		I	274	0	E0	P400		T22	TP2 TP7
2846	PYROPHORIC SOLID, ORGANIC, N.O.S.	4.2		I	274	0	E0	P404			
2849	3-CHLOROPROPANOL-1	6.1		III		5 L	E1	P001 IBC03 LP01		T4	TP1
2850	PROPYLENE TETRAMER	3		III		5 L	E1	P001 IBC03 LP01		T2	TP1

UN No.	Name and description	Class or division	Subsidiary hazard	UN packing group	Special provisions	Limited and excepted quantities		Packagings and IBCs		Portable tanks and bulk containers	
								Packing instruction	Special packing provisions	Instructions	Special provisions
(1)	(2)	(3)	(4)	(5)	(6)	(7a)	(7b)	(8)	(9)	(10)	(11)
-	3.1.2	2.0	2.0	2.0.1.3	3.3	3.4	3.5	4.1.4	4.1.4	4.2.5 / 4.3.2	4.2.5
2851	BORON TRIFLUORIDE DIHYDRATE	8		II		1 L	E2	P001 IBC02		T7	TP2
2852	DIPICRYL SULPHIDE, WETTED with not less than 10 % water, by mass	4.1		I	28	0	E0	P406	PP24		
2853	MAGNESIUM FLUOROSILICATE	6.1		III		5 kg	E1	P002 IBC08 LP02	B3	T1	TP33
2854	AMMONIUM FLUOROSILICATE	6.1		III		5 kg	E1	P002 IBC08 LP02	B3	T1	TP33
2855	ZINC FLUOROSILICATE	6.1		III		5 kg	E1	P002 IBC08 LP02	B3	T1	TP33
2856	FLUOROSILICATES, N.O.S.	6.1		III	274	5 kg	E1	P002 IBC08 LP02	B3	T1	TP33
2857	REFRIGERATING MACHINES containing non-flammable, non-toxic, gases or ammonia solutions (UN 2672)	2.2			119	0	E0	P003	PP32		
2858	ZIRCONIUM, DRY, coiled wire, finished metal sheets, strip (thinner than 254 microns but not thinner than 18 microns)	4.1		III		5 kg	E1	P002 LP02			
2859	AMMONIUM METAVANADATE	6.1		II		500 g	E4	P002 IBC08	B2, B4	T3	TP33
2861	AMMONIUM POLYVANADATE	6.1		II		500 g	E4	P002 IBC08	B2, B4	T3	TP33
2862	VANADIUM PENTOXIDE, non-fused form	6.1		III		5 kg	E1	P002 IBC08 LP02	B3	T1	TP33
2863	SODIUM AMMONIUM VANADATE	6.1		II		500 g	E4	P002 IBC08	B2, B4	T3	TP33
2864	POTASSIUM METAVANADATE	6.1		II		500 g	E4	P002 IBC08	B2, B4	T3	TP33
2865	HYDROXYLAMINE SULPHATE	8		III		5 kg	E1	P002 IBC08 LP02	B3	T1	TP33
2869	TITANIUM TRICHLORIDE MIXTURE	8		II		1 kg	E2	P002 IBC08	B2, B4	T3	TP33
2869	TITANIUM TRICHLORIDE MIXTURE	8		III	223	5 kg	E1	P002 IBC08 LP02	B3	T1	TP33
2870	ALUMINIUM BOROHYDRIDE	4.2	4.3	I		0	E0	P400		T21	TP7 TP33
2870	ALUMINIUM BOROHYDRIDE IN DEVICES	4.2	4.3			0	E0	P002	PP13		
2871	ANTIMONY POWDER	6.1		III		5 kg	E1	P002 IBC08 LP02	B3	T1	TP33
2872	DIBROMOCHLOROPROPANES	6.1		II		100 ml	E4	P001 IBC02		T7	TP2
2872	DIBROMOCHLOROPROPANES	6.1		III	223	5 L	E1	P001 IBC03 LP01		T4	TP1
2873	DIBUTYLAMINOETHANOL	6.1		III		5 L	E1	P001 IBC03 LP01		T4	TP1

UN No.	Name and description	Class or division	Subsidiary hazard	UN packing group	Special provisions	Limited and excepted quantities		Packagings and IBCs		Portable tanks and bulk containers	
						(7a)	(7b)	Packing instruction	Special packing provisions	Instructions	Special provisions
(1)	(2)	(3)	(4)	(5)	(6)	(7a)	(7b)	(8)	(9)	(10)	(11)
-	3.1.2	2.0	2.0	2.0.1.3	3.3	3.4	3.5	4.1.4	4.1.4	4.2.5 / 4.3.2	4.2.5
2874	FURFURYL ALCOHOL	6.1		III		5 L	E1	P001 IBC03 LP01		T4	TP1
2875	HEXACHLOROPHENE	6.1		III		5 kg	E1	P002 IBC08 LP02	B3	T1	TP33
2876	RESORCINOL	6.1		III		5 kg	E1	P002 IBC08 LP02	B3	T1	TP33
2878	TITANIUM SPONGE GRANULES or TITANIUM SPONGE POWDERS	4.1		III	223	5 kg	E1	P002 IBC08 LP02	B3	T1	TP33
2879	SELENIUM OXYCHLORIDE	8	6.1	I		0	E0	P001		T10	TP2 TP13
2880	CALCIUM HYPOCHLORITE, HYDRATED or CALCIUM HYPOCHLORITE, HYDRATED MIXTURE, with not less than 5.5 % but not more than 16 % water	5.1		II	314 322	1 kg	E2	P002 IBC08	PP85 B2, B4, B13		
2880	CALCIUM HYPOCHLORITE, HYDRATED or CALCIUM HYPOCHLORITE, HYDRATED MIXTURE, with not less than 5.5 % but not more than 16 % water	5.1		III	223 314	5 kg	E1	P002 IBC08	PP85 B4, B13		
2881	METAL CATALYST, DRY	4.2		I	274	0	E0	P404		T21	TP7 TP33
2881	METAL CATALYST, DRY	4.2		II	274	0	E0	P410 IBC06	B2	T3	TP33
2881	METAL CATALYST, DRY	4.2		III	223 274	0	E1	P002 IBC08 LP02	B3	T1	TP33
2900	INFECTIOUS SUBSTANCE, AFFECTING ANIMALS only	6.2			318 341	0	E0	P620		BK1 BK2	
2901	BROMINE CHLORIDE	2.3	5.1 8			0	E0	P200			
2902	PESTICIDE, LIQUID, TOXIC, N.O.S.	6.1		I	61 274	0	E5	P001		T14	TP2 TP13 TP27
2902	PESTICIDE, LIQUID, TOXIC, N.O.S.	6.1		II	61 274	100 ml	E4	P001 IBC02		T11	TP2 TP13 TP27
2902	PESTICIDE, LIQUID, TOXIC, N.O.S.	6.1		III	61 223 274	5 L	E1	P001 IBC03 LP01		T7	TP2 TP28
2903	PESTICIDE, LIQUID, TOXIC, FLAMMABLE, N.O.S., flash point not less than 23 °C	6.1	3	I	61 274	0	E5	P001		T14	TP2 TP13 TP27
2903	PESTICIDE, LIQUID, TOXIC, FLAMMABLE, N.O.S., flash point not less than 23 °C	6.1	3	II	61 274	100 ml	E4	P001 IBC02		T11	TP2 TP13 TP27
2903	PESTICIDE, LIQUID, TOXIC, FLAMMABLE, N.O.S., flash point not less than 23 °C	6.1	3	III	61 223 274	5 L	E1	P001 IBC03		T7	TP2
2904	CHLOROPHENOLATES, LIQUID or PHENOLATES, LIQUID	8		III		5 L	E1	P001 IBC03 LP01		T4	TP1
2905	CHLOROPHENOLATES, SOLID or PHENOLATES, SOLID	8		III		5 kg	E1	P002 IBC08 LP02	B3	T1	TP33

UN No.	Name and description	Class or division	Subsidiary hazard	UN packing group	Special provisions	Limited and excepted quantities		Packagings and IBCs		Portable tanks and bulk containers	
								Packing instruction	Special packing provisions	Instructions	Special provisions
(1)	(2)	(3)	(4)	(5)	(6)	(7a)	(7b)	(8)	(9)	(10)	(11)
-	3.1.2	2.0	2.0	2.0.1.3	3.3	3.4	3.5	4.1.4	4.1.4	4.2.5 / 4.3.2	4.2.5
2907	ISOSORBIDE DINITRATE MIXTURE with not less than 60 % lactose, mannose, starch or calcium hydrogen phosphate	4.1		II	28 127	0	E0	P406 IBC06	PP26 PP80 B2, B12		
2908	RADIOACTIVE MATERIAL, EXCEPTED PACKAGE - EMPTY PACKAGING	7			290 368	0	E0	See chapter 1.5			
2909	RADIOACTIVE MATERIAL, EXCEPTED PACKAGE - ARTICLES MANUFACTURED FROM NATURAL URANIUM or DEPLETED URANIUM or NATURAL THORIUM	7			290	0	E0	See chapter 1.5			
2910	RADIOACTIVE MATERIAL, EXCEPTED PACKAGE - LIMITED QUANTITY OF MATERIAL	7			290 368	0	E0	See chapter 1.5			
2911	RADIOACTIVE MATERIAL, EXCEPTED PACKAGE - INSTRUMENTS or ARTICLES	7			290	0	E0	See chapter 1.5			
2912	RADIOACTIVE MATERIAL, LOW SPECIFIC ACTIVITY (LSA-I), non-fissile or fissile-excepted	7			172 317 325	0	E0	See chapter 2.7 and section 4.1.9		T5	TP4
2913	RADIOACTIVE MATERIAL, SURFACE CONTAMINATED OBJECTS (SCO-I, SCO-II or SCO-III), non-fissile or fissile-excepted	7			172 317 325	0	E0	See chapter 2.7 and section 4.1.9		T5	TP4
2915	RADIOACTIVE MATERIAL, TYPE A PACKAGE, non-special form, non-fissile or fissile-excepted	7			172 317 325	0	E0	See chapter 2.7 and section 4.1.9			
2916	RADIOACTIVE MATERIAL, TYPE B(U) PACKAGE, non-fissile or fissile-excepted	7			172 317 325 337	0	E0	See chapter 2.7 and section 4.1.9			
2917	RADIOACTIVE MATERIAL, TYPE B(M) PACKAGE, non-fissile or fissile-excepted	7			172 317 325 337	0	E0	See chapter 2.7 and section 4.1.9			
2919	RADIOACTIVE MATERIAL, TRANSPORTED UNDER SPECIAL ARRANGEMENT, non-fissile or fissile-excepted	7			172 317 325	0	E0	See chapter 2.7 and section 4.1.9			
2920	CORROSIVE LIQUID, FLAMMABLE, N.O.S.	8	3	I	274	0	E0	P001		T14	TP2 TP27
2920	CORROSIVE LIQUID, FLAMMABLE, N.O.S.	8	3	II	274	1 L	E2	P001 IBC02		T11	TP2 TP27
2921	CORROSIVE SOLID, FLAMMABLE, N.O.S.	8	4.1	I	274	0	E0	P002 IBC99		T6	TP33
2921	CORROSIVE SOLID, FLAMMABLE, N.O.S.	8	4.1	II	274	1 kg	E2	P002 IBC08	B2, B4	T3	TP33
2922	CORROSIVE LIQUID, TOXIC, N.O.S.	8	6.1	I	274	0	E0	P001		T14	TP2 TP13 TP27
2922	CORROSIVE LIQUID, TOXIC, N.O.S.	8	6.1	II	274	1 L	E2	P001 IBC02		T7	TP2
2922	CORROSIVE LIQUID, TOXIC, N.O.S.	8	6.1	III	223 274	5 L	E1	P001 IBC03		T7	TP1 TP28

UN No.	Name and description	Class or division	Subsidiary hazard	UN packing group	Special provisions	Limited and excepted quantities		Packagings and IBCs		Portable tanks and bulk containers	
								Packing instruction	Special packing provisions	Instructions	Special provisions
(1)	(2)	(3)	(4)	(5)	(6)	(7a)	(7b)	(8)	(9)	(10)	(11)
-	3.1.2	2.0	2.0	2.0.1.3	3.3	3.4	3.5	4.1.4	4.1.4	4.2.5 / 4.3.2	4.2.5
2923	CORROSIVE SOLID, TOXIC, N.O.S.	8	6.1	I	274	0	E0	P002 IBC99		T6	TP33
2923	CORROSIVE SOLID, TOXIC, N.O.S.	8	6.1	II	274	1 kg	E2	P002 IBC08	B2, B4	T3	TP33
2923	CORROSIVE SOLID, TOXIC, N.O.S.	8	6.1	III	223 274	5 kg	E1	P002 IBC08	B3	T1	TP33
2924	FLAMMABLE LIQUID, CORROSIVE, N.O.S.	3	8	I	274	0	E0	P001		T14	TP2
2924	FLAMMABLE LIQUID, CORROSIVE, N.O.S.	3	8	II	274	1 L	E2	P001 IBC02		T11	TP2 TP27
2924	FLAMMABLE LIQUID, CORROSIVE, N.O.S.	3	8	III	223 274	5 L	E1	P001 IBC03		T7	TP1 TP28
2925	FLAMMABLE SOLID, CORROSIVE, ORGANIC, N.O.S.	4.1	8	II	274	1 kg	E2	P002 IBC06	B2	T3	TP33
2925	FLAMMABLE SOLID, CORROSIVE, ORGANIC, N.O.S.	4.1	8	III	223 274	5 kg	E1	P002 IBC06		T1	TP33
2926	FLAMMABLE SOLID, TOXIC, ORGANIC, N.O.S.	4.1	6.1	II	274	1 kg	E2	P002 IBC06	B2	T3	TP33
2926	FLAMMABLE SOLID, TOXIC, ORGANIC, N.O.S.	4.1	6.1	III	223 274	5 kg	E1	P002 IBC06		T1	TP33
2927	TOXIC LIQUID, CORROSIVE, ORGANIC, N.O.S.	6.1	8	I	274 315	0	E5	P001		T14	TP2 TP13 TP27
2927	TOXIC LIQUID, CORROSIVE, ORGANIC, N.O.S.	6.1	8	II	274	100 ml	E4	P001 IBC02		T11	TP2 TP27
2928	TOXIC SOLID, CORROSIVE, ORGANIC, N.O.S.	6.1	8	I	274	0	E5	P002 IBC99		T6	TP33
2928	TOXIC SOLID, CORROSIVE, ORGANIC, N.O.S.	6.1	8	II	274	500 g	E4	P002 IBC06	B2	T3	TP33
2929	TOXIC LIQUID, FLAMMABLE, ORGANIC, N.O.S.	6.1	3	I	274 315	0	E5	P001		T14	TP2 TP13 TP27
2929	TOXIC LIQUID, FLAMMABLE, ORGANIC, N.O.S.	6.1	3	II	274	100 ml	E4	P001 IBC02		T11	TP2 TP13 TP27
2930	TOXIC SOLID, FLAMMABLE, ORGANIC, N.O.S.	6.1	4.1	I	274	0	E5	P002 IBC99		T6	TP33
2930	TOXIC SOLID, FLAMMABLE, ORGANIC, N.O.S.	6.1	4.1	II	274	500 g	E4	P002 IBC08	B2, B4	T3	TP33
2931	VANADYL SULPHATE	6.1		II		500 g	E4	P002 IBC08	B2, B4	T3	TP33
2933	METHYL 2-CHLORO-PROPIONATE	3		III		5 L	E1	P001 IBC03 LP01		T2	TP1
2934	ISOPROPYL 2-CHLORO-PROPIONATE	3		III		5 L	E1	P001 IBC03 LP01		T2	TP1
2935	ETHYL 2-CHLOROPROPIONATE	3		III		5 L	E1	P001 IBC03 LP01		T2	TP1
2936	THIOLACTIC ACID	6.1		II		100 ml	E4	P001 IBC02		T7	TP2
2937	alpha-METHYLBENZYL ALCOHOL, LIQUID	6.1		III		5 L	E1	P001 IBC03 LP01		T4	TP1
2940	9-PHOSPHABICYCLO-NONANES (CYCLOOCTADIENE PHOSPHINES)	4.2		II		0	E2	P410 IBC06	B2	T3	TP33

UN No.	Name and description	Class or division	Subsidiary hazard	UN packing group	Special provisions	Limited and excepted quantities		Packagings and IBCs		Portable tanks and bulk containers	
								Packing instruction	Special packing provisions	Instructions	Special provisions
(1)	(2)	(3)	(4)	(5)	(6)	(7a)	(7b)	(8)	(9)	(10)	(11)
-	3.1.2	2.0	2.0	2.0.1.3	3.3	3.4	3.5	4.1.4	4.1.4	4.2.5 / 4.3.2	4.2.5
2941	FLUOROANILINES	6.1		III		5 L	E1	P001 IBC03 LP01		T4	TP1
2942	2-TRIFLUOROMETHYLANILINE	6.1		III		5 L	E1	P001 IBC03 LP01			
2943	TETRAHYDROFURFURYL-AMINE	3		III		5 L	E1	P001 IBC03 LP01		T2	TP1
2945	N-METHYLBUTYLAMINE	3	8	II		1 L	E2	P001 IBC02		T7	TP1
2946	2-AMINO-5-DIETHYLAMINO-PENTANE	6.1		III		5 L	E1	P001 IBC03 LP01		T4	TP1
2947	ISOPROPYL CHLOROACETATE	3		III		5 L	E1	P001 IBC03 LP01		T2	TP1
2948	3-TRIFLUOROMETHYL-ANILINE	6.1		II		100 ml	E4	P001 IBC02		T7	TP2
2949	SODIUM HYDROSULPHIDE, HYDRATED with not less than 25 % water of crystallization	8		II		1 kg	E2	P002 IBC08	B2, B4	T7	TP2
2950	MAGNESIUM GRANULES, COATED, particle size not less than 149 microns	4.3		III		1 kg	E1	P410 IBC08	B4	T1 BK2	TP33
2956	5-tert-BUTYL-2,4,6-TRINITRO-m-XYLENE (MUSK XYLENE)	4.1		III	132 133	5 kg	E0	P409			
2965	BORON TRIFLUORIDE DIMETHYL ETHERATE	4.3	3 8	I		0	E0	P401		T10	TP2 TP7 TP13
2966	THIOGLYCOL	6.1		II		100 ml	E4	P001 IBC02		T7	TP2
2967	SULPHAMIC ACID	8		III		5 kg	E1	P002 IBC08 LP02	B3	T1	TP33
2968	MANEB, STABILIZED or MANEB PREPARATION, STABILIZED against self-heating	4.3		III	223	1 kg	E1	P002 IBC08	B4	T1	TP33
2969	CASTOR BEANS or CASTOR MEAL or CASTOR POMACE or CASTOR FLAKE	9		II	141	5 kg	E2	P002 IBC08	PP34 B2, B4	T3 BK1 BK2	TP33
2977	RADIOACTIVE MATERIAL, URANIUM HEXAFLUORIDE, FISSILE	7	6.1 8			0	E0	See chapter 2.7 and section 4.1.9			
2978	RADIOACTIVE MATERIAL, URANIUM HEXAFLUORIDE, non-fissile or fissile-excepted	7	6.1 8		317	0	E0	See chapter 2.7 and section 4.1.9			
2983	ETHYLENE OXIDE AND PROPYLENE OXIDE MIXTURE, not more than 30 % ethylene oxide	3	6.1	I		0	E0	P001		T14	TP2 TP7 TP13
2984	HYDROGEN PEROXIDE, AQUEOUS SOLUTION with not less than 8 % but less than 20 % hydrogen peroxide (stabilized as necessary)	5.1		III	65	5 L	E1	P504 IBC02	B5	T4	TP1 TP6 TP24
2985	CHLOROSILANES, FLAMMABLE, CORROSIVE, N.O.S.	3	8	II		0	E0	P010		T14	TP2 TP7 TP13 TP27

UN No.	Name and description	Class or division	Subsi-diary hazard	UN packing group	Special provi-sions	Limited and excepted quantities		Packagings and IBCs		Portable tanks and bulk containers	
								Packing instruction	Special packing provisions	Instruc-tions	Special provisions
(1)	(2)	(3)	(4)	(5)	(6)	(7a)	(7b)	(8)	(9)	(10)	(11)
-	3.1.2	2.0	2.0	2.0.1.3	3.3	3.4	3.5	4.1.4	4.1.4	4.2.5 / 4.3.2	4.2.5
2986	CHLOROSILANES, CORROSIVE, FLAMMABLE, N.O.S.	8	3	II		0	E0	P010		T14	TP2 TP7 TP13 TP27
2987	CHLOROSILANES, CORROSIVE, N.O.S.	8		II		0	E0	P010		T14	TP2 TP7 TP13 TP27
2988	CHLOROSILANES, WATER-REACTIVE, FLAMMABLE, CORROSIVE, N.O.S.	4.3	3 8	I		0	E0	P401		T14	TP2 TP7 TP13
2989	LEAD PHOSPHITE, DIBASIC	4.1		II		1 kg	E2	P002 IBC08	B2, B4	T3	TP33
2989	LEAD PHOSPHITE, DIBASIC	4.1		III	223	5 kg	E1	P002 IBC08 LP02	B3	T1	TP33
2990	LIFE-SAVING APPLIANCES, SELF-INFLATING	9			296	0	E0	P905			
2991	CARBAMATE PESTICIDE, LIQUID, TOXIC, FLAMMABLE, flash point not less than 23 °C	6.1	3	I	61 274	0	E5	P001		T14	TP2 TP13 TP27
2991	CARBAMATE PESTICIDE, LIQUID, TOXIC, FLAMMABLE, flash point not less than 23 °C	6.1	3	II	61 274	100 ml	E4	P001 IBC02		T11	TP2 TP13 TP27
2991	CARBAMATE PESTICIDE, LIQUID, TOXIC, FLAMMABLE, flash point not less than 23 °C	6.1	3	III	61 223 274	5 L	E1	P001 IBC03		T7	TP2 TP28
2992	CARBAMATE PESTICIDE, LIQUID, TOXIC	6.1		I	61 274	0	E5	P001		T14	TP2 TP13 TP27
2992	CARBAMATE PESTICIDE, LIQUID, TOXIC	6.1		II	61 274	100 ml	E4	P001 IBC02		T11	TP2 TP13 TP27
2992	CARBAMATE PESTICIDE, LIQUID, TOXIC	6.1		III	61 223 274	5 L	E1	P001 IBC03 LP01		T7	TP2 TP28
2993	ARSENICAL PESTICIDE, LIQUID, TOXIC, FLAMMABLE, flash point not less than 23 °C	6.1	3	I	61 274	0	E5	P001		T14	TP2 TP13 TP27
2993	ARSENICAL PESTICIDE, LIQUID, TOXIC, FLAMMABLE, flash point not less than 23 °C	6.1	3	II	61 274	100 ml	E4	P001 IBC02		T11	TP2 TP13 TP27
2993	ARSENICAL PESTICIDE, LIQUID, TOXIC, FLAMMABLE, flash point not less than 23 °C	6.1	3	III	61 223 274	5 L	E1	P001 IBC03		T7	TP2 TP28
2994	ARSENICAL PESTICIDE, LIQUID, TOXIC	6.1		I	61 274	0	E5	P001		T14	TP2 TP13 TP27
2994	ARSENICAL PESTICIDE, LIQUID, TOXIC	6.1		II	61 274	100 ml	E4	P001 IBC02		T11	TP2 TP13 TP27
2994	ARSENICAL PESTICIDE, LIQUID, TOXIC	6.1		III	61 223 274	5 L	E1	P001 IBC03 LP01		T7	TP2 TP28
2995	ORGANOCHLORINE PESTICIDE, LIQUID, TOXIC, FLAMMABLE, flash point not less than 23 °C	6.1	3	I	61 274	0	E5	P001		T14	TP2 TP13 TP27
2995	ORGANOCHLORINE PESTICIDE, LIQUID, TOXIC, FLAMMABLE, flash point not less than 23 °C	6.1	3	II	61 274	100 ml	E4	P001 IBC02		T11	TP2 TP13 TP27

UN No.	Name and description	Class or division	Subsidiary hazard	UN packing group	Special provisions	Limited and excepted quantities		Packagings and IBCs		Portable tanks and bulk containers	
								Packing instruction	Special packing provisions	Instructions	Special provisions
(1)	(2)	(3)	(4)	(5)	(6)	(7a)	(7b)	(8)	(9)	(10)	(11)
-	3.1.2	2.0	2.0	2.0.1.3	3.3	3.4	3.5	4.1.4	4.1.4	4.2.5 / 4.3.2	4.2.5
2995	ORGANOCHLORINE PESTICIDE, LIQUID, TOXIC, FLAMMABLE, flash point not less than 23 °C	6.1	3	III	61 223 274	5 L	E1	P001 IBC03		T7	TP2 TP28
2996	ORGANOCHLORINE PESTICIDE, LIQUID, TOXIC	6.1		I	61 274	0	E5	P001		T14	TP2 TP13 TP27
2996	ORGANOCHLORINE PESTICIDE, LIQUID, TOXIC	6.1		II	61 274	100 ml	E4	P001 IBC02		T11	TP2 TP13 TP27
2996	ORGANOCHLORINE PESTICIDE, LIQUID, TOXIC	6.1		III	61 223 274	5 L	E1	P001 IBC03 LP01		T7	TP2 TP28
2997	TRIAZINE PESTICIDE, LIQUID, TOXIC, FLAMMABLE, flash point not less than 23 °C	6.1	3	I	61 274	0	E5	P001		T14	TP2 TP13 TP27
2997	TRIAZINE PESTICIDE, LIQUID, TOXIC, FLAMMABLE, flash point not less than 23 °C	6.1	3	II	61 274	100 ml	E4	P001 IBC02		T11	TP2 TP13 TP27
2997	TRIAZINE PESTICIDE, LIQUID, TOXIC, FLAMMABLE, flash point not less than 23 °C	6.1	3	III	61 223 274	5 L	E1	P001 IBC03		T7	TP2 TP28
2998	TRIAZINE PESTICIDE, LIQUID, TOXIC	6.1		I	61 274	0	E5	P001		T14	TP2 TP13 TP27
2998	TRIAZINE PESTICIDE, LIQUID, TOXIC	6.1		II	61 274	100 ml	E4	P001 IBC02		T11	TP2 TP13 TP27
2998	TRIAZINE PESTICIDE, LIQUID, TOXIC	6.1		III	61 223 274	5 L	E1	P001 IBC03 LP01		T7	TP2 TP28
3005	THIOCARBAMATE PESTICIDE, LIQUID, TOXIC, FLAMMABLE, flash point not less than 23 °C	6.1	3	I	61 274	0	E5	P001		T14	TP2 TP13
3005	THIOCARBAMATE PESTICIDE, LIQUID, TOXIC, FLAMMABLE, flash point not less than 23 °C	6.1	3	II	61 274	100 ml	E4	P001 IBC02		T11	TP2 TP13 TP27
3005	THIOCARBAMATE PESTICIDE, LIQUID, TOXIC, FLAMMABLE, flash point not less than 23 °C	6.1	3	III	61 223 274	5 L	E1	P001 IBC03		T7	TP2 TP28
3006	THIOCARBAMATE PESTICIDE, LIQUID, TOXIC	6.1		I	61 274	0	E5	P001		T14	TP2 TP13
3006	THIOCARBAMATE PESTICIDE, LIQUID, TOXIC	6.1		II	61 274	100 ml	E4	P001 IBC02		T11	TP2 TP13 TP27
3006	THIOCARBAMATE PESTICIDE, LIQUID, TOXIC	6.1		III	61 223 274	5 L	E1	P001 IBC03 LP01		T7	TP2 TP28
3009	COPPER BASED PESTICIDE, LIQUID, TOXIC, FLAMMABLE, flash point not less than 23 °C	6.1	3	I	61 274	0	E5	P001		T14	TP2 TP13 TP27
3009	COPPER BASED PESTICIDE, LIQUID, TOXIC, FLAMMABLE, flash point not less than 23 °C	6.1	3	II	61 274	100 ml	E4	P001 IBC02		T11	TP2 TP13 TP27
3009	COPPER BASED PESTICIDE, LIQUID, TOXIC, FLAMMABLE, flash point not less than 23 °C	6.1	3	III	61 223 274	5 L	E1	P001 IBC03		T7	TP2 TP28
3010	COPPER BASED PESTICIDE, LIQUID, TOXIC	6.1		I	61 274	0	E5	P001		T14	TP2 TP13 TP27

UN No.	Name and description	Class or division	Subsidiary hazard	UN packing group	Special provisions	Limited and excepted quantities		Packagings and IBCs		Portable tanks and bulk containers	
								Packing instruction	Special packing provisions	Instructions	Special provisions
(1)	(2)	(3)	(4)	(5)	(6)	(7a)	(7b)	(8)	(9)	(10)	(11)
-	3.1.2	2.0	2.0	2.0.1.3	3.3	3.4	3.5	4.1.4	4.1.4	4.2.5 / 4.3.2	4.2.5
3010	COPPER BASED PESTICIDE, LIQUID, TOXIC	6.1		II	61 274	100 ml	E4	P001 IBC02		T11	TP2 TP13 TP27
3010	COPPER BASED PESTICIDE, LIQUID, TOXIC	6.1		III	61 223 274	5 L	E1	P001 IBC03 LP01		T7	TP2 TP28
3011	MERCURY BASED PESTICIDE, LIQUID, TOXIC, FLAMMABLE, flash point not less than 23 °C	6.1	3	I	61 274	0	E5	P001		T14	TP2 TP13 TP27
3011	MERCURY BASED PESTICIDE, LIQUID, TOXIC, FLAMMABLE, flash point not less than 23 °C	6.1	3	II	61 274	100 ml	E4	P001 IBC02		T11	TP2 TP13 TP27
3011	MERCURY BASED PESTICIDE, LIQUID, TOXIC, FLAMMABLE, flash point not less than 23 °C	6.1	3	III	61 223 274	5 L	E1	P001 IBC03		T7	TP2 TP28
3012	MERCURY BASED PESTICIDE, LIQUID, TOXIC	6.1		I	61 274	0	E5	P001		T14	TP2 TP13 TP27
3012	MERCURY BASED PESTICIDE, LIQUID, TOXIC	6.1		II	61 274	100 ml	E4	P001 IBC02		T11	TP2 TP13 TP27
3012	MERCURY BASED PESTICIDE, LIQUID, TOXIC	6.1		III	61 223 274	5 L	E1	P001 IBC03 LP01		T7	TP2 TP28
3013	SUBSTITUTED NITROPHENOL PESTICIDE, LIQUID, TOXIC, FLAMMABLE, flash point not less than 23 °C	6.1	3	I	61 274	0	E5	P001		T14	TP2 TP13 TP27
3013	SUBSTITUTED NITROPHENOL PESTICIDE, LIQUID, TOXIC, FLAMMABLE, flash point not less than 23 °C	6.1	3	II	61 274	100 ml	E4	P001 IBC02		T11	TP2 TP13 TP27
3013	SUBSTITUTED NITROPHENOL PESTICIDE, LIQUID, TOXIC, FLAMMABLE, flash point not less than 23 °C	6.1	3	III	61 223 274	5 L	E1	P001 IBC03		T7	TP2 TP28
3014	SUBSTITUTED NITROPHENOL PESTICIDE, LIQUID, TOXIC	6.1		I	61 274	0	E5	P001		T14	TP2 TP13 TP27
3014	SUBSTITUTED NITROPHENOL PESTICIDE, LIQUID, TOXIC	6.1		II	61 274	100 ml	E4	P001 IBC02		T11	TP2 TP13 TP27
3014	SUBSTITUTED NITROPHENOL PESTICIDE, LIQUID, TOXIC	6.1		III	61 223 274	5 L	E1	P001 IBC03 LP01		T7	TP2 TP28
3015	BIPYRIDILIUM PESTICIDE, LIQUID, TOXIC, FLAMMABLE, flash point not less than 23 °C	6.1	3	I	61 274	0	E5	P001		T14	TP2 TP13 TP27
3015	BIPYRIDILIUM PESTICIDE, LIQUID, TOXIC, FLAMMABLE, flash point not less than 23 °C	6.1	3	II	61 274	100 ml	E4	P001 IBC02		T11	TP2 TP13 TP27
3015	BIPYRIDILIUM PESTICIDE, LIQUID, TOXIC, FLAMMABLE, flash point not less than 23 °C	6.1	3	III	61 223 274	5 L	E1	P001 IBC03		T7	TP2 TP28
3016	BIPYRIDILIUM PESTICIDE, LIQUID, TOXIC	6.1		I	61 274	0	E5	P001		T14	TP2 TP13 TP27
3016	BIPYRIDILIUM PESTICIDE, LIQUID, TOXIC	6.1		II	61 274	100 ml	E4	P001 IBC02		T11	TP2 TP13 TP27

UN No.	Name and description	Class or division	Subsidiary hazard	UN packing group	Special provisions	Limited and excepted quantities		Packagings and IBCs		Portable tanks and bulk containers	
								Packing instruction	Special packing provisions	Instructions	Special provisions
(1)	(2)	(3)	(4)	(5)	(6)	(7a)	(7b)	(8)	(9)	(10)	(11)
-	3.1.2	2.0	2.0	2.0.1.3	3.3	3.4	3.5	4.1.4	4.1.4	4.2.5 / 4.3.2	4.2.5
3016	BIPYRIDILIUM PESTICIDE, LIQUID, TOXIC	6.1		III	61 223 274	5 L	E1	P001 IBC03 LP01		T7	TP2 TP28
3017	ORGANOPHOSPHORUS PESTICIDE, LIQUID, TOXIC, FLAMMABLE, flash point not less than 23 °C	6.1	3	I	61 274	0	E5	P001		T14	TP2 TP13 TP27
3017	ORGANOPHOSPHORUS PESTICIDE, LIQUID, TOXIC, FLAMMABLE, flash point not less than 23 °C	6.1	3	II	61 274	100 ml	E4	P001 IBC02		T11	TP2 TP13 TP27
3017	ORGANOPHOSPHORUS PESTICIDE, LIQUID, TOXIC, FLAMMABLE, flash point not less than 23 °C	6.1	3	III	61 223 274	5 L	E1	P001 IBC03		T7	TP2 TP28
3018	ORGANOPHOSPHORUS PESTICIDE, LIQUID, TOXIC	6.1		I	61 274	0	E5	P001		T14	TP2 TP13 TP27
3018	ORGANOPHOSPHORUS PESTICIDE, LIQUID, TOXIC	6.1		II	61 274	100 ml	E4	P001 IBC02		T11	TP2 TP13 TP27
3018	ORGANOPHOSPHORUS PESTICIDE, LIQUID, TOXIC	6.1		III	61 223 274	5 L	E1	P001 IBC03 LP01		T7	TP2 TP28
3019	ORGANOTIN PESTICIDE, LIQUID, TOXIC, FLAMMABLE, flash point not less than 23 °C	6.1	3	I	61 274	0	E5	P001		T14	TP2 TP13 TP27
3019	ORGANOTIN PESTICIDE, LIQUID, TOXIC, FLAMMABLE, flash point not less than 23 °C	6.1	3	II	61 274	100 ml	E4	P001 IBC02		T11	TP2 TP13 TP27
3019	ORGANOTIN PESTICIDE, LIQUID, TOXIC, FLAMMABLE, flash point not less than 23 °C	6.1	3	III	61 223 274	5 L	E1	P001 IBC03		T7	TP2 TP28
3020	ORGANOTIN PESTICIDE, LIQUID, TOXIC	6.1		I	61 274	0	E5	P001		T14	TP2 TP13 TP27
3020	ORGANOTIN PESTICIDE, LIQUID, TOXIC	6.1		II	61 274	100 ml	E4	P001 IBC02		T11	TP2 TP13 TP27
3020	ORGANOTIN PESTICIDE, LIQUID, TOXIC	6.1		III	61 223 274	5 L	E1	P001 IBC03 LP01		T7	TP2 TP28
3021	PESTICIDE, LIQUID,FLAMMABLE, TOXIC, N.O.S., flash point less than 23 °C	3	6.1	I	61 274	0	E0	P001		T14	TP2 TP13 TP27
3021	PESTICIDE, LIQUID,FLAMMABLE, TOXIC, N.O.S., flash point less than 23 °C	3	6.1	II	61 274	1 L	E2	P001 IBC02		T11	TP2 TP13 TP27
3022	1,2-BUTYLENE OXIDE, STABILIZED	3		II	386	1 L	E2	P001 IBC02		T4	TP1
3023	2-METHYL-2-HEPTANETHIOL	6.1	3	I	354	0	E0	P602		T20	TP2 TP13
3024	COUMARIN DERIVATIVE PESTICIDE, LIQUID, FLAMMABLE, TOXIC, flash point less than 23 °C	3	6.1	I	61 274	0	E0	P001		T14	TP2 TP13 TP27
3024	COUMARIN DERIVATIVE PESTICIDE, LIQUID, FLAMMABLE, TOXIC, flash point less than 23 °C	3	6.1	II	61 274	1 L	E2	P001 IBC02		T11	TP2 TP13 TP27

UN No.	Name and description	Class or division	Subsidiary hazard	UN packing group	Special provisions	Limited and excepted quantities		Packagings and IBCs		Portable tanks and bulk containers	
								Packing instruction	Special packing provisions	Instructions	Special provisions
(1)	(2)	(3)	(4)	(5)	(6)	(7a)	(7b)	(8)	(9)	(10)	(11)
-	3.1.2	2.0	2.0	2.0.1.3	3.3	3.4	3.5	4.1.4	4.1.4	4.2.5 / 4.3.2	4.2.5
3025	COUMARIN DERIVATIVE PESTICIDE, LIQUID, TOXIC, FLAMMABLE, flash point not less than 23 °C	6.1	3	I	61 274	0	E5	P001		T14	TP2 TP13 TP27
3025	COUMARIN DERIVATIVE PESTICIDE, LIQUID, TOXIC, FLAMMABLE, flash point not less than 23 °C	6.1	3	II	61 274	100 ml	E4	P001 IBC02		T11	TP2 TP13 TP27
3025	COUMARIN DERIVATIVE PESTICIDE, LIQUID, TOXIC, FLAMMABLE, flash point not less than 23 °C	6.1	3	III	61 223 274	5 L	E1	P001 IBC03		T7	TP1 TP28
3026	COUMARIN DERIVATIVE PESTICIDE, LIQUID, TOXIC	6.1		I	61 274	0	E5	P001		T14	TP2 TP13 TP27
3026	COUMARIN DERIVATIVE PESTICIDE, LIQUID, TOXIC	6.1		II	61 274	100 ml	E4	P001 IBC02		T11	TP2 TP27
3026	COUMARIN DERIVATIVE PESTICIDE, LIQUID, TOXIC	6.1		III	61 223 274	5 L	E1	P001 IBC03 LP01		T7	TP1 TP28
3027	COUMARIN DERIVATIVE PESTICIDE, SOLID, TOXIC	6.1		I	61 274	0	E5	P002 IBC07	B1	T6	TP33
3027	COUMARIN DERIVATIVE PESTICIDE, SOLID, TOXIC	6.1		II	61 274	500 g	E4	P002 IBC08	B2, B4	T3	TP33
3027	COUMARIN DERIVATIVE PESTICIDE, SOLID, TOXIC	6.1		III	61 223 274	5 kg	E1	P002 IBC08 LP02	B3	T1	TP33
3028	BATTERIES, DRY, CONTAINING POTASSIUM HYDROXIDE SOLID, electric storage	8			295 304	2 kg	E0	P801			
3048	ALUMINIUM PHOSPHIDE PESTICIDE	6.1		I	153	0	E0	P002 IBC07	B1	T6	TP33
3054	CYCLOHEXYL MERCAPTAN	3		III		5 L	E1	P001 IBC03 LP01		T2	TP1
3055	2-(2-AMINOETHOXY)ETHANOL	8		III		5 L	E1	P001 IBC03 LP01		T4	TP1
3056	n-HEPTALDEHYDE	3		III		5 L	E1	P001 IBC03 LP01		T2	TP1
3057	TRIFLUOROACETYL CHLORIDE	2.3	8			0	E0	P200		T50	TP21
3064	NITROGLYCERIN, SOLUTION IN ALCOHOL with more than 1 % but not more than 5 % nitroglycerin	3		II	28 359	0	E0	P300			
3065	ALCOHOLIC BEVERAGES, with more than 70 % alcohol by volume	3		II	146	5 L	E2	P001 IBC02	PP2	T4	TP1
3065	ALCOHOLIC BEVERAGES, with more than 24 % but not more than 70 % alcohol by volume	3		III	144 145 247	5 L	E1	P001 IBC03	PP2	T2	TP1
3066	PAINT (including paint, lacquer, enamel, stain, shellac, varnish, polish, liquid filler and liquid lacquer base) or PAINT RELATED MATERIAL (including paint thinning or reducing compound)	8		II	163 367	1 L	E2	P001 IBC02		T7	TP2 TP28

UN No.	Name and description	Class or division	Subsidiary hazard	UN packing group	Special provisions	Limited and excepted quantities		Packagings and IBCs		Portable tanks and bulk containers	
								Packing instruction	Special packing provisions	Instructions	Special provisions
(1)	(2)	(3)	(4)	(5)	(6)	(7a)	(7b)	(8)	(9)	(10)	(11)
-	3.1.2	2.0	2.0	2.0.1.3	3.3	3.4	3.5	4.1.4	4.1.4	4.2.5 / 4.3.2	4.2.5
3066	PAINT (including paint, lacquer, enamel, stain, shellac, varnish, polish, liquid filler and liquid lacquer base) or PAINT RELATED MATERIAL (including paint thinning or reducing compound)	8		III	163 223 367	5 L	E1	P001 IBC03		T4	TP1 TP29
3070	ETHYLENE OXIDE AND DICHLORODIFLUORO-METHANE MIXTURE with not more than 12.5 % ethylene oxide	2.2			392	120 ml	E1	P200		T50	
3071	MERCAPTANS, LIQUID, TOXIC, FLAMMABLE, N.O.S. or MERCAPTAN MIXTURE, LIQUID, TOXIC, FLAMMABLE, N.O.S.	6.1	3	II	274	100 ml	E4	P001 IBC02		T11	TP2 TP13 TP27
3072	LIFE-SAVING APPLIANCES NOT SELF-INFLATING containing dangerous goods as equipment	9			296	0	E0	P905			
3073	VINYLPYRIDINES, STABILIZED	6.1	3 8	II	386	100 ml	E4	P001 IBC01		T7	TP2 TP13
3077	ENVIRONMENTALLY HAZARDOUS SUBSTANCE, SOLID, N.O.S.	9		III	274 331 335 375	5 kg	E1	P002 IBC08 LP02	PP12 B3	T1 BK2 BK3	TP33
3078	CERIUM, turnings or gritty powder	4.3		II		500 g	E2	P410 IBC07	B2	T3	TP33
3079	METHACRYLONITRILE, STABILIZED	6.1	3	I	354 386	0	E0	P602		T20	TP2 TP13
3080	ISOCYANATES, TOXIC, FLAMMABLE, N.O.S. or ISOCYANATE SOLUTION, TOXIC, FLAMMABLE, N.O.S.	6.1	3	II	274	100 ml	E4	P001 IBC02		T11	TP2 TP13 TP27
3082	ENVIRONMENTALLY HAZARDOUS SUBSTANCE, LIQUID, N.O.S.	9		III	274 331 335 375	5 L	E1	P001 IBC03 LP01	PP1	T4	TP1 TP29
3083	PERCHLORYL FLUORIDE	2.3	5.1			0	E0	P200			
3084	CORROSIVE SOLID, OXIDIZING, N.O.S.	8	5.1	I	274	0	E0	P002		T6	TP33
3084	CORROSIVE SOLID, OXIDIZING, N.O.S.	8	5.1	II	274	1 kg	E2	P002 IBC06	B2	T3	TP33
3085	OXIDIZING SOLID, CORROSIVE, N.O.S.	5.1	8	I	274	0	E0	P503			
3085	OXIDIZING SOLID, CORROSIVE, N.O.S.	5.1	8	II	274	1 kg	E2	P002 IBC06	B2	T3	TP33
3085	OXIDIZING SOLID, CORROSIVE, N.O.S.	5.1	8	III	223 274	5 kg	E1	P002 IBC08	B3	T1	TP33
3086	TOXIC SOLID, OXIDIZING, N.O.S.	6.1	5.1	I	274	0	E5	P002		T6	TP33
3086	TOXIC SOLID, OXIDIZING, N.O.S.	6.1	5.1	II	274	500 g	E4	P002 IBC06	B2	T3	TP33
3087	OXIDIZING SOLID, TOXIC, N.O.S.	5.1	6.1	I	274	0	E0	P503			
3087	OXIDIZING SOLID, TOXIC, N.O.S.	5.1	6.1	II	274	1 kg	E2	P002 IBC06	B2	T3	TP33
3087	OXIDIZING SOLID, TOXIC, N.O.S.	5.1	6.1	III	223 274	5 kg	E1	P002 IBC08	B3	T1	TP33
3088	SELF-HEATING SOLID, ORGANIC, N.O.S.	4.2		II	274	0	E2	P410 IBC06	B2	T3	TP33

UN No.	Name and description	Class or division	Subsidiary hazard	UN packing group	Special provisions	Limited and excepted quantities		Packagings and IBCs		Portable tanks and bulk containers	
								Packing instruction	Special packing provisions	Instructions	Special provisions
						(7a)	(7b)				
(1)	(2)	(3)	(4)	(5)	(6)	(7a)	(7b)	(8)	(9)	(10)	(11)
-	3.1.2	2.0	2.0	2.0.1.3	3.3	3.4	3.5	4.1.4	4.1.4	4.2.5 / 4.3.2	4.2.5
3088	SELF-HEATING SOLID, ORGANIC, N.O.S.	4.2		III	223 274	0	E1	P002 IBC08 LP02	B3	T1	TP33
3089	METAL POWDER, FLAMMABLE, N.O.S.	4.1		II		1 kg	E2	P002 IBC08	B2, B4	T3	TP33
3089	METAL POWDER, FLAMMABLE, N.O.S.	4.1		III	223	5 kg	E1	P002 IBC08	B2, B4	T1	TP33
3090	LITHIUM METAL BATTERIES (including lithium alloy batteries)	9			188 230 310 376 377 384 387	0	E0	P903 P908 P909 P910 P911 LP903 LP904 LP905 LP906			
3091	LITHIUM METAL BATTERIES CONTAINED IN EQUIPMENT or LITHIUM METAL BATTERIES PACKED WITH EQUIPMENT (including lithium alloy batteries)	9			188 230 310 360 376 377 384 387 390	0	E0	P903 P908 P909 P910 P911 LP903 LP904 LP905 LP906			
3092	1-METHOXY-2-PROPANOL	3		III		5 L	E1	P001 IBC03 LP01		T2	TP1
3093	CORROSIVE LIQUID, OXIDIZING, N.O.S.	8	5.1	I	274	0	E0	P001			
3093	CORROSIVE LIQUID, OXIDIZING, N.O.S.	8	5.1	II	274	1 L	E2	P001 IBC02			
3094	CORROSIVE LIQUID, WATER-REACTIVE, N.O.S.	8	4.3	I	274	0	E0	P001			
3094	CORROSIVE LIQUID, WATER-REACTIVE, N.O.S.	8	4.3	II	274	1 L	E2	P001			
3095	CORROSIVE SOLID, SELF-HEATING, N.O.S.	8	4.2	I	274	0	E0	P002		T6	TP33
3095	CORROSIVE SOLID, SELF-HEATING, N.O.S.	8	4.2	II	274	1 kg	E2	P002 IBC06	B2	T3	TP33
3096	CORROSIVE SOLID, WATER-REACTIVE, N.O.S.	8	4.3	I	274	0	E0	P002		T6	TP33
3096	CORROSIVE SOLID, WATER-REACTIVE, N.O.S.	8	4.3	II	274	1 kg	E2	P002 IBC06	B2	T3	TP33
3097	FLAMMABLE SOLID, OXIDIZING, N.O.S.	4.1	5.1	II	274	1 kg	E0	P099			
3097	FLAMMABLE SOLID, OXIDIZING, N.O.S.	4.1	5.1	III	223 274	5 kg	E0	P099		T1	TP33
3098	OXIDIZING LIQUID, CORROSIVE, N.O.S.	5.1	8	I	274	0	E0	P502			
3098	OXIDIZING LIQUID, CORROSIVE, N.O.S.	5.1	8	II	274	1 L	E2	P504 IBC01			
3098	OXIDIZING LIQUID, CORROSIVE, N.O.S.	5.1	8	III	223 274	5 L	E1	P504 IBC02			
3099	OXIDIZING LIQUID, TOXIC, N.O.S.	5.1	6.1	I	274	0	E0	P502			
3099	OXIDIZING LIQUID, TOXIC, N.O.S.	5.1	6.1	II	274	1 L	E2	P504 IBC01			
3099	OXIDIZING LIQUID, TOXIC, N.O.S.	5.1	6.1	III	223 274	5 L	E1	P504 IBC02			

UN No.	Name and description	Class or division	Subsidiary hazard	UN packing group	Special provisions	Limited and excepted quantities		Packagings and IBCs		Portable tanks and bulk containers	
								Packing instruction	Special packing provisions	Instructions	Special provisions
(1)	(2)	(3)	(4)	(5)	(6)	(7a)	(7b)	(8)	(9)	(10)	(11)
-	3.1.2	2.0	2.0	2.0.1.3	3.3	3.4	3.5	4.1.4	4.1.4	4.2.5 / 4.3.2	4.2.5
3100	OXIDIZING SOLID, SELF-HEATING, N.O.S.	5.1	4.2	I	274	0	E0	P099			
3100	OXIDIZING SOLID, SELF-HEATING, N.O.S.	5.1	4.2	II	274	0	E0	P099			
3101	ORGANIC PEROXIDE TYPE B, LIQUID	5.2			122 181 195 274	25 ml	E0	P520			
3102	ORGANIC PEROXIDE TYPE B, SOLID	5.2			122 181 195 274	100 g	E0	P520			
3103	ORGANIC PEROXIDE TYPE C, LIQUID	5.2			122 195 274	25 ml	E0	P520			
3104	ORGANIC PEROXIDE TYPE C, SOLID	5.2			122 195 274	100 g	E0	P520			
3105	ORGANIC PEROXIDE TYPE D, LIQUID	5.2			122 274	125 ml	E0	P520			
3106	ORGANIC PEROXIDE TYPE D, SOLID	5.2			122 274	500 g	E0	P520			
3107	ORGANIC PEROXIDE TYPE E, LIQUID	5.2			122 274	125 ml	E0	P520			
3108	ORGANIC PEROXIDE TYPE E, SOLID	5.2			122 274	500 g	E0	P520			
3109	ORGANIC PEROXIDE TYPE F, LIQUID	5.2			122 274	125 ml	E0	P520 IBC520		T23	
3110	ORGANIC PEROXIDE TYPE F, SOLID	5.2			122 274	500 g	E0	P520 IBC520		T23	TP33
3111	ORGANIC PEROXIDE TYPE B, LIQUID, TEMPERATURE CONTROLLED	5.2			122 181 195 274	0	E0	P520			
3112	ORGANIC PEROXIDE TYPE B, SOLID, TEMPERATURE CONTROLLED	5.2			122 181 195 274	0	E0	P520			
3113	ORGANIC PEROXIDE TYPE C, LIQUID, TEMPERATURE CONTROLLED	5.2			122 195 274	0	E0	P520			
3114	ORGANIC PEROXIDE TYPE C, SOLID, TEMPERATURE CONTROLLED	5.2			122 195 274	0	E0	P520			
3115	ORGANIC PEROXIDE TYPE D, LIQUID, TEMPERATURE CONTROLLED	5.2			122 274	0	E0	P520			
3116	ORGANIC PEROXIDE TYPE D, SOLID, TEMPERATURE CONTROLLED	5.2			122 274	0	E0	P520			
3117	ORGANIC PEROXIDE TYPE E, LIQUID, TEMPERATURE CONTROLLED	5.2			122 274	0	E0	P520			
3118	ORGANIC PEROXIDE TYPE E, SOLID, TEMPERATURE CONTROLLED	5.2			122 274	0	E0	P520			
3119	ORGANIC PEROXIDE TYPE F, LIQUID, TEMPERATURE CONTROLLED	5.2			122 274	0	E0	P520 IBC520		T23	

UN No.	Name and description	Class or division	Subsidiary hazard	UN packing group	Special provisions	Limited and excepted quantities		Packagings and IBCs		Portable tanks and bulk containers	
								Packing instruction	Special packing provisions	Instructions	Special provisions
(1)	(2)	(3)	(4)	(5)	(6)	(7a)	(7b)	(8)	(9)	(10)	(11)
-	3.1.2	2.0	2.0	2.0.1.3	3.3	3.4	3.5	4.1.4	4.1.4	4.2.5 / 4.3.2	4.2.5
3120	ORGANIC PEROXIDE TYPE F, SOLID, TEMPERATURE CONTROLLED	5.2			122 274	0	E0	P520 IBC520		T23	TP33
3121	OXIDIZING SOLID, WATER-REACTIVE, N.O.S.	5.1	4.3	I	274	0	E0	P099			
3121	OXIDIZING SOLID, WATER-REACTIVE, N.O.S.	5.1	4.3	II	274	1 kg	E0	P099			
3122	TOXIC LIQUID, OXIDIZING, N.O.S.	6.1	5.1	I	274 315	0	E0	P001			
3122	TOXIC LIQUID, OXIDIZING, N.O.S.	6.1	5.1	II	274	100 ml	E4	P001 IBC02			
3123	TOXIC LIQUID, WATER-REACTIVE, N.O.S.	6.1	4.3	I	274 315	0	E0	P099			
3123	TOXIC LIQUID, WATER-REACTIVE, N.O.S.	6.1	4.3	II	274	100 ml	E4	P001 IBC02			
3124	TOXIC SOLID, SELF-HEATING, N.O.S.	6.1	4.2	I	274	0	E5	P002		T6	TP33
3124	TOXIC SOLID, SELF-HEATING, N.O.S.	6.1	4.2	II	274	0	E4	P002 IBC06	B2	T3	TP33
3125	TOXIC SOLID, WATER-REACTIVE, N.O.S.	6.1	4.3	I	274	0	E5	P099		T6	TP33
3125	TOXIC SOLID, WATER-REACTIVE, N.O.S.	6.1	4.3	II	274	500 g	E4	P002 IBC06	B2	T3	TP33
3126	SELF-HEATING SOLID, CORROSIVE, ORGANIC, N.O.S.	4.2	8	II	274	0	E2	P410 IBC05	B2	T3	TP33
3126	SELF-HEATING SOLID, CORROSIVE, ORGANIC, N.O.S.	4.2	8	III	223 274	0	E1	P002 IBC08	B3	T1	TP33
3127	SELF-HEATING SOLID, OXIDIZING, N.O.S.	4.2	5.1	II	274	0	E0	P099		T3	TP33
3127	SELF-HEATING SOLID, OXIDIZING, N.O.S.	4.2	5.1	III	223 274	0	E0	P099		T1	TP33
3128	SELF-HEATING SOLID, TOXIC, ORGANIC, N.O.S.	4.2	6.1	II	274	0	E2	P410 IBC05	B2	T3	TP33
3128	SELF-HEATING SOLID, TOXIC, ORGANIC, N.O.S.	4.2	6.1	III	223 274	0	E1	P002 IBC08	B3	T1	TP33
3129	WATER-REACTIVE LIQUID, CORROSIVE, N.O.S.	4.3	8	I	274	0	E0	P402		T14	TP2 TP7 TP13
3129	WATER-REACTIVE LIQUID, CORROSIVE, N.O.S.	4.3	8	II	274	500 ml	E0	P402 IBC01		T11	TP2 TP7
3129	WATER-REACTIVE LIQUID, CORROSIVE, N.O.S.	4.3	8	III	223 274	1 L	E1	P001 IBC02		T7	TP2 TP7
3130	WATER-REACTIVE LIQUID, TOXIC, N.O.S.	4.3	6.1	I	274	0	E0	P402			
3130	WATER-REACTIVE LIQUID, TOXIC, N.O.S.	4.3	6.1	II	274	500 ml	E0	P402 IBC01			
3130	WATER-REACTIVE LIQUID, TOXIC, N.O.S.	4.3	6.1	III	223 274	1 L	E1	P001 IBC02			
3131	WATER-REACTIVE SOLID, CORROSIVE, N.O.S.	4.3	8	I	274	0	E0	P403		T9	TP7 TP33
3131	WATER-REACTIVE SOLID, CORROSIVE, N.O.S.	4.3	8	II	274	500 g	E2	P410 IBC06	B2	T3	TP33
3131	WATER-REACTIVE SOLID, CORROSIVE, N.O.S.	4.3	8	III	223 274	1 kg	E1	P410 IBC08	B4	T1	TP33
3132	WATER-REACTIVE SOLID, FLAMMABLE, N.O.S.	4.3	4.1	I	274	0	E0	P403 IBC99			
3132	WATER-REACTIVE SOLID, FLAMMABLE, N.O.S.	4.3	4.1	II	274	500 g	E2	P410 IBC04		T3	TP33

UN No.	Name and description	Class or division	Subsidiary hazard	UN packing group	Special provisions	Limited and excepted quantities		Packagings and IBCs		Portable tanks and bulk containers	
								Packing instruction	Special packing provisions	Instructions	Special provisions
(1)	(2)	(3)	(4)	(5)	(6)	(7a)	(7b)	(8)	(9)	(10)	(11)
-	3.1.2	2.0	2.0	2.0.1.3	3.3	3.4	3.5	4.1.4	4.1.4	4.2.5 / 4.3.2	4.2.5
3132	WATER-REACTIVE SOLID, FLAMMABLE, N.O.S.	4.3	4.1	III	223 274	1 kg	E1	P410 IBC06		T1	TP33
3133	WATER-REACTIVE SOLID, OXIDIZING, N.O.S.	4.3	5.1	II	274	500 g	E0	P099			
3133	WATER-REACTIVE SOLID, OXIDIZING, N.O.S.	4.3	5.1	III	223 274	1 kg	E0	P099			
3134	WATER-REACTIVE SOLID, TOXIC, N.O.S.	4.3	6.1	I	274	0	E0	P403			
3134	WATER-REACTIVE SOLID, TOXIC, N.O.S.	4.3	6.1	II	274	500 g	E2	P410 IBC05	B2	T3	TP33
3134	WATER-REACTIVE SOLID, TOXIC, N.O.S.	4.3	6.1	III	223 274	1 kg	E1	P410 IBC08	B4	T1	TP33
3135	WATER-REACTIVE SOLID, SELF-HEATING, N.O.S.	4.3	4.2	I	274	0	E0	P403			
3135	WATER-REACTIVE SOLID, SELF-HEATING, N.O.S.	4.3	4.2	II	274	0	E2	P410 IBC05	B2	T3	TP33
3135	WATER-REACTIVE SOLID, SELF-HEATING, N.O.S.	4.3	4.2	III	223 274	0	E1	P410 IBC08	B4	T1	TP33
3136	TRIFLUOROMETHANE, REFRIGERATED LIQUID	2.2				120 ml	E1	P203		T75	TP5
3137	OXIDIZING SOLID, FLAMMABLE, N.O.S.	5.1	4.1	I	274	0	E0	P099			
3138	ETHYLENE, ACETYLENE AND PROPYLENE MIXTURE, REFRIGERATED LIQUID containing at least 71.5 % ethylene with not more than 22.5 % acetylene and not more than 6 % propylene	2.1				0	E0	P203		T75	TP5
3139	OXIDIZING LIQUID, N.O.S.	5.1		I	274	0	E0	P502			
3139	OXIDIZING LIQUID, N.O.S.	5.1		II	274	1 L	E2	P504 IBC02			
3139	OXIDIZING LIQUID, N.O.S.	5.1		III	223 274	5 L	E1	P504 IBC02			
3140	ALKALOIDS, LIQUID, N.O.S. or ALKALOID SALTS, LIQUID, N.O.S.	6.1		I	43 274	0	E5	P001			
3140	ALKALOIDS, LIQUID, N.O.S. or ALKALOID SALTS, LIQUID, N.O.S.	6.1		II	43 274	100 ml	E4	P001 IBC02			
3140	ALKALOIDS, LIQUID, N.O.S. or ALKALOID SALTS, LIQUID, N.O.S.	6.1		III	43 223 274	5 L	E1	P001 IBC03 LP01			
3141	ANTIMONY COMPOUND, INORGANIC, LIQUID, N.O.S.	6.1		III	45 274	5 L	E1	P001 IBC03 LP01			
3142	DISINFECTANT, LIQUID, TOXIC, N.O.S.	6.1		I	274	0	E5	P001			
3142	DISINFECTANT, LIQUID, TOXIC, N.O.S.	6.1		II	274	100 ml	E4	P001 IBC02			
3142	DISINFECTANT, LIQUID, TOXIC, N.O.S.	6.1		III	223 274	5 L	E1	P001 IBC03 LP01			
3143	DYE, SOLID, TOXIC, N.O.S. or DYE INTERMEDIATE, SOLID, TOXIC, N.O.S.	6.1		I	274	0	E5	P002 IBC07	B1	T6	TP33
3143	DYE, SOLID, TOXIC, N.O.S. or DYE INTERMEDIATE, SOLID, TOXIC, N.O.S.	6.1		II	274	500 g	E4	P002 IBC08	B2, B4	T3	TP33

UN No.	Name and description	Class or division	Subsidiary hazard	UN packing group	Special provisions	Limited and excepted quantities		Packagings and IBCs		Portable tanks and bulk containers	
								Packing instruction	Special packing provisions	Instructions	Special provisions
(1)	(2)	(3)	(4)	(5)	(6)	(7a)	(7b)	(8)	(9)	(10)	(11)
-	3.1.2	2.0	2.0	2.0.1.3	3.3	3.4	3.5	4.1.4	4.1.4	4.2.5 / 4.3.2	4.2.5
3143	DYE, SOLID, TOXIC, N.O.S. or DYE INTERMEDIATE, SOLID, TOXIC, N.O.S.	6.1		III	223 274	5 kg	E1	P002 IBC08 LP02	B3	T1	TP33
3144	NICOTINE COMPOUND, LIQUID, N.O.S. or NICOTINE PREPARATION, LIQUID, N.O.S.	6.1		I	43 274	0	E5	P001			
3144	NICOTINE COMPOUND, LIQUID, N.O.S. or NICOTINE PREPARATION, LIQUID, N.O.S.	6.1		II	43 274	100 ml	E4	P001 IBC02			
3144	NICOTINE COMPOUND, LIQUID, N.O.S. or NICOTINE PREPARATION, LIQUID, N.O.S.	6.1		III	43 223 274	5 L	E1	P001 IBC03 LP01			
3145	ALKYLPHENOLS, LIQUID, N.O.S. (including C2-C12 homologues)	8		I		0	E0	P001		T14	TP2
3145	ALKYLPHENOLS, LIQUID, N.O.S. (including C2-C12 homologues)	8		II		1 L	E2	P001 IBC02		T11	TP2 TP27
3145	ALKYLPHENOLS, LIQUID, N.O.S. (including C2-C12 homologues)	8		III	223	5 L	E1	P001 IBC03 LP01		T7	TP1 TP28
3146	ORGANOTIN COMPOUND, SOLID, N.O.S.	6.1		I	43 274	0	E5	P002 IBC07	B1	T6	TP33
3146	ORGANOTIN COMPOUND, SOLID, N.O.S.	6.1		II	43 274	500 g	E4	P002 IBC08	B2, B4	T3	TP33
3146	ORGANOTIN COMPOUND, SOLID, N.O.S.	6.1		III	43 223 274	5 kg	E1	P002 IBC08 LP02	B3	T1	TP33
3147	DYE, SOLID, CORROSIVE, N.O.S. or DYE INTERMEDIATE, SOLID, CORROSIVE, N.O.S.	8		I	274	0	E0	P002 IBC07	B1	T6	TP33
3147	DYE, SOLID, CORROSIVE, N.O.S. or DYE INTERMEDIATE, SOLID, CORROSIVE, N.O.S.	8		II	274	1 kg	E2	P002 IBC08	B2, B4	T3	TP33
3147	DYE, SOLID, CORROSIVE, N.O.S. or DYE INTERMEDIATE, SOLID, CORROSIVE, N.O.S.	8		III	223 274	5 kg	E1	P002 IBC08 LP02	B3	T1	TP33
3148	WATER-REACTIVE LIQUID, N.O.S.	4.3		I	274	0	E0	P402		T13	TP2 TP7
3148	WATER-REACTIVE LIQUID, N.O.S.	4.3		II	274	500 ml	E2	P402 IBC01		T7	TP2 TP7
3148	WATER-REACTIVE LIQUID, N.O.S.	4.3		III	223 274	1 L	E1	P001 IBC02		T7	TP2 TP7
3149	HYDROGEN PEROXIDE AND PEROXYACETIC ACID MIXTURE with acid(s), water and not more than 5 % peroxyacetic acid, STABILIZED	5.1	8	II	196	1 L	E2	P504 IBC02	PP10 B5	T7	TP2 TP6 TP24
3150	DEVICES, SMALL, HYDROCARBON GAS POWERED or HYDROCARBON GAS REFILLS FOR SMALL DEVICES with release device	2.1				0	E0	P003			
3151	POLYHALOGENATED BIPHENYLS, LIQUID or HALOGENATED MONOMETHYLDIPHENYL-METHANES, LIQUID or POLYHALOGENATED TERPHENYLS, LIQUID	9		II	203 305	1 L	E2	P906 IBC02			

UN No.	Name and description	Class or division	Subsidiary hazard	UN packing group	Special provisions	Limited and excepted quantities		Packagings and IBCs		Portable tanks and bulk containers	
								Packing instruction	Special packing provisions	Instructions	Special provisions
(1)	(2)	(3)	(4)	(5)	(6)	(7a)	(7b)	(8)	(9)	(10)	(11)
-	3.1.2	2.0	2.0	2.0.1.3	3.3	3.4	3.5	4.1.4	4.1.4	4.2.5 / 4.3.2	4.2.5
3152	POLYHALOGENATED BIPHENYLS, SOLID or HALOGENATED MONOMETHYLDIPHENYL-METHANES, SOLID or POLYHALOGENATED TERPHENYLS, SOLID	9		II	203 305	1 kg	E2	P906 IBC08	B2, B4	T3	TP33
3153	PERFLUORO (METHYL VINYL ETHER)	2.1				0	E0	P200		T50	
3154	PERFLUORO (ETHYL VINYL ETHER)	2.1				0	E0	P200			
3155	PENTACHLOROPHENOL	6.1		II	43	500 g	E4	P002 IBC08	B2, B4	T3	TP33
3156	COMPRESSED GAS, OXIDIZING, N.O.S.	2.2	5.1		274	0	E0	P200			
3157	LIQUEFIED GAS, OXIDIZING, N.O.S.	2.2	5.1		274	0	E0	P200			
3158	GAS, REFRIGERATED LIQUID, N.O.S.	2.2			274	120 ml	E1	P203		T75	TP5
3159	1,1,1,2-TETRAFLUOROETHANE (REFRIGERANT GAS R 134a)	2.2				120 ml	E1	P200		T50	
3160	LIQUEFIED GAS, TOXIC, FLAMMABLE, N.O.S.	2.3	2.1		274	0	E0	P200			
3161	LIQUEFIED GAS, FLAMMABLE, N.O.S.	2.1			274	0	E0	P200		T50	
3162	LIQUEFIED GAS, TOXIC, N.O.S.	2.3			274	0	E0	P200			
3163	LIQUEFIED GAS, N.O.S.	2.2			274 392	120 ml	E1	P200		T50	
3164	ARTICLES, PRESSURIZED, PNEUMATIC or HYDRAULIC (containing non-flammable gas)	2.2			283 371	120 ml	E0	P003	PP32		
3165	AIRCRAFT HYDRAULIC POWER UNIT FUEL TANK (containing a mixture of anhydrous hydrazine and methylhydrazine) (M86 fuel)	3	6.1 8			0	E0	P301			
3166	VEHICLE, FLAMMABLE GAS POWERED or VEHICLE, FLAMMABLE LIQUID POWERED or VEHICLE, FUEL CELL, FLAMMABLE GAS POWERED or VEHICLE, FUEL CELL, FLAMMABLE LIQUID POWERED	9			123 356 388	0	E0	NONE			
3167	GAS SAMPLE, NON-PRESSURIZED, FLAMMABLE, N.O.S., not refrigerated liquid	2.1			209	0	E0	P201			
3168	GAS SAMPLE, NON-PRESSURIZED, TOXIC, FLAMMABLE, N.O.S., not refrigerated liquid	2.3	2.1		209	0	E0	P201			
3169	GAS SAMPLE, NON-PRESSURIZED, TOXIC, N.O.S., not refrigerated liquid	2.3			209	0	E0	P201			
3170	ALUMINIUM SMELTING BY-PRODUCTS or ALUMINIUM REMELTING BY-PRODUCTS	4.3		II	244	500 g	E2	P410 IBC07	B2	T3 BK2	TP33
3170	ALUMINIUM SMELTING BY-PRODUCTS or ALUMINIUM REMELTING BY-PRODUCTS	4.3		III	223 244	1 kg	E1	P002 IBC08	B4	T1 BK2	TP33

UN No.	Name and description	Class or division	Subsidiary hazard	UN packing group	Special provisions	Limited and excepted quantities		Packagings and IBCs		Portable tanks and bulk containers	
								Packing instruction	Special packing provisions	Instructions	Special provisions
(1)	(2)	(3)	(4)	(5)	(6)	(7a)	(7b)	(8)	(9)	(10)	(11)
-	3.1.2	2.0	2.0	2.0.1.3	3.3	3.4	3.5	4.1.4	4.1.4	4.2.5 / 4.3.2	4.2.5
3171	BATTERY-POWERED VEHICLE or BATTERY-POWERED EQUIPMENT	9			123 388	0	E0	NONE			
3172	TOXINS, EXTRACTED FROM LIVING SOURCES, LIQUID, N.O.S.	6.1		I	210 274	0	E5	P001			
3172	TOXINS, EXTRACTED FROM LIVING SOURCES, LIQUID, N.O.S.	6.1		II	210 274	100 ml	E4	P001 IBC02			
3172	TOXINS, EXTRACTED FROM LIVING SOURCES, LIQUID, N.O.S.	6.1		III	210 223 274	5 L	E1	P001 IBC03 LP01			
3174	TITANIUM DISULPHIDE	4.2		III		0	E1	P002 IBC08 LP02	B3	T1	TP33
3175	SOLIDS CONTAINING FLAMMABLE LIQUID, N.O.S.	4.1		II	216 274	1 kg	E2	P002 IBC06	PP9 B2	T3 BK1 BK2	TP33
3176	FLAMMABLE SOLID, ORGANIC, MOLTEN, N.O.S.	4.1		II	274	0	E0			T3	TP3 TP26
3176	FLAMMABLE SOLID, ORGANIC, MOLTEN, N.O.S.	4.1		III	223 274	0	E0	IBC01		T1	TP3 TP26
3178	FLAMMABLE SOLID, INORGANIC, N.O.S.	4.1		II	274	1 kg	E2	P002 IBC08	B2, B4	T3	TP33
3178	FLAMMABLE SOLID, INORGANIC, N.O.S.	4.1		III	223 274	5 kg	E1	P002 IBC08 LP02	B3	T1	TP33
3179	FLAMMABLE SOLID, TOXIC, INORGANIC, N.O.S.	4.1	6.1	II	274	1 kg	E2	P002 IBC06	B2	T3	TP33
3179	FLAMMABLE SOLID, TOXIC, INORGANIC, N.O.S.	4.1	6.1	III	223 274	5 kg	E1	P002 IBC06		T1	TP33
3180	FLAMMABLE SOLID, CORROSIVE, INORGANIC, N.O.S.	4.1	8	II	274	1 kg	E2	P002 IBC06	B2	T3	TP33
3180	FLAMMABLE SOLID, CORROSIVE, INORGANIC, N.O.S.	4.1	8	III	223 274	5 kg	E1	P002 IBC06		T1	TP33
3181	METAL SALTS OF ORGANIC COMPOUNDS, FLAMMABLE, N.O.S.	4.1		II	274	1 kg	E2	P002 IBC08	B2, B4	T3	TP33
3181	METAL SALTS OF ORGANIC COMPOUNDS, FLAMMABLE, N.O.S.	4.1		III	223 274	5 kg	E1	P002 IBC08 LP02	B3	T1	TP33
3182	METAL HYDRIDES, FLAMMABLE, N.O.S.	4.1		II	274	1 kg	E2	P410 IBC04	PP40	T3	TP33
3182	METAL HYDRIDES, FLAMMABLE, N.O.S.	4.1		III	223 274	5 kg	E1	P002 IBC04		T1	TP33
3183	SELF-HEATING LIQUID, ORGANIC, N.O.S.	4.2		II	274	0	E2	P001 IBC02			
3183	SELF-HEATING LIQUID, ORGANIC, N.O.S.	4.2		III	223 274	0	E1	P001 IBC02			
3184	SELF-HEATING LIQUID, TOXIC, ORGANIC, N.O.S.	4.2	6.1	II	274	0	E2	P402 IBC02			
3184	SELF-HEATING LIQUID, TOXIC, ORGANIC, N.O.S.	4.2	6.1	III	223 274	0	E1	P001 IBC02			
3185	SELF-HEATING LIQUID, CORROSIVE, ORGANIC, N.O.S.	4.2	8	II	274	0	E2	P402 IBC02			
3185	SELF-HEATING LIQUID, CORROSIVE, ORGANIC, N.O.S.	4.2	8	III	223 274	0	E1	P001 IBC02			

UN No.	Name and description	Class or division	Subsidiary hazard	UN packing group	Special provisions	Limited and excepted quantities		Packagings and IBCs		Portable tanks and bulk containers	
								Packing instruction	Special packing provisions	Instructions	Special provisions
(1)	(2)	(3)	(4)	(5)	(6)	(7a)	(7b)	(8)	(9)	(10)	(11)
-	3.1.2	2.0	2.0	2.0.1.3	3.3	3.4	3.5	4.1.4	4.1.4	4.2.5 / 4.3.2	4.2.5
3186	SELF-HEATING LIQUID, INORGANIC, N.O.S.	4.2		II	274	0	E2	P001 IBC02			
3186	SELF-HEATING LIQUID, INORGANIC, N.O.S.	4.2		III	223 274	0	E1	P001 IBC02			
3187	SELF-HEATING LIQUID, TOXIC, INORGANIC, N.O.S.	4.2	6.1	II	274	0	E2	P402 IBC02			
3187	SELF-HEATING LIQUID, TOXIC, INORGANIC, N.O.S.	4.2	6.1	III	223 274	0	E1	P001 IBC02			
3188	SELF-HEATING LIQUID, CORROSIVE, INORGANIC, N.O.S.	4.2	8	II	274	0	E2	P402 IBC02			
3188	SELF-HEATING LIQUID, CORROSIVE, INORGANIC, N.O.S.	4.2	8	III	223 274	0	E1	P001 IBC02			
3189	METAL POWDER, SELF-HEATING, N.O.S.	4.2		II	274	0	E2	P410 IBC06	B2	T3	TP33
3189	METAL POWDER, SELF-HEATING, N.O.S.	4.2		III	223 274	0	E1	P002 IBC08 LP02	B3	T1	TP33
3190	SELF-HEATING SOLID, INORGANIC, N.O.S.	4.2		II	274	0	E2	P410 IBC06	B2	T3	TP33
3190	SELF-HEATING SOLID, INORGANIC, N.O.S.	4.2		III	223 274	0	E1	P002 IBC08 LP02	B3	T1	TP33
3191	SELF-HEATING SOLID, TOXIC, INORGANIC, N.O.S.	4.2	6.1	II	274	0	E2	P410 IBC05	B2	T3	TP33
3191	SELF-HEATING SOLID, TOXIC, INORGANIC, N.O.S.	4.2	6.1	III	223 274	0	E1	P002 IBC08	B3	T1	TP33
3192	SELF-HEATING SOLID, CORROSIVE, INORGANIC, N.O.S.	4.2	8	II	274	0	E2	P410 IBC05	B2	T3	TP33
3192	SELF-HEATING SOLID, CORROSIVE, INORGANIC, N.O.S.	4.2	8	III	223 274	0	E1	P002 IBC08	B3	T1	TP33
3194	PYROPHORIC LIQUID, INORGANIC, N.O.S.	4.2		I	274	0	E0	P400			
3200	PYROPHORIC SOLID, INORGANIC, N.O.S.	4.2		I	274	0	E0	P404		T21	TP7 TP33
3205	ALKALINE EARTH METAL ALCOHOLATES, N.O.S.	4.2		II	183 274	0	E2	P410 IBC06	B2	T3	TP33
3205	ALKALINE EARTH METAL ALCOHOLATES, N.O.S.	4.2		III	183 223 274	0	E1	P002 IBC08 LP02	B3	T1	TP33
3206	ALKALI METAL ALCOHOLATES, SELF-HEATING, CORROSIVE, N.O.S.	4.2	8	II	182 274	0	E2	P410 IBC05	B2	T3	TP33
3206	ALKALI METAL ALCOHOLATES, SELF-HEATING, CORROSIVE, N.O.S.	4.2	8	III	182 223 274	0	E1	P002 IBC08	B3	T1	TP33
3208	METALLIC SUBSTANCE, WATER-REACTIVE, N.O.S.	4.3		I	274	0	E0	P403 IBC99			
3208	METALLIC SUBSTANCE, WATER-REACTIVE, N.O.S.	4.3		II	274	500 g	E2	P410 IBC07	B2	T3	TP33
3208	METALLIC SUBSTANCE, WATER-REACTIVE, N.O.S.	4.3		III	223 274	1 kg	E1	P410 IBC08	B4	T1	TP33
3209	METALLIC SUBSTANCE, WATER-REACTIVE, SELF-HEATING, N.O.S.	4.3	4.2	I	274	0	E0	P403			

UN No.	Name and description	Class or division	Subsidiary hazard	UN packing group	Special provisions	Limited and excepted quantities		Packagings and IBCs		Portable tanks and bulk containers	
								Packing instruction	Special packing provisions	Instructions	Special provisions
(1)	(2)	(3)	(4)	(5)	(6)	(7a)	(7b)	(8)	(9)	(10)	(11)
-	3.1.2	2.0	2.0	2.0.1.3	3.3	3.4	3.5	4.1.4	4.1.4	4.2.5 / 4.3.2	4.2.5
3209	METALLIC SUBSTANCE, WATER-REACTIVE, SELF-HEATING, N.O.S.	4.3	4.2	II	274	0	E0	P410 IBC05	B2	T3	TP33
3209	METALLIC SUBSTANCE, WATER-REACTIVE, SELF-HEATING, N.O.S.	4.3	4.2	III	223 274	0	E1	P410 IBC08	B4	T1	TP33
3210	CHLORATES, INORGANIC, AQUEOUS SOLUTION, N.O.S.	5.1		II	274 351	1 L	E2	P504 IBC02		T4	TP1
3210	CHLORATES, INORGANIC, AQUEOUS SOLUTION, N.O.S.	5.1		III	223 274 351	5 L	E1	P504 IBC02		T4	TP1
3211	PERCHLORATES, INORGANIC, AQUEOUS SOLUTION, N.O.S.	5.1		II		1 L	E2	P504 IBC02		T4	TP1
3211	PERCHLORATES, INORGANIC, AQUEOUS SOLUTION, N.O.S.	5.1		III	223	5 L	E1	P504 IBC02		T4	TP1
3212	HYPOCHLORITES, INORGANIC, N.O.S.	5.1		II	274 349	1 kg	E2	P002 IBC08	B2, B4	T3	TP33
3213	BROMATES, INORGANIC, AQUEOUS SOLUTION, N.O.S.	5.1		II	274 350	1 L	E2	P504 IBC02		T4	TP1
3213	BROMATES, INORGANIC, AQUEOUS SOLUTION, N.O.S.	5.1		III	223 274 350	5 L	E1	P504 IBC02		T4	TP1
3214	PERMANGANATES, INORGANIC, AQUEOUS SOLUTION, N.O.S.	5.1		II	206 274 353	1 L	E2	P504 IBC02		T4	TP1
3215	PERSULPHATES, INORGANIC, N.O.S.	5.1		III		5 kg	E1	P002 IBC08 LP02	B3	T1	TP33
3216	PERSULPHATES, INORGANIC, AQUEOUS SOLUTION, N.O.S.	5.1		III		5 L	E1	P504 IBC02		T4	TP1 TP29
3218	NITRATES, INORGANIC, AQUEOUS SOLUTION, N.O.S.	5.1		II	270	1 L	E2	P504 IBC02		T4	TP1
3218	NITRATES, INORGANIC, AQUEOUS SOLUTION, N.O.S.	5.1		III	223 270	5 L	E1	P504 IBC02		T4	TP1
3219	NITRITES, INORGANIC, AQUEOUS SOLUTION, N.O.S.	5.1		II	103 274	1 L	E2	P504 IBC01		T4	TP1
3219	NITRITES, INORGANIC, AQUEOUS SOLUTION, N.O.S.	5.1		III	103 223 274	5 L	E1	P504 IBC02		T4	TP1
3220	PENTAFLUOROETHANE (REFRIGERANT GAS R 125)	2.2				120 ml	E1	P200		T50	
3221	SELF-REACTIVE LIQUID TYPE B	4.1			181 274	25 ml	E0	P520	PP21		
3222	SELF-REACTIVE SOLID TYPE B	4.1			181 274	100 g	E0	P520	PP21		
3223	SELF-REACTIVE LIQUID TYPE C	4.1			274	25 ml	E0	P520	PP21 PP94 PP95		
3224	SELF-REACTIVE SOLID TYPE C	4.1			274	100 g	E0	P520	PP21 PP94 PP95		
3225	SELF-REACTIVE LIQUID TYPE D	4.1			274	125 ml	E0	P520			
3226	SELF-REACTIVE SOLID TYPE D	4.1			274	500 g	E0	P520			
3227	SELF-REACTIVE LIQUID TYPE E	4.1			274	125 ml	E0	P520			
3228	SELF-REACTIVE SOLID TYPE E	4.1			274	500 g	E0	P520			

UN No.	Name and description	Class or division	Subsidiary hazard	UN packing group	Special provisions	Limited and excepted quantities		Packagings and IBCs		Portable tanks and bulk containers	
						Packing instruction	Special packing provisions	Instructions	Special provisions
(1)	(2)	(3)	(4)	(5)	(6)	(7a)	(7b)	(8)	(9)	(10)	(11)
-	3.1.2	2.0	2.0	2.0.1.3	3.3	3.4	3.5	4.1.4	4.1.4	4.2.5 / 4.3.2	4.2.5
3229	SELF-REACTIVE LIQUID TYPE F	4.1			274	125 ml	E0	P520 IBC99		T23	
3230	SELF-REACTIVE SOLID TYPE F	4.1			274	500 g	E0	P520 IBC99		T23	
3231	SELF-REACTIVE LIQUID TYPE B, TEMPERATURE CONTROLLED	4.1			181 194 274	0	E0	P520	PP21		
3232	SELF-REACTIVE SOLID TYPE B, TEMPERATURE CONTROLLED	4.1			181 194 274	0	E0	P520	PP21		
3233	SELF-REACTIVE LIQUID TYPE C, TEMPERATURE CONTROLLED	4.1			194 274	0	E0	P520	PP21		
3234	SELF-REACTIVE SOLID TYPE C, TEMPERATURE CONTROLLED	4.1			194 274	0	E0	P520	PP21		
3235	SELF-REACTIVE LIQUID TYPE D, TEMPERATURE CONTROLLED	4.1			194 274	0	E0	P520			
3236	SELF-REACTIVE SOLID TYPE D, TEMPERATURE CONTROLLED	4.1			194 274	0	E0	P520			
3237	SELF-REACTIVE LIQUID TYPE E, TEMPERATURE CONTROLLED	4.1			194 274	0	E0	P520			
3238	SELF-REACTIVE SOLID TYPE E, TEMPERATURE CONTROLLED	4.1			194 274	0	E0	P520			
3239	SELF-REACTIVE LIQUID TYPE F, TEMPERATURE CONTROLLED	4.1			194 274	0	E0	P520		T23	
3240	SELF-REACTIVE SOLID TYPE F, TEMPERATURE CONTROLLED	4.1			194 274	0	E0	P520		T23	
3241	2-BROMO-2-NITROPROPANE-1,3-DIOL	4.1		III	246	5 kg	E1	P520 IBC08	PP22 B3		
3242	AZODICARBONAMIDE	4.1		II	215	1 kg	E0	P409		T3	TP33
3243	SOLIDS CONTAINING TOXIC LIQUID, N.O.S.	6.1		II	217 274	500 g	E4	P002 IBC02	PP9	T2 BK1 BK2	TP33
3244	SOLIDS CONTAINING CORROSIVE LIQUID, N.O.S.	8		II	218 274	1 kg	E2	P002 IBC05	PP9	T3 BK1 BK2	TP33
3245	GENETICALLY MODIFIED MICROORGANISMS or GENETICALLY MODIFIED ORGANISMS	9			219	0	E0	P904 IBC99			
3246	METHANESULPHONYL CHLORIDE	6.1	8	I	354	0	E0	P602		T20	TP2 TP13
3247	SODIUM PEROXOBORATE, ANHYDROUS	5.1		II		1 kg	E2	P002 IBC08	B2, B4	T3	TP33
3248	MEDICINE, LIQUID, FLAMMABLE, TOXIC, N.O.S.	3	6.1	II	220 221	1 L	E2	P001			
3248	MEDICINE, LIQUID, FLAMMABLE, TOXIC, N.O.S.	3	6.1	III	220 221 223	5 L	E1	P001			
3249	MEDICINE, SOLID, TOXIC, N.O.S.	6.1		II	221	500 g	E4	P002		T3	TP33
3249	MEDICINE, SOLID, TOXIC, N.O.S.	6.1		III	221 223	5 kg	E1	P002		T1	TP33
3250	CHLOROACETIC ACID, MOLTEN	6.1	8	II		0	E0	NONE		T7	TP3 TP28
3251	ISOSORBIDE-5-MONONITRATE	4.1		III	132 226	5 kg	E0	P409			

UN No.	Name and description	Class or division	Subsidiary hazard	UN packing group	Special provisions	Limited and excepted quantities		Packagings and IBCs		Portable tanks and bulk containers	
						(7a)	(7b)	Packing instruction	Special packing provisions	Instructions	Special provisions
(1)	(2)	(3)	(4)	(5)	(6)	(7a)	(7b)	(8)	(9)	(10)	(11)
-	3.1.2	2.0	2.0	2.0.1.3	3.3	3.4	3.5	4.1.4	4.1.4	4.2.5 / 4.3.2	4.2.5
3252	DIFLUOROMETHANE (REFRIGERANT GAS R 32)	2.1				0	E0	P200		T50	
3253	DISODIUM TRIOXOSILICATE	8		III		5 kg	E1	P002 IBC08 LP02	B3	T1	TP33
3254	TRIBUTYLPHOSPHANE	4.2		I		0	E0	P400		T21	TP2 TP7
3255	tert-BUTYL HYPOCHLORITE	4.2	8	I		0	E0	P099			
3256	ELEVATED TEMPERATURE LIQUID, FLAMMABLE, N.O.S. with flash point above 60 °C, at or above its flash point	3		III	274	0	E0	P099 IBC01		T3	TP3 TP29
3257	ELEVATED TEMPERATURE LIQUID, N.O.S., at or above 100 °C and below its flash point (including molten metals, molten salts, etc.)	9		III	232 274	0	E0	P099 IBC01		T3	TP3 TP29
3258	ELEVATED TEMPERATURE SOLID, N.O.S., at or above 240 °C	9		III	232 274	0	E0	P099			
3259	AMINES, SOLID, CORROSIVE, N.O.S. or POLYAMINES, SOLID, CORROSIVE, N.O.S.	8		I	274	0	E0	P002 IBC07	B1	T6	TP33
3259	AMINES, SOLID, CORROSIVE, N.O.S. or POLYAMINES, SOLID, CORROSIVE, N.O.S.	8		II	274	1 kg	E2	P002 IBC08	B2, B4	T3	TP33
3259	AMINES, SOLID, CORROSIVE, N.O.S. or POLYAMINES, SOLID, CORROSIVE, N.O.S.	8		III	223 274	5 kg	E1	P002 IBC08 LP02	B3	T1	TP33
3260	CORROSIVE SOLID, ACIDIC, INORGANIC, N.O.S.	8		I	274	0	E0	P002 IBC07	B1	T6	TP33
3260	CORROSIVE SOLID, ACIDIC, INORGANIC, N.O.S.	8		II	274	1 kg	E2	P002 IBC08	B2, B4	T3	TP33
3260	CORROSIVE SOLID, ACIDIC, INORGANIC, N.O.S.	8		III	223 274	5 kg	E1	P002 IBC08 LP02	B3	T1	TP33
3261	CORROSIVE SOLID, ACIDIC, ORGANIC, N.O.S.	8		I	274	0	E0	P002 IBC07	B1	T6	TP33
3261	CORROSIVE SOLID, ACIDIC, ORGANIC, N.O.S.	8		II	274	1 kg	E2	P002 IBC08	B2, B4	T3	TP33
3261	CORROSIVE SOLID, ACIDIC, ORGANIC, N.O.S.	8		III	223 274	5 kg	E1	P002 IBC08 LP02	B3	T1	TP33
3262	CORROSIVE SOLID, BASIC, INORGANIC, N.O.S.	8		I	274	0	E0	P002 IBC07	B1	T6	TP33
3262	CORROSIVE SOLID, BASIC, INORGANIC, N.O.S.	8		II	274	1 kg	E2	P002 IBC08	B2, B4	T3	TP33
3262	CORROSIVE SOLID, BASIC, INORGANIC, N.O.S.	8		III	223 274	5 kg	E1	P002 IBC08 LP02	B3	T1	TP33
3263	CORROSIVE SOLID, BASIC, ORGANIC, N.O.S.	8		I	274	0	E0	P002 IBC07	B1	T6	TP33
3263	CORROSIVE SOLID, BASIC, ORGANIC, N.O.S.	8		II	274	1 kg	E2	P002 IBC08	B2, B4	T3	TP33
3263	CORROSIVE SOLID, BASIC, ORGANIC, N.O.S.	8		III	223 274	5 kg	E1	P002 IBC08 LP02	B3	T1	TP33
3264	CORROSIVE LIQUID, ACIDIC, INORGANIC, N.O.S.	8		I	274	0	E0	P001		T14	TP2 TP27
3264	CORROSIVE LIQUID, ACIDIC, INORGANIC, N.O.S.	8		II	274	1 L	E2	P001 IBC02		T11	TP2 TP27

UN No.	Name and description	Class or division	Subsidiary hazard	UN packing group	Special provisions	Limited and excepted quantities		Packagings and IBCs		Portable tanks and bulk containers	
								Packing instruction	Special packing provisions	Instructions	Special provisions
(1)	(2)	(3)	(4)	(5)	(6)	(7a)	(7b)	(8)	(9)	(10)	(11)
-	3.1.2	2.0	2.0	2.0.1.3	3.3	3.4	3.5	4.1.4	4.1.4	4.2.5 / 4.3.2	4.2.5
3264	CORROSIVE LIQUID, ACIDIC, INORGANIC, N.O.S.	8		III	223 274	5 L	E1	P001 IBC03 LP01		T7	TP1 TP28
3265	CORROSIVE LIQUID, ACIDIC, ORGANIC, N.O.S.	8		I	274	0	E0	P001		T14	TP2 TP27
3265	CORROSIVE LIQUID, ACIDIC, ORGANIC, N.O.S.	8		II	274	1 L	E2	P001 IBC02		T11	TP2 TP27
3265	CORROSIVE LIQUID, ACIDIC, ORGANIC, N.O.S.	8		III	223 274	5 L	E1	P001 IBC03 LP01		T7	TP1 TP28
3266	CORROSIVE LIQUID, BASIC, INORGANIC, N.O.S.	8		I	274	0	E0	P001		T14	TP2 TP27
3266	CORROSIVE LIQUID, BASIC, INORGANIC, N.O.S.	8		II	274	1 L	E2	P001 IBC02		T11	TP2 TP27
3266	CORROSIVE LIQUID, BASIC, INORGANIC, N.O.S.	8		III	223 274	5 L	E1	P001 IBC03 LP01		T7	TP1 TP28
3267	CORROSIVE LIQUID, BASIC, ORGANIC, N.O.S.	8		I	274	0	E0	P001		T14	TP2 TP27
3267	CORROSIVE LIQUID, BASIC, ORGANIC, N.O.S.	8		II	274	1 L	E2	P001 IBC02		T11	TP2 TP27
3267	CORROSIVE LIQUID, BASIC, ORGANIC, N.O.S.	8		III	223 274	5 L	E1	P001 IBC03 LP01		T7	TP1 TP28
3268	SAFETY DEVICES, electrically initiated†	9			280 289	0	E0	P902 LP902			
3269	POLYESTER RESIN KIT, liquid base material	3		II	236 340	5 L	See SP 340 in chapter 3.3	P302			
3269	POLYESTER RESIN KIT, liquid base material	3		III	236 340	5 L	See SP 340 in chapter 3.3	P302			
3270	NITROCELLULOSE MEMBRANE FILTERS, with not more than 12.6 % nitrogen, by dry mass	4.1		II	237 286 403	1 kg	E2	P411			
3271	ETHERS, N.O.S.	3		II	274	1 L	E2	P001 IBC02		T7	TP1 TP8 TP28
3271	ETHERS, N.O.S.	3		III	223 274	5 L	E1	P001 IBC03 LP01		T4	TP1 TP29
3272	ESTERS, N.O.S.	3		II	274	1 L	E2	P001 IBC02		T7	TP1 TP8 TP28
3272	ESTERS, N.O.S.	3		III	223 274	5 L	E1	P001 IBC03 LP01		T4	TP1 TP29
3273	NITRILES, FLAMMABLE, TOXIC, N.O.S.	3	6.1	I	274	0	E0	P001		T14	TP2 TP13 TP27
3273	NITRILES, FLAMMABLE, TOXIC, N.O.S.	3	6.1	II	274	1 L	E2	P001 IBC02		T11	TP2 TP13 TP27
3274	ALCOHOLATES SOLUTION, N.O.S., in alcohol	3	8	II	274	1 L	E2	P001 IBC02			
3275	NITRILES, TOXIC, FLAMMABLE, N.O.S.	6.1	3	I	274 315	0	E5	P001		T14	TP2 TP13 TP27

UN No.	Name and description	Class or division	Subsidiary hazard	UN packing group	Special provisions	Limited and excepted quantities		Packagings and IBCs		Portable tanks and bulk containers	
								Packing instruction	Special packing provisions	Instructions	Special provisions
(1)	(2)	(3)	(4)	(5)	(6)	(7a)	(7b)	(8)	(9)	(10)	(11)
-	3.1.2	2.0	2.0	2.0.1.3	3.3	3.4	3.5	4.1.4	4.1.4	4.2.5 / 4.3.2	4.2.5
3275	NITRILES, TOXIC, FLAMMABLE, N.O.S.	6.1	3	II	274	100 ml	E4	P001 IBC02		T11	TP2 TP13 TP27
3276	NITRILES, LIQUID, TOXIC, N.O.S.	6.1		I	274 315	0	E5	P001		T14	TP2 TP13 TP27
3276	NITRILES, LIQUID, TOXIC, N.O.S.	6.1		II	274	100 ml	E4	P001 IBC02		T11	TP2 TP27
3276	NITRILES, LIQUID, TOXIC, N.O.S.	6.1		III	223 274	5 L	E1	P001 IBC03 LP01		T7	TP1 TP28
3277	CHLOROFORMATES, TOXIC, CORROSIVE, N.O.S.	6.1	8	II	274	100 ml	E4	P001 IBC02		T8	TP2 TP13 TP28
3278	ORGANOPHOSPHORUS COMPOUND, LIQUID, TOXIC, N.O.S.	6.1		I	43 274 315	0	E5	P001		T14	TP2 TP13 TP27
3278	ORGANOPHOSPHORUS COMPOUND, LIQUID, TOXIC, N.O.S.	6.1		II	43 274	100 ml	E4	P001 IBC02		T11	TP2 TP27
3278	ORGANOPHOSPHORUS COMPOUND, LIQUID, TOXIC, N.O.S.	6.1		III	43 223 274	5 L	E1	P001 IBC03 LP01		T7	TP1 TP28
3279	ORGANOPHOSPHORUS COMPOUND, TOXIC, FLAMMABLE, N.O.S.	6.1	3	I	43 274 315	0	E5	P001		T14	TP2 TP13 TP27
3279	ORGANOPHOSPHORUS COMPOUND, TOXIC, FLAMMABLE, N.O.S.	6.1	3	II	43 274	100 ml	E4	P001		T11	TP2 TP13 TP27
3280	ORGANOARSENIC COMPOUND, LIQUID, N.O.S.	6.1		I	274 315	0	E5	P001		T14	TP2 TP13 TP27
3280	ORGANOARSENIC COMPOUND, LIQUID, N.O.S.	6.1		II	274	100 ml	E4	P001 IBC02		T11	TP2 TP27
3280	ORGANOARSENIC COMPOUND, LIQUID, N.O.S.	6.1		III	223 274	5 L	E1	P001 IBC03 LP01		T7	TP1 TP28
3281	METAL CARBONYLS, LIQUID, N.O.S.	6.1		I	274 315	0	E5	P601		T14	TP2 TP13 TP27
3281	METAL CARBONYLS, LIQUID, N.O.S.	6.1		II	274	100 ml	E4	P001 IBC02		T11	TP2 TP27
3281	METAL CARBONYLS, LIQUID, N.O.S.	6.1		III	223 274	5 L	E1	P001 IBC03 LP01		T7	TP1 TP28
3282	ORGANOMETALLIC COMPOUND, LIQUID, TOXIC, N.O.S.	6.1		I	274	0	E5	P001		T14	TP2 TP13 TP27
3282	ORGANOMETALLIC COMPOUND, LIQUID, TOXIC, N.O.S.	6.1		II	274	100 ml	E4	P001 IBC02		T11	TP2 TP27
3282	ORGANOMETALLIC COMPOUND, LIQUID, TOXIC, N.O.S.	6.1		III	223 274	5 L	E1	P001 IBC03 LP01		T7	TP1 TP28
3283	SELENIUM COMPOUND, SOLID, N.O.S.	6.1		I	274	0	E5	P002 IBC07	B1	T6	TP33
3283	SELENIUM COMPOUND, SOLID, N.O.S.	6.1		II	274	500 g	E4	P002 IBC08	B2, B4	T3	TP33
3283	SELENIUM COMPOUND, SOLID, N.O.S.	6.1		III	223 274	5 kg	E1	P002 IBC08 LP02	B3	T1	TP33

UN No.	Name and description	Class or division	Subsi-diary hazard	UN packing group	Special provi-sions	Limited and excepted quantities		Packagings and IBCs		Portable tanks and bulk containers	
								Packing instruction	Special packing provisions	Instruc-tions	Special provisions
(1)	(2)	(3)	(4)	(5)	(6)	(7a)	(7b)	(8)	(9)	(10)	(11)
-	3.1.2	2.0	2.0	2.0.1.3	3.3	3.4	3.5	4.1.4	4.1.4	4.2.5 / 4.3.2	4.2.5
3284	TELLURIUM COMPOUND, N.O.S.	6.1		I	274	0	E5	P002 IBC07	B1	T6	TP33
3284	TELLURIUM COMPOUND, N.O.S.	6.1		II	274	500 g	E4	P002 IBC08	B2, B4	T3	TP33
3284	TELLURIUM COMPOUND, N.O.S.	6.1		III	223 274	5 kg	E1	P002 IBC08 LP02	B3	T1	TP33
3285	VANADIUM COMPOUND, N.O.S.	6.1		I	274	0	E5	P002 IBC07	B1	T6	TP33
3285	VANADIUM COMPOUND, N.O.S.	6.1		II	274	500 g	E4	P002 IBC08	B2, B4	T3	TP33
3285	VANADIUM COMPOUND, N.O.S.	6.1		III	223 274	5 kg	E1	P002 IBC08 LP02	B3	T1	TP33
3286	FLAMMABLE LIQUID, TOXIC, CORROSIVE, N.O.S.	3	6.1 8	I	274	0	E0	P001		T14	TP2 TP13 TP27
3286	FLAMMABLE LIQUID, TOXIC, CORROSIVE, N.O.S.	3	6.1 8	II	274	1 L	E2	P001 IBC99		T11	TP2 TP13 TP27
3287	TOXIC LIQUID, INORGANIC, N.O.S.	6.1		I	274 315	0	E5	P001		T14	TP2 TP13 TP27
3287	TOXIC LIQUID, INORGANIC, N.O.S.	6.1		II	274	100 ml	E4	P001 IBC02		T11	TP2 TP27
3287	TOXIC LIQUID, INORGANIC, N.O.S.	6.1		III	223 274	5 L	E1	P001 IBC03 LP01		T7	TP1 TP28
3288	TOXIC SOLID, INORGANIC, N.O.S.	6.1		I	274	0	E5	P002 IBC99		T6	TP33
3288	TOXIC SOLID, INORGANIC, N.O.S.	6.1		II	274	500 g	E4	P002 IBC08	B2, B4	T3	TP33
3288	TOXIC SOLID, INORGANIC, N.O.S.	6.1		III	223 274	5 kg	E1	P002 IBC08 LP02	B3	T1	TP33
3289	TOXIC LIQUID, CORROSIVE, INORGANIC, N.O.S.	6.1	8	I	274 315	0	E5	P001		T14	TP2 TP13 TP27
3289	TOXIC LIQUID, CORROSIVE, INORGANIC, N.O.S.	6.1	8	II	274	100 ml	E4	P001 IBC02		T11	TP2 TP27
3290	TOXIC SOLID, CORROSIVE, INORGANIC, N.O.S.	6.1	8	I	274	0	E5	P002 IBC99		T6	TP33
3290	TOXIC SOLID, CORROSIVE, INORGANIC, N.O.S.	6.1	8	II	274	500 g	E4	P002 IBC06	B2	T3	TP33
3291	CLINICAL WASTE, UNSPECIFIED, N.O.S. or (BIO) MEDICAL WASTE, N.O.S. or REGULATED MEDICAL WASTE, N.O.S.	6.2				0	E0	P621 IBC620 LP621		BK2	
3292	BATTERIES, CONTAINING METALLIC SODIUM OR SODIUM ALLOY, or CELLS, CONTAINING METALLIC SODIUM OR SODIUM ALLOY	4.3			239 401	0	E0	P408			
3293	HYDRAZINE, AQUEOUS SOLUTION with not more than 37 % hydrazine, by mass	6.1		III	223	5 L	E1	P001 IBC03 LP01		T4	TP1
3294	HYDROGEN CYANIDE, SOLUTION IN ALCOHOL with not more than 45 % hydrogen cyanide	6.1	3	I		0	E0	P601		T14	TP2 TP13

UN No.	Name and description	Class or division	Subsidiary hazard	UN packing group	Special provisions	Limited and excepted quantities		Packagings and IBCs		Portable tanks and bulk containers	
								Packing instruction	Special packing provisions	Instructions	Special provisions
(1)	(2)	(3)	(4)	(5)	(6)	(7a)	(7b)	(8)	(9)	(10)	(11)
-	3.1.2	2.0	2.0	2.0.1.3	3.3	3.4	3.5	4.1.4	4.1.4	4.2.5 / 4.3.2	4.2.5
3295	HYDROCARBONS, LIQUID, N.O.S.	3		I		500 ml	E3	P001		T11	TP1 TP8 TP28
3295	HYDROCARBONS, LIQUID, N.O.S.	3		II		1 L	E2	P001 IBC02		T7	TP1 TP8 TP28
3295	HYDROCARBONS, LIQUID, N.O.S.	3		III	223	5 L	E1	P001 IBC03 LP01		T4	TP1 TP29
3296	HEPTAFLUOROPROPANE (REFRIGERANT GAS R 227)	2.2				120 ml	E1	P200		T50	
3297	ETHYLENE OXIDE AND CHLOROTETRAFLUORO-ETHANE MIXTURE with not more than 8.8 % ethylene oxide	2.2			392	120 ml	E1	P200		T50	
3298	ETHYLENE OXIDE AND PENTAFLUOROETHANE MIXTURE with not more than 7.9 % ethylene oxide	2.2			392	120 ml	E1	P200		T50	
3299	ETHYLENE OXIDE AND TETRAFLUOROETHANE MIXTURE with not more than 5.6 % ethylene oxide	2.2			392	120 ml	E1	P200		T50	
3300	ETHYLENE OXIDE AND CARBON DIOXIDE MIXTURE with more than 87 % ethylene oxide	2.3	2.1			0	E0	P200			
3301	CORROSIVE LIQUID, SELF-HEATING, N.O.S.	8	4.2	I	274	0	E0	P001			
3301	CORROSIVE LIQUID, SELF-HEATING, N.O.S.	8	4.2	II	274	0	E2	P001			
3302	2-DIMETHYLAMINOETHYL ACRYLATE, STABILIZED	6.1		II	386	100 ml	E4	P001 IBC02		T7	TP2
3303	COMPRESSED GAS, TOXIC, OXIDIZING, N.O.S.	2.3	5.1		274	0	E0	P200			
3304	COMPRESSED GAS, TOXIC, CORROSIVE, N.O.S.	2.3	8		274	0	E0	P200			
3305	COMPRESSED GAS, TOXIC, FLAMMABLE, CORROSIVE, N.O.S.	2.3	2.1 8		274	0	E0	P200			
3306	COMPRESSED GAS, TOXIC, OXIDIZING, CORROSIVE, N.O.S.	2.3	5.1 8		274	0	E0	P200			
3307	LIQUEFIED GAS, TOXIC, OXIDIZING, N.O.S.	2.3	5.1		274	0	E0	P200			
3308	LIQUEFIED GAS, TOXIC, CORROSIVE, N.O.S.	2.3	8		274	0	E0	P200			
3309	LIQUEFIED GAS, TOXIC, FLAMMABLE, CORROSIVE, N.O.S.	2.3	2.1 8		274	0	E0	P200			
3310	LIQUEFIED GAS, TOXIC, OXIDIZING, CORROSIVE, N.O.S.	2.3	5.1 8		274	0	E0	P200			
3311	GAS, REFRIGERATED LIQUID, OXIDIZING, N.O.S.	2.2	5.1		274	0	E0	P203		T75	TP5 TP22
3312	GAS, REFRIGERATED LIQUID, FLAMMABLE, N.O.S.	2.1			274	0	E0	P203		T75	TP5
3313	ORGANIC PIGMENTS, SELF-HEATING	4.2		II		0	E2	P002 IBC08	B2, B4	T3	TP33
3313	ORGANIC PIGMENTS, SELF-HEATING	4.2		III	223	0	E1	P002 IBC08 LP02	B3	T1	TP33

UN No.	Name and description	Class or division	Subsidiary hazard	UN packing group	Special provisions	Limited and excepted quantities		Packagings and IBCs		Portable tanks and bulk containers	
								Packing instruction	Special packing provisions	Instructions	Special provisions
(1)	(2)	(3)	(4)	(5)	(6)	(7a)	(7b)	(8)	(9)	(10)	(11)
-	3.1.2	2.0	2.0	2.0.1.3	3.3	3.4	3.5	4.1.4	4.1.4	4.2.5 / 4.3.2	4.2.5
3314	PLASTICS MOULDING COMPOUND in dough, sheet or extruded rope form evolving flammable vapour	9		III	207	5 kg	E1	P002 IBC08	PP14 B3, B6		
3315	CHEMICAL SAMPLE, TOXIC	6.1		I	250	0	E0	P099			
3316	CHEMICAL KIT or FIRST AID KIT	9			251 340	See SP 251 in chapter 3.3	See SP 340 in chapter 3.3	P901			
3317	2-AMINO-4,6-DINITROPHENOL, WETTED with not less than 20 % water, by mass	4.1		I	28	0	E0	P406	PP26		
3318	AMMONIA SOLUTION, relative density less than 0.880 at 15 °C in water, with more than 50 % ammonia	2.3	8		23	0	E0	P200		T50	
3319	NITROGLYCERIN MIXTURE, DESENSITIZED, SOLID, N.O.S. with more than 2 % but not more than 10 % nitroglycerin, by mass	4.1		II	28 272 274	0	E0	P099			
3320	SODIUM BOROHYDRIDE AND SODIUM HYDROXIDE SOLUTION, with not more than 12 % sodium borohydride and not more than 40 % sodium hydroxide by mass	8		II		1 L	E2	P001 IBC02		T7	TP2
3320	SODIUM BOROHYDRIDE AND SODIUM HYDROXIDE SOLUTION, with not more than 12 % sodium borohydride and not more than 40 % sodium hydroxide by mass	8		III	223	5 L	E1	P001 IBC03 LP01		T4	TP2
3321	RADIOACTIVE MATERIAL, LOW SPECIFIC ACTIVITY (LSA-II), non fissile or fissile-excepted	7			172 317 325 336	0	E0	See chapter 2.7 and section 4.1.9		T5	TP4
3322	RADIOACTIVE MATERIAL, LOW SPECIFIC ACTIVITY (LSA-III), non fissile or fissile-excepted	7			172 317 325 336	0	E0	See chapter 2.7 and section 4.1.9		T5	TP4
3323	RADIOACTIVE MATERIAL, TYPE C PACKAGE, non fissile or fissile-excepted	7			172 317 325	0	E0	See chapter 2.7 and section 4.1.9			
3324	RADIOACTIVE MATERIAL, LOW SPECIFIC ACTIVITY (LSA-II), FISSILE	7			172 326 336	0	E0	See chapter 2.7 and section 4.1.9			
3325	RADIOACTIVE MATERIAL, LOW SPECIFIC ACTIVITY, (LSA-III), FISSILE	7			172 326 336	0	E0	See chapter 2.7 and section 4.1.9			
3326	RADIOACTIVE MATERIAL, SURFACE CONTAMINATED OBJECTS (SCO-I or SCO-II), FISSILE	7			172 326	0	E0	See chapter 2.7 and section 4.1.9			
3327	RADIOACTIVE MATERIAL, TYPE A PACKAGE, FISSILE, non-special form	7			172 326	0	E0	See chapter 2.7 and section 4.1.9			
3328	RADIOACTIVE MATERIAL, TYPE B(U) PACKAGE, FISSILE	7			172 326 337	0	E0	See chapter 2.7 and section 4.1.9			

UN No.	Name and description	Class or division	Subsidiary hazard	UN packing group	Special provisions	Limited and excepted quantities		Packagings and IBCs		Portable tanks and bulk containers	
								Packing instruction	Special packing provisions	Instructions	Special provisions
(1)	(2)	(3)	(4)	(5)	(6)	(7a)	(7b)	(8)	(9)	(10)	(11)
-	3.1.2	2.0	2.0	2.0.1.3	3.3	3.4	3.5	4.1.4	4.1.4	4.2.5 / 4.3.2	4.2.5
3329	RADIOACTIVE MATERIAL, TYPE B(M) PACKAGE, FISSILE	7			172 326 337	0	E0	See chapter 2.7 and section 4.1.9			
3330	RADIOACTIVE MATERIAL, TYPE C PACKAGE, FISSILE	7			172 326	0	E0	See chapter 2.7 and section 4.1.9			
3331	RADIOACTIVE MATERIAL, TRANSPORTED UNDER SPECIAL ARRANGEMENT, FISSILE	7			172 326	0	E0	See chapter 2.7 and section 4.1.9			
3332	RADIOACTIVE MATERIAL, TYPE A PACKAGE, SPECIAL FORM, non fissile or fissile-excepted	7			172 317	0	E0	See chapter 2.7 and section 4.1.9			
3333	RADIOACTIVE MATERIAL, TYPE A PACKAGE, SPECIAL FORM, FISSILE	7			172	0	E0	See chapter 2.7 and section 4.1.9			
3334	AVIATION REGULATED LIQUID, N.O.S.	9			106 274 276	0	E1	N/A			
3335	AVIATION REGULATED SOLID, N.O.S.	9			106 274 276	0	E1	N/A			
3336	MERCAPTANS, LIQUID, FLAMMABLE, N.O.S. or MERCAPTAN MIXTURE, LIQUID, FLAMMABLE, N.O.S.	3		I	274	0	E0	P001		T11	TP2
3336	MERCAPTANS, LIQUID, FLAMMABLE, N.O.S. or MERCAPTAN MIXTURE, LIQUID, FLAMMABLE, N.O.S.	3		II	274	1 L	E2	P001 IBC02		T7	TP1 TP8 TP28
3336	MERCAPTANS, LIQUID, FLAMMABLE, N.O.S. or MERCAPTAN MIXTURE, LIQUID, FLAMMABLE, N.O.S.	3		III	223 274	5 L	E1	P001 IBC03 LP01		T4	TP1 TP29
3337	REFRIGERANT GAS R 404A	2.2				120 ml	E1	P200		T50	
3338	REFRIGERANT GAS R 407A	2.2				120 ml	E1	P200		T50	
3339	REFRIGERANT GAS R 407B	2.2				120 ml	E1	P200		T50	
3340	REFRIGERANT GAS R 407C	2.2				120 ml	E1	P200		T50	
3341	THIOUREA DIOXIDE	4.2		II		0	E2	P002 IBC06	B2	T3	TP33
3341	THIOUREA DIOXIDE	4.2		III	223	0	E1	P002 IBC08 LP02	B3	T1	TP33
3342	XANTHATES	4.2		II		0	E2	P002 IBC06	B2	T3	TP33
3342	XANTHATES	4.2		III	223	0	E1	P002 IBC08 LP02	B3	T1	TP33
3343	NITROGLYCERIN MIXTURE, DESENSITIZED, LIQUID, FLAMMABLE, N.O.S. with not more than 30 % nitroglycerin, by mass	3			28 274 278	0	E0	P099			
3344	PENTAERYTHRITE TETRANITRATE (PENTAERYTHRITOL TETRANITRATE; PETN) MIXTURE, DESENSITIZED, SOLID, N.O.S. with more than 10 % but not more than 20 % PETN, by mass	4.1		II	28 272 274	0	E0	P406	PP26 PP80		

UN No.	Name and description	Class or division	Subsidiary hazard	UN packing group	Special provisions	Limited and excepted quantities		Packagings and IBCs		Portable tanks and bulk containers	
								Packing instruction	Special packing provisions	Instructions	Special provisions
(1)	(2)	(3)	(4)	(5)	(6)	(7a)	(7b)	(8)	(9)	(10)	(11)
-	3.1.2	2.0	2.0	2.0.1.3	3.3	3.4	3.5	4.1.4	4.1.4	4.2.5 / 4.3.2	4.2.5
3345	PHENOXYACETIC ACID DERIVATIVE PESTICIDE, SOLID, TOXIC	6.1		I	61 274	0	E5	P002 IBC07	B1	T6	TP33
3345	PHENOXYACETIC ACID DERIVATIVE PESTICIDE, SOLID, TOXIC	6.1		II	61 274	500 g	E4	P002 IBC08	B2, B4	T3	TP33
3345	PHENOXYACETIC ACID DERIVATIVE PESTICIDE, SOLID, TOXIC	6.1		III	61 223 274	5 kg	E1	P002 IBC08 LP02	B3	T1	TP33
3346	PHENOXYACETIC ACID DERIVATIVE PESTICIDE, LIQUID, FLAMMABLE, TOXIC, flash point less than 23 °C	3	6.1	I	61 274	0	E0	P001		T14	TP2 TP13 TP27
3346	PHENOXYACETIC ACID DERIVATIVE PESTICIDE, LIQUID, FLAMMABLE, TOXIC, flash point less than 23 °C	3	6.1	II	61 274	1 L	E2	P001 IBC02		T11	TP2 TP13 TP27
3347	PHENOXYACETIC ACID DERIVATIVE PESTICIDE, LIQUID, TOXIC, FLAMMABLE, flash point not less than 23 °C	6.1	3	I	61 274	0	E5	P001		T14	TP2 TP13 TP27
3347	PHENOXYACETIC ACID DERIVATIVE PESTICIDE, LIQUID, TOXIC, FLAMMABLE, flash point not less than 23 °C	6.1	3	II	61 274	100 ml	E4	P001 IBC02		T11	TP2 TP13 TP27
3347	PHENOXYACETIC ACID DERIVATIVE PESTICIDE, LIQUID, TOXIC, FLAMMABLE, flash point not less than 23 °C	6.1	3	III	61 223 274	5 L	E1	P001 IBC03		T7	TP2 TP28
3348	PHENOXYACETIC ACID DERIVATIVE PESTICIDE, LIQUID, TOXIC	6.1		I	61 274	0	E5	P001		T14	TP2 TP13 TP27
3348	PHENOXYACETIC ACID DERIVATIVE PESTICIDE, LIQUID, TOXIC	6.1		II	61 274	100 ml	E4	P001 IBC02		T11	TP2 TP27
3348	PHENOXYACETIC ACID DERIVATIVE PESTICIDE, LIQUID, TOXIC	6.1		III	61 223 274	5 L	E1	P001 IBC03 LP01		T7	TP2 TP28
3349	PYRETHROID PESTICIDE, SOLID, TOXIC	6.1		I	61 274	0	E5	P002 IBC07	B1	T6	TP33
3349	PYRETHROID PESTICIDE, SOLID, TOXIC	6.1		II	61 274	500 g	E4	P002 IBC08	B2, B4	T3	TP33
3349	PYRETHROID PESTICIDE, SOLID, TOXIC	6.1		III	61 223 274	5 kg	E1	P002 IBC08 LP02	B3	T1	TP33
3350	PYRETHROID PESTICIDE, LIQUID, FLAMMABLE, TOXIC, flash point less than 23 °C	3	6.1	I	61 274	0	E0	P001		T14	TP2 TP13 TP27
3350	PYRETHROID PESTICIDE, LIQUID, FLAMMABLE, TOXIC, flash point less than 23 °C	3	6.1	II	61 274	1 L	E2	P001 IBC02		T11	TP2 TP13 TP27
3351	PYRETHROID PESTICIDE, LIQUID, TOXIC, FLAMMABLE, flash point not less than 23 °C	6.1	3	I	61 274	0	E5	P001		T14	TP2 TP13 TP27
3351	PYRETHROID PESTICIDE, LIQUID, TOXIC, FLAMMABLE, flash point not less than 23 °C	6.1	3	II	61 274	100 ml	E4	P001 IBC02		T11	TP2 TP13 TP27
3351	PYRETHROID PESTICIDE, LIQUID, TOXIC, FLAMMABLE, flash point not less than 23 °C	6.1	3	III	61 223 274	5 L	E1	P001 IBC03		T7	TP2 TP28

UN No.	Name and description	Class or division	Subsidiary hazard	UN packing group	Special provisions	Limited and excepted quantities		Packagings and IBCs		Portable tanks and bulk containers	
						(7a)	(7b)	Packing instruction	Special packing provisions	Instructions	Special provisions
(1)	(2)	(3)	(4)	(5)	(6)	(7a)	(7b)	(8)	(9)	(10)	(11)
-	3.1.2	2.0	2.0	2.0.1.3	3.3	3.4	3.5	4.1.4	4.1.4	4.2.5 / 4.3.2	4.2.5
3352	PYRETHROID PESTICIDE, LIQUID, TOXIC	6.1		I	61 274	0	E5	P001		T14	TP2 TP13 TP27
3352	PYRETHROID PESTICIDE, LIQUID, TOXIC	6.1		II	61 274	100 ml	E4	P001 IBC02		T11	TP2 TP27
3352	PYRETHROID PESTICIDE, LIQUID, TOXIC	6.1		III	61 223 274	5 L	E1	P001 IBC03 LP01		T7	TP2 TP28
3354	INSECTICIDE GAS, FLAMMABLE, N.O.S.	2.1			274	0	E0	P200			
3355	INSECTICIDE GAS, TOXIC, FLAMMABLE, N.O.S.	2.3	2.1		274	0	E0	P200			
3356	OXYGEN GENERATOR, CHEMICAL†	5.1			284	0	E0	P500			
3357	NITROGLYCERIN MIXTURE, DESENSITIZED, LIQUID, N.O.S. with not more than 30 % nitroglycerin, by mass	3		II	28 274 288	0	E0	P099			
3358	REFRIGERATING MACHINES containing flammable, non-toxic, liquefied gas	2.1			291	0	E0	P003	PP32		
3359	FUMIGATED CARGO TRANSPORT UNIT	9			302	0	E0	NONE			
3360	FIBRES, VEGETABLE, DRY	4.1			29 123 299	0	E0	P003	PP19		
3361	CHLOROSILANES, TOXIC, CORROSIVE, N.O.S.	6.1	8	II	274	0	E0	P010		T14	TP2 TP7 TP13 TP27
3362	CHLOROSILANES, TOXIC, CORROSIVE, FLAMMABLE, N.O.S.	6.1	3 8	II	274	0	E0	P010		T14	TP2 TP7 TP13 TP27
3363	DANGEROUS GOODS IN ARTICLES or DANGEROUS GOODS IN MACHINERY or DANGEROUS GOODS IN APPARATUS	9			301	0	E0	P907			
3364	TRINITROPHENOL (PICRIC ACID), WETTED, with not less than 10 % water by mass	4.1		I	28	0	E0	P406	PP24		
3365	TRINITROCHLOROBENZENE (PICRYL CHLORIDE), WETTED, with not less than 10 % water by mass	4.1		I	28	0	E0	P406	PP24		
3366	TRINITROTOLUENE (TNT), WETTED, with not less than 10 % water by mass	4.1		I	28	0	E0	P406	PP24		
3367	TRINITROBENZENE, WETTED, with not less than 10 % water by mass	4.1		I	28	0	E0	P406	PP24		
3368	TRINITROBENZOIC ACID, WETTED, with not less than 10 % water by mass	4.1		I	28	0	E0	P406	PP24		
3369	SODIUM DINITRO-o-CRESOLATE, WETTED, with not less than 10 % water by mass	4.1		I	28	0	E0	P406	PP24		
3370	UREA NITRATE, WETTED, with not less than 10 % water by mass	4.1		I	28	0	E0	P406	PP78		

UN No.	Name and description	Class or division	Subsidiary hazard	UN packing group	Special provisions	Limited and excepted quantities		Packagings and IBCs		Portable tanks and bulk containers	
						Packing instruction	Special packing provisions	Instructions	Special provisions
(1)	(2)	(3)	(4)	(5)	(6)	(7a)	(7b)	(8)	(9)	(10)	(11)
-	3.1.2	2.0	2.0	2.0.1.3	3.3	3.4	3.5	4.1.4	4.1.4	4.2.5 / 4.3.2	4.2.5
3371	2-METHYLBUTANAL	3		II		1 L	E2	P001 IBC02		T4	TP1
3373	BIOLOGICAL SUBSTANCE, CATEGORY B	6.2			319 341	0	E0	P650		T1 BK1 BK2	TP1
3374	ACETYLENE, SOLVENT FREE	2.1				0	E0	P200			
3375	AMMONIUM NITRATE EMULSION or SUSPENSION or GEL, intermediate for blasting explosives	5.1		II	309	0	E2	P505 IBC02	B16	T1	TP1 TP9 TP17 TP32
3376	4-NITROPHENYLHYDRAZINE, with not less than 30 % water, by mass	4.1		I	28	0	E0	P406	PP26		
3377	SODIUM PERBORATE MONOHYDRATE	5.1		III		5 kg	E1	P002 IBC08 LP02	B3	T1 BK1 BK2 BK3	TP33
3378	SODIUM CARBONATE PEROXYHYDRATE	5.1		II		1 kg	E2	P002 IBC08	B2, B4	T3 BK1 BK2	TP33
3378	SODIUM CARBONATE PEROXYHYDRATE	5.1		III		5 kg	E1	P002 IBC08 LP02	B3	T1 BK1 BK2 BK3	TP33
3379	DESENSITIZED EXPLOSIVE, LIQUID, N.O.S.	3		I	274 311	0	E0	P099			
3380	DESENSITIZED EXPLOSIVE, SOLID, N.O.S.	4.1		I	274 311 394	0	E0	P099			
3381	TOXIC BY INHALATION LIQUID, N.O.S. with an LC_{50} lower than or equal to 200 ml/m^3 and saturated vapour concentration greater than or equal to 500 LC_{50}	6.1		I	274	0	E0	P601		T22	TP2 TP13
3382	TOXIC BY INHALATION LIQUID, N.O.S. with an LC_{50} lower than or equal to 1000 ml/m^3 and saturated vapour concentration greater than or equal to 10 LC_{50}	6.1		I	274	0	E0	P602		T20	TP2 TP13
3383	TOXIC BY INHALATION LIQUID, FLAMMABLE, N.O.S. with an LC_{50} lower than or equal to 200 ml/m^3 and saturated vapour concentration greater than or equal to 500 LC_{50}	6.1	3	I	274	0	E0	P601		T22	TP2 TP13
3384	TOXIC BY INHALATION LIQUID, FLAMMABLE, N.O.S. with an LC_{50} lower than or equal to 1000 ml/m^3 and saturated vapour concentration greater than or equal to 10 LC_{50}	6.1	3	I	274	0	E0	P602		T20	TP2 TP13
3385	TOXIC BY INHALATION LIQUID, WATER-REACTIVE, N.O.S. with an LC_{50} lower than or equal to 200 ml/m^3 and saturated vapour concentration greater than or equal to 500 LC_{50}	6.1	4.3	I	274	0	E0	P601		T22	TP2 TP13
3386	TOXIC BY INHALATION LIQUID, WATER-REACTIVE, N.O.S. with an LC_{50} lower than or equal to 1000 ml/m^3 and saturated vapour concentration greater than or equal to 10 LC_{50}	6.1	4.3	I	274	0	E0	P602		T20	TP2 TP13

UN No.	Name and description	Class or division	Subsidiary hazard	UN packing group	Special provisions	Limited and excepted quantities		Packagings and IBCs		Portable tanks and bulk containers	
								Packing instruction	Special packing provisions	Instructions	Special provisions
(1)	(2)	(3)	(4)	(5)	(6)	(7a)	(7b)	(8)	(9)	(10)	(11)
-	3.1.2	2.0	2.0	2.0.1.3	3.3	3.4	3.5	4.1.4	4.1.4	4.2.5 / 4.3.2	4.2.5
3387	TOXIC BY INHALATION LIQUID, OXIDIZING, N.O.S. with an LC_{50} lower than or equal to 200 ml/m^3 and saturated vapour concentration greater than or equal to 500 LC_{50}	6.1	5.1	I	274	0	E0	P601		T22	TP2 TP13
3388	TOXIC BY INHALATION LIQUID, OXIDIZING, N.O.S. with an LC_{50} lower than or equal to 1000 ml/m^3 and saturated vapour concentration greater than or equal to 10 LC_{50}	6.1	5.1	I	274	0	E0	P602		T20	TP2 TP13
3389	TOXIC BY INHALATION LIQUID, CORROSIVE, N.O.S. with an LC_{50} lower than or equal to 200 ml/m^3 and saturated vapour concentration greater than or equal to 500 LC_{50}	6.1	8	I	274	0	E0	P601		T22	TP2 TP13
3390	TOXIC BY INHALATION LIQUID, CORROSIVE, N.O.S. with an LC_{50} lower than or equal to 1000 ml/m^3 and saturated vapour concentration greater than or equal to 10 LC_{50}	6.1	8	I	274	0	E0	P602		T20	TP2 TP13
3391	ORGANOMETALLIC SUBSTANCE, SOLID, PYROPHORIC	4.2		I	274	0	E0	P404	PP86	T21	TP7 TP33 TP36
3392	ORGANOMETALLIC SUBSTANCE, LIQUID, PYROPHORIC	4.2		I	274	0	E0	P400	PP86	T21	TP2 TP7 TP36
3393	ORGANOMETALLIC SUBSTANCE, SOLID, PYROPHORIC, WATER-REACTIVE	4.2	4.3	I	274	0	E0	P404	PP86	T21	TP7 TP33 TP36 TP41
3394	ORGANOMETALLIC SUBSTANCE, LIQUID, PYROPHORIC, WATER-REACTIVE	4.2	4.3	I	274	0	E0	P400	PP86	T21	TP2 TP7 TP36 TP41
3395	ORGANOMETALLIC SUBSTANCE, SOLID, WATER-REACTIVE	4.3		I	274	0	E0	P403		T9	TP7 TP33 TP36 TP41
3395	ORGANOMETALLIC SUBSTANCE, SOLID, WATER-REACTIVE	4.3		II	274	500 g	E2	P410 IBC04		T3	TP33 TP36 TP41
3395	ORGANOMETALLIC SUBSTANCE, SOLID, WATER-REACTIVE	4.3		III	223 274	1 kg	E1	P410 IBC06		T1	TP33 TP36 TP41
3396	ORGANOMETALLIC SUBSTANCE, SOLID, WATER-REACTIVE, FLAMMABLE	4.3	4.1	I	274	0	E0	P403		T9	TP7 TP33 TP36 TP41
3396	ORGANOMETALLIC SUBSTANCE, SOLID, WATER-REACTIVE, FLAMMABLE	4.3	4.1	II	274	500 g	E2	P410 IBC04		T3	TP33 TP36 TP41
3396	ORGANOMETALLIC SUBSTANCE, SOLID, WATER-REACTIVE, FLAMMABLE	4.3	4.1	III	223 274	1 kg	E1	P410 IBC06		T1	TP33 TP36 TP41
3397	ORGANOMETALLIC SUBSTANCE, SOLID, WATER-REACTIVE, SELF-HEATING	4.3	4.2	I	274	0	E0	P403		T9	TP7 TP33 TP36 TP41

UN No.	Name and description	Class or division	Subsidiary hazard	UN packing group	Special provisions	Limited and excepted quantities		Packagings and IBCs		Portable tanks and bulk containers	
								Packing instruction	Special packing provisions	Instructions	Special provisions
(1)	(2)	(3)	(4)	(5)	(6)	(7a)	(7b)	(8)	(9)	(10)	(11)
-	3.1.2	2.0	2.0	2.0.1.3	3.3	3.4	3.5	4.1.4	4.1.4	4.2.5 / 4.3.2	4.2.5
3397	ORGANOMETALLIC SUBSTANCE, SOLID, WATER-REACTIVE, SELF-HEATING	4.3	4.2	II	274	500 g	E2	P410 IBC04		T3	TP33 TP36 TP41
3397	ORGANOMETALLIC SUBSTANCE, SOLID, WATER-REACTIVE, SELF-HEATING	4.3	4.2	III	223 274	1 kg	E1	P410 IBC06		T1	TP33 TP36 TP41
3398	ORGANOMETALLIC SUBSTANCE, LIQUID, WATER-REACTIVE	4.3		I	274	0	E0	P402		T13	TP2 TP7 TP36 TP41
3398	ORGANOMETALLIC SUBSTANCE, LIQUID, WATER-REACTIVE	4.3		II	274	500 ml	E2	P001 IBC01		T7	TP2 TP7 TP36 TP41
3398	ORGANOMETALLIC SUBSTANCE, LIQUID, WATER-REACTIVE	4.3		III	223 274	1 L	E1	P001 IBC02		T7	TP2 TP7 TP36 TP41
3399	ORGANOMETALLIC SUBSTANCE, LIQUID, WATER-REACTIVE, FLAMMABLE	4.3	3	I	274	0	E0	P402		T13	TP2 TP7 TP36 TP41
3399	ORGANOMETALLIC SUBSTANCE, LIQUID, WATER-REACTIVE, FLAMMABLE	4.3	3	II	274	500 ml	E2	P001 IBC01		T7	TP2 TP7 TP36 TP41
3399	ORGANOMETALLIC SUBSTANCE, LIQUID, WATER-REACTIVE, FLAMMABLE	4.3	3	III	223 274	1 L	E1	P001 IBC02		T7	TP2 TP7 TP36 TP41
3400	ORGANOMETALLIC SUBSTANCE, SOLID, SELF-HEATING	4.2		II	274	500 g	E2	P410 IBC06		T3	TP33 TP36
3400	ORGANOMETALLIC SUBSTANCE, SOLID, SELF-HEATING	4.2		III	223 274	1 kg	E1	P002 IBC08		T1	TP33 TP36
3401	ALKALI METAL AMALGAM, SOLID	4.3		I	182	0	E0	P403		T9	TP7 TP33
3402	ALKALINE EARTH METAL AMALGAM, SOLID	4.3		I	183	0	E0	P403		T9	TP7 TP33
3403	POTASSIUM METAL ALLOYS, SOLID	4.3		I		0	E0	P403		T9	TP7 TP33
3404	POTASSIUM SODIUM ALLOYS, SOLID	4.3		I		0	E0	P403		T9	TP7 TP33
3405	BARIUM CHLORATE SOLUTION	5.1	6.1	II		1 L	E2	P504 IBC02		T4	TP1
3405	BARIUM CHLORATE SOLUTION	5.1	6.1	III	223	5 L	E1	P001 IBC02		T4	TP1
3406	BARIUM PERCHLORATE SOLUTION	5.1	6.1	II		1 L	E2	P504 IBC02		T4	TP1
3406	BARIUM PERCHLORATE SOLUTION	5.1	6.1	III	223	5 L	E1	P001 IBC02		T4	TP1
3407	CHLORATE AND MAGNESIUM CHLORIDE MIXTURE SOLUTION	5.1		II		1 L	E2	P504 IBC02		T4	TP1
3407	CHLORATE AND MAGNESIUM CHLORIDE MIXTURE SOLUTION	5.1		III	223	5 L	E1	P504 IBC02		T4	TP1
3408	LEAD PERCHLORATE SOLUTION	5.1	6.1	II		1 L	E2	P504 IBC02		T4	TP1

UN No.	Name and description	Class or division	Subsidiary hazard	UN packing group	Special provisions	Limited and excepted quantities		Packagings and IBCs		Portable tanks and bulk containers	
								Packing instruction	Special packing provisions	Instructions	Special provisions
(1)	(2)	(3)	(4)	(5)	(6)	(7a)	(7b)	(8)	(9)	(10)	(11)
-	3.1.2	2.0	2.0	2.0.1.3	3.3	3.4	3.5	4.1.4	4.1.4	4.2.5 / 4.3.2	4.2.5
3408	LEAD PERCHLORATE SOLUTION	5.1	6.1	III	223	5 L	E1	P001 IBC02		T4	TP1
3409	CHLORONITROBENZENES, LIQUID	6.1		II	279	100 ml	E4	P001 IBC02		T7	TP2
3410	4-CHLORO-o-TOLUIDINE HYDROCHLORIDE SOLUTION	6.1		III	223	5 L	E1	P001 IBC03		T4	TP1
3411	beta-NAPHTHYLAMINE SOLUTION	6.1		II		100 ml	E4	P001 IBC02		T7	TP2
3411	beta-NAPHTHYLAMINE SOLUTION	6.1		III	223	5 L	E1	P001 IBC02		T7	TP2
3412	FORMIC ACID with not less than 10 % but not more than 85 % acid by mass	8		II		1 L	E2	P001 IBC02		T7	TP2
3412	FORMIC ACID with not less than 5 % but less than 10 % acid by mass	8		III		5 L	E1	P001 IBC03 LP01		T4	TP1
3413	POTASSIUM CYANIDE SOLUTION	6.1		I		0	E5	P001		T14	TP2 TP13
3413	POTASSIUM CYANIDE SOLUTION	6.1		II		100 ml	E4	P001 IBC02		T11	TP2 TP13 TP27
3413	POTASSIUM CYANIDE SOLUTION	6.1		III	223	5 L	E1	P001 IBC03 LP01		T7	TP2 TP13 TP28
3414	SODIUM CYANIDE SOLUTION	6.1		I		0	E5	P001		T14	TP2 TP13
3414	SODIUM CYANIDE SOLUTION	6.1		II		100 ml	E4	P001 IBC02		T11	TP2 TP13 TP27
3414	SODIUM CYANIDE SOLUTION	6.1		III	223	5 L	E1	P001 IBC03 LP01		T7	TP2 TP13 TP28
3415	SODIUM FLUORIDE SOLUTION	6.1		III	223	5 L	E1	P001 IBC03 LP01		T4	TP1
3416	CHLOROACETOPHENONE, LIQUID	6.1		II		0	E0	P001 IBC02		T7	TP2 TP13
3417	XYLYL BROMIDE, SOLID	6.1		II		0	E4	P002 IBC08	B2, B4	T3	TP33
3418	2,4-TOLUYLENEDIAMINE SOLUTION	6.1		III	223	5 L	E1	P001 IBC03 LP01		T4	TP1
3419	BORON TRIFLUORIDE ACETIC ACID COMPLEX, SOLID	8		II		1 kg	E2	P002 IBC08	B2, B4	T3	TP33
3420	BORON TRIFLUORIDE PROPIONIC ACID COMPLEX, SOLID	8		II		1 kg	E2	P002 IBC08	B2, B4	T3	TP33
3421	POTASSIUM HYDROGEN DIFLUORIDE SOLUTION	8	6.1	II		1 L	E2	P001 IBC02		T7	TP2
3421	POTASSIUM HYDROGEN DIFLUORIDE SOLUTION	8	6.1	III	223	5 L	E1	P001 IBC03		T4	TP1
3422	POTASSIUM FLUORIDE SOLUTION	6.1		III	223	5 L	E1	P001 IBC03 LP01		T4	TP1
3423	TETRAMETHYLAMMONIUM HYDROXIDE, SOLID	6.1	8	I	279 409	0	E5	P002 IBC99		T6	TP33
3424	AMMONIUM DINITRO-o-CRESOLATE, SOLUTION	6.1		II		100 ml	E4	P001 IBC02		T7	TP2
3424	AMMONIUM DINITRO-o-CRESOLATE, SOLUTION	6.1		III	223	5 L	E1	P001 IBC02		T7	TP2

UN No.	Name and description	Class or division	Subsidiary hazard	UN packing group	Special provisions	Limited and excepted quantities		Packagings and IBCs		Portable tanks and bulk containers	
								Packing instruction	Special packing provisions	Instructions	Special provisions
(1)	(2)	(3)	(4)	(5)	(6)	(7a)	(7b)	(8)	(9)	(10)	(11)
-	3.1.2	2.0	2.0	2.0.1.3	3.3	3.4	3.5	4.1.4	4.1.4	4.2.5 / 4.3.2	4.2.5
3425	BROMOACETIC ACID, SOLID	8		II		1 kg	E2	P002 IBC08	B2, B4	T3	TP33
3426	ACRYLAMIDE SOLUTION	6.1		III	223	5 L	E1	P001 IBC03 LP01		T4	TP1
3427	CHLOROBENZYL CHLORIDES, SOLID	6.1		III		5 kg	E1	P002 IBC08 LP02	B3	T1	TP33
3428	3-CHLORO-4-METHYLPHENYL ISOCYANATE, SOLID	6.1		II		500 g	E4	P002 IBC08	B2, B4	T3	TP33
3429	CHLOROTOLUIDINES, LIQUID	6.1		III		5 L	E1	P001 IBC03 LP01		T4	TP1
3430	XYLENOLS, LIQUID	6.1		II		100 ml	E4	P001 IBC02		T7	TP2
3431	NITROBENZOTRIFLUORIDES, SOLID	6.1		II		500 g	E4	P002 IBC08	B2, B4	T3	TP33
3432	POLYCHLORINATED BIPHENYLS, SOLID	9		II	305	1 kg	E2	P906 IBC08	B2, B4	T3	TP33
3434	NITROCRESOLS, LIQUID	6.1		III		5 L	E1	P001 IBC03 LP01		T4	TP1
3436	HEXAFLUOROACETONE HYDRATE, SOLID	6.1		II		500 g	E4	P002 IBC08	B2, B4	T3	TP33
3437	CHLOROCRESOLS, SOLID	6.1		II		500 g	E4	P002 IBC08	B2, B4	T3	TP33
3438	alpha-METHYLBENZYL ALCOHOL, SOLID	6.1		III		5 kg	E1	P002 IBC08 LP02	B3	T1	TP33
3439	NITRILES, SOLID, TOXIC, N.O.S.	6.1		I	274	0	E5	P002 IBC07	B1	T6	TP33
3439	NITRILES, SOLID, TOXIC, N.O.S.	6.1		II	274	500 g	E4	P002 IBC08	B2, B4	T3	TP33
3439	NITRILES, SOLID, TOXIC, N.O.S.	6.1		III	223 274	5 kg	E1	P002 IBC08 LP02	B3	T1	TP33
3440	SELENIUM COMPOUND, LIQUID, N.O.S.	6.1		I	274	0	E5	P001		T14	TP2 TP27
3440	SELENIUM COMPOUND, LIQUID, N.O.S.	6.1		II	274	100 ml	E4	P001 IBC02		T11	TP2 TP27
3440	SELENIUM COMPOUND, LIQUID, N.O.S.	6.1		III	223 274	5 L	E1	P001 IBC03		T7	TP1 TP28
3441	CHLORODINITROBENZENES, SOLID	6.1		II	279	500 g	E4	P002 IBC08	B2, B4	T3	TP33
3442	DICHLOROANILINES, SOLID	6.1		II	279	500 g	E4	P002 IBC08	B2, B4	T3	TP33
3443	DINITROBENZENES, SOLID	6.1		II		500 g	E4	P002 IBC08	B2, B4	T3	TP33
3444	NICOTINE HYDROCHLORIDE, SOLID	6.1		II	43	500 g	E4	P002 IBC08	B2, B4	T3	TP33
3445	NICOTINE SULPHATE, SOLID	6.1		II		500 g	E4	P002 IBC08	B2, B4	T3	TP33
3446	NITROTOLUENES, SOLID	6.1		II		500 g	E4	P002 IBC08	B2, B4	T3	TP33
3447	NITROXYLENES, SOLID	6.1		II		500 g	E4	P002 IBC08	B2, B4	T3	TP33
3448	TEAR GAS SUBSTANCE, SOLID, N.O.S.	6.1		I	274	0	E0	P002		T6	TP33

UN No.	Name and description	Class or division	Subsidiary hazard	UN packing group	Special provisions	Limited and excepted quantities		Packagings and IBCs		Portable tanks and bulk containers	
								Packing instruction	Special packing provisions	Instructions	Special provisions
(1)	(2)	(3)	(4)	(5)	(6)	(7a)	(7b)	(8)	(9)	(10)	(11)
-	3.1.2	2.0	2.0	2.0.1.3	3.3	3.4	3.5	4.1.4	4.1.4	4.2.5 / 4.3.2	4.2.5
3448	TEAR GAS SUBSTANCE, SOLID, N.O.S.	6.1		II	274	0	E0	P002 IBC08	B2, B4	T3	TP33
3449	BROMOBENZYL CYANIDES, SOLID	6.1		I	138	0	E5	P002		T6	TP33
3450	DIPHENYLCHLOROARSINE, SOLID	6.1		I		0	E0	P002 IBC07	B1	T6	TP33
3451	TOLUIDINES, SOLID	6.1		II	279	500 g	E4	P002 IBC08	B2, B4	T3	TP33
3452	XYLIDINES, SOLID	6.1		II		500 g	E4	P002 IBC08	B2, B4	T3	TP33
3453	PHOSPHORIC ACID, SOLID	8		III		5 kg	E1	P002 IBC08 LP02	B3	T1	TP33
3454	DINITROTOLUENES, SOLID	6.1		II		500 g	E4	P002 IBC08	B2, B4	T3	TP33
3455	CRESOLS, SOLID	6.1	8	II		500 g	E4	P002 IBC08	B2, B4	T3	TP33
3456	NITROSYLSULPHURIC ACID, SOLID	8		II		1 kg	E2	P002 IBC08	B2, B4	T3	TP33
3457	CHLORONITROTOLUENES, SOLID	6.1		III		5 kg	E1	P002 IBC08 LP02	B3	T1	TP33
3458	NITROANISOLES, SOLID	6.1		III	279	5 kg	E1	P002 IBC08 LP02	B3	T1	TP33
3459	NITROBROMOBENZENES, SOLID	6.1		III		5 kg	E1	P002 IBC08 LP02	B3	T1	TP33
3460	N-ETHYLBENZYLTOLUIDINES, SOLID	6.1		III		5 kg	E1	P002 IBC08 LP02	B3	T1	TP33
3462	TOXINS, EXTRACTED FROM LIVING SOURCES, SOLID, N.O.S.	6.1		I	210 274	0	E5	P002 IBC07	B1	T6	TP33
3462	TOXINS, EXTRACTED FROM LIVING SOURCES, SOLID, N.O.S.	6.1		II	210 274	500 g	E4	P002 IBC08	B2, B4	T3	TP33
3462	TOXINS, EXTRACTED FROM LIVING SOURCES, SOLID, N.O.S.	6.1		III	210 223 274	5 kg	E1	P002 IBC08	B3	T1	TP33
3463	PROPIONIC ACID with not less than 90 % acid by mass	8	3	II		1 L	E2	P001 IBC02		T7	TP2
3464	ORGANOPHOSPHORUS COMPOUND, SOLID, TOXIC, N.O.S.	6.1		I	43 274	0	E5	P002 IBC07	B1	T6	TP33
3464	ORGANOPHOSPHORUS COMPOUND, SOLID, TOXIC, N.O.S.	6.1		II	43 274	500 g	E4	P002 IBC08	B2, B4	T3	TP33
3464	ORGANOPHOSPHORUS COMPOUND, SOLID, TOXIC, N.O.S.	6.1		III	43 223 274	5 kg	E1	P002 IBC08 LP02	B3	T1	TP33
3465	ORGANOARSENIC COMPOUND, SOLID, N.O.S.	6.1		I	274	0	E5	P002 IBC07	B1	T6	TP33
3465	ORGANOARSENIC COMPOUND, SOLID, N.O.S.	6.1		II	274	500 g	E4	P002 IBC08	B2, B4	T3	TP33
3465	ORGANOARSENIC COMPOUND, SOLID, N.O.S.	6.1		III	223 274	5 kg	E1	P002 IBC08 LP02	B3	T1	TP33
3466	METAL CARBONYLS, SOLID, N.O.S.	6.1		I	274	0	E5	P002 IBC07	B1	T6	TP33

UN No.	Name and description	Class or division	Subsidiary hazard	UN packing group	Special provisions	Limited and excepted quantities		Packagings and IBCs		Portable tanks and bulk containers	
								Packing instruction	Special packing provisions	Instructions	Special provisions
(1)	(2)	(3)	(4)	(5)	(6)	(7a)	(7b)	(8)	(9)	(10)	(11)
-	3.1.2	2.0	2.0	2.0.1.3	3.3	3.4	3.5	4.1.4	4.1.4	4.2.5 / 4.3.2	4.2.5
3466	METAL CARBONYLS, SOLID, N.O.S.	6.1		II	274	500 g	E4	P002 IBC08	B2, B4	T3	TP33
3466	METAL CARBONYLS, SOLID, N.O.S.	6.1		III	223 274	5 kg	E1	P002 IBC08 LP02	B3	T1	TP33
3467	ORGANOMETALLIC COMPOUND, SOLID, TOXIC, N.O.S.	6.1		I	274	0	E5	P002 IBC07	B1	T6	TP33
3467	ORGANOMETALLIC COMPOUND, SOLID, TOXIC, N.O.S.	6.1		II	274	500 g	E4	P002 IBC08	B2, B4	T3	TP33
3467	ORGANOMETALLIC COMPOUND, SOLID, TOXIC, N.O.S.	6.1		III	223 274	5 kg	E1	P002 IBC08 LP02	B3	T1	TP33
3468	HYDROGEN IN A METAL HYDRIDE STORAGE SYSTEM or HYDROGEN IN A METAL HYDRIDE STORAGE SYSTEM CONTAINED IN EQUIPMENT or HYDROGEN IN A METAL HYDRIDE STORAGE SYSTEM PACKED WITH EQUIPMENT	2.1			321 356	0	E0	P205			
3469	PAINT, FLAMMABLE, CORROSIVE (including paint, lacquer, enamel, stain, shellac, varnish, polish, liquid filler and liquid lacquer base) or PAINT RELATED MATERIAL, FLAMMABLE, CORROSIVE (including paint thinning or reducing compound)	3	8	I	163 367	0	E0	P001		T11	TP2 TP27
3469	PAINT, FLAMMABLE, CORROSIVE (including paint, lacquer, enamel, stain, shellac, varnish, polish, liquid filler and liquid lacquer base) or PAINT RELATED MATERIAL, FLAMMABLE, CORROSIVE (including paint thinning or reducing compound)	3	8	II	163 367	1 L	E2	P001 IBC02		T7	TP2 TP8 TP28
3469	PAINT, FLAMMABLE, CORROSIVE (including paint, lacquer, enamel, stain, shellac, varnish, polish, liquid filler and liquid lacquer base) or PAINT RELATED MATERIAL, FLAMMABLE, CORROSIVE (including paint thinning or reducing compound)	3	8	III	163 223 367	5 L	E1	P001 IBC03		T4	TP1 TP29
3470	PAINT, CORROSIVE, FLAMMABLE (including paint, lacquer, enamel, stain, shellac, varnish, polish, liquid filler and liquid lacquer base) or PAINT RELATED MATERIAL CORROSIVE, FLAMMABLE (including paint thinning or reducing compound)	8	3	II	163 367	1 L	E2	P001 IBC02		T7	TP2 TP8 TP28
3471	HYDROGENDIFLUORIDES SOLUTION, N.O.S.	8	6.1	II		1 L	E2	P001 IBC02		T7	TP2
3471	HYDROGENDIFLUORIDES SOLUTION, N.O.S.	8	6.1	III	223	5 L	E1	P001 IBC03		T4	TP1

UN No.	Name and description	Class or division	Subsidiary hazard	UN packing group	Special provisions	Limited and excepted quantities		Packagings and IBCs		Portable tanks and bulk containers	
								Packing instruction	Special packing provisions	Instructions	Special provisions
(1)	(2)	(3)	(4)	(5)	(6)	(7a)	(7b)	(8)	(9)	(10)	(11)
-	3.1.2	2.0	2.0	2.0.1.3	3.3	3.4	3.5	4.1.4	4.1.4	4.2.5 / 4.3.2	4.2.5
3472	CROTONIC ACID, LIQUID	8		III		5 L	E1	P001 IBC03 LP01		T4	TP1
3473	FUEL CELL CARTRIDGES or FUEL CELL CARTRIDGES CONTAINED IN EQUIPMENT or FUEL CELL CARTRIDGES PACKED WITH EQUIPMENT, containing flammable liquids	3			328	1 L	E0	P004			
3474	1-HYDROXYBENZOTRIAZOLE MONOHYDRATE	4.1		I		0	E0	P406	PP48		
3475	ETHANOL AND GASOLINE MIXTURE or ETHANOL AND MOTOR SPIRIT MIXTURE or ETHANOL AND PETROL MIXTURE, with more than 10 % ethanol	3		II	333	1 L	E2	P001 IBC02		T4	TP1
3476	FUEL CELL CARTRIDGES or FUEL CELL CARTRIDGES CONTAINED IN EQUIPMENT or FUEL CELL CARTRIDGES PACKED WITH EQUIPMENT, containing water-reactive substances	4.3			328 334	500 ml or 500 g	E0	P004			
3477	FUEL CELL CARTRIDGES or FUEL CELL CARTRIDGES CONTAINED IN EQUIPMENT or FUEL CELL CARTRIDGES PACKED WITH EQUIPMENT, containing corrosive substances	8			328 334	1 l or 1 kg	E0	P004			
3478	FUEL CELL CARTRIDGES or FUEL CELL CARTRIDGES CONTAINED IN EQUIPMENT or FUEL CELL CARTRIDGES PACKED WITH EQUIPMENT, containing liquefied flammable gas	2.1			328 338	120 ml	E0	P004			
3479	FUEL CELL CARTRIDGES or FUEL CELL CARTRIDGES CONTAINED IN EQUIPMENT or FUEL CELL CARTRIDGES PACKED WITH EQUIPMENT, containing hydrogen in metal hydride	2.1			328 339	120 ml	E0	P004			
3480	LITHIUM ION BATTERIES (including lithium ion polymer batteries)	9			188 230 310 348 376 377 384 387	0	E0	P903 P908 P909 P910 P911 LP903 LP904 LP905 LP906			
3481	LITHIUM ION BATTERIES CONTAINED IN EQUIPMENT or LITHIUM ION BATTERIES PACKED WITH EQUIPMENT (including lithium ion polymer batteries)	9			188 230 310 348 360 376 377 384 387 390	0	E0	P903 P908 P909 P910 P911 LP903 LP904 LP905 LP906			
3482	ALKALI METAL DISPERSION, FLAMMABLE or ALKALINE EARTH METAL DISPERSION, FLAMMABLE	4.3	3	I	182 183	0	E0	P402		T13	TP2 TP7 TP42

UN No.	Name and description	Class or division	Subsidiary hazard	UN packing group	Special provisions	Limited and excepted quantities		Packagings and IBCs		Portable tanks and bulk containers	
								Packing instruction	Special packing provisions	Instructions	Special provisions
(1)	(2)	(3)	(4)	(5)	(6)	(7a)	(7b)	(8)	(9)	(10)	(11)
-	3.1.2	2.0	2.0	2.0.1.3	3.3	3.4	3.5	4.1.4	4.1.4	4.2.5 / 4.3.2	4.2.5
3483	MOTOR FUEL ANTI-KNOCK MIXTURE, FLAMMABLE	6.1	3	I		0	E0	P602		T14	TP2 TP13
3484	HYDRAZINE AQUEOUS SOLUTION, FLAMMABLE with more than 37 % hydrazine, by mass	8	3 6.1	I		0	E0	P001		T10	TP2 TP13
3485	CALCIUM HYPOCHLORITE, DRY, CORROSIVE or CALCIUM HYPOCHLORITE MIXTURE, DRY, CORROSIVE with more than 39 % available chlorine (8.8 % available oxygen)	5.1	8	II	314	1 kg	E2	P002 IBC08	PP85 B2, B4, B13		
3486	CALCIUM HYPOCHLORITE MIXTURE, DRY, CORROSIVE with more than 10 % but not more than 39 % available chlorine	5.1	8	III	314	5 kg	E1	P002 IBC08 LP02	PP85 B3, B13 L3		
3487	CALCIUM HYPOCHLORITE, HYDRATED, CORROSIVE or CALCIUM HYPOCHLORITE, HYDRATED MIXTURE, CORROSIVE with not less than 5.5 % but not more than 16 % water	5.1	8	II	314 322	1 kg	E2	P002 IBC08	PP85 B2, B4, B13		
3487	CALCIUM HYPOCHLORITE, HYDRATED, CORROSIVE or CALCIUM HYPOCHLORITE, HYDRATED MIXTURE, CORROSIVE with not less than 5.5 % but not more than 16 % water	5.1	8	III	223 314	5 kg	E1	P002 IBC08	PP85 B4, B13		
3488	TOXIC BY INHALATION LIQUID, FLAMMABLE, CORROSIVE, N.O.S. with an LC_{50} lower than or equal to 200 ml/m^3 and saturated vapour concentration greater than or equal to 500 LC_{50}	6.1	3 8	I	274	0	E0	P601		T22	TP2 TP13
3489	TOXIC BY INHALATION LIQUID, FLAMMABLE, CORROSIVE, N.O.S. with an LC_{50} lower than or equal to 1000 ml/m^3 and saturated vapour concentration greater than or equal to 10 LC_{50}	6.1	3 8	I	274	0	E0	P602		T20	TP2 TP13
3490	TOXIC BY INHALATION LIQUID, WATER-REACTIVE, FLAMMABLE, N.O.S. with an LC_{50} lower than or equal to 200 ml/m^3 and saturated vapour concentration greater than or equal to 500 LC_{50}	6.1	4.3 3	I	274	0	E0	P601		T22	TP2 TP13
3491	TOXIC BY INHALATION LIQUID, WATER-REACTIVE, FLAMMABLE, N.O.S. with an LC_{50} lower than or equal to 1000 ml/m^3 and saturated vapour concentration greater than or equal to 10 LC_{50}	6.1	4.3 3	I	274	0	E0	P602		T20	TP2 TP13
3494	PETROLEUM SOUR CRUDE OIL, FLAMMABLE, TOXIC	3	6.1	I	343	0	E0	P001		T14	TP2 TP13
3494	PETROLEUM SOUR CRUDE OIL, FLAMMABLE, TOXIC	3	6.1	II	343	1 L	E2	P001 IBC02		T7	TP2
3494	PETROLEUM SOUR CRUDE OIL, FLAMMABLE, TOXIC	3	6.1	III	343	5 L	E1	P001 IBC03		T4	TP1
3495	IODINE	8	6.1	III	279	5 kg	E1	P002 IBC08	B3	T1	TP33
3496	BATTERIES, NICKEL-METAL HYDRIDE	9			117	0	E0	N/A			

UN No.	Name and description	Class or division	Subsidiary hazard	UN packing group	Special provisions	Limited and excepted quantities		Packagings and IBCs		Portable tanks and bulk containers	
								Packing instruction	Special packing provisions	Instructions	Special provisions
(1)	(2)	(3)	(4)	(5)	(6)	(7a)	(7b)	(8)	(9)	(10)	(11)
-	3.1.2	2.0	2.0	2.0.1.3	3.3	3.4	3.5	4.1.4	4.1.4	4.2.5 / 4.3.2	4.2.5
3497	KRILL MEAL	4.2		II	300	0	E2	P410 IBC06	B2	T3	TP33
3497	KRILL MEAL	4.2		III	223 300	0	E1	P002 IBC08 LP02	B3	T1	TP33
3498	IODINE MONOCHLORIDE, LIQUID	8		II		1 L	E0	P001 IBC02		T7	TP2
3499	CAPACITOR, ELECTRIC DOUBLE LAYER (with an energy storage capacity greater than 0.3Wh)	9			361	0	E0	P003			
3500	CHEMICAL UNDER PRESSURE, N.O.S.	2.2			274 362	0	E0	P206	PP97	T50	TP4 TP40
3501	CHEMICAL UNDER PRESSURE, FLAMMABLE, N.O.S.	2.1			274 362	0	E0	P206	PP89	T50	TP4 TP40
3502	CHEMICAL UNDER PRESSURE, TOXIC, N.O.S.	2.2	6.1		274 362	0	E0	P206	PP89	T50	TP4 TP40
3503	CHEMICAL UNDER PRESSURE, CORROSIVE, N.O.S.	2.2	8		274 362	0	E0	P206	PP89	T50	TP4 TP40
3504	CHEMICAL UNDER PRESSURE, FLAMMABLE, TOXIC, N.O.S.	2.1	6.1		274 362	0	E0	P206	PP89	T50	TP4 TP40
3505	CHEMICAL UNDER PRESSURE, FLAMMABLE, CORROSIVE, N.O.S.	2.1	8		274 362	0	E0	P206	PP89	T50	TP4 TP40
3506	MERCURY CONTAINED IN MANUFACTURED ARTICLES	8	6.1		366	5 kg	E0	P003	PP90		
3507	URANIUM HEXAFLUORIDE, RADIOACTIVE MATERIAL, EXCEPTED PACKAGE, less than 0.1 kg per package, non-fissile or fissile-excepted	6.1	7 8	I	317 369	0	E0	P603			
3508	CAPACITOR, ASYMMETRIC (with an energy storage capacity greater than 0.3Wh)	9			372	0	E0	P003			
3509	PACKAGINGS, DISCARDED, EMPTY, UNCLEANED	9			374	0	E0				
3510	ADSORBED GAS, FLAMMABLE, N.O.S.	2.1			274	0	E0	P208			
3511	ADSORBED GAS, N.O.S.	2.2			274	0	E0	P208			
3512	ADSORBED GAS, TOXIC, N.O.S.	2.3			274	0	E0	P208			
3513	ADSORBED GAS, OXIDIZING, N.O.S.	2.2	5.1		274	0	E0	P208			
3514	ADSORBED GAS, TOXIC, FLAMMABLE, N.O.S.	2.3	2.1		274	0	E0	P208			
3515	ADSORBED GAS, TOXIC, OXIDIZING, N.O.S.	2.3	5.1		274	0	E0	P208			
3516	ADSORBED GAS, TOXIC, CORROSIVE, N.O.S.	2.3	8		274 379	0	E0	P208			
3517	ADSORBED GAS, TOXIC, FLAMMABLE, CORROSIVE, N.O.S.	2.3	2.1 8		274	0	E0	P208			
3518	ADSORBED GAS, TOXIC, OXIDIZING, CORROSIVE, N.O.S.	2.3	5.1 8		274	0	E0	P208			
3519	BORON TRIFLUORIDE, ADSORBED	2.3	8			0	E0	P208			
3520	CHLORINE, ADSORBED	2.3	5.1 8			0	E0	P208			

UN No.	Name and description	Class or division	Subsidiary hazard	UN packing group	Special provisions	Limited and excepted quantities		Packagings and IBCs		Portable tanks and bulk containers	
								Packing instruction	Special packing provisions	Instructions	Special provisions
(1)	(2)	(3)	(4)	(5)	(6)	(7a)	(7b)	(8)	(9)	(10)	(11)
-	3.1.2	2.0	2.0	2.0.1.3	3.3	3.4	3.5	4.1.4	4.1.4	4.2.5 / 4.3.2	4.2.5
3521	SILICON TETRAFLUORIDE, ADSORBED	2.3	8			0	E0	P208			
3522	ARSINE, ADSORBED	2.3	2.1			0	E0	P208			
3523	GERMANE, ADSORBED	2.3	2.1			0	E0	P208			
3524	PHOSPHORUS PENTAFLUORIDE, ADSORBED	2.3	8			0	E0	P208			
3525	PHOSPHINE, ADSORBED	2.3	2.1			0	E0	P208			
3526	HYDROGEN SELENIDE, ADSORBED	2.3	2.1			0	E0	P208			
3527	POLYESTER RESIN KIT, solid base material	4.1		II	236 340	5 kg	See SP 340 in chapter 3.3	P412			
3527	POLYESTER RESIN KIT, solid base material	4.1		III	236 340	5 kg	See SP 340 in chapter 3.3	P412			
3528	ENGINE, INTERNAL COMBUSTION, FLAMMABLE LIQUID POWERED or ENGINE, FUEL CELL, FLAMMABLE LIQUID POWERED or MACHINERY, INTERNAL COMBUSTION, FLAMMABLE LIQUID POWERED or MACHINERY, FUEL CELL, FLAMMABLE LIQUID POWERED	3			363	0	E0	P005			
3529	ENGINE, INTERNAL COMBUSTION, FLAMMABLE GAS POWERED or ENGINE, FUEL CELL, FLAMMABLE GAS POWERED or MACHINERY, INTERNAL COMBUSTION, FLAMMABLE GAS POWERED or MACHINERY, FUEL CELL, FLAMMABLE GAS POWERED	2.1			356 363	0	E0	P005			
3530	ENGINE, INTERNAL COMBUSTION or MACHINERY, INTERNAL COMBUSTION	9			363	0	E0	P005			
3531	POLYMERIZING SUBSTANCE, SOLID, STABILIZED, N.O.S.	4.1		III	274 386	0	E0	P002 IBC07	PP92 B18	T7	TP4 TP6 TP33
3532	POLYMERIZING SUBSTANCE, LIQUID, STABILIZED, N.O.S.	4.1		III	274 386	0	E0	P001 IBC03	PP93 B19	T7	TP4 TP6
3533	POLYMERIZING SUBSTANCE, SOLID, TEMPERATURE CONTROLLED, N.O.S.	4.1		III	274 386	0	E0	P002 IBC07	PP92 B18	T7	TP4 TP6 TP33
3534	POLYMERIZING SUBSTANCE, LIQUID, TEMPERATURE CONTROLLED, N.O.S.	4.1		III	274 386	0	E0	P001 IBC03	PP93 B19	T7	TP4 TP6
3535	TOXIC SOLID, FLAMMABLE, INORGANIC, N.O.S.	6.1	4.1	I	274	0	E5	P002 IBC99		T6	TP33
3535	TOXIC SOLID, FLAMMABLE, INORGANIC, N.O.S.	6.1	4.1	II	274	500 g	E4	P002 IBC08	B2, B4	T3	TP33
3536	LITHIUM BATTERIES INSTALLED IN CARGO TRANSPORT UNIT lithium ion batteries or lithium metal batteries	9			389	0	E0				
3537	ARTICLES CONTAINING FLAMMABLE GAS, N.O.S.	2.1	See 2.0.5.6		274 310 391	0	E0	P006 LP03			

UN No.	Name and description	Class or division	Subsidiary hazard	UN packing group	Special provisions	Limited and excepted quantities		Packagings and IBCs		Portable tanks and bulk containers	
								Packing instruction	Special packing provisions	Instructions	Special provisions
(1)	(2)	(3)	(4)	(5)	(6)	(7a)	(7b)	(8)	(9)	(10)	(11)
-	3.1.2	2.0	2.0	2.0.1.3	3.3	3.4	3.5	4.1.4	4.1.4	4.2.5 / 4.3.2	4.2.5
3538	ARTICLES CONTAINING NON-FLAMMABLE, NON TOXIC GAS, N.O.S.	2.2	See 2.0.5.6		274 310 391 396	0	E0	P006 LP03			
3539	ARTICLES CONTAINING TOXIC GAS, N.O.S.	2.3	See 2.0.5.6		274 391	0	E0				
3540	ARTICLES CONTAINING FLAMMABLE LIQUID, N.O.S.	3	See 2.0.5.6		274 310 391	0	E0	P006 LP03			
3541	ARTICLES CONTAINING FLAMMABLE SOLID, N.O.S.	4.1	See 2.0.5.6		274 310 391	0	E0	P006 LP03			
3542	ARTICLES CONTAINING A SUBSTANCE LIABLE TO SPONTANEOUS COMBUSTION, N.O.S.	4.2	See 2.0.5.6		274 391	0	E0				
3543	ARTICLES CONTAINING A SUBSTANCE WHICH IN CONTACT WITH WATER EMITS FLAMMABLE GASES, N.O.S.	4.3	See 2.0.5.6		274 391	0	E0				
3544	ARTICLES CONTAINING OXIDIZING SUBSTANCE, N.O.S.	5.1	See 2.0.5.6		274 391	0	E0				
3545	ARTICLES CONTAINING ORGANIC PEROXIDE, N.O.S.	5.2	See 2.0.5.6		274 391	0	E0				
3546	ARTICLES CONTAINING TOXIC SUBSTANCE, N.O.S.	6.1	See 2.0.5.6		274 310 391	0	E0	P006 LP03			
3547	ARTICLES CONTAINING CORROSIVE SUBSTANCE, N.O.S.	8	See 2.0.5.6		274 310 391	0	E0	P006 LP03			
3548	ARTICLES CONTAINING MISCELLANEOUS DANGEROUS GOODS, N.O.S.	9	See 2.0.5.6		274 310 391	0	E0	P006 LP03			
3549	MEDICAL WASTE, CATEGORY A, AFFECTING HUMANS, solid or MEDICAL WASTE, CATEGORY A, AFFECTING ANIMALS only, solid	6.2			395	0	E0	P622 LP622			
3550	COBALT DIHYDROXIDE POWDER, containing not less than 10 % respirable particles	6.1		I		0	E5	P002 IBC07	B1, B20	T6	TP33
3551	SODIUM ION BATTERIES with organic electrolyte	9			188 230 310 348 376 377 384 400 401	0	E0	P903 P908 P909 P910 P911 LP903 LP904 LP905 LP906			
3552	SODIUM ION BATTERIES CONTAINED IN EQUIPMENT or SODIUM ION BATTERIES PACKED WITH EQUIPMENT, with organic electrolyte	9			188 230 310 348 360 376 377 384 400 401	0	E0	P903 P908 P909 P910 P911 LP903 LP904 LP905 LP906			
3553	DISILANE	2.1				0	E0	P200			

UN No.	Name and description	Class or division	Subsidiary hazard	UN packing group	Special provisions	Limited and excepted quantities		Packagings and IBCs		Portable tanks and bulk containers	
								Packing instruction	Special packing provisions	Instructions	Special provisions
(1)	(2)	(3)	(4)	(5)	(6)	(7a)	(7b)	(8)	(9)	(10)	(11)
-	3.1.2	2.0	2.0	2.0.1.3	3.3	3.4	3.5	4.1.4	4.1.4	4.2.5 / 4.3.2	4.2.5
3554	GALLIUM CONTAINED IN MANUFACTURED ARTICLES	8			366	5 kg	E0	P003	PP90		
3555	TRIFLUOROMETHYLTETRAZOLE-SODIUM SALT IN ACETONE, with not less than 68 % acetone, by mass	3		II	28 132	0	E0	P303	PP26		
3556	VEHICLE, LITHIUM ION BATTERY POWERED	9			384 388 405	0	E0	P912			
3557	VEHICLE, LITHIUM METAL BATTERY POWERED	9			384 388 405	0	E0	P912			
3558	VEHICLE, SODIUM ION BATTERY POWERED	9			384 388 404 405	0	E0	P912			
3559	FIRE SUPPRESSANT DISPERSING DEVICES†	9			407	0	E0	P902			
3560	TETRAMETHYLAMMONIUM HYDROXIDE AQUEOUS SOLUTION with not less than 25 % tetramethylammonium hydroxide	6.1	8	I	279 408 409	0	E5	P001		T14	TP2

CHAPTER 3.3

SPECIAL PROVISIONS APPLICABLE TO CERTAIN ARTICLES OR SUBSTANCES

3.3.1 When Column 6 of the Dangerous Goods List of chapter 3.2 indicates that a special provision is relevant to a substance or article, the meaning and requirements of that special provision are as set forth below. Where a special provision includes a requirement for package marking, the provisions of 5.2.1.2 (a) to (d) shall be met. If the required mark is in the form of specific wording indicated in quotation marks, such as "LITHIUM BATTERIES FOR DISPOSAL", the size of the mark shall be at least 12 mm, unless otherwise indicated in the special provision or elsewhere in these Regulations.

16 Samples of new or existing explosive substances or articles may be transported as directed by the competent authorities for purposes including: testing, classification, research and development, quality control, or as a commercial sample. Explosive samples which are not wetted or desensitized shall be limited to 10 kg in small packages as specified by the competent authorities. Explosive samples which are wetted or desensitized shall be limited to 25 kg.

23 Even though this substance has a flammability hazard, it only exhibits such hazard under extreme fire conditions in confined areas.

26 This substance is not permitted for transport in portable tanks, or intermediate bulk containers with a capacity exceeding 450 litres, due to potential initiation of explosion when transported in large volumes.

28 This substance may be transported under the provisions of Class 3 or Division 4.1 only if it is so packed that the percentage of diluent will not fall below that stated, at any time during transport (see 2.3.1.4 and 2.4.2.4). In cases where the diluent is not stated, the substance shall be packed so that the amount of explosive substance does not exceed the stated value.

29 This substance is exempt from labelling, but shall be marked with the appropriate class or division.

32 This substance is not subject to these Regulations when in any other form.

37 This substance is not subject to these Regulations when coated.

38 This substance is not subject to these Regulations when it contains not more than 0.1 % calcium carbide.

39 This substance is not subject to these Regulations when it contains less than 30 % or not less than 90 % silicon.

43 When offered for carriage as pesticides, these substances shall be carried under the relevant pesticide entry and in accordance with the relevant pesticide provisions (see 2.6.2.3 and 2.6.2.4).

45 Antimony sulphides and oxides which contain not more than 0.5 % of arsenic calculated on the total mass are not subject to these Regulations.

47 Ferricyanides and ferrocyanides are not subject to these Regulations.

48 The transport of this substance, when it contains more than 20 % hydrocyanic acid, is prohibited except with special authorization granted by the competent authorities.

59 These substances are not subject to these Regulations when they contain not more than 50 % magnesium.

60 If the concentration is more than 72 %, the transport of this substance is prohibited except with special authorization granted by the competent authorities.

61 The technical name which shall supplement the proper shipping name shall be the ISO common name, other name listed in the WHO Recommended Classification of Pesticides by Hazard and Guidelines to Classification or the name of the active substance (see also 3.1.2.8.1.1).

62 This substance is not subject to these Regulations when it contains not more than 4 % sodium hydroxide.

63 The division of Class 2 and the subsidiary hazards depend on the nature of the contents of the aerosol dispenser. The following provisions shall apply:

   (a) Division 2.1 applies if the contents include 85 % by mass or more flammable components and the chemical heat of combustion is 30 kJ/g or more;

   (b) Division 2.2 applies if the contents contain 1 % by mass or less flammable components and the heat of combustion is less than 20 kJ/g;

   (c) Otherwise the product shall be classified as tested by the tests described in the *Manual of Tests and Criteria*, part III, section 31. Extremely flammable and flammable aerosols shall be classified in Division 2.1; non-flammable in Division 2.2;

   (d) Gases of Division 2.3 shall not be used as a propellant in an aerosol dispenser;

   (e) Where the contents other than the propellant of aerosol dispensers to be ejected are classified as Division 6.1 packing groups II or III or Class 8 packing groups II or III, the aerosol shall have a subsidiary hazard of Division 6.1 or Class 8;

   (f) Aerosols with contents meeting the criteria for packing group I for toxicity or corrosivity shall be prohibited from transport;

   (g) Subsidiary hazard labels may be required for air transport.

   Flammable components are flammable liquids, flammable solids or flammable gases and gas mixtures as defined in notes 1 to 3 of sub-section 31.1.3 of part III of the *Manual of Tests and Criteria*. This designation does not cover pyrophoric, self-heating or water-reactive substances. The chemical heat of combustion shall be determined by one of the following methods ASTM D 240, ISO/FDIS 13943: 1999 (E/F) 86.1 to 86.3 or NFPA 30B.

65 Hydrogen peroxide aqueous solutions with less than 8 % hydrogen peroxide are not subject to these Regulations.

66 Cinnabar is not subject to these Regulations.

103 Ammonium nitrites and mixtures of an inorganic nitrite with an ammonium salt are prohibited.

105 Nitrocellulose meeting the descriptions of UN Nos. 2556 or 2557 may be classified in Division 4.1.

106 Subject to these Regulations only when transported by air.

113 The carriage of chemically unstable mixtures is prohibited.

117   Subject to these Regulations only when transported by sea.

119   Refrigerating machines include machines or other appliances which have been designed for the specific purpose of keeping food or other items at a low temperature in an internal compartment, and air conditioning units. Refrigerating machines and refrigerating machine components are not subject to these Regulations if they contain less than 12 kg of gas in Division 2.2 or less than 12 litres ammonia solution (UN 2672).

122   The subsidiary hazards, control and emergency temperatures if any, and the generic entry number for each of the currently assigned organic peroxide formulations are given in 2.5.3.2.4, 4.1.4.2 packing instruction IBC520 and 4.2.5.2.6 portable tank instruction T23.

123   Subject to these Regulations only when transported by air or by sea.

127   Other inert material or inert material mixture may be used at the discretion of the competent authority, provided this inert material has identical phlegmatizing properties.

131   The phlegmatized substance shall be significantly less sensitive than dry PETN.

132   During the course of transport, this substance shall be protected from direct sunshine and stored (or kept) in a cool and well-ventilated place, away from all sources of heat.

133   If over-confined in packagings, this substance may exhibit explosive behaviour. Packagings authorized under packing instruction P409 are intended to prevent over-confinement. When a packaging other than those prescribed under packing instruction P409 is authorized by the competent authority of the country of origin in accordance with 4.1.3.7, the package shall bear an "EXPLOSIVE" subsidiary hazard label (Model No 1, see 5.2.2.2.2) unless the competent authority of the country of origin has permitted this label to be dispensed with for the specific packaging employed because test data have proved that the substance in this packaging does not exhibit explosive behaviour (see 5.4.1.5.5.1). The provisions of 7.1.3.1 shall also be then considered.

135   The dihydrated sodium salt of dichloroisocyanuric acid does not meet the criteria for inclusion in Division 5.1 and is not subject to these Regulations unless meeting the criteria for inclusion in another Class or Division.

138   p-Bromobenzyl cyanide is not subject to these Regulations.

141   Products which have undergone sufficient heat treatment so that they present no hazard during transport are not subject to these Regulations.

142   Solvent extracted soya bean meal containing not more than 1.5 % oil and 11 % moisture, which is substantially free of flammable solvent, is not subject to these Regulations.

144   An aqueous solution containing not more than 24 % alcohol by volume is not subject to these Regulations.

145   Other than for air transport, alcoholic beverages of packing group III, when carried in receptacles of 250 litres or less, are not subject to these Regulations.

146   Other than for air and sea transport, alcoholic beverages of packing group II, when carried in receptacles of 5 litres or less, are not subject to these Regulations.

152   The classification of this substance will vary with particle size and packaging, but borderlines have not been experimentally determined. Appropriate classifications shall be made as required by 2.1.3.

153 This entry applies only if it is demonstrated, on the basis of tests, that the substances when in contact with water are not combustible nor show a tendency to auto-ignition and that the mixture of gases evolved is not flammable.

163 A substance specifically listed by name in the Dangerous Goods List of chapter 3.2 shall not be transported under this entry. Materials transported under this entry may contain 20 % or less nitrocellulose provided the nitrocellulose contains not more than 12.6 % nitrogen (by dry mass).

168 Asbestos which is immersed or fixed in a natural or artificial binder (such as cement, plastics, asphalt, resins or mineral ore) in such a way that no escape of hazardous quantities of respirable asbestos fibres can occur during transport is not subject to these Regulations. Manufactured articles containing asbestos and not meeting this provision are nevertheless not subject to these Regulations when packed so that no escape of hazardous quantities of respirable asbestos fibres can occur during transport.

169 Phthalic anhydride in the solid state and tetrahydrophthalic anhydrides, with not more than 0.05 % maleic anhydride, are not subject to these Regulations. Phthalic anhydride molten at a temperature above its flash point, with not more than 0.05 % maleic anhydride, shall be classified under UN 3256.

172 Where a radioactive material has (a) subsidiary hazard(s):

(a) The substance shall be allocated to Packing Group I, II or III, if appropriate, by application of the packing group criteria provided in part 2 corresponding to the nature of the predominant subsidiary hazard;

(b) Packages shall be labelled with subsidiary hazard labels corresponding to each subsidiary hazard exhibited by the material; corresponding placards shall be affixed to cargo transport units in accordance with the relevant provisions of 5.3.1;

(c) For the purposes of documentation and package marking, the proper shipping name shall be supplemented with the name of the constituents which most predominantly contribute to this (these) subsidiary hazard(s) and which shall be enclosed in parenthesis;

(d) The dangerous goods transport document shall indicate the class or division of the subsidiary hazard and, where assigned the packing group as required by 5.4.1.4.1(d) and (e).

For packing, see also 4.1.9.1.5.

177 Barium sulphate is not subject to these Regulations.

178 This designation shall be used only when no other appropriate designation exists in the Dangerous Goods List of chapter 3.2, and only with the approval of the competent authority of the country of origin.

179 *Deleted.*

181 Packages containing this type of substance shall bear the "EXPLOSIVE" subsidiary hazard label (Model No 1, see 5.2.2.2.2) unless the competent authority of the country of origin has permitted this label to be dispensed with for the specific packaging employed because test data have proved that the substance in this packaging does not exhibit explosive behaviour (see 5.4.1.5.5.1). The provisions of 7.1.3.1 shall also be considered.

182 The group of alkali metals includes lithium, sodium, potassium, rubidium and caesium.

183 The group of alkaline earth metals includes magnesium, calcium, strontium and barium.

186 *Deleted.*

188 Cells and batteries offered for transport are not subject to other provisions of these Regulations if they meet the following:

    (a)   For a lithium metal or lithium alloy cell, the lithium content is not more than 1 g, and for a lithium ion or sodium ion cell, the watt-hour rating is not more than 20 Wh;

    (b)   For a lithium metal or lithium alloy battery the aggregate lithium content is not more than 2 g, and for a lithium ion or sodium ion battery, the watt-hour rating is not more than 100 Wh. Lithium ion and sodium ion batteries subject to this provision shall be marked with the watt-hour rating on the outside case, except lithium ion batteries manufactured before 1 January 2009;

    (c)   Each lithium cell or battery meets the provisions of 2.9.4 (a), (e), (f) if applicable and (g) or for sodium ion cells or batteries, the provisions of 2.9.5 (a), (e) and (f) shall apply;

    (d)   Cells and batteries, except when installed in equipment, shall be packed in inner packagings that completely enclose the cell or battery. Cells and batteries shall be protected so as to prevent short circuits. This includes protection against contact with electrically conductive material within the same packaging that could lead to a short circuit. The inner packagings shall be packed in strong outer packagings which conform to the provisions of 4.1.1.1, 4.1.1.2, and 4.1.1.5;

    (e)   Cells and batteries when installed in equipment shall be protected from damage and short circuit, and the equipment shall be equipped with an effective means of preventing accidental activation. This requirement does not apply to devices which are intentionally active in transport (radio frequency identification (RFID) transmitters, watches, sensors, etc.) and which are not capable of generating a dangerous evolution of heat. When batteries are installed in equipment, the equipment shall be packed in strong outer packagings constructed of suitable material of adequate strength and design in relation to the packaging's capacity and its intended use unless the battery is afforded equivalent protection by the equipment in which it is contained;

    (f)   Each package shall be marked with the appropriate lithium or sodium battery mark, as illustrated at 5.2.1.9;

    NOTE: *Packages containing lithium batteries packed in conformity with the provisions of part 4, chapter 11, packing instructions 965 or 968, section IB of the ICAO Technical Instructions for the Safe Transport of Dangerous Goods by Air that bear the mark as shown in 5.2.1.9 (lithium battery mark) and the label shown in 5.2.2.2.2, Model No.9A shall be deemed to meet the provisions of this special provision.*

    This requirement does not apply to:

        (i)   packages containing only button cell batteries installed in equipment (including circuit boards); and

        (ii)   packages containing no more than four cells or two batteries installed in equipment, where there are not more than two packages in the consignment.

    When packages are placed in an overpack, the lithium or sodium battery mark shall either be clearly visible or be reproduced on the outside of the overpack and the overpack shall be marked with the word "OVERPACK". The lettering of the "OVERPACK" mark shall be at least 12 mm high.

(g) Except when cells or batteries are installed in equipment, each package shall be capable of withstanding a 1.2 m drop test in any orientation without damage to cells or batteries contained therein, without shifting of the contents so as to allow battery to battery (or cell to cell) contact and without release of contents; and

(h) Except when cells or batteries are installed in or packed with equipment, packages shall not exceed 30 kg gross mass.

As used above and elsewhere in these Regulations, "lithium content" means the mass of lithium in the anode of a lithium metal or lithium alloy cell. As used in this special provision "equipment" means apparatus for which the cells or batteries will provide electrical power for its operation.

Separate entries exist for lithium metal batteries and lithium ion batteries to facilitate the transport of these batteries for specific modes of transport and to enable the application of different emergency response actions.

A single cell battery as defined in part III, sub-section 38.3.2.3 of the *Manual of Tests and Criteria* is considered a "cell" and shall be transported according to the requirements for "cells" for the purpose of this special provision.

190 Aerosol dispensers shall be provided with protection against inadvertent discharge. Aerosols with a capacity not exceeding 50 ml containing only non-toxic constituents are not subject to these Regulations.

191 Receptacles, small, containing gas are not fitted with a release device. Receptacles with a capacity not exceeding 50 ml containing only non-toxic constituents are not subject to these Regulations.

193 This entry may only be used for ammonium nitrate based compound fertilizers. They shall be classified in accordance with the procedure as set out in the *Manual of Tests and Criteria*, part III, section 39. Fertilizers meeting the criteria for this UN number are only subject to these Regulations when transported by air or sea.

194 The control and emergency temperatures, if any, and the generic entry number for each of the currently assigned self-reactive substances are given in 2.4.2.3.2.3.

195 For certain organic peroxides types B or C, a smaller packaging than that allowed by packing methods OP5 or OP6 respectively has to be used (see 4.1.7 and 2.5.3.2.4).

196 Formulations which in laboratory testing neither detonate in the cavitated state nor deflagrate, which show no effect when heated under confinement and which exhibit no explosive power may be transported under this entry. The formulation must also be thermally stable (i.e. the SADT is 60 °C or higher for a 50 kg package). Formulations not meeting these criteria shall be transported under the provisions of Division 5.2; see 2.5.3.2.4.

198 Nitrocellulose solutions containing not more than 20 % nitrocellulose may be transported as paint, perfumery products or printing ink, as applicable. See UN Nos. 1210, 1263, 1266, 3066, 3469 and 3470.

199 Lead compounds which, when mixed in a ratio of 1:1000 with 0.07M hydrochloric acid and stirred for one hour at a temperature of 23 °C ± 2 °C, exhibit a solubility of 5 % or less (see ISO 3711:1990 *"Lead chromate pigments and lead chromate-molybdate pigments – Specifications and methods of test"*) are considered insoluble and are not subject to these Regulations unless they meet the criteria for inclusion in another hazard class or division.

201 Lighters and lighter refills shall comply with the provisions of the country in which they were filled. They shall be provided with protection against inadvertent discharge. The

liquid portion of the gas shall not exceed 85 % of the capacity of the receptacle at 15 °C. The receptacles, including the closures, shall be capable of withstanding an internal pressure of twice the pressure of the liquefied petroleum gas at 55 °C. The valve mechanisms and ignition devices shall be securely sealed, taped or otherwise fastened or designed to prevent operation or leakage of the contents during transport. Lighters shall not contain more than 10 g of liquefied petroleum gas. Lighter refills shall not contain more than 65 g of liquefied petroleum gas.

203 This entry shall not be used for polychlorinated biphenyls, UN 2315.

204 Articles containing smoke-producing substance(s) corrosive according to the criteria for Class 8 shall be labelled with a "CORROSIVE" subsidiary hazard label (Model No 8, see 5.2.2.2.2).

Articles containing smoke-producing substance(s) toxic by inhalation according to the criteria for Division 6.1 shall be labelled with a "TOXIC" subsidiary hazard label (Model No 6.1, see 5.2.2.2.2).

205 This entry shall not be used for UN 3155 PENTACHLOROPHENOL.

206 This entry is not intended to include ammonium permanganate, the transport of which is prohibited except with special authorization granted by the competent authorities.

207 Plastics moulding compounds may be made from polystyrene, poly (methyl methacrylate) or other polymeric material.

208 The commercial grade of calcium nitrate fertilizer, when consisting mainly of a double salt (calcium nitrate and ammonium nitrate) containing not more than 10 % ammonium nitrate and at least 12 % water of crystallization, is not subject to these Regulations.

209 The gas shall be at a pressure corresponding to ambient atmospheric pressure at the time the containment system is closed and this shall not exceed 105 kPa absolute.

210 Toxins from plant, animal or bacterial sources which contain infectious substances, or toxins that are contained in infectious substances, shall be classified in Division 6.2.

215 This entry only applies to the technically pure substance or to formulations derived from it having an SADT higher than 75 °C and therefore does not apply to formulations which are self-reactive substances. (For self-reactive substances, see 2.4.2.3.2.3). Homogeneous mixtures containing not more than 35 % by mass of azodicarbonamide and at least 65 % of inert substance are not subject to these Regulations unless criteria of other classes or divisions are met.

216 Mixtures of solids which are not subject to these Regulations and flammable liquids may be transported under this entry without first applying the classification criteria of Division 4.1, provided there is no free liquid visible at the time the substance is loaded or at the time the packaging or cargo transport unit is closed. Each cargo transport unit shall be leakproof when used as a bulk packaging. Sealed packets and articles containing less than 10 ml of a packing group II or III flammable liquid absorbed into a solid material are not subject to these Regulations provided there is no free liquid in the packet or article.

217 Mixtures of solids which are not subject to these Regulations and toxic liquids may be transported under this entry without first applying the classification criteria of Division 6.1, provided there is no free liquid visible at the time the substance is loaded or at the time the packaging or cargo transport unit is closed. Each cargo transport unit shall be leakproof when used as a bulk packaging. This entry shall not be used for solids containing a packing group I liquid.

218 Mixtures of solids which are not subject to these Regulations and corrosive liquids may be transported under this entry without first applying the classification criteria of

Class 8, provided there is no free liquid visible at the time the substance is loaded or at the time the packaging or cargo transport unit is closed. Each cargo transport unit shall be leakproof when used as a bulk packaging.

219 Genetically modified microorganisms (GMMOs) and genetically modified organisms (GMOs) packed and marked in accordance with packing instruction P904 are not subject to any other requirements in these Regulations.

If GMMOs or GMOs meet the definition in chapter 2.6 of a toxic substance or an infectious substance and the criteria for inclusion in Division 6.1 or 6.2 the requirements in these Regulations for transporting toxic substances or infectious substances apply.

220 The technical name of the flammable liquid component only of this solution or mixture shall be shown in parentheses immediately following the proper shipping name.

221 Substances included under this entry shall not be of packing group I.

223 If the chemical or physical properties of a substance covered by this description are such that when tested it does not meet the established defining criteria for the class or division listed in Column 3 of the Dangerous Goods List of chapter 3.2, or any other class or division, it is not subject to these Regulations.

224 Unless it can be demonstrated by testing that the sensitivity of the substance in its frozen state is no greater than in its liquid state, the substance shall remain liquid during normal transport conditions. It shall not freeze at temperatures above -15 °C.

225 Fire extinguishers under this entry may include installed actuating cartridges (cartridges, power device of Division 1.4C or 1.4S), without changing the classification of Division 2.2 provided the total quantity of deflagrating (propellant) explosives does not exceed 3.2 g per extinguishing unit. Fire extinguishers shall be manufactured, tested, approved and labelled according to the provisions applied in the country of manufacture.

NOTE: *"Provisions applied in the country of manufacture" means the provisions applicable in the country of manufacture or those applicable in the country of use.*

Fire extinguishers under this entry include:

(a) Portable fire extinguishers for manual handling and operation;

NOTE: *This entry applies to portable fire extinguishers, even if some components that are necessary for their proper functioning (e.g. hoses and nozzles) are temporarily detached, as long as the safety of the pressurized extinguishing agent containers is not compromised and the fire extinguishers continue to be identified as a portable fire extinguisher.*

(b) Fire extinguishers for installation in aircraft;

(c) Fire extinguishers mounted on wheels for manual handling;

(d) Fire extinguishing equipment or machinery mounted on wheels or wheeled platforms or units transported similar to (small) trailers, and

(e) Fire extinguishers composed of a non-rollable pressure drum and equipment, and handled e.g. by fork lift or crane when loaded or unloaded.

NOTE: *Pressure receptacles which contain gases for use in the above-mentioned extinguishers or for use in stationary fire-fighting installations shall meet the requirements in chapter 6.2 and all requirements applicable to the relevant dangerous goods when these pressure receptacles are transported separately.*

226 Formulations of these substances containing not less than 30 % non-volatile, non-flammable phlegmatizer are not subject to these Regulations.

227 When phlegmatized with water and inorganic inert material the content of urea nitrate may not exceed 75 % by mass and the mixture shall not be capable of being detonated by the Series 1, type (a), test in the *Manual of Tests and Criteria*, part I.

228 Mixtures not meeting the criteria for flammable gases (Division 2.1) shall be transported under UN 3163.

230 Lithium cells and batteries may be transported under this entry if they meet the provisions of 2.9.4. Sodium ion cells and batteries may be transported under this entry if they meet the provisions of 2.9.5.

232 This designation shall only be used when the substance does not meet the criteria of any other class. Transport in cargo transport units other than in multimodal tanks shall be in accordance with standards specified by the competent authorities of the country of origin.

235 This entry applies to articles which contain Class 1 explosive substances and which may also contain dangerous goods of other classes. These articles are used to enhance safety in vehicles, vessels or aircraft – e.g. air bag inflators, air bag modules, seat-belt pretensioners, and pyromechanical devices.

236 Polyester resin kits consist of two components: a base material (either Class 3 or Division 4.1, packing group II or III) and an activator (organic peroxide). The organic peroxide shall be type D, E, or F, not requiring temperature control. The packing group shall be II or III, according to the criteria of either Class 3 or Division 4.1, as appropriate, applied to the base material. The quantity limit shown in column 7a of the Dangerous Goods List of chapter 3.2 applies to the base material.

237 The membrane filters, including paper separators, coating or backing materials, etc., that are present in transport, shall not be liable to propagate a detonation as tested by one of the tests described in the *Manual of Tests and Criteria*, part I, test series 1(a).

In addition, the competent authority may determine, on the basis of the results of suitable burning rate tests taking account of the standard tests in the *Manual of Tests and Criteria*, part III, sub-section 33.2, that nitrocellulose membrane filters in the form in which they are to be transported are not subject to the provisions of these Regulations applicable to flammable solids in Division 4.1.

238 (a) Batteries can be considered as non-spillable provided that they are capable of withstanding the vibration and pressure differential tests given below, without leakage of battery fluid.

Vibration test: The battery is rigidly clamped to the platform of a vibration machine and a simple harmonic motion having an amplitude of 0.8 mm (1.6 mm maximum total excursion) is applied. The frequency is varied at the rate of 1 Hz/min between the limits of 10 Hz and 55 Hz. The entire range of frequencies and return is traversed in 95 ± 5 minutes for each mounting position (direction of vibration) of the battery. The battery is tested in three mutually perpendicular positions (to include testing with fill openings and vents, if any, in an inverted position) for equal time periods.

Pressure differential test: Following the vibration test, the battery is stored for six hours at 24 °C ± 4 °C while subjected to a pressure differential of at least 88 kPa. The battery is tested in three mutually perpendicular positions (to include testing with fill openings and vents, if any, in an inverted position) for at least six hours in each position.

> *NOTE: Non-spillable type batteries which are an integral part of and necessary for the operation of mechanical or electronic equipment, shall be securely fastened in the battery holder on the equipment and protected in such a manner as to prevent damage and short circuits.*

    (b)   Non-spillable batteries are not subject to these Regulations if, at a temperature of 55 °C, the electrolyte will not flow from a ruptured or cracked case and there is no free liquid to flow and if, when packaged for transport, the terminals are protected from short circuit.

239   Batteries or cells shall not contain dangerous goods other than sodium, sulphur or sodium compounds (e.g. sodium polysulphides and sodium tetrachloroaluminate). Batteries or cells shall not be offered for transport at a temperature such that liquid elemental sodium is present in the battery or cell unless approved and under the conditions established by the competent authority.

Cells shall consist of hermetically sealed metal casings which fully enclose the dangerous goods and which are so constructed and closed as to prevent the release of the dangerous goods under normal conditions of transport.

Batteries shall consist of cells secured within and fully enclosed by a metal casing so constructed and closed as to prevent the release of the dangerous goods under normal conditions of transport.

240   *Deleted.*

241   The formulation shall be prepared so that it remains homogeneous and does not separate during transport. Formulations with low nitrocellulose contents and not showing dangerous properties when tested for their liability to detonate, deflagrate or explode when heated under defined confinement by tests of test series 1 (a), 2 (b) and 2 (c) respectively in the *Manual of Tests and Criteria*, part I and not being a flammable solid when tested in accordance with test N.1 in the *Manual of Tests and Criteria*, part III, sub-section 33.2.4 (chips, if necessary, crushed and sieved to a particle size of less than 1.25 mm) are not subject to these Regulations.

242   Sulphur is not subject to these Regulations when it has been formed to a specific shape (e.g. prills, granules, pellets, pastilles or flakes).

243   Gasoline, motor spirit and petrol for use in spark-ignition engines (e.g. in automobiles, stationary engines and other engines) shall be assigned to this entry regardless of variations in volatility.

244   This entry includes e.g. aluminium dross, aluminium skimmings, spent cathodes, spent potliner, and aluminium salt slags.

Before loading, these by-products shall be cooled to ambient temperature, unless they have been calcined to remove moisture. Cargo transport units containing bulk loads shall be adequately ventilated and protected against ingress of water throughout the journey.

Notwithstanding the provisions of 4.3.2.2, sheeted bulk containers (BK1) may be used for inland transport.

246   This substance shall be packed in accordance with packing method OP6 (see applicable packing instruction). During transport, it shall be protected from direct sunshine and stored (or kept) in a cool and well-ventilated place, away from all sources of heat.

247   Alcoholic beverages containing more than 24 % alcohol but not more than 70 % by volume, when transported as part of the manufacturing process, may be transported in wooden barrels with a capacity of more than 250 litres and not more than 500 litres meeting the general requirements of 4.1.1, as appropriate, on the following conditions:

(a) The wooden barrels shall be checked and tightened before filling;

(b) Sufficient ullage (not less than 3 %) shall be left to allow for the expansion of the liquid;

(c) The wooden barrels shall be transported with the bungholes pointing upwards;

(d) The wooden barrels shall be transported in containers meeting the requirements of the International Convention for Safe Containers (CSC), 1972, as amended. Each wooden barrel shall be secured in custom-made cradles and be wedged by appropriate means to prevent it from being displaced in any way during transport.

249 Ferrocerium, stabilized against corrosion, with a minimum iron content of 10 % is not subject to these Regulations.

250 This entry may only be used for samples of chemicals taken for analysis in connection with the implementation of the Convention on the Prohibition of the Development, Production, Stockpiling and Use of Chemical Weapons and on their Destruction. The transport of substances under this entry shall be in accordance with the chain of custody and security procedures specified by the Organisation for the Prohibition of Chemical Weapons.

The chemical sample may only be transported providing prior approval has been granted by the competent authority or the Director General of the Organisation for the Prohibition of Chemical Weapons and providing the sample complies with the following provisions:

(a) It shall be packed according to Packing Instruction 623 in the International Civil Aviation Organization's Technical Instructions for the Safe Transport of Dangerous Goods by Air; and

(b) During transport it shall be accompanied by a copy of the document of approval for transport, showing the quantity limitations and the packing provisions.

251 The entry CHEMICAL KIT or FIRST AID KIT is intended to apply to boxes, cases etc. containing small quantities of various dangerous goods which are used for example for medical, analytical or testing or repair purposes.

Such kits shall only contain dangerous goods that are permitted as:

(a) Excepted quantities not exceeding the quantity indicated by the code in column (7b) of the Dangerous Goods List of chapter 3.2, provided that the net quantity per inner packaging and net quantity per package are as prescribed in 3.5.1.2 and 3.5.1.3; or;

(b) Limited quantities as indicated in column (7a) of the Dangerous Goods List of chapter 3.2, provided that the net quantity per inner packaging does not exceed 250 ml or 250 g.

Components shall not react dangerously (see 4.1.1.6). The total quantity of dangerous goods in any one kit shall not exceed either 1 l or 1 kg.

For the purposes of completion of the dangerous goods transport document as set out in 5.4.1.4.1, the packing group shown on the document shall be the most stringent packing group assigned to any individual substance in the kit. Where the kit contains only dangerous goods to which no packing group is assigned, no packing group need be indicated on the dangerous goods transport document.

Kits which are carried on board vehicles for first-aid or operating purposes are not subject to these Regulations.

Chemical kits and first aid kits containing dangerous goods in inner packagings which do not exceed the quantity limits for limited quantities applicable to individual substances as specified in Column 7a of the Dangerous Goods List of chapter 3.2 may be transported in accordance with chapter 3.4.

252 (1) Ammonium nitrate hot concentrated solutions can be transported under this entry provided:

    (a) The solution contains not more than 93 % ammonium nitrate;

    (b) The solution contains at least 7 % water;

    (c) The solution contains not more than 0.2 % combustible material;

    (d) The solution contains no chlorine compounds in quantities such that the chloride ion level exceeds 0.02 %;

    (e) The pH of an aqueous solution of 10 % of the substance is between 5 and 7, measured at 25 °C; and

    (f) The maximum allowable transport temperature of the solution is 140 °C.

(2) Additionally, ammonium nitrate hot concentrate solutions are not subject to these Regulations provided:

    (a) The solution contains not more than 80 % ammonium nitrate;

    (b) The solution contains not more than 0.2 % combustible material;

    (c) The ammonium nitrate remains in solution under all conditions of transport; and

    (d) The solution does not meet the criteria of any other class or division.

266 This substance, when containing less alcohol, water or phlegmatizer than specified, shall not be transported unless specifically authorized by the competent authority.

267 Any explosives, blasting, type C containing chlorates shall be segregated from explosives containing ammonium nitrate or other ammonium salts.

270 Aqueous solutions of Division 5.1 inorganic solid nitrate substances are considered as not meeting the criteria of Division 5.1 if the concentration of the substances in solution at the minimum temperature encountered in transport is not greater than 80 % of the saturation limit.

271 Lactose or glucose or similar materials, may be used as a phlegmatizer provided that the substance contains not less than 90 %, by mass, of phlegmatizer. The competent authority may authorize these mixtures to be classified in Division 4.1 on the basis of a test series 6(c) of section 16 of part I of the *Manual of Tests and Criteria* on at least three packages as prepared for transport. Mixtures containing at least 98 %, by mass, of phlegmatizer are not subject to these Regulations. Packages containing mixtures with not less than 90 %, by mass, of phlegmatizer need not bear a TOXIC subsidiary hazard label.

272 This substance shall not be transported under the provisions of Division 4.1 unless specifically authorized by the competent authority (see UN Nos. 0143 or 0150 as appropriate).

273 Maneb and maneb preparations stabilized against self-heating need not be classified in Division 4.2 when it can be demonstrated by testing that a cubic volume of 1 m^3 of substance does not self-ignite and that the temperature at the centre of the sample does

not exceed 200 °C, when the sample is maintained at a temperature of not less than 75 °C ± 2 °C for a period of 24 hours.

274 For the purposes of documentation and package marking, the proper shipping name shall be supplemented with the technical name (see 3.1.2.8).

For UN Nos. 3077 and 3082 only, the technical name may be a name shown in capital letters in column 2 of the Dangerous Goods List, provided that this name does not include "N.O.S." and that special provision 274 is not assigned. The name which most appropriately describes the substance or mixture shall be used, e.g.:

UN 3082, ENVIRONMENTALLY HAZARDOUS SUBSTANCE, LIQUID, N.O.S. (PAINT)

UN 3082, ENVIRONMENTALLY HAZARDOUS SUBSTANCE, LIQUID, N.O.S. (PERFUMERY PRODUCTS)

276 This includes any substance which is not covered by any of the other classes but which has narcotic, noxious or other properties such that, in the event of spillage or leakage on an aircraft, annoyance or discomfort could be caused to crew members so as to prevent the correct performance of assigned duties.

277 For aerosols or receptacles containing toxic substances the limited quantity value is 120 ml. For all other aerosols or receptacles the limited quantity value is 1 000 ml.

278 These substances shall not be classified and transported unless authorized by the competent authority on the basis of results from Series 2 tests and a Series 6(c) test of part I of the *Manual of Tests and Criteria* on packages as prepared for transport (see 2.1.3.1). The competent authority shall assign the packing group on the basis of the chapter 2.3 criteria and the package type used for the Series 6(c) test.

279 The substance is assigned to this classification or packing group based on human experience rather than the strict application of classification criteria set out in these regulations.

280 This entry applies to safety devices for vehicles, vessels or aircraft, e.g. air bag inflators, air bag modules, seat-belt pretensioners, and pyromechanical devices, which contain dangerous goods of Class 1 or of other classes, when transported as component parts and if these articles as presented for transport have been tested in accordance with test series 6(c) of part 1 of the *Manual of Tests and Criteria*, with no explosion of the device, no fragmentation of device casing or pressure receptacle, and no projection hazard nor thermal effect which would significantly hinder fire-fighting or emergency response efforts in the immediate vicinity. This entry does not apply to life saving appliances described in special provision 296 (UN Nos. 2990 and 3072) or to fire suppressant dispersing devices described in special provision 407 (UN Nos. 0514 and 3559).

281 The transport by sea of hay, straw or bhusa, wet, damp or contaminated with oil shall be prohibited. Transport by other modes is also prohibited except with special authorization by the competent authorities.

Hay, straw and bhusa, when not wet, damp or contaminated with oil, are subject to these Regulations only when transported by sea.

283 Articles, containing gas, intended to function as shock absorbers, including impact energy-absorbing devices, or pneumatic springs are not subject to these Regulations provided:

(a) Each article has a gas space capacity not exceeding 1.6 litres and a charge pressure not exceeding 280 bar where the product of the capacity (litres) and charge pressure (bars) does not exceed 80 (i.e. 0.5 litre gas space and 160 bar charge pressure, 1 litre gas space and 80 bar charge pressure, 1.6 litre gas space and 50 bar charge pressure, 0.28 litre gas space and 280 bar charge pressure);

 (b) Each article has a minimum burst pressure of 4 times the charge pressure at 20°C for products not exceeding 0.5 litre gas space capacity and 5 times charge pressure for products greater than 0.5 litre gas space capacity;

 (c) Each article is manufactured from material which will not fragment upon rupture;

 (d) Each article is manufactured in accordance with a quality assurance standard acceptable to the competent authority; and

 (e) The design type has been subjected to a fire test demonstrating that pressure in the article is relieved by means of a fire degradable seal or other pressure relief device, such that the article will not fragment and that the article does not rocket.

284 An oxygen generator, chemical, containing oxidizing substances shall meet the following conditions:

 (a) The generator when containing an explosive actuating device shall only be transported under this entry when excluded from Class 1 in accordance with 2.1.1.1 (b) of these Regulations;

 (b) The generator, without its packaging, shall be capable of withstanding a 1.8 m drop test onto a rigid, non-resilient, flat and horizontal surface, in the position most likely to cause damage, without loss of its contents and without actuation; and

 (c) When a generator is equipped with an actuating device, it shall have at least two positive means of preventing unintentional actuation.

286 Nitrocellulose membrane filters covered by this entry, each with a mass not exceeding 0.5 g, are not subject to these Regulations when contained individually in an article or a sealed packet.

288 These substances shall not be classified and transported unless authorized by the competent authority on the basis of results from Series 2 tests and a Series 6(c) test of the *Manual of Tests and Criteria* on packages as prepared for transport (see 2.1.3.1).

289 Safety devices, electrically initiated and safety devices, pyrotechnic installed in vehicles, vessels or aircraft or in completed components such as steering columns, door panels, seats, etc. are not subject to these Regulations.

290 When this radioactive material meets the definitions and criteria of other classes or divisions as defined in part 2, it shall be classified in accordance with the following:

 (a) Where the substance meets the criteria for dangerous goods in excepted quantities as set out in chapter 3.5, the packagings shall be in accordance with 3.5.2 and meet the testing requirements of 3.5.3. All other requirements applicable to radioactive material, excepted packages as set out in 1.5.1.5 shall apply without reference to the other class or division;

 (b) Where the quantity exceeds the limits specified in 3.5.1.2 the substance shall be classified in accordance with the predominant subsidiary hazard. The dangerous goods transport document shall describe the substance with the UN number and proper shipping name applicable to the other class supplemented with the name applicable to the radioactive excepted package according to Column 2 in the Dangerous Goods List of chapter 3.2, and the substance shall be transported in accordance with the provisions applicable to that UN number. An example of the information shown on the dangerous goods transport document is:

UN 1993, Flammable liquid, n.o.s. (ethanol and toluene mixture), Radioactive material, excepted package – limited quantity of material, Class 3, PG II.

In addition, the requirements of 2.7.2.4.1 shall apply.

(c) The provisions of chapter 3.4 for the transport of dangerous goods packed in limited quantities shall not apply to substances classified in accordance with sub-paragraph (b);

(d) When the substance meets a special provision that exempts this substance from all dangerous goods provisions of the other classes it shall be classified in accordance with the applicable UN number of class 7 and all requirements specified in 1.5.1.5 shall apply.

291 Flammable liquefied gases shall be contained within refrigerating machine components. These components shall be designed and tested to at least three times the working pressure of the machinery. The refrigerating machines shall be designed and constructed to contain the liquefied gas and preclude the risk of bursting or cracking of the pressure retaining components during normal conditions of transport. Refrigerating machines and refrigerating-machine components are considered not subject to these Regulations if they contain less than 12 kg of gas.

292 *Deleted.*

293 The following definitions apply to matches:

(a) Fusee matches are matches the heads of which are prepared with a friction-sensitive igniter composition and a pyrotechnic composition which burns with little or no flame, but with intense heat;

(b) Safety matches are matches that combined with or attached to the box, book or card that can be ignited by friction only on a prepared surface;

(c) Strike anywhere matches are matches that can be ignited by friction on a solid surface;

(d) Wax Vesta matches are matches that can be ignited by friction either on a prepared surface or on a solid surface.

294 Safety matches and wax "Vesta" matches in outer packagings not exceeding 25 kg net mass are not subject to any other requirement (except marking) of these Regulations when packaged in accordance with packing instruction P407.

295 Batteries need not be individually marked and labelled if the pallet bears the appropriate mark and label.

296 These entries apply for life-saving appliances such as life rafts, personal flotation devices and self-inflating slides. UN 2990 applies for self-inflating appliances and UN 3072 applies for life-saving appliances that are not self-inflating. Life-saving appliances may contain:

(a) Signal devices (Class 1) which may include smoke and illumination signal flares packed in packagings that prevent them from being inadvertently activated;

(b) For UN 2990 only, cartridges, power device of Division 1.4, compatibility group S, may be contained for purposes of the self-inflating mechanism and provided that the quantity of explosives per appliance does not exceed 3.2 g;

(c) Division 2.2 compressed or liquefied gases;

(d) Electric storage batteries (Class 8) and lithium or sodium ion batteries (Class 9);

(e) First aid kits or repair kits containing small quantities of dangerous goods (e.g.: Class 3, Division 4.1, Division 5.2, Class 8 or Class 9 substances); or

(f) "Strike anywhere" matches packed in packagings that prevent them from being inadvertently activated.

Life-saving appliances packed in strong rigid outer packagings with a total maximum gross mass of 40 kg, containing no dangerous goods other than Division 2.2 compressed or liquefied gases with no subsidiary risk in receptacles with a capacity not exceeding 120 ml, installed solely for the purpose of the activation of the appliance, are not subject to these Regulations.

297 *Deleted.*

299 Consignments of COTTON, DRY having a density not less than 360 kg/m^3 according to ISO 8115:1986 "Cotton bales – Dimensions and density" are not subject to these Regulations when transported in closed cargo transport units.

300 Fish meal, fish scrap and krill meal shall not be transported if the temperature at the time of loading exceeds 35 °C or 5 °C above the ambient temperature whichever is higher.

301 This entry only applies to articles such as machinery, apparatus or devices containing dangerous goods as a residue or an integral element of the articles. It shall not be used for articles for which a proper shipping name already exists in the Dangerous Goods List of chapter 3.2. Articles transported under this entry shall only contain dangerous goods which are authorized to be transported in accordance with the provisions of chapter 3.4 (Limited quantities). The quantity of dangerous goods in articles shall not exceed the quantity specified in Column 7a of the Dangerous Goods List of chapter 3.2 for each item of dangerous goods contained. If the articles contain more than one item of dangerous goods, the individual dangerous goods shall be enclosed to prevent them reacting dangerously with one another during transport (see 4.1.1.6). When it is required to ensure liquid dangerous goods remain in their intended orientation, orientation arrows shall be displayed on at least two opposite vertical sides with the arrows pointing in the correct direction in accordance with 5.2.1.7.1.

The competent authority may exempt from regulation articles which would otherwise be transported under this entry.

302 Fumigated cargo transport units containing no other dangerous goods are only subject to the provisions of 5.5.2.

303 Receptacles shall be assigned to the division and, if any, subsidiary hazard of the gas or mixture of gases contained therein determined in accordance with the provisions of chapter 2.2.

304 This entry may only be used for the transport of non-activated batteries which contain dry potassium hydroxide and which are intended to be activated prior to use by the addition of an appropriate amount of water to the individual cells.

305 These substances are not subject to these Regulations when in concentrations of not more than 50 mg/kg.

306 This entry may only be used for substances that are too insensitive for acceptance into Class 1 when tested in accordance with test series 2 (see *Manual of Tests and Criteria*, part I).

307 This entry may only be used for ammonium nitrate based fertilizers. They shall be classified in accordance with the procedure as set out in the *Manual of Tests and Criteria*, part III, section 39.

308 Stabilization of fishmeal shall be achieved to prevent spontaneous combustion by effective application of ethoxyquin, BHT (butylated hydroxytoluene) or tocopherols (also used in a blend with rosemary extract) at the time of production. The said application shall occur within twelve months prior to shipment. Fish scrap or fish meal shall contain at least 50 ppm (mg/kg) of ethoxyquin, 100 ppm (mg/kg) of BHT or 250 ppm (mg/kg) of tocopherol based antioxidant at the time of consignment.

309 This entry applies to non sensitized emulsions, suspensions and gels consisting primarily of a mixture of ammonium nitrate and fuel, intended to produce a Type E blasting explosive only after further processing prior to use.

The mixture for emulsions typically has the following composition: 60-85 % ammonium nitrate; 5-30 % water; 2-8 % fuel; 0.5-4 % emulsifier agent; 0-10 % soluble flame supressants and trace additives. Other inorganic nitrate salts may replace part of the ammonium nitrate.

The mixture for suspensions and gels typically has the following composition: 60-85 % ammonium nitrate, 0-5 % sodium or potassium perchlorate, 0-17 % hexamine nitrate or monomethylamine nitrate, 5-30 % water, 2-15 % fuel, 0.5-4 % thickening agent, 0-10 % soluble flame suppressants, and trace additives. Other inorganic nitrate salts may replace part of the ammonium nitrate.

Substances shall satisfy the criteria for classification as an ammonium nitrate emulsion, suspension or gel, intermediate for blasting explosives (ANE) of test series 8 of the *Manual of Tests and Criteria*, part I, section 18 and be approved by the competent authority.

310 Cells or batteries from production runs of not more than 100 cells or batteries, or pre-production prototypes of cells or batteries when these prototypes are transported for testing, shall meet the provisions of 2.9.4 with the exception of 2.9.4 (a), (e) (vii), (f) (iii) if applicable, (f) (iv) if applicable and (g).

NOTE: *"Transported for testing" includes, but is not limited to, testing described in the "Manual of Tests and Criteria", part III, sub-section 38.3, integration testing and product performance testing.*

These cells and batteries shall be packaged in accordance with packing instruction P910 of 4.1.4.1 or LP905 of 4.1.4.3, as applicable.

Articles (UN Nos. 3537, 3538, 3540, 3541, 3546, 3547 or 3548) may contain such cells or batteries provided that the applicable parts of packing instruction P006 of 4.1.4.1 or LP03 of 4.1.4.3, as applicable, are met.

The transport document shall include the following statement: "Transport in accordance with special provision 310".

Damaged or defective cells, batteries, or cells and batteries contained in equipment shall be transported in accordance with special provision 376.

Cells, batteries or cells and batteries contained in equipment transported for disposal or recycling may be packaged in accordance with special provision 377 and packing instruction P909 of 4.1.4.1.

311 Substances shall not be transported under this entry unless approved by the competent authority on the basis of the results of appropriate tests according to part I of the *Manual of Tests and Criteria*. Packaging shall ensure that the percentage of diluent does not fall below that stated in the competent authority approval, at any time during transport.

312 *Deleted.*

313 *Deleted.*

314 (a) These substances are liable to exothermic decomposition at elevated temperatures. Decomposition can be initiated by heat or by impurities (e.g. powdered metals (iron, manganese, cobalt, magnesium) and their compounds);

(b) During the course of transport, these substances shall be shaded from direct sunlight and all sources of heat and be placed in adequately ventilated areas.

315 This entry shall not be used for Division 6.1 substances which meet the inhalation toxicity criteria for packing group I described in 2.6.2.2.4.3.

316 This entry applies only to calcium hypochlorite, dry, when transported in non friable tablet form.

317 "Fissile-excepted" applies only to those fissile material and packages containing fissile material which are excepted in accordance with 2.7.2.3.5.

318 For the purposes of documentation, the proper shipping name shall be supplemented with the technical name (see 3.1.2.8). Technical names need not be shown on the package. When the infectious substances to be transported are unknown, but suspected of meeting the criteria for inclusion in category A and assignment to UN 2814 or UN 2900, the words "suspected category A infectious substance" shall be shown, in parentheses, following the proper shipping name on the transport document, but not on the outer packagings.

319 Substances packed and marked in accordance with packing instruction P650 are not subject to any other requirements in these Regulations.

320 *Deleted.*

321 These storage systems shall always be considered as containing hydrogen.

322 When transported in non-friable tablet form, these goods are assigned to packing group III.

323 *Deleted.*

324 This substance needs to be stabilized when in concentrations of not more than 99 %.

325 In the case of non-fissile or fissile excepted uranium hexafluoride, the material shall be classified under UN 2978.

326 In the case of fissile uranium hexafluoride, the material shall be classified under UN 2977.

327 Waste aerosols and waste gas cartridges consigned in accordance with 5.4.1.4.3 (c) may be transported under UN Nos. 1950 or 2037, as appropriate, for the purposes of reprocessing or disposal. They need not be protected against movement and inadvertent discharge provided that measures to prevent dangerous build up of pressure and dangerous atmospheres are addressed. Waste aerosols, other than those leaking or severely deformed, shall be packed in accordance with packing instruction P207 and special provision PP87, or packing instruction LP200 and special packing provision L2. Waste gas cartridges, other than those leaking or severely deformed, shall be packed in accordance with packing instruction P003 and special packing provisions PP17 and PP96, or packing instruction LP200 and special packing provision L2. Leaking or severely deformed aerosols and gas cartridges shall be transported in salvage pressure receptacles or salvage packagings provided appropriate measures are taken to ensure there is no dangerous build up of pressure. Waste aerosols and waste gas cartridges shall not be transported in closed freight containers.

Waste gas cartridges that were filled with gases of Division 2.2 and have been pierced are not subject to these Regulations.

328 This entry applies to fuel cell cartridges including when contained in equipment or packed with equipment. Fuel cell cartridges installed in or integral to a fuel cell system are regarded as contained in equipment. Fuel cell cartridge means an article that stores fuel for discharge into the fuel cell through a valve(s) that controls the discharge of fuel into the fuel cell. Fuel cell cartridges, including when contained in equipment, shall be designed and constructed to prevent fuel leakage under normal conditions of transport.

Fuel cell cartridge design types using liquids as fuels shall pass an internal pressure test at a pressure of 100 kPa (gauge) without leakage.

Except for fuel cell cartridges containing hydrogen in metal hydride which shall be in compliance with special provision 339, each fuel cell cartridge design type shall be shown to pass a 1.2 metre drop test onto an unyielding surface in the orientation most likely to result in failure of the containment system with no loss of contents.

When lithium metal, lithium ion or sodium ion batteries are contained in the fuel cell system, the consignment shall be consigned under this entry and under the appropriate entries for UN 3091 LITHIUM METAL BATTERIES CONTAINED IN EQUIPMENT, UN 3481 LITHIUM ION BATTERIES CONTAINED IN EQUIPMENT or UN 3552 SODIUM ION BATTERIES CONTAINED IN EQUIPMENT.

329 *Deleted.*

330 *Deleted.*

331 For environmentally hazardous substances meeting the criteria of 2.9.3, an additional mark as specified in 5.2.1.6 and 5.3.2.3 shall be applied.

332 Magnesium nitrate hexahydrate is not subject to these Regulations.

333 Ethanol and gasoline, motor spirit or petrol mixtures for use in spark-ignition engines (e.g. in automobiles, stationary engines and other engines) shall be assigned to this entry regardless of variations in volatility.

334 A fuel cell cartridge may contain an activator provided it is fitted with two independent means of preventing unintended mixing with the fuel during transport.

335 Mixtures of solids which are not subject to these Regulations and environmentally hazardous liquids or solids shall be classified as UN 3077 and may be transported under this entry, provided there is no free liquid visible at the time the substance is loaded or at the time the packaging or cargo transport unit is closed. Each cargo transport unit shall be leakproof when used as a bulk container. If free liquid is visible at the time the mixture is loaded or at the time the packaging or cargo transport unit is closed, the mixture shall be classified as UN 3082. Sealed packets and articles containing less than 10 ml of an environmentally hazardous liquid, absorbed into a solid material but with no free liquid in the packet or article, or containing less than 10 g of an environmentally hazardous solid, are not subject to these Regulations.

336 A single package of non-combustible solid LSA-II or LSA-III material, if carried by air, shall not contain an activity greater than 3 000 A_2.

337 Type B(U) and Type B(M) packages, if transported by air, shall not contain activities greater than the following:

(a) For low dispersible radioactive material: as authorized for the package design as specified in the certificate of approval;

(b) For special form radioactive material: 3 000 A_1 or 100 000 A_2, whichever is the lower; or

(c) For all other radioactive material: 3 000 A_2.

338 Each fuel cell cartridge transported under this entry and designed to contain a liquefied flammable gas shall:

(a) Be capable of withstanding, without leakage or bursting, a pressure of at least two times the equilibrium pressure of the contents at 55 °C;

(b) Not contain more than 200 ml liquefied flammable gas, the vapour pressure of which shall not exceed 1 000 kPa at 55 °C; and

(c) Pass the hot water bath test prescribed in 6.2.4.1.

339 Fuel cell cartridges containing hydrogen in a metal hydride transported under this entry shall have a water capacity less than or equal to 120 ml.

The pressure in the fuel cell cartridge shall not exceed 5 MPa at 55 °C. The design type shall withstand, without leaking or bursting, a pressure of two times the design pressure of the cartridge at 55 °C or 200 kPa more than the design pressure of the cartridge at 55 °C, whichever is greater. The pressure at which this test is conducted is referred to in the Drop Test and the Hydrogen Cycling Test as the "minimum shell burst pressure".

Fuel cell cartridges shall be filled in accordance with procedures provided by the manufacturer. The manufacturer shall provide the following information with each fuel cell cartridge:

(a) Inspection procedures to be carried out before initial filling and before refilling of the fuel cell cartridge;

(b) Safety precautions and potential hazards to be aware of;

(c) Method for determining when the rated capacity has been achieved;

(d) Minimum and maximum pressure range;

(e) Minimum and maximum temperature range; and

(f) Any other requirements to be met for initial filling and refilling including the type of equipment to be used for initial filling and refilling.

The fuel cell cartridges shall be designed and constructed to prevent fuel leakage under normal conditions of transport. Each cartridge design type, including cartridges integral to a fuel cell, shall be subjected to and shall pass the following tests:

<u>Drop test</u>

A 1.8 metre drop test onto an unyielding surface in four different orientations:

(a) Vertically, on the end containing the shut-off valve assembly;

(b) Vertically, on the end opposite to the shut-off valve assembly;

(c) Horizontally, onto a steel apex with a diameter of 38 mm, with the steel apex in the upward position; and

(d) At a 45° angle on the end containing the shut-off valve assembly.

There shall be no leakage, determined by using a soap bubble solution or other equivalent means on all possible leak locations, when the cartridge is charged to its rated charging pressure. The fuel cell cartridge shall then be hydrostatically pressurized to destruction. The recorded burst pressure shall exceed 85 % of the minimum shell burst pressure.

Fire test

A fuel cell cartridge filled to rated capacity with hydrogen shall be subjected to a fire engulfment test. The cartridge design, which may include a vent feature integral to it, is deemed to have passed the fire test if :

(a) The internal pressure vents to zero gauge pressure without rupture of the cartridge; or

(b) The cartridge withstands the fire for a minimum of 20 minutes without rupture.

Hydrogen cycling test

This test is intended to ensure that fuel cell cartridge design stress limits are not exceeded during use.

The fuel cell cartridge shall be cycled from not more than 5 % rated hydrogen capacity to not less than 95 % rated hydrogen capacity and back to not more than 5 % rated hydrogen capacity. The rated charging pressure shall be used for charging and temperatures shall be held within the operating temperature range. The cycling shall be continued for at least 100 cycles.

Following the cycling test, the fuel cell cartridge shall be charged and the water volume displaced by the cartridge shall be measured. The cartridge design is deemed to have passed the hydrogen cycling test if the water volume displaced by the cycled cartridge does not exceed the water volume displaced by an uncycled cartridge charged to 95 % rated capacity and pressurized to 75 % of its minimum shell burst pressure.

Production leak test

Each fuel cell cartridge shall be tested for leaks at 15 °C ± 5 °C, while pressurized to its rated charging pressure. There shall be no leakage, determined by using a soap bubble solution or other equivalent means on all possible leak locations.

Each fuel cell cartridge shall be permanently marked with the following information:

(a) The rated charging pressure in megapascals (MPa);

(b) The manufacturer's serial number of the fuel cell cartridges or unique identification number; and

(c) The date of expiry based on the maximum service life (year in four digits; month in two digits).

340 Chemical kits, first aid kits and polyester resin kits containing dangerous substances in inner packagings which do not exceed the quantity limits for excepted quantities applicable to individual substances as specified in column 7b of the Dangerous Goods List of chapter 3.2 may be transported in accordance with chapter 3.5. Division 5.2 substances, although not individually authorized as excepted quantities in the Dangerous Goods List of chapter 3.2, are authorized in such kits and are assigned Code E2 (see 3.5.1.2).

341 Bulk transport of infectious substances in BK1 and BK2 bulk containers is only permitted for infectious substances contained in animal material as defined in 1.2.1 (see 4.3.2.4.1).

342 Glass inner receptacles (such as ampoules or capsules) intended only for use in sterilization devices, when containing less than 30 ml of ethylene oxide per inner packaging with not more than 300 ml per outer packaging, may be transported in accordance with the provisions in chapter 3.5, irrespective of the indication of "E0" in column 7b of the Dangerous Goods List provided that:

(a) After filling, each glass inner receptacle has been determined to be leak-tight by placing the glass inner receptacle in a hot water bath at a temperature, and for a period of time, sufficient to ensure that an internal pressure equal to the vapour pressure of ethylene oxide at 55 °C is achieved. Any glass inner receptacle showing evidence of leakage, distortion or other defect under this test shall not be transported under the terms of this special provision;

(b) In addition to the packaging required by 3.5.2, each glass inner receptacle is placed in a sealed plastics bag compatible with ethylene oxide and capable of containing the contents in the event of breakage or leakage of the glass inner receptacle; and

(c) Each glass inner receptacle is protected by a means of preventing puncture of the plastics bag (e.g. sleeves or cushioning) in the event of damage to the packaging (e.g. by crushing).

343 This entry applies to crude oil containing hydrogen sulphide in sufficient concentration that vapours evolved from the crude oil can present an inhalation hazard. The packing group assigned shall be determined by the flammability hazard and inhalation hazard, in accordance with the degree of danger presented.

344 The provisions of 6.2.4 shall be met.

345 This gas contained in open cryogenic receptacles with a maximum capacity of 1 litre constructed with glass double walls having the space between the inner and outer wall evacuated (vacuum insulated) is not subject to these Regulations provided each receptacle is transported in an outer packaging with suitable cushioning or absorbent materials to protect it from impact damage.

346 Open cryogenic receptacles conforming to the requirements of packing instruction P203 and containing no dangerous goods except for UN 1977, nitrogen, refrigerated liquid, which is fully absorbed in a porous material are not subject to any other requirements of these Regulations.

347 This entry shall only be used if the results of test series 6 (d) of part I of the *Manual of Tests and Criteria* have demonstrated that any hazardous effects arising from functioning are confined within the package.

348 Lithium batteries manufactured after 31 December 2011 and sodium ion batteries manufactured after 31 December 2025 shall be marked with the watt-hour rating on the outside case.

349 Mixtures of a hypochlorite with an ammonium salt are not to be accepted for transport. UN 1791 hypochlorite solution is a substance of Class 8.

350 Ammonium bromate and its aqueous solutions and mixtures of a bromate with an ammonium salt are not to be accepted for transport.

351 Ammonium chlorate and its aqueous solutions and mixtures of a chlorate with an ammonium salt are not to be accepted for transport.

352 Ammonium chlorite and its aqueous solutions and mixtures of a chlorite with an ammonium salt are not to be accepted for transport.

353 Ammonium permanganate and its aqueous solutions and mixtures of a permanganate with an ammonium salt are not to be accepted for transport.

354 This substance is toxic by inhalation.

355 Oxygen cylinders for emergency use transported under this entry may include installed actuating cartridges (cartridges, power device of Division 1.4, Compatibility Group C or S), without changing the classification of Division 2.2 provided the total quantity of deflagrating (propellant) explosives does not exceed 3.2 g per oxygen cylinder. The cylinders with the installed actuating cartridges as prepared for transport shall have an effective means of preventing inadvertent activation.

356 Metal hydride storage systems installed in vehicles, vessels, machinery, engines or aircraft or in completed components or intended to be installed in vehicles, vessels, machinery, engines or aircraft shall be approved by the competent authority before acceptance for transport. The transport document shall include an indication that the package was approved by the competent authority or a copy of the competent authority approval shall accompany each consignment.

357 Petroleum crude oil containing hydrogen sulphide in sufficient concentration that vapours evolved from the crude oil can present an inhalation hazard shall be consigned under the entry UN 3494 PETROLEUM SOUR CRUDE OIL, FLAMMABLE, TOXIC.

358 Nitroglycerin solution in alcohol with more than 1 % but not more than 5 % nitroglycerin may be classified in Class 3 and assigned to UN 3064 provided all the requirements of packing instruction P300 are complied with.

359 Nitroglycerin solution in alcohol with more than 1 % but not more than 5 % nitroglycerin shall be classified in Class 1 and assigned to UN 0144 if not all the requirements of packing instruction P300 are complied with.

360 Vehicles only powered by lithium metal, lithium ion or sodium ion batteries shall be assigned to the entries UN 3556 VEHICLE, LITHIUM ION BATTERY POWERED or UN 3557 VEHICLE, LITHIUM METAL BATTERY POWERED or UN 3558 VEHICLE, SODIUM ION BATTERY POWERED, as applicable. Lithium batteries installed in cargo transport units, designed only to provide power external to the transport unit shall be assigned to entry UN 3536 LITHIUM BATTERIES INSTALLED IN CARGO TRANSPORT UNIT.

361 This entry applies to electric double layer capacitors with an energy storage capacity greater than 0.3 Wh. Capacitors with an energy storage capacity of 0.3 Wh or less are not subject to these Regulations. Energy storage capacity means the energy held by a capacitor, as calculated using the nominal voltage and capacitance. All capacitors to which this entry applies, including capacitors containing an electrolyte that does not meet the classification criteria of any class or division of dangerous goods, shall meet the following conditions:

(a) Capacitors not installed in equipment shall be transported in an uncharged state. Capacitors installed in equipment shall be transported either in an uncharged state or protected against short circuit;

(b) Each capacitor shall be protected against a potential short circuit hazard in transport as follows:

(i) When a capacitor's energy storage capacity is less than or equal to 10Wh or when the energy storage capacity of each capacitor in a module is less than or equal to 10 Wh, the capacitor or module shall be protected against short circuit or be fitted with a metal strap connecting the terminals; and

(ii) When the energy storage capacity of a capacitor or a capacitor in a module is more than 10 Wh, the capacitor or module shall be fitted with a metal strap connecting the terminals;

(c) Capacitors containing dangerous goods shall be designed to withstand a 95 kPa pressure differential;

(d) Capacitors shall be designed and constructed to safely relieve pressure that may build up in use, through a vent or a weak point in the capacitor casing. Any liquid which is released upon venting shall be contained by the packaging or by the equipment in which a capacitor is installed; and

(e) Capacitors manufactured after 31 December 2013, shall be marked with the energy storage capacity in Wh.

Capacitors containing an electrolyte not meeting the classification criteria of any class or division of dangerous goods, including when installed in equipment, are not subject to other provisions of these Regulations.

Capacitors containing an electrolyte meeting the classification criteria of any class or division of dangerous goods, with an energy storage capacity of 10 Wh or less are not subject to other provisions of these Regulations when they are capable of withstanding a 1.2 metre drop test unpackaged on an unyielding surface without loss of contents.

Capacitors containing an electrolyte meeting the classification criteria of any class or division of dangerous goods that are not installed in equipment and with an energy storage capacity of more than 10 Wh are subject to these Regulations.

Capacitors installed in equipment and containing an electrolyte meeting the classification criteria of any class or division of dangerous goods, are not subject to other provisions of these Regulations provided the equipment is packaged in a strong outer packaging constructed of suitable material, and of adequate strength and design in relation to the packaging's intended use and in such a manner as to prevent accidental functioning of capacitors during transport. Large robust equipment containing capacitors may be offered for transport unpackaged or on pallets when capacitors are afforded equivalent protection by the equipment in which they are contained.

NOTE: *Capacitors which by design maintain a terminal voltage (e.g. asymmetrical capacitors) do not belong to this entry.*

362 This entry applies to liquids, pastes or powders, pressurized with a propellant which meets the definition of a gas in 2.2.1.1 and 2.2.1.2 (a) or (b).

NOTE: *A chemical under pressure in an aerosol dispenser shall be transported under UN 1950.*

The following provisions shall apply:

(a) The chemical under pressure shall be classified based on the hazard characteristics of the components in the different states:

- The propellant;

- The liquid; or

- The solid.

If one of these components, which can be a pure substance or a mixture, needs to be classified as flammable, the chemical under pressure shall be classified as flammable in Division 2.1. Flammable components are flammable liquids and liquid mixtures, flammable solids and solid mixtures or flammable gases and gas mixtures meeting the following criteria:

(i) A flammable liquid is a liquid having a flashpoint of not more than 93 °C;

(ii) A flammable solid is a solid which meets the criteria in 2.4.2.2 of these Regulations;

(iii) A flammable gas is a gas which meets the criteria in 2.2.2.1 of these Regulations;

(b) Gases of Division 2.3 and gases with a subsidiary hazard of 5.1 shall not be used as a propellant in a chemical under pressure;

(c) Where the liquid or solid components are classified as dangerous goods of Division 6.1, packing groups II or III, or Class 8, packing groups II or III, the chemical under pressure shall be assigned a subsidiary hazard of Division 6.1 or Class 8 and the appropriate UN number shall be assigned. Components classified in Division 6.1, packing group I, or Class 8, packing group I, shall not be used for transport under this proper shipping name;

(d) In addition, chemicals under pressure with components meeting the properties of: Class 1, explosives; Class 3, liquid desensitized explosives; Division 4.1, self-reactive substances and solid desensitized explosives; Division 4.2, substances liable to spontaneous combustion; Division 4.3, substances which, in contact with water, emit flammable gases; Division 5.1 oxidizing substances; Division 5.2, organic peroxides; Division 6.2, Infectious substances or Class 7, Radioactive material, shall not be used for transport under this proper shipping name;

(e) Substances to which PP86 or TP7 are assigned in Column 9 and Column 11 of the Dangerous Goods List in chapter 3.2 and therefore require air to be eliminated from the vapour space, shall not be used for transport under this UN number but shall be transported under their respective UN numbers as listed in the Dangerous Goods List of chapter 3.2.

363 This entry may only be used when the conditions of this special provision are met. No other requirements of these Regulations apply.

(a) This entry applies to engines or machinery, powered by fuels classified as dangerous goods via internal combustion systems or fuel cells (e.g. combustion engines, generators, compressors, turbines, heating units, etc.), except those which are assigned under UN Nos. 3166 or 3363.

(b) Engines or machinery which are empty of liquid or gaseous fuels and which do not contain other dangerous goods, are not subject to these Regulations.

NOTE 1: An engine or machinery is considered to be empty of liquid fuel when the liquid fuel tank has been drained and the engine or machinery cannot be operated due to a lack of fuel. Engine or machinery components such as fuel lines, fuel filters and injectors do not need to be cleaned, drained or purged to be considered empty of liquid fuels. In addition, the liquid fuel tank does not need to be cleaned or purged.

NOTE 2: An engine or machinery is considered to be empty of gaseous fuels when the gaseous fuel tanks are empty of liquid (for liquefied gases), the positive pressure in the tanks does not exceed 2 bar and the fuel shut-off or isolation valve is closed and secured.

(c) Engines and machinery containing fuels meeting the classification criteria of Class 3, shall be consigned under the entries UN 3528 ENGINE, INTERNAL

COMBUSTION, FLAMMABLE LIQUID POWERED or UN 3528 ENGINE, FUEL CELL, FLAMMABLE LIQUID POWERED or UN 3528 MACHINERY, INTERNAL COMBUSTION, FLAMMABLE LIQUID POWERED or UN 3528 MACHINERY, FUEL CELL, FLAMMABLE LIQUID POWERED, as appropriate.

(d) Engines and machinery containing fuels meeting the classification criteria of Division 2.1, shall be consigned under the entries UN 3529 ENGINE, INTERNAL COMBUSTION, FLAMMABLE GAS POWERED or UN 3529 ENGINE, FUEL CELL, FLAMMABLE GAS POWERED or UN 3529 MACHINERY, INTERNAL COMBUSTION, FLAMMABLE GAS POWERED or UN 3529 MACHINERY, FUEL CELL, FLAMMABLE GAS POWERED, as appropriate.

Engines and machinery powered by both a flammable gas and a flammable liquid shall be consigned under the appropriate UN 3529 entry.

(e) Engines and machinery containing liquid fuels meeting the classification criteria of 2.9.3 for environmentally hazardous substances and not meeting the classification criteria of any other Class or Division, shall be consigned under the entries UN 3530 ENGINE, INTERNAL COMBUSTION or UN 3530 MACHINERY, INTERNAL COMBUSTION, as appropriate.

(f) Engines or machinery may contain other dangerous goods than fuels (e.g. batteries, fire extinguishers, compressed gas accumulators or safety devices) required for their functioning or safe operation without being subject to any additional requirements for these other dangerous goods, unless otherwise specified in these Regulations. However, lithium batteries shall meet the provisions of 2.9.4, except that 2.9.4 (a), (e) (vii), (f) (iii) if applicable, (f) (iv) if applicable and (g) do not apply when batteries of a production run of not more than 100 cells or batteries, or pre-production prototypes of cells or batteries when these prototypes are transported for testing, are installed in machinery or engines.

Where a lithium battery installed in a machinery or an engine is damaged or defective, the machinery or engine shall be transported as defined by the competent authority.

(g) The engine or machinery, including the means of containment containing dangerous goods, shall be in compliance with the construction requirements specified by the competent authority;

(h) Any valves or openings (e.g. venting devices) shall be closed during transport;

(i) The engines or machinery shall be oriented to prevent inadvertent leakage of dangerous goods and secured by means capable of restraining the engines or machinery to prevent any movement during transport which would change the orientation or cause them to be damaged;

(j) For UN Nos. 3528 and 3530:

Where the engine or machinery contains more than 60 *l* of liquid fuel and has a capacity of not more than 450 *l*, the labelling requirements of 5.2.2 shall apply.

Where the engine or machinery contains more than 60 *l* of liquid fuel and has a capacity of more than 450 *l* but not more than 3 000 *l*, it shall be labelled on two opposing sides in accordance with 5.2.2.

Where the engine or machinery contains more than 60 *l* of liquid fuel and has a capacity of more than 3 000 *l*, it shall be placarded on two opposing sides. Placards shall correspond to the class indicated in Column 3 of the Dangerous

Goods List of chapter 3.2 and shall conform to the specifications given in 5.3.1.2.1;

(k) For UN 3529:

Where the fuel tank of the engine or machinery has a water capacity of not more than 450 *l*, the labelling requirements of 5.2.2 shall apply.

Where the fuel tank of the engine or machinery has a water capacity of more than 450 *l* but not more than 1 000 *l*, it shall be labelled on two opposing sides in accordance with 5.2.2.

Where the fuel tank of the engine or machinery has a water capacity of more than 1 000 *l*, it shall be placarded on two opposing sides. Placards shall correspond to the class indicated in Column 3 of the Dangerous Goods List in chapter 3.2 and shall conform to the specifications given in 5.3.1.2.1;

(l) A transport document in accordance with 5.4 is required, except for UN 3528 and UN 3530, where a transport document is only required when the engine or machinery contains more than 60 *l* of liquid fuels. This transport document shall contain the following additional statement "Transport in accordance with special provision 363";

(m) The requirements specified in packing instruction P005 of 4.1.4.1 shall be met.

364 This article may only be transported under the provisions of chapter 3.4 if, as presented for transport, the package is capable of passing the test in accordance with test series 6 (d) of part I of the *Manual of Tests and Criteria* as determined by the competent authority.

365 For manufactured instruments and articles containing mercury or gallium, see UN Nos. 3506 or 3554, as appropriate.

366 For land and sea transport, manufactured instruments and articles containing not more than 1 kg of mercury or gallium are not subject to these Regulations. For air transport, articles containing not more than 15 g of mercury or gallium are not subject to these Regulations.

367 For the purposes of documentation and package marking:

The proper shipping name "Paint related material" may be used for consignments of packages containing "Paint" and "Paint related material" in the same package;

The proper shipping name "Paint related material, corrosive, flammable" may be used for consignments of packages containing "Paint, corrosive, flammable" and "Paint related material, corrosive, flammable" in the same package;

The proper shipping name "Paint related material, flammable, corrosive" may be used for consignments of packages containing "Paint, flammable, corrosive" and "Paint related material, flammable, corrosive" in the same package; and

The proper shipping name "Printing ink related material" may be used for consignments of packages containing "Printing Ink" and "Printing ink related material" in the same package.

368 In the case of non-fissile or fissile-excepted uranium hexafluoride, the material shall be classified under UN Nos. 3507 or 2978.

369 In accordance with 2.0.3.2, this radioactive material in an excepted package possessing toxic and corrosive properties is classified in Division 6.1 with radioactivity and corrosivity subsidiary hazards.

Uranium hexafluoride may be classified under this entry only if the conditions of 2.7.2.4.1.2, 2.7.2.4.1.5, 2.7.2.4.5.2 and, for fissile-excepted material, of 2.7.2.3.5 are met.

In addition to the provisions applicable to the transport of Division 6.1 substances with a corrosivity subsidiary hazard, the provisions of 5.1.3.2, 5.1.5.2.2, 5.1.5.4.1 (b), 7.1.8.5.1 to 7.1.8.5.4 and 7.1.8.6.1 shall apply.

No Class 7 label is required to be displayed.

370 This entry only applies to ammonium nitrate that meets one of the following criteria:

(a) Ammonium nitrate with more than 0.2 % combustible substances, including any organic substance calculated as carbon, to the exclusion of any added substance; or

(b) Ammonium nitrate with not more than 0.2 % combustible substances, including any organic substance calculated as carbon, to the exclusion of any added substance, that gives a positive result when tested in accordance with test series 2 (see *Manual of Tests and Criteria*, part I). See also UN 1942.

This entry shall not be used for ammonium nitrate for which a proper shipping name already exists in the Dangerous Goods List of chapter 3.2 including ammonium nitrate mixed with fuel oil (ANFO) or any of the commercial grades of ammonium nitrate.

371 (1) This entry also applies to articles, containing a small pressure receptacle with a release device. Such articles shall comply with the following requirements:

    (a) The water capacity of the pressure receptacle shall not exceed 0.5 litres and the working pressure shall not exceed 25 bar at 15 °C;

    (b) The minimum burst pressure of the pressure receptacle shall be at least four times the pressure of the gas at 15 °C;

    (c) Each article shall be manufactured in such a way that unintentional firing or release is avoided under normal conditions of handling, packing, transport and use. This may be fulfilled by an additional locking device linked to the activator;

    (d) Each article shall be manufactured in such a way as to prevent hazardous projections of the pressure receptacle or parts of the pressure receptacle;

    (e) Each pressure receptacle shall be manufactured from material which will not fragment upon rupture;

    (f) The design type of the article shall be subjected to a fire test. For this test, the provisions of paragraphs 16.6.1.2 except letter g, 16.6.1.3.1 to 16.6.1.3.4, 16.6.1.3.6, 16.6.1.3.7 (b) and 16.6.1.3.8 of the *Manual of Tests and Criteria* shall be applied. It shall be demonstrated that the article relieves its pressure by means of a fire degradable seal or other pressure relief device, in such a way that the pressure receptacle will not fragment and that the article or fragments of the article do not rocket more than 10 metres;

    (g) The design type of the article shall be subjected to the following test. A stimulating mechanism shall be used to initiate one article in the middle of the packaging. There shall be no hazardous effects outside the package such as disruption of the package, metal fragments or a receptacle which passes through the packaging.

(2) The manufacturer shall produce technical documentation of the design type, manufacture as well as the tests and their results. The manufacturer shall apply procedures to ensure that articles produced in series are made of good quality,

conform to the design type and are able to meet the requirements in (1). The manufacturer shall provide such information to the competent authority on request.

372 This entry applies to asymmetric capacitors with an energy storage capacity greater than 0.3 Wh. Capacitors with an energy storage capacity of 0.3 Wh or less are not subject to these Regulations.

Energy storage capacity means the energy stored in a capacitor, as calculated according to the following equation,

$$Wh = 1/2 C_N (U_R^2 - U_L^2) \times (1/3600),$$

using the nominal capacitance (C_N), rated voltage (U_R) and rated lower limit voltage (U_L).

All asymmetric capacitors to which this entry applies shall meet the following conditions:

(a) Capacitors or modules shall be protected against short circuit;

(b) Capacitors shall be designed and constructed to safely relieve pressure that may build up in use, through a vent or a weak point in the capacitor casing. Any liquid which is released upon venting shall be contained by packaging or by equipment in which a capacitor is installed;

(c) Capacitors manufactured after 31 December 2015, shall be marked with the energy storage capacity in Wh.

(d) Capacitors containing an electrolyte meeting the classification criteria of any class or division of dangerous goods shall be designed to withstand a 95 kPa pressure differential;

Capacitors containing an electrolyte not meeting the classification criteria of any class or division of dangerous goods, including when configured in a module or when installed in equipment are not subject to other provisions of these Regulations.

Capacitors containing an electrolyte meeting the classification criteria of any class or division of dangerous goods, with an energy storage capacity of 20 Wh or less, including when configured in a module, are not subject to other provisions of these Regulations when the capacitors are capable of withstanding a 1.2 metre drop test unpackaged on an unyielding surface without loss of contents.

Capacitors containing an electrolyte meeting the classification criteria of any class or division of dangerous goods that are not installed in equipment and with an energy storage capacity of more than 20 Wh are subject to these Regulations.

Capacitors installed in equipment and containing an electrolyte meeting the classification criteria of any class or division of dangerous goods, are not subject to other provisions of these Regulations provided that the equipment is packaged in a strong outer packaging constructed of suitable material, and of adequate strength and design, in relation to the packaging's intended use and in such a manner as to prevent accidental functioning of capacitors during transport. Large robust equipment containing capacitors may be offered for transport unpackaged or on pallets when capacitors are afforded equivalent protection by the equipment in which they are contained.

NOTE: *Notwithstanding the provisions of this special provision, nickel-carbon asymmetric capacitors containing Class 8 alkaline electrolytes shall be transported as UN 2795, BATTERIES, WET, FILLED WITH ALKALI, electric storage.*

373 Neutron radiation detectors containing non-pressurized boron trifluoride gas may be transported under this entry provided that the following conditions are met.

(a) Each radiation detector shall meet the following conditions.

   (i) The pressure in each detector shall not exceed 105 kPa absolute at 20°C;

   (ii) The amount of gas shall not exceed 13 g per detector;

   (iii) Each detector shall be manufactured under a registered quality assurance programme;

   NOTE: The application of ISO 9001:2008 may be considered acceptable for this purpose.

   (iv) Each neutron radiation detector shall be of welded metal construction with brazed metal to ceramic feed through assemblies. These detectors shall have a minimum burst pressure of 1800 kPa as demonstrated by design type qualification testing; and

   (v) Each detector shall be tested to a 1×10^{-10} cm³/s leaktightness standard before filling.

(b) Radiation detectors transported as individual components shall be transported as follows:

   (i) Detectors shall be packed in a sealed intermediate plastics liner with sufficient absorbent or adsorbent material to absorb or adsorb the entire gas contents;

   (ii) They shall be packed in strong outer packaging. The completed package shall be capable of withstanding a 1.8 m drop test without leakage of gas contents from detectors;

   (iii) The total amount of gas from all detectors per outer packaging shall not exceed 52 g.

(c) Completed neutron radiation detection systems containing detectors meeting the conditions of paragraph (a) shall be transported as follows:

   (i) The detectors shall be contained in a strong sealed outer casing;

   (ii) The casing shall contain sufficient absorbent or adsorbent material to absorb or adsorb the entire gas contents;

   (iii) The completed systems shall be packed in strong outer packagings capable of withstanding a 1.8 m drop test without leakage unless a system's outer casing affords equivalent protection.

Packing instruction P200 of 4.1.4.1 is not applicable.

The transport document shall include the following statement "Transport in accordance with special provision 373".

Neutron radiation detectors containing not more than 1 g of boron trifluoride, including those with solder glass joints, are not subject to these Regulations provided they meet the requirements in paragraph (a) and are packed in accordance with paragraph (b). Radiation detection systems containing such detectors are not subject to these Regulations provided they are packed in accordance with paragraph (c).

374 This entry may only be used, as authorized by the competent authority, for packagings, large packagings or intermediate bulk containers (IBC), or parts thereof, which have contained dangerous goods, other than radioactive material, which are transported for disposal, recycling or recovery of their material, other than reconditioning, repair, routine

maintenance, remanufacturing or reuse, and which have been emptied to the extent that only residues of dangerous goods adhering to the packaging parts are present when they are handed over for transport.

375 These substances when transported in single or combination packagings containing a net quantity per single or inner packaging of 5 *l* or less for liquids or having a net mass per single or inner packaging of 5 kg or less for solids, are not subject to any other provisions of these Regulations provided the packagings meet the general provisions of 4.1.1.1, 4.1.1.2 and 4.1.1.4 to 4.1.1.8.

376 Lithium ion, lithium metal or sodium ion cells or batteries identified as being damaged or defective such that they do not conform to the type tested according to the applicable provisions of the *Manual of Tests and Criteria* shall comply with the requirements of this special provision.

For the purposes of this special provision, these may include, but are not limited to:

- Cells or batteries identified as being defective for safety reasons;
- Cells or batteries that have leaked or vented;
- Cells or batteries that cannot be diagnosed prior to transport; or
- Cells or batteries that have sustained physical or mechanical damage.

NOTE: *In assessing a cell or battery as damaged or defective, an assessment or evaluation shall be performed based on safety criteria from the cell, battery or product manufacturer or by a technical expert with knowledge of the cell's or battery's safety features. An assessment or evaluation may include, but is not limited to, the following criteria:*

(a) *Acute hazard, such as gas, fire, or electrolyte leaking;*

(b) *The use or misuse of the cell or battery;*

(c) *Signs of physical damage, such as deformation to cell or battery casing, or colours on the casing;*

(d) *External and internal short circuit protection, such as voltage or isolation measures;*

(e) *The condition of the cell or battery safety features; or*

(f) *Damage to any internal safety components, such as the battery management system.*

Cells and batteries shall be transported according to the provisions applicable to UN Nos. 3090, 3091, 3480, 3481, 3551 and 3552, as appropriate, except special provision 230 and as otherwise stated in this special provision.

Cells and batteries shall be packed in accordance with packing instructions P908 of 4.1.4.1 or LP904 of 4.1.4.3, as applicable.

Cells and batteries identified as damaged or defective and liable to rapidly disassemble, dangerously react, produce a flame or a dangerous evolution of heat or a dangerous emission of toxic, corrosive or flammable gases or vapours under normal conditions of transport shall be packed and transported in accordance with packing instruction P911 of 4.1.4.1 or LP906 of 4.1.4.3, as applicable. Alternative packing and/or transport conditions may be authorized by the competent authority.

Packages shall be marked "DAMAGED/DEFECTIVE" in addition to the proper shipping name, as stated in 5.2.1.

The transport document shall include the following statement "Transport in accordance with special provision 376".

If applicable, a copy of the competent authority approval shall accompany the transport.

377 Lithium ion, lithium metal or sodium ion cells and batteries and equipment containing such cells and batteries transported for disposal or recycling, either packed together with or packed without non-lithium or non-sodium batteries, may be packaged in accordance with packing instruction P909 of 4.1.4.1.

These cells and batteries are not subject to the requirements of section 2.9.4 or 2.9.5. Additional exemptions may be provided under the conditions defined by modal transport regulations.

Packages shall be marked "LITHIUM BATTERIES FOR DISPOSAL", "SODIUM ION BATTERIES FOR DISPOSAL", "LITHIUM BATTERIES FOR RECYCLING" or "SODIUM ION BATTERIES FOR RECYCLING", as appropriate.

Identified damaged or defective batteries shall be transported in accordance with special provision 376.

378 Radiation detectors containing this gas in non-refillable pressure receptacles not meeting the requirements of chapter 6.2 and packing instruction P200 of 4.1.4.1 may be transported under this entry provided:

(a) The working pressure in each receptacle does not exceed 50 bar;

(b) The receptacle capacity does not exceed 12 litres;

(c) Each receptacle has a minimum burst pressure of at least 3 times the working pressure when a relief device is fitted and at least 4 times the working pressure when no relief device is fitted;

(d) Each receptacle is manufactured from material which will not fragment upon rupture;

(e) Each detector is manufactured under a registered quality assurance programme;

NOTE: ISO 9001:2008 may be used for this purpose.

(f) Detectors are transported in strong outer packagings. The complete package shall be capable of withstanding a 1.2 metre drop test without breakage of the detector or rupture of the outer packaging. Equipment that includes a detector shall be packed in a strong outer packaging unless the detector is afforded equivalent protection by the equipment in which it is contained; and

(g) The transport document includes the following statement "Transport in accordance with special provision 378".

Radiation detectors, including detectors in radiation detection systems, are not subject to any other requirements of these Regulations if the detectors meet the requirements in (a) to (f) above and the capacity of detector receptacles does not exceed 50 ml.

379 Anhydrous ammonia adsorbed or absorbed on a solid contained in ammonia dispensing systems or receptacles intended to form part of such systems are not subject to the other provisions of these Regulations if the following conditions are observed:

(a) The adsorption or absorption presents the following properties:

       (i)   The pressure at a temperature of 20 °C in the receptacle is less than 0.6 bar;

       (ii)   The pressure at a temperature of 35 °C in the receptacle is less than 1 bar;

       (iii)   The pressure at a temperature of 85 °C in the receptacle is less than 12 bar.

(b) The adsorbent or absorbent material shall not have dangerous properties listed in Classes 1 to 8;

(c) The maximum contents of a receptacle shall be 10 kg of ammonia; and

(d) Receptacles containing adsorbed or absorbed ammonia shall meet the following conditions:

       (i)   Receptacles shall be made of a material compatible with ammonia as specified in ISO 11114-1:2020;

       (ii)   Receptacles and their means of closure shall be hermetically sealed and able to contain the generated ammonia;

       (iii)   Each receptacle shall be able to withstand the pressure generated at 85 °C with a volumetric expansion no greater than 0.1 %;

       (iv)   Each receptacle shall be fitted with a device that allows for gas evacuation once pressure exceeds 15 bar without violent rupture, explosion or projection; and

       (v)   Each receptacle shall be able to withstand a pressure of 20 bar without leakage when the pressure relief device is deactivated.

When transported in an ammonia dispenser, the receptacles shall be connected to the dispenser in such a way that the assembly is guaranteed to have the same strength as a single receptacle.

The properties of mechanical strength mentioned in this special provision shall be tested using a prototype of a receptacle and/or dispenser filled to nominal capacity, by increasing the temperature until the specified pressures are reached.

The test results shall be documented, shall be traceable and shall be communicated to the relevant authorities upon request.

380   *Deleted.*

381   Large packagings conforming to the packing group III performance level used in accordance with packing instruction LP02 of 4.1.4.3, as prescribed in the 18th revised edition of the United Nations Recommendations on the Transport of Dangerous Goods, Model Regulations, may be used until 31 December 2022.

382   Polymeric beads may be made from polystyrene, poly (methyl methacrylate) or other polymeric material. When it can be demonstrated that no flammable vapour, resulting in a flammable atmosphere, is evolved according to test U1 (Test method for substances liable to evolve flammable vapours) of part III, sub-section 38.4.4 of the *Manual of Tests and Criteria*, polymeric beads, expandable need not be classified under this UN number. This test should only be performed when de-classification of a substance is considered.

383   Table tennis balls manufactured from celluloid are not subject to these Regulations where the net mass of each table tennis ball does not exceed 3.0 g and the total net mass of table tennis balls does not exceed 500 g per package.

384 The label to be used is Model No 9A, see 5.2.2.2.2. However, for placarding of cargo transport units, the placard shall correspond to Model No 9.

385 *Deleted.*

386 When substances are stabilized by temperature control, the provisions of 7.1.5 apply. When chemical stabilization is employed, the person offering the packaging, IBC or tank for transport shall ensure that the level of stabilization is sufficient to prevent the substance in the packaging, IBC or tank from dangerous polymerization at a bulk mean temperature of 50 °C, or, in the case of a portable tank, 45 °C. Where chemical stabilization becomes ineffective at lower temperatures within the anticipated duration of transport, temperature control is required. In making this determination factors to be taken into consideration include, but are not limited to, the capacity and geometry of the packaging, IBC or tank and the effect of any insulation present, the temperature of the substance when offered for transport, the duration of the journey and the ambient temperature conditions typically encountered in the journey (considering also the season of year), the effectiveness and other properties of the stabilizer employed, applicable operational controls imposed by regulation (e.g. requirements to protect from sources of heat, including other cargo transported at a temperature above ambient) and any other relevant factors.

387 Lithium batteries in conformity with 2.9.4 (f) containing both primary lithium metal cells and rechargeable lithium ion cells shall be assigned to UN Nos. 3090 or 3091 as appropriate. When such batteries are transported in accordance with special provision 188, the total lithium content of all lithium metal cells contained in the battery shall not exceed 1.5 g and the total capacity of all lithium ion cells contained in the battery shall not exceed 10 Wh.

388 UN 3166 entries apply to vehicles powered by flammable liquid or gas internal combustion engines or fuel cells.

Vehicles powered by a fuel cell engine shall be assigned to the entries UN 3166 VEHICLE, FUEL CELL, FLAMMABLE GAS POWERED or UN 3166 VEHICLE, FUEL CELL, FLAMMABLE LIQUID POWERED, as appropriate. These entries include hybrid electric vehicles powered by both a fuel cell and an internal combustion engine with wet batteries, sodium batteries, lithium metal batteries or lithium ion batteries, transported with the battery(ies) installed.

Other vehicles which contain an internal combustion engine shall be assigned to the entries UN 3166 VEHICLE, FLAMMABLE GAS POWERED or UN 3166 VEHICLE, FLAMMABLE LIQUID POWERED, as appropriate. These entries include hybrid electric vehicles powered by both an internal combustion engine and wet batteries, sodium batteries, lithium metal batteries or lithium ion batteries, transported with the battery(ies) installed.

If a vehicle is powered by a flammable liquid and a flammable gas internal combustion engine, it shall be assigned to UN 3166 VEHICLE, FLAMMABLE GAS POWERED.

Entry UN 3171 only applies to vehicles and equipment powered by wet batteries, metallic sodium batteries or sodium alloy batteries, transported with these batteries installed.

UN 3556 VEHICLE, LITHIUM ION BATTERY POWERED, UN 3557 VEHICLE, LITHIUM METAL BATTERY POWERED and UN 3558 VEHICLE, SODIUM ION BATTERY POWERED, as applicable, apply to vehicles powered by lithium ion, lithium metal or sodium ion batteries transported with the batteries installed.

For the purpose of this special provision, vehicles are self-propelled apparatus designed to carry one or more persons or goods. Examples of such vehicles are cars, motorcycles, scooters, three- and four-wheeled vehicles or motorcycles, trucks, locomotives, bicycles (pedal cycles with a motor) and other vehicles of this type (e.g. self-balancing vehicles or vehicles not equipped with at least one seating position), wheelchairs, lawn tractors, self-propelled farming and construction equipment, boats and aircraft. When vehicles are transported in a packaging, some parts of the vehicle, other than the battery, may be detached from its frame to fit into the packaging.

Examples of equipment are lawnmowers, cleaning machines or model boats and model aircraft. Equipment powered by lithium metal batteries or lithium ion batteries shall be assigned to the entries UN 3091 LITHIUM METAL BATTERIES CONTAINED IN EQUIPMENT or UN 3091 LITHIUM METAL BATTERIES PACKED WITH EQUIPMENT or UN 3481 LITHIUM ION BATTERIES CONTAINED IN EQUIPMENT or UN 3481 LITHIUM ION BATTERIES PACKED WITH EQUIPMENT, as appropriate. Lithium ion batteries or lithium metal batteries installed in a cargo transport unit and designed only to provide power external to the cargo transport unit shall be assigned to the entry UN 3536 LITHIUM BATTERIES INSTALLED IN CARGO TRANSPORT UNIT lithium ion batteries or lithium metal batteries.

Dangerous goods, such as batteries, airbags, fire extinguishers, compressed gas accumulators, safety devices and other integral components of the vehicle that are necessary for the operation of the vehicle or for the safety of its operator or passengers, shall be securely installed in the vehicle and are not otherwise subject to these Regulations. However, lithium batteries shall meet the provisions of 2.9.4, except that 2.9.4 (a), (e) (vii), (f) (iii) if applicable, (f) (iv) if applicable and (g) do not apply when batteries of a production run of not more than 100 cells or batteries, or pre-production prototypes of cells or batteries when these prototypes are transported for testing, are installed in vehicles or equipment.

Where a lithium battery installed in a vehicle is damaged or defective, the vehicle shall be transported as defined by the competent authority.

389   This entry only applies to lithium ion batteries or lithium metal batteries installed in a cargo transport unit and designed only to provide power external to the cargo transport unit. The lithium batteries shall meet the requirements of 2.9.4 (a) to (g) and contain the necessary systems to prevent overcharge and over discharge between the batteries.

The batteries shall be securely attached to the interior structure of the cargo transport unit (e.g., by means of placement in racks, cabinets, etc.) in such a manner as to prevent short circuits, accidental operation, and significant movement relative to the cargo transport unit under the shocks, loadings and vibrations normally incident to transport. Dangerous goods necessary for the safe and proper operation of the cargo transport unit (e.g., fire extinguishing systems and air conditioning systems), shall be properly secured to or installed in the cargo transport unit and are not otherwise subject to these Regulations. Dangerous goods not necessary for the safe and proper operation of the cargo transport unit shall not be transported within the cargo transport unit.

The batteries inside the cargo transport unit are not subject to marking or labelling requirements. The cargo transport unit shall display the UN number in accordance with 5.3.2.1.2 and be placarded on two opposing sides in accordance with 5.3.1.1.2.

390   When a package contains a combination of lithium batteries contained in equipment and lithium batteries packed with equipment, the following requirements apply for the purposes of package marking and documentation:

(a)   the package shall be marked "UN 3091 Lithium metal batteries packed with equipment", or "UN 3481 Lithium ion batteries packed with equipment", as appropriate. If a package contains both lithium ion batteries and lithium metal batteries packed with and contained in equipment, the package shall be marked as required for both battery types. However, button cell batteries installed in equipment (including circuit boards) need not be considered.

(b) the transport document shall indicate "UN 3091 Lithium metal batteries packed with equipment" or "UN 3481 Lithium ion batteries packed with equipment", as appropriate. If a package contains both lithium metal batteries and lithium ion batteries packed with and contained in equipment, then the transport document shall indicate both "UN 3091 Lithium metal batteries packed with equipment" and "UN 3481 Lithium ion batteries packed with equipment".

391 Articles containing dangerous goods of Division 2.3, or Division 4.2, or Division 4.3, or Division 5.1, or Division 5.2 or Division 6.1 for substances of inhalation toxicity requiring Packing Group I and articles containing more than one of the hazards listed in 2.0.3.1 (b), (c), or (d) shall be transported under conditions approved by the competent authority.

392 For the transport of fuel gas containment systems designed and approved to be fitted in motor vehicles containing this gas the provisions of sub-section 4.1.4.1 and chapter 6.2 of these Regulations need not be applied when transported for disposal, recycling, repair, inspection, maintenance or from where they are manufactured to a vehicle assembly plant, provided the following conditions are met:

(a) The fuel gas containment systems shall meet the requirements of the standards or regulations for fuel tanks for vehicles, as applicable. Examples of applicable standards and regulations are:

LPG tanks	
ECE Regulation No. 67 Revision 2	Uniform provisions concerning: I. Approval of specific equipment of vehicles of category M and N using liquefied petroleum gases in their propulsion system; II. Approval of vehicles of category M and N fitted with specific equipment for the use of liquefied petroleum gases in their propulsion system with regard to the installation of such equipment
ECE Regulation No. 115	Uniform provisions concerning the approval of: I. Specific LPG (liquefied petroleum gases) retrofit systems to be installed in motor vehicles for the use of LPG in their propulsion systems; II Specific CNG (compressed natural gas) retrofit systems to be installed in motor vehicles for the use of CNG in their propulsion system
CNG tanks	
ECE Regulation No. 110	Uniform provisions concerning the approval of: I. Specific components of motor vehicles using compressed natural gas (CNG) and/or liquefied natural gas (LNG) in their propulsion system; II. Vehicles with regard to the installation of specific components of an approved type for the use of compressed natural gas (CNG) and/or liquefied natural gas (LNG) in their propulsion system
ECE Regulation No. 115	(Uniform provisions concerning the approval of: I. Specific LPG (liquefied petroleum gases) retrofit systems to be installed in motor vehicles for the use of LPG in their propulsion systems; II Specific CNG (compressed natural gas) retrofit systems to be installed in motor vehicles for the use of CNG in their propulsion system)
ISO 11439:2013	Gas cylinders — High pressure cylinders for the on-board storage of natural gas as a fuel for automotive vehicles
ISO 15500-Series	ISO 15500: Road vehicles -- Compressed natural gas (CNG) fuel system components – several parts as applicable
ANSI NGV 2	Compressed natural gas vehicle fuel containers

CSA B51 Part 2: 2014	Boiler, pressure vessel, and pressure piping code, part 2: Requirements for high-pressure cylinders for on-board storage of fuels for automotive vehicles
Hydrogen pressure tanks	
Global Technical Regulation (GTR) No. 13	Global technical regulation on hydrogen and fuel cell vehicles (ECE/TRANS/180/Add.13).
ISO/TS 15869:2009	Gaseous hydrogen and hydrogen blends – Land vehicle fuel tanks
Regulation (EC) No.79/2009	Regulation (EC) No. 79/2009 of the European Parliament and of the Council of 14 January 2009 on type approval of hydrogen-powered motor vehicles, and amending Directive 2007/46/EC
Regulation (EU) No. 406/2010	Commission Regulation (EU) No 406/2010 of 26 April 2010 implementing Regulation (EC) No 79/2009 of the European Parliament and of the Council on type-approval of hydrogen-powered motor vehicles
ECE Regulation No. 134	Uniform provisions concerning the approval of motor vehicles and their components with regards to the safety-related performance of hydrogen and fuel cell vehicles (HFCV)
CSA B51 Part 2: 2014	Boiler, pressure vessel, and pressure piping code, part 2: Requirements for high-pressure cylinders for on-board storage of fuels for automotive vehicles

Gas tanks designed and constructed in accordance with previous versions of relevant standards or regulations for gas tanks for motor vehicles, which were applicable at the time of the certification of the vehicles for which the gas tanks were designed and constructed may continue to be transported;

(b) The fuel gas containment systems shall be leakproof and shall not exhibit any signs of external damage which may affect their safety;

NOTE 1: Criteria may be found in standard ISO 11623:2015 Gas cylinders – Composite construction – Periodic inspection and testing (or ISO 19078:2013 Gas cylinders – Inspection of the cylinder installation, and requalification of high pressure cylinders for the on-board storage of natural gas as a fuel for automotive vehicles).

NOTE 2: If the fuel gas containment systems are not leakproof or are overfilled or if they exhibit damage that could affect their safety (e.g. in case of a safety related recall), they shall only be carried in salvage pressure receptacles in conformity with these Regulations.

(c) If a fuel gas containment system is equipped with two valves or more integrated in line, the two valves shall be closed as to be gastight under normal conditions of transport. If only one valve exists or only one valve works, all openings with the exception of the opening of the pressure relief device shall be closed as to be gastight under normal conditions of transport;

(d) Fuel gas containment systems shall be transported in such a way as to prevent obstruction of the pressure relief device or any damage to the valves and any other pressurised part of the fuel gas containment systems and unintentional release of the gas under normal conditions of transport. The fuel gas containment system shall be secured in order to prevent slipping, rolling or vertical movement;

(e) Valves shall be protected by one of the methods described in 4.1.6.1.8 (a) to (e);

(f) Except for the case of fuel gas containment systems removed for disposal, recycling, repair, inspection or maintenance, they shall be filled with not more than 20 % of their nominal filling ratio or nominal working pressure, as applicable;

(g) Notwithstanding the provisions of chapter 5.2, when fuel gas containment systems are consigned in a handling device, markings and labels may be affixed to the handling device; and

(h) Notwithstanding the provisions of 5.4.1.5 the information on the total quantity of dangerous goods may be replaced by the following information:

(i) The number of fuel gas containment systems; and

(ii) In the case of liquefied gases the total net mass (kg) of gas of each fuel gas containment system and, in the case of compressed gases, the total water capacity (l) of each fuel gas containment system followed by the nominal working pressure.

Examples for information in the transport document:

Example 1: "UN 1971 natural gas, compressed, 2.1, 1 fuel gas containment system of 50 *l* in total, 200 bar".

Example 2: "UN 1965 hydrocarbon gas mixture, liquefied, n.o.s., 2.1, 3 fuel gas containment systems, each of 15 kg net mass of gas".

393 The nitrocellulose shall meet the criteria of the Bergmann-Junk test or methyl violet paper test in the *Manual of Tests and Criteria,* appendix 10. Tests of type 3 (c) need not be applied.

394 The nitrocellulose shall meet the criteria of the Bergmann-Junk test or methyl violet paper test in the *Manual of Tests and Criteria,* appendix 10.

395 This entry shall only be used for solid medical waste of Category A transported for disposal.

396 Large and robust articles may be transported with connected gas cylinders with the valves open regardless of 4.1.6.1.5 provided:

(a) The gas cylinders contain nitrogen of UN 1066 or compressed gas of UN 1956 or compressed air of UN 1002;

(b) The gas cylinders are connected with the article through pressure regulators and fixed piping in such a way that the pressure of the gas (gauge pressure) in the article does not exceed 35 kPa (0.35 bar);

(c) The gas cylinders are properly secured so that they cannot move in relation to the article and are fitted with strong and pressure resistant hoses and pipes;

(d) The gas cylinders, pressure regulators, piping and other components are protected from damage and impacts during transport by wooden crates or other suitable means;

(e) The transport document includes the following statement "Transport in accordance with special provision 396";

(f) Cargo transport units containing articles transported with cylinders with open valves containing a gas presenting a risk of asphyxiation are well ventilated and marked in accordance with 5.5.3.6.

397 Mixtures of nitrogen and oxygen containing not less than 19.5 % and not more than 23.5 % oxygen by volume may be transported under this entry when no other oxidizing gases are present. A Division 5.1 subsidiary hazard label is not required for any concentrations within this limit.

398   This entry applies to mixtures of butylenes, 1-butylene, cis-2-butylene and trans-2-butylene. For isobutylene, see UN 1055.

399   For articles that meet the definition for DETONATORS, ELECTRONIC as described in appendix B and assigned to UN Nos. 0511, 0512 and 0513, the entries for DETONATORS, ELECTRIC (UN Nos. 0030, 0255 and 0456) may continue to be used until 30 June 2025.

400   Sodium ion cells and batteries and sodium ion cells and batteries contained in or packed with equipment, prepared and offered for transport, are not subject to other provisions of these Regulations if they meet the following:

- (a) The cell or battery is short-circuited, in a way that the cell or battery does not contain electrical energy. The short-circuiting of the cell or battery shall be easily verifiable (e.g., busbar between terminals);

- (b) Each cell or battery meets the provisions of 2.9.5 (a), (b), (d), (e) and (f);

- (c) Each package shall be marked according to 5.2.1.9;

- (d) Except when cells or batteries are installed in equipment, each package shall be capable of withstanding a 1.2 m drop test in any orientation without damage to cells or batteries contained therein, without shifting of the contents so as to allow battery to battery (or cell to cell) contact and without release of contents;

- (e) Cells and batteries, when installed in equipment shall be protected from damage. When batteries are installed in equipment, the equipment shall be packed in strong outer packagings constructed of suitable material of adequate strength and design in relation to the packaging's capacity and its intended use unless the battery is afforded equivalent protection by the equipment in which it is contained;

- (f) Each cell, including when it is a component of a battery, shall only contain dangerous goods that are authorized to be transported in accordance with the provisions of chapter 3.4 and in a quantity not exceeding the quantity specified in column 7a of the Dangerous Goods List of chapter 3.2.

401   Sodium ion cells and batteries with organic electrolyte shall be transported as UN Nos. 3551 or 3552, as appropriate. Sodium ion cells and batteries with aqueous alkali electrolyte shall be transported as UN 2795 BATTERIES, WET, FILLED WITH ALKALI, electric storage.

402   Substances transported under this entry shall have a vapour pressure at 70 °C not exceeding 1.1 MPa (11 bar) and a density at 50 °C not lower than 0.525 kg/l.

403   Nitrocellulose (NC) membrane filters covered by this entry with NC content not exceeding 53 g/m² and an NC net mass not exceeding 300 g per inner packaging, are not subject to the requirements of this regulation if they meet the following conditions:

- (a) They are packed with paper separators of minimum 80 g/m² placed between each layer of NC membrane filters;

- (b) They are packed to maintain the alignment of the NC membrane filters and the paper separators in any of the following configurations:

  - (i) Rolls tightly wound and packed in plastic foil of minimum 80 g/m² or aluminium pouches with an oxygen permeability of equal or less than 0.1 % according to standard ISO 15105-1:2007;

(ii) Sheets packed in cardboard of minimum 250 g/m² or aluminium pouches with an oxygen permeability of equal or less than 0.1 % according to standard ISO 15105-1:2007;

(iii) Round filters packed in disc holders or cardboard packaging of minimum 250 g/m² or single packed in pouches of paper and plastic material of total minimum 100 g/m².

404 Vehicles powered by sodium ion batteries, containing no other dangerous goods, are not subject to other provisions of these Regulations, if the battery is short-circuited in a way that the battery does not contain electrical energy. The short-circuiting of the battery shall be easily verifiable (e.g., busbar between terminals).

405 Vehicles are not subject to the marking or labelling requirements of chapter 5.2 when they are not fully enclosed by packagings, crates or other means that prevent ready identification.

406 This entry may be transported in accordance with the limited quantity provisions of chapter 3.4 when transported in pressure receptacles containing not more than 1 000 ml. The pressure receptacles shall meet the requirements of packing instruction P200 of 4.1.4.1 and have a test pressure capacity product not exceeding 15.2 MPa·l (152 bar·l). The pressure receptacles shall not be packed together with other dangerous goods.

407 Fire suppressant dispersing devices are articles which contain a pyrotechnic substance, which are intended to disperse a fire extinguishing agent (or aerosol) when activated, and which do not contain any other dangerous goods. These articles, as packaged for transport, shall fulfil the criteria for Division 1.4S, when tested in accordance with test series 6(c) of section 16 of part I of the *Manual of Tests and Criteria*. The device shall be transported with either the means of activation removed or equipped with at least two independent means to prevent accidental activation.

Fire suppressant dispersing devices shall only be assigned to Class 9, UN 3559 if the following additional conditions are met:

(a) The device meets the exclusion criteria in 2.1.3.6.4 (b), (c) and (d);

(b) The suppressant shall be deemed safe for normally occupied spaces in compliance with international or regional standards (e.g. NFPA2010);

(c) The article shall be packaged in a manner such that when activated, temperatures of the outside of the package shall not exceed 200 °C;

(d) This entry shall be used only with the approval of the competent authority of the country of manufacture.

This entry does not apply to "SAFETY DEVICES, electrically initiated" described in special provision 280 (UN 3268).

408 This entry applies only to aqueous solutions comprised of water, tetramethylammonium hydroxide (TMAH), and no more than 1 % of other constituents. Other formulations containing tetramethylammonium hydroxide must be assigned to an appropriate generic or N.O.S. entry (e.g., UN 2927, TOXIC LIQUID, CORROSIVE, ORGANIC, N.O.S., etc.), except as follows:

(a) Other formulations containing a surfactant in a concentration > 1 % and with not less than 8.75 % tetramethylammonium hydroxide must be assigned to UN 2927, TOXIC LIQUID, CORROSIVE, ORGANIC, N.O.S., PG I; and

(b) Other formulations containing a surfactant in a concentration > 1 % and with more than 2.38 % but less than 8.75 % tetramethylammonium hydroxide must be assigned to UN 2927, TOXIC LIQUID, CORROSIVE, ORGANIC, N.O.S., PG II.

409 The provisions of chapter 3.2 from the twenty-second revised edition of the Recommendations on the Transport of Dangerous Goods, Model Regulations may continue to be applied until 31 December 2026.

CHAPTER 3.4

DANGEROUS GOODS PACKED IN LIMITED QUANTITIES

3.4.1　　　　This chapter provides the provisions applicable to the transport of dangerous goods of certain classes packed in limited quantities. The applicable quantity limit for the inner packaging or article is specified for each substance in Column 7a of the Dangerous Goods List of chapter 3.2. In addition, the quantity "0" has been indicated in this column for each entry not permitted to be transported in accordance with this chapter.

Limited quantities of dangerous goods packed in such limited quantities, meeting the provisions of this chapter, are not subject to any other provisions of these Regulations except the relevant provisions of:

(a)　Part 1, chapters 1.1, 1.2 and 1.3;

(b)　Part 2;

(c)　Part 3, chapters 3.1, 3.2, 3.3;

(d)　Part 4, paragraphs 4.1.1.1, 4.1.1.2 and 4.1.1.4 to 4.1.1.8;

NOTE: For air transport, additional provisions apply; refer to part 3, chapter 4 of the ICAO Technical Instructions for the Safe Transport of Dangerous Goods by Air.

(e)　Part 5:

　　(i)　For air transport: chapters 5.1, 5.2 and 5.4;

　　(ii)　For sea transport: 5.1.1.2, 5.1.2.3, 5.2.1.7 and chapter 5.4;

　　(iii)　For transport by road, rail or inland waterway: 5.1.1.2, 5.1.2.3, 5.2.1.7 and section 5.4.2.

(f)　Part 6, construction requirements of 6.1.4, paragraph 6.2.1.2 and section 6.2.4;

(g)　Part 7, section 7.1.1 except first sentence of 7.1.1.7, paragraph 7.1.3.1.4 and sub-section 7.1.3.2.

3.4.2　　　　Dangerous goods shall be packed only in inner packagings placed in suitable outer packagings. Intermediate packagings may be used. In addition, for articles of Division 1.4, Compatibility Group S, the provisions of section 4.1.5 shall be fully complied with. The use of inner packagings is not necessary for the transport of articles such as aerosols or "receptacles, small, containing gas". The total gross mass of the package shall not exceed 30 kg.

3.4.3　　　　Except for articles of Division 1.4, Compatibility Group S, shrink-wrapped or stretch-wrapped trays meeting the conditions of 4.1.1.1, 4.1.1.2 and 4.1.1.4 to 4.1.1.8 are acceptable as outer packagings for articles or inner packagings containing dangerous goods transported in accordance with this chapter. Inner packagings that are liable to break or be easily punctured, such as those made of glass, porcelain, stoneware or certain plastics, shall be placed in suitable intermediate packagings meeting the provisions of 4.1.1.1, 4.1.1.2 and 4.1.1.4 to 4.1.1.8, and be so designed that they meet the construction requirements of 6.1.4. The total gross mass of the package shall not exceed 20 kg.

3.4.4　　　　Liquid goods of Class 8, packing group II in glass, porcelain or stoneware inner packagings shall be enclosed in a compatible and rigid intermediate packaging.

3.4.5 and 3.4.6 *Deleted.*

3.4.7   Marking of packages containing limited quantities

3.4.7.1   Except for air transport, packages containing dangerous goods in limited quantities shall bear the mark shown in figure 3.4.1:

Figure 3.4.1: Mark for packages containing limited quantities

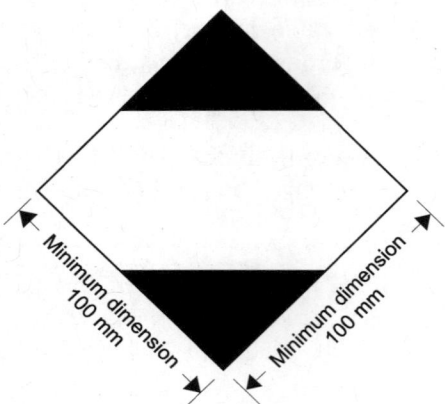

The mark shall be readily visible, legible and able to withstand open weather exposure without a substantial reduction in effectiveness.

The mark shall be in the form of a square set at an angle of 45 degrees (diamond-shaped). The top and bottom portions and the surrounding line shall be black. The centre area shall be white or a suitable contrasting background. The minimum dimensions shall be 100 mm × 100 mm and the minimum width of line forming the diamond shall be 2 mm. Where dimensions are not specified, all features shall be in approximate proportion to those shown.

3.4.7.2   If the size of the package so requires, the minimum outer dimensions shown in figure 3.4.1 may be reduced to be not less than 50 mm × 50 mm provided the mark remains clearly visible. The minimum width of the line forming the diamond may be reduced to a minimum of 1 mm.

3.4.8   Marking of packages containing limited quantities conforming to part 3, chapter 4 of the ICAO Technical Instructions for the Safe Transport of Dangerous Goods by Air

3.4.8.1   Packages containing dangerous goods packed in conformity with the provisions of part 3, chapter 4 of the ICAO Technical Instructions for the Transport of Dangerous Goods may bear the mark shown in figure 3.4.2 to certify conformity with these provisions:

Figure 3.4.2: Mark for packages containing limited quantities conforming to part 3, chapter 4 of the ICAO Technical Instructions for the Safe Transport of Dangerous Goods by Air

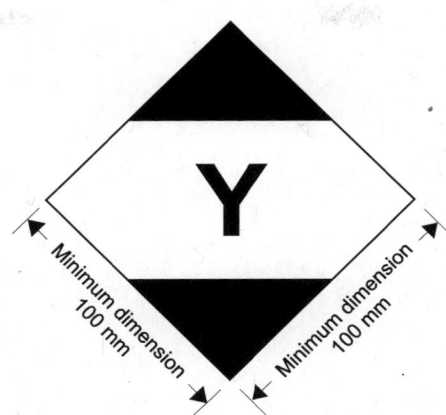

The mark shall be readily visible, legible and able to withstand open weather exposure without a substantial reduction in effectiveness.

The mark shall be in the form of a square set at an angle of 45 degrees (diamond-shaped). The top and bottom portions and the surrounding line shall be black. The centre area shall be white or a suitable contrasting background. The minimum dimensions shall be 100 mm × 100 mm and the minimum width of the line forming the diamond shall be 2 mm. The symbol "Y" shall be placed in the centre of the mark and shall be clearly visible. Where dimensions are not specified, all features shall be in approximate proportion to those shown.

3.4.8.2 If the size of the package so requires, the minimum outer dimensions shown in figure 3.4.2 may be reduced to be not less than 50 mm × 50 mm provided the mark remains clearly visible. The minimum width of the line forming the diamond may be reduced to a minimum of 1 mm. The symbol "Y" shall remain in approximate proportion to that shown in figure 3.4.2.

3.4.9 Packages containing dangerous goods bearing the mark shown in 3.4.8 with or without the additional labels and marks for air transport shall be deemed to meet the provisions of section 3.4.1 as appropriate and of sections 3.4.2 to 3.4.4 of this chapter and need not bear the mark shown in 3.4.7.

3.4.10 Packages containing dangerous goods in limited quantities bearing the mark shown in 3.4.7 and conforming with the provisions of the ICAO Technical Instructions for the Safe Transport of Dangerous Goods by Air, including all necessary marks and labels specified in parts 5 and 6, shall be deemed to meet the provisions of section 3.4.1 as appropriate and of sections 3.4.2 to 3.4.4 when transported by land or by sea.

3.4.11 Use of overpacks

For an overpack containing dangerous goods packed in limited quantities, the following applies:

Unless the marks representative of all dangerous goods in an overpack are visible, the overpack shall be:

(a) marked with the word "OVERPACK". The lettering of the "OVERPACK" mark shall be at least 12 mm high; and

(b) marked with the marks required by this chapter.

Except for air transport, the other provisions of 5.1.2.1 apply only if other dangerous goods which are not packed in limited quantities are contained in the overpack and only in relation to these other dangerous goods.

CHAPTER 3.5

DANGEROUS GOODS PACKED IN EXCEPTED QUANTITIES

3.5.1 Excepted quantities

3.5.1.1 Excepted quantities of dangerous goods of certain classes, other than articles, meeting the provisions of this chapter are not subject to any other provisions of these Regulations except for:

(a) The training requirements in chapter 1.3;

(b) The classification procedures and packing group criteria in part 2;

(c) The packaging requirements of 4.1.1.1, 4.1.1.2, 4.1.1.4, 4.1.1.4.1 and 4.1.1.6.

NOTE: *In the case of radioactive material, the requirements for radioactive material in excepted packages in 1.5.1.5 apply.*

3.5.1.2 Dangerous goods which may be carried as excepted quantities in accordance with the provisions of this chapter are shown in column 7b of the dangerous goods list of chapter 3.2 by means of an alphanumeric code as follows:

Code	Maximum net quantity per inner packaging (in grams for solids and ml for liquids and gases)	Maximum net quantity per outer packaging (in grams for solids and ml for liquids and gases, or sum of grams and ml in the case of mixed packing)
E0	Not permitted as Excepted Quantity	
E1	30	1000
E2	30	500
E3	30	300
E4	1	500
E5	1	300

For gases, the volume indicated for inner packagings refers to the water capacity of the inner receptacle and the volume indicated for outer packagings refers to the combined water capacity of all inner packagings within a single outer packaging.

3.5.1.3 Where dangerous goods in excepted quantities for which different codes are assigned are packaged together the total quantity per outer packaging shall be limited to that corresponding to the most restrictive code.

3.5.1.4 Excepted quantities of dangerous goods assigned to codes E1, E2, E4 and E5 are not subject to these Regulations provided that:

(a) The maximum net quantity of material per inner packaging is limited to 1 ml for liquids and gases and 1 g for solids;

(b) The provisions of 3.5.2 are met, except that an intermediate packaging is not required if the inner packagings are securely packed in an outer packaging with cushioning material in such a way that, under normal conditions of transport, they cannot break, be punctured, or leak their contents; and for liquids, the outer packaging contains sufficient absorbent material to absorb the entire contents of the inner packagings;

(c) The provisions of 3.5.3 are complied with; and

(d) The maximum net quantity of dangerous goods per outer packaging does not exceed 100 g for solids or 100 ml for liquids and gases.

3.5.2 **Packagings**

Packagings used for the transport of dangerous goods in excepted quantities shall be in compliance with the following:

(a) There shall be an inner packaging and each inner packaging shall be constructed of plastic (when used for liquid dangerous goods it shall have a thickness of not less than 0.2 mm), or of glass, porcelain, stoneware, earthenware or metal (see also 4.1.1.2) and the closure of each inner packaging shall be held securely in place with wire, tape or other positive means; any receptacle having a neck with moulded screw threads shall have a leak proof threaded type cap. The closure shall be resistant to the contents;

(b) Each inner packaging shall be securely packed in an intermediate packaging with cushioning material in such a way that, under normal conditions of transport, it cannot break, be punctured or leak its contents. For liquid dangerous goods, the intermediate or outer packaging shall contain sufficient absorbent material to absorb the entire contents of the inner packagings. When placed in the intermediate packaging, the absorbent material may be the cushioning material. Dangerous goods shall not react dangerously with cushioning, absorbent material and packaging material or reduce the integrity or function of the materials. Regardless of its orientation, the package shall completely contain the contents in case of breakage or leakage;

(c) The intermediate packaging shall be securely packed in a strong, rigid outer packaging (wooden, fibreboard or other equally strong material);

(d) Each package type shall be in compliance with the provisions in 3.5.3;

(e) Each package shall be of such a size that there is adequate space to apply all necessary marks; and

(f) Overpacks may be used and may also contain packages of dangerous goods or goods not subject to these Regulations.

3.5.3 **Tests for packages**

3.5.3.1 The complete package as prepared for transport, with inner packagings filled to not less than 95 % of their capacity for solids or 98 % for liquids, shall be capable of withstanding, as demonstrated by testing which is appropriately documented, without breakage or leakage of any inner packaging and without significant reduction in effectiveness:

(a) Drops onto a rigid, non-resilient, flat and horizontal surface from a height of 1.8 m:

   (i) Where the sample is in the shape of a box, it shall be dropped in each of the following orientations:

   - flat on the base;
   - flat on the top;
   - flat on the longest side;
   - flat on the shortest side;
   - on a corner;

(ii) Where the sample is in the shape of a drum, it shall be dropped in each of the following orientations:

- diagonally on the top chime, with the centre of gravity directly above the point of impact;

- diagonally on the base chime;

- flat on the side.

NOTE: Each of the above drops may be performed on different but identical packages.

(b) A force applied to the top surface for a duration of 24 hours, equivalent to the total weight of identical packages if stacked to a height of 3 m (including the sample).

3.5.3.2 For the purposes of testing, the substances to be transported in the packaging may be replaced by other substances except where this would invalidate the results of the tests. For solids, when another substance is used, it must have the same physical characteristics (mass, grain size, etc.) as the substance to be carried. In the drop tests for liquids, when another substance is used, its relative density (specific gravity) and viscosity should be similar to those of the substance to be transported.

3.5.4 Marking of packages

3.5.4.1 Packages containing excepted quantities of dangerous goods prepared in accordance with this chapter shall be durably and legibly marked with the mark shown in figure 3.5.1. The primary hazard class or, when assigned, the division of each of the dangerous goods contained in the package shall be shown in the mark. Where the name of the consignor or consignee is not shown elsewhere on the package this information shall be included within the mark.

3.5.4.2 *Excepted quantities mark*

Figure 3.5.1: Excepted quantities mark

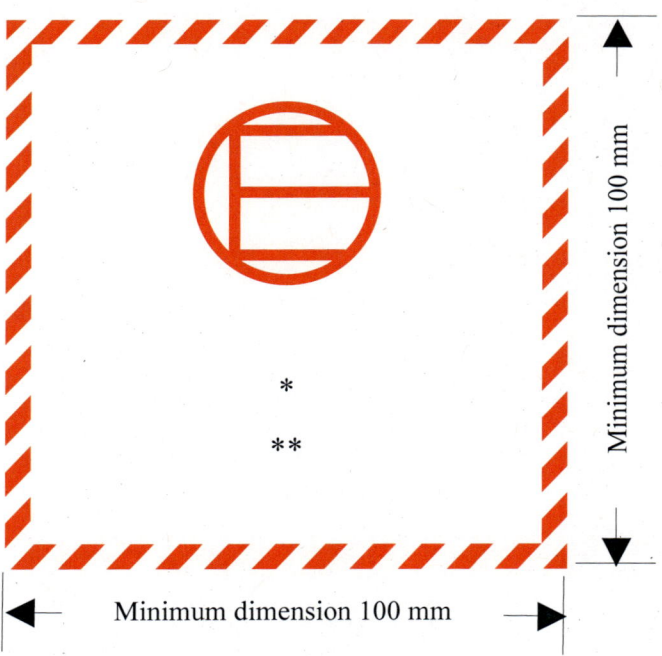

* The Class or, when assigned, the Division number(s) shall be shown in this location

** The name of the consignor or of the consignee shall be shown in this location if not shown elsewhere on the package

The mark shall be in the form of a square. The hatching and symbol shall be of the same colour, black or red, on white or suitable contrasting background. The minimum dimensions shall be 100 mm × 100 mm. Where dimensions are not specified, all features shall be in approximate proportion to those shown.

3.5.4.3   *Use of overpacks*

For an overpack containing dangerous goods packed in excepted quantities, the following applies:

Unless the marks representative of all dangerous goods in an overpack are visible, the overpack shall be:

(a)   Marked with the word "OVERPACK". The lettering of the "OVERPACK" mark shall be at least 12 mm high; and

(b)   Marked with the marks required by this chapter.

The other provisions of 5.1.2.1 apply only if other dangerous goods which are not packed in excepted quantities are contained in the overpack and only in relation to these other dangerous goods.

3.5.5   **Maximum number of packages in any cargo transport unit**

The number of packages in any cargo transport unit shall not exceed 1 000.

3.5.6   **Documentation**

If a document (such as a bill of lading or air waybill) accompanies dangerous goods in excepted quantities, it shall include the statement "Dangerous Goods in Excepted Quantities" and indicate the number of packages.

APPENDICES

APPENDIX A

LIST OF GENERIC
AND
N.O.S. PROPER SHIPPING NAMES

Substances or articles not mentioned specifically by name in the Dangerous Goods List in chapter 3.2 must be classified in accordance with 3.1.1.2. Thus the name in the Dangerous Goods List which most appropriately describes the substance or article shall be used as the Proper Shipping Name. The main generic entries and all the N.O.S. entries given in the Dangerous Goods List are listed below. This proper shipping name shall be supplemented by the technical name when special provision 274 has been assigned to the entry in Column 6 of the Dangerous Goods List.

In this list generic and N.O.S. names are grouped according to their hazard class or division. Within each hazard class or division the names have been placed into three groups as follows:

- specific entries covering a group of substances or articles of a particular chemical or technical nature;

- pesticide entries, for Class 3 and Division 6.1;

- general entries covering a group of substances or articles having one or more general dangerous properties.

THE MOST SPECIFIC APPLICABLE NAME MUST ALWAYS BE USED.

Class or Division	Subsidiary Hazard	UN No	Proper Shipping Name
			CLASS 1
1		0190	SAMPLES, EXPLOSIVE, other than initiating explosive
			Division 1.1
1.1A		0473	SUBSTANCES, EXPLOSIVE, N.O.S.
1.1B		0461	COMPONENTS, EXPLOSIVE TRAIN, N.O.S.
1.1C		0462	ARTICLES, EXPLOSIVE, N.O.S.
1.1C		0474	SUBSTANCES, EXPLOSIVE, N.O.S.
1.1C		0497	PROPELLANT, LIQUID
1.1C		0498	PROPELLANT, SOLID
1.1D		0463	ARTICLES, EXPLOSIVE, N.O.S.
1.1D		0475	SUBSTANCES, EXPLOSIVE, N.O.S.
1.1E		0464	ARTICLES, EXPLOSIVE, N.O.S.
1.1F		0465	ARTICLES, EXPLOSIVE, N.O.S.
1.1G		0476	SUBSTANCES, EXPLOSIVE, N.O.S.
1.1L		0354	ARTICLES, EXPLOSIVE, N.O.S.
1.1L		0357	SUBSTANCES, EXPLOSIVE, N.O.S.
			Division 1.2
1.2B		0382	COMPONENTS, EXPLOSIVE TRAIN, N.O.S.
1.2C		0466	ARTICLES, EXPLOSIVE, N.O.S.
1.2D		0467	ARTICLES, EXPLOSIVE, N.O.S.
1.2E		0468	ARTICLES, EXPLOSIVE, N.O.S.
1.2F		0469	ARTICLES, EXPLOSIVE, N.O.S.
1.2K	6.1	0020	AMMUNITION, TOXIC with burster, expelling charge or propelling charge
1.2L		0248	CONTRIVANCES, WATER-ACTIVATED with burster, expelling charge or propelling charge
1.2L		0355	ARTICLES, EXPLOSIVE, N.O.S.
1.2L		0358	SUBSTANCES, EXPLOSIVE, N.O.S.
			Division 1.3
1.3C		0132	DEFLAGRATING METAL SALTS OF AROMATIC NITRODERIVATIVES, N.O.S.
1.3C		0470	ARTICLES, EXPLOSIVE, N.O.S.
1.3C		0477	SUBSTANCES, EXPLOSIVE, N.O.S.
1.3C		0495	PROPELLANT, LIQUID
1.3C		0499	PROPELLANT, SOLID
1.3G		0478	SUBSTANCES, EXPLOSIVE, N.O.S.
1.3K	6.1	0021	AMMUNITION, TOXIC with burster, expelling charge or propelling charge
1.3L		0249	CONTRIVANCES, WATER-ACTIVATED with burster, expelling charge or propelling charge
1.3L		0356	ARTICLES, EXPLOSIVE, N.O.S.
1.3L		0359	SUBSTANCES, EXPLOSIVE, N.O.S.

Class or Division	Subsidiary Hazard	UN No	Proper Shipping Name
			Division 1.4
1.4B		0350	ARTICLES, EXPLOSIVE, N.O.S.
1.4B		0383	COMPONENTS, EXPLOSIVE TRAIN, N.O.S.
1.4C		0351	ARTICLES, EXPLOSIVE, N.O.S.
1.4C		0479	SUBSTANCES, EXPLOSIVE, N.O.S.
1.4C		0501	PROPELLANT, SOLID
1.4D		0352	ARTICLES, EXPLOSIVE, N.O.S.
1.4D		0480	SUBSTANCES, EXPLOSIVE, N.O.S.
1.4E		0471	ARTICLES, EXPLOSIVE, N.O.S.
1.4F		0472	ARTICLES, EXPLOSIVE, N.O.S.
1.4G		0353	ARTICLES, EXPLOSIVE, N.O.S.
1.4G		0485	SUBSTANCES, EXPLOSIVE, N.O.S.
1.4S		0349	ARTICLES, EXPLOSIVE, N.O.S.
1.4S		0384	COMPONENTS, EXPLOSIVE TRAIN, N.O.S.
1.4S		0481	SUBSTANCES, EXPLOSIVE, N.O.S.
			Division 1.5
1.5D		0482	SUBSTANCES, EXPLOSIVE, VERY INSENSITIVE (SUBSTANCES, EVI), N.O.S.
			Division 1.6
1.6N		0486	ARTICLES, EXPLOSIVE, EXTREMELY INSENSITIVE (ARTICLES, EEI)

Class or Division	Subsidiary Hazard	UN No	Proper Shipping Name
			CLASS 2
			Division 2.1
			Specific entries
2.1		1964	HYDROCARBON GAS MIXTURE, COMPRESSED, N.O.S.
2.1		1965	HYDROCARBON GAS MIXTURE, LIQUEFIED, N.O.S.
2.1		3354	INSECTICIDE GAS, FLAMMABLE, N.O.S.
			General entries
2.1		1954	COMPRESSED GAS, FLAMMABLE, N.O.S.
2.1		3161	LIQUEFIED GAS, FLAMMABLE, N.O.S.
2.1		3167	GAS SAMPLE, NON-PRESSURIZED, FLAMMABLE, N.O.S., not refrigerated liquid
2.1		3312	GAS, REFRIGERATED LIQUID, FLAMMABLE, N.O.S.
2.1		3501	CHEMICAL UNDER PRESSURE, FLAMMABLE, N.O.S.
2.1	6.1	3504	CHEMICAL UNDER PRESSURE, FLAMMABLE, TOXIC, N.O.S.
2.1	8	3505	CHEMICAL UNDER PRESSURE, FLAMMABLE, CORROSIVE, N.O.S.
2.1		3510	ADSORBED GAS, FLAMMABLE, N.O.S.
2.1	See 2.0.5.6	3537	ARTICLES CONTAINING FLAMMABLE GAS, N.O.S.
			Division 2.2
			Specific entries
2.2		1078	REFRIGERANT GAS, N.O.S.
2.2		1968	INSECTICIDE GAS, N.O.S.
			General entries
2.2		1956	COMPRESSED GAS, N.O.S.
2.2		3163	LIQUEFIED GAS, N.O.S.
2.2		3158	GAS, REFRIGERATED LIQUID, N.O.S.
2.2		3500	CHEMICAL UNDER PRESSURE, N.O.S.
2.2	5.1	3156	COMPRESSED GAS, OXIDIZING, N.O.S.
2.2	5.1	3157	LIQUEFIED GAS, OXIDIZING, N.O.S.
2.2	5.1	3311	GAS, REFRIGERATED LIQUID, OXIDIZING, N.O.S.
2.2	6.1	3502	CHEMICAL UNDER PRESSURE, TOXIC, N.O.S.
2.2	8	3503	CHEMICAL UNDER PRESSURE, CORROSIVE, N.O.S.
2.2		3511	ADSORBED GAS, N.O.S.
2.2	5.1	3513	ADSORBED GAS, OXIDIZING, N.O.S.
2.2	See 2.0.5.6	3538	ARTICLES CONTAINING NON-FLAMMABLE, NON TOXIC GAS, N.O.S.

Class or Division	Subsidiary Hazard	UN No	Proper Shipping Name
			Division 2.3
			Specific entries
2.3		1967	INSECTICIDE GAS, TOXIC, N.O.S.
2.3	2.1	3355	INSECTICIDE GAS, TOXIC, FLAMMABLE, N.O.S.
			General entries
2.3		1955	COMPRESSED GAS, TOXIC, N.O.S.
2.3		3162	LIQUEFIED GAS, TOXIC, N.O.S.
2.3		3169	GAS SAMPLE, NON-PRESSURIZED, TOXIC, N.O.S., not refrigerated liquid
2.3	2.1	1953	COMPRESSED GAS, TOXIC, FLAMMABLE, N.O.S.
2.3	2.1	3160	LIQUEFIED GAS, TOXIC, FLAMMABLE, N.O.S.
2.3	2.1	3168	GAS SAMPLE, NON-PRESSURIZED, TOXIC, FLAMMABLE, N.O.S., not refrigerated liquid
2.3	2.1 + 8	3305	COMPRESSED GAS, TOXIC, FLAMMABLE, CORROSIVE, N.O.S.
2.3	2.1 + 8	3309	LIQUEFIED GAS, TOXIC, FLAMMABLE, CORROSIVE, N.O.S.
2.3	5.1	3303	COMPRESSED GAS, TOXIC, OXIDIZING, N.O.S.
2.3	5.1	3307	LIQUEFIED GAS, TOXIC, OXIDIZING, N.O.S.
2.3	5.1 + 8	3306	COMPRESSED GAS, TOXIC, OXIDIZING, CORROSIVE, N.O.S.
2.3	5.1 + 8	3310	LIQUEFIED GAS, TOXIC, OXIDIZING, CORROSIVE, N.O.S.
2.3	8	3304	COMPRESSED GAS, TOXIC, CORROSIVE, N.O.S.
2.3	8	3308	LIQUEFIED GAS, TOXIC, CORROSIVE, N.O.S.
2.3		3512	ADSORBED GAS, TOXIC, N.O.S.
2.3	2.1	3514	ADSORBED GAS, TOXIC, FLAMMABLE, N.O.S.
2.3	5.1	3515	ADSORBED GAS, TOXIC, OXIDIZING, N.O.S.
2.3	8	3516	ADSORBED GAS, TOXIC, CORROSIVE, N.O.S.
2.3	2.1 + 8	3517	ADSORBED GAS, TOXIC, FLAMMABLE, CORROSIVE, N.O.S.
2.3	5.1 + 8	3518	ADSORBED GAS, TOXIC, OXIDIZING, CORROSIVE, N.O.S.
2.3	See 2.0.5.6	3539	ARTICLES CONTAINING TOXIC GAS, N.O.S.

Class or Division	Subsidiary Hazard	UN No	Proper Shipping Name
			CLASS 3
			Specific entries
3		1224	KETONES, LIQUID, N.O.S.
3		1268	PETROLEUM DISTILLATES, N.O.S. or PETROLEUM PRODUCTS, N.O.S.
3		1987	ALCOHOLS, N.O.S.
3		1989	ALDEHYDES, N.O.S.
3		2319	TERPENE HYDROCARBONS, N.O.S.
3		3271	ETHERS, N.O.S.
3		3272	ESTERS, N.O.S.
3		3295	HYDROCARBONS, LIQUID, N.O.S.
3		3336	MERCAPTANS, LIQUID, FLAMMABLE, N.O.S. or MERCAPTAN MIXTURE, LIQUID, FLAMMABLE, N.O.S.
3		3343	NITROGLYCERIN MIXTURE, DESENSITIZED, LIQUID, FLAMMABLE, N.O.S. with not more than 30 % nitroglycerin, by mass
3		3357	NITROGLYCERIN MIXTURE, DESENSITIZED, LIQUID, N.O.S. with not more than 30 % nitroglycerin, by mass
3	6.1	1228	MERCAPTANS, LIQUID, FLAMMABLE, TOXIC, N.O.S. or MERCAPTAN MIXTURE, LIQUID, FLAMMABLE, TOXIC, N.O.S.
3	6.1	1986	ALCOHOLS, FLAMMABLE, TOXIC, N.O.S.
3	6.1	1988	ALDEHYDES, FLAMMABLE, TOXIC, N.O.S.
3	6.1	2478	ISOCYANATES, FLAMMABLE, TOXIC, N.O.S. or ISOCYANATE SOLUTION, FLAMMABLE, TOXIC, N.O.S.
3	6.1	3248	MEDICINE, LIQUID, FLAMMABLE, TOXIC, N.O.S.
3	6.1	3273	NITRILES, FLAMMABLE, TOXIC, N.O.S.
3	8	2733	AMINES, FLAMMABLE, CORROSIVE, N.O.S. or POLYAMINES, FLAMMABLE, CORROSIVE, N.O.S.
3	8	2985	CHLOROSILANES, FLAMMABLE, CORROSIVE, N.O.S.
3	8	3274	ALCOHOLATES SOLUTION, N.O.S., in alcohol
3		3379	DESENSITIZED EXPLOSIVE, LIQUID, N.O.S.

Class or Division	Subsidiary Hazard	UN No	Proper Shipping Name
			Pesticides
3	6.1	2758	CARBAMATE PESTICIDE, LIQUID, FLAMMABLE, TOXIC, flash point < 23 °C
3	6.1	2760	ARSENICAL PESTICIDE, LIQUID, FLAMMABLE, TOXIC, flash point < 23 °C
3	6.1	2762	ORGANOCHLORINE PESTICIDE, LIQUID, FLAMMABLE, TOXIC, flash point < 23 °C
3	6.1	2764	TRIAZINE PESTICIDE, LIQUID, FLAMMABLE, TOXIC, flash point < 23 °C
3	6.1	2772	THIOCARBAMATE PESTICIDE, LIQUID, FLAMMABLE, TOXIC, flash point < 23 °C
3	6.1	2776	COPPER BASED PESTICIDE, LIQUID, FLAMMABLE, TOXIC, flash point < 23 °C
3	6.1	2778	MERCURY BASED PESTICIDE, LIQUID, FLAMMABLE, TOXIC, flash point < 23 °C
3	6.1	2780	SUBSTITUTED NITROPHENOL PESTICIDE, LIQUID, FLAMMABLE, TOXIC, flash point < 23 °C
3	6.1	2782	BIPYRIDILIUM PESTICIDE, LIQUID, FLAMMABLE, TOXIC, flash point < 23 °C
3	6.1	2784	ORGANOPHOSPHORUS PESTICIDE, LIQUID, FLAMMABLE, TOXIC, flash point < 23 °C
3	6.1	2787	ORGANOTIN PESTICIDE, LIQUID, FLAMMABLE, TOXIC, flash point < 23 °C
3	6.1	3021	PESTICIDE, LIQUID, FLAMMABLE, TOXIC, N.O.S., flash point < 23 °C
3	6.1	3024	COUMARIN DERIVATIVE PESTICIDE, LIQUID, FLAMMABLE, TOXIC, flash point < 23 °C
3	6.1	3346	PHENOXYACETIC ACID DERIVATIVE PESTICIDE, LIQUID, FLAMMABLE, TOXIC, flash point < 23 °C
3	6.1	3350	PYRETHROID PESTICIDE, LIQUID, FLAMMABLE, TOXIC, flash point < 23 °C
			General entries
3		1993	FLAMMABLE LIQUID, N.O.S.
3		3256	ELEVATED TEMPERATURE LIQUID, FLAMMABLE, N.O.S., with flash point above 60 °C, at or above its flash point
3	6.1	1992	FLAMMABLE LIQUID, TOXIC, N.O.S.
3	6.1+8	3286	FLAMMABLE LIQUID, TOXIC, CORROSIVE, N.O.S.
3	8	2924	FLAMMABLE LIQUID, CORROSIVE, N.O.S.
3	See 2.0.5.6	3540	ARTICLES CONTAINING FLAMMABLE LIQUID, N.O.S.

Class or Division	Subsidiary Hazard	UN No	Proper Shipping Name
			CLASS 4
			Division 4.1
			Specific entries
4.1		1353	FIBRES or FABRICS IMPREGNATED WITH WEAKLY NITRATED NITROCELLULOSE, N.O.S.
4.1		3089	METAL POWDER, FLAMMABLE, N.O.S.
4.1		3182	METAL HYDRIDES, FLAMMABLE, N.O.S.
4.1		3221	SELF-REACTIVE LIQUID TYPE B
4.1		3222	SELF-REACTIVE SOLID TYPE B
4.1		3223	SELF-REACTIVE LIQUID TYPE C
4.1		3224	SELF-REACTIVE SOLID TYPE C
4.1		3225	SELF-REACTIVE LIQUID TYPE D
4.1		3226	SELF-REACTIVE SOLID TYPE D
4.1		3227	SELF-REACTIVE LIQUID TYPE E
4.1		3228	SELF-REACTIVE SOLID TYPE E
4.1		3229	SELF-REACTIVE LIQUID TYPE F
4.1		3230	SELF-REACTIVE SOLID TYPE F
4.1		3231	SELF-REACTIVE LIQUID TYPE B, TEMPERATURE CONTROLLED
4.1		3232	SELF-REACTIVE SOLID TYPE B, TEMPERATURE CONTROLLED
4.1		3233	SELF-REACTIVE LIQUID TYPE C, TEMPERATURE CONTROLLED
4.1		3234	SELF-REACTIVE SOLID TYPE C, TEMPERATURE CONTROLLED
4.1		3235	SELF-REACTIVE LIQUID TYPE D, TEMPERATURE CONTROLLED
4.1		3236	SELF-REACTIVE SOLID TYPE D, TEMPERATURE CONTROLLED
4.1		3237	SELF-REACTIVE LIQUID TYPE E, TEMPERATURE CONTROLLED
4.1		3238	SELF-REACTIVE SOLID TYPE E, TEMPERATURE CONTROLLED
4.1		3239	SELF-REACTIVE LIQUID TYPE F, TEMPERATURE CONTROLLED
4.1		3240	SELF-REACTIVE SOLID TYPE F, TEMPERATURE CONTROLLED
4.1		3319	NITROGLYCERIN MIXTURE, DESENSITIZED, SOLID, N.O.S. with more than 2 % but not more than 10 % nitroglycerin, by mass
4.1		3344	PENTAERYTHRITE TETRANITRATE (PENTAERYTHRITOL TETRANITRATE; PETN) MIXTURE, DESENSITIZED, SOLID, N.O.S. with more than 10 % but not more than 20 % PETN, by mass
4.1		3380	DESENSITIZED EXPLOSIVE, SOLID, N.O.S.
			General entries
4.1		1325	FLAMMABLE SOLID, ORGANIC, N.O.S.
4.1		3175	SOLIDS CONTAINING FLAMMABLE LIQUID, N.O.S.
4.1		3176	FLAMMABLE SOLID, ORGANIC, MOLTEN, N.O.S.
4.1		3178	FLAMMABLE SOLID, INORGANIC, N.O.S.
4.1		3181	METAL SALTS OF ORGANIC COMPOUNDS, FLAMMABLE, N.O.S.
4.1	5.1	3097	FLAMMABLE SOLID, OXIDIZING, N.O.S.
4.1	6.1	2926	FLAMMABLE SOLID, TOXIC, ORGANIC, N.O.S.
4.1	6.1	3179	FLAMMABLE SOLID, TOXIC, INORGANIC, N.O.S.
4.1	8	2925	FLAMMABLE SOLID, CORROSIVE, ORGANIC, N.O.S.
4.1	8	3180	FLAMMABLE SOLID, CORROSIVE, INORGANIC, N.O.S.
4.1	See 2.0.5.6	3541	ARTICLES CONTAINING FLAMMABLE SOLID, N.O.S

Class or Division	Subsidiary Hazard	UN No	Proper Shipping Name
			Division 4.2
			Specific entries
4.2		1373	FIBRES or FABRICS, ANIMAL or VEGETABLE or SYNTHETIC, N.O.S., with oil
4.2		1378	METAL CATALYST, WETTED with a visible excess of liquid
4.2		1383	PYROPHORIC METAL, N.O.S. or PYROPHORIC ALLOY, N.O.S.
4.2		2006	PLASTICS, NITROCELLULOSE-BASED, SELF-HEATING, N.O.S.
4.2		2881	METAL CATALYST, DRY
4.2		3189	METAL POWDER, SELF-HEATING, N.O.S.
4.2		3205	ALKALINE EARTH METAL ALCOHOLATES, N.O.S.
4.2		3313	ORGANIC PIGMENTS, SELF-HEATING
4.2		3342	XANTHATES
4.2		3391	ORGANOMETALLIC SUBSTANCE, SOLID, PYROPHORIC
4.2		3392	ORGANOMETALLIC SUBSTANCE, LIQUID, PYROPHORIC
4.2		3400	ORGANOMETALLIC SUBSTANCE, SOLID, SELF-HEATING
4.2	4.3	3393	ORGANOMETALLIC SUBSTANCE, SOLID, PYROPHORIC, WATER REACTIVE
4.2	4.3	3394	ORGANOMETALLIC SUBSTANCE, LIQUID, PYROPHORIC, WATER REACTIVE
4.2	8	3206	ALKALI METAL ALCOHOLATES, SELF-HEATING, CORROSIVE, N.O.S.
			General entries
4.2		2845	PYROPHORIC LIQUID, ORGANIC, N.O.S.
4.2		2846	PYROPHORIC SOLID, ORGANIC, N.O.S.
4.2		3088	SELF-HEATING SOLID, ORGANIC, N.O.S.
4.2		3183	SELF-HEATING LIQUID, ORGANIC, N.O.S.
4.2		3186	SELF-HEATING LIQUID, INORGANIC, N.O.S.
4.2		3190	SELF-HEATING SOLID, INORGANIC, N.O.S.
4.2		3194	PYROPHORIC LIQUID, INORGANIC, N.O.S.
4.2		3200	PYROPHORIC SOLID, INORGANIC, N.O.S.
4.2	5.1	3127	SELF-HEATING SOLID, OXIDIZING, N.O.S.
4.2	6.1	3128	SELF-HEATING SOLID, TOXIC, ORGANIC, N.O.S.
4.2	6.1	3184	SELF-HEATING LIQUID, TOXIC, ORGANIC, N.O.S.
4.2	6.1	3187	SELF-HEATING LIQUID, TOXIC, INORGANIC, N.O.S.
4.2	6.1	3191	SELF-HEATING SOLID, TOXIC, INORGANIC, N.O.S.
4.2	8	3126	SELF-HEATING SOLID, CORROSIVE, ORGANIC, N.O.S.
4.2	8	3185	SELF-HEATING LIQUID, CORROSIVE, ORGANIC, N.O.S.
4.2	8	3188	SELF-HEATING LIQUID, CORROSIVE, INORGANIC, N.O.S.
4.2	8	3192	SELF-HEATING SOLID, CORROSIVE, INORGANIC, N.O.S.
4.2	See 2.0.5.6	3542	ARTICLES CONTAINING A SUBSTANCE LIABLE TO SPONTANEOUS COMBUSTION, N.O.S.

Class or Division	Subsidiary Hazard	UN No	Proper Shipping Name
			Division 4.3
			Specific entries
4.3		1389	ALKALI METAL AMALGAM, LIQUID
4.3		1390	ALKALI METAL AMIDES
4.3		1391	ALKALI METAL DISPERSION or ALKALI EARTH METAL DISPERSION
4.3		1392	ALKALINE EARTH METAL AMALGAM, LIQUID
4.3		1393	ALKALINE EARTH METAL ALLOY, N.O.S.
4.3		1409	METAL HYDRIDES, WATER-REACTIVE, N.O.S.
4.3		1421	ALKALI METAL ALLOY, LIQUID, N.O.S.
4.3		3208	METALLIC SUBSTANCE, WATER-REACTIVE, N.O.S.
4.3		3395	ORGANOMETALLIC SUBSTANCE, SOLID, WATER REACTIVE
4.3		3398	ORGANOMETALLIC SUBSTANCE, LIQUID, WATER REACTIVE
4.3		3401	ALKALI METAL AMALGAM, SOLID
4.3		3402	ALKALINE EARTH METAL AMALGAM, SOLID
4.3	3	3399	ORGANOMETALLIC SUBSTANCE, LIQUID, WATER REACTIVE, FLAMMABLE
4.3	3	3482	ALKALI METAL DISPERSION, FLAMMABLE or ALKALINE EARTH METAL DISPERSION, FLAMMABLE
4.3	3+8	2988	CHLOROSILANES, WATER-REACTIVE, FLAMMABLE, CORROSIVE, N.O.S.
4.3	4.1	3396	ORGANOMETALLIC SUBSTANCE, SOLID, WATER REACTIVE, FLAMMABLE
4.3	4.2	3209	METALLIC SUBSTANCE, WATER-REACTIVE, SELF-HEATING, N.O.S.
4.3	4.2	3397	ORGANOMETALLIC SUBSTANCE, SOLID, WATER REACTIVE, SELF-HEATING
			General entries
4.3		3148	WATER-REACTIVE LIQUID, N.O.S.
4.3		2813	WATER-REACTIVE SOLID, N.O.S.
4.3	4.1	3132	WATER-REACTIVE SOLID, FLAMMABLE, N.O.S.
4.3	4.2	3135	WATER-REACTIVE SOLID, SELF-HEATING, N.O.S.
4.3	5.1	3133	WATER-REACTIVE SOLID, OXIDIZING, N.O.S.
4.3	6.1	3130	WATER-REACTIVE LIQUID, TOXIC, N.O.S.
4.3	6.1	3134	WATER-REACTIVE SOLID, TOXIC, N.O.S.
4.3	8	3129	WATER-REACTIVE LIQUID, CORROSIVE, N.O.S.
4.3	8	3131	WATER-REACTIVE SOLID, CORROSIVE, N.O.S.
4.3	See 2.0.5.6	3543	ARTICLES CONTAINING A SUBSTANCE WHICH IN CONTACT WITH WATER EMITS FLAMMABLE GASES, N.O.S.

Class or Division	Subsidiary Hazard	UN No	Proper Shipping Name
			CLASS 5
			Division 5.1
			Specific entries
5.1		1450	BROMATES, INORGANIC, N.O.S.
5.1		1461	CHLORATES, INORGANIC, N.O.S.
5.1		1462	CHLORITES, INORGANIC, N.O.S.
5.1		1477	NITRATES, INORGANIC, N.O.S.
5.1		1481	PERCHLORATES, INORGANIC, N.O.S.
5.1		1482	PERMANGANATES, INORGANIC, N.O.S.
5.1		1483	PEROXIDES, INORGANIC, N.O.S.
5.1		2627	NITRITES, INORGANIC, N.O.S.
5.1		3210	CHLORATES, INORGANIC, AQUEOUS SOLUTION, N.O.S.
5.1		3211	PERCHLORATES, INORGANIC, AQUEOUS SOLUTION, N.O.S.
5.1		3212	HYPOCHLORITES, INORGANIC, N.O.S.
5.1		3213	BROMATES, INORGANIC, AQUEOUS SOLUTION, N.O.S.
5.1		3214	PERMANGANATES, INORGANIC, AQUEOUS SOLUTION, N.O.S.
5.1		3215	PERSULPHATES, INORGANIC, N.O.S.
5.1		3216	PERSULPHATES, INORGANIC, AQUEOUS SOLUTION, N.O.S.
5.1		3218	NITRATES, INORGANIC, AQUEOUS SOLUTION, N.O.S.
5.1		3219	NITRITES, INORGANIC, AQUEOUS SOLUTION, N.O.S.
			General entries
5.1		1479	OXIDIZING SOLID, N.O.S.
5.1		3139	OXIDIZING LIQUID, N.O.S.
5.1	4.1	3137	OXIDIZING SOLID, FLAMMABLE, N.O.S.
5.1	4.2	3100	OXIDIZING SOLID, SELF-HEATING, N.O.S.
5.1	4.3	3121	OXIDIZING SOLID, WATER-REACTIVE, N.O.S.
5.1	6.1	3087	OXIDIZING SOLID, TOXIC, N.O.S.
5.1	6.1	3099	OXIDIZING LIQUID, TOXIC, N.O.S.
5.1	8	3085	OXIDIZING SOLID, CORROSIVE, N.O.S.
5.1	8	3098	OXIDIZING LIQUID, CORROSIVE, N.O.S.
5.1	See 2.0.5.6	3544	ARTICLES CONTAINING OXIDIZING SUBSTANCE, N.O.S.

Class or Division	Subsidiary Hazard	UN No	Proper Shipping Name
			Division 5.2
			Specific entries
5.2		3101	ORGANIC PEROXIDE TYPE B, LIQUID
5.2		3102	ORGANIC PEROXIDE TYPE B, SOLID
5.2		3103	ORGANIC PEROXIDE TYPE C, LIQUID
5.2		3104	ORGANIC PEROXIDE TYPE C, SOLID
5.2		3105	ORGANIC PEROXIDE TYPE D, LIQUID
5.2		3106	ORGANIC PEROXIDE TYPE D, SOLID
5.2		3107	ORGANIC PEROXIDE TYPE E, LIQUID
5.2		3108	ORGANIC PEROXIDE TYPE E, SOLID
5.2		3109	ORGANIC PEROXIDE TYPE F, LIQUID
5.2		3110	ORGANIC PEROXIDE TYPE F, SOLID
5.2		3111	ORGANIC PEROXIDE TYPE B, LIQUID, TEMPERATURE CONTROLLED
5.2		3112	ORGANIC PEROXIDE TYPE B, SOLID, TEMPERATURE CONTROLLED
5.2		3113	ORGANIC PEROXIDE TYPE C, LIQUID, TEMPERATURE CONTROLLED
5.2		3114	ORGANIC PEROXIDE TYPE C, SOLID, TEMPERATURE CONTROLLED
5.2		3115	ORGANIC PEROXIDE TYPE D, LIQUID, TEMPERATURE CONTROLLED
5.2		3116	ORGANIC PEROXIDE TYPE D, SOLID, TEMPERATURE CONTROLLED
5.2		3117	ORGANIC PEROXIDE TYPE E, LIQUID, TEMPERATURE CONTROLLED
5.2		3118	ORGANIC PEROXIDE TYPE E, SOLID, TEMPERATURE CONTROLLED
5.2		3119	ORGANIC PEROXIDE TYPE F, LIQUID, TEMPERATURE CONTROLLED
5.2		3120	ORGANIC PEROXIDE TYPE F, SOLID, TEMPERATURE CONTROLLED
			General entries
5.2	See 2.0.5.6	3545	ARTICLES CONTAINING ORGANIC PEROXIDE, N.O.S.

Class or Division	Subsidiary Hazard	UN No	Proper Shipping Name
			CLASS 6
			Division 6.1
			Specific entries
6.1		1544	ALKALOIDS, SOLID, N.O.S. or ALKALOID SALTS, SOLID, N.O.S.
6.1		1549	ANTIMONY COMPOUND, INORGANIC, SOLID, N.O.S.
6.1		1556	ARSENIC COMPOUND, LIQUID, N.O.S.
6.1		1557	ARSENIC COMPOUND, SOLID, N.O.S.
6.1		1564	BARIUM COMPOUND, N.O.S.
6.1		1566	BERYLLIUM COMPOUND, N.O.S.
6.1		1583	CHLOROPICRIN MIXTURE, N.O.S.
6.1		1588	CYANIDES, INORGANIC, SOLID, N.O.S.
6.1		1601	DISINFECTANT, SOLID, TOXIC, N.O.S.
6.1		1602	DYE, LIQUID, TOXIC, N.O.S. or DYE INTERMEDIATE, LIQUID, TOXIC, N.O.S.
6.1		1655	NICOTINE COMPOUND, SOLID, N.O.S. or NICOTINE PREPARATION, SOLID, N.O.S.
6.1		1693	TEAR GAS SUBSTANCE, LIQUID, N.O.S.
6.1		1707	THALLIUM COMPOUND, N.O.S.
6.1		1851	MEDICINE, LIQUID, TOXIC, N.O.S.
6.1		1935	CYANIDE SOLUTION, N.O.S.
6.1		2024	MERCURY COMPOUND, LIQUID, N.O.S.
6.1		2025	MERCURY COMPOUND, SOLID, N.O.S.
6.1		2026	PHENYLMERCURIC COMPOUND, N.O.S.
6.1		2206	ISOCYANATES, TOXIC, N.O.S. or ISOCYANATE SOLUTION, TOXIC, N.O.S.
6.1		2291	LEAD COMPOUND, SOLUBLE, N.O.S.
6.1		2570	CADMIUM COMPOUND
6.1		2788	ORGANOTIN COMPOUND, LIQUID, N.O.S.
6.1		2856	FLUOROSILICATES, N.O.S.
6.1		3140	ALKALOIDS, LIQUID, N.O.S. or ALKALOID SALTS, LIQUID, N.O.S.
6.1		3141	ANTIMONY COMPOUND, INORGANIC, LIQUID, N.O.S.
6.1		3142	DISINFECTANT, LIQUID, TOXIC, N.O.S.
6.1		3143	DYE, SOLID, TOXIC, N.O.S. or DYE INTERMEDIATE, SOLID, TOXIC, N.O.S.
6.1		3144	NICOTINE COMPOUND, LIQUID, N.O.S. or NICOTINE PREPARATION, LIQUID, N.O.S.
6.1		3146	ORGANOTIN COMPOUND, SOLID, N.O.S.
6.1		3249	MEDICINE, SOLID, TOXIC, N.O.S.
6.1		3276	NITRILES, LIQUID, TOXIC, N.O.S.
6.1		3278	ORGANOPHOSPHORUS COMPOUND, LIQUID, TOXIC, N.O.S.
6.1		3280	ORGANOARSENIC COMPOUND LIQUID, N.O.S.
6.1		3281	METAL CARBONYLS LIQUID, N.O.S.

Class or Division	Subsidiary Hazard	UN No	Proper Shipping Name
6.1		3282	ORGANOMETALLIC COMPOUND, LIQUID, TOXIC, N.O.S.
6.1		3283	SELENIUM COMPOUND, SOLID, N.O.S.
6.1		3284	TELLURIUM COMPOUND, N.O.S.
6.1		3285	VANADIUM COMPOUND, N.O.S.
6.1		3439	NITRILES, SOLID, TOXIC, N.O.S.
6.1		3440	SELENIUM COMPOUND, LIQUID, N.O.S.
6.1		3448	TEAR GAS SUBSTANCE, SOLID, N.O.S.
6.1		3464	ORGANOPHOSPHORUS COMPOUND, SOLID, TOXIC, N.O.S.
6.1		3465	ORGANOARSENIC COMPOUND SOLID, N.O.S.
6.1		3466	METAL CARBONYLS SOLID, N.O.S.
6.1		3467	ORGANOMETALLIC COMPOUND, SOLID, TOXIC, N.O.S.
6.1	3	3071	MERCAPTANS, LIQUID, TOXIC, FLAMMABLE, N.O.S. or MERCAPTAN MIXTURE, LIQUID, TOXIC, FLAMMABLE, N.O.S.
6.1	3	3080	ISOCYANATES, TOXIC, FLAMMABLE, N.O.S. or ISOCYANATE SOLUTION, TOXIC, FLAMMABLE, N.O.S.
6.1	3	3275	NITRILES, TOXIC, FLAMMABLE, N.O.S.
6.1	3	3279	ORGANOPHOSPHORUS COMPOUND, TOXIC, FLAMMABLE, N.O.S.
6.1	3 + 8	2742	CHLOROFORMATES, TOXIC, CORROSIVE, FLAMMABLE, N.O.S.
6.1	3 + 8	3362	CLOROSILANES, TOXIC, CORROSIVE, FLAMMABLE, N.O.S.
6.1	8	3277	CHLOROFORMATES, TOXIC, CORROSIVE, N.O.S.
6.1	8	3361	CLOROSILANES, TOXIC, CORROSIVE, N.O.S.
			Pesticides (solid)
6.1		2588	PESTICIDE, SOLID, TOXIC, N.O.S.
6.1		2757	CARBAMATE PESTICIDE, SOLID, TOXIC
6.1		2759	ARSENICAL PESTICIDE, SOLID, TOXIC
6.1		2761	ORGANOCHLORINE PESTICIDE, SOLID, TOXIC
6.1		2763	TRIAZINE PESTICIDE, SOLID, TOXIC
6.1		2771	THIOCARBAMATE PESTICIDE, SOLID, TOXIC
6.1		2775	COPPER BASED PESTICIDE, SOLID, TOXIC
6.1		2777	MERCURY BASED PESTICIDE, SOLID, TOXIC
6.1		2779	SUBSTITUTED NITROPHENOL PESTICIDE, SOLID, TOXIC
6.1		2781	BIPYRIDILIUM PESTICIDE, SOLID, TOXIC
6.1		2783	ORGANOPHOSPHORUS PESTICIDE, SOLID, TOXIC
6.1		2786	ORGANOTIN PESTICIDE, SOLID, TOXIC
6.1		3027	COUMARIN DERIVATIVE PESTICIDE, SOLID, TOXIC
6.1		3345	PHENOXYACETIC ACID DERIVATIVE PESTICIDE, SOLID, TOXIC
6.1		3349	PYRETHROID PESTICIDE, SOLID, TOXIC

Class or Division	Subsidiary Hazard	UN No	Proper Shipping Name
			Pesticides (liquid)
6.1		2902	PESTICIDE, LIQUID, TOXIC, N.O.S.
6.1		2992	CARBAMATE PESTICIDE, LIQUID, TOXIC
6.1		2994	ARSENICAL PESTICIDE, LIQUID, TOXIC
6.1		2996	ORGANOCHLORINE PESTICIDE, LIQUID, TOXIC
6.1		2998	TRIAZINE PESTICIDE, LIQUID, TOXIC
6.1		3006	THIOCARBAMATE PESTICIDE, LIQUID, TOXIC
6.1		3010	COPPER BASED PESTICIDE, LIQUID, TOXIC
6.1		3012	MERCURY BASED PESTICIDE, LIQUID, TOXIC
6.1		3014	SUBSTITUTED NITROPHENOL PESTICIDE, LIQUID, TOXIC
6.1		3016	BIPYRIDILIUM PESTICIDE, LIQUID, TOXIC
6.1		3018	ORGANOPHOSPHORUS PESTICIDE, LIQUID, TOXIC
6.1		3020	ORGANOTIN PESTICIDE, LIQUID, TOXIC
6.1		3026	COUMARIN DERIVATIVE PESTICIDE, LIQUID, TOXIC
6.1		3348	PHENOXYACETIC ACID DERIVATIVE PESTICIDE, LIQUID, TOXIC
6.1		3352	PYRETHROID PESTICIDE, LIQUID, TOXIC
6.1	3	2903	PESTICIDE, LIQUID, TOXIC, FLAMMABLE, N.O.S., flash point 23 °C
6.1	3	2991	CARBAMATE PESTICIDE, LIQUID, TOXIC, FLAMMABLE, flash point 23 °C
6.1	3	2993	ARSENICAL PESTICIDE, LIQUID, TOXIC, FLAMMABLE, flash point 23 °C
6.1	3	2995	ORGANOCHLORINE PESTICIDE, LIQUID, TOXIC, FLAMMABLE, flash point 23 °C
6.1	3	2997	TRIAZINE PESTICIDE, LIQUID, TOXIC, FLAMMABLE, flash point 23 °C
6.1	3	3005	THIOCARBAMATE PESTICIDE, LIQUID, TOXIC, FLAMMABLE, flash point 23 °C
6.1	3	3009	COPPER BASED PESTICIDE, LIQUID, TOXIC, FLAMMABLE, flash point 23 °C
6.1	3	3011	MERCURY BASED PESTICIDE, LIQUID, TOXIC, FLAMMABLE, flash point 23 °C
6.1	3	3013	SUBSTITUTED NITROPHENOL PESTICIDE, LIQUID, TOXIC, FLAMMABLE, flash point 23 °C
6.1	3	3015	BIPYRIDILIUM PESTICIDE, LIQUID, TOXIC, FLAMMABLE, flash point 23 °C
6.1	3	3017	ORGANOPHOSPHORUS PESTICIDE, LIQUID, TOXIC, FLAMMABLE, flash point 23 °C
6.1	3	3019	ORGANOTIN PESTICIDE, LIQUID, TOXIC, FLAMMABLE, flash point 23 °C
6.1	3	3025	COUMARIN DERIVATIVE PESTICIDE, LIQUID, TOXIC, FLAMMABLE, flash point 23 °C
6.1	3	3347	PHENOXYACETIC ACID DERIVATIVE PESTICIDE, LIQUID, TOXIC, FLAMMABLE, flash point 23 °C
6.1	3	3351	PYRETHROID PESTICIDE, LIQUID, TOXIC, FLAMMABLE, flash point 23 °C

Class or Division	Subsidiary Hazard	UN No	Proper Shipping Name
			General entries
6.1		2810	TOXIC LIQUID, ORGANIC, N.O.S.
6.1		2811	TOXIC SOLID, ORGANIC, N.O.S.
6.1		3172	TOXINS, EXTRACTED FROM LIVING SOURCES, LIQUID, N.O.S.
6.1		3243	SOLIDS CONTAINING TOXIC LIQUID, N.O.S.
6.1		3287	TOXIC LIQUID, INORGANIC, N.O.S.
6.1		3288	TOXIC SOLID, INORGANIC, N.O.S.
6.1		3315	CHEMICAL SAMPLE, TOXIC
6.1		3381	TOXIC BY INHALATION LIQUID, N.O.S. with an LC_{50} lower than or equal to 200 ml/m³ and saturated vapour concentration greater than or equal to 500 LC_{50}
6.1		3382	TOXIC BY INHALATION LIQUID, N.O.S. with an LC_{50} lower than or equal to 1000 ml/m³ and saturated vapour concentration greater than or equal to 10 LC_{50}
6.1		3462	TOXINS, EXTRACTED FROM LIVING SOURCES, SOLID, N.O.S.
6.1	3	2929	TOXIC LIQUID, FLAMMABLE, ORGANIC, N.O.S.
6.1	3	3383	TOXIC BY INHALATION LIQUID, FLAMMABLE, N.O.S. with an LC_{50} lower than or equal to 200 ml/m³ and saturated vapour concentration greater than or equal to 500 LC_{50}
6.1	3	3384	TOXIC BY INHALATION LIQUID, FLAMMABLE, N.O.S. with an LC_{50} lower than or equal to 1000 ml/m³ and saturated vapour concentration greater than or equal to 10 LC_{50}
6.1	3 + 8	3488	TOXIC BY INHALATION LIQUID, FLAMMABLE, CORROSIVE, N.O.S. with an LC_{50} lower than or equal to 200 ml/m³ and saturated vapour concentration greater than or equal to 500 LC_{50}
6.1	3 + 8	3489	TOXIC BY INHALATION LIQUID, FLAMMABLE, CORROSIVE, N.O.S. with an LC_{50} lower than or equal to 1000 ml/m³ and saturated vapour concentration greater than or equal to 10 LC_{50}
6.1	4.1	2930	TOXIC SOLID, FLAMMABLE, ORGANIC, N.O.S.
6.1	4.1	3535	TOXIC SOLID, FLAMMABLE, INORGANIC, N.O.S.
6.1	4.2	3124	TOXIC SOLID, SELF-HEATING, N.O.S.
6.1	4.3	3123	TOXIC LIQUID, WATER-REACTIVE, N.O.S.
6.1	4.3	3125	TOXIC SOLID, WATER-REACTIVE, N.O.S.
6.1	4.3	3385	TOXIC BY INHALATION LIQUID, WATER-REACTIVE, N.O.S. with an LC_{50} lower than or equal to 200 ml/m³ and saturated vapour concentration greater than or equal to 500 LC_{50}
6.1	4.3	3386	TOXIC BY INHALATION LIQUID, WATER-REACTIVE, N.O.S. with an LC_{50} lower than or equal to 1000 ml/m³ and saturated vapour concentration greater than or equal to 10 LC_{50}
6.1	4.3 + 3	3490	TOXIC BY INHALATION LIQUID, WATER-REACTIVE, FLAMMABLE, N.O.S. with an LC_{50} lower than or equal to 200 ml/m³ and saturated vapour concentration greater than or equal to 500 LC_{50}
6.1	4.3 + 3	3491	TOXIC BY INHALATION LIQUID, WATER-REACTIVE, FLAMMABLE, N.O.S. with an LC_{50} lower than or equal to 1000 ml/m³ and saturated vapour concentration greater than or equal to 10 LC_{50}
6.1	5.1	3122	TOXIC LIQUID, OXIDIZING, N.O.S.
6.1	5.1	3086	TOXIC SOLID, OXIDIZING, N.O.S.
6.1	5.1	3387	TOXIC BY INHALATION LIQUID, OXIDIZING, N.O.S. with an LC_{50} lower than or equal to 200 ml/m³ and saturated vapour concentration greater than or equal to 500 LC_{50}

Class or Division	Subsidiary Hazard	UN No	Proper Shipping Name
6.1	5.1	3388	TOXIC BY INHALATION LIQUID, OXIDIZING, N.O.S. with an LC_{50} lower than or equal to 1000 ml/m³ and saturated vapour concentration greater than or equal to 10 LC_{50}
6.1	8	2927	TOXIC LIQUID, CORROSIVE, ORGANIC, N.O.S.
6.1	8	2928	TOXIC SOLID, CORROSIVE, ORGANIC, N.O.S.
6.1	8	3289	TOXIC LIQUID, CORROSIVE, INORGANIC, N.O.S.
6.1	8	3290	TOXIC SOLID, CORROSIVE, INORGANIC, N.O.S.
6.1	8	3389	TOXIC BY INHALATION LIQUID, CORROSIVE, N.O.S. with an LC_{50} lower than or equal to 200 ml/m³ and saturated vapour concentration greater than or equal to 500 LC_{50}
6.1	8	3390	TOXIC BY INHALATION LIQUID, CORROSIVE, N.O.S. with an LC_{50} lower than or equal to 1000 ml/m³ and saturated vapour concentration greater than or equal to 10 LC_{50}
6.1	See 2.0.5.6	3546	ARTICLES CONTAINING TOXIC SUBSTANCE, N.O.S.
			Division 6.2
			Specific entries
6.2		3291	CLINICAL WASTE, UNSPECIFIED, N.O.S. or (BIO) MEDICAL WASTE, N.O.S. or REGULATED MEDICAL WASTE, N.O.S.
6.2		3373	BIOLOGICAL SUBSTANCE, CATEGORY B
6.2		3549	MEDICAL WASTE, CATEGORY A, AFFECTING HUMANS, solid
6.2		3549	MEDICAL WASTE, CATEGORY A, AFFECTING ANIMALS only, solid
			General entries
6.2		2814	INFECTIOUS SUBSTANCE, AFFECTING HUMANS
6.2		2900	INFECTIOUS SUBSTANCE, AFFECTING ANIMALS only

Class or Division	Subsidiary Hazard	UN No	Proper Shipping Name
			CLASS 7
			General entries
7		2908	RADIOACTIVE MATERIAL, EXCEPTED PACKAGE – EMPTY PACKAGING
7		2909	RADIOACTIVE MATERIAL, EXCEPTED PACKAGE – ARTICLES MANUFACTURED FROM NATURAL URANIUM or DEPLETED URANIUM or NATURAL THORIUM
7		2910	RADIOACTIVE MATERIAL, EXCEPTED PACKAGE – LIMITED QUANTITY OF MATERIAL
7		2911	RADIOACTIVE MATERIAL, EXCEPTED PACKAGE - INSTRUMENTS or ARTICLES
7		2912	RADIOACTIVE MATERIAL, LOW SPECIFIC ACTIVITY (LSA-I), non fissile or fissile-excepted
7		2913	RADIOACTIVE MATERIAL, SURFACE CONTAMINATED OBJECTS (SCO-I, SCO-II or SCO-III), non fissile or fissile-excepted
7		2915	RADIOACTIVE MATERIAL, TYPE A PACKAGE, non-special form, non fissile or fissile-excepted
7		2916	RADIOACTIVE MATERIAL, TYPE B(U) PACKAGE, non fissile or fissile-excepted
7		2917	RADIOACTIVE MATERIAL, TYPE B(M) PACKAGE, non fissile or fissile-excepted
7		2919	RADIOACTIVE MATERIAL, TRANSPORTED UNDER SPECIAL ARRANGEMENT, non fissile or fissile-excepted
7		3321	RADIOACTIVE MATERIAL, LOW SPECIFIC ACTIVITY (LSA-II), non fissile or fissile-excepted
7		3322	RADIOACTIVE MATERIAL, LOW SPECIFIC ACTIVITY (LSA-III), non fissile or fissile-excepted
7		3323	RADIOACTIVE MATERIAL, TYPE C PACKAGE, non fissile or fissile-excepted
7		3324	RADIOACTIVE MATERIAL, LOW SPECIFIC ACTIVITY (LSA-II), FISSILE
7		3325	RADIOACTIVE MATERIAL, LOW SPECIFIC ACTIVITY (LSA-III), FISSILE
7		3326	RADIOACTIVE MATERIAL, SURFACE CONTAMINATED OBJECTS (SCO-I or SCO-II), FISSILE
7		3327	RADIOACTIVE MATERIAL, TYPE A PACKAGE, FISSILE, non-special form
7		3328	RADIOACTIVE MATERIAL, TYPE B(U) PACKAGE, FISSILE
7		3329	RADIOACTIVE MATERIAL, TYPE B(M) PACKAGE, FISSILE
7		3330	RADIOACTIVE MATERIAL, TYPE C PACKAGE, FISSILE
7		3331	RADIOACTIVE MATERIAL, TRANSPORTED UNDER SPECIAL ARRANGEMENT, FISSILE
7		3332	RADIOACTIVE MATERIAL, TYPE A PACKAGE, SPECIAL FORM, non fissile or fissile-excepted
7		3333	RADIOACTIVE MATERIAL, TYPE A PACKAGE, SPECIAL FORM, FISSILE

Class or Division	Subsidiary Hazard	UN No	Proper Shipping Name
			CLASS 8
			Specific entries
8		1719	CAUSTIC ALKALI LIQUID, N.O.S.
8		1740	HYDROGENDIFLUORIDES, SOLID, N.O.S.
8		1903	DISINFECTANT, LIQUID, CORROSIVE, N.O.S.
8		2430	ALKYLPHENOLS, SOLID, N.O.S.(including C2-C12 homologues)
8		2693	BISULPHITES, AQUEOUS SOLUTION, N.O.S.
8		2735	AMINES, LIQUID, CORROSIVE, N.O.S. or POLYAMINES, LIQUID, CORROSIVE, N.O.S.
8		2801	DYE, LIQUID, CORROSIVE, N.O.S. or DYE INTERMEDIATE, LIQUID, CORROSIVE, N.O.S.
8		2837	BISULPHATES, AQUEOUS SOLUTION
8		2987	CHLOROSILANES, CORROSIVE, N.O.S.
8		3145	ALKYLPHENOLS, LIQUID, N.O.S.(including C2-C12 homologues)
8		3147	DYE, SOLID, CORROSIVE, N.O.S. or DYE INTERMEDIATE, SOLID, CORROSIVE, N.O.S.
8		3259	AMINES, SOLID, CORROSIVE, N.O.S. or POLYAMINES, SOLID, CORROSIVE, N.O.S.
8	3	2734	AMINES, LIQUID, CORROSIVE, FLAMMABLE, N.O.S. or POLYAMINES, LIQUID, CORROSIVE, FLAMMABLE, N.O.S.
8	3	2986	CHLOROSILANES, CORROSIVE, FLAMMABLE, N.O.S.
8	6.1	3471	HYDROGENDIFLUORIDES SOLUTION, N.O.S.
			General entries
8		1759	CORROSIVE SOLID, N.O.S.
8		1760	CORROSIVE LIQUID, N.O.S.
8		3244	SOLIDS CONTAINING CORROSIVE LIQUID, N.O.S.
8		3260	CORROSIVE SOLID, ACIDIC, INORGANIC, N.O.S.
8		3261	CORROSIVE SOLID, ACIDIC, ORGANIC, N.O.S.
8		3262	CORROSIVE SOLID, BASIC, INORGANIC, N.O.S.
8		3263	CORROSIVE SOLID, BASIC, ORGANIC, N.O.S.
8		3264	CORROSIVE LIQUID, ACIDIC, INORGANIC, N.O.S.
8		3265	CORROSIVE LIQUID, ACIDIC, ORGANIC, N.O.S.
8		3266	CORROSIVE LIQUID, BASIC, INORGANIC, N.O.S.
8		3267	CORROSIVE LIQUID, BASIC, ORGANIC, N.O.S.
8	3	2920	CORROSIVE LIQUID, FLAMMABLE, N.O.S.
8	4.1	2921	CORROSIVE SOLID, FLAMMABLE, N.O.S.
8	4.2	3095	CORROSIVE SOLID, SELF-HEATING, N.O.S.
8	4.2	3301	CORROSIVE LIQUID, SELF-HEATING, N.O.S.
8	4.3	3094	CORROSIVE LIQUID, WATER-REACTIVE, N.O.S.
8	4.3	3096	CORROSIVE SOLID, WATER-REACTIVE, N.O.S.
8	5.1	3084	CORROSIVE SOLID, OXIDIZING, N.O.S.
8	5.1	3093	CORROSIVE LIQUID, OXIDIZING, N.O.S.
8	6.1	2922	CORROSIVE LIQUID, TOXIC, N.O.S.
8	6.1	2923	CORROSIVE SOLID, TOXIC, N.O.S.
8	See 2.0.5.6	3547	ARTICLES CONTAINING CORROSIVE SUBSTANCE, N.O.S.

Class or Division	Subsidiary Hazard	UN No	Proper Shipping Name
			CLASS 9
			General entries
9		3077	ENVIRONMENTALLY HAZARDOUS SUBSTANCE, SOLID, N.O.S.
9		3082	ENVIRONMENTALLY HAZARDOUS SUBSTANCE, LIQUID, N.O.S.
9		3245	GENETICALLY MODIFIED MICROORGANISMS or GENETICALLY MODIFIED ORGANISMS
9		3257	ELEVATED TEMPERATURE LIQUID, N.O.S., at or above 100 °C and below its flash point (including molten metals, molten salts, etc.)
9		3258	ELEVATED TEMPERATURE SOLID, N.O.S., at or above 240 °C
9		3334	AVIATION REGULATED LIQUID, N.O.S.
9		3335	AVIATION REGULATED SOLID, N.O.S.
9	See 2.0.5.6	3548	ARTICLES CONTAINING MISCELLANEOUS DANGEROUS GOODS, N.O.S

APPENDIX B

GLOSSARY OF TERMS

Caution: The explanations in this Glossary are for information only and are not to be used for purposes of hazard classification.

Ammunition

Generic term related mainly to articles of military application consisting of all kind of bombs, grenades, rockets, mines, projectiles and other similar devices or contrivances.

AMMUNITION, ILLUMINATING with or without burster, expelling charge or propelling charge

Ammunition designed to produce a single source of intense light for lighting up an area. The term includes illuminating cartridges, grenades and projectiles; and illuminating and target identification bombs. The term excludes the following articles which are listed separately: CARTRIDGES, SIGNAL; SIGNAL DEVICES, HAND; SIGNALS, DISTRESS; FLARES, AERIAL and FLARES, SURFACE.

AMMUNITION, INCENDIARY

Ammunition containing incendiary substances which may be a solid, liquid or gel including white phosphorus. Except when the composition is an explosive per se, it also contains one or more of the following: a propelling charge with primer and igniter charge; a fuze with burster or expelling charge. The term includes:

> AMMUNITION, INCENDIARY, liquid or gel, with burster, expelling charge or propelling charge;
> AMMUNITION, INCENDIARY with or without burster, expelling charge or propelling charge;
> AMMUNITION, INCENDIARY, WHITE PHOSPHORUS with burster, expelling charge or propelling charge.

AMMUNITION, PRACTICE

Ammunition without a main bursting charge, containing a burster or expelling charge. Normally it also contains a fuze and a propelling charge. The term excludes the following articles which are listed separately: GRENADES, PRACTICE.

AMMUNITION, PROOF

Ammunition containing pyrotechnic substances, used to test the performance or strength of new ammunition, weapon component or assemblies.

AMMUNITION, SMOKE

Ammunition containing smoke-producing substance such as chlorosulphonic acid mixture, titanium tetrachloride or white phosphorus; or smoke-producing pyrotechnic composition based on hexachloroethane or red phosphorus. Except when the substance is an explosive per se, the ammunition also contains one or more of the following: a propelling charge with primer and igniter charge; a fuze with burster or expelling charge. The term includes grenades, smoke but excludes SIGNALS, SMOKE which are listed separately. The term includes:

> AMMUNITION, SMOKE with or without burster, expelling charge or propelling charge;
> AMMUNITION, SMOKE, WHITE PHOSPHORUS with burster, expelling charge or propelling charge.

AMMUNITION, TEAR-PRODUCING with burster, expelling charge or propelling charge

Ammunition containing tear-producing substance. It also contains one or more of the following: a pyrotechnic substance; a propelling charge with primer and igniter charge; a fuze with burster or expelling charge.

AMMUNITION, TOXIC with burster, expelling charge or propelling charge

Ammunition containing toxic agent. It also contains one or more of the following: a pyrotechnic substance; a propelling charge with primer and igniter charge; a fuze with burster or expelling charge.

ARTICLES, EXPLOSIVE, EXTREMELY INSENSITIVE (ARTICLES, EEI)

Articles that predominantly contain extremely insensitive substances and which demonstrate a negligible probability of accidental initiation or propagation (under normal conditions of transport) and which have passed test series 7.

ARTICLES, PYROPHORIC

Articles which contain a pyrophoric substance (capable of spontaneous ignition when exposed to air) and an explosive substance or component. The term excludes articles containing white phosphorus.

ARTICLES, PYROTECHNIC for technical purposes

Articles which contain pyrotechnic substances and are used for technical purposes such as heat generation, gas generation, theatrical effects, etc. The term excludes the following articles which are listed separately: all ammunition; CARTRIDGES, SIGNAL; CUTTERS, CABLE, EXPLOSIVE; FIREWORKS; FLARES, AERIAL; FLARES, SURFACE; RELEASE DEVICES, EXPLOSIVE; RIVETS, EXPLOSIVE; SIGNAL DEVICES, HAND; SIGNALS, DISTRESS; SIGNALS, RAILWAY TRACK, EXPLOSIVE; SIGNALS, SMOKE.

Auxiliary explosive component, isolated

An "isolated auxiliary explosive component" is a small device that explosively performs an operation related to the article's functioning, other than its main explosive loads' performance. Functioning of the component does not cause any reaction of the main explosive loads contained within the article.

BLACK POWDER (GUNPOWDER)

Substance consisting of an intimate mixture of charcoal or other carbon and either potassium nitrate or sodium nitrate, with or without sulphur. It may be meal, granular, compressed or pelletized.

Bombs

Explosive articles which are dropped from aircraft. They may contain a flammable liquid with bursting charge, a photo-flash composition or a bursting charge. The term excludes torpedoes (aerial) and includes:

BOMBS, PHOTO-FLASH;
BOMBS with bursting charge;
BOMBS WITH FLAMMABLE LIQUID with bursting charge.

BOOSTERS

Articles consisting of a charge of detonating explosive with or without means of initiation. They are used to increase the initiating power of detonators or detonating cord.

BURSTERS, explosive

Articles consisting of a small charge of explosive used to open projectiles, or other ammunition in order to disperse their contents.

Cartridges, blank

Articles which consist of a cartridge case with a centre or rim fire primer and a confined charge of smokeless or black powder but no projectile. Used for training, saluting or in starter pistols, tools, etc.

CARTRIDGES, FLASH

Articles consisting of a casing, a primer and flash powder, all assembled in one piece ready for firing.

Cartridges for Weapons

(1) Fixed (assembled) or semi-fixed (partially-assembled) ammunition designed to be fired from weapons. Each cartridge includes all the components necessary to function the weapon once. The name and description shall be used for small arms cartridges that cannot be described as "cartridges, small arms". Separate loading ammunition is included under this name and description when the propelling charge and projectile are packed together (see also "Cartridges, blank").

(2) Incendiary, smoke, toxic and tear-producing cartridges are described in this Glossary under AMMUNITION, INCENDIARY etc.

CARTRIDGES FOR WEAPONS, INERT PROJECTILE

Ammunition consisting of a projectile without bursting charge but with a propelling charge. The presence of a tracer can be disregarded for classification purposes provided that the predominant hazard is that of the propelling charge.

CARTRIDGES, OIL WELL

Articles consisting of a casing of thin fibre, metal or other material containing only propellant which projects a hardened projectile. The term excludes the following articles which are listed separately: CHARGES, SHAPED.

CARTRIDGES, POWER DEVICE

Articles designed to accomplish mechanical actions. They consist of a casing with a charge of deflagrating explosive and a means of ignition. The gaseous products of the deflagration produce inflation, or linear or rotary motion, or activate diaphragms, valves or switches or project fastening devices or extinguishing agents.

CARTRIDGES, SIGNAL

Articles designed to fire coloured flares or other signals from signal pistols, etc.

CARTRIDGES, SMALL ARMS

Ammunition consisting of a cartridge case fitted with a centre or rim fire primer and containing both a propelling charge and a solid projectile. They are designed to be fired in weapons of calibre not larger than 19.1 mm. Shot-gun cartridges of any calibre are included in this description. The term excludes: CARTRIDGES, SMALL ARMS, BLANK listed separately in the Dangerous Goods List; and some small arms cartridges which are listed under CARTRIDGES FOR WEAPONS, INERT PROJECTILE.

CASES, CARTRIDGE, EMPTY, WITH PRIMER

Articles consisting of a cartridge case made from metal, plastics or other non-flammable material, in which the only explosive component is the primer.

CASES, COMBUSTIBLE, EMPTY, WITHOUT PRIMER

Articles consisting of cartridge cases made partly or entirely from nitrocellulose.

Charges, bursting

Articles consisting of a charge of detonating explosive such as hexolite, octolite or plastics bonded explosive designed to produce effect by blast or fragmentation.

CHARGES, DEMOLITION

Articles containing a charge of a detonating explosive in a casing of fibreboard, plastics, metal or other material. The term excludes the following articles which are listed separately: bombs, mines, etc.

CHARGES, DEPTH

Articles consisting of a charge of detonating explosive contained in a drum or projectile. They are designed to detonate under water.

Charges, expelling

A charge of deflagrating explosive designed to eject the payload from the parent articles without damage.

CHARGES, EXPLOSIVE, COMMERCIAL without detonator

Articles consisting of a charge of detonating explosive without means of initiation, used for explosive welding, jointing, forming and other metallurgical processes.

CHARGES, PROPELLING

Articles consisting of a propellant charge in any physical form, with or without a casing, for use as a component of rocket motors or for reducing the drag of projectiles.

CHARGES, PROPELLING FOR CANNON

Articles consisting of a propellant charge in any physical form, with or without a casing, for use in a cannon.

CHARGES, SHAPED, without detonator

Articles consisting of a casing containing a charge of detonating explosive with a cavity lined with rigid material, without means of initiation. They are designed to produce a powerful, penetrating jet effect.

CHARGES, SHAPED, FLEXIBLE, LINEAR

Articles consisting of a V-shaped core of a detonating explosive clad by a flexible metal sheath.

CHARGES, SUPPLEMENTARY, EXPLOSIVE

Articles consisting of a small removable booster used in the cavity of a projectile between the fuze and the bursting charge.

COMPONENTS, EXPLOSIVE TRAIN, N.O.S.

Articles containing an explosive designed to transmit the detonation or deflagration within an explosive train.

CONTRIVANCES, WATER-ACTIVATED with burster, expelling charge or propelling charge

Articles whose functioning depends upon physico-chemical reaction of their contents with water.

CORD, DETONATING, flexible

Article consisting of a core of detonating explosive enclosed in spun fabric, with plastics or other covering unless the spun fabric is sift-proof.

CORD (FUSE), DETONATING, metal clad

Article consisting of a core of detonating explosive clad by a soft metal tube with or without protective covering. When the core contains a sufficiently small quantity of explosive, the words "MILD EFFECT" are added.

CORD, IGNITER

Article consisting of textile yarns covered with black powder or another fast burning pyrotechnic composition and of a flexible protective covering; or it consists of a core of black powder surrounded by a flexible woven fabric. It burns progressively along its length with an external flame and is used to transmit ignition from a device to a charge or primer.

CUTTERS, CABLE, EXPLOSIVE

Articles consisting of a knife-edged device which is driven by a small charge of deflagrating explosive into an anvil.

DETONATOR ASSEMBLIES, NON-ELECTRIC for blasting

Non-electric detonators assembled with and activated by such means as safety fuse, shock tube, flash tube or detonating cord. They may be of instantaneous design or incorporate delay elements. Detonating relays incorporating detonating cord are included. Other detonating relays are included in "Detonators, non-electric".

Detonators

Articles consisting of a small metal or plastics tube containing explosives such as lead azide, PETN or combinations of explosives. They are designed to start a detonation train. They may be constructed to detonate instantaneously, or may contain a delay element. The term includes:

DETONATORS FOR AMMUNITION and
DETONATORS for blasting, ELECTRIC, NON-ELECTRIC and ELECTRONIC
    programmable.

Detonating relays without flexible detonating cord are included.

DETONATORS, ELECTRONIC programmable for blasting

Detonators with enhanced safety and security features, utilizing electronic components to transmit a firing signal with validated commands and secure communications. Detonators of this type cannot be initiated by other means.

Entire load and total contents

The phrases "entire load" and "total contents" mean such a substantial proportion that the practical hazard shall be assessed by assuming simultaneous explosion of the whole of the explosive content of the load or package.

Explode

The verb used to indicate those explosive effects capable of endangering life and property through blast, heat and projection of missiles. It encompasses both deflagration and detonation.

Explosion of the total contents

The phrase "explosion of the total contents" is used in testing a single article or package or a small stack of articles or packages.

Explosive, blasting

Detonating explosive substances used in mining, construction and similar tasks. Blasting explosives are assigned to one of five types. In addition to the ingredients listed, blasting explosives may also contain inert components such as kieselguhr, and minor ingredients such as colouring agents and stabilizers.

EXPLOSIVE, BLASTING, TYPE A

Substances consisting of liquid organic nitrates such as nitroglycerin or a mixture of such ingredients with one or more of the following: nitrocellulose; ammonium nitrate or other inorganic nitrates; aromatic nitro-derivatives, or combustible materials, such as wood-meal and aluminium powder. Such explosives shall be in powdery, gelatinous or elastic form.

The term includes dynamite gelatine, blasting and gelatine dynamites.

EXPLOSIVE, BLASTING, TYPE B

Substances consisting of (a) a mixture of ammonium nitrate or other inorganic nitrates with an explosive such as trinitrotoluene, with or without other substances such as wood-meal and aluminium powder, or (b) a mixture of ammonium nitrate or other inorganic nitrates with other combustible substances which are not explosive ingredients. Such explosives shall not contain nitroglycerin, similar liquid organic nitrates, or chlorates.

EXPLOSIVE, BLASTING, TYPE C

Substances consisting of a mixture of either potassium or sodium chlorate or potassium, sodium or ammonium perchlorate with organic nitro-derivatives or combustible materials such as wood-meal or aluminium powder or a hydrocarbon. Such explosives shall not contain nitroglycerin or similar liquid organic nitrates.

EXPLOSIVE, BLASTING, TYPE D

Substances consisting of a mixture of organic nitrated compounds and combustible materials such as hydrocarbons and aluminium powder. Such explosives shall not contain nitroglycerin, similar liquid organic nitrates, chlorates or ammonium nitrate. The term generally includes plastic explosives.

EXPLOSIVE, BLASTING, TYPE E

Substances consisting of water as an essential ingredient and high proportions of ammonium nitrate or other oxidizers, some or all of which are in solution. The other constituents may include nitro-derivatives such as trinitrotoluene, hydrocarbons or aluminium powder.

The term includes explosives, emulsion; explosives slurry and explosives, water gel.

Explosive, deflagrating

A substance, e.g. propellant, which reacts by deflagration rather than detonation when ignited and used in its normal manner.

Explosive, detonating

A substance which reacts by detonation rather than deflagration when initiated and used in its normal manner.

Explosive, extremely insensitive substances (EIS)

A substance which has demonstrated through tests that it is so insensitive that there is very little probability of accidental initiation.

Explosive, primary

Explosive substance manufactured with a view to producing a practical effect by explosion which is very sensitive to heat, impact or friction and which, even in very small quantities, either detonates or burns very rapidly. It is able to transmit detonation (in the case of initiating explosive) or deflagration to secondary explosives close to it. The main primary explosives are mercury fulminate, lead azide and lead styphnate.

Explosive, secondary

Explosive substance which is relatively insensitive (when compared to primary explosives), which is usually initiated by primary explosives with or without the aid of boosters or supplementary charges. Such an explosive may react as a deflagrating or as a detonating explosive.

FIRE SUPPRESSANT DISPERSING DEVICES

Articles which contain a pyrotechnic substance, which are intended to disperse a fire extinguishing agent (or aerosol) when activated, and which do not contain any other dangerous goods.

FIREWORKS

Pyrotechnic articles designed for entertainment.

Flares

Articles containing pyrotechnic substances which are designed for use to illuminate, identify, signal or warn. The term includes:

FLARES, AERIAL;
FLARES, SURFACE.

FLASH POWDER

Pyrotechnic substance which, when ignited, produces an intense light.

FRACTURING DEVICES, EXPLOSIVE *for oil wells, without detonator*

Articles consisting of a charge of detonating explosive contained in a casing without means of initiation. They are used to fracture the rock around a drill shaft to assist the flow of crude oil from the rock.

Fuse/Fuze (English text only)

Although these two words have a common origin (French fusée, fusil) and are sometimes considered to be different spellings, it is useful to maintain the convention that <u>fuse</u> refers to a cord-like igniting device whereas <u>fuze</u> refers to a device used in ammunition which incorporates mechanical, electrical, chemical or hydrostatic components to initiate a train by deflagration or detonation.

FUSE, IGNITER, tubular, metal clad

Article consisting of a metal tube with a core of deflagrating explosive.

FUSE, INSTANTANEOUS, NON-DETONATING (QUICKMATCH)

Article consisting of cotton yarns impregnated with fine black powder (Quickmatch). It burns with an external flame and is used in ignition trains for fireworks, etc.

FUSE, SAFETY

Article consisting of a core of fine-grained black powder surrounded by a flexible woven fabric with one or more protective outer coverings. When ignited, it burns at a predetermined rate without any external explosive effect.

Fuzes

Articles designed to start a detonation or a deflagration in ammunition. They incorporate mechanical, electrical, chemical or hydrostatic components and generally protective features. The term includes:

FUZES, DETONATING;
FUZES, DETONATING with protective features;
FUZES, IGNITING.

GRENADES, hand or rifle

Articles which are designed to be thrown by hand or to be projected by a rifle. The term includes:

GRENADES, hand or rifle, with bursting charge;
GRENADES, PRACTICE, hand or rifle.

The term excludes grenades, smoke which are listed under AMMUNITION, SMOKE.

IGNITERS

Articles containing one or more explosive substances used to start deflagration in an explosive train. They may be actuated chemically, electrically or mechanically. This term excludes the following articles which are listed separately: CORD, IGNITER; FUSE, IGNITER; FUSE, NON-DETONATING; FUZES, IGNITING; LIGHTERS, FUSE; PRIMERS, CAP TYPE; PRIMERS, TUBULAR.

Ignition, means of

A general term used in connection with the method employed to ignite a deflagrating train of explosive or pyrotechnic substances (for example: a primer for a propelling charge; an igniter for a rocket motor; an igniting fuze).

Initiation, means of

(1) A device intended to cause the detonation of an explosive (for example: detonator; detonator for ammunition; detonating fuze).

(2) The term "with its own means of initiation" means that the contrivance has its normal initiating device assembled to it and this device is considered to present a significant risk during transport but not one great enough to be unacceptable. The term does not apply, however, to a contrivance packed together with its means of initiation provided

the device is packaged so as to eliminate the risk of causing detonation of the contrivance in the event of accidental functioning of the initiating device. The means of initiating can even be assembled to the contrivance provided there are protective features such that the device is very unlikely to cause detonation of the contrivance in conditions which are associated with transport.

(3) For the purposes of classification any means of initiation without two effective protective features shall be regarded as Compatibility Group B; an article with its own means of initiation, without two effective protective features, would be Compatibility Group F. On the other hand a means of initiation which itself possesses two effective protective features would be Compatibility Group D; and an article with a means of initiation which possesses two effective protective features would be Compatibility Group D or E. Means of initiation adjudged as having two effective protective features shall have been approved by the competent national authority. A common and effective way of achieving the necessary degree of protection is to use a means of initiation which incorporates two or more independent safety features.

JET PERFORATING GUNS, CHARGED, oil well, without detonator

Articles consisting of a steel tube or metallic strip, into which are inserted shaped charges connected by detonating cord, without means of initiation.

LIGHTERS, FUSE

Articles of various design actuated by friction, percussion or electricity and used to ignite a safety fuse.

Mass explosion

Explosion which affects almost the entire load virtually instantaneously.

MINES

Articles consisting normally of metal or composition receptacles and a bursting charge. They are designed to be operated by the passage of ships, vehicles or personnel. The term includes "Bangalore torpedoes".

OXYGEN GENERATORS, CHEMICAL

Oxygen generators, chemical, are devices containing chemicals which upon activation release oxygen as a product of chemical reaction. Chemical oxygen generators are used for the generation of oxygen for respiratory support, e.g. in aircraft, submarines, spacecraft, bomb shelters and breathing apparatus. Oxidizing salts such as chlorates and perchlorates of lithium, sodium and potassium, which are used in chemical oxygen generators, evolve oxygen when heated. These salts are mixed (compounded) with a fuel, usually iron powder, to form a chlorate candle, which produces oxygen by continuous reaction. The fuel is used to generate heat by oxidation. Once the reaction begins, oxygen is released from the hot salt by thermal decomposition (a thermal shield is used around the generator). A portion of the oxygen reacts with the fuel to produce more heat which produces more oxygen, and so on. Initiation of the reaction can be achieved by a percussion device, friction device or electric wire.

POWDER CAKE (POWDER PASTE), WETTED

Substance consisting of nitrocellulose impregnated with not more than 60 % of nitroglycerin or other liquid organic nitrates or a mixture of these.

POWDER, SMOKELESS

Substance based on nitrocellulose used as propellant. The term includes propellants with a single base (nitrocellulose (NC) alone), those with a double base (such as NC and nitroglycerin (NG)) and those with a triple base (such as NC/NG/nitroguanidine). Cast, pressed or bag-charges of smokeless powder are listed under "CHARGES, PROPELLING" or "CHARGES, PROPELLING FOR CANNON".

PRIMERS, CAP TYPE

Articles consisting of a metal or plastics cap containing a small amount of primary explosive mixture that is readily ignited by impact. They serve as igniting elements in small arms cartridges, and in percussion primers for propelling charges.

PRIMERS, TUBULAR

Articles consisting of a primer for ignition and an auxiliary charge of deflagrating explosive such as black powder used to ignite the propelling charge in a cartridge case for cannon, etc.

PROJECTILES

Articles such as a shell or bullet which are projected from a cannon or other artillery gun, rifle or other small arm. They may be inert, with or without tracer, or may contain a burster or expelling charge or a bursting charge. The term includes:

PROJECTILES, inert, with tracer;
PROJECTILES with burster or expelling charge;
PROJECTILES with bursting charge.

PROPELLANTS

Deflagrating explosive used for propulsion or for reducing the drag of projectiles.

PROPELLANTS, LIQUID

Substances consisting of a deflagrating liquid explosive, used for propulsion.

PROPELLANTS, SOLID

Substances consisting of a deflagrating solid explosive, used for propulsion.

RELEASE DEVICES, EXPLOSIVE

Articles consisting of a small charge of explosive with means of initiation. They sever rods or links to release equipment quickly.

ROCKET MOTORS

Articles consisting of a solid, liquid or hypergolic fuel contained in a cylinder fitted with one or more nozzles. They are designed to propel a rocket or a guided missile. The term includes:

ROCKET MOTORS;
ROCKET MOTORS WITH HYPERGOLIC LIQUIDS with or without expelling charge;
ROCKET MOTORS, LIQUID FUELLED.

ROCKETS

Articles consisting of a rocket motor and a payload which may be an explosive warhead or other device. The term includes guided missiles and:

ROCKETS, LINE-THROWING;
ROCKETS, LIQUID FUELLED with bursting charge;
ROCKETS with bursting charge;
ROCKETS with expelling charge;
ROCKETS with inert head.

SAFETY DEVICES, electrically initiated

Articles which contain pyrotechnic substances or dangerous goods of other classes and are used in vehicles, vessels or aircraft to enhance safety to persons. Examples are: air bag inflators, air bag modules, seat-belt pretensioners and pyromechanical devices. These pyromechanical devices are assembled components for tasks such as but not limited to separation, locking, or release-and-drive or occupant restraint. The term includes "SAFETY DEVICES, PYROTECHNIC".

SIGNALS

Articles containing pyrotechnic substances designed to produce signals by means of sound, flame or smoke or any combinations thereof. The term includes:

SIGNAL DEVICES, HAND;
SIGNALS, DISTRESS, ship;
SIGNALS, RAILWAY TRACK, EXPLOSIVE;
SIGNALS, SMOKE.

SOUNDING DEVICES, EXPLOSIVE

Articles consisting of a charge of detonating explosive. They are dropped from ships and function when they reach a predetermined depth or the sea-bed.

STABILIZED

Stabilized means that the substance is in a condition that precludes uncontrolled reaction. This may be achieved by methods such as the addition of an inhibiting chemical, degassing the substance to remove dissolved oxygen and inerting the air space in the package, or maintaining the substance under temperature control.

SUBSTANCES, EXPLOSIVE, VERY INSENSITIVE (SUBSTANCES, EVI), N.O.S.

Substances which present a mass explosion hazard but which are so insensitive that there is very little probability of initiation, or of transition from burning to detonation (under normal conditions of transport) and which have passed test series 5.

TORPEDOES

Articles containing an explosive or non-explosive propulsion system and designed to be propelled through water. They may contain an inert head or a warhead. The term includes:

TORPEDOES, LIQUID FUELLED with inert head;
TORPEDOES, LIQUID FUELLED with or without bursting charge;
TORPEDOES with bursting charge.

TRACERS FOR AMMUNITION

Sealed articles containing pyrotechnic substances, designed to reveal the trajectory of a projectile.

Warheads

Articles consisting of detonating explosives. They are designed to be fitted to a rocket, guided missile or torpedo. They may contain a burster or expelling charge or bursting charge. The term includes:

WARHEADS, ROCKET with burster or expelling charge;
WARHEADS, ROCKET with bursting charge;
WARHEADS, TORPEDO with bursting charge.

ALPHABETICAL INDEX

OF

SUBSTANCES
AND ARTICLES

NOTES TO THE INDEX

1. This index is an alphabetical list of the substances and articles which are listed in numerical order in the Dangerous Goods List in chapter 3.2.

2. For the purpose of determining the alphabetical order the following information has been ignored even when it forms part of the proper shipping name: numbers; Greek letters; the abbreviations "sec" and "tert"; the prefixes "cis" and "trans"; and the letters "N" (nitrogen), "n" (normal), "o" (ortho) "m" (meta), "p" (para) and "N.O.S." (not otherwise specified).

3. The name of a substance or article in block capital letters indicates a proper shipping name.

4. The name of a substance or article in block capital letters followed by the word "see" indicates an alternative proper shipping name or part of a proper shipping name (except for PCBs).

5. An entry in lower case letters followed by the word "see" indicates that the entry is not a proper shipping name; it is a synonym.

6. Where an entry is partly in block capital letters and partly in lower case letters, the latter part is considered not to be part of the proper shipping name.

7. A proper shipping name may be used in the singular or plural, as appropriate, for the purposes of documentation and package marking.

INDEX

Name and description	Class	UN No.
Accumulators, electric, see	4.3	3292
	8	2794
	8	2795
	8	2800
	8	3028
ACETAL	3	1088
ACETALDEHYDE	3	1089
ACETALDEHYDE AMMONIA	9	1841
ACETALDEHYDE OXIME	3	2332
ACETIC ACID, GLACIAL	8	2789
ACETIC ACID SOLUTION, more than 10 % but not more than 80 % acid, by mass	8	2790
ACETIC ACID SOLUTION, more than 80 % acid, by mass	8	2789
ACETIC ANHYDRIDE	8	1715
Acetoin, see	3	2621
ACETONE	3	1090
ACETONE CYANOHYDRIN, STABILIZED	6.1	1541
ACETONE OILS	3	1091
ACETONITRILE	3	1648
ACETYL BROMIDE	8	1716
ACETYL CHLORIDE	3	1717
ACETYLENE, DISSOLVED	2.1	1001
ACETYLENE, SOLVENT FREE	2.1	3374
Acetylene tetrabromide, see	6.1	2504
Acetylene tetrachloride, see	6.1	1702
ACETYL IODIDE	8	1898
ACETYL METHYL CARBINOL	3	2621
Acid butyl phosphate, see	8	1718
Acid mixture, hydrofluoric and sulphuric, see	8	1786
Acid mixture, nitrating acid, see	8	1796
Acid mixture, spent, nitrating acid, see	8	1826
Acraldehyde, inhibited, see	6.1	1092

Name and description	Class	UN No.
ACRIDINE	6.1	2713
ACROLEIN DIMER, STABILIZED	3	2607
ACROLEIN, STABILIZED	6.1	1092
ACRYLAMIDE, SOLID	6.1	2074
ACRYLAMIDE SOLUTION	6.1	3426
ACRYLIC ACID, STABILIZED	8	2218
ACRYLONITRILE, STABILIZED	3	1093
Actinolite, see	9	2212
Activated carbon, see	4.2	1362
Activated charcoal, see	4.2	1362
ADHESIVES containing flammable liquid	3	1133
ADIPONITRILE	6.1	2205
Aeroplane flares, see	1.1G	0420
	1.2G	0421
	1.3G	0093
	1.4G	0403
	1.4S	0404
ADSORBED GAS, FLAMMABLE, N.O.S.	2.1	3510
ADSORBED GAS, N.O.S.	2.2	3511
ADSORBED GAS, OXIDIZING, N.O.S.	2.2	3513
ADSORBED GAS, TOXIC, CORROSIVE, N.O.S.	2.3	3516
ADSORBED GAS, TOXIC, FLAMMABLE, CORROSIVE, N.O.S.	2.3	3517
ADSORBED GAS, TOXIC, FLAMMABLE, N.O.S.	2.3	3514
ADSORBED GAS, TOXIC, N.O.S.	2.3	3512
ADSORBED GAS, TOXIC, OXIDIZING, CORROSIVE, N.O.S.	2.3	3518
ADSORBED GAS, TOXIC, OXIDIZING, N.O.S.	2.3	3515
AEROSOLS	2	1950
AGENT, BLASTING, TYPE B, see	1.5D	0331
AGENT, BLASTING, TYPE E, see	1.5D	0332

Name and description	Class	UN No.
Air bag inflators, see	1.4G	0503
	9	3268
Air bag modules, see	1.4G	0503
	9	3268
AIR, COMPRESSED	2.2	1002
Aircraft evacuation slides, see	9	2990
AIRCRAFT HYDRAULIC POWER UNIT FUEL TANK (containing a mixture of anhydrous hydrazine and methylhydrazine) (M86 fuel)	3	3165
Aircraft survival kits, see	9	2990
AIR, REFRIGERATED LIQUID	2.2	1003
ALCOHOLATES SOLUTION, N.O.S., in alcohol	3	3274
Alcohol, denatured, see	3	1986
		1987
Alcohol, industrial, see	3	1986
		1987
ALCOHOLS, N.O.S.	3	1987
ALCOHOLS, FLAMMABLE, TOXIC, N.O.S.	3	1986
ALCOHOLIC BEVERAGES, with more than 70 % alcohol by volume	3	3065
ALCOHOLIC BEVERAGES, with more than 24 % but not more than 70 % alcohol by volume	3	3065
Aldehyde, see	3	1989
ALDEHYDES, N.O.S.	3	1989
ALDEHYDES, FLAMMABLE, TOXIC, N.O.S.	3	1988
ALDOL	6.1	2839
ALKALI METAL ALCOHOLATES, SELF-HEATING, CORROSIVE, N.O.S.	4.2	3206
ALKALI METAL ALLOY, LIQUID, N.O.S.	4.3	1421
ALKALI METAL AMALGAM, LIQUID	4.3	1389
ALKALI METAL AMALGAM, SOLID	4.3	3401
ALKALI METAL AMIDES	4.3	1390
ALKALI METAL DISPERSION	4.3	1391
ALKALI METAL DISPERSION, FLAMMABLE	4.3	3482
Alkaline corrosive battery fluid, see	8	2797
ALKALINE EARTH METAL ALCOHOLATES, N.O.S.	4.2	3205
ALKALINE EARTH METAL ALLOY, N.O.S.	4.3	1393
ALKALINE EARTH METAL AMALGAM, LIQUID	4.3	1392
ALKALINE EARTH METAL AMALGAM, SOLID	4.3	3402
ALKALINE EARTH METAL DISPERSION	4.3	1391
ALKALINE EARTH METAL DISPERSION, FLAMMABLE	4.3	3482
ALKALOID SALTS, LIQUID, N.O.S.	6.1	3140
ALKALOID SALTS, SOLID, N.O.S.	6.1	1544
ALKALOIDS, LIQUID, N.O.S.	6.1	3140
ALKALOIDS, SOLID, N.O.S.	6.1	1544
Alkyl aluminium halides, see	4.2	3393
		3394
ALKYLPHENOLS, LIQUID, N.O.S. (including C_2-C_{12} homologues)	8	3145
ALKYLPHENOLS, SOLID, N.O.S. (including C_2-C_{12} homologues)	8	2430
ALKYLSULPHONIC ACIDS, LIQUID with more than 5 % free sulphuric acid	8	2584
ALKYLSULPHONIC ACIDS, LIQUID with not more than 5 % free sulphuric acid	8	2586
ALKYLSULPHONIC ACIDS, SOLID with more than 5 % free sulphuric acid	8	2583
ALKYLSULPHONIC ACIDS, SOLID with not more than 5 % free sulphuric acid	8	2585
ALKYLSULPHURIC ACIDS	8	2571
Allene, see	2.1	2200
ALLYL ACETATE	3	2333
ALLYL ALCOHOL	6.1	1098

Name and description	Class	UN No.
ALLYLAMINE	6.1	2334
ALLYL BROMIDE	3	1099
ALLYL CHLORIDE	3	1100
Allyl chlorocarbonate, see	6.1	1722
ALLYL CHLOROFORMATE	6.1	1722
ALLYL ETHYL ETHER	3	2335
ALLYL FORMATE	3	2336
ALLYL GLYCIDYL ETHER	3	2219
ALLYL IODIDE	3	1723
ALLYL ISOTHIOCYANATE, STABILIZED	6.1	1545
ALLYLTRICHLOROSILANE, STABILIZED	8	1724
Aluminium alkyl halides, liquid, see	4.2	3394
Aluminium alkyl halides, solid, see	4.2	3393
Aluminium alkyl hydrides, see	4.2	3394
Aluminium alkyls, see	4.2	3394
ALUMINIUM BOROHYDRIDE	4.2	2870
ALUMINIUM BOROHYDRIDE IN DEVICES	4.2	2870
ALUMINIUM BROMIDE, ANHYDROUS	8	1725
ALUMINIUM BROMIDE SOLUTION	8	2580
ALUMINIUM CARBIDE	4.3	1394
ALUMINIUM CHLORIDE, ANHYDROUS	8	1726
ALUMINIUM CHLORIDE SOLUTION	8	2581
Aluminium dross, see	4.3	3170
ALUMINIUM FERROSILICON POWDER	4.3	1395
ALUMINIUM HYDRIDE	4.3	2463
ALUMINIUM NITRATE	5.1	1438
ALUMINIUM PHOSPHIDE	4.3	1397
ALUMINIUM PHOSPHIDE PESTICIDE	6.1	3048

Name and description	Class	UN No.
ALUMINIUM POWDER, COATED	4.1	1309
ALUMINIUM POWDER, UNCOATED	4.3	1396
ALUMINIUM REMELTING BY-PRODUCTS	4.3	3170
ALUMINIUM RESINATE	4.1	2715
ALUMINIUM SILICON POWDER, UNCOATED	4.3	1398
ALUMINIUM SMELTING BY-PRODUCTS	4.3	3170
Amatols, see	1.1D	0082
AMINES, FLAMMABLE, CORROSIVE, N.O.S.	3	2733
AMINES, LIQUID, CORROSIVE, N.O.S.	8	2735
AMINES, LIQUID, CORROSIVE, FLAMMABLE, N.O.S.	8	2734
AMINES, SOLID, CORROSIVE, N.O.S.	8	3259
Aminobenzene, see	6.1	1547
2-Aminobenzotrifluoruride, see	6.1	2942
3-Aminobenzotrifluoruride, see	6.1	2948
Aminobutane, see	3	1125
2-AMINO-4-CHLOROPHENOL	6.1	2673
2-AMINO-5-DIETHYL-AMINOPENTANE	6.1	2946
2-AMINO-4,6-DINITROPHENOL, WETTED with not less than 20 % water, by mass	4.1	3317
2-(2-AMINOETHOXY)ETHANOL	8	3055
N-AMINOETHYLPIPERAZINE	8	2815
1-Amino-2-nitrobenzene, see	6.1	1661
1-Amino-3-nitrobenzene, see	6.1	1661
1-Amino-4-nitrobenzene, see	6.1	1661
AMINOPHENOLS (o-, m-, p-)	6.1	2512
AMINOPYRIDINES (o-, m-, p-)	6.1	2671
AMMONIA, ANHYDROUS	2.3	1005

Name and description	Class	UN No.
AMMONIA SOLUTION relative density between 0.880 and 0.957 at 15 °C in water, with more than 10 % but not more than 35 % ammonia	8	2672
AMMONIA SOLUTION, relative density less than 0.880 at 15 °C in water, with more than 35 % but not more than 50 % ammonia	2.2	2073
AMMONIA SOLUTION, relative density less than 0.880 at 15 °C in water, with more than 50 % ammonia	2.3	3318
AMMONIUM ARSENATE	6.1	1546
Ammonium bichromate, see	5.1	1439
Ammonium bifluoride solid, see	8	1727
Ammonium bifluoride solution, see	8	2817
Ammonium bisulphate, see	8	2506
Ammonium bisulphite solution, see	8	2693
AMMONIUM DICHROMATE	5.1	1439
AMMONIUM DINITRO-o-CRESOLATE, SOLID	6.1	1843
AMMONIUM DINITRO-o-CRESOLATE, SOLUTION	6.1	3424
AMMONIUM FLUORIDE	6.1	2505
AMMONIUM FLUOROSILICATE	6.1	2854
Ammonium hexafluorosilicate, see	6.1	2854
AMMONIUM HYDROGEN-DIFLUORIDE, SOLID	8	1727
AMMONIUM HYDROGEN-DIFLUORIDE SOLUTION	8	2817
AMMONIUM HYDROGEN SULPHATE	8	2506
Ammonium hydrosulphide solution (treat as ammonium sulphide solution), see	8	2683
AMMONIUM METAVANADATE	6.1	2859
AMMONIUM NITRATE BASED FERTILIZER	5.1 9	2067 2071
AMMONIUM NITRATE EMULSION, intermediate for blasting explosives	5.1	3375
Ammonium nitrate explosive, see	1.1D 1.5D	0082 0331

Name and description	Class	UN No.
AMMONIUM NITRATE GEL, intermediate for blasting explosives	5.1	3375
AMMONIUM NITRATE, LIQUID (hot concentrated solution)	5.1	2426
AMMONIUM NITRATE SUSPENSION, intermediate for blasting explosives	5.1	3375
AMMONIUM NITRATE	1.1D	0222
AMMONIUM NITRATE, with not more than 0.2 % combustible substances, including any organic substance calculated as carbon, to the exclusion of any other added substance	5.1	1942
AMMONIUM PERCHLORATE	1.1D 5.1	0402 1442
Ammonium permanganate, see	5.1	1482
AMMONIUM PERSULPHATE	5.1	1444
AMMONIUM PICRATE dry or wetted with less than 10 % water, by mass	1.1D	0004
AMMONIUM PICRATE, WETTED with not less than 10 % water, by mass	4.1	1310
AMMONIUM POLYSULPHIDE SOLUTION	8	2818
AMMONIUM POLYVANADATE	6.1	2861
Ammonium silicofluoride, see	6.1	2854
AMMONIUM SULPHIDE SOLUTION	8	2683
Ammunition, blank, see	1.1C 1.2C 1.3C 1.4C 1.4S	0326 0413 0327 0338 0014
Ammunition, fixed; Ammunition, semi-fixed; or Ammunition, separate loading; see	1.1E 1.1F 1.2E 1.2F 1.4E 1.4F	0006 0005 0321 0007 0412 0348
AMMUNITION, ILLUMINATING with or without burster, expelling charge or propelling charge	1.2G 1.3G 1.4G	0171 0254 0297
AMMUNITION, INCENDIARY, liquid or gel, with burster, expelling charge or propelling charge	1.3J	0247

Name and description	Class	UN No.
AMMUNITION, INCENDIARY with or without burster, expelling charge or propelling charge	1.2G 1.3G 1.4G	0009 0010 0300
Ammunition, incendiary (water-activated contrivances) with burster, expelling charge or propelling charge, see	1.2L 1.3L	0248 0249
AMMUNITION, INCENDIARY, WHITE PHOSPHORUS with burster, expelling charge or propelling charge	1.2H 1.3H	0243 0244
Ammunition, industrial, see	1.2C 1.3C 1.3C 1.4C 1.4C 1.4S	0381 0275 0277 0276 0278 0323
Ammunition, lachrymatory, see	1.2G 1.3G 1.4G 6.1	0018 0019 0301 2017
AMMUNITION, PRACTICE	1.3G 1.4G	0488 0362
AMMUNITION, PROOF	1.4G	0363
AMMUNITION, SMOKE with or without burster, expelling charge or propelling charge	1.2G 1.3G 1.4G	0015 0016 0303
Ammunition, smoke (water-activated contrivances), white phosphorus with burster, expelling charge or propelling charge, see	1.2L	0248
Ammunition, smoke (water-activated contrivances), without white phosphorus or phosphides with burster, expelling charge or propelling charge, see	1.3L	0249
AMMUNITION, SMOKE, WHITE PHOSPHORUS with burster, expelling charge or propelling charge	1.2H 1.3H	0245 0246
Ammunition, sporting, see	1.2C 1.3C 1.4C 1.4S	0328 0417 0339 0012
AMMUNITION, TEAR-PRODUCING, NON-EXPLOSIVE without burster or expelling charge, non-fuzed	6.1	2017
AMMUNITION, TEAR-PRODUCING with burster, expelling charge or propelling charge	1.2G 1.3G 1.4G	0018 0019 0301

Name and description	Class	UN No.
AMMUNITION, TOXIC with burster, expelling charge or propelling charge	1.2K 1.3K	0020 0021
Ammunition, toxic (water-activated contrivances) with burster, expelling charge or propelling charge, see	1.2L 1.3L	0248 0249
AMMUNITION, TOXIC, NON-EXPLOSIVE without burster or expelling charge, non-fuzed	6.1	2016
Amosite, see	9	2212
Amphibole asbestos, see	9	2212
AMYL ACETATES	3	1104
AMYL ACID PHOSPHATE	8	2819
Amyl aldehyde, see	3	2058
AMYLAMINE	3	1106
AMYL BUTYRATES	3	2620
AMYL CHLORIDE	3	1107
n-AMYLENE, see	3	1108
AMYL FORMATES	3	1109
AMYL MERCAPTAN	3	1111
n-AMYL METHYL KETONE	3	1110
AMYL NITRATE	3	1112
AMYL NITRITE	3	1113
AMYLTRICHLOROSILANE	8	1728
Anaesthetic ether, see	3	1155
ANILINE	6.1	1547
Aniline chloride, see	6.1	1548
ANILINE HYDROCHLORIDE	6.1	1548
Aniline oil, see	6.1	1547
Aniline salt, see	6.1	1548
ANISIDINES	6.1	2431
ANISOLE	3	2222
ANISOYL CHLORIDE	8	1729
Anthophyllite, see	9	2212
Antimonous chloride, see	8	1733

Name and description	Class	UN No.
ANTIMONY COMPOUND, INORGANIC, LIQUID, N.O.S.	6.1	3141
ANTIMONY COMPOUND, INORGANIC, SOLID, N.O.S.	6.1	1549
Antimony hydride, see	2.3	2676
ANTIMONY LACTATE	6.1	1550
Antimony (III) lactate, see	6.1	1550
ANTIMONY PENTACHLORIDE, LIQUID	8	1730
ANTIMONY PENTACHLORIDE SOLUTION	8	1731
ANTIMONY PENTAFLUORIDE	8	1732
Antimony perchloride, liquid, see	8	1730
ANTIMONY POTASSIUM TARTRATE	6.1	1551
ANTIMONY POWDER	6.1	2871
ANTIMONY TRICHLORIDE	8	1733
A.n.t.u., see	6.1	1651
ARGON, COMPRESSED	2.2	1006
ARGON, REFRIGERATED LIQUID	2.2	1951
Arsenates, n.o.s., see	6.1	1556
	6.1	1557
ARSENIC	6.1	1558
ARSENIC ACID, LIQUID	6.1	1553
ARSENIC ACID, SOLID	6.1	1554
ARSENICAL DUST	6.1	1562
Arsenical flue dust, see	6.1	1562
ARSENICAL PESTICIDE, LIQUID, FLAMMABLE, TOXIC, flash-point less than 23 °C	3	2760
ARSENICAL PESTICIDE, LIQUID, TOXIC	6.1	2994
ARSENICAL PESTICIDE, LIQUID, TOXIC, FLAMMABLE, flash-point not less than 23 °C	6.1	2993
ARSENICAL PESTICIDE, SOLID, TOXIC	6.1	2759
ARSENIC BROMIDE	6.1	1555
Arsenic (III) bromide, see	6.1	1555
Arsenice chloride, see	6.1	1560
ARSENIC COMPOUND, LIQUID, N.O.S., inorganic, including: Arsenates, n.o.s.; Arsenites, n.o.s.; and Arsenic sulphides, n.o.s.	6.1	1556
ARSENIC COMPOUND, SOLID, N.O.S., inorganic, including: Arsenates, n.o.s.; Arsenites, n.o.s.; and Arsenic sulphides, n.o.s.	6.1	1557
Arsenic (III) oxide, see	6.1	1561
Arsenic (V) oxide, see	6.1	1559
ARSENIC PENTOXIDE	6.1	1559
Arsenic sulphides, see	6.1	1556
	6.1	1557
ARSENIC TRICHLORIDE	6.1	1560
ARSENIC TRIOXIDE	6.1	1561
Arsenious chloride, see	6.1	1560
Arsenites, n.o.s., see	6.1	1556
	6.1	1557
Arsenous chloride, see	6.1	1560
ARSINE	2.3	2188
ARSINE, ADSORBED	2.3	3522
ARTICLES CONTAINING FLAMMABLE GAS, N.O.S.	2.1	3537
ARTICLES CONTAINING NON-FLAMMABLE, NON TOXIC GAS, N.O.S.	2.2	3538
ARTICLES CONTAINING TOXIC GAS, N.O.S.	2.3	3539
ARTICLES CONTAINING FLAMMABLE LIQUID, N.O.S.	3	3540
ARTICLES CONTAINING FLAMMABLE SOLID, N.O.S.	4.1	3541
ARTICLES CONTAINING A SUBSTANCE LIABLE TO SPONTANEOUS COMBUSTION, N.O.S.	4.2	3542

Name and description	Class	UN No.	Name and description	Class	UN No.
ARTICLES CONTAINING A SUBSTANCE WHICH IN CONTACT WITH WATER EMITS FLAMMABLE GASES, N.O.S.	4.3	3543	ARYLSULPHONIC ACIDS, LIQUID with more than 5 % free sulphuric acid	8	2584
			ARYLSULPHONIC ACIDS, LIQUID with not more than 5 % free sulphuric acid	8	2586
ARTICLES CONTAINING OXIDIZING SUBSTANCE, N.O.S.	5.1	3544			
			ARYLSULPHONIC ACIDS, SOLID with more than 5 % free sulphuric acid	8	2583
ARTICLES CONTAINING ORGANIC PEROXIDE, N.O.S.	5.2	3545			
			ARYLSULPHONIC ACIDS, SOLID with not more than 5 % free sulphuric acid	8	2585
ARTICLES CONTAINING TOXIC SUBSTANCE, N.O.S.	6.1	3546			
ARTICLES CONTAINING CORROSIVE SUBSTANCE, N.O.S.	8	3547	ASBESTOS, AMPHIBOLE	9	2212
			ASBESTOS, CHRYSOTILE	9	2590
ARTICLES CONTAINING MISCELLANEOUS DANGEROUS GOODS, N.O.S.	9	3548	AVIATION REGULATED LIQUID, N.O.S.	9	3334
ARTICLES, EEI, see	1.6N	0486	AVIATION REGULATED SOLID, N.O.S.	9	3335
ARTICLES, EXPLOSIVE, EXTREMELY INSENSITIVE	1.6N	0486	AZODICARBONAMIDE	4.1	3242
ARTICLES, EXPLOSIVE, N.O.S.	1.1C	0462	Bag charges, see	1.1C	0279
	1.1D	0463		1.2C	0414
	1.1E	0464		1.3C	0242
	1.1F	0465			
	1.1L	0354	Ballistite, see	1.1C	0160
	1.2C	0466		1.3C	0161
	1.2D	0467			
	1.2E	0468	Bangalore torpedoes, see	1.1D	0137
	1.2F	0469		1.1F	0136
	1.2L	0355		1.2D	0138
	1.3C	0470		1.2F	0294
	1.3L	0356			
	1.4B	0350	BARIUM	4.3	1400
	1.4C	0351	BARIUM ALLOYS, PYROPHORIC	4.2	1854
	1.4D	0352			
	1.4E	0471	BARIUM AZIDE, dry or wetted with less than 50 % water, by mass	1.1A	0224
	1.4F	0472			
	1.4G	0353			
	1.4S	0349	BARIUM AZIDE, WETTED with not less than 50 % water, by mass	4.1	1571
ARTICLES, PRESSURIZED, HYDRAULIC (containing non flammable gas)	2.2	3164	Barium binoxide, see	5.1	1449
			BARIUM BROMATE	5.1	2719
ARTICLES, PRESSURIZED, PNEUMATIC (containing non flammable gas)	2.2	3164	BARIUM CHLORATE, SOLID	5.1	1445
			BARIUM CHLORATE SOLUTION	5.1	3405
ARTICLES, PYROPHORIC	1.2L	0380	BARIUM COMPOUND, N.O.S.	6.1	1564
ARTICLES, PYROTECHNIC for technical purposes	1.1G	0428			
	1.2G	0429	BARIUM CYANIDE	6.1	1565
	1.3G	0430			
	1.4G	0431	Barium dioxide, see	5.1	1449
	1.4S	0432			

Name and description	Class	UN No.
BARIUM HYPOCHLORITE with more than 22 % available chlorine	5.1	2741
BARIUM NITRATE	5.1	1446
BARIUM OXIDE	6.1	1884
BARIUM PERCHLORATE, SOLID	5.1	1447
BARIUM PERCHLORATE SOLUTION	5.1	3406
BARIUM PERMANGANATE	5.1	1448
BARIUM PEROXIDE	5.1	1449
Barium selenate, see	6.1	2630
Barium selenite, see	6.1	2630
Barium superoxide, see	5.1	1449
BATTERIES, CONTAINING METALLIC SODIUM OR SODIUM ALLOY	4.3	3292
BATTERIES, DRY, CONTAINING POTASSIUM HYDROXIDE SOLID, electric storage	8	3028
BATTERIES, NICKEL-METAL HYDRIDE	9	3496
Batteries, sodium nickel chloride, see	4.3	3292
BATTERIES, WET, FILLED WITH ACID, electric storage	8	2794
BATTERIES, WET, FILLED WITH ALKALI, electric storage	8	2795
BATTERIES, WET, NON-SPILLABLE, electric storage	8	2800
BATTERY FLUID, ACID	8	2796
BATTERY FLUID, ALKALI	8	2797
Battery, lithium ion, see	9	3480
	9	3481
Battery, lithium metal, see	9	3090
	9	3091
BATTERY-POWERED EQUIPMENT	9	3171
BATTERY-POWERED VEHICLE	9	3171
BENZALDEHYDE	9	1990
BENZENE	3	1114
BENZENESULPHONYL CHLORIDE	8	2225

Name and description	Class	UN No.
Benzenethiol, see	6.1	2337
BENZIDINE	6.1	1885
Benzol, see	3	1114
Benzolene, see	3	1268
BENZONITRILE	6.1	2224
BENZOQUINONE	6.1	2587
Benzosulphochloride, see	8	2225
BENZOTRICHLORIDE	8	2226
BENZOTRIFLUORIDE	3	2338
BENZOYL CHLORIDE	8	1736
BENZYL BROMIDE	6.1	1737
BENZYL CHLORIDE	6.1	1738
Benzyl chlorocarbonate, see	8	1739
BENZYL CHLOROFORMATE	8	1739
Benzyl cyanide, see	6.1	2470
BENZYLDIMETHYLAMINE	8	2619
BENZYLIDENE CHLORIDE	6.1	1886
BENZYL IODIDE	6.1	2653
BERYLLIUM COMPOUND, N.O.S.	6.1	1566
BERYLLIUM NITRATE	5.1	2464
BERYLLIUM POWDER	6.1	1567
BHUSA	4.1	1327
BICYCLO[2.2.1]HEPTA-2,5-DIENE, STABILIZED	3	2251
Bifluorides, n.o.s., see	8	1740
BIOLOGICAL SUBSTANCE, CATEGORY B	6.2	3373
(BIO) MEDICAL WASTE, N.O.S.	6.2	3291
BIPYRIDILIUM PESTICIDE, LIQUID, FLAMMABLE, TOXIC, flash-point less than 23 °C	3	2782
BIPYRIDILIUM PESTICIDE, LIQUID, TOXIC	6.1	3016

Name and description	Class	UN No.
BIPYRIDILIUM PESTICIDE, LIQUID, TOXIC, FLAMMABLE, flash-point not less than 23 °C	6.1	3015
BIPYRIDILIUM PESTICIDE, SOLID, TOXIC	6.1	2781
BISULPHATES, AQUEOUS SOLUTION	8	2837
BISULPHITES, AQUEOUS SOLUTION, N.O.S.	8	2693
BLACK POWDER, COMPRESSED	1.1D	0028
BLACK POWDER, granular or as a meal	1.1D	0027
BLACK POWDER, IN PELLETS	1.1D	0028
Blasting cap assemblies, see	1.1B	0360
	1.4B	0361
Blasting caps, electric, see	1.1B	0030
	1.4B	0255
	1.4S	0456
Blasting caps, non electric, see	1.1B	0029
	1.4B	0267
	1.4S	0455
Bleaching powder, see	5.1	2208
BOMBS with bursting charge	1.1D	0034
	1.1F	0033
	1.2D	0035
	1.2F	0291
Bombs, illuminating, see	1.3G	0254
BOMBS, PHOTO-FLASH	1.1D	0038
	1.1F	0037
	1.2G	0039
	1.3G	0299
BOMBS, SMOKE, NON-EXPLOSIVE with corrosive liquid, without initiating device	8	2028
Bombs, target identification, see	1.2G	0171
	1.3G	0254
	1.4G	0297
BOMBS WITH FLAMMABLE LIQUID with bursting charge	1.1J	0399
	1.2J	0400
BOOSTERS without detonator	1.1D	0042
	1.2D	0283
BOOSTERS WITH DETONATOR	1.1B	0225
	1.2B	0268

Name and description	Class	UN No.
Borate and chlorate mixture, see	5.1	1458
BORNEOL	4.1	1312
BORON TRIBROMIDE	8	2692
BORON TRICHLORIDE	2.3	1741
BORON TRIFLUORIDE	2.3	1008
BORON TRIFLUORIDE ACETIC ACID COMPLEX, LIQUID	8	1742
BORON TRIFLUORIDE ACETIC ACID COMPLEX, SOLID	8	3419
BORON TRIFLUORIDE, ADSORBED	2.3	3519
BORON TRIFLUORIDE DIETHYL ETHERATE	8	2604
BORON TRIFLUORIDE DIHYDRATE	8	2851
BORON TRIFLUORIDE DIMETHYL ETHERATE	4.3	2965
BORON TRIFLUORIDE PROPIONIC ACID COMPLEX, LIQUID	8	1743
BORON TRIFLUORIDE PROPIONIC ACID COMPLEX, SOLID	8	3420
BROMATES, INORGANIC, N.O.S.	5.1	1450
BROMATES, INORGANIC, AQUEOUS SOLUTION, N.O.S	5.1	3213
BROMINE	8	1744
BROMINE CHLORIDE	2.3	2901
BROMINE PENTAFLUORIDE	5.1	1745
BROMINE SOLUTION	8	1744
BROMINE TRIFLUORIDE	5.1	1746
BROMOACETIC ACID SOLUTION	8	1938
BROMOACETIC ACID, SOLID	8	3425
BROMOACETONE	6.1	1569
omega-Bromoacetone, see	6.1	2645
BROMOACETYL BROMIDE	8	2513
BROMOBENZENE	3	2514
BROMOBENZYL CYANIDES, LIQUID	6.1	1694
BROMOBENZYL CYANIDES, SOLID	6.1	3449

Name and description	Class	UN No.
1-BROMOBUTANE	3	1126
2-BROMOBUTANE	3	2339
BROMOCHLOROMETHANE	6.1	1887
1-BROMO-3-CHLOROPROPANE	6.1	2688
1-Bromo-2,3-epoxypropane, see	6.1	2558
Bromoethane, see	6.1	1891
2-BROMOETHYL ETHYL ETHER	3	2340
BROMOFORM	6.1	2515
Bromomethane, see	2.3	1062
1-BROMO-3-METHYLBUTANE	3	2341
BROMOMETHYLPROPANES	3	2342
2-BROMO-2-NITROPROPANE-1,3-DIOL	4.1	3241
2-BROMOPENTANE	3	2343
BROMOPROPANES	3	2344
3-BROMOPROPYNE	3	2345
BROMOTRIFLUOROETHYLENE	2.1	2419
BROMOTRIFLUOROMETHANE	2.2	1009
BRUCINE	6.1	1570
BURSTERS, explosive	1.1D	0043
BUTADIENES, STABILIZED	2.1	1010
BUTADIENES AND HYDROCARBON MIXTURE, STABILIZED, containing more than 20 % butadienes	2.1	1010
BUTANE	2.1	1011
BUTANEDIONE	3	2346
Butane-1-thiol, see	3	2347
1-Butanol, see	3	1120
Butan-2-ol, see	3	1120
BUTANOLS	3	1120
Butanol, secondary, see	3	1120
Butanol, tertiary, see	3	1120
Butanone, see	3	1193
2-Butenal, see	6.1	1143

Name and description	Class	UN No.
Butene, see	2.1	1012
But-1-ene-3-one, see	6.1	1251
1,2-Buteneoxide, see	3	3022
2-Buten-1-ol, see	3	2614
BUTYL ACETATES	3	1123
Butyl acetate, secondary, see	3	1123
BUTYL ACID PHOSPHATE	8	1718
BUTYL ACRYLATES, STABILIZED	3	2348
Butyl alcohols, see	3	1120
n-BUTYLAMINE	3	1125
N-BUTYLANILINE	6.1	2738
sec-Butyl benzene, see	3	2709
BUTYLBENZENES	3	2709
n-Butyl bromide, see	3	1126
n-Butyl chloride, see	3	1127
n-BUTYL CHLOROFORMATE	6.1	2743
tert-BUTYLCYCLOHEXYL CHLOROFORMATE	6.1	2747
BUTYLENE	2.1	1012
1-butylene, see	2.1	1012
cis-2-butylene, see	2.1	1012
trans-2-butylene, see	2.1	1012
1,2-BUTYLENE OXIDE, STABILIZED	3	3022
Butylenes mixture, see	2.1	1012
Butyl ethers, see	3	1149
Butyl ethyl ether, see	3	1179
n-BUTYL FORMATE	3	1128
tert-BUTYL HYPOCHLORITE	4.2	3255
N,n-BUTYLIMIDAZOLE	6.1	2690
N,n-Butyliminazole, see	6.1	2690
n-BUTYL ISOCYANATE	6.1	2485
tert-BUTYL ISOCYANATE	6.1	2484
Butyl lithium, see	4.2	3394

Name and description	Class	UN No.
BUTYL MERCAPTAN	3	2347
n-BUTYL METHACRYLATE, STABILIZED	3	2227
BUTYL METHYL ETHER	3	2350
BUTYL NITRITES	3	2351
Butylphenols, liquid, see	8	3145
Butylphenols, solid, see	8	2430
BUTYL PROPIONATES	3	1914
p-tert-Butyltoluene, see	6.1	2667
BUTYLTOLUENES	6.1	2667
BUTYLTRICHLOROSILANE	8	1747
5-tert-BUTYL-2,4,6-TRINITRO-m XYLENE	4.1	2956
BUTYL VINYL ETHER, STABILIZED	3	2352
But-1-yne, see	2.1	2452
1,4-BUTYNEDIOL	6.1	2716
2-Butyne-1,4-diol, see	6.1	2716
BUTYRALDEHYDE	3	1129
BUTYRALDOXIME	3	2840
BUTYRIC ACID	8	2820
BUTYRIC ANHYDRIDE	8	2739
Butyrone, see	3	2710
BUTYRONITRILE	3	2411
Butyroyl chloride, see	3	2353
BUTYRYL CHLORIDE	3	2353
Cable cutters, explosive, see	1.4S	0070
CACODYLIC ACID	6.1	1572
CADMIUM COMPOUND	6.1	2570
CAESIUM	4.3	1407
CAESIUM HYDROXIDE	8	2682
CAESIUM HYDROXIDE SOLUTION	8	2681
CAESIUM NITRATE	5.1	1451
Caffeine, see	6.1	1544
Cajeputene, see	3	2052
CALCIUM	4.3	1401
CALCIUM ALLOYS, PYROPHORIC	4.2	1855
CALCIUM ARSENATE	6.1	1573
CALCIUM ARSENATE AND CALCIUM ARSENITE MIXTURE, SOLID	6.1	1574
Calcium bisulphite solution, see	8	2693
CALCIUM CARBIDE	4.3	1402
CALCIUM CHLORATE	5.1	1452
CALCIUM CHLORATE, AQUEOUS SOLUTION	5.1	2429
CALCIUM CHLORITE	5.1	1453
CALCIUM CYANAMIDE with more than 0.1 % calcium carbide	4.3	1403
CALCIUM CYANIDE	6.1	1575
CALCIUM DITHIONITE	4.2	1923
CALCIUM HYDRIDE	4.3	1404
CALCIUM HYDROSULPHITE, see	4.2	1923
CALCIUM HYPOCHLORITE, DRY with more than 39 % available chlorine (8.8 % available oxygen)	5.1	1748
CALCIUM HYPOCHLORITE, DRY, CORROSIVE with more than 39 % available chlorine (8.8 % available oxygen)	5.1	3485
CALCIUM HYPOCHLORITE, HYDRATED with not less than 5.5 % but not more than 16 % water	5.1	2880
CALCIUM HYPOCHLORITE, HYDRATED, CORROSIVE with not less than 5.5 % but not more than 16 % water	5.1	3487
CALCIUM HYPOCHLORITE, HYDRATED MIXTURE with not less than 5.5 % but not more than 16 % water	5.1	2880
CALCIUM HYPOCHLORITE, HYDRATED MIXTURE, CORROSIVE with not less than 5.5 % but not more than 16 % water	5.1	3487

Name and description	Class	UN No.
CALCIUM HYPOCHLORITE MIXTURE, DRY with more than 39 % available chlorine (8.8 % available oxygen)	5.1	1748
CALCIUM HYPOCHLORITE MIXTURE, DRY, CORROSIVE with more than 39 % available chlorine (8.8 % available oxygen)	5.1	3485
CALCIUM HYPOCHLORITE MIXTURE, DRY with more than 10 % but not more than 39 % available chlorine	5.1	2208
CALCIUM HYPOCHLORITE MIXTURE, DRY, CORROSIVE with more than 10 % but not more than 39 % available chlorine	5.1	3486
CALCIUM MANGANESE SILICON	4.3	2844
CALCIUM NITRATE	5.1	1454
CALCIUM OXIDE	8	1910
CALCIUM PERCHLORATE	5.1	1455
CALCIUM PERMANGANATE	5.1	1456
CALCIUM PEROXIDE	5.1	1457
CALCIUM PHOSPHIDE	4.3	1360
CALCIUM, PYROPHORIC	4.2	1855
CALCIUM RESINATE	4.1	1313
CALCIUM RESINATE, FUSED	4.1	1314
Calcium selenate, see	6.1	2630
CALCIUM SILICIDE	4.3	1405
Calcium silicon, see	4.3	1405
Calcium superoxide, see	5.1	1457
Camphanone, see	4.1	2717
CAMPHOR OIL	3	1130
CAMPHOR, synthetic	4.1	2717
CAPACITOR, ASYMMETRIC, (with an energy storage capacity greater than 0.3Wh)	9	3508
CAPACITOR, ELECTRIC DOUBLE LAYER (with an energy storage capacity greater than 0.3Wh)	9	3499
CAPROIC ACID	8	2829

Name and description	Class	UN No.
CARBAMATE PESTICIDE, LIQUID, FLAMMABLE, TOXIC, flash-point less than 23 °C	3	2758
CARBAMATE PESTICIDE, LIQUID, TOXIC	6.1	2992
CARBAMATE PESTICIDE, LIQUID, TOXIC, FLAMMABLE, flash-point not less than 23 °C	6.1	2991
CARBAMATE PESTICIDE, SOLID, TOXIC	6.1	2757
Carbolic acid, see	6.1	1671
	6.1	2312
	6.1	2821
CARBON, animal or vegetable origin	4.2	1361
CARBON, ACTIVATED	4.2	1362
Carbon bisulphide, see	3	1131
Carbon black (animal or vegetable origin), see	4.2	1361
CARBON DIOXIDE	2.2	1013
Carbon dioxide and ethylene oxide mixture, see	2.1	1041
	2.2	1952
	2.3	3300
CARBON DIOXIDE, REFRIGERATED LIQUID	2.2	2187
CARBON DIOXIDE, SOLID	9	1845
CARBON DISULPHIDE	3	1131
Carbonic anhydride, see	2.2	1013
	9	1845
	2.2	2187
CARBON MONOXIDE, COMPRESSED	2.3	1016
Carbon oxysulphide, see	2.3	2204
CARBON TETRABROMIDE	6.1	2516
CARBON TETRACHLORIDE	6.1	1846
Carbonyl chloride, see	2.3	1076
CARBONYL FLUORIDE	2.3	2417
CARBONYL SULPHIDE	2.3	2204
Cartridge cases, empty, primed, see	1.4C	0379
	1.4S	0055

Name and description	Class	UN No.
Cartridges, actuating, for fire extinguisher or apparatus valve, see	1.2C 1.3C 1.4C 1.4S	0381 0275 0276 0323
Cartridges, explosive, see	1.1D	0048
CARTRIDGES, FLASH	1.1G 1.3G	0049 0050
CARTRIDGES FOR TOOLS, BLANK	1.4S	0014
CARTRIDGES FOR WEAPONS with bursting charge	1.1E 1.1F 1.2E 1.2F 1.4E 1.4F	0006 0005 0321 0007 0412 0348
CARTRIDGES FOR WEAPONS, BLANK	1.1C 1.2C 1.3C 1.4C 1.4S	0326 0413 0327 0338 0014
CARTRIDGES FOR WEAPONS, INERT PROJECTILE	1.2C 1.3C 1.4C 1.4S	0328 0417 0339 0012
Cartridges, illuminating, see	1.2G 1.3G 1.4G	0171 0254 0297
CARTRIDGES, OIL WELL	1.3C 1.4C	0277 0278
CARTRIDGES, POWER DEVICE	1.2C 1.3C 1.4C 1.4S	0381 0275 0276 0323
CARTRIDGES, SIGNAL	1.3G 1.4G 1.4S	0054 0312 0405
CARTRIDGES, SMALL ARMS	1.3C 1.4C 1.4S	0417 0339 0012
CARTRIDGES, SMALL ARMS, BLANK	1.3C 1.4C 1.4S	0327 0338 0014
Cartridges, starter, jet engine, see	1.2C 1.3C 1.4C 1.4S	0381 0275 0276 0323
CASES, CARTRIDGE, EMPTY, WITH PRIMER	1.4C 1.4S	0379 0055

Name and description	Class	UN No.
CASES, COMBUSTIBLE, EMPTY, WITHOUT PRIMER	1.3C 1.4C	0447 0446
Casinghead gasoline, see	3	1203
CASTOR BEANS	9	2969
CASTOR FLAKE	9	2969
CASTOR MEAL	9	2969
CASTOR POMACE	9	2969
CAUSTIC ALKALI LIQUID, N.O.S.	8	1719
Caustic potash, see	8	1814
Caustic soda, see	8	1824
Caustic soda liquor, see	8	1824
CELLS, CONTAINING METALLIC SODIUM OR SODIUM ALLOY	4.3	3292
CELLULOID in block, rods, rolls, sheets, tubes, etc., except scrap	4.1	2000
CELLULOID, SCRAP	4.2	2002
Cement, see	3	1133
CERIUM, slabs, ingots or rods	4.1	1333
CERIUM, turnings or gritty powder	4.3	3078
Cer mishmetall, see	4.1	1323
Charcoal, activated, see	4.2	1362
Charcoal, non-activated, see	4.2	1361
CHARGES, BURSTING, PLASTICS BONDED	1.1D 1.2D 1.4D 1.4S	0457 0458 0459 0460
CHARGES, DEMOLITION	1.1D	0048
CHARGES, DEPTH	1.1D	0056
Charges, expelling, explosive, for fire extinguishers, see	1.2C 1.3C 1.4C 1.4S	0381 0275 0276 0323
CHARGES, EXPLOSIVE, COMMERCIAL without detonator	1.1D 1.2D 1.4D 1.4S	0442 0443 0444 0445

Name and description	Class	UN No.
CHARGES, PROPELLING	1.1C	0271
	1.2C	0415
	1.3C	0272
	1.4C	0491
CHARGES, PROPELLING, FOR CANNON	1.1C	0279
	1.2C	0414
	1.3C	0242
CHARGES, SHAPED, FLEXIBLE, LINEAR	1.1D	0288
	1.4D	0237
CHARGES, SHAPED, without detonator	1.1D	0059
	1.2D	0439
	1.4D	0440
	1.4S	0441
CHARGES, SUPPLEMENTARY, EXPLOSIVE	1.1D	0060
CHEMICAL KIT	9	3316
CHEMICAL SAMPLE, TOXIC	6.1	3315
CHEMICAL UNDER PRESSURE, N.O.S.	2.2	3500
CHEMICAL UNDER PRESSURE, CORROSIVE, N.O.S.	2.2	3503
CHEMICAL UNDER PRESSURE, FLAMMABLE, N.O.S.	2.1	3501
CHEMICAL UNDER PRESSURE, FLAMMABLE, CORROSIVE, N.O.S.	2.1	3505
CHEMICAL UNDER PRESSURE, FLAMMABLE, TOXIC, N.O.S.	2.1	3504
CHEMICAL UNDER PRESSURE, TOXIC, N.O.S.	2.2	3502
Chile saltpetre, see	5.1	1498
CHLORAL, ANHYDROUS, STABILIZED	6.1	2075
CHLORATE AND BORATE MIXTURE	5.1	1458
CHLORATE AND MAGNESIUM CHLORIDE MIXTURE, SOLID	5.1	1459
CHLORATE AND MAGNESIUM CHLORIDE MIXTURE SOLUTION	5.1	3407
CHLORATES, INORGANIC, N.O.S.	5.1	1461
CHLORATES, INORGANIC, AQUEOUS SOLUTION, N.O.S.	5.1	3210
CHLORIC ACID, AQUEOUS SOLUTION with not more than 10 % chloric acid	5.1	2626
CHLORINE	2.3	1017
CHLORINE, ADSORBED	2.3	3520
CHLORINE PENTAFLUORIDE	2.3	2548
CHLORINE TRIFLUORIDE	2.3	1749
CHLORITES, INORGANIC, N.O.S.	5.1	1462
CHLORITE SOLUTION	8	1908
Chloroacetaldehyde, see	6.1	2232
CHLOROACETIC ACID, MOLTEN	6.1	3250
CHLOROACETIC ACID, SOLID	6.1	1751
CHLOROACETIC ACID SOLUTION	6.1	1750
CHLOROACETONE, STABILIZED	6.1	1695
CHLOROACETONITRILE	6.1	2668
CHLOROACETOPHENONE, SOLID	6.1	1697
CHLOROACETOPHENONE, LIQUID	6.1	3416
CHLOROACETYL CHLORIDE	6.1	1752
CHLOROANILINES, LIQUID	6.1	2019
CHLOROANILINES, SOLID	6.1	2018
CHLOROANISIDINES	6.1	2233
CHLOROBENZENE	3	1134
CHLOROBENZOTRIFLUORIDES	3	2234
CHLOROBENZYL CHLORIDES, LIQUID	6.1	2235
CHLOROBENZYL CHLORIDES, SOLID	6.1	3427
1-Chloro-3-bromopropane, see	6.1	2688
1-Chlorobutane, see	3	1127
2-Chlorobutane, see	3	1127
CHLOROBUTANES	3	1127
CHLOROCRESOLS SOLUTION	6.1	2669
CHLOROCRESOLS, SOLID	6.1	3437

Name and description	Class	UN No.
CHLORODIFLUOROBROMO METHANE	2.3	1974
1-CHLORO-1,1-DIFLUOROETHANE	2.1	2517
CHLORODIFLUOROMETHANE	2.2	1018
CHLORODIFLUOROMETHANE AND CHLOROPENTAFLUORO-ETHANE MIXTURE with fixed boiling point, with approximately 49 % chlorodifluoromethane	2.2	1973
3-Chloro-1,2-dihydroxypropane, see	6.1	2689
Chlorodimethyl ether, see	6.1	1239
CHLORODINITROBENZENES, LIQUID	6.1	1577
CHLORODINITROBENZENES, SOLID	6.1	3441
2-CHLOROETHANAL	6.1	2232
Chloroethane, see	2.1	1037
Chloroethane nitrile, see	6.1	2668
2-Chloroethanol, see	6.1	1135
CHLOROFORM	6.1	1888
CHLOROFORMATES, TOXIC, CORROSIVE, N.O.S.	6.1	3277
CHLOROFORMATES, TOXIC, CORROSIVE, FLAMMABLE, N.O.S.	6.1	2742
Chloromethane, see	2.1	1063
1-Chloro-3-methylbutane, see	3	1107
2-Chloro-2-methylbutane, see	3	1107
CHLOROMETHYL CHLOROFORMATE	6.1	2745
Chloromethyl cyanide, see	6.1	2668
CHLOROMETHYL ETHYL ETHER	3	2354
Chloromethyl methyl ether, see	6.1	1239
3-CHLORO-4-METHYLPHENYL ISOCYANATE, LIQUID	6.1	2236
3-CHLORO-4-METHYLPHENYL ISOCYANATE, SOLID	6.1	3428
3-Chloro-2-methylprop-1-ene, see	3	2554
CHLORONITROANILINES	6.1	2237
CHLORONITROBENZENES, SOLID	6.1	1578
CHLORONITROBENZENES, LIQUID	6.1	3409
CHLORONITROTOLUENES, LIQUID	6.1	2433
CHLORONITROTOLUENES, SOLID	6.1	3457
CHLOROPENTAFLUOROETHANE	2.2	1020
CHLOROPHENOLATES, LIQUID	8	2904
CHLOROPHENOLATES, SOLID	8	2905
CHLOROPHENOLS, LIQUID	6.1	2021
CHLOROPHENOLS, SOLID	6.1	2020
CHLOROPHENYL-TRICHLOROSILANE	8	1753
CHLOROPICRIN	6.1	1580
CHLOROPICRIN AND METHYL CHLORIDE MIXTURE	2.3	1582
CHLOROPICRIN AND METHYL BROMIDE MIXTURE with more than 2 % chloropicrin	2.3	1581
CHLOROPICRIN MIXTURE, N.O.S.	6.1	1583
CHLOROPLATINIC ACID, SOLID	8	2507
CHLOROPRENE, STABILIZED	3	1991
1-CHLOROPROPANE	3	1278
2-CHLOROPROPANE	3	2356
3-Chloro-propanediol-1,2, see	6.1	2689
3-CHLOROPROPANOL-1	6.1	2849
2-CHLOROPROPENE	3	2456
3-Chloropropene, see	3	1100
3-Chloroprop-1-ene, see	3	1100
2-CHLOROPROPIONIC ACID	8	2511
2-CHLOROPYRIDINE	6.1	2822
CHLOROSILANES, CORROSIVE, N.O.S.	8	2987
CHLOROSILANES, CORROSIVE, FLAMMABLE, N.O.S.	8	2986

Name and description	Class	UN No.
CHLOROSILANES, FLAMMABLE, CORROSIVE, N.O.S.	3	2985
CHLOROSILANES, TOXIC, CORROSIVE, N.O.S.	6.1	3361
CHLOROSILANES, TOXIC, CORROSIVE, FLAMMABLE, N.O.S.	6.1	3362
CHLOROSILANES, WATER-REACTIVE, FLAMMABLE, CORROSIVE, N.O.S.	4.3	2988
CHLOROSULPHONIC ACID (with or without sulphur trioxide)	8	1754
1-CHLORO-1,2,2,2-TETRAFLUOROETHANE	2.2	1021
CHLOROTOLUENES	3	2238
4-CHLORO-o-TOLUIDINE HYDROCHLORIDE, SOLID	6.1	1579
4-CHLORO-ortho-TOLUIDINE HYDROCHLORIDE SOLUTION	6.1	3410
CHLOROTOLUIDINES, SOLID	6.1	2239
CHLOROTOLUIDINES, LIQUID	6.1	3429
1-CHLORO-2,2,2-TRIFLUORO-ETHANE	2.2	1983
Chlorotrifluoroethylene, see	2.3	1082
CHLOROTRIFLUOROMETHANE	2.2	1022
CHLOROTRIFLUOROMETHANE AND TRIFLUOROMETHANE AZEOTROPIC MIXTURE with approximately 60 % chlorotrifluoromethane	2.2	2599
Chromic acid, solid, see	5.1	1463
CHROMIC ACID SOLUTION	8	1755
Chromic anhydride, solid, see	5.1	1463
CHROMIC FLUORIDE, SOLID	8	1756
CHROMIC FLUORIDE SOLUTION	8	1757
Chromic nitrate, see	5.1	2720
Chromium (VI) dichloride dioxide, see	8	1758
Chromium (III) fluoride, solid, see	8	1756
CHROMIUM NITRATE	5.1	2720
Chromium (III) nitrate, see	5.1	2720
CHROMIUM OXYCHLORIDE	8	1758
CHROMIUM TRIOXIDE, ANHYDROUS	5.1	1463
CHROMOSULPHURIC ACID	8	2240
Chrysotile, see	9	2590
Cinene, see	3	2052
Cinnamene, see	3	2055
Cinnamol, see	3	2055
CLINICAL WASTE, UNSPECIFIED, N.O.S.	6.2	3291
COAL GAS, COMPRESSED	2.3	1023
COAL TAR DISTILLATES, FLAMMABLE	3	1136
Coal tar naphtha, see	3	1268
Coal tar oil, see	3	1136
COATING SOLUTION (includes surface treatment or coatings used for industrial or other purposes such as vehicle under coating, drum or barrel lining)	3	1139
COBALT DIHYDROXIDE POWDER, containing not less than 10 % respirable particles	6.1	3550
COBALT NAPHTHENATES, POWDER	4.1	2001
COBALT RESINATE, PRECIPITATED	4.1	1318
Cocculus, see	6.1	3172
Collodion cottons, see	1.1D	0340
	1.1D	0341
	1.3C	0342
	3	2059
	4.1	2555
	4.1	2556
	4.1	2557
COMPONENTS, EXPLOSIVE TRAIN, N.O.S.	1.1B	0461
	1.2B	0382
	1.4B	0383
	1.4S	0384
Composition B, see	1.1D	0118
COMPRESSED GAS, N.O.S.	2.2	1956

Name and description	Class	UN No.
COMPRESSED GAS, FLAMMABLE, N.O.S.	2.1	1954
COMPRESSED GAS, OXIDIZING, N.O.S.	2.2	3156
COMPRESSED GAS, TOXIC, N.O.S.	2.3	1955
COMPRESSED GAS, TOXIC, CORROSIVE, N.O.S.	2.3	3304
COMPRESSED GAS, TOXIC, FLAMMABLE, N.O.S.	2.3	1953
COMPRESSED GAS, TOXIC, FLAMMABLE, CORROSIVE, N.O.S.	2.3	3305
COMPRESSED GAS, TOXIC, OXIDIZING, N.O.S.	2.3	3303
COMPRESSED GAS, TOXIC, OXIDIZING, CORROSIVE, N.O.S.	2.3	3306
CONTRIVANCES, WATER-ACTIVATED with burster, expelling charge or propelling charge	1.2L 1.3L	0248 0249
COPPER ACETOARSENITE	6.1	1585
COPPER ARSENITE	6.1	1586
Copper (II) arsenite, see	6.1	1586
COPPER BASED PESTICIDE, LIQUID, FLAMMABLE, TOXIC, flash-point less than 23 °C	3	2776
COPPER BASED PESTICIDE, LIQUID, TOXIC	6.1	3010
COPPER BASED PESTICIDE, LIQUID, TOXIC, FLAMMABLE, flash-point not less than 23 °C	6.1	3009
COPPER BASED PESTICIDE, SOLID, TOXIC	6.1	2775
COPPER CHLORATE	5.1	2721
Copper (II) chlorate, see	5.1	2721
COPPER CHLORIDE	8	2802
COPPER CYANIDE	6.1	1587
Copper selenate, see	6.1	2630
Copper selenite, see	6.1	2630
COPRA	4.2	1363
CORD, DETONATING, flexible	1.1D 1.4D	0065 0289

Name and description	Class	UN No.
CORD, DETONATING, metal clad	1.1D 1.2D	0290 0102
CORD, DETONATING, MILD EFFECT, metal clad	1.4D	0104
CORD, IGNITER	1.4G	0066
Cordite, see	1.1C 1.3C	0160 0161
CORROSIVE LIQUID, N.O.S.	8	1760
CORROSIVE LIQUID, ACIDIC, INORGANIC, N.O.S.	8	3264
CORROSIVE LIQUID, ACIDIC, ORGANIC, N.O.S.	8	3265
CORROSIVE LIQUID, BASIC, INORGANIC, N.O.S.	8	3266
CORROSIVE LIQUID, BASIC, ORGANIC, N.O.S.	8	3267
CORROSIVE LIQUID, FLAMMABLE, N.O.S.	8	2920
CORROSIVE LIQUID, OXIDIZING, N.O.S.	8	3093
CORROSIVE LIQUID, SELF-HEATING, N.O.S.	8	3301
CORROSIVE LIQUID, TOXIC, N.O.S.	8	2922
CORROSIVE LIQUID, WATER-REACTIVE, N.O.S.	8	3094
CORROSIVE SOLID, N.O.S.	8	1759
CORROSIVE SOLID, ACIDIC, INORGANIC, N.O.S.	8	3260
CORROSIVE SOLID, ACIDIC, ORGANIC, N.O.S.	8	3261
CORROSIVE SOLID, BASIC, INORGANIC, N.O.S.	8	3262
CORROSIVE SOLID, BASIC, ORGANIC, N.O.S.	8	3263
CORROSIVE SOLID, FLAMMABLE, N.O.S.	8	2921
CORROSIVE SOLID, OXIDIZING, N.O.S.	8	3084
CORROSIVE SOLID, SELF-HEATING, N.O.S.	8	3095
CORROSIVE SOLID, TOXIC, N.O.S.	8	2923

Name and description	Class	UN No.
CORROSIVE SOLID, WATER-REACTIVE, N.O.S.	8	3096
COTTON WASTE, OILY	4.2	1364
COTTON, WET	4.2	1365
COUMARIN DERIVATIVE PESTICIDE, LIQUID, FLAMMABLE, TOXIC, flash-point less than 23 °C	3	3024
COUMARIN DERIVATIVE PESTICIDE, LIQUID, TOXIC	6.1	3026
COUMARIN DERIVATIVE PESTICIDE, LIQUID, TOXIC, FLAMMABLE, flash-point not less than 23 °C	6.1	3025
COUMARIN DERIVATIVE PESTICIDE, SOLID, TOXIC	6.1	3027
Creosote, see	6.1	2810
Creosote salts, see	4.1	1334
CRESOLS, LIQUID	6.1	2076
CRESOLS, SOLID	6.1	3455
CRESYLIC ACID	6.1	2022
Crocidolite, see	9	2212
CROTONALDEHYDE	6.1	1143
CROTONALDEHYDE, STABILIZED	6.1	1143
CROTONIC ACID, SOLID	8	2823
CROTONIC ACID, LIQUID	8	3472
Crotonic aldehyde, stabilized, see	6.1	1143
CROTONYLENE	3	1144
Crude naphtha, see	3	1268
Cumene, see	3	1918
Cupric chlorate, see	5.1	2721
CUPRIETHYLENEDIAMINE SOLUTION	8	1761
CUTTERS, CABLE, EXPLOSIVE	1.4S	0070
CYANIDE SOLUTION, N.O.S.	6.1	1935
CYANIDES, INORGANIC, SOLID, N.O.S.	6.1	1588
Cyanides, organic, flammable, toxic, n.o.s., see	3	3273
Cyanides, organic, toxic, n.o.s., see	6.1	3276
	6.1	3439
Cyanides, organic, toxic, flammable, n.o.s., see	6.1	3275
Cyanoacetonitrile, see	6.1	2647
CYANOGEN	2.3	1026
CYANOGEN BROMIDE	6.1	1889
CYANOGEN CHLORIDE, STABILIZED	2.3	1589
CYANURIC CHLORIDE	8	2670
CYCLOBUTANE	2.1	2601
CYCLOBUTYL CHLOROFORMATE	6.1	2744
1,5,9-CYCLODODECATRIENE	6.1	2518
CYCLOHEPTANE	3	2241
CYCLOHEPTATRIENE	3	2603
1,3,5-Cycloheptatriene, see	3	2603
CYCLOHEPTENE	3	2242
1,4-Cyclohexadienedione, see	6.1	2587
CYCLOHEXANE	3	1145
Cyclehexanethiol, see	3	3054
CYCLOHEXANONE	3	1915
CYCLOHEXENE	3	2256
CYCLOHEXENYLTRICHLOROSILANE	8	1762
CYCLOHEXYL ACETATE	3	2243
CYCLOHEXYLAMINE	8	2357
CYCLOHEXYL ISOCYANATE	6.1	2488
CYCLOHEXYL MERCAPTAN	3	3054
CYCLOHEXYLTRICHLOROSILANE	8	1763
CYCLONITE, see	1.1D	0072
	1.1D	0391
	1.1D	0483
CYCLOOCTADIENE PHOSPHINES, see	4.2	2940

Name and description	Class	UN No.
CYCLOOCTADIENES	3	2520
CYCLOOCTATETRAENE	3	2358
CYCLOPENTANE	3	1146
CYCLOPENTANOL	3	2244
CYCLOPENTANONE	3	2245
CYCLOPENTENE	3	2246
CYCLOPROPANE	2.1	1027
CYCLOTETRAMETHYLENE-TETRANITRAMINE, DESENSITIZED	1.1D	0484
CYCLOTETRAMETHYLENE-TETRANITRAMINE, WETTED with not less than 15 % water, by mass	1.1D	0226
CYCLOTRIMETHYLENE TRINITRAMINE AND CYCLOTETRAMETHYLENE-TETRANITRAMINE MIXTURE, DESENSITIZED with not less than 10 % phlegmatizer, by mass	1.1D	0391
CYCLOTRIMETHYLENETRI-NITRAMINE AND CYCLOTETRAMETHYLENE-TETRANITRAMINE MIXTURE, WETTED with not less than 15 % water, by mass	1.1D	0391
CYCLOTRIMETHYLENE-TRINITRAMINE, DESENSITIZED	1.1D	0483
CYCLOTRIMETHYLENE-TRINITRAMINE, WETTED with not less than 15 % water, by mass	1.1D	0072
CYMENES	3	2046
Cymol, see	3	2046
DANGEROUS GOODS IN APPARATUS	9	3363
DANGEROUS GOODS IN ARTICLES	9	3363
DANGEROUS GOODS IN MACHINERY	9	3363
Deanol, see	8	2051
DECABORANE	4.1	1868
DECAHYDRONAPHTHALENE	3	1147
Decalin, see	3	1147

Name and description	Class	UN No.
n-DECANE	3	2247
DEFLAGRATING METAL SALTS OF AROMATIC NITRODERIVATIVES, N.O.S.	1.3C	0132
Depth charge, see	1.1D	0056
DESENSITIZED EXPLOSIVE, LIQUID, N.O.S.	3	3379
DESENSITIZED EXPLOSIVE, SOLID, N.O.S.	4.1	3380
Detonating relays, see	1.1B	0029
	1.1B	0360
	1.4B	0267
	1.4B	0361
	1.4S	0455
	1.4S	0500
DETONATOR ASSEMBLIES, NON-ELECTRIC for blasting	1.1B	0360
	1.4B	0361
	1.4S	0500
DETONATORS FOR AMMUNITION	1.1B	0073
	1.2B	0364
	1.4B	0365
	1.4S	0366
DETONATORS, ELECTRIC for blasting	1.1B	0030
	1.4B	0255
	1.4S	0456
DETONATORS, ELECTRONIC programmable for blasting	1.1B	0511
	1.4B	0512
	1.4S	0513
DETONATORS, NON-ELECTRIC for blasting	1.1B	0029
	1.4B	0267
	1.4S	0455
DEUTERIUM, COMPRESSED	2.1	1957
DEVICES, SMALL, HYDROCARBON GAS POWERED with release device	2.1	3150
DIACETONE ALCOHOL	3	1148
DIALLYLAMINE	3	2359
DIALLYL ETHER	3	2360
4,4'-DIAMINODIPHENYLMETHANE	6.1	2651
1,2-Diaminoethane, see	8	1604
Diaminopropylamine, see	8	2269
DI-n-AMYLAMINE	3	2841

- 422 -

Name and description	Class	UN No.
DIAZODINITROPHENOL, WETTED with not less than 40 % water, or mixture of alcohol and water, by mass	1.1A	0074
Dibenzopyridine, see	6.1	2713
DIBENZYLDICHLOROSILANE	8	2434
DIBORANE	2.3	1911
1,2-DIBROMOBUTAN-3-ONE	6.1	2648
DIBROMOCHLOROPROPANES	6.1	2872
1,2-Dibromo-3-chloropropane, see	6.1	2872
DIBROMODIFLUOROMETHANE	9	1941
DIBROMOMETHANE	6.1	2664
DI-n-BUTYLAMINE	8	2248
DIBUTYLAMINOETHANOL	6.1	2873
2-Dibutylaminoethanol, see	6.1	2873
N,N-Di-n-butylaminoethanol, see	6.1	2873
DIBUTYL ETHERS	3	1149
DICHLOROACETIC ACID	8	1764
1,3-DICHLOROACETONE	6.1	2649
DICHLOROACETYL CHLORIDE	8	1765
DICHLOROANILINES, LIQUID	6.1	1590
DICHLOROANILINES, SOLID	6.1	3442
o-DICHLOROBENZENE	6.1	1591
2,2'-DICHLORODIETHYL ETHER	6.1	1916
DICHLORODIFLUOROMETHANE	2.2	1028
DICHLORODIFLUOROMETHANE AND DIFLUOROETHANE AZEOTROPIC MIXTURE with approximately 74 % dichlorodifluoromethane	2.2	2602
Dichlorodifluoromethane and ethylene oxide mixture, see	2.2	3070
DICHLORODIMETHYL ETHER, SYMMETRICAL	6.1	2249
1,1-DICHLOROETHANE	3	2362
1,2-Dichloroethane, see	3	1184
1,2-DICHLOROETHYLENE	3	1150

Name and description	Class	UN No.
Di(2-chloroethyl) ether, see	6.1	1916
DICHLOROFLUOROMETHANE	2.2	1029
alpha-Dichlorohydrin, see	6.1	2750
DICHLOROISOCYANURIC ACID, DRY	5.1	2465
DICHLOROISOCYANURIC ACID SALTS	5.1	2465
DICHLOROISOPROPYL ETHER	6.1	2490
DICHLOROMETHANE	6.1	1593
1,1-DICHLORO-1-NITROETHANE	6.1	2650
DICHLOROPENTANES	3	1152
Dichlorophenol, see	6.1	2020
	6.1	2021
DICHLOROPHENYL ISOCYANATES	6.1	2250
DICHLOROPHENYLTRICHLORO-SILANE	8	1766
1,2-DICHLOROPROPANE	3	1279
1,3-DICHLOROPROPANOL-2	6.1	2750
1,3-Dichloro-2-propanone, see	6.1	2649
DICHLOROPROPENES	3	2047
DICHLOROSILANE	2.3	2189
1,2-DICHLORO-1,1,2,2-TETRAFLUOROETHANE	2.2	1958
Dichloro-s-triazine-2,4,6-trione, see	5.1	2465
1,4-Dicyanobutane, see	6.1	2205
Dicycloheptadiene, see	3	2251
DICYCLOHEXYLAMINE	8	2565
Dicyclohexylamine nitrite, see	4.1	2687
DICYCLOHEXYLAMMONIUM NITRITE	4.1	2687
DICYCLOPENTADIENE	3	2048
1,2-DI-(DIMETHYLAMINO) ETHANE	3	2372
DIDYMIUM NITRATE	5.1	1465
DIESEL FUEL	3	1202
1,1-Diethoxyethane, see	3	1088

Name and description	Class	UN No.
1,2-Diethoxyethane, see	3	1153
DIETHOXYMETHANE	3	2373
3,3-DIETHOXYPROPENE	3	2374
DIETHYLAMINE	3	1154
2-DIETHYLAMINOETHANOL	8	2686
3-DIETHYLAMINOPROPYLAMINE	3	2684
N,N-DIETHYLANILINE	6.1	2432
DIETHYLBENZENE	3	2049
Diethylcarbinol, see	3	1105
DIETHYL CARBONATE	3	2366
DIETHYLDICHLOROSILANE	8	1767
Diethylenediamine, see	8	2579
DIETHYLENEGLYCOL DINITRATE, DESENSITIZED with not less than 25 % non-volatile, water-insoluble phlegmatizer, by mass	1.1D	0075
DIETHYLENETRIAMINE	8	2079
N,N-Diethylethanolamine, see	8	2686
DIETHYL ETHER	3	1155
N,N-DIETHYLETHYLENEDIAMINE	8	2685
Di-(2-ethylhexyl) phosphoric acid, see	8	1902
DIETHYL KETONE	3	1156
DIETHYL SULPHATE	6.1	1594
DIETHYL SULPHIDE	3	2375
DIETHYLTHIOPHOSPHORYL CHLORIDE	8	2751
Diethylzinc, see	4.2	3394
2,4-Difluoroaniline, see	6.1	2941
Difluorochloroethane, see	2.1	2517
1,1-DIFLUOROETHANE	2.1	1030
1,1-DIFLUOROETHYLENE	2.1	1959
DIFLUOROMETHANE	2.1	3252

Name and description	Class	UN No.
Difluoromethane, pentafluoroethane, and 1,1,1,2-tetrafluoroethane zeotropic mixture with approximately 23 % difluoromethane and 25 % pentafluoroethane, see	2.2	3340
Difluoromethane, pentafluoroethane, and 1,1,1,2-tetrafluoroethane zeotropic mixture with approximately 20 % difluoromethane and 40 % pentafluoroethane, see	2.2	3338
Difluoromethane, pentafluoroethane, and 1,1,1,2-tetrafluoroethane zeotropic mixture with approximately 10 % difluoromethane and 70 % pentafluoroethane, see	2.2	3339
DIFLUOROPHOSPHORIC ACID, ANHYDROUS	8	1768
2,3-DIHYDROPYRAN	3	2376
DIISOBUTYLAMINE	3	2361
DIISOBUTYLENE, ISOMERIC COMPOUNDS	3	2050
alpha-Diisobutylene, see	3	2050
beta-Diisobutylene, see	3	2050
DIISOBUTYL KETONE	3	1157
DIISOOCTYL ACID PHOSPHATE	8	1902
DIISOPROPYLAMINE	3	1158
DIISOPROPYL ETHER	3	1159
DIKETENE, STABILIZED	6.1	2521
1,1-DIMETHOXYETHANE	3	2377
1,2-DIMETHOXYETHANE	3	2252
Dimethoxystrychnine, see	6.1	1570
DIMETHYLAMINE, ANHYDROUS	2.1	1032
DIMETHYLAMINE AQUEOUS SOLUTION	3	1160
2-DIMETHYLAMINO-ACETONITRILE	3	2378
2-DIMETHYLAMINOETHANOL	8	2051
2-DIMETHYLAMINOETHYL ACRYLATE, STABILIZED	6.1	3302
2-DIMETHYLAMINOETHYL METHACRYLATE, STABILIZED	6.1	2522

Name and description	Class	UN No.
N,N-DIMETHYLANILINE	6.1	2253
Dimethylarsenic acid, see	6.1	1572
N,N-Dimethylbenzylamine, see	8	2619
2,3-DIMETHYLBUTANE	3	2457
1,3-DIMETHYLBUTYLAMINE	3	2379
DIMETHYLCARBAMOYL CHLORIDE	8	2262
DIMETHYL CARBONATE	3	1161
DIMETHYLCYCLOHEXANES	3	2263
N,N-DIMETHYLCYCLO-HEXYLAMINE	8	2264
DIMETHYLDICHLOROSILANE	3	1162
DIMETHYLDIETHOXYSILANE	3	2380
DIMETHYLDIOXANES	3	2707
DIMETHYL DISULPHIDE	3	2381
Dimethylethanolamine, see	8	2051
DIMETHYL ETHER	2.1	1033
N,N-DIMETHYLFORMAMIDE	3	2265
DIMETHYLHYDRAZINE, SYMMETRICAL	6.1	2382
DIMETHYLHYDRAZINE, UNSYMMETRICAL	6.1	1163
1,1-Dimethylhydrazine, see	6.1	1163
N,N-Dimethyl-4-nitrosoaniline, see	4.2	1369
2,2-DIMETHYLPROPANE	2.1	2044
DIMETHYL-N-PROPYLAMINE	3	2266
DIMETHYL SULPHATE	6.1	1595
DIMETHYL SULPHIDE	3	1164
DIMETHYL THIOPHOSPHORYL CHLORIDE	6.1	2267
Dimethylzinc, see	4.2	3394
DINGU, see	1.1D	0489
DINITROANILINES	6.1	1596
DINITROBENZENES, SOLID	6.1	3443

Name and description	Class	UN No.
DINITROBENZENES LIQUID	6.1	1597
Dinitrochlorobenzene, see	6.1	1577
DINITRO-o-CRESOL	6.1	1598
DINITROGEN TETROXIDE	2.3	1067
DINITROGLYCOLURIL	1.1D	0489
DINITROPHENOL, dry or wetted with less than 15 % water, by mass	1.1D	0076
DINITROPHENOL SOLUTION	6.1	1599
DINITROPHENOL, WETTED with not less than 15 % water, by mass	4.1	1320
DINITROPHENOLATES, alkali metals, dry or wetted with less than 15 % water, by mass	1.3C	0077
DINITROPHENOLATES, WETTED with not less than 15 % water, by mass	4.1	1321
DINITRORESORCINOL, dry or wetted with less than 15 % water, by mass	1.1D	0078
DINITRORESORCINOL, WETTED with not less than 15 % water, by mass	4.1	1322
DINITROSOBENZENE	1.3C	0406
Dinitrotoluene mixed with sodium chlorate, see	1.1D	0083
DINITROTOLUENES, LIQUID	6.1	2038
DINITROTOLUENES, MOLTEN	6.1	1600
DINITROTOLUENES, SOLID	6.1	3454
DIOXANE	3	1165
DIOXOLANE	3	1166
DIPENTENE	3	2052
DIPHENYLAMINE CHLOROARSINE	6.1	1698
DIPHENYLCHLOROARSINE, LIQUID	6.1	1699
DIPHENYLCHLOROARSINE, SOLID	6.1	3450
DIPHENYLDICHLOROSILANE	8	1769
DIPHENYLMETHYL BROMIDE	8	1770
DIPICRYLAMINE, see	1.1D	0079
DIPICRYL SULPHIDE, dry or wetted with less than 10 % water, by mass	1.1D	0401

Name and description	Class	UN No.
DIPICRYL SULPHIDE, WETTED with not less than 10 % water, by mass	4.1	2852
DIPROPYLAMINE	3	2383
Dipropylene triamine, see	8	2269
DI-n-PROPYL ETHER	3	2384
DIPROPYL KETONE	3	2710
DISILANE	2.1	3553
DISINFECTANT, LIQUID, CORROSIVE, N.O.S.	8	1903
DISINFECTANT, LIQUID, TOXIC, N.O.S.	6.1	3142
DISINFECTANT, SOLID, TOXIC, N.O.S.	6.1	1601
DISODIUM TRIOXOSILICATE	8	3253
DIVINYL ETHER, STABILIZED	3	1167
DODECYLTRICHLOROSILANE	8	1771
DRY ICE, see	9	1845
DYE INTERMEDIATE, LIQUID, CORROSIVE, N.O.S.	8	2801
DYE INTERMEDIATE, LIQUID, TOXIC, N.O.S.	6.1	1602
DYE INTERMEDIATE, SOLID, CORROSIVE, N.O.S.	8	3147
DYE INTERMEDIATE, SOLID, TOXIC, N.O.S.	6.1	3143
Dynamite, see	1.1D	0081
Electric storage batteries, see	8	2794
	8	2795
	8	2800
	8	3028
Electrolyte (acid or alkaline) for batteries, see	8	2796
	8	2797
ELEVATED TEMPERATURE LIQUID, N.O.S., at or above 100 °C and below its flash-point (including molten metals, molten salts, etc.)	9	3257
ELEVATED TEMPERATURE LIQUID, FLAMMABLE, N.O.S. with flash-point above 60 °C, at or above its flash-point	3	3256
ELEVATED TEMPERATURE SOLID, N.O.S., at or above 240 °C	9	3258

Name and description	Class	UN No.
ENGINE, FUEL CELL, FLAMMABLE GAS POWERED	2.1	3529
ENGINE, FUEL CELL, FLAMMABLE LIQUID POWERED	3	3528
ENGINE, INTERNAL COMBUSTION	9	3530
ENGINE, INTERNAL COMBUSTION, FLAMMABLE GAS POWERED	2.1	3529
ENGINE, INTERNAL COMBUSTION, FLAMMABLE LIQUID POWERED	3	3528
Engines, rocket, see	1.2L	0322
	1.3L	0250
ENVIRONMENTALLY HAZARDOUS SUBSTANCE, LIQUID, N.O.S.	9	3082
ENVIRONMENTALLY HAZARDOUS SUBSTANCE, SOLID, N.O.S.	9	3077
EPIBROMOHYDRIN	6.1	2558
EPICHLOROHYDRIN	6.1	2023
1,2-Epoxybutane, stabilized, see	3	3022
Epoxyethane, see	2.3	1040
1,2-EPOXY-3-ETHOXYPROPANE	3	2752
2,3-Epoxy-1-propanal, see	3	2622
2,3-Epoxypropyl ethyl ether, see	3	2752
ESTERS, N.O.S.	3	3272
ETHANE	2.1	1035
ETHANE, REFRIGERATED LIQUID	2.1	1961
Ethanethiol, see	3	2363
ETHANOL	3	1170
ETHANOL AND GASOLINE MIXTURE	3	3475
ETHANOL AND MOTOR SPIRIT MIXTURE	3	3475
ETHANOL AND PETROL MIXTURE	3	3475
ETHANOL SOLUTION	3	1170
ETHANOLAMINE	8	2491
ETHANOLAMINE SOLUTION	8	2491
Ether, see	3	1155

Name and description	Class	UN No.
ETHERS, N.O.S.	3	3271
2-Ethoxyethanol, see	3	1171
2-Ethoxyethyl acetate, see	3	1172
Ethoxy propane-1, see	3	2615
ETHYL ACETATE	3	1173
ETHYLACETYLENE, STABILIZED	2.1	2452
ETHYL ACRYLATE, STABILIZED	3	1917
ETHYL ALCOHOL, see	3	1170
ETHYL ALCOHOL SOLUTION, see	3	1170
ETHYLAMINE	2.1	1036
ETHYLAMINE, AQUEOUS SOLUTION with not less than 50 % but not more than 70 % ethylamine	3	2270
ETHYL AMYL KETONE	3	2271
N-ETHYLANILINE	6.1	2272
2-ETHYLANILINE	6.1	2273
ETHYLBENZENE	3	1175
N-ETHYL-N-BENZYLANILINE	6.1	2274
N-ETHYLBENZYLTOLUIDINES, LIQUID	6.1	2753
N-ETHYLBENZYLTOLUIDINES, SOLID	6.1	3460
ETHYL BORATE	3	1176
ETHYL BROMIDE	6.1	1891
ETHYL BROMOACETATE	6.1	1603
2-ETHYLBUTANOL	3	2275
2-ETHYLBUTYL ACETATE	3	1177
2-Ethylbutyl acetate, see	3	1177
ETHYL BUTYL ETHER	3	1179
2-ETHYLBUTYRALDEHYDE	3	1178
ETHYL BUTYRATE	3	1180
ETHYL CHLORIDE	2.1	1037
ETHYL CHLOROACETATE	6.1	1181
Ethyl chlorocarbonate, see	6.1	1182
ETHYL CHLOROFORMATE	6.1	1182
ETHYL 2-CHLOROPROPIONATE	3	2935
Ethyl-alpha-chloropropionate, see	3	2935
ETHYL CHLOROTHIOFORMATE	8	2826
ETHYL CROTONATE	3	1862
ETHYLDICHLOROARSINE	6.1	1892
ETHYLDICHLOROSILANE	4.3	1183
ETHYLENE, ACETYLENE AND PROPYLENE MIXTURE, REFRIGERATED LIQUID containing at least 71.5 % ethylene with not more than 22.5 % acetylene and not more than 6 % propylene	2.1	3138
ETHYLENE CHLOROHYDRIN	6.1	1135
ETHYLENE	2.1	1962
ETHYLENEDIAMINE	8	1604
ETHYLENE DIBROMIDE	6.1	1605
Ethylene dibromide and methyl bromide, liquid mixture, see	6.1	1647
ETHYLENE DICHLORIDE	3	1184
ETHYLENE GLYCOL DIETHYL ETHER	3	1153
ETHYLENE GLYCOL MONOETHYL ETHER	3	1171
ETHYLENE GLYCOL MONOETHYL ETHER ACETATE	3	1172
ETHYLENE GLYCOL MONOMETHYL ETHER	3	1188
ETHYLENE GLYCOL MONOMETHYL ETHER ACETATE	3	1189
ETHYLENEIMINE, STABILIZED	6.1	1185
ETHYLENE OXIDE	2.3	1040
ETHYLENE OXIDE AND CARBON DIOXIDE MIXTURE with more than 87 % ethylene oxide	2.3	3300
ETHYLENE OXIDE AND CARBON DIOXIDE MIXTURE with more than 9 % but not more than 87 % ethylene oxide	2.1	1041

Name and description	Class	UN No.
ETHYLENE OXIDE AND CARBON DIOXIDE MIXTURE with not more than 9 % ethylene oxide	2.2	1952
ETHYLENE OXIDE AND CHLOROTETRAFLUORO-ETHANE MIXTURE with not more than 8.8 % ethylene oxide	2.2	3297
ETHYLENE OXIDE AND DICHLORODIFLUOROMETHANE MIXTURE with not more than 12.5 % ethylene oxide	2.2	3070
ETHYLENE OXIDE AND PENTAFLUOROETHANE MIXTURE with not more than 7.9 % ethylene oxide	2.2	3298
ETHYLENE OXIDE AND PROPYLENE OXIDE MIXTURE, not more than 30 % ethylene oxide	3	2983
ETHYLENE OXIDE AND TETRAFLUOROETHANE MIXTURE with not more than 5.6 % ethylene oxide	2.2	3299
ETHYLENE OXIDE WITH NITROGEN up to a total pressure of 1 MPa (10 bar) at 50 °C	2.3	1040
ETHYLENE, REFRIGERATED LIQUID	2.1	1038
ETHYL ETHER, see	3	1155
ETHYL FLUORIDE	2.1	2453
ETHYL FORMATE	3	1190
2-ETHYLHEXYLAMINE	3	2276
2-ETHYLHEXYL CHLOROFORMATE	6.1	2748
Ethylidene chloride, see	3	2362
ETHYL ISOBUTYRATE	3	2385
ETHYL ISOCYANATE	3	2481
ETHYL LACTATE	3	1192
ETHYL MERCAPTAN	3	2363
ETHYL METHACRYLATE, STABILIZED	3	2277
ETHYL METHYL ETHER	2.1	1039
ETHYL METHYL KETONE	3	1193
ETHYL NITRITE SOLUTION	3	1194
ETHYL ORTHOFORMATE	3	2524
ETHYL OXALATE	6.1	2525
ETHYLPHENYLDICHLOROSILANE	8	2435
1-ETHYLPIPERIDINE	3	2386
ETHYL PROPIONATE	3	1195
ETHYL PROPYL ETHER	3	2615
Ethyl silicate, see	3	1292
Ethyl sulphate, see	6.1	1594
N-ETHYLTOLUIDINES	6.1	2754
ETHYLTRICHLOROSILANE	3	1196
EXPLOSIVE, BLASTING, TYPE A	1.1D	0081
EXPLOSIVE, BLASTING, TYPE B	1.1D 1.5D	0082 0331
EXPLOSIVE, BLASTING, TYPE C	1.1D	0083
EXPLOSIVE, BLASTING, TYPE D	1.1D	0084
EXPLOSIVE, BLASTING, TYPE E	1.1D 1.5D	0241 0332
Explosives, emulsion, see	1.1D 1.5D	0241 0332
Explosive, seismic, see	1.1D 1.1D 1.1D 1.5D	0081 0082 0083 0331
Explosive, slurry, see	1.1D 1.5D	0241 0332
Explosive, water gel, see	1.1D 1.5D	0241 0332
Extracts, aromatic, liquid, see	3	1197
Extracts, flavouring, liquid, see	3	1197
EXTRACTS, LIQUID, for flavour or aroma	3	1197
FABRICS, ANIMAL, N.O.S. with oil	4.2	1373
FABRICS IMPREGNATED WITH WEAKLY NITRATED NITROCELLULOSE, N.O.S.	4.1	1353
FABRICS, SYNTHETIC, N.O.S. with oil	4.2	1373

Name and description	Class	UN No.
FABRICS, VEGETABLE, N.O.S. with oil	4.2	1373
FERRIC ARSENATE	6.1	1606
FERRIC ARSENITE	6.1	1607
FERRIC CHLORIDE, ANHYDROUS	8	1773
FERRIC CHLORIDE SOLUTION	8	2582
FERRIC NITRATE	5.1	1466
FERROCERIUM	4.1	1323
FERROSILICON with 30 % or more but less than 90 % silicon	4.3	1408
FERROUS ARSENATE	6.1	1608
FERROUS METAL BORINGS in a form liable to self-heating	4.2	2793
FERROUS METAL CUTTINGS in a form liable to self-heating	4.2	2793
FERROUS METAL SHAVINGS in a form liable to self-heating	4.2	2793
FERROUS METAL TURNINGS in a form liable to self-heating	4.2	2793
FERTILIZER AMMONIATING SOLUTION with free ammonia	2.2	1043
Fertilizer with ammonium nitrate, n.o.s., see	5.1 9	2067 2071
FIBRES, ANIMAL burnt, wet or damp	4.2	1372
FIBRES, ANIMAL, N.O.S. with oil	4.2	1373
FIBRES IMPREGNATED WITH WEAKLY NITRATED NITROCELLULOSE, N.O.S.	4.1	1353
FIBRES, SYNTHETIC, N.O.S. with oil	4.2	1373
FIBRES, VEGETABLE burnt, wet or damp	4.2	1372
FIBRES, VEGETABLE, DRY	4.1	3360
FIBRES, VEGETABLE, N.O.S. with oil	4.2	1373
Films, nitrocellulose base, from which gelatin has been removed; film scrap, see	4.2	2002
FILMS, NITROCELLULOSE BASE, gelatin coated, except scrap	4.1	1324

Name and description	Class	UN No.
FIRE EXTINGUISHER CHARGES, corrosive liquid	8	1774
Fire extinguisher charges, expelling, explosive, see	1.2C 1.3C 1.4C 1.4S	0381 0275 0276 0323
FIRE EXTINGUISHERS with compressed or liquefied gas	2.2	1044
FIRELIGHTERS, SOLID with flammable liquid	4.1	2623
FIRE SUPPRESSANT DISPERSING DEVICES	1.4S 9	0514 3559
FIREWORKS	1.1G 1.2G 1.3G 1.4G 1.4S	0333 0334 0335 0336 0337
FIRST AID KIT	9	3316
Fish meal, stabilized	9	2216
FISH MEAL, UNSTABILIZED	4.2	1374
Fish scrap, stabilized, see	9	2216
FISH SCRAP, UNSTABILIZED, see	4.2	1374
Flammable gas in lighters, see	2.1	1057
FLAMMABLE LIQUID, N.O.S	3	1993
FLAMMABLE LIQUID, CORROSIVE, N.O.S.	3	2924
FLAMMABLE LIQUID, TOXIC, N.O.S.	3	1992
FLAMMABLE LIQUID, TOXIC, CORROSIVE, N.O.S.	3	3286
FLAMMABLE SOLID, CORROSIVE, INORGANIC, N.O.S.	4.1	3180
FLAMMABLE SOLID, CORROSIVE, ORGANIC, N.O.S.	4.1	2925
FLAMMABLE SOLID, INORGANIC, N.O.S.	4.1	3178
FLAMMABLE SOLID, ORGANIC, N.O.S.	4.1	1325
FLAMMABLE SOLID, ORGANIC, MOLTEN, N.O.S.	4.1	3176

Name and description	Class	UN No.
FLAMMABLE SOLID, OXIDIZING, N.O.S.	4.1	3097
FLAMMABLE SOLID, TOXIC, INORGANIC, N.O.S.	4.1	3179
FLAMMABLE SOLID, TOXIC, ORGANIC, N.O.S.	4.1	2926
FLARES, AERIAL	1.1G	0420
	1.2G	0421
	1.3G	0093
	1.4G	0403
	1.4S	0404
Flares, aeroplane, see	1.1G	0420
	1.2G	0421
	1.3G	0093
	1.4G	0403
	1.4S	0404
Flares, highway,; Flares, distress, small,; or Flares, railway or highway; see	1.4G	0191
	1.4S	0373
FLARES, SURFACE	1.1G	0418
	1.2G	0419
	1.3G	0092
Flares, water-activated, see	1.2L	0248
	1.3L	0249
FLASH POWDER	1.1G	0094
	1.3G	0305
Flue dusts, toxic, see	6.1	1562
Fluoric acid, see	8	1790
FLUORINE, COMPRESSED	2.3	1045
FLUOROACETIC ACID	6.1	2642
FLUOROANILINES	6.1	2941
2-Fluoroaniline, see	6.1	2941
4-Fluoroaniline, see	6.1	2941
o-Fluoroaniline, see	6.1	2941
p-Fluoroaniline, see	6.1	2941
FLUOROBENZENE	3	2387
FLUOROBORIC ACID	8	1775
Fluoroethane, see	2.1	2453
Fluoroform, see	2.2	1984
Fluoromethane, see	2.1	2454

Name and description	Class	UN No.
FLUOROPHOSPHORIC ACID, ANHYDROUS	8	1776
FLUOROSILICATES, N.O.S.	6.1	2856
FLUOROSILICIC ACID	8	1778
FLUOROSULPHONIC ACID	8	1777
FLUOROTOLUENES	3	2388
FORMALDEHYDE SOLUTION with not less than 25 % formaldehyde	8	2209
FORMALDEHYDE SOLUTION, FLAMMABLE	3	1198
Formalin, see	3	1198
	8	2209
Formamidine sulphinic acid, see	4.2	3341
FORMIC ACID with more than 85 % acid by mass	8	1779
FORMIC ACID with not less than 10 % but not more than 85 % acid by mass	8	3412
FORMIC ACID with not less than 5 % but less than 10 % acid by mass	8	3412
Formic aldehyde, see	3	1198
	8	2209
2-Formyl-3,4-dihydro-2H-pyran, see	3	2607
FRACTURING DEVICES, EXPLOSIVE without detonator, for oil wells	1.1D	0099
FUEL, AVIATION, TURBINE ENGINE	3	1863
FUEL CELL CARTRIDGES containing corrosive substances	8	3477
FUEL CELL CARTRIDGES CONTAINED IN EQUIPMENT containing corrosive substances	8	3477
FUEL CELL CARTRIDGES PACKED WITH EQUIPMENT containing corrosive substances	8	3477
FUEL CELL CARTRIDGES containing flammable liquids	3	3473
FUEL CELL CARTRIDGES CONTAINED IN EQUIPMENT containing flammable liquids	3	3473

Name and description	Class	UN No.
FUEL CELL CARTRIDGES PACKED WITH EQUIPMENT containing flammable liquids	3	3473
FUEL CELL CARTRIDGES containing hydrogen in metal hydride	2.1	3479
FUEL CELL CARTRIDGES CONTAINED IN EQUIPMENT containing hydrogen in metal hydride	2.1	3479
FUEL CELL CARTRIDGES PACKED WITH EQUIPMENT containing hydrogen in metal hydride	2.1	3479
FUEL CELL CARTRIDGES containing liquefied flammable gas	2.1	3478
FUEL CELL CARTRIDGES CONTAINED IN EQUIPMENT containing liquefied flammable gas	2.1	3478
FUEL CELL CARTRIDGES PACKED WITH EQUIPMENT containing liquefied flammable gas	2.1	3478
FUEL CELL CARTRIDGES containing water-reactive substances	4.3	3476
FUEL CELL CARTRIDGES CONTAINED IN EQUIPMENT containing water-reactive substances	4.3	3476
FUEL CELL CARTRIDGES PACKED WITH EQUIPMENT containing water-reactive substances	4.3	3476
Fumaroyl dichloride, see	8	1780
FUMARYL CHLORIDE	8	1780
FUMIGATED CARGO TRANSPORT UNIT	9	3359
FURALDEHYDES	6.1	1199
FURAN	3	2389
FURFURYL ALCOHOL	6.1	2874
FURFURYLAMINE	3	2526
Furyl carbinol, see	6.1	2874
FUSE, DETONATING, metal clad, see	1.1D 1.2D	0290 0102
FUSE, DETONATING, MILD EFFECT, metal clad, see	1.4D	0104
FUSE, IGNITER, tubular, metal clad	1.4G	0103

Name and description	Class	UN No.
FUSE, NON-DETONATING	1.3G	0101
FUSEL OIL	3	1201
FUSE, SAFETY	1.4S	0105
Fuze, combination, percussion or time, see	1.1B 1.2B 1.3G 1.4B 1.4G 1.4S 1.4S	0106 0107 0316 0257 0317 0367 0368
FUZES, DETONATING	1.1B 1.2B 1.4B 1.4S	0106 0107 0257 0367
FUZES, DETONATING with protective features	1.1D 1.2D 1.4D	0408 0409 0410
FUZES, IGNITING	1.3G 1.4G 1.4S	0316 0317 0368
GALLIUM	8	2803
GALLIUM CONTAINED IN MANUFACTURED ARTICLES	8	3554
GAS CARTRIDGES without a release device, non-refillable, see	2	2037
Gas drips, hydrocarbon, see	3	3295
GAS OIL	3	1202
GASOLINE	3	1203
Gasoline, casinghead, see	3	1203
GASOLINE AND ETHANOL MIXTURE	3	3475
GAS, REFRIGERATED LIQUID, N.O.S.	2.2	3158
GAS, REFRIGERATED LIQUID, FLAMMABLE, N.O.S.	2.1	3312
GAS, REFRIGERATED LIQUID, OXIDIZING, N.O.S.	2.2	3311
GAS SAMPLE, NON-PRESSURIZED, FLAMMABLE, N.O.S., not refrigerated liquid	2.1	3167
GAS SAMPLE, NON-PRESSURIZED, TOXIC, N.O.S., not refrigerated liquid	2.3	3169

Name and description	Class	UN No.
GAS SAMPLE, NON-PRESSURIZED, TOXIC, FLAMMABLE, N.O.S., not refrigerated liquid	2.3	3168
Gelatin, blasting, see	1.1D	0081
Gelatin, dynamites, see	1.1D	0081
GENETICALLY MODIFIED MICROORGANISMS	9	3245
GENETICALLY MODIFIED ORGANISMS	9	3245
GERMANE	2.3	2192
GERMANE, ADSORBED	2.3	3523
Germanium hydride, see	2.3	2192
Glycer-1,3-dichlorohydrin, see	6.1	2750
GLYCEROL alpha-MONOCHLOROHYDRIN	6.1	2689
Glyceryl trinitrate, see	1.1D	0143
	1.1D	0144
	3	1204
	3	3064
GLYCIDALDEHYDE	3	2622
GRENADES, hand or rifle, with bursting charge	1.1D	0284
	1.1F	0292
	1.2D	0285
	1.2F	0293
Grenades, illuminating, see	1.2G	0171
	1.3G	0254
	1.4G	0297
GRENADES, PRACTICE, hand or rifle	1.2G	0372
	1.3G	0318
	1.4G	0452
	1.4S	0110
Grenades, smoke, see	1.2G	0015
	1.2H	0245
	1.3G	0016
	1.3H	0246
	1.4G	0303
GUANIDINE NITRATE	5.1	1467
GUANYLNITROSAMINO-GUANYLIDENE HYDRAZINE, WETTED with not less than 30 % water, by mass	1.1A	0113

Name and description	Class	UN No.
GUANYLNITROSAMINO-GUANYLTETRAZENE, WETTED with not less than 30 % water, or mixture of alcohol and water, by mass	1.1A	0114
GUNPOWDER, COMPRESSED, see	1.1D	0028
GUNPOWDER, granular or as a meal, see	1.1D	0027
GUNPOWDER, IN PELLETS, see	1.1D	0028
Gutta percha solution, see	3	1287
HAFNIUM POWDER, DRY	4.2	2545
HAFNIUM POWDER, WETTED with not less than 25 % water (a visible excess of water must be present) (a) mechanically produced, particle size less than 53 microns; (b) chemically produced, particle size less than 840 microns	4.1	1326
HALOGENATED MONOMETHYLDIPHENYL-METHANES, LIQUID	9	3151
HALOGENATED MONOMETHYLDIPHENYL-METHANES, SOLID	9	3152
HAY	4.1	1327
HEATING OIL, LIGHT	3	1202
Heavy hydrogen, see	2.1	1957
HELIUM, COMPRESSED	2.2	1046
HELIUM, REFRIGERATED LIQUID	2.2	1963
HEPTAFLUOROPROPANE	2.2	3296
n-HEPTALDEHYDE	3	3056
n-Heptanal, see	3	3056
HEPTANES	3	1206
4-Heptanone, see	3	2710
n-HEPTENE	3	2278
HEXACHLOROACETONE	6.1	2661
HEXACHLOROBENZENE	6.1	2729
HEXACHLOROBUTADIENE	6.1	2279
Hexachloro-1,3-butadiene, see	6.1	2279

Name and description	Class	UN No.
HEXACHLOROCYCLO-PENTADIENE	6.1	2646
HEXACHLOROPHENE	6.1	2875
Hexachloro-2-propanone, see	6.1	2661
HEXADECYLTRICHLOROSILANE	8	1781
HEXADIENE	3	2458
HEXAETHYL TETRAPHOSPHATE	6.1	1611
HEXAETHYL TETRAPHOSPHATE AND COMPRESSED GAS MIXTURE	2.3	1612
HEXAFLUOROACETONE	2.3	2420
HEXAFLUOROACETONE HYDRATE, LIQUID	6.1	2552
HEXAFLUOROACETONE HYDRATE, SOLID	6.1	3436
HEXAFLUOROETHANE	2.2	2193
HEXAFLUOROPHOSPHORIC ACID	8	1782
HEXAFLUOROPROPYLENE	2.2	1858
Hexahydrocresol, see	3	2617
Hexahydromethyl phenol, see	3	2617
HEXALDEHYDE	3	1207
HEXAMETHYLENEDIAMINE, SOLID	8	2280
HEXAMETHYLENEDIAMINE SOLUTION	8	1783
HEXAMETHYLENE DIISOCYANATE	6.1	2281
HEXAMETHYLENEIMINE	3	2493
HEXAMETHYLENETETRAMINE	4.1	1328
Hexamine, see	4.1	1328
HEXANES	3	1208
HEXANITRODIPHENYLAMINE	1.1D	0079
HEXANITROSTILBENE	1.1D	0392
Hexanoic acid, see	8	2829
HEXANOLS	3	2282
1-HEXENE	3	2370

Name and description	Class	UN No.
HEXOGEN, see	1.1D	0072
	1.1D	0391
	1.1D	0483
HEXOLITE, dry or wetted with less than 15 % water, by mass	1.1D	0118
HEXOTOL, see	1.1D	0118
HEXOTONAL	1.1D	0393
HEXOTONAL, cast, see	1.1D	0393
HEXYL, see	1.1D	0079
HEXYLTRICHLOROSILANE	8	1784
HMX, see	1.1D	0226
	1.1D	0391
	1.1D	0484
HYDRAZINE, ANHYDROUS	8	2029
HYDRAZINE, AQUEOUS SOLUTION with more than 37 % hydrazine, by mass	8	2030
HYDRAZINE, AQUEOUS SOLUTION with not more than 37 % hydrazine, by mass	6.1	3293
HYDRAZINE AQUEOUS SOLUTION, FLAMMABLE with more than 37 % hydrazine, by mass	8	3484
Hydrazine hydrate	8	2030
Hydrides, metal, water-reactive, n.o.s., see	4.3	1409
Hydriodic acid, anhydrous, see	2.3	2197
HYDRIODIC ACID	8	1787
HYDROBROMIC ACID	8	1788
HYDROCARBON GAS MIXTURE, COMPRESSED, N.O.S.	2.1	1964
HYDROCARBON GAS MIXTURE, LIQUEFIED, N.O.S. such as mixtures A, A01, A02, A0, A1, B1, B2, B or C	2.1	1965
HYDROCARBON GAS REFILLS FOR SMALL DEVICES with release device	2.1	3150
HYDROCARBONS, LIQUID, N.O.S.	3	3295
HYDROCHLORIC ACID	8	1789
HYDROCYANIC ACID, AQUEOUS SOLUTION with not more than 20 % hydrogen cyanide	6.1	1613

Name and description	Class	UN No.
HYDROFLUORIC ACID, with more than 60 % hydrogen fluoride	8	1790
HYDROFLUORIC ACID, with not more than 60 % hydrogen fluoride	8	1790
HYDROFLUORIC ACID AND SULPHURIC ACID MIXTURE	8	1786
Hydrofluoroboric acid, see	8	1775
Hydrofluorosilicic acid, see	8	1778
HYDROGEN AND METHANE MIXTURE, COMPRESSED	2.1	2034
Hydrogen arsenide, see	2.3	2188
HYDROGEN BROMIDE, ANHYDROUS	2.3	1048
Hydrogen bromide solution, see	8	1788
HYDROGEN CHLORIDE, ANHYDROUS	2.3	1050
HYDROGEN CHLORIDE, REFRIGERATED LIQUID	2.3	2186
HYDROGEN, COMPRESSED	2.1	1049
HYDROGEN CYANIDE, AQUEOUS SOLUTION with not more than 20 % hydrogen cyanide, see	6.1	1613
HYDROGEN CYANIDE, SOLUTION IN ALCOHOL with not more than 45 % hydrogen cyanide	6.1	3294
HYDROGEN CYANIDE, STABILIZED containing less than 3 % water	6.1	1051
HYDROGEN CYANIDE, STABILIZED, containing less than 3 % water and absorbed in a porous inert material	6.1	1614
HYDROGENDIFLUORIDES, SOLID, N.O.S.	8	1740
HYDROGENDIFLUORIDES, SOLUTION, N.O.S.	8	3471
HYDROGEN FLUORIDE, ANHYDROUS	8	1052
Hydrogen fluoride solution, see	8	1790
HYDROGEN IN A METAL HYDRIDE STORAGE SYSTEM	2.1	3468
HYDROGEN IN A METAL HYDRIDE STORAGE SYSTEM CONTAINED IN EQUIPMENT	2.1	3468
HYDROGEN IN A METAL HYDRIDE STORAGE SYSTEM PACKED WITH EQUIPMENT	2.1	3468
HYDROGEN IODIDE, ANHYDROUS	2.3	2197
Hydrogen iodide solution, see	8	1787
HYDROGEN PEROXIDE AND PEROXYACETIC ACID MIXTURE with acid(s), water and not more than 5 % peroxyacetic acid, STABILIZED	5.1	3149
HYDROGEN PEROXIDE, AQUEOUS SOLUTION with not less than 8 % but less than 20 % hydrogen peroxide (stabilized as necessary)	5.1	2984
HYDROGEN PEROXIDE, AQUEOUS SOLUTION with not less than 20 % but not more than 60 % hydrogen peroxide (stabilized as necessary)	5.1	2014
HYDROGEN PEROXIDE, AQUEOUS SOLUTION, STABILIZED with more than 60 % hydrogen peroxide	5.1	2015
HYDROGEN PEROXIDE, STABILIZED	5.1	2015
HYDROGEN, REFRIGERATED LIQUID	2.1	1966
HYDROGEN SELENIDE, ADSORBED	2.3	3526
HYDROGEN SELENIDE, ANHYDROUS	2.3	2202
Hydrogen silicide, see	2.1	2203
HYDROGEN SULPHIDE	2.3	1053
Hydroselenic acid, see	2.3	2202
Hydrosilicofluoric acid, see	8	1778
1-HYDROXYBENZOTRIAZOLE, ANHYDROUS, dry or wetted with less than 20 % water, by mass	1.3C	0508
1-HYDROXYBENZOTRIAZOLE-MONOHYDRATE	4.1	3474
3-Hydroxybutan-2-one, see	3	2621
HYDROXYLAMINE SULPHATE	8	2865
1-Hydroxy-3-methyl-2-penten-4-yne, see	8	2705

Name and description	Class	UN No.
3-Hydroxyphenol, see	6.1	2876
HYPOCHLORITES, INORGANIC, N.O.S.	5.1	3212
HYPOCHLORITE SOLUTION	8	1791
IGNITERS	1.1G	0121
	1.2G	0314
	1.3G	0315
	1.4G	0325
	1.4S	0454
3,3'-IMINODIPROPYLAMINE	8	2269
Indiarubber, see	3	1287
INFECTIOUS SUBSTANCE, AFFECTING ANIMALS only	6.2	2900
INFECTIOUS SUBSTANCE, AFFECTING HUMANS	6.2	2814
Ink, printer's, flammable, see	3	1210
INSECTICIDE GAS, N.O.S.	2.2	1968
INSECTICIDE GAS, FLAMMABLE, N.O.S.	2.1	3354
INSECTICIDE GAS, TOXIC, N.O.S.	2.3	1967
INSECTICIDE GAS, TOXIC, FLAMMABLE, N.O.S.	2.3	3355
IODINE	8	3495
IODINE MONOCHLORIDE, LIQUID	8	3498
IODINE MONOCHLORIDE, SOLID	8	1792
IODINE PENTAFLUORIDE	5.1	2495
2-IODOBUTANE	3	2390
Iodomethane, see	6.1	2644
IODOMETHYLPROPANES	3	2391
IODOPROPANES	3	2392
alpha-Iodotoluene, see	6.1	2653
I.p.d.i., see	6.1	2290
Iron chloride, anhydrous, see	8	1773
Iron (III) chloride, anhydrous, see	8	1773
Iron chloride solution, see	8	2582
IRON OXIDE, SPENT obtained from coal gas purification	4.2	1376

Name and description	Class	UN No.
IRON PENTACARBONYL	6.1	1994
Iron perchloride, anhydrous, see	8	1773
Iron powder, pyrophoric, see	4.2	1383
Iron sesquichloride, anhydrous, see	8	1773
IRON SPONGE, SPENT obtained from coal gas purification	4.2	1376
Iron swarf, see	4.2	2793
ISOBUTANE	2.1	1969
ISOBUTANOL	3	1212
Isobutene, see	2.1	1055
ISOBUTYL ACETATE	3	1213
ISOBUTYL ACRYLATE, STABILIZED	3	2527
ISOBUTYL ALCOHOL, see	3	1212
ISOBUTYL ALDEHYDE, see	3	2045
ISOBUTYLAMINE	3	1214
ISOBUTYLENE	2.1	1055
ISOBUTYL FORMATE	3	2393
ISOBUTYL ISOBUTYRATE	3	2528
ISOBUTYL ISOCYANATE	3	2486
ISOBUTYL METHACRYLATE, STABILIZED	3	2283
ISOBUTYL PROPIONATE	3	2394
ISOBUTYRALDEHYDE	3	2045
ISOBUTYRIC ACID	3	2529
ISOBUTYRONITRILE	3	2284
ISOBUTYRYL CHLORIDE	3	2395
ISOCYANATES, FLAMMABLE, TOXIC, N.O.S.	3	2478
ISOCYANATES, TOXIC, N.O.S.	6.1	2206
ISOCYANATES, TOXIC, FLAMMABLE, N.O.S.	6.1	3080
ISOCYANATE SOLUTION, FLAMMABLE, TOXIC, N.O.S.	3	2478

Name and description	Class	UN No.
ISOCYANATE SOLUTION, TOXIC, N.O.S.	6.1	2206
ISOCYANATE SOLUTION, TOXIC, FLAMMABLE, N.O.S.	6.1	3080
ISOCYANATOBENZOTRI-FLUORIDES	6.1	2285
3-Isocyanatomethyl-3,5,5-tri-methylcyclohexyl isocyanate, see	6.1	2290
Isododecane, see	3	2286
ISOHEPTENES	3	2287
ISOHEXENES	3	2288
Isooctane, see	3	1262
ISOOCTENES	3	1216
Isopentane, see	3	1265
ISOPENTENES	3	2371
Isopentylamine, see	3	1106
Isopentyl nitrite, see	3	1113
ISOPHORONEDIAMINE	8	2289
ISOPHORONE DIISOCYANATE	6.1	2290
ISOPRENE, STABILIZED	3	1218
ISOPROPANOL	3	1219
ISOPROPENYL ACETATE	3	2403
ISOPROPENYLBENZENE	3	2303
ISOPROPYL ACETATE	3	1220
ISOPROPYL ACID PHOSPHATE	8	1793
ISOPROPYL ALCOHOL, see	3	1219
ISOPROPYLAMINE	3	1221
ISOPROPYLBENZENE	3	1918
ISOPROPYL BUTYRATE	3	2405
Isopropyl chloride, see	3	2356
ISOPROPYL CHLOROACETATE	3	2947
ISOPROPYL CHLOROFORMATE	6.1	2407
ISOPROPYL 2-CHLOROPROPIONATE	3	2934

Name and description	Class	UN No.
Isopropyl-alpha-chloropropionate, see	3	2934
Isopropyl ether, see	3	1159
Isopropylethylene, see	3	2561
Isopropyl formate, see	3	1281
ISOPROPYL ISOBUTYRATE	3	2406
ISOPROPYL ISOCYANATE	3	2483
Isopropyl mercaptan, see	3	2402
ISOPROPYL NITRATE	3	1222
ISOPROPYL PROPIONATE	3	2409
Isolpropyltoluene, see	3	2046
Isopropyltoluol, see	3	2046
ISOSORBIDE DINITRATE MIXTURE with not less than 60 % lactose, mannose, starch or calcium hydrogen phosphate	4.1	2907
ISOSORBIDE-5-MONONITRATE	4.1	3251
Isovaleraldehyde, see	3	2058
JET PERFORATING GUNS, CHARGED, oil well, without detonator	1.1D 1.4D	0124 0494
Jet tappers, without detonator, see	1.1D	0059
KEROSENE	3	1223
KETONES, LIQUID, N.O.S.	3	1224
KRILL MEAL	4.2	3497
KRYPTON, COMPRESSED	2.2	1056
KRYPTON, REFRIGERATED LIQUID	2.2	1970
Lacquer base or lacquer chips, nitrocellulose, dry, see	4.1	2557
Lacquer base or lacquer chips, plastic, wet with alcohol or solvent, see	3 3 4.1 4.1	1263 2059 2555 2556
LEAD ACETATE	6.1	1616
Lead (II) acetate, see	6.1	1616
LEAD ARSENATES	6.1	1617
LEAD ARSENITES	6.1	1618

Name and description	Class	UN No.
LEAD AZIDE, WETTED with not less than 20 % water, or mixture of alcohol and water, by mass	1.1A	0129
Lead chloride, solid, see	6.1	2291
LEAD COMPOUND, SOLUBLE, N.O.S.	6.1	2291
LEAD CYANIDE	6.1	1620
Lead (II) cyanide	6.1	1620
LEAD DIOXIDE	5.1	1872
LEAD NITRATE	5.1	1469
Lead (II) nitrate	5.1	1469
LEAD PERCHLORATE, SOLID	5.1	1470
Lead (II) perchlorate	5.1	1470
	5.1	3408
LEAD PERCHLORATE SOLUTION	5.1	3408
Lead peroxide, see	5.1	1872
LEAD PHOSPHITE, DIBASIC	4.1	2989
LEAD STYPHNATE, WETTED with not less than 20 % water, or mixture of alcohol and water, by mass	1.1A	0130
LEAD SULPHATE with more than 3 % free acid	8	1794
Lead tetraethyl, see	6.1	1649
Lead tetramethyl, see	6.1	1649
LEAD TRINITRORESORCINATE, WETTED, see	1.1A	0130
LIFE-SAVING APPLIANCES NOT SELF-INFLATING containing dangerous goods as equipment	9	3072
LIFE-SAVING APPLIANCES, SELF-INFLATING	9	2990
LIGHTER REFILLS containing flammable gas	2.1	1057
LIGHTERS containing flammable gas	2.1	1057
LIGHTERS, FUSE	1.4S	0131
Limonene, inactive, see	3	2052
LIQUEFIED GAS, N.O.S.	2.2	3163

Name and description	Class	UN No.
LIQUEFIED GASES, non-flammable, charged with nitrogen, carbon dioxide or air	2.2	1058
LIQUEFIED GAS, FLAMMABLE, N.O.S.	2.1	3161
LIQUEFIED GAS, OXIDIZING, N.O.S.	2.2	3157
LIQUEFIED GAS, TOXIC, N.O.S.	2.3	3162
LIQUEFIED GAS, TOXIC, CORROSIVE, N.O.S.	2.3	3308
LIQUEFIED GAS, TOXIC, FLAMMABLE, N.O.S.	2.3	3160
LIQUEFIED GAS, TOXIC, FLAMMABLE, CORROSIVE, N.O.S.	2.3	3309
LIQUEFIED GAS, TOXIC, OXIDIZING, N.O.S.	2.3	3307
LIQUEFIED GAS, TOXIC, OXIDIZING, CORROSIVE, N.O.S.	2.3	3310
Liquefied petroleum gas, see	2.1	1075
LITHIUM	4.3	1415
Lithium alkyls, liquid, see	4.2	3394
Lithium alkyls, solid, see	4.2	3393
Lithium alloy batteries	9	3090
	9	3091
LITHIUM ALUMINIUM HYDRIDE	4.3	1410
LITHIUM ALUMINIUM HYDRIDE, ETHEREAL	4.3	1411
LITHIUM BATTERIES INSTALLED IN CARGO TRANSPORT UNIT lithium ion batteries or lithium metal batteries	9	3536
LITHIUM BOROHYDRIDE	4.3	1413
LITHIUM FERROSILICON	4.3	2830
LITHIUM HYDRIDE	4.3	1414
LITHIUM HYDRIDE, FUSED SOLID	4.3	2805
LITHIUM HYDROXIDE	8	2680
LITHIUM HYDROXIDE SOLUTION	8	2679
LITHIUM HYPOCHLORITE, DRY	5.1	1471
LITHIUM HYPOCHLORITE MIXTURE	5.1	1471

Name and description	Class	UN No.
Lithium in cartouches, see	4.3	1415
LITHIUM ION BATTERIES	9	3480
LITHIUM ION BATTERIES CONTAINED IN EQUIPMENT	9	3481
LITHIUM BATTERIES INSTALLED IN CARGO TRANSPORT UNIT lithium ion batteries or lithium metal batteries	9	3536
LITHIUM ION BATTERIES PACKED WITH EQUIPMENT	9	3481
Lithium ion polymer batteries	9	3480
	9	3481
LITHIUM METAL BATTERIES	9	3090
LITHIUM METAL BATTERIES CONTAINED IN EQUIPMENT	9	3091
LITHIUM METAL BATTERIES PACKED WITH EQUIPMENT	9	3091
LITHIUM NITRATE	5.1	2722
LITHIUM NITRIDE	4.3	2806
LITHIUM PEROXIDE	5.1	1472
Lithium silicide, see	4.3	1417
LITHIUM SILICON	4.3	1417
L.n.g., see	2.1	1972
LONDON PURPLE	6.1	1621
L.p.g., see	2.1	1075
Lye, see	8	1823
Lythene, see	3	1268
MACHINERY, FUEL CELL, FLAMMABLE GAS POWERED	2.1	3529
MACHINERY, FUEL CELL, FLAMMABLE LIQUID POWERED	3	3528
MACHINERY, INTERNAL COMBUSTION	9	3530
ENGINE, INTERNAL COMBUSTION, FLAMMABLE GAS POWERED	2.1	3529
MACHINERY, INTERNAL COMBUSTION, FLAMMABLE LIQUID POWERED	3	3528

Name and description	Class	UN No.
MAGNESIUM in pellets, turnings or ribbons	4.1	1869
Magnesium alkyls, see	4.2	3394
MAGNESIUM ALLOYS with more than 50 % magnesium in pellets, turnings or ribbons	4.1	1869
MAGNESIUM ALLOYS POWDER	4.3	1418
MAGNESIUM ALUMINIUM PHOSPHIDE	4.3	1419
MAGNESIUM ARSENATE	6.1	1622
Magnesium bisulphite solution, see	8	2693
MAGNESIUM BROMATE	5.1	1473
MAGNESIUM CHLORATE	5.1	2723
Magnesium chloride and chlorate mixture, see	5.1	1459
	5.1	3407
MAGNESIUM DIAMIDE	4.2	2004
Magnesium diphenyl, see	4.2	3393
MAGNESIUM FLUOROSILICATE	6.1	2853
MAGNESIUM GRANULES, COATED, particle size not less than 149 microns	4.3	2950
MAGNESIUM HYDRIDE	4.3	2010
MAGNESIUM NITRATE	5.1	1474
MAGNESIUM PERCHLORATE	5.1	1475
MAGNESIUM PEROXIDE	5.1	1476
MAGNESIUM PHOSPHIDE	4.3	2011
MAGNESIUM POWDER	4.3	1418
Magnesium scrap, see	4.1	1869
MAGNESIUM SILICIDE	4.3	2624
Magnesium silicofluoride, see	6.1	2853
Magnetized material	9	2807
MALEIC ANHYDRIDE	8	2215
MALEIC ANHYDRIDE, MOLTEN	8	2215
Malonic dinitrile, see	6.1	2647
Malonodinitrile, see	6.1	2647
MALONONITRILE	6.1	2647

Name and description	Class	UN No.
MANEB	4.2	2210
MANEB PREPARATION with not less than 60 % maneb	4.2	2210
MANEB PREPARATION, STABILIZED against self-heating	4.3	2968
MANEB, STABILIZED against self-heating	4.3	2968
Manganese ethylene-di-dithiocarbamate, see	4.2	2210
Manganese ethylene-1,2-dithiocarbamate, see	4.2	2210
MANGANESE NITRATE	5.1	2724
Manganese (II) nitrate, see	5.1	2724
MANGANESE RESINATE	4.1	1330
Manganous nitrate, see	5.1	2724
MANNITOL HEXANITRATE, WETTED with not less than 40 % water, or mixture of alcohol and water, by mass	1.1D	0133
MATCHES, FUSEE	4.1	2254
MATCHES, SAFETY (book, card or strike on box)	4.1	1944
MATCHES, "STRIKE ANYWHERE"	4.1	1331
MATCHES, WAX "VESTA"	4.1	1945
MEDICAL WASTE, CATEGORY A, AFFECTING HUMANS, solid	6.2	3549
MEDICAL WASTE, CATEGORY A, AFFECTING ANIMALS only, solid	6.2	3549
MEDICAL WASTE, N.O.S.	6.2	3291
MEDICINE, LIQUID, FLAMMABLE, TOXIC, N.O.S.	3	3248
MEDICINE, LIQUID, TOXIC, N.O.S.	6.1	1851
MEDICINE, SOLID, TOXIC, N.O.S.	6.1	3249
p-Mentha-1,8-diene, see	3	2052
MERCAPTANS, LIQUID, FLAMMABLE, N.O.S.	3	3336
MERCAPTANS, LIQUID, FLAMMABLE, TOXIC, N.O.S.	3	1228
MERCAPTANS, LIQUID, TOXIC, FLAMMABLE, N.O.S.	6.1	3071
MERCAPTAN MIXTURE, LIQUID, FLAMMABLE, N.O.S.	3	3336
MERCAPTAN MIXTURE, LIQUID, FLAMMABLE, TOXIC, N.O.S.	3	1228
MERCAPTAN MIXTURE, LIQUID, TOXIC, FLAMMABLE, N.O.S.	6.1	3071
2-Mercaptoethanol, see	6.1	2966
2-Mercaptopropionic acid, see	6.1	2936
5-MERCAPTOTETRAZOL-1-ACETIC ACID	1.4C	0448
MERCURIC ARSENATE	6.1	1623
MERCURIC CHLORIDE	6.1	1624
MERCURIC NITRATE	6.1	1625
MERCURIC POTASSIUM CYANIDE	6.1	1626
Mercuric sulphate, see	6.1	1645
Mercurol, see	6.1	1639
Mercurous bisulphate, see	6.1	1645
Mercurous chloride, see	6.1	2025
MERCUROUS NITRATE	6.1	1627
Mercurous sulphate, see	6.1	1645
MERCURY	8	2809
MERCURY ACETATE	6.1	1629
MERCURY AMMONIUM CHLORIDE	6.1	1630
MERCURY BASED PESTICIDE, LIQUID, FLAMMABLE, TOXIC, flash-point less than 23 °C	3	2778
MERCURY BASED PESTICIDE, LIQUID, TOXIC	6.1	3012
MERCURY BASED PESTICIDE, LIQUID, TOXIC, FLAMMABLE, flash-point not less than 23 °C	6.1	3011
MERCURY BASED PESTICIDE, SOLID, TOXIC	6.1	2777
MERCURY BENZOATE	6.1	1631
Mercury bichloride, see	6.1	1624

Name and description	Class	UN No.
MERCURY BROMIDES	6.1	1634
MERCURY COMPOUND, LIQUID, N.O.S.	6.1	2024
MERCURY COMPOUND, SOLID, N.O.S.	6.1	2025
MERCURY CONTAINED IN MANUFACTURED ARTICLES	8	3506
MERCURY CYANIDE	6.1	1636
MERCURY FULMINATE, WETTED with not less than 20 % water, or mixture of alcohol and water, by mass	1.1A	0135
MERCURY GLUCONATE	6.1	1637
MERCURY IODIDE	6.1	1638
MERCURY NUCLEATE	6.1	1639
MERCURY OLEATE	6.1	1640
MERCURY OXIDE	6.1	1641
MERCURY OXYCYANIDE, DESENSITIZED	6.1	1642
MERCURY POTASSIUM IODIDE	6.1	1643
MERCURY SALICYLATE	6.1	1644
MERCURY SULPHATE	6.1	1645
MERCURY THIOCYANATE	6.1	1646
Mesitylene, see	3	2325
MESITYL OXIDE	3	1229
METAL CARBONYLS, LIQUID, N.O.S.	6.1	3281
METAL CARBONYLS, SOLID, N.O.S.	6.1	3466
METAL CATALYST, DRY	4.2	2881
METAL CATALYST, WETTED with a visible excess of liquid	4.2	1378
METALDEHYDE	4.1	1332
METAL HYDRIDES, FLAMMABLE, N.O.S.	4.1	3182
METAL HYDRIDES, WATER-REACTIVE, N.O.S.	4.3	1409
METALLIC SUBSTANCE, WATER-REACTIVE, N.O.S.	4.3	3208

Name and description	Class	UN No.
METALLIC SUBSTANCE, WATER-REACTIVE, SELF-HEATING, N.O.S.	4.3	3209
METAL POWDER, FLAMMABLE, N.O.S.	4.1	3089
METAL POWDER, SELF-HEATING, N.O.S.	4.2	3189
METAL SALTS OF ORGANIC COMPOUNDS, FLAMMABLE, N.O.S.	4.1	3181
METHACRYLALDEHYDE, STABILIZED	3	2396
METHACRYLIC ACID, STABILIZED	8	2531
METHACRYLONITRILE, STABILIZED	3	3079
METHALLYL ALCOHOL	3	2614
Methanal, see	3	1198
	8	2209
Methane and hydrogen mixture, see	2.1	2034
METHANE, COMPRESSED	2.1	1971
METHANE, REFRIGERATED LIQUID	2.1	1972
METHANESULPHONYL CHLORIDE	6.1	3246
METHANOL	3	1230
2-Methoxyethyl acetate, see	3	1189
METHOXYMETHYL ISOCYANATE	3	2605
4-METHOXY-4-METHYLPENTAN-2-ONE	3	2293
1-Methoxy-2-nitrobenzene, see	6.1	2730
	6.1	3458
1-Methoxy-3-nitrobenzene, see	6.1	2730
	6.1	3458
1-Methoxy-4-nitrobenzene, see	6.1	2730
	6.1	3458
1-METHOXY-2-PROPANOL	3	3092
METHYL ACETATE	3	1231
METHYLACETYLENE AND PROPADIENE MIXTURE, STABILIZED	2.1	1060
beta-Methyl acrolein, see	6.1	1143
METHYL ACRYLATE, STABILIZED	3	1919

Name and description	Class	UN No.
METHYLAL	3	1234
Methyl alcohol, see	3	1230
Methyl allyl alcohol, see	3	2614
METHYLALLYL CHLORIDE	3	2554
METHYLAMINE, ANHYDROUS	2.1	1061
METHYLAMINE, AQUEOUS SOLUTION	3	1235
METHYLAMYL ACETATE	3	1233
Methyl amyl alcohol, see	3	2053
Methyl amyl ketone, see	3	1110
N-METHYLANILINE	6.1	2294
Methylated spirit, see	3	1986
	3	1987
alpha-METHYLBENZYL ALCOHOL, LIQUID	6.1	2937
alpha-METHYLBENZYL ALCOHOL, SOLID	6.1	3438
METHYL BROMIDE with not more than 2 % chloropicrin	2.3	1062
Methyl bromide and chloropicrin mixture, see	2.3	1581
METHYL BROMIDE AND ETHYLENE DIBROMIDE MIXTURE, LIQUID	6.1	1647
METHYL BROMOACETATE	6.1	2643
2-METHYLBUTANAL	3	3371
3-METHYLBUTAN-2-ONE	3	2397
2-METHYL-1-BUTENE	3	2459
2-METHYL-2-BUTENE	3	2460
3-METHYL-1-BUTENE	3	2561
N-METHYLBUTYLAMINE	3	2945
METHYL tert-BUTYL ETHER	3	2398
METHYL BUTYRATE	3	1237
METHYL CHLORIDE	2.1	1063
Methyl chloride and chloropicrin mixture, see	2.3	1582

Name and description	Class	UN No.
METHYL CHLORIDE AND METHYLENE CHLORIDE MIXTURE	2.1	1912
METHYL CHLOROACETATE	6.1	2295
Methyl chlorocarbonate, see	6.1	1238
Methyl chloroform, see	6.1	2831
METHYL CHLOROFORMATE	6.1	1238
METHYL CHLOROMETHYL ETHER	6.1	1239
METHYL 2-CHLOROPROPIONATE	3	2933
Methyl alpha-chloropropionate, see	3	2933
METHYLCHLOROSILANE	2.3	2534
Methyl cyanide, see	3	1648
METHYLCYCLOHEXANE	3	2296
METHYLCYCLOHEXANOLS, flammable	3	2617
METHYLCYCLOHEXANONE	3	2297
METHYLCYCLOPENTANE	3	2298
METHYL DICHLOROACETATE	6.1	2299
METHYLDICHLOROSILANE	4.3	1242
Methylene bromide, see	6.1	2664
Methylene chloride, see	6.1	1593
Methylene chloride and methyl chloride mixture, see	2.1	1912
Methylene cyanide, see	6.1	2647
p,p'-Methylene dianiline, see	6.1	2651
Methylene dibromide, see	6.1	2664
2,2'-Methylene-di-(3,4,6-trichlorophenol), see	6.1	2875
Methyl ethyl ether, see	2.1	1039
METHYL ETHYL KETONE, see	3	1193
2-METHYL-5-ETHYLPYRIDINE	6.1	2300
METHYL FLUORIDE	2.1	2454
METHYL FORMATE	3	1243
2-METHYLFURAN	3	2301

Name and description	Class	UN No.
Methyl glycol, see	3	1188
Methyl glycol acetate, see	3	1189
2-METHYL-2-HEPTANETHIOL	6.1	3023
5-METHYLHEXAN-2-ONE	3	2302
METHYLHYDRAZINE	6.1	1244
METHYL IODIDE	6.1	2644
METHYL ISOBUTYL CARBINOL	3	2053
METHYL ISOBUTYL KETONE	3	1245
METHYL ISOCYANATE	6.1	2480
METHYL ISOPROPENYL KETONE, STABILIZED	3	1246
METHYL ISOTHIOCYANATE	6.1	2477
METHYL ISOVALERATE	3	2400
METHYL MAGNESIUM BROMIDE IN ETHYL ETHER	4.3	1928
METHYL MERCAPTAN	2.3	1064
Methyl mercaptopropionaldehyde, see	6.1	2785
METHYL METHACRYLATE MONOMER, STABILIZED	3	1247
4-METHYLMORPHOLINE	3	2535
N-METHYLMORPHOLINE, see	3	2535
METHYL NITRITE	2.2	2455
METHYL ORTHOSILICATE	6.1	2606
METHYLPENTADIENE	3	2461
Methylpentanes, see	3	1208
2-METHYLPENTAN-2-OL	3	2560
4-Methylpentan-2-ol, see	3	2053
3-Methyl-2-penten-4ynol, see	8	2705
METHYLPHENYLDICHLORO-SILANE	8	2437
2-Methyl-2-phenylpropane, see	3	2709
1-METHYLPIPERIDINE	3	2399
METHYL PROPIONATE	3	1248
Methylpropylbenzene, see	3	2046
METHYL PROPYL ETHER	3	2612
METHYL PROPYL KETONE	3	1249
Methyl pyridines, see	3	2313
Methylstyrene, inhibited, see	3	2618
alpha-Methylstyrene, see	3	2303
Methyl sulphate, see	6.1	1595
Methyl sulphide, see	3	1164
METHYLTETRAHYDROFURAN	3	2536
METHYL TRICHLOROACETATE	6.1	2533
METHYLTRICHLOROSILANE	3	1250
alpha-METHYLVALERALDEHYDE	3	2367
Methyl vinyl benzene, inhibited, see	3	2618
METHYL VINYL KETONE, STABILIZED	6.1	1251
M.i.b.c., see	3	2053
MINES with bursting charge	1.1D	0137
	1.1F	0136
	1.2D	0138
	1.2F	0294
Mirbane oil, see	6.1	1662
Missiles, guided, see	1.1E	0181
	1.1F	0180
	1.1J	0397
	1.2C	0436
	1.2E	0182
	1.2F	0295
	1.2J	0398
	1.3C	0183
	1.3C	0437
	1.4C	0438
MOLYBDENUM PENTACHLORIDE	8	2508
Monochloroacetic acid, see	6.1	1750
	6.1	1751
Monochlorobenzene, see	3	1134
Monochlorodifluoromethane, see	2.2	1018
Monochlorodifluoromethane and monochloropentafluoroethane mixture, see	2.2	1973
Monochlorodifluoromono-bromomethane, see	2.2	1974

Name and description	Class	UN No.
Monochloropentafluoroethane and monochlorodifluoromethane mixture, see	2.2	1973
Monoethylamine, see	2.1	1036
MONONITROTOLUIDINES, see	6.1	2660
Monopropylamine, see	3	1277
MORPHOLINE	8	2054
MOTOR FUEL ANTI-KNOCK MIXTURE	6.1	1649
MOTOR FUEL ANTI-KNOCK MIXTURE, FLAMMABLE	6.1	3483
MOTOR SPIRIT	3	1203
MOTOR SPIRIT AND ETHANOL MIXTURE	3	3475
Muriatic acid, see	8	1789
MUSK XYLENE, see	4.1	2956
Mysorite, see	9	2212
Naphta, see	3	1268
Naphta, petroleum, see	3	1268
Naphta, solvent, see	3	1268
NAPHTHALENE, CRUDE	4.1	1334
NAPHTHALENE, MOLTEN	4.1	2304
NAPHTHALENE, REFINED	4.1	1334
alpha-NAPHTHYLAMINE	6.1	2077
beta-NAPHTHYLAMINE, SOLID	6.1	1650
beta-NAPHTHYLAMINE SOLUTION	6.1	3411
NAPHTHYLTHIOUREA	6.1	1651
1-Naphthylthiourea, see	6.1	1651
NAPHTHYLUREA	6.1	1652
NATURAL GAS, COMPRESSED with high methane content	2.1	1971
NATURAL GAS, REFRIGERATED LIQUID with high methane content	2.1	1972
Natural gasoline, see	3	1203
Neohexane, see	3	1208
NEON, COMPRESSED	2.2	1065
NEON, REFRIGERATED LIQUID	2.2	1913
Neothyl, see	3	2612
NICKEL CARBONYL	6.1	1259
NICKEL CYANIDE	6.1	1653
Nickel (II) cyanide, see	6.1	1653
NICKEL NITRATE	5.1	2725
Nickel (II) nitrate, see	5.1	2725
NICKEL NITRITE	5.1	2726
Nickel (II) nitrite, see	5.1	2726
Nickelous nitrate, see	5.1	2725
Nickelous nitrite, see	5.1	2726
Nickel tetracarbonyl, see	6.1	1259
NICOTINE	6.1	1654
NICOTINE COMPOUND, LIQUID, N.O.S	6.1	3144
NICOTINE COMPOUND, SOLID, N.O.S	6.1	1655
NICOTINE HYDROCHLORIDE, LIQUID	6.1	1656
NICOTINE HYDROCHLORIDE, SOLID	6.1	3444
NICOTINE HYDROCHLORIDE SOLUTION	6.1	1656
NICOTINE PREPARATION, LIQUID, N.O.S.	6.1	3144
NICOTINE PREPARATION, SOLID, N.O.S.	6.1	1655
NICOTINE SALICYLATE	6.1	1657
NICOTINE SULPHATE, SOLID	6.1	3445
NICOTINE SULPHATE SOLUTION	6.1	1658
NICOTINE TARTRATE	6.1	1659
NITRATES, INORGANIC, N.O.S.	5.1	1477
NITRATES, INORGANIC, AQUEOUS SOLUTION, N.O.S.	5.1	3218

Name and description	Class	UN No.
NITRATING ACID MIXTURE with more than 50 % nitric acid	8	1796
NITRATING ACID MIXTURE with not more than 50 % nitric acid	8	1796
NITRATING ACID MIXTURE, SPENT, with more than 50 % nitric acid	8	1826
NITRATING ACID MIXTURE, SPENT, with not more than 50 % nitric acid	8	1826
NITRIC ACID, other than red fuming	8	2031
NITRIC ACID, RED FUMING	8	2032
NITRIC OXIDE, COMPRESSED	2.3	1660
NITRIC OXIDE AND DINITROGEN TETROXIDE MIXTURE	2.3	1975
NITRIC OXIDE AND NITROGEN DIOXIDE MIXTURE, see	2.3	1975
NITRILES, FLAMMABLE, TOXIC, N.O.S.	3	3273
NITRILES, LIQUID, TOXIC, N.O.S.	6.1	3276
NITRILES, SOLID, TOXIC, N.O.S.	6.1	3439
NITRILES, TOXIC, FLAMMABLE, N.O.S.	6.1	3275
NITRITES, INORGANIC, N.O.S.	5.1	2627
NITRITES, INORGANIC, AQUEOUS SOLUTION, N.O.S.	5.1	3219
NITROANILINES (o-, m-, p-)	6.1	1661
NITROANISOLES, LIQUID	6.1	2730
NITROANISOLES, SOLID	6.1	3458
NITROBENZENE	6.1	1662
Nitrobenzene bromide, see	6.1	2732
NITROBENZENESULPHONIC ACID	8	2305
Nitrobenzol, see	6.1	1662
5-NITROBENZOTRIAZOL	1.1D	0385
NITROBENZOTRIFLUORIDES, liquid	6.1	2306
NITROBENZOTRIFLUORIDES, SOLID	6.1	3431
NITROBROMOBENZENES, LIQUID	6.1	2732
NITROBROMOBENZENES, SOLID	6.1	3459
NITROCELLULOSE, dry or wetted with less than 25 % water (or alcohol), by mass	1.1D	0340
NITROCELLULOSE, unmodified or plasticized with less than 18 % plasticizing substance, by mass	1.1D	0341
NITROCELLULOSE MEMBRANE FILTERS, with not more than 12.6 % nitrogen, by dry mass	4.1	3270
NITROCELLULOSE, with not more than 12.6 % nitrogen, by dry mass, MIXTURE WITH PLASTICIZER, WITH PIGMENT	4.1	2557
NITROCELLULOSE, with not more than 12.6 % nitrogen, by dry mass, MIXTURE WITH PLASTICIZER, WITHOUT PIGMENT	4.1	2557
NITROCELLULOSE, with not more than 12.6 % nitrogen, by dry mass, MIXTURE WITHOUT PLASTICIZER, WITH PIGMENT	4.1	2557
NITROCELLULOSE, with not more than 12.6 % nitrogen, by dry mass, MIXTURE WITHOUT PLASTICIZER, WITHOUT PIGMENT	4.1	2557
NITROCELLULOSE, PLASTICIZED with not less than 18 % plasticizing substance, by mass	1.3C	0343
NITROCELLULOSE SOLUTION, FLAMMABLE with not more than 12.6 % nitrogen, by dry mass, and not more than 55 % nitrocellulose	3	2059
NITROCELLULOSE, WETTED with not less than 25 % alcohol, by mass	1.3C	0342
NITROCELLULOSE WITH ALCOHOL (not less than 25 % alcohol, by mass, and not more than 12.6 % nitrogen, by dry mass)	4.1	2556
NITROCELLULOSE WITH WATER (not less than 25 % water, by mass)	4.1	2555
Nitrochlorobenzenes, see	6.1	1578
3-NITRO-4-CHLOROBENZOTRI-FLUORIDE	6.1	2307
NITROCRESOLS, SOLID	6.1	2446
NITROCRESOLS, LIQUID	6.1	3434

Name and description	Class	UN No.
NITROETHANE	3	2842
NITROGEN, COMPRESSED	2.2	1066
NITROGEN DIOXIDE, see	2.3	1067
NITROGEN, REFRIGERATED LIQUID	2.2	1977
NITROGEN TRIFLUORIDE	2.2	2451
NITROGEN TRIOXIDE	2.3	2421
NITROGLYCERIN, DESENSITIZED with not less than 40 % non-volatile water-insoluble phlegmatizer, by mass	1.1D	0143
NITROGLYCERIN MIXTURE, DESENSITIZED, LIQUID, N.O.S. with not more than 30 % nitroglycerin, by mass	3	3357
NITROGLYCERIN MIXTURE, DESENSITIZED, LIQUID, FLAMMABLE, N.O.S. with not more than 30 % nitroglycerin, by mass	3	3343
NITROGLYCERIN MIXTURE, DESENSITIZED, SOLID, N.O.S. with more than 2 % but not more than 10 % nitroglycerin, by mass	4.1	3319
NITROGLYCERIN, SOLUTION IN ALCOHOL with more than 1 % but not more than 5 % nitroglycerin	3	3064
NITROGLYCERIN SOLUTION IN ALCOHOL with more than 1 % but not more than 10 % nitroglycerin	1.1D	0144
NITROGLYCERIN SOLUTION IN ALCOHOL with not more than 1 % nitroglycerin	3	1204
NITROGUANIDINE, dry or wetted with less than 20 % water, by mass	1.1D	0282
NITROGUANIDINE, WETTED with not less than 20 % water, by mass	4.1	1336
NITROHYDROCHLORIC ACID	8	1798
NITROMANNITE, WETTED, see	1.1D	0133
NITROMETHANE	3	1261
Nitromuriatic acid, see	8	1798
NITRONAPHTHALENE	4.1	2538
NITROPHENOLS (o-, m-, p-)	6.1	1663

Name and description	Class	UN No.
4-NITROPHENYLHYDRAZINE, with not less than 30 % water, by mass	4.1	3376
NITROPROPANES	3	2608
p-NITROSODIMETHYLANILINE	4.2	1369
NITROSTARCH, dry or wetted with less than 20 % water, by mass	1.1D	0146
NITROSTARCH, WETTED with not less than 20 % water, by mass	4.1	1337
NITROSYL CHLORIDE	2.3	1069
NITROSYLSULPHURIC ACID, LIQUID	8	2308
NITROSYLSULPHURIC ACID, SOLID	8	3456
NITROTOLUENES, LIQUID	6.1	1664
NITROTOLUENES, SOLID	6.1	3446
NITROTOLUIDINES	6.1	2660
NITROTRIAZOLONE	1.1D	0490
NITRO UREA	1.1D	0147
NITROUS OXIDE	2.2	1070
NITROUS OXIDE, REFRIGERATED LIQUID	2.2	2201
NITROXYLENES, LIQUID	6.1	1665
NITROXYLENES, SOLID	6.1	3447
Non-activated carbon, see	4.2	1361
Non-activated charcoal, see	4.2	1361
NONANES	3	1920
NONYLTRICHLOROSILANE	8	1799
2,5-NORBORNADIENE, STABILIZED, see	3	2251
Normal propyl alcohol, see	3	1274
NTO, see	1.1D	0490
OCTADECYLTRICHLOROSILANE	8	1800
OCTADIENE	3	2309
OCTAFLUOROBUT-2-ENE	2.2	2422
OCTAFLUOROCYCLOBUTANE	2.2	1976
OCTAFLUOROPROPANE	2.2	2424

Name and description	Class	UN No.
OCTANES	3	1262
OCTOGEN, see	1.1D	0226
	1.1D	0391
	1.1D	0484
OCTOL, dry or wetted with less than 15 % water, by mass, see	1.1D	0266
OCTOLITE, dry or wetted with less than 15 % water, by mass	1.1D	0266
OCTONAL	1.1D	0496
OCTYL ALDEHYDES	3	1191
tert-Octyl mercaptan, see	6.1	3023
OCTYLTRICHLOROSILANE	8	1801
Oenanthol, see	3	3056
OIL GAS, COMPRESSED	2.3	1071
Oleum, see	8	1831
ORGANIC PEROXIDE TYPE B, LIQUID	5.2	3101
ORGANIC PEROXIDE TYPE B, LIQUID, TEMPERATURE CONTROLLED	5.2	3111
ORGANIC PEROXIDE TYPE B, SOLID	5.2	3102
ORGANIC PEROXIDE TYPE B, SOLID, TEMPERATURE CONTROLLED	5.2	3112
ORGANIC PEROXIDE TYPE C, LIQUID	5.2	3103
ORGANIC PEROXIDE TYPE C, LIQUID, TEMPERATURE CONTROLLED	5.2	3113
ORGANIC PEROXIDE TYPE C, SOLID	5.2	3104
ORGANIC PEROXIDE TYPE C, SOLID, TEMPERATURE CONTROLLED	5.2	3114
ORGANIC PEROXIDE TYPE D, LIQUID	5.2	3105
ORGANIC PEROXIDE TYPE D, LIQUID, TEMPERATURE CONTROLLED	5.2	3115
ORGANIC PEROXIDE TYPE D, SOLID	5.2	3106
ORGANIC PEROXIDE TYPE D, SOLID, TEMPERATURE CONTROLLED	5.2	3116
ORGANIC PEROXIDE TYPE E, LIQUID	5.2	3107
ORGANIC PEROXIDE TYPE E, LIQUID, TEMPERATURE CONTROLLED	5.2	3117
ORGANIC PEROXIDE TYPE E, SOLID	5.2	3108
ORGANIC PEROXIDE TYPE E, SOLID, TEMPERATURE CONTROLLED	5.2	3118
ORGANIC PEROXIDE TYPE F, LIQUID	5.2	3109
ORGANIC PEROXIDE TYPE F, LIQUID, TEMPERATURE CONTROLLED	5.2	3119
ORGANIC PEROXIDE TYPE F, SOLID	5.2	3110
ORGANIC PEROXIDE TYPE F, SOLID, TEMPERATURE CONTROLLED	5.2	3120
Organic peroxides, see 2.5.3.2.4 for a list of currently assigned organic peroxides	5.2	3101 to 3120
ORGANIC PIGMENTS, SELF-HEATING	4.2	3313
ORGANOARSENIC COMPOUND, LIQUID, N.O.S.	6.1	3280
ORGANOARSENIC COMPOUND, SOLID, N.O.S.	6.1	3465
ORGANOCHLORINE PESTICIDE, LIQUID, FLAMMABLE, TOXIC, flash-point less than 23 °C	3	2762
ORGANOCHLORINE PESTICIDE, LIQUID, TOXIC	6.1	2996
ORGANOCHLORINE PESTICIDE, LIQUID, TOXIC, FLAMMABLE, flash-point not less than 23 °C	6.1	2995
ORGANOCHLORINE PESTICIDE, SOLID, TOXIC	6.1	2761

Name and description	Class	UN No.
ORGANOMETALLIC COMPOUND, LIQUID, TOXIC, N.O.S.	6.1	3282
ORGANOMETALLIC COMPOUND, SOLID, TOXIC, N.O.S.	6.1	3467
ORGANOMETALLIC SUBSTANCE, LIQUID, PYROPHORIC	4.2	3392
ORGANOMETALLIC SUBSTANCE, LIQUID, PYROPHORIC, WATER-REACTIVE	4.2	3394
ORGANOMETALLIC SUBSTANCE, LIQUID, WATER-REACTIVE	4.3	3398
ORGANOMETALLIC SUBSTANCE, LIQUID, WATER-REACTIVE, FLAMMABLE	4.3	3399
ORGANOMETALLIC SUBSTANCE, SOLID, PYROPHORIC	4.2	3391
ORGANOMETALLIC SUBSTANCE, SOLID, PYROPHORIC, WATER-REACTIVE	4.2	3393
ORGANOMETALLIC SUBSTANCE, SOLID, SELF-HEATING	4.2	3400
ORGANOMETALLIC SUBSTANCE, SOLID, WATER-REACTIVE, FLAMMABLE	4.3	3396
ORGANOMETALLIC SUBSTANCE, SOLID, WATER-REACTIVE	4.3	3395
ORGANOMETALLIC SUBSTANCE, SOLID, WATER-REACTIVE, SELF-HEATING	4.3	3397
ORGANOPHOSPHORUS COMPOUND, TOXIC, FLAMMABLE, N.O.S.	6.1	3279
ORGANOPHOSPHORUS COMPOUND, LIQUID, TOXIC, N.O.S.	6.1	3278
ORGANOPHOSPHORUS COMPOUND, SOLID, TOXIC, N.O.S.	6.1	3464
ORGANOPHOSPHORUS PESTICIDE, LIQUID, FLAMMABLE, TOXIC, flash-point less than 23 °C	3	2784
ORGANOPHOSPHORUS PESTICIDE, LIQUID, TOXIC	6.1	3018
ORGANOPHOSPHORUS PESTICIDE, LIQUID, TOXIC, FLAMMABLE, flash-point not less than 23 °C	6.1	3017
ORGANOPHOSPHORUS PESTICIDE, SOLID, TOXIC	6.1	2783
ORGANOTIN COMPOUND, LIQUID, N.O.S.	6.1	2788
ORGANOTIN COMPOUND, SOLID, N.O.S.	6.1	3146
ORGANOTIN PESTICIDE, LIQUID, FLAMMABLE, TOXIC, flash-point less than 23 °C	3	2787
ORGANOTIN PESTICIDE, LIQUID, TOXIC	6.1	3020
ORGANOTIN PESTICIDE, LIQUID, TOXIC, FLAMMABLE, flash-point not less than 23 °C	6.1	3019
ORGANOTIN PESTICIDE, SOLID, TOXIC	6.1	2786
Orthophospohoric acid, see	8	1805
	8	3453
OSMIUM TETROXIDE	6.1	2471
OXIDIZING LIQUID, N.O.S.	5.1	3139
OXIDIZING LIQUID, CORROSIVE, N.O.S.	5.1	3098
OXIDIZING LIQUID, TOXIC, N.O.S.	5.1	3099
OXIDIZING SOLID, N.O.S.	5.1	1479
OXIDIZING SOLID, CORROSIVE, N.O.S.	5.1	3085
OXIDIZING SOLID, FLAMMABLE, N.O.S.	5.1	3137
OXIDIZING SOLID, SELF-HEATING, N.O.S.	5.1	3100
OXIDIZING SOLID, TOXIC, N.O.S.	5.1	3087
OXIDIZING SOLID, WATER-REACTIVE, N.O.S.	5.1	3121
Oxirane, see	2.3	1040
OXYGEN, COMPRESSED	2.2	1072
OXYGEN DIFLUORIDE, COMPRESSED	2.3	2190
OXYGEN GENERATOR, CHEMICAL	5.1	3356
OXYGEN, REFRIGERATED LIQUID	2.2	1073
1-Oxy-4-nitrobenzene, see	6.1	1663

Name and description	Class	UN No.
PACKAGING DISCARDED, EMPTY, UNCLEANED	9	3509
PAINT (including paint, lacquer, enamel, stain, shellac, varnish, polish, liquid filler and liquid lacquer base)	3 8	1263 3066
PAINT, CORROSIVE, FLAMMABLE (including paint, lacquer, enamel, stain, shellac, varnish, polish, liquid filler and liquid lacquer base)	8	3470
PAINT, FLAMMABLE, CORROSIVE (including paint, lacquer, enamel, stain, shellac, varnish, polish, liquid filler and liquid lacquer base)	3	3469
PAINT RELATED MATERIAL (including paint thinning and reducing compound)	3 8	1263 3066
PAINT RELATED MATERIAL CORROSIVE, FLAMMABLE (including paint thinning or reducing compound)	8	3470
PAINT RELATED MATERIAL, FLAMMABLE, CORROSIVE (including paint thinning or reducing compound)	3	3469
PAPER, UNSATURATED OIL TREATED, incompletely dried (including carbon paper)	4.2	1379
Paraffin, see	3	1223
PARAFORMALDEHYDE	4.1	2213
PARALDEHYDE	3	1264
PCBs, see	9 9	2315 3432
PENTABORANE	4.2	1380
PENTACHLOROETHANE	6.1	1669
PENTACHLOROPHENOL	6.1	3155
PENTAERYTHRITE TETRANITRATE with not less than 7 % wax, by mass	1.1D	0411
PENTAERYTHRITE TETRANITRATE, DESENSITIZED with not less than 15 % phlegmatizer, by mass	1.1D	0150
PENTAERYTHRITE TETRANITRATE MIXTURE, DESENSITIZED, SOLID, N.O.S. with more than 10 % but not more than 20 % PETN, by mass	4.1	3344
PENTAERYTHRITE TETRANITRATE, WETTED with not less than 25 % water, by mass	1.1D	0150
PENTAERYTHRITOL TETRANITRATE, see	1.1D 1.1D	0150 0411
PENTAERYTHRITOL TETRANITRATE MIXTURE, DESENSITIZED, see	4.1	3344
PENTAFLUOROETHANE	2.2	3220
Pentafluoroethane, 1,1,1-trifluoroethane, and 1,1,1,2-tetrafluoroethane zeotropic mixture with approximately 44 % pentafluoroethane and 52 % 1,1,1-trifluoroethane, see	2.2	3337
PENTAMETHYLHEPTANE	3	2286
Pentanal, see	3	2058
PENTANE-2,4-DIONE	3	2310
PENTANES, liquid	3	1265
n-Pentane, see	3	1265
PENTANOLS	3	1105
3-Pentanol, see	3	1105
1-PENTENE	3	1108
1-PENTOL	8	2705
PENTOLITE, dry or wetted with less than 15 % water, by mass	1.1D	0151
Pentyl nitrite, see	3	1113
PERCHLORATES, INORGANIC, N.O.S.	5.1	1481
PERCHLORATES, INORGANIC, AQUEOUS SOLUTION, N.O.S.	5.1	3211
PERCHLORIC ACID with more than 50 % but not more than 72 % acid, by mass	5.1	1873
PERCHLORIC ACID with not more than 50 % acid, by mass	8	1802
Perchlorobenzene, see	6.1	2729
Perchlorocyclopentadiene, see	6.1	2646
Perchloroethylene, see	6.1	1897
PERCHLOROMETHYL MERCAPTAN	6.1	1670

Name and description	Class	UN No.
PERCHLORYL FLUORIDE	2.3	3083
Perfluoroacetylchloride, see	2.3	3057
PERFLUORO(ETHYL VINYL ETHER)	2.1	3154
PERFLUORO(METHYL VINYL ETHER)	2.1	3153
Perfluoropropane, see	2.2	2424
PERFUMERY PRODUCTS with flammable solvents	3	1266
PERMANGANATES, INORGANIC, N.O.S.	5.1	1482
PERMANGANATES, INORGANIC, AQUEOUS SOLUTION, N.O.S.	5.1	3214
PEROXIDES, INORGANIC, N.O.S.	5.1	1483
PERSULPHATES, INORGANIC, N.O.S.	5.1	3215
PERSULPHATES, INORGANIC, AQUEOUS SOLUTION, N.O.S.	5.1	3216
PESTICIDE, LIQUID, FLAMMABLE, TOXIC, N.O.S., flash-point less than 23 °C	3	3021
PESTICIDE, LIQUID, TOXIC, N.O.S.	6.1	2902
PESTICIDE, LIQUID, TOXIC, FLAMMABLE, N.O.S., flash-point not less than 23 °C	6.1	2903
PESTICIDE, SOLID, TOXIC, N.O.S.	6.1	2588
Pesticide, toxic, under compressed gas, n.o.s, see	2	1950
PETN, see	1.1D	0150
	1.1D	0411
PETN, MIXTURE DESENSITIZED, see	4.1	3344
PETN/TNT, see	1.1D	0151
PETROL	3	1203
MOTOR SPIRIT AND ETHANOL MIXTURE	3	3475
PETROLEUM CRUDE OIL	3	1267
PETROLEUM SOUR CRUDE OIL, FLAMMABLE, TOXIC	3	3494
PETROLEUM DISTILLATES, N.O.S.	3	1268
Petroleum ether, see	3	1268
PETROLEUM GASES, LIQUEFIED	2.1	1075
Petroleum naphtha, see	3	1268
Petroleum oil, see	3	1268
PETROLEUM PRODUCTS, N.O.S.	3	1268
Petroleum raffinate, see	3	1268
Petroleum spirit, see	3	1268
PHENACYL BROMIDE	6.1	2645
PHENETIDINES	6.1	2311
PHENOLATES, LIQUID	8	2904
PHENOLATES, SOLID	8	2905
PHENOL, MOLTEN	6.1	2312
PHENOL, SOLID	6.1	1671
PHENOL SOLUTION	6.1	2821
PHENOLSULPHONIC ACID, LIQUID	8	1803
PHENOXYACETIC ACID DERIVATIVE PESTICIDE, LIQUID, FLAMMABLE, TOXIC, flash-point less than 23 °C	3	3346
PHENOXYACETIC ACID DERIVATIVE PESTICIDE, LIQUID, TOXIC	6.1	3348
PHENOXYACETIC ACID DERIVATIVE PESTICIDE, LIQUID, TOXIC, FLAMMABLE, flash-point not less than 23 °C	6.1	3347
PHENOXYACETIC ACID DERIVATIVE PESTICIDE, SOLID, TOXIC	6.1	3345
PHENYLACETONITRILE, LIQUID	6.1	2470
PHENYLACETYL CHLORIDE	8	2577
Phenylamine, see	6.1	1547
1-Phenylbutane, see	3	2709
2-Phenylbutane, see	3	2709
PHENYLCARBYLAMINE CHLORIDE	6.1	1672
PHENYL CHLOROFORMATE	6.1	2746
Phenyl cyanide, see	6.1	2224
PHENYLENEDIAMINES (o-, m-, p-)	6.1	1673

Name and description	Class	UN No.
Phenylethylene, see	3	2055
PHENYLHYDRAZINE	6.1	2572
PHENYL ISOCYANATE	6.1	2487
Phenylisocyanodichloride, see	6.1	1672
PHENYL MERCAPTAN	6.1	2337
PHENYLMERCURIC ACETATE	6.1	1674
PHENYLMERCURIC COMPOUND, N.O.S.	6.1	2026
PHENYLMERCURIC HYDROXIDE	6.1	1894
PHENYLMERCURIC NITRATE	6.1	1895
PHENYLPHOSPHORUS DICHLORIDE	8	2798
PHENYLPHOSPHORUS THIODICHLORIDE	8	2799
2-Phenylpropene, see	3	2303
PHENYLTRICHLOROSILANE	8	1804
PHOSGENE	2.3	1076
9-PHOSPHABICYCLONONANES	4.2	2940
PHOSPHINE	2.3	2199
PHOSPHINE, ADSORBED	2.3	3525
Phosphoretted hydrogen, see	2.3	2199
PHOSPHORIC ACID, SOLUTION	8	1805
PHOSPHORIC ACID, SOLID	8	3453
Phosphoric acid, anhydrous, see	8	1807
PHOSPHOROUS ACID	8	2834
PHOSPHORUS, AMORPHOUS	4.1	1338
Phosphorus bromide, see	8	1808
Phosphorus chloride, see	6.1	1809
PHOSPHORUS HEPTASULPHIDE, free from yellow and white phosphorus	4.1	1339
PHOSPHORUS OXYBROMIDE	8	1939
PHOSPHORUS OXYBROMIDE, MOLTEN	8	2576
PHOSPHORUS OXYCHLORIDE	8	1810

Name and description	Class	UN No.
PHOSPHORUS PENTABROMIDE	8	2691
PHOSPHORUS PENTACHLORIDE	8	1806
PHOSPHORUS PENTAFLUORIDE	2.3	2198
PHOSPHORUS PENTAFLUORIDE, ADSORBED	2.3	3524
PHOSPHORUS PENTASULPHIDE, free from yellow and white phosphorus	4.3	1340
PHOSPHORUS PENTOXIDE	8	1807
PHOSPHORUS SESQUISULPHIDE, free from yellow and white phosphorus	4.1	1341
Phosphorus (V) sulphide, free from yellow and white phosphorus, see	4.3	1340
Phosphorus sulphochloride, see	8	1837
PHOSPHORUS TRIBROMIDE	8	1808
PHOSPHORUS TRICHLORIDE	6.1	1809
PHOSPHORUS TRIOXIDE	8	2578
PHOSPHORUS TRISULPHIDE, free from yellow and white phosphorus	4.1	1343
PHOSPHORUS, WHITE, DRY	4.2	1381
PHOSPHORUS, WHITE IN SOLUTION	4.2	1381
PHOSPHORUS, WHITE, MOLTEN	4.2	2447
PHOSPHORUS, WHITE, UNDER WATER	4.2	1381
PHOSPHORUS, YELLOW, DRY	4.2	1381
PHOSPHORUS, YELLOW, IN SOLUTION	4.2	1381
PHOSPHORUS, YELLOW, UNDER WATER	4.2	1381
Phosphoryl chloride, see	8	1810
PHTHALIC ANHYDRIDE with more than 0.05 % of maleic anhydride	8	2214
PICOLINES	3	2313
PICRAMIDE, see	1.1D	0153
PICRIC ACID, see	1.1D	0154
PICRIC ACID, WETTED see	4.1	1344
	4.1	3364

Name and description	Class	UN No.
PICRITE, see	1.1D	0282
PICRITE, WETTED, see	4.1	1336
Picrotoxin, see	6.1	3172
	6.1	3462
PICRYL CHLORIDE, see	1.1D	0155
PICRYLCHLORIDE, WETTED see	4.1	3365
alpha-PINENE	3	2368
PINE OIL	3	1272
PIPERAZINE	8	2579
PIPERIDINE	8	2401
Pivaloyl chloride, see	6.1	2438
Plastic explosives, see	1.1D	0084
PLASTICS MOULDING COMPOUND in dough, sheet or extruded rope form evolving flammable vapour	9	3314
PLASTICS, NITROCELLULOSE-BASED, SELF-HEATING, N.O.S.	4.2	2006
POLYAMINES, FLAMMABLE, CORROSIVE, N.O.S.	3	2733
POLYAMINES, LIQUID, CORROSIVE, N.O.S.	8	2735
POLYAMINES, LIQUID, CORROSIVE, FLAMMABLE, N.O.S.	8	2734
POLYAMINES, SOLID, CORROSIVE, N.O.S.	8	3259
POLYCHLORINATED BIPHENYLS, LIQUID	9	2315
POLYCHLORINATED BIPHENYLS, SOLID	9	3432
POLYESTER RESIN KIT, liquid base material	3	3269
POLYESTER RESIN KIT, solid base material	4.1	3527
POLYHALOGENATED BIPHENYLS, LIQUID	9	3151
POLYHALOGENATED BIPHENYLS, SOLID	9	3152
POLYHALOGENATED TERPHENYLS, LIQUID	9	3151
POLYHALOGENATED TERPHENYLS, SOLID	9	3152
POLYMERIC BEADS, EXPANDABLE, evolving flammable vapour	9	2211
POLYMERIZING SUBSTANCE, LIQUID, STABILIZED, N.O.S.	4.1	3532
POLYMERIZING SUBSTANCE, LIQUID, TEMPERATURE CONTROLLED, N.O.S.	4.1	3534
POLYMERIZING SUBSTANCE, SOLID, STABILIZED, N.O.S.	4.1	3531
POLYMERIZING SUBSTANCE, SOLID, TEMPERATURE CONTROLLED, N.O.S.	4.1	3533
Polystyrene beads, expandable, see	9	2211
POTASSIUM	4.3	2257
POTASSIUM ARSENATE	6.1	1677
POTASSIUM ARSENITE	6.1	1678
Potassium bifluoride, see	8	1811
Potassium bisulphate, see	8	2509
Potassium bisulphite solution, see	8	2693
POTASSIUM BOROHYDRIDE	4.3	1870
POTASSIUM BROMATE	5.1	1484
POTASSIUM CHLORATE	5.1	1485
POTASSIUM CHLORATE, AQUEOUS SOLUTION	5.1	2427
Potassium chlorate mixed with mineral oil, see	1.1D	0083
POTASSIUM CUPROCYANIDE	6.1	1679
POTASSIUM CYANIDE, SOLID	6.1	1680
POTASSIUM CYANIDE SOLUTION	6.1	3413
Potassium dicyanocuprate (I), see	6.1	1679
POTASSIUM DITHIONITE	4.2	1929
POTASSIUM FLUORIDE, SOLID	6.1	1812
POTASSIUM FLUORIDE SOLUTION	6.1	3422
POTASSIUM FLUOROACETATE	6.1	2628
POTASSIUM FLUOROSILICATE	6.1	2655

Name and description	Class	UN No.
Potassium hexafluorosilicate, see	6.1	2655
Potassium hydrate, see	8	1814
POTASSIUM HYDROGENDIFLUORIDE SOLID	8	1811
POTASSIUM HYDROGENDIFLUORIDE SOLUTION	8	3421
POTASSIUM HYDROGEN SULPHATE	8	2509
POTASSIUM HYDROSULPHITE, see	4.2	1929
Potassium hydroxide, liquid, see	8	1814
POTASSIUM HYDROXIDE, SOLID	8	1813
POTASSIUM HYDROXIDE SOLUTION	8	1814
POTASSIUM METAL ALLOYS, LIQUID	4.3	1420
POTASSIUM METAL ALLOYS, SOLID	4.3	3403
POTASSIUM METAVANADATE	6.1	2864
POTASSIUM MONOXIDE	8	2033
POTASSIUM NITRATE	5.1	1486
Potassium nitrate and sodium nitrate mixture, see	5.1	1499
POTASSIUM NITRATE AND SODIUM NITRITE MIXTURE	5.1	1487
POTASSIUM NITRITE	5.1	1488
POTASSIUM PERCHLORATE	5.1	1489
POTASSIUM PERMANGANATE	5.1	1490
POTASSIUM PEROXIDE	5.1	1491
POTASSIUM PERSULPHATE	5.1	1492
POTASSIUM PHOSPHIDE	4.3	2012
Potassium selenate, see	6.1	2630
Potassium selenite, see	6.1	2630
Potassium silicofluoride, see	6.1	2655
POTASSIUM SODIUM ALLOYS, LIQUID	4.3	1422
POTASSIUM SODIUM ALLOYS, SOLID	4.3	3404
POTASSIUM SULPHIDE with less than 30 % water of crystallization	4.2	1382
POTASSIUM SULPHIDE, ANHYDROUS	4.2	1382
POTASSIUM SULPHIDE, HYDRATED with not less than 30 % water of crystallization	8	1847
POTASSIUM SUPEROXIDE	5.1	2466
Potassium tetracyanomercurate (II), see	6.1	1626
POWDER CAKE, WETTED with not less than 17 % alcohol, by mass	1.1C	0433
POWDER CAKE, WETTED with not less than 25 % water, by mass	1.3C	0159
POWDER PASTE, see	1.1C	0433
	1.3C	0159
POWDER, SMOKELESS	1.1C	0160
	1.3C	0161
	1.4C	0509
Power devices, explosive, see	1.2C	0381
	1.3C	0275
	1.4C	0276
	1.4S	0323
PRIMERS, CAP TYPE	1.1B	0377
	1.4B	0378
	1.4S	0044
Primers, small arms, see	1.4S	0044
PRIMERS, TUBULAR	1.3G	0319
	1.4G	0320
	1.4S	0376
PRINTING INK, flammable or PRINTING INK RELATED MATERIAL (including printing ink thinning or reducing compound), flammable	3	1210
Projectiles, illuminating, seee	1.2G	0171
	1.3G	0254
	1.4G	0297
PROJECTILES, inert with tracer	1.3G	0424
	1.4G	0425
	1.4S	0345

Name and description	Class	UN No.
PROJECTILES with burster or expelling charge	1.2D	0346
	1.2F	0426
	1.2G	0434
	1.4D	0347
	1.4F	0427
	1.4G	0435
PROJECTILES with bursting charge	1.1D	0168
	1.1F	0167
	1.2D	0169
	1.2F	0324
	1.4D	0344
PROPADIENE, STABILIZED	2.1	2200
Propadiene and methyl acetylene mixture, stabilized, see	2.1	1060
PROPANE	2.1	1978
PROPANETHIOLS	3	2402
n-PROPANOL	3	1274
PROPELLANT, LIQUID	1.1C	0497
	1.3C	0495
PROPELLANT, SOLID	1.1C	0498
	1.3C	0499
	1.4C	0501
Propellant with a single base; Propellant with a double base; or Propellant with a triple base; see	1.1C	0160
	1.3C	0161
Propene, see	2.1	1077
PROPIONALDEHYDE	3	1275
PROPIONIC ACID with not less than 10 % and less than 90 % acid by mass	8	1848
PROPIONIC ACID with not less than 90 % acid by mass	8	3463
PROPIONIC ANHYDRIDE	8	2496
PROPIONITRILE	3	2404
PROPIONYL CHLORIDE	3	1815
n-PROPYL ACETATE	3	1276
PROPYL ALCOHOL, NORMAL, see	3	1274
PROPYLAMINE	3	1277
n-PROPYLBENZENE	3	2364
Propyl chloride, see	3	1278
n-PROPYL CHLOROFORMATE	6.1	2740

Name and description	Class	UN No.
PROPYLENE	2.1	1077
PROPYLENE CHLOROHYDRIN	6.1	2611
1,2-PROPYLENEDIAMINE	8	2258
Propylene dichloride, see	3	1279
PROPYLENEIMINE, STABILIZED	3	1921
PROPYLENE OXIDE	3	1280
PROPYLENE TETRAMER	3	2850
Propylene trimer, see	3	2057
PROPYL FORMATES	3	1281
n-PROPYL ISOCYANATE	6.1	2482
Propyl mercaptan, see	3	2402
n-PROPYL NITRATE	3	1865
PROPYLTRICHLOROSILANE	8	1816
Pyrazine hexahydride, see	8	2579
PYRETHROID PESTICIDE, LIQUID, FLAMMABLE, TOXIC, flash-point less than 23 °C	3	3350
PYRETHROID PESTICIDE, LIQUID, TOXIC	6.1	3352
PYRETHROID PESTICIDE, LIQUID, TOXIC, FLAMMABLE, flash-point not less than 23 °C	6.1	3351
PYRETHROID PESTICIDE, SOLID, TOXIC	6.1	3349
PYRIDINE	3	1282
PYROPHORIC ALLOY, N.O.S.	4.2	1383
PYROPHORIC LIQUID, INORGANIC, N.O.S.	4.2	3194
PYROPHORIC LIQUID, ORGANIC, N.O.S.	4.2	2845
PYROPHORIC METAL, N.O.S.	4.2	1383
PYROPHORIC SOLID, INORGANIC, N.O.S.	4.2	3200
PYROPHORIC SOLID, ORGANIC, N.O.S.	4.2	2846
PYROSULPHURYL CHLORIDE	8	1817
Pyroxylin solution, see	3	2059

Name and description	Class	UN No.
PYRROLIDINE	3	1922
QUINOLINE	6.1	2656
Quinone, see	6.1	2587
RADIOACTIVE MATERIAL, EXCEPTED PACKAGE - ARTICLES MANUFACTURED FROM NATURAL URANIUM or DEPLETED URANIUM or NATURAL THORIUM	7	2909
RADIOACTIVE MATERIAL, EXCEPTED PACKAGE - EMPTY PACKAGING	7	2908
RADIOACTIVE MATERIAL, EXCEPTED PACKAGE - INSTRUMENTS or ARTICLES	7	2911
RADIOACTIVE MATERIAL, EXCEPTED PACKAGE - LIMITED QUANTITY OF MATERIAL	7	2910
RADIOACTIVE MATERIAL, LOW SPECIFIC ACTIVITY (LSA-I), non fissile or fissile-excepted	7	2912
RADIOACTIVE MATERIAL, LOW SPECIFIC ACTIVITY (LSA-II), FISSILE	7	3324
RADIOACTIVE MATERIAL, LOW SPECIFIC ACTIVITY (LSA-II), non fissile or fissile-excepted	7	3321
RADIOACTIVE MATERIAL, LOW SPECIFIC ACTIVITY, (LSA-III), FISSILE	7	3325
RADIOACTIVE MATERIAL, LOW SPECIFIC ACTIVITY (LSA-III), non fissile or fissile-excepted	7	3322
RADIOACTIVE MATERIAL, SURFACE CONTAMINATED OBJECTS (SCO-I or SCO-II), FISSILE	7	3326
RADIOACTIVE MATERIAL, SURFACE CONTAMINATED OBJECTS (SCO-I, SCO-II or SCO-III), non fissile or fissile-excepted	7	2913
RADIOACTIVE MATERIAL, TRANSPORTED UNDER SPECIAL ARRANGEMENT, FISSILE	7	3331
RADIOACTIVE MATERIAL, TRANSPORTED UNDER SPECIAL ARRANGEMENT, non fissile or fissile-excepted	7	2919
RADIOACTIVE MATERIAL, TYPE A PACKAGE, FISSILE, non-special form	7	3327
RADIOACTIVE MATERIAL, TYPE A PACKAGE, non-special form, non fissile or fissile-excepted	7	2915
RADIOACTIVE MATERIAL, TYPE A PACKAGE, SPECIAL FORM, FISSILE	7	3333
RADIOACTIVE MATERIAL, TYPE A PACKAGE, SPECIAL FORM, non fissile or fissile-excepted	7	3332
RADIOACTIVE MATERIAL, TYPE B(M) PACKAGE, FISSILE	7	3329
RADIOACTIVE MATERIAL, TYPE B(M) PACKAGE, non fissile or fissile-excepted	7	2917
RADIOACTIVE MATERIAL, TYPE B(U) PACKAGE, FISSILE	7	3328
RADIOACTIVE MATERIAL, TYPE B(U) PACKAGE, non fissile or fissile-excepted	7	2916
RADIOACTIVE MATERIAL, TYPE C PACKAGE, FISSILE	7	3330
RADIOACTIVE MATERIAL, TYPE C PACKAGE, non fissile or fissile-excepted	7	3323
RADIOACTIVE MATERIAL, URANIUM HEXAFLUORIDE, FISSILE	7	2977
RADIOACTIVE MATERIAL, URANIUM HEXAFLUORIDE, non fissile or fissile-excepted	7	2978
RAGS, OILY	4.2	1856
RDX, see	1.1D	0072
	1.1D	0391
	1.1D	0483
RECEPTACLES, SMALL, CONTAINING GAS without a release device, non-refillable	2	2037
Red phosphorus, see	4.1	1338
REFRIGERANT GAS, N.O.S.	2.2	1078
REFRIGERANT GAS R 12, see	2.2	1028
REFRIGERANT GAS R 12B1, see	2.2	1974

Name and description	Class	UN No.
REFRIGERANT GAS R 13, see	2.2	1022
REFRIGERANT GAS R 13B1, see	2.2	1009
REFRIGERANT GAS R 14, see	2.2	1982
REFRIGERANT GAS R 21, see	2.2	1029
REFRIGERANT GAS R 22, see	2.2	1018
REFRIGERANT GAS R 23, see	2.2	1984
REFRIGERANT GAS R 32, see	2.1	3252
REFRIGERANT GAS R 40, see	2.1	1063
REFRIGERANT GAS R 41, see	2.1	2454
REFRIGERANT GAS R 114, see	2.2	1958
REFRIGERANT GAS R 115, see	2.2	1020
REFRIGERANT GAS R 116, see	2.2	2193
REFRIGERANT GAS R 124, see	2.2	1021
REFRIGERANT GAS R 125, see	2.2	3220
REFRIGERANT GAS R 133a, see	2.2	1983
REFRIGERANT GAS R 134a, see	2.2	3159
REFRIGERANT GAS R 142b, see	2.1	2517
REFRIGERANT GAS R 143a, see	2.1	2035
REFRIGERANT GASR 152a, see	2.1	1030
REFRIGERANT GAS R 161, see	2.1	2453
REFRIGERANT GAS R 218, see	2.2	2424
REFRIGERANT GAS R 227, see	2.2	3296
REFRIGERANT GAS R 404A	2.2	3337
REFRIGERANT GAS R 407A	2.2	3338
REFRIGERANT GAS R 407B	2.2	3339
REFRIGERANT GAS R 407C	2.2	3340
REFRIGERANT GAS R 500, see	2.2	2602
REFRIGERANT GAS R 502, see	2.2	1973
REFRIGERANT GAS R 503, see	2.2	2599
REFRIGERANT GAS R 1132a, see	2.1	1959
REFRIGERANT GAS R 1216, see	2.2	1858
REFRIGERANT GAS R 1318, see	2.2	2422

Name and description	Class	UN No.
REFRIGERANT GAS RC 318, see	2.2	1976
REFRIGERATING MACHINES containing flammable, non-toxic, liquefied gas	2.1	3358
REFRIGERATING MACHINES containing non-flammable, non-toxic, gases or ammonia solutions (UN 2672)	2.2	2857
REGULATED MEDICAL WASTE, N.O.S.	6.2	3291
RELEASE DEVICES, EXPLOSIVE	1.4S	0173
RESIN SOLUTION, flammable	3	1866
Resorcin, see	6.1	2876
RESORCINOL	6.1	2876
RIVETS, EXPLOSIVE	1.4S	0174
ROCKET MOTORS	1.1C 1.2C 1.3C 1.4C	0280 0281 0186 0510
ROCKET MOTORS, LIQUID FUELLED	1.2J 1.3J	0395 0396
ROCKET MOTORS WITH HYPERGOLIC LIQUIDS with or without expelling charge	1.2L 1.3L	0322 0250
ROCKETS with bursting charge	1.1E 1.1F 1.2E 1.2F	0181 0180 0182 0295
ROCKETS with expelling charge	1.2C 13C 1.4C	0436 0437 0438
ROCKETS with inert head	1.3C 1.2C	0183 0502
ROCKETS, LINE-THROWING	1.2G 1.3G 1.4G	0238 0240 0453
ROCKETS, LIQUID FUELLED with bursting charge	1.1J 1.2J	0397 0398
ROSIN OIL	3	1286
RUBBER SCRAP, powdered or granulated, not exceeding 840 microns and rubber content exceeding 45 %	4.1	1345

Name and description	Class	UN No.	Name and description	Class	UN No.
RUBBER SHODDY, powdered or granulated, not exceeding 840 microns and rubber content exceeding 45 %	4.1	1345	SELF-HEATING LIQUID, ORGANIC, N.O.S.	4.2	3183
RUBBER SOLUTION	3	1287	SELF-HEATING LIQUID, TOXIC, INORGANIC, N.O.S.	4.2	3187
RUBIDIUM	4.3	1423	SELF-HEATING LIQUID, TOXIC, ORGANIC, N.O.S.	4.2	3184
RUBIDIUM HYDROXIDE	8	2678	SELF-HEATING SOLID, CORROSIVE, INORGANIC, N.O.S.	4.2	3192
RUBIDIUM HYDROXIDE SOLUTION	8	2677			
Rubidium nitrate, see	5.1	1477	SELF-HEATING SOLID, CORROSIVE, ORGANIC, N.O.S.	4.2	3126
SAFETY DEVICES, electrically initiated	9	3268	SELF-HEATING SOLID, INORGANIC, N.O.S.	4.2	3190
SAFETY DEVICES, PYROTECHNIC	1.4G	0503			
Saltpetre, see	5.1	1486	SELF-HEATING SOLID, ORGANIC, N.O.S.	4.2	3088
SAMPLES, EXPLOSIVE, other than initiating explosive		0190	SELF-HEATING SOLID, OXIDIZING, N.O.S	4.2	3127
Sand acid, see	8	1778	SELF-HEATING SOLID, TOXIC, INORGANIC, N.O.S.	4.2	3191
Seat-belt pretensioners, see	1.4G 9	0503 3268	SELF-HEATING SOLID, TOXIC, ORGANIC, N.O.S.	4.2	3128
SEED CAKE with more than 1.5 % oil and not more than 11 % moisture	4.2	1386	SELF-REACTIVE LIQUID TYPE B	4.1	3221
SEED CAKE with not more than 1.5 % oil and not more than 11 % moisture	4.2	2217	SELF-REACTIVE LIQUID TYPE B, TEMPERATURE CONTROLLED	4.1	3231
Seed expellers, see	4.2 4.2	1386 2217	SELF-REACTIVE LIQUID TYPE C	4.1	3223
SELENATES	6.1	2630	SELF-REACTIVE LIQUID TYPE C, TEMPERATURE CONTROLLED	4.1	3233
SELENIC ACID	8	1905	SELF-REACTIVE LIQUID TYPE D	4.1	3225
SELENITES	6.1	2630			
SELENIUM COMPOUND, N.O.S.	6.1	3283	SELF-REACTIVE LIQUID TYPE D, TEMPERATURE CONTROLLED	4.1	3235
SELENIUM COMPOUND, LIQUID, N.O.S.	6.1	3440	SELF-REACTIVE LIQUID TYPE E	4.1	3227
SELENIUM DISULPHIDE	6.1	2657	SELF-REACTIVE LIQUID TYPE E, TEMPERATURE CONTROLLED	4.1	3237
SELENIUM HEXAFLUORIDE	2.3	2194	SELF-REACTIVE LIQUID TYPE F	4.1	3229
SELENIUM OXYCHLORIDE	8	2879	SELF-REACTIVE LIQUID TYPE F, TEMPERATURE CONTROLLED	4.1	3239
SELF-HEATING LIQUID, CORROSIVE, INORGANIC, N.O.S.	4.2	3188	SELF-REACTIVE SOLID TYPE B	4.1	3222
SELF-HEATING LIQUID, CORROSIVE, ORGANIC, N.O.S.	4.2	3185	SELF-REACTIVE SOLID TYPE B, TEMPERATURE CONTROLLED	4.1	3232
SELF-HEATING LIQUID, INORGANIC, N.O.S.	4.2	3186	SELF-REACTIVE SOLID TYPE C	4.1	3224

Name and description	Class	UN No.
SELF-REACTIVE SOLID TYPE C, TEMPERATURE CONTROLLED	4.1	3234
SELF-REACTIVE SOLID TYPE D	4.1	3226
SELF-REACTIVE SOLID TYPE D, TEMPERATURE CONTROLLED	4.1	3236
SELF-REACTIVE SOLID TYPE E	4.1	3228
SELF-REACTIVE SOLID TYPE E, TEMPERATURE CONTROLLED	4.1	3238
SELF-REACTIVE SOLID TYPE F	4.1	3230
SELF-REACTIVE SOLID TYPE F, TEMPERATURE CONTROLLED	4.1	3240
SHALE OIL	3	1288
Shaped charges, see	1.1D	0059
	1.2D	0439
	1.4D	0440
	1.4S	0441
SIGNAL DEVICES, HAND	1.4G	0191
	1.4S	0373
SIGNALS, DISTRESS, ship	1.1G	0194
	1.3G	0195
	1.4G	0505
	1.4S	0506
Signals, distress, ship, water-activated, see	1.3L	0249
SIGNALS, RAILWAY TRACK, EXPLOSIVE	1.1G	0192
	1.3G	0492
	1.4G	0493
	1.4S	0193
SIGNALS, SMOKE	1.1G	0196
	1.2G	0313
	1.3G	0487
	1.4G	0197
	1.4S	0507
SILANE	2.1	2203
Silicofluoric acid, see	8	1778
Silicofluorides, n.o.s., see	6.1	2856
Silicon chloride, see	8	1818
SILICON POWDER, AMORPHOUS	4.1	1346
SILICON TETRACHLORIDE	8	1818
SILICON TETRAFLUORIDE	2.3	1859

Name and description	Class	UN No.
SILICON TETRAFLUORIDE, ADSORBED	2.3	3521
SILVER ARSENITE	6.1	1683
SILVER CYANIDE	6.1	1684
SILVER NITRATE	5.1	1493
SILVER PICRATE, WETTED with not less than 30 % water, by mass	4.1	1347
SLUDGE ACID	8	1906
SODA LIME with more than 4 % sodium hydroxide	8	1907
SODIUM	4.3	1428
Sodium aluminate, solid	8	2812
SODIUM ALUMINATE SOLUTION	8	1819
SODIUM ALUMINIUM HYDRIDE	4.3	2835
SODIUM AMMONIUM VANADATE	6.1	2863
SODIUM ARSANILATE	6.1	2473
SODIUM ARSENATE	6.1	1685
SODIUM ARSENITE, AQUEOUS SOLUTION	6.1	1686
SODIUM ARSENITE, SOLID	6.1	2027
SODIUM AZIDE	6.1	1687
Sodium bifluoride, see	8	2439
Sodium binoxide, see	5.1	1504
Sodium bisulphite solution, see	8	2693
SODIUM BOROHYDRIDE	4.3	1426
SODIUM BOROHYDRIDE AND SODIUM HYDROXIDE SOLUTION, with not more than 12 % sodium borohydride and not more than 40 % sodium hydroxide, by mass	8	3320
SODIUM BROMATE	5.1	1494
SODIUM CACODYLATE	6.1	1688
SODIUM CARBONATE PEROXYHYDRATE	5.1	3378
SODIUM CHLORATE	5.1	1495
SODIUM CHLORATE, AQUEOUS SOLUTION	5.1	2428

Name and description	Class	UN No.
Sodium chlorate mixed with dinitrotoluene, see	1.1D	0083
SODIUM CHLORITE	5.1	1496
SODIUM CHLOROACETATE	6.1	2659
SODIUM CUPROCYANIDE, SOLID	6.1	2316
SODIUM CUPROCYANIDE SOLUTION	6.1	2317
SODIUM CYANIDE, SOLID	6.1	1689
SODIUM CYANIDE SOLUTION	6.1	3414
Sodium dicyanocuprate (I), solid, see	6.1	2316
Sodium dicyanocuprate (I) solution, see	6.1	2317
Sodium dimethylarsenate, see	6.1	1688
SODIUM DINITRO-o-CRESOLATE, dry or wetted with less than 15 % water, by mass	1.3C	0234
SODIUM DINITRO-o-CRESOLATE, WETTED, with not less than 10 % water, by mass	4.1	3369
SODIUM DINITRO-o-CRESOLATE, WETTED with not less than 15 % water, by mass	4.1	1348
Sodium dioxide, see	5.1	1504
SODIUM DITHIONITE	4.2	1384
SODIUM FLUORIDE, SOLID	6.1	1690
SODIUM FLUORIDE SOLUTION	6.1	3415
SODIUM FLUOROACETATE	6.1	2629
SODIUM FLUOROSILICATE	6.1	2674
Sodium hexafluorosilicate, see	6.1	2674
Sodium hydrate, see	8	1824
SODIUM HYDRIDE	4.3	1427
Sodium hydrogen 4-amino-phenylarsenate, see	6.1	2473
SODIUM HYDROGENDIFLUORIDE	8	2439
SODIUM HYDROSULPHIDE with less than 25 % water of crystallization	4.2	2318
SODIUM HYDROSULPHIDE, HYDRATED with not less than 25 % water of crystallization	8	2949
SODIUM HYDROSULPHITE, see	4.2	1384
SODIUM HYDROXIDE, SOLID	8	1823
SODIUM HYDROXIDE SOLUTION	8	1824
SODIUM ION BATTERIES with organic electrolyte	9	3551
SODIUM ION BATTERIES CONTAINED IN EQUIPMENT, with organic electrolyte	9	3552
SODIUM ION BATTERIES PACKED WITH EQUIPMENT, with organic electrolyte	9	3552
Sodium metasilicate pentahydrate, see	8	3253
SODIUM METHYLATE	4.2	1431
SODIUM METHYLATE SOLUTION in alcohol	3	1289
SODIUM MONOXIDE	8	1825
SODIUM NITRATE	5.1	1498
SODIUM NITRATE AND POTASSIUM NITRATE MIXTURE	5.1	1499
SODIUM NITRITE	5.1	1500
Sodium nitrite and potassium nitrate mixture, see	5.1	1487
SODIUM PENTACHLOROPHENATE	6.1	2567
SODIUM PERBORATE MONOHYDRATE	5.1	3377
SODIUM PERCHLORATE	5.1	1502
SODIUM PERMANGANATE	5.1	1503
SODIUM PEROXIDE	5.1	1504
SODIUM PEROXOBORATE, ANHYDROUS	5.1	3247
SODIUM PERSULPHATE	5.1	1505
SODIUM PHOSPHIDE	4.3	1432
SODIUM PICRAMATE, dry or wetted with less than 20 % water, by mass	1.3C	0235
SODIUM PICRAMATE, WETTED with not less than 20 % water, by mass	4.1	1349
Sodium potassium alloys, see	4.3 4.3	1422 3404

Name and description	Class	UN No.
Sodium selenate, see	6.1	2630
Sodium selenite, see	6.1	2630
Sodium silicofluoride, see	6.1	2674
SODIUM SULPHIDE, ANHYDROUS	4.2	1385
SODIUM SULPHIDE with less than 30 % water of crystallization	4.2	1385
SODIUM SULPHIDE, HYDRATED with not less than 30 % water	8	1849
SODIUM SUPEROXIDE	5.1	2547
SOLIDS CONTAINING CORROSIVE LIQUID, N.O.S.	8	3244
SOLIDS CONTAINING FLAMMABLE LIQUID, N.O.S.	4.1	3175
SOLIDS CONTAINING TOXIC LIQUID, N.O.S.	6.1	3243
Solvents, flammable, n.o.s., see	3	1993
Solvents, flammable, toxic, n.o.s., see	3	1992
SOUNDING DEVICES, EXPLOSIVE	1.1D	0374
	1.1F	0296
	1.2D	0375
	1.2F	0204
Squibs, see	1.4G	0325
	1.4S	0454
STANNIC CHLORIDE, ANHYDROUS	8	1827
STANNIC CHLORIDE PENTAHYDRATE	8	2440
STANNIC PHOSPHIDES	4.3	1433
Steel swarf, see	4.2	2793
STIBINE	2.3	2676
STRAW	4.1	1327
Strontium alloys, pyrophoric, see	4.2	1383
STRONTIUM ARSENITE	6.1	1691
STRONTIUM CHLORATE	5.1	1506
Strontium dioxide, see	5.1	1509
STRONTIUM NITRATE	5.1	1507
STRONTIUM PERCHLORATE	5.1	1508
STRONTIUM PEROXIDE	5.1	1509
STRONTIUM PHOSPHIDE	4.3	2013
STRYCHNINE	6.1	1692
STRYCHNINE SALTS	6.1	1692
STYPHNIC ACID, see	1.1D	0219
	1.1D	0394
STYRENE MONOMER, STABILIZED	3	2055
SUBSTANCES, EVI, N.O.S., see	1.5D	0482
SUBSTANCES, EXPLOSIVE, N.O.S.	1.1A	0473
	1.1C	0474
	1.1D	0475
	1.1G	0476
	1.1L	0357
	1.2L	0358
	1.3C	0477
	1.3G	0478
	1.3L	0359
	1.4C	0479
	1.4D	0480
	1.4G	0485
	1.4S	0481
SUBSTANCES, EXPLOSIVE, VERY INSENSITIVE, N.O.S.	1.5D	0482
Substances liable to spontaneous combustion, n.o.s., see	4.2	2845
	4.2	2846
	4.2	3194
	4.2	3200
SUBSTITUTED NITROPHENOL PESTICIDE, LIQUID, FLAMMABLE, TOXIC, flash-point less than 23 °C	3	2780
SUBSTITUTED NITROPHENOL PESTICIDE, LIQUID, TOXIC	6.1	3014
SUBSTITUTED NITROPHENOL PESTICIDE, LIQUID, TOXIC, FLAMMABLE, flash-point not less than 23 °C	6.1	3013
SUBSTITUTED NITROPHENOL PESTICIDE, SOLID, TOXIC	6.1	2779
SULPHAMIC ACID	8	2967
SULPHUR	4.1	1350
SULPHUR CHLORIDES	8	1828
Sulphur dichloride, see	8	1828
SULPHUR DIOXIDE	2.3	1079
Sulphuretted hydrogen, see	2.3	1053

Name and description	Class	UN No.
SULPHUR HEXAFLUORIDE	2.2	1080
SULPHURIC ACID with more than 51 % acid	8	1830
SULPHURIC ACID with not more than 51 % acid	8	2796
SULPHURIC ACID, FUMING	8	1831
SULPHURIC ACID, SPENT	8	1832
Sulphuric and hydrofluoric acid mixture, see	8	1786
SULPHUR, MOLTEN	4.1	2448
Sulphur monochloride, see	8	1828
SULPHUROUS ACID	8	1833
SULPHUR TETRAFLUORIDE	2.3	2418
SULPHUR TRIOXIDE, STABILIZED	8	1829
SULPHURYL CHLORIDE	8	1834
SULPHURYL FLUORIDE	2.3	2191
Table tennis balls, see	4.1	2000
Talcum with tremolite and/or actinolite, see	9	2212
TARS, LIQUID, including road oils, and cutback bitumens	3	1999
Tartar emetic, see	6.1	1551
TEAR GAS CANDLES	6.1	1700
TEAR GAS SUBSTANCE, LIQUID, N.O.S.	6.1	1693
TEAR GAS SUBSTANCE, SOLID, N.O.S.	6.1	3448
TELLURIUM COMPOUND, N.O.S.	6.1	3284
TELLURIUM HEXAFLUORIDE	2.3	2195
TERPENE HYDROCARBONS, N.O.S.	3	2319
TERPINOLENE	3	2541
TETRABROMOETHANE	6.1	2504
1,1,2,2-TETRACHLOROETHANE	6.1	1702
TETRACHLOROETHYLENE	6.1	1897
TETRAETHYL DITHIOPYROPHOSPHATE	6.1	1704
TETRAETHYLENEPENTAMINE	8	2320
Tetraethyl lead, see	6.1	1649
TETRAETHYL SILICATE	3	1292
Tetraethyoxysilane, see	3	1292
Tetrafluorodichloroethane, see	2.2	1958
1,1,1,2-TETRAFLUOROETHANE	2.2	3159
TETRAFLUOROETHYLENE, STABILIZED	2.1	1081
TETRAFLUOROMETHANE	2.2	1982
1,2,3,6-TETRAHYDRO-BENZALDEHYDE	3	2498
TETRAHYDROFURAN	3	2056
TETRAHYDROFURFURYLAMINE	3	2943
Tetrahydro-1,4-oxazine, see	8	2054
TETRAHYDROPHTHALIC ANHYDRIDES with more than 0.05 % of maleic anhydride	8	2698
1,2,3,6-TETRAHYDROPYRIDINE	3	2410
TETRAHYDROTHIOPHENE	3	2412
Tetramethoxysilane, see	6.1	2606
TETRAMETHYLAMMONIUM HYDROXIDE AQUEOUS SOLUTION	6.1 8	3560 1835
TETRAMETHYLAMMONIUM HYDROXIDE, SOLID	6.1	3423
Tetramethylene, see	2.1	2601
Tetramethylene cyanide, see	6.1	2205
Tetramethyl lead, see	6.1	1649
TETRAMETHYLSILANE	3	2749
TETRANITROANILINE	1.1D	0207
TETRANITROMETHANE	5.1	1510
TETRAPROPYL ORTHOTITANATE	3	2413
TETRAZENE, WETTED see	1.1A	0114
TETRAZOL-1-ACETIC ACID	1.4C	0407
1H-TETRAZOLE	1.1D	0504

Name and description	Class	UN No.
TETRYL, see	1.1D	0208
TEXTILE WASTE, WET	4.2	1857
THALLIUM CHLORATE	5.1	2573
Thallium (I) chlorate, see	5.1	2573
THALLIUM COMPOUND, N.O.S.	6.1	1707
THALLIUM NITRATE	6.1	2727
Thallium (I) nitrate, see	6.1	2727
Thallous chlorate, see	5.1	2573
4-THIAPENTANAL	6.1	2785
Thia-4-pentanal, see	6.1	2785
THIOACETIC ACID	3	2436
THIOCARBAMATE PESTICIDE, LIQUID, FLAMMABLE, TOXIC, flash-point less than 23 °C	3	2772
THIOCARBAMATE PESTICIDE, LIQUID, TOXIC	6.1	3006
THIOCARBAMATE PESTICIDE, LIQUID, TOXIC, FLAMMABLE, flash-point not less than 23 °C	6.1	3005
THIOCARBAMATE PESTICIDE, SOLID, TOXIC	6.1	2771
THIOGLYCOL	6.1	2966
THIOGLYCOLIC ACID	8	1940
THIOLACTIC ACID	6.1	2936
THIONYL CHLORIDE	8	1836
THIOPHENE	3	2414
Thiophenol, see	6.1	2337
THIOPHOSGENE	6.1	2474
THIOPHOSPHORYL CHLORIDE	8	1837
THIOUREA DIOXIDE	4.2	3341
Tin (IV) chloride, anhydrous, see	8	1827
Tin (IV) chloride pentahydrate, see	8	2440
TINCTURES, MEDICINAL	3	1293
Tin tetrachloride, see	8	1827
TITANIUM DISULPHIDE	4.2	3174
TITANIUM HYDRIDE	4.1	1871
TITANIUM POWDER, DRY	4.2	2546
TITANIUM POWDER, WETTED with not less than 25 % water (a visible excess of water must be present) mechanically produced, particle size less than 53 microns; chemically produced, particle size less than 840 microns	4.1	1352
TITANIUM SPONGE GRANULES	4.1	2878
TITANIUM SPONGE POWDERS	4.1	2878
TITANIUM TETRACHLORIDE	8	1838
TITANIUM TRICHLORIDE MIXTURE	8	2869
TITANIUM TRICHLORIDE MIXTURE, PYROPHORIC	4.2	2441
TITANIUM TRICHLORIDE, PYROPHORIC	4.2	2441
TNT, see	1.1D 1.1D 1.1D	0209 0388 0389
TNT, WETTED, see	4.1 4.1	1356 3366
TNT mixed with aluminium, see	1.1D	0390
Toe puffs, nitrocellulose base, see	4.1	1353
TOLUENE	3	1294
TOLUENE DIISOCYANATE	6.1	2078
TOLUIDINES, LIQUID	6.1	1708
TOLUIDINES, SOLID	6.1	3451
Toluol, see	3	1294
2,4-TOLUYLENEDIAMINE, SOLID	6.1	1709
2,4-TOLUYLENEDIAMINE SOLUTION	6.1	3418
Toluylene diisocyanate, see	6.1	2078
Tolylene diisocyanate, see	6.1	2078
Tolylethylene, inhibited, see	3	2618
TORPEDOES with bursting charge	1.1D 1.1E 1.1F	0451 0329 0330

Name and description	Class	UN No.	Name and description	Class	UN No.
TORPEDOES, LIQUID FUELLED with inert head	1.3J	0450	TOXIC BY INHALATION LIQUID, WATER-REACTIVE, FLAMMABLE, N.O.S. with an LC_{50} lower than or equal to 200 ml/m^3 and saturated vapour concentration greater than or equal to 500 LC_{50}	6.1	3490
TORPEDOES, LIQUID FUELLED with or without bursting charge	1.1J	0449			
TOXIC BY INHALATION LIQUID, N.O.S. with an LC_{50} lower than or equal to 200 ml/m^3 and saturated vapour concentration greater than or equal to 500 LC_{50}	6.1	3381	TOXIC BY INHALATION LIQUID, WATER-REACTIVE, FLAMMABLE, N.O.S. with an LC_{50} lower than or equal to 1000 ml/m^3 and saturated vapour concentration greater than or equal to 10 LC_{50}	6.1	3491
TOXIC BY INHALATION LIQUID, N.O.S. with an LC_{50} lower than or equal to 1000 ml/m^3 and saturated vapour concentration greater than or equal to 10 LC_{50}	6.1	3382	TOXIC BY INHALATION LIQUID, OXIDIZING, N.O.S. with an LC_{50} lower than or equal to 200 ml/m^3 or less and saturated vapour concentration greater than or equal to 500 LC_{50}	6.1	3387
TOXIC BY INHALATION LIQUID, FLAMMABLE, N.O.S. with an LC_{50} lower than or equal to 200 ml/m^3 and saturated vapour concentration greater than or equal to 500 LC_{50}	6.1	3383	TOXIC BY INHALATION LIQUID, OXIDIZING, N.O.S. with an LC_{50} lower than or equal to 1000 ml/m^3 or less and saturated vapour concentration greater than or equal to 10 LC_{50}	6.1	3388
TOXIC BY INHALATION LIQUID, FLAMMABLE, N.O.S. with an LC_{50} lower than or equal to 1000 ml/m^3 and saturated vapour concentration greater than or equal to 10 LC_{50}	6.1	3384	TOXIC BY INHALATION LIQUID, CORROSIVE, N.O.S. with an LC_{50} lower than or equal to 200 ml/m^3 and saturated vapour concentration greater than or equal to 500 LC_{50}	6.1	3389
TOXIC BY INHALATION LIQUID, FLAMMABLE, CORROSIVE, N.O.S. with an LC_{50} lower than or equal to 200 ml/m^3 and saturated vapour concentration greater than or equal to 500 LC_{50}	6.1	3488	TOXIC BY INHALATION LIQUID, CORROSIVE, N.O.S. with an LC_{50} lower than or equal to 1000 ml/m^3 and saturated vapour concentration greater than or equal to 10 LC_{50}	6.1	3390
TOXIC BY INHALATION LIQUID, FLAMMABLE, CORROSIVE, N.O.S. with an LC_{50} lower than or equal to 1000 ml/m^3 and saturated vapour concentration greater than or equal to 10 LC_{50}	6.1	3489	TOXIC LIQUID, CORROSIVE, INORGANIC, N.O.S.	6.1	3289
			TOXIC LIQUID, CORROSIVE, ORGANIC, N.O.S.	6.1	2927
TOXIC BY INHALATION LIQUID, WATER-REACTIVE, N.O.S. with an LC_{50} lower than or equal to 200 ml/m^3 and saturated vapour concentration greater than or equal to 500 LC_{50}	6.1	3385	TOXIC LIQUID, FLAMMABLE, ORGANIC, N.O.S.	6.1	2929
			TOXIC LIQUID, INORGANIC, N.O.S.	6.1	3287
			TOXIC LIQUID, ORGANIC, N.O.S.	6.1	2810
TOXIC BY INHALATION LIQUID, WATER-REACTIVE, N.O.S. with an LC_{50} lower than or equal to 1000 ml/m^3 and saturated vapour concentration greater than or equal to 10 LC_{50}	6.1	3386	TOXIC LIQUID, OXIDIZING, N.O.S.	6.1	3122
			TOXIC LIQUID, WATER-REACTIVE, N.O.S.	6.1	3123
			TOXIC SOLID, CORROSIVE, INORGANIC, N.O.S.	6.1	3290
			TOXIC SOLID, CORROSIVE, ORGANIC, N.O.S.	6.1	2928

Name and description	Class	UN No.
TOXIC SOLID, FLAMMABLE, INORGANIC, N.O.S.	6.1	3535
TOXIC SOLID, FLAMMABLE, ORGANIC, N.O.S.	6.1	2930
TOXIC SOLID, INORGANIC, N.O.S.	6.1	3288
TOXIC SOLID, ORGANIC, N.O.S.	6.1	2811
TOXIC SOLID, OXIDIZING, N.O.S.	6.1	3086
TOXIC SOLID, SELF-HEATING, N.O.S.	6.1	3124
TOXIC SOLID, WATER-REACTIVE, N.O.S.	6.1	3125
TOXINS, EXTRACTED FROM LIVING SOURCES, LIQUID, N.O.S.	6.1	3172
TOXINS, EXTRACTED FROM LIVING SOURCES, SOLID, N.O.S.	6.1	3462
TRACERS FOR AMMUNITION	1.3G	0212
	1.4G	0306
Tremolite, see	9	2212
TRIALLYLAMINE	3	2610
TRIALLYL BORATE	6.1	2609
TRIAZINE PESTICIDE, LIQUID, FLAMMABLE, TOXIC, flash-point less than 23 °C	3	2764
TRIAZINE PESTICIDE, LIQUID, TOXIC	6.1	2998
TRIAZINE PESTICIDE, LIQUID, TOXIC, FLAMMABLE, flash-point not less than 23 °C	6.1	2997
TRIAZINE PESTICIDE, SOLID, TOXIC	6.1	2763
Tribromoborane, see	8	2692
TRIBUTYLAMINE	6.1	2542
TRIBUTYLPHOSPHANE	4.2	3254
Trichloroacetaldehyde, see	6.1	2075
TRICHLOROACETIC ACID	8	1839
TRICHLOROACETIC ACID SOLUTION	8	2564
Trichlororaceticaldehyde, see	6.1	2075
TRICHLOROACETYL CHLORIDE	8	2442
TRICHLOROBENZENES, LIQUID	6.1	2321
TRICHLOROBUTENE	6.1	2322
1,1,1-TRICHLOROETHANE	6.1	2831
TRICHLOROETHYLENE	6.1	1710
TRICHLOROISOCYANURIC ACID, DRY	5.1	2468
Trichloronitromethane, see	6.1	1580
TRICHLOROSILANE	4.3	1295
1,3,5-Trichloro-s-triazine-2,4,6-trione, see	5.1	2468
2,4,6-Trichloro-1,3,5- triazine, see	8	2670
TRICRESYL PHOSPHATE with more than 3 % ortho isomer	6.1	2574
TRIETHYLAMINE	3	1296
Triethyl borate, see	3	1176
TRIETHYLENETETRAMINE	8	2259
Triethyl orthoformate, see	3	2524
TRIETHYL PHOSPHITE	3	2323
TRIFLUOROACETIC ACID	8	2699
TRIFLUOROACETYL CHLORIDE	2.3	3057
Trifluorobromomethane, see	2.2	1009
Trifluorochloroethane, see	2.2	1983
TRIFLUOROCHLOROETHYLENE, STABILIZED, REFRIGERANT GAS R 1113	2.3	1082
Trifluorochloromethane, see	2.2	1022
1,1,1-TRIFLUOROETHANE	2.1	2035
TRIFLUOROMETHANE	2.2	1984
TRIFLUOROMETHANE, REFRIGERATED LIQUID	2.2	3136
2-TRIFLUOROMETHYLANILINE	6.1	2942
3-TRIFLUOROMETHYLANILINE	6.1	2948
TRIFLUOROMETHYLTETRAZOLE-SODIUM SALT IN ACETONE, with not less than 68 % acetone, by mass	3	3555
TRIISOBUTYLENE	3	2324

Name and description	Class	UN No.
TRIISOPROPYL BORATE	3	2616
TRIMETHYLACETYL CHLORIDE	6.1	2438
TRIMETHYLAMINE, ANHYDROUS	2.1	1083
TRIMETHYLAMINE, AQUEOUS SOLUTION, not more than 50 % trimethylamine, by mass	3	1297
1,3,5-TRIMETHYLBENZENE	3	2325
TRIMETHYL BORATE	3	2416
TRIMETHYLCHLOROSILANE	3	1298
TRIMETHYLCYCLOHEXYLAMINE	8	2326
Trimethylene chlorobromide, see	6.1	2688
TRIMETHYLHEXA-METHYLENEDIAMINES	8	2327
TRIMETHYLHEXAMETHYLENE DIISOCYANATE	6.1	2328
2,4,4-Trimethylpentene-1, see	3	2050
2,4,4-Trimethylpentene-2, see	3	2050
TRIMETHYL PHOSPHITE	3	2329
TRINITROANILINE	1.1D	0153
TRINITROANISOLE	1.1D	0213
TRINITROBENZENE, dry or wetted with less than 30 % water, by mass	1.1D	0214
TRINITROBENZENE, WETTED, with not less than 10 % water, by mass	4.1	3367
TRINITROBENZENE, WETTED with not less than 30 % water, by mass	4.1	1354
TRINITROBENZENESULPHONIC ACID	1.1D	0386
TRINITROBENZOIC ACID, dry or wetted with less than 30 % water, by mass	1.1D	0215
TRINITROBENZOIC ACID, WETTED, with not less than 10 % water by mass	4.1	3368
TRINITROBENZOIC ACID, WETTED with not less than 30 % water, by mass	4.1	1355
TRINITROCHLOROBENZENE	1.1D	0155
TRINITROCHLOROBENZENE, WETTED, with not less than 10 % water by mass	4.1	3365
TRINITRO-m-CRESOL	1.1D	0216
TRINITROFLUORENONE	1.1D	0387
TRINITRONAPHTHALENE	1.1D	0217
TRINITROPHENETOLE	1.1D	0218
TRINITROPHENOL, dry or wetted with less than 30 % water, by mass	1.1D	0154
TRINITROPHENOL, WETTED, with not less than 10 % water by mass	4.1	3364
TRINITROPHENOL, WETTED with not less than 30 % water, by mass	4.1	1344
TRINITROPHENYLMETHYL-NITRAMINE	1.1D	0208
TRINITRORESORCINOL, dry or wetted with less than 20 % water, or mixture of alcohol and water, by mass	1.1D	0219
TRINITRORESORCINOL, WETTED with not less than 20 % water, or mixture of alcohol and water, by mass	1.1D	0394
TRINITROTOLUENE, dry or wetted with less than 30 % water, by mass	1.1D	0209
TRINITROTOLUENE AND HEXA-NITROSTILBENE MIXTURE	1.1D	0388
TRINITROTOLUENE AND TRINITROBENZENE MIXTURE	1.1D	0388
TRINITROTOLUENE MIXTURE CONTAINING TRINITRO-BENZENE AND HEXANITROSTILBENE	1.1D	0389
TRINITROTOLUENE, WETTED, with not less than 10 % water by mass	4.1	3366
TRINITROTOLUENE, WETTED with not less than 30 % water, by mass	4.1	1356
TRIPROPYLAMINE	3	2260
TRIPROPYLENE	3	2057
TRIS-(1-AZIRIDINYL) PHOSPHINE OXIDE SOLUTION	6.1	2501
TRITONAL	1.1D	0390
Tropilidene, see	3	2603
TUNGSTEN HEXAFLUORIDE	2.3	2196
TURPENTINE	3	1299
TURPENTINE SUBSTITUTE	3	1300

Name and description	Class	UN No.
UNDECANE	3	2330
URANIUM HEXAFLUORIDE, RADIOACTIVE MATERIAL, EXCEPTED PACKAGE, less than 0.1 kg per package, non-fissile or fissile-excepted	6.1	3507
UREA HYDROGEN PEROXIDE	5.1	1511
UREA NITRATE, dry or wetted with less than 20 % water, by mass	1.1D	0220
UREA NITRATE, WETTED with not less than 10 % water, by mass	4.1	3370
UREA NITRATE, WETTED with not less than 20 % water, by mass	4.1	1357
Valeral, see	3	2058
VALERALDEHYDE	3	2058
n-Valeraldehyde, see	3	2058
Valeric aldehyde, see	3	2058
VALERYL CHLORIDE	8	2502
VANADIUM COMPOUND, N.O.S.	6.1	3285
Vanadium (IV) oxide sulphate, see	6.1	2931
Vanadium oxysulphate, see	6.1	2931
VANADIUM OXYTRICHLORIDE	8	2443
VANADIUM PENTOXIDE, non-fused form	6.1	2862
VANADIUM TETRACHLORIDE	8	2444
VANADIUM TRICHLORIDE	8	2475
VANADYL SULPHATE	6.1	2931
VEHICLE, FLAMMABLE GAS POWERED	9	3166
VEHICLE, FLAMMABLE LIQUID POWERED	9	3166
VEHICLE, FUEL CELL, FLAMMABLE GAS POWERED	9	3166
VEHICLE, FUEL CELL, FLAMMABLE LIQUID POWERED	9	3166
VEHICLE, LITHIUM ION BATTERY POWERED	9	3556
VEHICLE, LITHIUM METAL BATTERY POWERED	9	3557
VEHICLE, SODIUM ION BATTERY POWERED	9	3558
Villiaumite, see	6.1	1690
VINYL ACETATE, STABILIZED	3	1301
Vinylbenzene, see	3	2055
VINYL BROMIDE, STABILIZED	2.1	1085
VINYL BUTYRATE, STABILIZED	3	2838
VINYL CHLORIDE, STABILIZED	2.1	1086
VINYL CHLOROACETATE	6.1	2589
VINYL ETHYL ETHER, STABILIZED	3	1302
VINYL FLUORIDE, STABILIZED	2.1	1860
VINYLIDENE CHLORIDE, STABILIZED	3	1303
VINYL ISOBUTYL ETHER, STABILIZED	3	1304
VINYL METHYL ETHER, STABILIZED	2.1	1087
VINYLPYRIDINES, STABILIZED	6.1	3073
VINYLTOLUENES, STABILIZED	3	2618
VINYLTRICHLOROSILANE	3	1305
Warheads for guided missiles, see	1.1D	0286
	1.1F	0369
	1.2D	0287
	1.4D	0370
	1.4F	0371
WARHEADS, ROCKET with burster or expelling charge	1.4D	0370
	1.4F	0371
WARHEADS, ROCKET with bursting charge	1.1D	0286
	1.1F	0369
	1.2D	0287
WARHEADS, TORPEDO with bursting charge	1.1D	0221
WATER-REACTIVE LIQUID, N.O.S.	4.3	3148
WATER-REACTIVE LIQUID, CORROSIVE, N.O.S.	4.3	3129
WATER-REACTIVE LIQUID, TOXIC, N.O.S.	4.3	3130
WATER-REACTIVE SOLID, N.O.S	4.3	2813

Name and description	Class	UN No.
WATER-REACTIVE SOLID, CORROSIVE, N.O.S	4.3	3131
WATER-REACTIVE SOLID, FLAMMABLE, N.O.S	4.3	3132
WATER-REACTIVE SOLID, OXIDIZING, N.O.S	4.3	3133
WATER-REACTIVE SOLID, SELF-HEATING, N.O.S	4.3	3135
WATER-REACTIVE SOLID, TOXIC, N.O.S.	4.3	3134
White arsenic, see	6.1	1561
White spirit, see	3	1300
WOOD PRESERVATIVES, LIQUID	3	1306
WOOL WASTE, WET	4.2	1387
XANTHATES	4.2	3342
XENON	2.2	2036
XENON, REFRIGERATED LIQUID	2.2	2591
XYLENES	3	1307
XYLENOLS, SOLID	6.1	2261
XYLENOLS, LIQUID	6.1	3430
XYLIDINES, LIQUID	6.1	1711
XYLIDINES, SOLID	6.1	3452
Xylols, see	3	1307
XYLYL BROMIDE, LIQUID	6.1	1701
XYLYL BROMIDE, SOLID	6.1	3417
ZINC AMMONIUM NITRITE	5.1	1512
ZINC ARSENATE	6.1	1712
ZINC ARSENATE AND ZINC ARSENITE MIXTURE	6.1	1712
ZINC ARSENITE	6.1	1712
ZINC ASHES	4.3	1435
Zinc bisulphite solution, see	8	2693
ZINC BROMATE	5.1	2469
ZINC CHLORATE	5.1	1513
ZINC CHLORIDE, ANHYDROUS	8	2331
ZINC CHLORIDE SOLUTION	8	1840
ZINC CYANIDE	6.1	1713
ZINC DITHIONITE	9	1931
ZINC DUST	4.3	1436
ZINC FLUOROSILICATE	6.1	2855
Zinc hexafluorosilicate, see	6.1	2855
ZINC HYDROSULPHITE, see	9	1931
ZINC NITRATE	5.1	1514
ZINC PERMANGANATE	5.1	1515
ZINC PEROXIDE	5.1	1516
ZINC PHOSPHIDE	4.3	1714
ZINC POWDER	4.3	1436
ZINC RESINATE	4.1	2714
Zinc selenate, see	6.1	2630
Zinc selenite, see	6.1	2630
Zinc silicofluoride, see	6.1	2855
ZIRCONIUM, DRY, coiled wire, finished metal sheets, strip (thinner than 254 microns but not thinner than 18 microns)	4.1	2858
ZIRCONIUM, DRY, finished sheets, strip or coiled wire	4.2	2009
ZIRCONIUM HYDRIDE	4.1	1437
ZIRCONIUM NITRATE	5.1	2728
ZIRCONIUM PICRAMATE, dry or wetted with less than 20 % water, by mass	1.3C	0236
ZIRCONIUM PICRAMATE, WETTED with not less than 20 % water, by mass	4.1	1517
ZIRCONIUM POWDER, DRY	4.2	2008
ZIRCONIUM POWDER, WETTED with not less than 25 % water (a visible excess of water must be present) (a) mechanically produced, particle size less than 53 microns; (b) chemically produced, particle size less than 840 microns	4.1	1358
ZIRCONIUM SCRAP	4.2	1932

Name and description	Class	UN No.	Name and description	Class	UN No.
ZIRCONIUM SUSPENDED IN A FLAMMABLE LIQUID	3	1308	ZIRCONIUM TETRACHLORIDE	8	2503